BUSINESS
AND
SOCIETY
A Strategic Approach
to Social Responsibility

BUSINESS
AND
SOCIETY

A Strategic Approach
to Social Responsibility
Second Edition

DEBBIE THORNE McALISTER
Texas State University–San Marcos

O. C. FERRELL
Colorado State University

LINDA FERRELL
University of Wyoming

Houghton Mifflin Company
Boston   New York

This book is dedicated to:

Catherine Thorne
Debbie Thorne McAlister

Kathlene Ferrell
O. C. Ferrell

Norlan and Phyllis Nafziger
Linda Ferrell

Vice President, Editor-in-Chief: *George Hoffman*
Associate Sponsoring Editor: *Susan M. Kahn*
Assistant Editor: *Julia M. Perez*
Editorial Assistant: *Kira Robinson-Kates*
Senior Project Editors: *Fred Burns, Nancy Blodget*
Editorial Assistants: *Lisa Goodman, Sean McGann*
Senior Production/Design Coordinator: *Sarah Ambrose*
Senior Art/Design Coordinator: *Jill Haber*
Senior Manufacturing Coordinator: *Priscilla Bailey*
Senior Marketing Manager: *Steven W. Mikels*

Cover photos:
Plato and Aristotle, detail from the fresco *The School of Athens* by Raphael (1483–1520). Stanza della Segnatura, Vatican Palace/Scala/Art Resource, NY.
B.F. Skinner in his laboratory. Photograph. B.F. Skinner Foundation.
Galton Anthropometric Laboratory, opened 1884. Photograph. © The Grant Museum of Zoology and Comparative Anatomy, University College, London, UK.
Title page, Rene Descartes, *Les Meditations* . . . . Rare Book Room, Cambridge University Library, Cambridge, UK.
Mockup title page, Charles Darwin, *Origin of the Species*. American Philosophical Society, Philadelphia, PA.

Printed in the U.S.A.

Library of Congress Control Number: 2003110152

ISBN: 0-618-41596-3

23456789-MV-08 07 06 05 04

Contents

PREFACE xiii

CHAPTER 1:   **Social Responsibility Framework**   1

Social Responsibility Defined 3
  Social Responsibility Applies to All Types of Businesses... 4
  Social Responsibility Adopts a Strategic Focus... 5
  Social Responsibility Fulfills Society's Expectations... 8
  Social Responsibility Requires a Stakeholder Orientation ... 11
Development of Social Responsibility 12
Global Nature of Social Responsibility 15
**Global Initiatives: Global Business and the World Trade
Organization... 18**
Benefits of Social Responsibility 18
  Trust... 20
  Customer Satisfaction... 21
  Employee Commitment... 21
  Investor Loyalty... 22
  The Bottom Line: Profits... 23
  National Economy... 23
Framework for Studying Social Responsibility 24
  Strategic Management of Stakeholder Relationships... 26
  Legal, Regulatory, and Political Issues... 27
  Business Ethics... 27
  Corporate Governance... 27
  Consumer and Community Relations... 27
  Employee Relations... 28
  Environmental Issues... 28
  Technology Issues... 28
  Strategic Philanthropy... 29
  The Social Audit... 29
Summary 30 • Key Terms 31 • Discussion Questions 31 • Experiential Exercise 31
• What Would You Do? 32

CHAPTER 2:   **Strategic Management of Stakeholder Relationships**   **33**

Stakeholders Defined 35

Stakeholder Identification and Importance 38

  Primary and Secondary Stakeholders... 38

  Stakeholders Around the World... 40

  Legal and Regulatory Challenges: Satisfying Regulatory Stakeholders Around

  the World... 42

    Stakeholder Attributes... 43

      • *Power 44*

      • *Legitimacy 45*

      • *Urgency 45*

Performance with Stakeholders 46

  Reputation Management... 46

  Crisis Management... 49

Development of Stakeholder Relationships 52

Link Between Stakeholder Relationships and Social Reponsibility 56

Summary 58 • Key Terms 60 • Discussion Questions 60 • Experiential Exercise 60
• What Would You Do? 60

CHAPTER 3:   **Legal, Regulatory, and Political Issues**   **62**

Government's Influence on Business 64

  The Rationale for Regulation... 65

      • *Economic and Competitive Reasons for Regulation 66*

      • *Social Reasons for Regulation 67*

  Laws and Regulations... 69

      • *Sherman Antitrust Act 69*

      • *Clayton Antitrust Act 69*

      • *Federal Trade Commission Act 71*

      • *Enforcement of the Laws 72*

  Global Regulation... 73

  Costs and Benefits of Regulation... 74

      • *Costs of Regulation 74*

  Benefits of Regulation... 76

      • *Regulatory Reform 76*

      • *Self-Regulation 77*

Business's Influence on Government 78

  The Contemporary Political Environment... 79

      • *Changes in Congress 80*

      • *Rise of Special-Interest Groups 80*

  Corporate Approaches to Influencing Government... 81

      • *Lobbying 81*

      • *Political Action Committees 82*

      • *Campaign Contributions 82*

Global Initiatives: Royal Ahold Illustrates That Accounting Irregularities Are a Global Issue... 84

The Government's Approach for Legal and Ethical Compliance 85
Federal Sentencing Guidelines for Organizations... 85
Sarbanes-Oxley Act... 88
Summary 89 • Key Terms 91 • Discussion Questions 91 • Experiential Exercise 92 • What Would You Do? 92

CHAPTER 4:   **Business Ethics and Ethical Decision Making**   **94**

The Nature of Business Ethics 96
Foundations of Business Ethics 98
Ethical Issues in Business 101
Classification of Ethical Issues... 101
Honesty and Fairness... 101
Conflict of Interest... 103
Fraud... 105
    • *Accounting Fraud 105*

Legal and Regulatory Challenges: Qwest Struggles with Both Accounting and Marketing Ethics... 106
    • *Marketing Fraud 107*
Discrimination... 109
Information Technology... 111
Recognizing an Ethical Issue... 111
Understanding the Ethical Decision-Making Process 112
Individual Factors... 113
    • *Moral Philosophy 113*
    • *Stage of Moral Development 115*
    • *Motivation 119*
Organizational Relationships... 120
    • *Organizational Culture 120*
    • *Significant Others 122*
Opportunity... 123
Summary 124 • Key Terms 125 • Discussion Questions 126 • Experiential Exercise 126 • What Would You Do? 126

CHAPTER 5:   **Strategic Approaches to Improving Ethical Behavior**   **127**

The Need for Organizational Ethics Programs 129
Codes of Conduct 132
Ethics Officers 137
Ethics Training and Communication 138
Establishing Systems to Monitor and Enforce Ethical Standards 143

Help or Assistance Lines... 143

Observation and Feedback... 144

Whistle-blowing... 145

Continuous Improvement of the Ethics Program 147

Implementing Organizational Ethics Programs 149

The Role of Leadership... 149

• *Transformational Leadership 149*

Legal and Regulatory Challenges: Unethical Leadership at Kmart?... 150

• *Transactional Leadership 150*

The Role of an Ethical Corporate Culture... 151

Summary 153 • Key Terms 154 • Discussion Questions 154 • Experiential Exercise 154 • What Would You Do? 154

CHAPTER 6: **Corporate Governance** **156**

Corporate Governance Defined 158

Corporate Governance and Social Responsibility 161

History of Corporate Governance 163

Issues in Corporate Governance Systems 165

Boards of Directors... 165

• *Independence 166*

• *Quality 166*

• *Performance 167*

Shareholders and Investors... 168

• *Shareholder Activism 169*

Legal and Regulatory Challenges: Governance Reform at Cendant... 170

• *Social Investing 171*

• *Investor Confidence 175*

Internal Control and Risk Management... 177

• *Internal and External Audits 178*

• *Control Systems 178*

• *Risk Management 179*

Executive Compensation... 180

Corporate Governance Around the World 182

Future of Corporate Governance 185

Summary 188 • Key Terms 189 • Discussion Questions 189 • Experiential Exercise 190 • What Would You Do? 190

CHAPTER 7: **Consumer and Community Relations** **191**

Consumer Stakeholders 193

Responsibilities to Consumers 193

Economic Issues... 194

Legal Issues... 196

• *Health and Safety 197*

* *Credit and Ownership 197*
* *Marketing, Advertising, and Packaging 199*
* *Sales and Warranties 200*

Global Initiatives: Consumer Credit in Mexico... 201

* *Product Liability 202*
* *International Issues 203*

Ethical Issues... 203

* *Right to Choose 205*
* *Right to Safety 205*
* *Right to Be Informed 206*
* *Right to Be Heard 207*
* *Right to Seek Redress 207*
* *Right to Privacy 207*

Philanthropic Issues... 210

Community Stakeholders 210

Responsibilities to the Community 214

Economic Issues... 217

Legal Issues... 219

Ethical Issues... 219

Philanthropic Issues... 221

Strategic Implementation of Responsibilities to Consumers
and the Community 222

Summary 222 • Key Terms 224 • Discussion Questions 224 • Experiential
Exercise 224 • What Would You Do? 224

CHAPTER 8: **Employee Relations** **226**

Employee Stakeholders 228

Responsibilities to Employees 228

Economic... 229

* *Employee–Employer Contract 229*
* *Workforce Reduction 231*

Legal... 234

* *Wages and Benefits 234*
* *Labor Unions 236*
* *Health and Safety 236*
* *Equal Opportunity 239*
* *Sexual Harassment 240*
* *Whistle-blowing 242*

Ethical... 243

* *Training and Development 243*

Legal and Regulatory Challenges: The Whistle-blower Phenomenon... 244

* *Diversity 246*
* *Work/Life Balance 249*

Philanthropic... 251

Strategic Implementation of Responsibilities to Employees 252

Summary 254 • Key Terms 255 • Discussion Questions 255 • Experiential
Exercise 256 • What Would You Do? 256

CHAPTER 9:   **Environmental Issues**   257

Global Environmental Issues 259
  Atmospheric Issues... 260
      • *Air Pollution 260*
      • *Acid Rain 260*
      • *Global Warming 261*
  Water Issues... 262
      • *Water Pollution 262*
      • *Water Quantity 264*
  Land Issues... 265
      • *Land Pollution 265*
      • *Waste Management 265*
      • *Deforestation 265*
      • *Urban Sprawl 265*
  Biodiversity... 267
  Genetically Modified Foods... 268
Environmental Policy and Regulation 269
  Environmental Protection Agency... 269
  Environmental Legislation... 271
      • *Clean Air Act 271*
      • *Federal Insecticide, Fungicide, and Rodenticide Act 271*
      • *Endangered Species Act 271*
      • *Toxic Substances Control Act 273*
      • *Clean Water Act 274*
      • *Emergency Planning and Community Right-to-Know Act 274*
      • *Pollution Prevention Act 274*
      • *Food Quality Protection Act 274*
Business Response to Environmental Issues 274
  Green Marketing... 275
  Recycling Initiatives... 277
  Emissions Reduction Initiatives... 279
  Legal and Regulatory Challenges: Single-Use Camera Recycling Issues... 280
  Socially Responsible Buying... 280
Strategic Implementation of Environmental Responsibility 281
  Stakeholder Assessment... 282
  Risk Analysis... 283
  The Strategic Environmental Audit... 284
Summary 285 • Key Terms 287 • Discussion Questions 287 • Experiential
Exercise 287 • What Would You Do? 287

CHAPTER 10: **Technology Issues** 289

The Nature of Technology 291
  Characteristics of Technology... 291
  Effects of Technology... 293
Technology's Influence on the Economy 295
  Economic Growth and Employment... 295
  Economic Concerns About the Use of Technology... 298
Technology's Influence on Society 299
  The Internet... 299
  Legal and Regulatory Challenges: Cybercrime... 304
  Privacy... 304
    • *International Initiatives on Privacy 308*
    • *Privacy Officers and Certification 311*
  Intellectual Property... 312
  Health and Biotechnology... 315
    • *Biotechnology 316*
    • *Genetically Modified Foods 318*
Strategic Implementation of Responsibility for Technology 321
  The Role of Government... 321
  The Role of Business... 323
  Strategic Technology Assessment... 324
Summary 326 • Key Terms 327 • Discussion Questions 327 • Experiential
Exercise 327 • What Would You Do? 328

CHAPTER 11: **Strategic Philanthropy** 329

Strategic Philanthropy Defined 331
Strategic Philanthropy and Social Responsibility 333
  History of Corporate Philanthropy... 336
  Strategic Philanthropy Versus Cause-Related Marketing... 339
Stakeholders in Strategic Philanthropy 342
  Employees... 342
  Customers... 343
  Business Partners... 344
  Community and Society... 345
Global Initiatives: Global Change Through Social Venture Capital
and Entrepreneurship... 346
    • *Natural Environment 348*
Benefits of Strategic Philanthropy 348
Implementation of Strategic Philanthropy 350
  Top Management Support... 351
  Planning and Evaluating Strategic Philanthropy... 352
Summary 354 • Key Terms 355 • Discussion Questions 355 • Experiential
Exercise 356 • What Would You Do? 356

CHAPTER 12: **The Social Audit** 357

The Nature of Social Auditing 359
  Reasons for Social Audits... 360
  Benefits of Social Auditing... 360
  Risks of Social Auditing... 363
  Crisis Management and Recovery... 364
  Social Auditing Versus Financial Auditing... 366
The Auditing Process 370
  Secure Commitment of Top Management and/or Board of Directors... 373
  Establish an Audit Committee... 374
  Define the Scope of the Audit Process... 374
  Review Organizational Mission, Policies, Goals, and Objectives... 376
  Define the Organization's Social Priorities... 376
  Identify Tools or Methods for Accurate Measurement of Social Objectives... 377
  Collect Relevant Information... 378
  Analyze the Data... 381
  Verify the Results... 382
  Global Initiatives: Social Reporting at Johnson & Johnson... 384
  Report the Findings... 384
Strategic Importance of Social Auditing 387
Summary 389 • Key Terms 390 • Discussion Questions 390 • Experiential Exercise 390 • What Would You Do? 391

CASES 393

PART I
Successful Management of Social Responsibility

CASE 1: Coca-Cola Company: Crisis and Reputation Management 394
CASE 2: Wainwright Bank & Trust: Banking on Values .403
CASE 3: Conoco's Decision: The First Annual President's Award for Business Ethics 412
CASE 4: Home Depot: Commitment to Social Responsibility 431
CASE 5: New Belgium Brewing Company: Environmental and Social Concerns . .437
CASE 6: DoubleClick: Privacy on the Internet 442

PART II
Challenges in Social Responsibility

CASE 7: Enron: Questionable Accounting Leads to Collapse 449
CASE 8: WorldCom: Actions Lead to Corporate Reform 459
CASE 9: Martha Stewart: Insider-Trading Scandal 467
CASE 10: Arthur Andersen: Questionable Accounting Practices 474
CASE 11: Tyco International: Leadership Crisis 483
CASE 12: Global Crossing: Inflated Sales Lead to Bankruptcy 491

APPENDIX: *Role-Play Exercises* 499

NOTES 507

INDEX 537

Preface

Because of the dramatic changes in corporate responsibility issues over the last several years, the second edition of *Business and Society: A Strategic Approach to Social Responsibility* is designed to reflect these changes. Corporate responsibility issues related to business ethics, corporate governance, regulation of business, and other stakeholder considerations are now a major concern of society. Confidence in business has reached a new low, and public expectations for responsible behavior are increasing.

Business and Society is a highly readable and teachable text that focuses on the reality of social responsibility in the workplace. We have revised the second edition to be the most practical and applied business and society text available. A differentiating feature of this book is its focus on the role that social responsibility takes in strategic business decisions. We demonstrate that studying social responsibility provides knowledge and insights that positively contribute to organizational performance and professional success. This text prepares students for the social responsibility challenges and opportunities they will face throughout their careers. We provide the latest examples and cases that help students capture the reality of social responsibility.

Although there is no universal agreement on the responsibilities, stakeholders, and programs that are required, expected, and desired of business, all businesspeople make decisions related to social responsibility. These actions have consequences for many groups, including employees, consumers, business partners, the community, and many others. Students and instructors like this book because it presents examples, tools, and practices needed to actually develop and implement a socially responsible business strategy. We have been diligent in this revision about discussing the most current knowledge and describing best practices related to social responsibility.

Philosophy of This Text

Business and Society: A Strategic Approach to Social Responsibility 2e introduces a new strategic social responsibility framework for courses that address the role of business in society. Social responsibility is concerned with issues related to values and expectations, as well as the rights of members of society. We view social responsibility as the extent to which a business adopts a strategic focus for fulfilling the economic, legal, ethical, and philanthropic responsibilities expected by all its stakeholders.

The compact format of this book provides twelve chapters on the topics that professors view as essential in a course on business and society. We have developed manageable teaching materials that are flexible enough to incorporate current areas of interest. We provide a complete teaching and learning package that includes traditional resources for effectively using the book, diverse cases, role-play exercises, an example of a social audit, experiential exercises, "What Would You Do?" scenarios, videos, and student and instructor web sites.

The relationship between business and society is inherently controversial and complex, yet the intersection of its components, such as corporate governance, workplace ethics, the natural environment, government institutions, business objectives, community needs, and technology, is felt in every organization. For this reason, we developed this text to effectively assist decision making and inspire the application of social responsibility principles to a variety of situations and organizations. In sum, we demonstrate and help the instructor prove that social responsibility is a theoretically grounded, yet highly actionable and practical, field of interest.

A Relevant and Engaging Approach

Our book provides cutting-edge knowledge, based on research, best practices, and the latest developments in social responsibility. Reviewers inform us that our book takes a fresh look at real-world issues in an engaging, readable way that connects students to reality. We integrate emerging developments in the field of corporate governance, business ethics, and information technology as well as environmental and social issues throughout the text. We balance our coverage by avoiding overemphasis of some topics and providing enough depth on key content areas so students receive the background they need in order to learn more about the relevant topics. For example, the internal and external environments of business changed tremendously with the corporate scandals of the early 2000s. These events shocked millions of Americans into reevaluating our economic system and their expectations of business. Today, organizational stakeholders are more concerned about business ethics, governance, and accountability—key concepts discussed throughout the book. This text was revised to incorporate both the subtle and obvious long-term ramifications of these and other recent events on social responsibility.

A business and society course provides the necessary grounding for discussing the interactions, effects, and changes to social responsibility that we experience every day as new events occur. For this reason, our goal is to make *Business and Society: A Strategic Approach to Social Responsibility 2e* as interesting, timely, thought provoking, and useful as possible. To accomplish this goal, we incorporate historical, current, and emerging concepts and theories, draw on current news and corporate events from around the world, take an active and experiential learning perspective, and encourage our readers to contemplate their understanding of social responsibility and the challenges and opportunities it poses for executives, communities, employees, governments, consumers, and other constituents.

Content and Organization

Professors who teach business and society courses come from diverse backgrounds, including law, management, marketing, philosophy, and many others. Such diversity affords great opportunities to the field of business and society and showcases the central role that social responsibility has, and will continue to have, within various academic, professional, work, and community circles. Because of the widespread interest and multiplicity of stakeholders, the philosophy and practice of social responsibility is both exciting and debatable; it is in a constant state of development—just like all important business concepts and practices.

The term *social responsibility* came into widespread use during the 1990s, but many other terms, like those mentioned at the beginning of the preface, are also often used. In Chapter 1, "Social Responsibility Framework," we define social responsibility as the adoption by a business of a strategic focus for fulfilling the economic, legal, ethical, and philanthropic responsibilities expected of it by its stakeholders. Social responsibility must be fully valued and championed by top managers and granted the same planning time, priority, and management attention as any company initiative. Our framework begins with the social responsibility philosophy, includes the four types of responsibilities, involves many types of stakeholders, and ultimately results in both short- and long-term performance gains. We take a strategic orientation to social responsibility, so students develop knowledge, skills, and attitudes for understanding how organizations achieve many benefits through social responsibility. This chapter also offers evidence that resources invested in social responsibility contribute to improved corporate reputation and financial performance. We explore the central role of trust in maintaining positive relationships with stakeholders, particularly employees, customers, and shareholders. By fostering a high level of trust in stakeholder relationships, companies receive a variety of benefits including lower operating costs and long-term relationships. Misconduct can harm a firm's reputation, sales, and stock price, but addressing stakeholder concerns through a strategic responsibility program can improve a firm's bottom line.

To gain the benefits of social responsibility, effective and mutually beneficial relationships must be developed with customers, employees, investors, competitors, government, the community, and others who have a stake in the company. Chapter 2, "Strategic Management of Stakeholder Relationships," examines the types and attributes of stakeholders, how stakeholders become influential, and the processes for integrating and managing their influence on a firm. The impact of corporate reputation and crisis situations on stakeholder relationships is also examined in detail.

Chapter 3, "Legal, Regulatory, and Political Issues," explores the complex relationship between business and government. Every business must be aware of and abide by the laws and regulations that dictate required business conduct. This chapter also examines how business can participate in the public policy process to influence government. A strategic approach for legal compliance, based on the Federal Sentencing Guidelines for Organizations, is also provided. Chapter 4, "Business Ethics and Ethical Decision Making," and Chapter 5, "Strategic Approaches to Improving Ethical Behavior," are devoted to exploring the role of ethics in business decision making. Business ethics relates to responsibilities and expectations that exist beyond legally prescribed levels. We examine the factors that influence ethical decision making and consider how companies can apply this understanding to improve ethical conduct. We fully describe the components of an organizational ethics program and detail the implementation plans needed for effectiveness.

Because both daily and strategic decisions affect a variety of stakeholders, companies must maintain a governance structure for ensuring proper control and responsibility for their actions. Chapter 6, "Corporate Governance," examines the rights of shareholders, the accountability of top management for corporate actions, executive compensation, and strategic-level processes for ensuring that economic, legal, ethical, and philanthropic responsibilities are satisfied. Corporate governance is an emerging subfield and important process for business and society, which, until the recent scandals, had not received the same level of emphasis as issues such as the environment and human rights.

Chapter 7, "Consumer and Community Relations," and Chapter 8, "Employee Relations," explore relationships with important stakeholders, including consumers, the community, and employees. These constituencies, although different by definition, have similar expectations of the economic, legal, ethical, and philanthropic responsibilities that must be addressed by business. Chapter 9, "Environmental Issues," explores some of the significant environmental issues business and society face today, including air pollution, global warming, water pollution and water quantity, land pollution, waste management, deforestation, urban sprawl, biodiversity, and genetically modified foods. This chapter also considers the impact of government environmental policy and regulation, and examines how some companies are going beyond these laws to address environmental issues and act in an environmentally responsible manner.

Thanks to the Internet and other technological advances, communication is faster than ever before, information can be found about almost anything, and people are living longer, healthier lives. Chapter 10, "Technology Issues" provides cutting-edge information on the unique issues that arise as a result of enhanced technology in the workplace and business environment, including its effects on privacy, intellectual property, and health. The strategic direction for technology depends on the government's and business's ability to plan, implement, and audit the influence of technology on society. Chapter 11, "Strategic Philanthropy," examines companies' synergistic use of organizational core competencies and resources to address key stakeholders' interests and achieve both organizational and social benefits. While traditional benevolent philanthropy involves donating a percentage of sales to social causes, a strategic approach aligns employees and organizational resources and expertise with the needs and concerns of stakeholders. Strategic philanthropy involves both financial and nonfinancial contributions (employee time, goods and services, technology and equipment, as well as facilities) to stakeholders, but it also benefits the company.

Regardless of an organization's particular situation, without reliable measurements of the achievement of objectives, a company has no concrete way to verify their importance, link them to organizational performance, justify expenditures, or adequately address stakeholder concerns. Chapter 12, "The Social Audit," describes an auditing procedure that can be used to measure and improve the social responsibility effort. This chapter takes a complete strategic perspective on social responsibility, including stakeholder relations, legal and ethical issues, and philanthropy. This audit is important for demonstrating commitment and ensuring the continuous improvement of the social responsibility effort. An example of a company's social responsibility or social audit is included in the book's web site. Since many instructors use the audit as a class project or organizing mechanism for the course, the chapter and web site serve as important additions to instructor resources.

Special Features

Business and Society: A Strategic Approach to Social Responsibility 2e has a highly visible practical orientation. This text provides a variety of features to aid students in understanding the relevance and seeing the real-world application of key concepts, in identifying key points and recalling important ideas, and in applying their knowledge to realistic situations. The purpose of all these tools is to take students through a complete strategic planning and implementation perspective on business and society concerns by incorporating an active and team-based learning perspective.

Examples from companies and circumstances all over the world are found throughout the text. Every chapter opens with a vignette and includes numerous boxed and in-text examples that shed more light on how social responsibility works in today's business. Chapter opening objectives, a chapter summary, boldfaced key terms, and discussion questions at the end of the chapter help direct students' attention to key points.

Experiential exercises at the end of each chapter help students apply social responsibility concepts and ideas to business practice. Most of the exercises involve research on the activities, programs, and philosophies that companies and organizations are using to implement social responsibility today. These exercises are designed for higher-level learning and require students to apply, analyze, synthesize, and evaluate knowledge, concepts, practices, and possibilities for social responsibility. At the same time, the instructor can generate rich and complex discussions from student responses to the exercises. For example, the experiential exercise for Chapter 1 asks students to examine *Fortune* magazine's annual list of the Most Admired Companies. This exercise sets the stage for a discussion on the broad context in which stakeholders, business objectives, and responsibilities converge. The experiential exercise for Chapter 10 requires students to visit web sites targeted at children. In visiting the site, students take on the perspective of a child and then assess the site for any persuasion, potentially worrisome content, privacy issues, and guidelines of the Children's Online Privacy Protection Act. The exercise for Chapter 10 requires knowledge of government policy, strong analytical skills, and the ability to verify information and recognize subjectivity.

"What Would You Do?" exercises are new with the second edition. These exercises depict people in real-world scenarios who are faced with a decision about social responsibility in the workplace. The exercise in Chapter 11 discusses the dilemma of a newly named Vice President of Corporate Philanthropy. His charge over the next year is to develop a stronger reputation for philanthropy and social responsibility with the company's stakeholders, including employees, customers, and the community. At the end of the scenario, students are asked to help the VP develop a plan for gaining internal support for the office and its philanthropic efforts. The exercise in Chapter 4 describes ethical conflict that occurs when an employee discovers that a coworker is using company resources for personal consulting jobs. He confronts his coworker and learns that she is using the resources after normal work hours and on the weekends. He is also concerned that the intellectual capital generated by company projects is getting used in these consulting jobs. Students are asked to help the employee decide what to do with this information.

So that students learn more about specific practices, problems, and opportunities in social responsibility, twelve cases are provided at the end of this book. Additional cases are found within the *Instructor's Resource Manual*. The cases comprise a comprehensive collection for examining social responsibility in a multidimensional way. The recent travails and successes of high-profile companies and people, like Enron, WorldCom, Tyco, Coca-Cola, Martha Stewart, Conoco, Home Depot, Arthur Andersen, and Global Crossing, allow students to consider the effects of stakeholders and responsibility expectations on larger and well-known businesses. Cases on smaller organizations, including DoubleClick, New Belgium Brewing Company, and Wainwright Bank, exemplify the many forms of social responsibility that shape today's business environment.

Six additional cases are located in the *Instructor's Resource Manual*. These cases give professors additional resources to use for testing and other course projects. Cases on the PlaySkool Travel-Lite Crib, Ethics Officer Association, Henry Lyons and the National Baptist Convention, Jack-in-the-Box *e. coli* Crisis, Texas A & M Bonfire Collapse, and the Coalition for Environmentally Responsible Economies (CERES) provide additional diversity to the twelve cases presented in the text. These cases address issues in the nonprofit sector, crisis situations, and the role of nongovernmental organizations and associations in developing social responsibility standards.

In addition to many examples, end-of-chapter exercises, and the cases, several role-play exercises are provided in the *Instructor's Resource Manual*. The role-play exercises are built around a fictitious yet plausible scenario or case, support higher-level learning objectives, require group decision-making skills, and can be used in classes of any size. Implementation of the exercises can be customized to the time frame, course objectives, student population, and other unique characteristics of a course. These exercises are aligned with trends in higher education toward teamwork, active learning, and student experiences in handling real-world business issues. For example, the National Farm & Garden exercise places students in a crisis situation that requires an immediate response and consideration of changes over the long term. The role-play simulations (1) give students the opportunity to practice making decisions that have consequences for social responsibility, (2) utilize a team-based approach, (3) recreate the pressures, power, information flows, and other factors that affect decision making in the workplace, and (4) incorporate a debriefing and feedback period for maximum learning and linkages to course objectives. We developed the role-play exercises to enhance more traditional learning tools and to complement the array of resources provided to users of this text. Few textbooks offer this level of teaching support and proprietary learning devices.

A Complete Supplements Package

The comprehensive *Instructor's Resource Manual with Test Bank* includes chapter outlines, answers to the discussion questions at the end of each chapter, comments on the experiential exercises at the end of each chapter, comments on each case, a sample syllabus, and a test bank. The test bank provides multiple-choice and essay questions for each chapter and includes a mix of descriptive and application questions. HM Testing, a computerized version of the Test Bank, is also available. The role-play exercises are included in the manual, along with specific suggestions for using and implementing them in class.

- The *Student Web Site* includes links to a variety of web sites related to social responsibility as well as links to organizations mentioned in the text. The student site also includes practice test questions and decision-making scenarios.

- The password-protected *Instructor Web Site* includes, among other assets, PowerPoint slides and files from the *Instructor's Resource Manual,* which can be downloaded and customized to fit any instructor's specific needs.

- Finally, several *Videos* are available for instructors wishing to bring real-world examples into the classroom. A video guide presents overviews and questions for discussion and suggested uses for the videos.

Acknowledgments

A number of individuals provided reviews and suggestions that helped improve the text and related materials. We sincerely appreciate their time, expertise, and interest in the project.

Frank Barber,
Cuyahoga Community College

Wendy S. Becker,
State University of New York at Albany

Lehman Benson,
University of Arizona

Sandra Christensen,
Eastern Washington University

Richard Coughlan,
University of Richmond

Anne C. Cowden,
California State University, Sacramento

Peggy Cunningham,
Queens University

Dawn Elm,
University of St. Thomas

Andrew Forman,
Hofstra University

John Fraedrich,
Southern Illinois University–Carbondale

Virginia Gerde,
University of New Mexico

Kathleen A. Getz,
American University

Neil Herndon,
University of Missouri

David Hess,
Rutgers Business School

Kenneth Hoffman,
Emporia State University

Susan Key,
University of Alabama at Birmingham

Terry Loe,
Kennesaw State University

Isabelle Maignan,
Vrige Universiteit–Amsterdam

Alan N. Miller,
University of Nevada, Las Vegas

Jan Morgan,
Colorado State University

David W. Murphy,
Madisonville Community College

Larry Overlan,
Stonehill College

Kurt H. Parkum,
Penn State, Harrisburg

Mark Puclik,
University of Illinois at Springfield

Beverly Ross,
Wilmington College

Becky Smith,
York College of Pennsylvania

Barry Shollenberger,
Virginia College

Gary Sokolow,
College of the Redwoods

Diane Scott,
Wichita State University

Marta Szabo White,
Georgia State University

We wish to acknowledge the many people who played an important role in the development of this book. Gwyneth Walters and Barbara Gilmer, educational consultants with whom we have worked for many years, were pivotal to the project. Heather Stein and Sarah Scott assisted with research and provided support in revising several chapters. Leyla Baykal, Reneé Galvin, J. Brooke Hamilton, Neil Herndon, Linda Mullen, Kevin Sample, Timothy Sellnow, Steve Sheck, Nichole Scheele, Mark Smith, Robyn Smith, Heather Stein, Tracy Suter, Jane Swoboda, Robert Ulmer, and David Zivan wrote timely and thought-provoking cases. Kelly Padden and Yvonne Karel assisted with several aspects of the *IRM*. Finally, we express much appreciation to our colleagues and the administration at Colorado State University, Texas State University–San Marcos, and the University of Wyoming.

Our goal is to provide materials and resources that enhance and strengthen both teaching and learning about social responsibility. We invite your comments, concerns, and questions. Your suggestions will be sincerely appreciated and utilized.

DEBBIE THORNE McALISTER
O. C. FERRELL
LINDA FERRELL

Chapter 1

Social Responsibility Framework

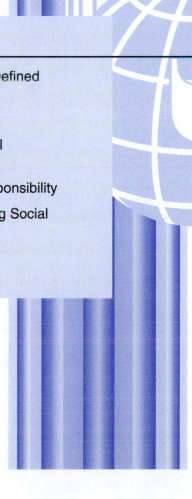

CHAPTER OBJECTIVES

- To define the concept of social responsibility
- To trace the development of social responsibility
- To examine the global nature of social responsibility
- To discuss the benefits of social responsibility
- To discuss the framework for understanding social responsibility

CHAPTER OUTLINE

Social Responsibility Defined

Development of Social Responsibility

Global Nature of Social Responsibility

Benefits of Social Responsibility

Framework for Studying Social Responsibility

Like many organizations, Cummins Engine Company of Columbus, Indiana, has faced a number of challenges over the past several decades. Cummins is currently the world leader in the design and manufacture of diesel engines, and its customers include a variety of industrial companies, including the automotive industry. Cummins, founded in 1919, was Columbus's largest employer for many years. Now, the company employs over 24,000 people in 131 countries and territories and has been a multinational business since 1956. In the tradition of the era in which it was founded, Cummins provided many benefits to the community, including job opportunities and economic growth. For example, its top executives provided the funding for architectural designs for public buildings in the city of Columbus. Thanks to that largess, the American Institute of Architects ranks Columbus sixth in the United States for outstanding and innovative architecture.

Throughout its first sixty years of business, Cummins also performed well for its shareholders. The company enjoyed increased profits for forty-three consecutive years, until 1979. Cummins suffered during the 1980s, however, and it had to fend off the threat of hostile takeovers from several overseas companies. Its stock price plummeted, and stock owners demanded short-run profits at the expense of the company's long-term goals. The founding family repelled one takeover attempt with a large infusion of capital and thwarted another attempt by expanding the firm's shareholder-rights program. Despite its financial woes, Cummins remained focused on research and development, managed to produce a more environmentally friendly diesel engine, and even engaged in limited charitable giving. These actions were consistent with the personality and beliefs of Henry Schacht, Cummins's CEO for more than twenty years, who believed that the company should not aim solely at profit, but rather should develop a balanced set of values.

Although Schacht's beliefs provided a strong foundation, Cummins did not always achieve its social and economic goals. In 1983, for example, for the first time ever, the company was forced to lay off some employees. Later in the decade, the company closed plants and laid off even more people. To reverse these trends, Schacht adopted a new business plan that included cooperation with unions, former employees, and other firms to spur economic development. Negotiations with unions, for example, made it possible for Cummins to re-hire former employees and ultimately to reopen a Columbus plant that had been shuttered in 1987. Although the plant offered lower wages and fewer benefits than Cummins's plants in other locations, its reopening was the culmination of an eleven-year labor negotiation that helped the company reduce costs and boost productivity, allowing Cummins to become a formidable competitor once again. Expansion into Japan, India, and China soon followed.

Throughout this difficult period, Cummins still managed to donate to charities and participate in civic activities. The company partnered with Arvin Industries, another leading Columbus employer, to fund an economic development program that attracted several firms to the city, resulting in three thousand to four thousand new jobs. In 2001, Cummins built a child development center in Columbus for its employees' children. This is Cummins's third such facility; the others are located in Iowa and Brazil. In discussing this latest employee benefit, Tim Solso, the current CEO, noted that in addition to satisfying shareholders, Cummins also considered its obligations to employees and the community. Its efforts were recognized in late 2002, when Cummins received a Business Childcare award from the state of Indiana. By the end of the twentieth century, Cummins was back on track financially, with sales topping $6.6 billion, up 6 percent from the prior year. Sales in the tumultuous year of 2001 slipped to $5.7 billion, but the company rebounded in 2002. Cummins's drive to build positive relationships with its employees, its customers, and its community led *Business Ethics* to rank the firm seventh on the magazine's list of the "100 Best Corporate Citizens."[1]

Businesses today face increasingly complex, and often competing, motives and incentives in their decision making. In a recent *Business Week*–Harris Poll survey of the general population, 95 percent of respondents agreed with the following statement: "U.S. corporations should have more than one purpose. They also owe something to their workers and the communities in which they operate, and they should sometimes sacrifice some profit for the sake of making things better for their workers and communities."[2] In an era of intense global competition and increasing media scrutiny, consumer activism, and government regulation, all types of organizations need to become adept at fulfilling these expectations. Like Cummins Engine Company, many companies are trying, with varying results, to meet the many economic, legal, ethical, and philanthropic responsibilities they now face. Satisfying the expectations of social responsibility is a never-ending process of continuous improvement that requires leadership from top management, buy-in from employees, and good relationships across the community, industry, market, and government. Companies must properly plan, allocate, and use resources to satisfy the demands placed on them by investors, employees, customers, business partners, the government, the community, and others.

In this chapter, we examine the concept of social responsibility and how it relates to today's complex business environment. First, we define social responsibility. Next, we consider the development of social responsibility, its benefits to organizations, and the changing nature of expectations in our increasingly global economy. Finally, we introduce the framework for studying social responsibility used by this text, which includes such elements as strategic management for stakeholder relations; legal, regulatory, and political issues; business ethics; corporate governance; consumer and community relations; employee relations; environmental issues; technology issues; strategic philanthropy; and the social audit.

Social Responsibility Defined

Business ethics, corporate volunteerism, compliance, corporate citizenship, reputation management—these are terms you may have heard used, or even used yourself, to describe the various rights and responsibilities of business organizations. You may have pondered what these terms actually mean for business practice. You may also have wondered what expectations of business these phrases describe. In this chapter, we clarify some of the confusion that exists in the terminology that people use when they talk about expectations for business conduct. To this end, we begin by defining social responsibility.

In most societies, businesses are granted a license to operate and the right to exist through a combination of social and legal mechanisms. Businesses are expected to pay taxes, abide by laws and regulations, treat employees fairly, follow through on contracts, protect the natural environment, meet warranty obligations, and adhere to many other standards. Companies that continuously meet and exceed these standards are rewarded with customer satisfaction, employee dedication, investor loyalty, strong relationships in the community, and the time and energy to continue focusing on business-related concerns. Firms that fail to meet these responsibilities can face penalties, both formal and informal, and may have their attention diverted away from core business issues. For example, a restaurant that delivers poor food quality and shoddy service may be informally sanctioned by customers who decide to take their business elsewhere. These same customers often tell friends and family to avoid the restaurant, thus creating a spiral of effects that eventually shutters the restaurant's doors. On the other hand, a large multinational corporation may be faced with protestors who use physical means to destroy or deface one of its retail stores. In this case, the company is not permanently harmed, but must allocate resources to remodel the store and answer criticism. Finally, a company engaged in deceptive practices may face formal investigation by a government agency. This investigation could lead to legal charges and penalties, perhaps severe enough to significantly alter the company's products and practices or close the business. For example, Conseco Inc., a large insurance and finance company, filed for Chapter 11 bankruptcy protection amidst a federal investigation into its accounting practices and investor lawsuits. Before the filing, Conseco reported $52.3 billion in assets, making its bankruptcy the third largest in U.S. history.[3]

Businesses today are expected to look beyond self-interest and recognize that they belong to a larger group, or society, that expects responsible participation. Thus, if any group, society, or institution is to function, there must be a delicate interplay between rights (i.e., what people expect to get) and responsibilities (i.e., what people are expected to contribute) for the common good. The old adage "no man is an island" describes the relational and integrative nature of society. Although businesses are not human beings, they plan, develop goals, allocate resources, and act and behave purposefully. Thus, society grants them both benefits and responsibilities.

The term *social responsibility* came into widespread use in the business world during the last several decades, but there remains some confusion over the term's exact meaning. Table 1.1 lists some of the different ways in which people commonly use the term to describe business responsibilities. Many of these characterizations have elements in common, such as focusing on the achievement of both corporate and social goals and recognizing the broad groups to which business has an obligation. Only the sixth characterization, which describes social responsibility as an oxymoron, is distinctly different from the others. This view of social responsibility, articulated in the famous economist Milton Friedman's 1962 *Capitalism and Freedom,* asserts that business has one purpose; satisfying its investors or stockholders, and that any other considerations are outside its scope.[4] Although this view still exists today, it has lost some credence as more and more companies have assumed the social responsibility orientation.[5] We define **social responsibility** as the adoption by a business of a strategic focus for fulfilling the economic, legal, ethical, and philanthropic responsibilities expected of it by its stakeholders. This definition encompasses a wide range of objectives and activities, including both historical views of business and perceptions that have emerged in the last decade. Let's take a closer look at the parts of this definition.

social responsibility
the adoption by a business of a strategic focus for fulfilling the economic, legal, ethical, and philanthropic responsibilities expected of it by its stakeholders

Social Responsibility Applies to All Types of Businesses

It is important to recognize that all types of businesses—small and large, sole proprietorships and partnerships as well as large corporations—implement social responsibility initiatives to further their relationships with their customers, their employees, and their community at large. For example, RunTex, a store in Austin, Texas, which

TABLE 1.1	Six Characterizations of Social Responsibility

CHARACTERIZATION	DESCRIPTION
1. License to operate	Social responsibility is a condition for doing business, and as with customer requirements, a firm should find the most efficient way to meet requirements from the government and other external groups.
2. Long-term business investment	Like research and development, social responsibility is designed to improve the business environment for future progress.
3. Vehicle for achieving goals and reputation	Companies that focus on social responsibility will have stronger customer loyalty, more committed employees, better government relations, and, ultimately, stronger reputations.
4. Activity to avoid exposure and risk	Responsible activities help companies avoid being singled out or exposed to unnecessary outsider intrusion.
5. Economic and constructive	Companies should reinforce the economic foundation and viability of the communities in which they operate.
6. Oxymoron	Companies are designed to increase shareholder wealth.

Sources: Barbara W. Altman, "Transformed Corporate Community Relations: A Management Tool for Achieving Corporate Citizenship," *Business and Society Review,* March 22, 1999, p. 43; Melissa A. Berman, "New Ideas, Big Ideas, Fake Ideas," *Across the Board* 36 (January 1999): 28–32; Archie Carroll, "A Three-Dimensional Conceptual Model of Corporate Social Performance," *Academy of Management Review* 4 (1979): 497–505; Kim Davenport, "Corporate Citizenship: A Stakeholder Approach for Defining Corporate Social Performance and Identifying Measures for Assessing It," *Business and Society* 39 (June 2000): 210–219.

sells athletic shoes, clothing, and accessories, donates used shoes (which customers have traded in for discounts on new shoes) to the community's poor and homeless. The company also cosponsors walk/run events that generate funds for local and national social causes. Thus, the ideas advanced in this book are equally relevant and applicable across a broad spectrum of business firms.

Although the social responsibility efforts of large corporations usually receive the most attention, the activities of small businesses may have a greater impact on local communities.[6] Owners of small businesses often serve as community leaders, provide goods and services for customers in smaller markets that larger corporations are not interested in serving, create jobs, and donate resources to local community causes. Medium-sized businesses and their employees have similar roles and functions on both a local and a regional level. Although larger firms produce a large portion of the gross national output of the United States, companies with less than 100 employees account for nearly one-half of total employment.[7] Thus, it is vital that all businesses consider the relationships and expectations that our definition of social responsibility suggests.

Social Responsibility Adopts a Strategic Focus

Social responsibility is not just an academic term; it involves action and measurement, or the "extent" to which a firm embraces the philosophy of social responsibility and then follows through with the implementation of initiatives. Our definition of social responsibility requires a formal commitment, or way of communicating the company's social responsibility philosophy and commitment. For example, Herman Miller, a multinational provider of office, residential, and health care furniture and

Starbucks' Fair Trade Policy is one aspect of this coffee purveyor's strategic commitment to social responsibility. (Mark Richards/ PhotoEdit)

services, has crafted a statement that it calls the Blueprint for Corporate Community (shown in Figure 1.1). This statement declares Herman Miller's philosophy and the way it will fulfill its responsibilities to its customers, its shareholders, its employees, the community, and the natural environment. Because this statement takes into account all of Herman Miller's constituents and applies directly to all of the company's operations, products, markets, and business relationships, it demonstrates the company's strategic focus on social responsibility. Other companies that embrace social responsibility have incorporated similar elements into their strategic communications, including mission and vision statements, annual reports, and web sites. For example, the web site and annual report of the Shimizu Corporation of Japan notes a companywide commitment to constructing high-quality buildings that create social and cultural value and are in harmony with the environment.[8]

In addition to a company's verbal and written commitment to social responsibility, our definition requires action and results. To implement its social responsibility philosophy, Herman Miller has developed and implemented several corporatewide strategic initiatives, including research on improving work furniture and environments, innovation in the area of ergonomically correct products, progressive employee development opportunities, and an environmental stewardship program. These efforts have earned the company many accolades, such as being named the "Most Admired" furniture manufacturer in America by *Fortune* magazine, and a place on numerous prestigious lists, including *Fortune* magazine's "100 Best Companies to Work for in America," *Forbes* magazine's "Platinum List" of America's 400 best-managed large companies, *Business Ethics* magazine's "100 Best Corporate Citi-

| **FIGURE 1.1** | **Herman Miller, Inc.'s, Blueprint for Corporate Community** |

Herman Miller, Inc., is more than just a legal entity. It combines the talents, hopes, and dreams of thousands of people. At its best, it is a high-performance, values-driven community of people tied together by a common purpose. Herman Miller has always stood apart from the crowd because of what we believed, and we have always believed that what we stand for matters. Our strategies will change as the needs of our business change. Our core values will not. We build our business on them. How well we live up to these values will determine whether we are to be trusted by others.

What We Believe in:

- **Making a meaningful contribution to our customers**
- **Cultivating community, participation, and people development**
- **Creating economic value for shareholders and employee-owners**
- **Responding to change through design and innovation**
- **Living with integrity and respecting the environment**

— *A Different Kind of Company* —

Source: "Blueprint for Corporate Community," Herman Miller, Inc., www.hermanmiller.com/CDA/category/aboutus/0,1243,c18,00.html, accessed December 18, 2002. Courtesy of Herman Miller, Inc.

zens," and *Industry Week* magazine's "100 Best-Managed Manufacturers" in the world.[9] As this example demonstrates, effective social responsibility requires both words and action.

If any such initiative is to have strategic importance, it must be fully valued and championed by top management. Executives must believe in and support the integration of constituent interests and economic, legal, ethical, and philanthropic responsibilities into every corporate decision. For example, company objectives for brand awareness and loyalty can be developed and measured from both a marketing and a social responsibility standpoint, because researchers have documented a relationship between consumers' perceptions of a firm's social responsibility and their intentions to purchase that company's brands.[10] Likewise, engineers can integrate consumers' desires for reduced negative environmental impact in product designs, and marketers can ensure that a brand's advertising campaign incorporates this product benefit. Finally, consumers' desires for an environmentally sound product may stimulate a stronger company interest in assuming environmental leadership in all aspects of its operations. Home Depot, for example, responded to demands by consumers and environmentalists for environmentally friendly wood products by launching a new initiative that gives preference to wood products certified as having been harvested responsibly over those taken from endangered forests.[11] With this action, the company, which has long touted its environmental principles, has chosen to take a leadership role in the campaign for environmental responsibility in the home-improvement industry. Although social responsibility depends on collaboration and coordination across many parts of the business and among its constituencies, it also produces effects throughout these same groups. We discuss some of these benefits in a later section of this chapter.

Because of the need for coordination, a large company that is committed to social responsibility often creates specific positions or departments to spearhead the various components of its program. For example, Target, the national retailer, uses a decentralized approach to manage employee volunteerism. Each Target store has a "good neighbor captain" who coordinates employees' efforts with a local charity or cause. The Sara Lee Corporation, whose brands include Bryan Meats, L'Eggs, Coach, Kiwi, and Champion, has established an office of public responsibility to oversee its citizenship efforts.[12] The Japanese firm Toto Ltd., the largest toilet manufacturer in the world, created an office and management structure for its social responsibility effort. Toto's manager of social and cultural promotion recently commented on his firm's social responsibility philosophy, saying, "Toto believes it owes a lot to society. As a good citizen, we need to reciprocate and support the local society."[13] A smaller firm may give an executive, perhaps in human resources or corporate communications, the additional task of overseeing social responsibility. In either structure, this department or executive should ensure that formal social responsibility initiatives are aligned with the company's corporate culture, integrated with companywide goals and plans, fully communicated within and outside the company, and measured to determine their effectiveness and strategic impact. In sum, social responsibility must be given the same planning time, priority, and management attention as is given to any other company initiative, such as continuous improvement, cost management, investor relations, research and development, human resources, or marketing research.

Social Responsibility Fulfills Society's Expectations

Another element of our definition of social responsibility involves society's expectations of business conduct. Many people believe that businesses should accept and abide by four types of responsibility—economic, legal, ethical, and philanthropic (see Figure 1.2). To varying degrees, the four types are required, expected, and/or desired by society.[14]

At the lowest level of the pyramid, businesses have a responsibility to be economically viable so that they can provide a return on investment for their owners, create jobs for the community, and contribute goods and services to the economy. The economy is influenced by the ways in which organizations relate to their stockholders, their customers, their employees, their suppliers, their competitors, their community, and even the natural environment. For example, in nations with corrupt businesses and industries, the negative effects often pervade the entire society. Transparency International, a German organization dedicated to curbing national and international corruption, has conducted research on the effects of business and government corruption on a country's economic growth and prospects. The organization reports that corruption reduces economic growth, inhibits foreign investment, and often channels investment and funds into "pet projects" that may create little benefit other than high returns to the corrupt decision makers.[15] Thus, although

| FIGURE 1.2 | **Pyramid of Responsibility** |

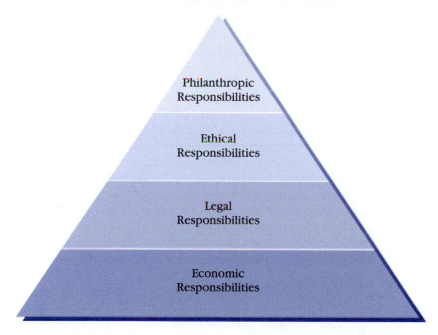

business and society may be theoretically distinct, business has the opportunity to have an economic impact on many people.

At the next level of the pyramid, companies are required to obey laws and regulations that specify what is responsible business conduct. Society enforces its expectations regarding the behavior of businesses through the legal system. If a business chooses to behave in a way that customers, special-interest groups, or other businesses perceive as irresponsible, these groups may ask their elected representatives to draft legislation to regulate the firm's behavior, or they may sue the firm in a court of law in an effort to force it to "play by the rules." For example, many businesses have complained that Microsoft Corporation effectively had a monopoly in the computer operating system and Web browser markets and that the company acted illegally to maintain this dominance. Their complaints were validated in 2000 when U.S. District Judge Thomas Penfield Jackson ruled in a federal lawsuit that Microsoft had indeed used anticompetitive tactics to maintain its Windows monopoly in operating-system software and to attempt to dominate the Web browser market by illegally bundling its Internet Explorer Web browser into its Windows operating system. Microsoft, which vehemently denied the charges, appealed that decision. The election of George W. Bush and a court of appeal's ruling to overturn Jackson's decision shifted the focus to settlement talks, away from an earlier suggestion to break up the company. Microsoft began implementing the provisions of the antitrust settlement agreement in late 2002, including hiring a compliance officer.[16]

Beyond the economic and legal dimensions of social responsibility, companies must decide what they consider to be just, fair, and right—the realm of business ethics. Business ethics refers to the principles and standards that guide behavior in the world of business. These principles are determined and expected by the public, government regulators, special-interest groups, consumers, industry, and individual organizations. The most basic of these principles have been codified into laws and regulations to require that companies conduct themselves in ways that conform to society's expectations. Many firms and industries have chosen to go beyond these basic laws in an effort to act responsibly. The Direct Selling Association (DSA), for example, has established a code of ethics that applies to all individual and company members of the association. Because direct selling, such as door-to-door selling, involves personal contact with consumers, there are many ethical issues that can arise. For this reason, the DSA code directs the association's members to go beyond legal standards of conduct in areas such as product representation, appropriate ways of contacting consumers, and warranties and guarantees. In addition, the DSA actively works with government agencies and consumer groups to ensure that ethical standards are pervasive in the direct selling industry. The World Federation of Direct Selling Associations (WFDSA) also maintains two codes of conduct, one for dealing with consumers and the other for interactions within the industry, that provide guidance for direct sellers around the world, in countries as diverse as Argentina, Canada, Finland, Taiwan, and Poland.[17]

At the top of the pyramid are philanthropic activities, which promote human welfare and goodwill. By making voluntary donations of money, time, and other resources, companies can contribute to their communities and society and improve the quality of life. For example, Hitachi, Ltd., of Tokyo, Japan, established the Hitachi Foundation, a nonprofit philanthropic organization that invests in increasing the well-being of underserved people and communities. With annual contributions of $2.5 million, the foundation is considered a pioneer of global social responsibility.[18] Although Hitachi is not required to support the community, similar corporate actions are increasingly desired and expected by people around the world.

When the pyramid was first introduced, many people assumed that there was a natural progression from economic to philanthropic responsibilities, meaning that a firm had to be economically viable before it could properly consider the other three elements. Today, the pyramid is viewed in a more holistic fashion, with all four responsibilities being seen as related and integrated, and this is the view we will use in this book.[19] In fact, companies demonstrate varying degrees of social responsibility at different points in time, as illustrated by the Cummins opening vignette. Figure 1.3 depicts the social responsibility continuum. Companies' fulfillment of their economic, legal, ethical, and philanthropic responsibilities can range from minimal to strategic responsibility. Firms that focus only on those expectations required by laws and contracts demonstrate minimal responsibility. Strategic responsibility is realized when a company has integrated a range of expectations, desires, and constituencies into its strategic direction and planning processes.[20] In this book, we will give many examples of firms that are at different places along this continuum to show how the pursuit of social responsibility is never-ending. For example, Coca-Cola, the world's largest beverage firm, dropped out of the top ten in *Fortune* magazine's annual list of "America's Most Admired Companies" in 2000 and out of the top one hundred

FIGURE 1.3	Social Responsibility Continuum

Minimal   **Strategic**

⟵――――――――――――――――――――――――――――――――⟶

Economic and
legal considerations
focusing on contractual
stakeholders

Economic, legal, ethical,
and philanthropic
considerations focusing
on all stakeholders

Source: Based on ideas presented in Malcolm McIntosh, Deborah Leipziger, Keith Jones, and Gill Coleman, *Corporate Citizenship: Successful Strategies for Responsible Companies* (London: Financial Times Management, 2000).

in *Business Ethics* magazine's annual list of "100 Best Corporate Citizens" in 2001. For a company that had spent years on both lists, this was disappointing, but perhaps it was not unexpected, as the company was planning to eliminate six thousand jobs, was facing a racial discrimination lawsuit, was still recovering from a product contamination scare in Europe, and was trying to salvage its relationships with its bottlers. Then in 2002, Coca-Cola scored highest in the beverage industry on *Fortune* magazine's measure of social responsibility and the *Business Ethics* magazine survey highlighted Coca-Cola's relationships with stakeholders. These gains are an important step in the company's efforts to reclaim its top rankings.[21]

Social Responsibility Requires a Stakeholder Orientation

The final element of our definition involves those to whom an organization is responsible, including customers, employees, investors and shareholders, suppliers, governments, communities, and many others. These constituents have a stake in, or claim on, some aspect of a company's products, operations, markets, industry, and outcomes, and thus are known as **stakeholders.** We explore the roles and expectations of stakeholders in Chapter 2. Companies that consider the diverse perspectives of these constituents in their daily operations and strategic planning are said to have a stakeholder orientation, meaning that they are focused on stakeholders' concerns. Adopting this orientation is part of the social responsibility philosophy, which implies that business is fundamentally connected to other parts of society and must take responsibility for its effects in those areas.[22]

stakeholders
constituents that have a stake in, or claim on, some aspect of a company's products, operations, markets, industry, and outcomes

R. E. Freeman, one of the earliest writers on stakeholder theory, maintains that business and society are "interpenetrating systems," in that each both affects and is affected by the other.[23] For example, the British home-improvement and garden retailer B&Q has developed a formal process for securing stakeholder input on a variety of issues, including child labor, fair wages, environmental impact, and equal opportunity. To develop a vision and key objectives in these areas, B&Q conferred with suppliers, store managers, employees, customers, and government representatives. On the basis of these consultations, the retailer now recognizes and measures its progress on all four levels of corporate social responsibility.[24] B&Q strengthened its efforts in the 1990s, a period in which social responsibility and the requisite stakeholder orientation became more popular and more generally accepted within the corporate community. Many events have led to this era of increasing accountability and responsibility.

Development of Social Responsibility

In 1959, the Harvard economist Edward Mason asserted that business corporations are "the most important economic institutions."[25] His declaration implied that companies probably affect the community and society as much, or perhaps more, in social terms as in monetary, or financial, terms. For example, most businesses use advertising to convey messages that have an economic impact but also have a social meaning. As an extreme example, when Benetton decided to use convicted felons who had been given death sentences in an advertising campaign, many people were outraged. The Italian clothier had a history of using cutting-edge advertising to comment on social ideas and problems, but some people felt that this campaign went too far. Benetton's original goal was to open up a dialog on the controversial issue of the death penalty, but criticism of the campaign was rampant and Sears dropped its contract with Benetton as a result.[26]

Although most companies do not go to the extremes that Benetton does, companies do influence many aspects of our lives, from the workplace to the natural environment. This influence has led many people to conclude that companies' actions should be designed to benefit employees, customers, business partners, and the community as well as shareholders. Social responsibility has become a benchmark for companies today.[27] However, these expectations have evolved over time. For example, the first corporations in the United States were granted charters by various state governments because they were needed to serve an important function in society, such as transportation, insurance, water, or banking services. In addition to serving as a "license to operate," these charters specified the internal structure of these firms, allowing their actions to be more closely monitored.[28] During this period, corporate charters were often granted for a limited period of time because many people, including legislators, feared the power that corporations could potentially wield. It was not until the mid-1800s that profit and responsibility to stockholders became a major corporate goal.[29]

After World War II, as many large U.S. firms came to dominate the global economy, their actions inspired imitation in other nations. The definitive external characteristic of these firms was their economic dominance. Internally, they were marked by the virtually unlimited autonomy afforded to their top managers. This total discretion meant that the top managers of these firms had the luxury of not having to answer much for their actions.[30] In the current business mind-set, such total autonomy would be viewed as a hindrance to social responsibility because there is no effective system of checks and balances. In Chapter 6, we elaborate on corporate governance, the process of control and accountability in organizations that is necessary for social responsibility.

In the 1950s, the 130 or so largest companies in the United States provided more than half of the country's manufacturing output. The top 500 firms accounted for almost two-thirds of the country's nonagricultural economic activity.[31] U.S. productivity and technological advancements also dramatically outpaced those of global competitors, such as Japan and Western Europe. For example, the level of production in the United States was twice as high as that in Europe and quadruple that in Japan. The level of research and development carried out by U.S. corporations was also well ahead of that of overseas firms. For these reasons, the United States was perceived as setting a global standard for other nations to emulate.

The power of these large U.S. corporations was largely mirrored by the autonomy of their top managers.[32] This autonomy could be characterized as "largely unchecked," as most such managers had the authority to make whatever decisions they thought necessary. Because of the relative lack of global competition and shareholder input during the 1950s and 1960s, there were few formal governance procedures to restrain management's actions. However, this laxity permitted management to focus not just on profit margins but also on a wide variety of discretionary activities, including charitable giving. Thus, it is interesting to note that although top managers' actions were rarely questioned or scrutinized, these managers did use their company's resources to address broader concerns than self-interest. Although the general public was sometimes suspicious of the power held by top managers in large corporations, it also recognized the gains it received from these corporations, such as better products, more choices, good employee salaries, and other such benefits. During this period, many corporations put money into their communities. Although these firms had high executive pay, organizational inefficiencies, high overhead costs, and various other problems, they were quick to share their gains. Employees in the lower echelons of these large corporations received substantially higher wages and better benefits than the national average. This practice has continued into the present; for example, what major automobile manufacturers pay their workers is 50 percent above the national average and 40 percent above the manufacturing national average.[33]

During the 1950s and 1960s, these companies also provided other benefits that are often overlooked. Their contributions to charities, the arts, culture, and other community activities were often quite generous. They spent considerable sums of money on research that was more beneficial to the industry or to society than to the companies' own profitability. For example, the lack of competition meant that companies had the profits to invest in higher-quality products for consumer and industrial use. Although the government passed laws that required companies to take actions to protect the natural environment, make products safer, and promote equity and diversity in the workplace, many companies voluntarily adopted responsible practices and did not constantly fight government regulations and taxes. These corporations once provided many of the services that are now provided by the government in the United States. For example, during this period, the U.S. government spent less than the government of any other industrialized nation on such things as pensions and health benefits, as these were provided by companies rather than by the government.[34] In the 1960s and 1970s, however, the business landscape changed.

Economic turmoil during the 1970s and 1980s almost eliminated the old corporations. Venerable firms that had dominated the economy in the 1950s and 1960s became extinct or ineffective as a result of bankruptcies, takeovers, or other threats, including high energy prices and an influx of foreign competitors. The stability experienced by the U.S. firms of mid-century dissolved. During the 1960s and 1970s, the *Fortune* 500 had a relatively low turnover of about 4 percent. By 1990, however, one-third of the companies in the *Fortune* 500 of 1980 had disappeared, primarily as a result of takeovers and bankruptcies. The threats and instability led companies to protect themselves from business cycles by becoming more focused on their core competencies and reducing their product diversity. To combat takeovers, many companies adopted flatter organizational hierarchies. Flatter organizations meant workforce reduction, but also entailed increasing empowerment of lower-level employees.

Thus, the 1980s and 1990s brought a new focus on profitability and economies of scale. Efficiency and productivity became the primary objectives of business. This fostered a wave of downsizing and restructuring that left some people and communities without financial security. Before 1970, large corporations employed about one of every five Americans, but by the 1990s, they employed only one in ten. The familial relationship between employee and employer disappeared, and along with it went employee loyalty and company promises of lifetime employment. Companies slashed their payrolls to reduce costs, and employees changed jobs more often. Workforce reductions and "job hopping" were almost unheard of in the 1960s, but had become commonplace two decades later. These trends made temporary employment and contract work the fastest-growing forms of employment throughout the 1990s.[35]

Along with these changes, top managers were stripped of their former freedom. Competition heated up, and both consumers and stockholders grew more demanding. The increased competition led business managers to worry more and more about the bottom line and about protecting the company. Escalating use of the Internet provided unprecedented access to information about corporate decisions and conduct and fostered communication among once unconnected groups, furthering consumer awareness and shareholder activism. Consumer demands put more pressure on companies and their employees. The education and activism of stockholders had top management fearing for their jobs. Throughout the last two decades of the twentieth century, legislators and regulators initiated more and more regulatory requirements every year. These factors resulted in difficult trade-offs for management.

The benefits of the corporations of old were largely forgotten in the 1980s, but concern for corporate responsibilities was renewed in the 1990s. Partly as a result of business scandals and Wall Street excesses in the 1980s, many industries and companies decided to pursue and expect more responsible and respectable business practices. Many of these practices focused on creating value for stakeholders through more effective processes and decreased the narrow and sole emphasis on corporate profitability. At the same time, consumers and employees became less interested in making money for its own sake and turned toward intrinsic rewards and a more holistic approach to life and work.[36] This resulted in increased interest in the development of human and intellectual capital; the installation of corporate ethics programs; the development of programs to promote employee volunteerism in the community, strategic philanthropy efforts, and trust in the workplace; and the initiation of a more open dialog between companies and their stakeholders.

Despite major advances in the 1990s, the sheer number of corporate scandals in 2001 and 2002 prompted a new era of social responsibility. The downfall of Enron, WorldCom, and other corporate stalwarts caused regulators, former employees, investors, nongovernmental organizations, and ordinary citizens to question the role and integrity of big business and the underlying economic system. Federal legislators passed the Sarbanes-Oxley Act to overhaul securities laws and governance structures. The new Public Company Accounting Oversight Board was implemented to regulate the accounting and auditing profession. Harvey Pitt, the Securities and Exchange Commission Chairman, resigned after a series of gaffes reduced his ability to lead in turbulent times. America's home decorating guru, Martha Stewart, was indicted on charges related to the sale of ImClone stock. The ImClone CEO, Sam Waksal, lost his job amid insider trading and securities fraud charges and began serving a seven-year sentence in mid-2003. Newspapers, business magazines, and news web sites devoted entire sections—often labeled as Corporate Scandal, Year of the Apology, or Year of the Scandal—to the trials and tribulations of executives, their companies and auditors, and stock analysts.

Mark Lilla, a professor of politics, notes that perceptions of business and society often represent the confluence of the ideas of two decades, the 1960s and 1980s. From the 1960s, we gained a stronger interest in social issues and in how all parts of society can help prevent these issues from arising and resolve them when they do. The economic upheaval and excess of the 1980s alerted many people to the influence that companies have on society when the desire to make money profoundly dominates their activities.[37] The economic growth and gains of the 1990s brought sharp reminders of the 1980s, involving both exorbitant executive salaries and exorbitant executive personal wealth, which eventually took their toll on markets and companies.[38] Events of the past and the scandalous start to the twenty-first century brought calls for a stronger balance between the global market economy and social responsibility, social justice, and cohesion. This is evident on a global scale as special-interest groups, companies, human rights activists, and governments strive to balance worldwide economic growth and spending with social, environmental, technological, and cultural issues.

Global Nature of Social Responsibility

Although many forces have shaped the debate on social responsibility, the increasing globalization of business has made it an international concern. For example, as people around the world celebrated the year 2000, there was also a growing backlash against big business, particularly multinational corporations. A wide variety of protests were held around the globe, but their common theme was criticism of the increasing power and scope of business. The scandals of 2001 and 2002 fortified this criticism and awoke even the staunchest of business advocates. Questions of corruption, environmental protection, fair wages, safe working conditions, and the income gap between rich and poor were posed. Many critics and protesters believe that global business involves exploitation of the working poor, destruction of the planet, and a rise in inequality.[39] Ruy Teixeira, a pollster from the Century Foundation, says, "There's a widespread sense of unfairness and distrust today, where people think companies are not quite playing by the rules." Even *Business Week* weighed in with a cover story entitled "Too Much Corporate Power?"[40] In addition, a 2002 Gallup poll showed that Americans were highly distrustful of executives in large businesses. Thirty-eight percent felt that big business had become a threat to the United States's future and nearly 80 percent believed that executives would take improper actions to benefit themselves.[41]

The globalization of business is fodder for many critics, who believe the movement is detrimental because it destroys the unique cultural elements of individual countries, concentrates power within developed nations and their corporations, abuses natural resources, and takes advantage of people in developing countries. Multinational corporations are perhaps most subject to criticism because of their size and scope. Over 50 of the world's top 100 economies are not national economies at all; they are corporations like Wal-Mart and Royal Dutch Shell. For example, General Motor's revenues are roughly the size of the combined revenues of Hungary, Ireland, and New Zealand. The actions of large, multinational companies are under scrutiny by many stakeholders. For example, a victims' advocate group has charged that Unocal, a large U.S.-based oil and gas exploration and production firm, knew the government of Burma forced peasants to help build a pipeline for the company. Peasants who resisted the military government were tortured or killed. Unocal has denied knowing of the oppression, but faces charges under a 1789 U.S. law called the Alien Tort Claims Act.[42] Most allegations by antiglobalization protestors are not this extreme, but the issues are still of consequence. For example, the pharmaceutical industry has long been criticized for excessive pricing, interference with clinical evaluations, some disregard for developing nations, and aggressive promotional practices. Critics have called on governments, as well as public health organizations, to influence the industry in changing some of its practices.[43]

Advocates of the global economy counter these allegations by pointing to increases in overall economic growth, new jobs, new and more effective products, and other positive effects of global business. Although these differences of opinion provide fuel for debate and discussion, the global economy probably, in the words of author John Dalla Costa, "holds much greater potential than its critics think, and much more disruption than its advocates admit. By definition, a global economy is as big as it can get. This means that the scale of both the opportunity and the consequences are at an apex."[44] Thus, companies around the world are increasingly implementing

Wages paid in the clothing manufacturing business are a source of controversy for many large retailers, including The Gap. (AP Photo/ Richard Drew)

programs and practices that strive to achieve a balance between economic responsibilities and other social responsibilities. The Nestlé Company, a global foods manufacturer and marketer, published the Nestlé Corporate Business Principles in 1998 and revised them in 2002. These principles serve as a management tool for decision making at Nestlé and have been translated into over forty languages. The updated principles are consistent with the United Nations's Global Compact, an accord that covers environmental standards, human rights, and labor conditions.[45]

In most developed countries, social responsibility involves stakeholder accountability and the economic, legal, ethical, and philanthropic dimensions discussed earlier in the chapter. However, a key question for implementing social responsibility on a global scale is, "Who decides on these responsibilities?" Many executives and managers face the challenge of doing business in diverse countries while attempting to maintain their employers' corporate culture and satisfy their expectations. Some companies have adopted an approach in which broad corporate standards can be adapted at a local level. For example, a corporate goal of demonstrating environmental leadership could be met in a number of different ways, depending on local conditions and needs. The Compaq Computer Corporation, which merged with Hewlett-Packard in 2002, implemented its goal of environmental responsibility in different ways depending on the needs in various regions of the world. In North America, Compaq focused on recycling and reducing waste. In Latin America, corporate resources were devoted to wastewater treatment and cleanup of contaminated soil. Efforts in the firm's Asia-Pacific division included the distribution of "green kits" to educate managers, employees, and other stakeholders about Compaq's commitment to environmental leadership.[46]

Global social responsibility also involves the confluence of government, business, trade associations, and other groups. For example, countries that belong to the Asia-Pacific Economic Cooperation (APEC) are responsible for half the world's annual production and trade volume. As APEC works to reduce trade barriers and tariffs, it has also developed meaningful projects in the areas of sustainable development, clean technologies, workplace safety, management of human resources, and the health of the marine environment. This powerful trade group has demonstrated that economic, social, and ethical concerns can be tackled simultaneously.[47] Like APEC, other trade groups are also exploring ways to enhance economic productivity within the context of legal, ethical, and philanthropic responsibilities.

In sum, progressive global businesses recognize the "shared bottom line" that results from the partnership among business, communities, government, customers, and the natural environment. In the Millennium Poll, a survey of more than 25,000 citizens in 23 countries, 66 percent of the respondents indicated that they want companies to go beyond their traditional role of making a profit, paying taxes, and providing jobs. More than half the respondents said that they believe their national government and companies should focus more on social and environmental goals than on economic goals in the first decade of the new millennium.[48] This survey reiterates our philosophy that business is now accountable to a variety of stakeholders and has a number of responsibilities. Thus, our concept of social responsibility is applicable to businesses around the world, although adaptations of implementation and other details on the local level are definitely required. In companies around the world, there is also a recognition of the relationship between strategic social responsibility and benefits to society and organizational performance.

Global Initiatives

Global Business and the World Trade Organization

Ordinary citizens may have obtained little knowledge of the World Trade Organization (WTO), mainly because they have not become aware of the far-reaching power and influence the organization has on business. The International Chamber of Commerce describes the WTO as "the most prominent symbol of globalization and the complex changes that are driving the world economy." The WTO was formed to develop and monitor a set of rules governing international trade and investment around the world. Most large companies and countries, and many others, are in favor of the WTO because the organization has helped liberalize and smooth trading among countries. Proponents point to the stability, consensus, predictability, and promise that the WTO has created for doing business globally.

The organization boasts member countries from different parts of the world, representing large developed countries as well as emerging economies. Member nations of the WTO number over 140, with an additional 30 nations listed as observers or under consideration for membership. The economies of WTO members account for over 90 percent of all world trade. While the most economically progressive and successful nations are WTO members, the majority of members are from developing countries, including over 25 nations categorized as least-developed by the United Nations.

The WTO came into being on January 1, 1995, as the successor to the General Agreement on Tariffs and Trade (GATT), which had regulated tariffs worldwide since the mid-1940s. Its member governments run the WTO and major decisions are the result of input from the entire membership. In fact, most decisions have been made by consensus, not just a majority vote. The WTO promotes the concept of equality and fair representation, regardless of a particular country's level of economic success and power. The world's economic trading system is governed by various WTO agreements, some of which constrain or modify the role that member countries' governments may have in developing law and regulation of the environment, technology, health and safety, and other areas.

Despite the benefits of the WTO, news articles often highlight the stories of various protesting groups and associations that vehemently oppose the WTO and its effect on trading relations, consumer issues, and other political and social concerns. To date, the most-publicized and -organized protests took place in late 1999 in Seattle, Washington, during the WTO ministerial meetings. More than 1,400 organizations signed a declaration opposing the WTO. These organizations represented widespread interests, including agriculture, employment and labor, human rights, the natural environment, democracy, and others. Protestors carried signs with phrases such as "Fair Trade Not Free Trade," "WTO Trades Away Our Forests," "Cancel Debts of Poor Countries," "Trade Is Not a Race to the Bottom," and "WTO: Hands Off Our Bananas."

Over the years, critics have raised serious questions about the WTO. These comments center on

Benefits of Social Responsibility

The importance of social responsibility initiatives in enhancing stakeholder relationships, improving performance, and creating other benefits has been debated from many different perspectives.[49] Many business managers view such programs as costly activities that provide rewards only to society at the expense of the bottom line. Another view holds that some costs of social responsibility cannot be recovered through improved performance. Although it is true that some aspects of social responsibility

the potentially negative environmental, social, cultural, and political impacts of corporate and economic globalization. Demonstrators are often concerned about the seeming priority of money and profit over all other concerns, such as people, animals, and the environment. For example, some people believe that the WTO helps large and powerful nations but puts developing countries at a disadvantage and at risk in the global economic arena. These critics point to the severe debt, poverty, corruption, and social ills that may exist in poor countries striving for a capitalistic economy. Whereas a small group of people and leaders may become wealthy, the rest of the country's citizens are left destitute or unaffected by the promises of global trade.

Other concerns are directed at the survival of specific industries. For example, Taiwan's local film industry was threatened by that country's decision to enter the WTO. While the WTO could open many economic doors, Taiwanese filmmakers were concerned about the number of U.S.-based and other foreign films that already made screenings and showings of Taiwanese films harder and harder to secure. One Taiwanese filmmaker lamented, "All the theaters were occupied with Hollywood films, and even if I managed to get one theater, my film may still be pulled off once a big-cast movie is showing." In this case, trade liberalization was viewed as threatening the local film industry, endangering the livelihood of people in the industry, and potentially destroying cultural and symbolic representations of the Taiwanese people.

For developing nations, there may be concerns about the true level of equality that exists in the WTO and various negotiations. Although equality is an admirable goal, some writers have warned developing nations that the uniformity of rules in WTO agreements does not favor developing nations. Since larger economies have more to give and take and developing countries still rely on them tremendously, developed nations may still have the upper hand in negotiation and implementation of trade rules. Some critics have encouraged the WTO to modify its "trade creates wealth" mantra to one focused on the developmental needs of nations. This philosophical shift would put emphasis on domestic economies, self-sufficiency, standards of living, sustainable environments, and many other issues at the heart of current criticisms.

In summary, the WTO deserves serious consideration by businesspeople, governments, and citizens. While the benefits are clear, the criticisms need to be understood so that future decisions limit potentially damaging effects, increase cultural, social, and political prospects, and reduce the tension that seems to exist between economic concerns and all others.

Sources:
Kyle Bagwell and Robert Staiger, "Economic Theory and the Interpretation of GATT/WTO," *American Economist* 46 (Fall 2002): 31–19; "Finance and Economics: Weighing Up the WTO," *The Economist,* November 30, 2002, p. 96; Jeffrey Garten, "Can the WTO's New Leader Make It a Force For Change?" *Business Week,* October 27, 2002, p. 28; Aileen Kwa, "WTO and Developing Countries," www.foreignpolicy-infocus.org/, accessed November 1998; Yu Sen-lun, "Taiwan's Film Industry Threatened by WTO Entry," *Taipei Times,* November 23, 1999; World Trade Organization, http://www.wto.org/, accessed December 19, 2002; "WTO History Project," http://depts.washington.edu/wtohist/, accessed December 19, 2002.

may not accrue directly to the bottom line, we believe that organizations benefit indirectly over the long run from these activities. Moreover, ample research and anecdotal evidence demonstrate that there are many rewards for those companies that implement such programs. Some of these rewards include increased efficiency in daily operations, greater employee commitment, higher product quality, improved decision making, increased customer loyalty, and improved financial performance. In short, companies that establish a reputation for trust, fairness, and integrity develop a valuable resource that fosters success, which then translates to greater financial

---

FIGURE 1.4 The Role of Social Responsibility in Performance

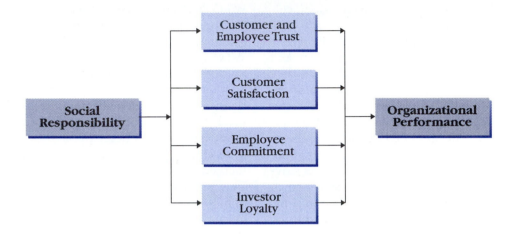

performance (see Figure 1.4). This section provides evidence that resources invested in social responsibility programs reap benefits for organizations and stakeholders.

Trust

Trust is the glue that holds organizations together and allows them to focus on efficiency, productivity, and profits. According to Stephen R. Covey, author of *The 7 Habits of Highly Effective People,* "Trust lies at the very core of effective human interactions. Compelling trust is the highest form of human motivation. It brings out the very best in people, but it takes time and patience, and it doesn't preclude the necessity to train and develop people so their competency can rise to that level of trust." When trust is low, organizations decay and relationships deteriorate, resulting in infighting, playing politics within the organization, and general inefficiency. Employee commitment to the organization declines, product quality suffers, employee turnover skyrockets, and customers turn to trustworthier competitors.[50]

In a trusting work environment, however, employees can reasonably expect to be treated with respect and consideration by both their peers and their superiors. They are also more willing to rely and act on the decisions and actions of their coworkers. Thus, trusting relationships between managers and their subordinates contribute to greater decision-making efficiencies. Research by the Ethics Resource Center indicates that trust also contributes to employee satisfaction. The study reported that 93 percent of surveyed employees who said that trust was frequently evident in their organizations indicated satisfaction with their employers.[51]

Trust is also essential for a company to maintain positive long-term relationships with customers. A study by Cone-Roper reported that three out of four consumers say they avoid or refuse to buy from certain businesses. Poor service was the number one reason cited for refusing to buy, but business conduct was the second reason that consumers gave for avoiding specific companies.[52] After the *Exxon Valdez* oil spill in 1989, certain groups and individual citizens aggressively boycotted Exxon because of its response to the environmental disaster.

Customer Satisfaction

The prevailing business philosophy about customer relationships is that a company should strive to market products that satisfy customers' needs through a coordinated effort that also allows the company to achieve its own objectives. It is well accepted that customer satisfaction is one of the most important factors for business success. Although companies must continue to develop and adapt products to keep pace with consumers' changing desires, it is also crucial to develop long-term relationships with customers. Relationships built on mutual respect and cooperation facilitate the repeat purchases that are essential for success. By focusing on customer satisfaction, a business can continually strengthen its customers' trust in the company, and as their confidence grows, this in turn increases the firm's understanding of their requirements.

In a 2001 Cone-Roper national survey of consumer attitudes, 81 percent of consumers indicated they would be likely to switch to brands associated with a good cause if price and quality were equal. These results were up 11 percent from the same study in 1997 and show that consumers take for granted that they can buy high-quality products at low prices; therefore, companies need to stand out as doing something—something that demonstrates their commitment to society. The 2001 survey also indicated that consumers believed companies should continue supporting causes, even during an economic downturn.[53] A study by Harris Interactive Inc. and the Reputation Institute reported that one-quarter of the respondents had boycotted a firm's products or lobbied others to do so when they did not agree with the firm's policies or activities.[54] Another way of looking at these results is that irresponsible behavior could trigger disloyalty and refusals to buy, whereas good social responsibility initiatives could draw customers to a company's products. For example, many firms use cause-related marketing programs to donate part of a product's sales revenue to a charity that is meaningful to the product's target market. Among the most well-known cause-related marketing programs is Avon's "pink ribbon," which we discuss in Chapter 11.

Employee Commitment

Employee commitment stems from employees who believe their future is tied to that of the organization and are willing to make personal sacrifices for the organization.[55] Hershey Foods is an example of a business that historically drew substantial benefits from its long-lasting commitment to social responsibility. Every year, Hershey employees receive a booklet entitled *Key Corporate Policies,* which describes the values—fairness, integrity, honesty, respect—at the heart of the company's way of doing business. Employees are asked to sign the booklet and are made aware of procedures for reporting concerns about proper conduct or policies in the workplace. These efforts help employees understand the importance of developing and maintaining respectful relationships with both colleagues and customers. Because they support the idea that customers should receive full value for their money, employees are also committed to delivering the highest-quality standards possible. Today, Hershey claims about 43 percent of the U.S. chocolate market.[56]

When companies fail to provide value for their employees, loyalty and commitment suffer. A survey by Walker Information Global Network found low levels of employee loyalty and commitment worldwide. The study, which surveyed thousands of employees in thirty-two countries, found that only one in three workers is "truly loyal" to the organization for which he or she works.[57] Employees spend much of their waking hours at work; thus, an organization's commitment to goodwill and respect of its employees usually results in increased employee loyalty and support of the company's objectives.

Investor Loyalty

Investors look at a corporation's bottom line for profits or the potential for increased stock prices. To be successful, relationships with stockholders and other investors must rest on dependability, trust, and commitment. But investors also look for potential cracks or flaws in a company's performance. Companies perceived by their employees as having a high degree of honesty and integrity had an average three-year total return to shareholders of 101 percent, whereas companies perceived as having a low degree of honesty and integrity had a three-year total return to shareholders of just 69 percent.[58] When the Securities and Exchange Commission investigated Sunbeam for improprieties in accounting procedures, the company's stock plummeted from a high of $54 to almost worthless. The negative publicity associated with the alleged misconduct had an enormous impact on investors' confidence in Sunbeam—a previously trusted and respected U.S. brand.[59]

Many shareholders are also concerned about the reputation of companies in which they invest. Investors have even been known to avoid buying the stock of firms they view as irresponsible. For example, fifteen mutual fund managers announced a boycott of Mitsubishi stock after the Japanese firm refused to cancel a plan to build a salt factory on a Mexican lagoon that is also a major breeding site for gray whales.[60] Many socially responsible mutual funds and asset management firms are available to help concerned investors purchase stock in responsible companies. These investors recognize that corporate responsibility is the foundation for efficiency, productivity, and profits. On the other hand, investors know that fines or negative publicity can decrease a company's stock price, customer loyalty, and long-term viability. Consequently, many chief executives spend a great deal of time communicating with investors about their firms' reputations and financial performance and trying to attract them to their stock.

The issue of drawing and retaining investors is a critical one for CEOs, as roughly 50 percent of investors sell their stock in companies within one year, and the average household replaces 80 percent of its common stock portfolio each year.[61] This focus on short-term gains subjects corporate managers to tremendous pressure to boost short-term earnings, often at the expense of long-term strategic plans. The resulting pressure for short-term gains deprives corporations of stable capital and forces decision makers into a "quarterly" mentality. Conversely, those shareholders willing to hold onto their investments are more willing to sacrifice short-term gains for long-term income. Attracting these long-term investors shields companies from the vagaries of the stock market and gives them flexibility and stability in long-term strategic planning. In the aftermath of the Enron scandal, however, trust and confidence in financial audits and published financial statements were severely shaken. Membership in grass-roots investment clubs declined, retail stock investments declined, and investors called for increased transparency in company operations and reports.[62] Gaining investors' trust and confidence is vital for sustaining a firm's financial stability.

The Bottom Line: Profits

Social responsibility is positively associated with return on investment, return on assets, and sales growth.[63] A company cannot be continuously socially responsible and nurture and develop an ethical organizational culture unless it has achieved financial performance in terms of profits. Businesses with greater resources—regardless of their staff size—have the ability to promote their social responsibility along with serving their customers, valuing their employees, and establishing trust with the public.

Many studies have identified a positive relationship between social responsibility and financial performance.[64] For example, a survey of the 500 largest public corporations in the United States found that those that commit to responsible behavior and emphasize compliance with codes of conduct show better financial performance.[65] A managerial focus on stakeholder interests can affect financial performance, although the relationships between stakeholders and financial performance vary and are very complex.[66] A meta-analysis of twenty-five years of research identified thirty-three studies (63 percent) demonstrating a positive relationship between corporate social performance and corporate financial performance, five studies (about 10 percent) indicating a negative relationship, and fourteen studies (27 percent) yielding an inconclusive result or no relationship.[67] Research on the effects of legal infractions suggests that the negative effect of misconduct does not appear until the third year following a conviction, with multiple convictions being more harmful than a single one.[68]

National Economy

An often-asked question is whether business conduct has any bearing on a nation's overall economic performance. Many economists have wondered why some market-based economies are productive and provide a high standard of living for their citizens, whereas other market-based economies lack the kinds of social institutions that foster productivity and economic growth. Perhaps a society's economic problems can be explained by a lack of social responsibility. As the glue that holds organizations and relationships together, trust stems from principles of morality and serves as an important "lubricant of the social system."[69] Many descriptions of market economies fail to take into account the role of such institutions as family, education, and social systems in explaining standards of living and economic success. Perhaps some countries do a better job of developing because of the social structure of their economic relationships.

Social institutions, particularly those that promote trust, are important for the economic well-being of a society.[70] Society has become economically successful over time "because of the underlying institutional framework persistently reinforcing incentives for organizations to engage in productive activity."[71] In some developing countries, opportunities for political and economic development have been stifled by activities that promote monopolies, graft, and corruption and by restrictions on opportunities to advance individual, as well as collective, well-being. Author

L. E. Harrison offers four fundamental factors that promote economic well-being: "(1) The degree of identification with others in a society—the radius of trust, or the sense of community; (2) the rigor of the ethical system; (3) the way authority is exercised within the society; and (4) attitudes about work, innovation, saving, and profit."[72]

Countries with strong trust-based institutions foster a productivity-enhancing environment because they have ethical systems in place that reduce transaction costs and make competitive processes more efficient and effective. In market-based systems where there is a great degree of trust, such as Japan, Great Britain, Canada, the United States, and Sweden, highly successful enterprises can develop through a spirit of cooperation and the ease in conducting business.[73]

Superior financial performance at the firm level within a society is measured as profits, earnings per share, return on investment, and capital appreciation. Businesses must achieve a certain level of financial performance in order to survive and reinvest in the various institutions in society that provide support. On the other hand, at the institutional or societal level, a key factor distinguishing societies with high standards of living is trust-promoting institutions. The challenge is to articulate the process by which institutions that support social responsibility can contribute to firm-level superior financial performance.[74]

A comparison of countries that have high levels of corruption and underdeveloped social institutions with countries that have low levels of corruption reveals differences in the economic well-being of the country's citizens. According to Transparency International's Corruption Perceptions Index, countries such as Nigeria and Bangladesh rank high on corruption, whereas countries such as Denmark and Finland rank low.[75] The differences in these countries' economic well-being and stability offer evidence that the social institutions that support ethics and responsibility play a vital role in economic development. Conducting business in an ethical and responsible manner generates trust and leads to relationships that promote productivity and innovativeness.

Framework for Studying Social Responsibility

The framework we developed for this text is designed to help you understand how businesses fulfill social expectations. Figure 1.5 illustrates the concept that social responsibility is a process. It begins with the social responsibility philosophy, includes the four levels of social responsibilities, involves many types of stakeholders, and ultimately results in both short- and long-term performance benefits. As we discussed earlier, social responsibility must have the support of top management—both in words and in deeds—before it can become an organizational reality. For example, in 2000 the Ford Motor Company released its inaugural social responsibility report, entitled "Connecting with Society." This report was partly commissioned by William Clay Ford, Jr., the company's chairman of the board, who is recognized as an advocate for environmental and social initiatives. The chairman's leadership in this area was a primary driver of this report, which included the admission that sport utility vehicles (SUVs) have poor fuel efficiency and emit high levels of air pollutants.[76] Once the social responsibility philosophy is accepted, the four aspects of corporate social responsibility are defined and implemented through programs that incorporate stakeholder input and feedback. For example, in response to William Clay Ford's

FIGURE 1.5	Social Responsibility Model

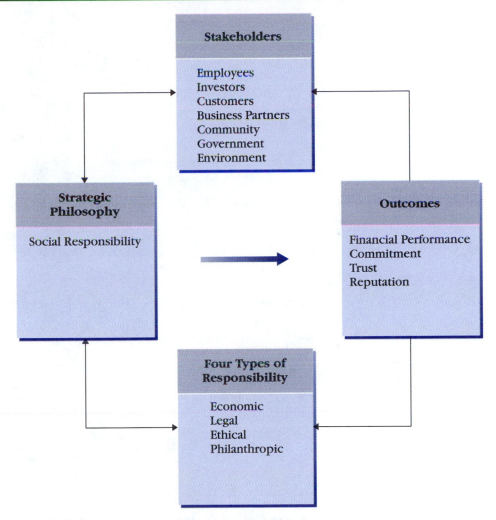

Source: Adapted from Charles J. Fombrun, "Three Pillars of Corporate Citizenship," in *Corporate Global Citizenship,* ed. Noel M. Tichy, Andrew R. McGill, and Lynda St. Clair (San Francisco: New Lexington Press, 1997), pp. 27–42.

social responsibility philosophy, criticism from environmental groups, and the recognition that SUVs are harmful to the environment, Ford announced plans to address the issue. However, the company is aware of the potential costs associated with addressing this issue. As Ford will discover, when social responsibility programs are put into action, they have both immediate and delayed outcomes.

Figure 1.6 depicts how the chapters of this book fit into our framework. This framework begins with a look at the importance of working with stakeholders to achieve social responsibility objectives. The framework also includes an examination of the influence on business decisions and actions of the legal, regulatory, and political

FIGURE 1.6   An Overview of This Book

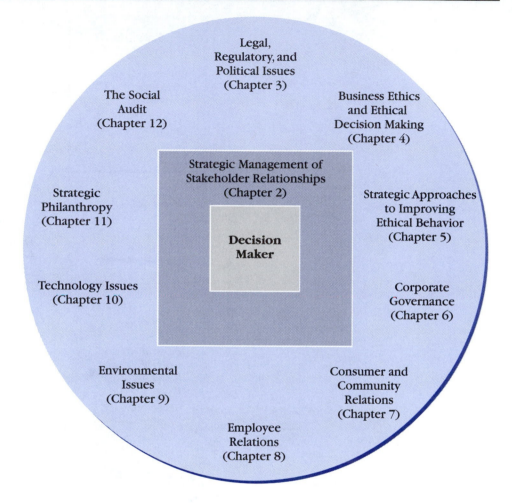

environment; business ethics; and corporate governance. The remaining chapters of the book explore the responsibilities associated with specific stakeholders and issues that confront business decision makers today, including the process of implementing a social responsibility audit.

Strategic Management of Stakeholder Relationships

Social responsibility is grounded in effective and mutually beneficial relationships with customers, employees, investors, competitors, government, the community, and others who have a stake in the company. Increasingly, companies are recognizing that these constituents both affect and are affected by their actions. For this reason, many companies attempt to address the concerns of stakeholder groups, recognizing that failure to do so can have serious long-term consequences. For example, the Connecticut Better Business Bureau revoked the membership of Priceline.com after the Internet company failed to address complaints related to misrepresentation of products, billing problems, and refunds.[77] Chapter 2 examines the types of stakeholders and their attributes, how stakeholders become influential, and the processes for integrating and managing stakeholders' influence on a firm. The impact of corporate reputation and crisis situations on stakeholder relationships is also examined.

Legal, Regulatory, and Political Issues

In Chapter 3, we explore the complex relationship between business and government. Every business must be aware of and abide by the laws and regulations that dictate acceptable business conduct. This chapter also examines how business can influence government by participating in the public policy process. A strategic approach for legal compliance is also provided.

Business Ethics

Because individual values are a component of organizational conduct, these findings raise concerns about the ethics of future business leaders. Chapters 4 and 5 are devoted to exploring the role of ethics in business decision making. These chapters explore business responsibilities that go beyond the conduct that is legally prescribed. We also examine the factors that influence ethical decision making and consider how companies can apply this understanding to increase their ethical conduct.

Corporate Governance

Because both daily and strategic decisions affect a variety of stakeholders, companies must maintain a governance structure to ensure proper control of their actions and assign responsibility for those actions. In Chapter 6, we define corporate governance and discuss its role in achieving strategic social responsibility. Key governance issues addressed include the rights of shareholders, the accountability of top management for corporate actions, executive compensation, and strategic-level processes for ensuring that economic, legal, ethical, and philanthropic responsibilities are satisfied.

Consumer and Community Relations

Chapter 7 explores companies' relationships with two important stakeholders: consumers and the community. These constituencies, although different by definition, have similar expectations concerning the economic, legal, ethical, and philanthropic responsibilities of business that companies must address. Chapter 7 therefore considers the obligations that companies have toward their customers, including health and safety issues, honesty in marketing, and consumer rights. The chapter also examines the larger community by exploring issues that have a profound impact on the communities in which businesses operate. For example, many communities fear that they will lose their unique character when large national chain retailers such as Starbucks, Wal-Mart, and Home Depot move to town, especially when the presence of these firms contributes to the failure of longtime local businesses. These fears have prompted passionate activism that in some cases has resulted in ordinances that restrict the types and sizes of new businesses.[78]

Employee Relations

In today's business environment, most organizations want to build long-term relationships with a variety of stakeholders, but particularly with employees—the focus of Chapter 8. Employees today want fair treatment, excellent compensation and benefits, and assistance in balancing work and family obligations. Raytheon has developed a computer program called SilentRunner that can detect patterns of data activity that may reflect employee fraud, insider trading, espionage, or other unauthorized activity.[79] Critics, however, question whether the use of such software contributes to an environment of trust and commitment. Research has shown that committed and satisfied employees are more productive, serve customers better, and are less likely to leave their employers. These benefits are important to successful business performance, but organizations must be proactive in their human resources programs if they are to receive them.

Environmental Issues

In Chapter 9, we explore some of the significant environmental issues that business and society face today, including air pollution, global warming, water pollution and water quantity, land pollution, waste management, deforestation, urban sprawl, biodiversity, and genetically modified foods. For example, consumers around the world have expressed fears about the safety of food products that contain genetically modified crops. Although current research suggests that these products pose no threat to health or to the environment, the debate surrounding their use has grown increasingly bitter. Many companies are beginning to rethink their use of these crops in response to consumer concerns. Among these is J. R. Simplot Co., which has asked its farmers to stop growing genetically modified potatoes that may be used in the French fries it supplies to McDonald's.[80] Chapter 9 also considers the impact of government environmental policy and regulation and examines how some companies are going beyond these laws to address environmental issues and act in an environmentally responsible manner.

Technology Issues

Thanks to the Internet and other technological advances, we can communicate faster than ever before, find information about just about anything, and live longer, healthier lives. However, not all of the changes that occur as a result of new technologies are positive. For example, because shopping via the Internet does not require a signature to verify transactions, online credit-card fraud is now more than three and a half times greater than credit-card fraud through mail-order catalogs and almost nine times higher than for traditional storefront retailers. A major identity theft ring in New York was uncovered in late 2002, with the scam affecting thousands of people and losses totaling nearly $3 million. Members of the theft ring illegally obtained the credit records of consumers and then sold them to criminals for about $60 per record. The criminals used the credit records to obtain loans, drain bank accounts, and perform other fraudulent activities.[81] In Chapter 10, we examine the unique issues that arise as a result of enhanced technology in the workplace and business environment, including the effects of new technology on privacy, intellectual property, and health. The strategic direction for technology depends on government, as well as on business's ability to plan the implementation of new technology and to audit the influence of that technology on society.

Strategic Philanthropy

Chapter 11 examines strategic philanthropy, the synergistic use of organizational core competencies and resources to address key stakeholders' interests and to achieve both organizational and social benefits. Whereas traditional benevolent philanthropy involves donating a percentage of sales to social causes, a strategic approach aligns employees and organizational resources and expertise with the needs and concerns of stakeholders. Strategic philanthropy involves both financial and nonfinancial contributions (employee time, goods and services, technology and equipment, and facilities) to stakeholders, but it also benefits the company.

The Social Audit

Without reliable measurements of the achievement of social responsibility goals, a company has no concrete way to verify the importance of these objectives, link them to organizational performance, justify expenditures on them to stockholders and investors, or address any stakeholder concerns involving them. Chapter 12 describes an auditing procedure that can be used to measure and improve the social responsibility effort. This chapter takes you through a complete strategic perspective on social responsibility, including stakeholder relations, legal and ethical issues, and philanthropy. Such an audit is important for demonstrating commitment and ensuring the continuous improvement of the social responsibility effort.

We hope this framework provides you with a way of understanding the range of concepts, ideas, and practices that are involved in an effective social responsibility initiative. So that you can learn more about the practices of specific companies, a number of cases are provided at the end of the book. In addition, every chapter includes an opening vignette and other examples that shed more light on how social responsibility works in today's businesses. Every chapter also includes a real-life scenario and experiential exercise to help you apply concepts and examine your own decision-making process. As you will soon see, the concept of social responsibility is both exciting and controversial; it is in a constant state of development—just like all important business concepts and practices. A recent survey of thought leaders in the area of social responsibility found that a majority believes social responsibility is making steady progress into conventional business thinking. Much like the social responsibility continuum introduced in this chapter, the thought leaders described several stages of commitment to corporate social responsibility. These stages range from lite, where companies are concerned about responding to complaints, to deep, where companies are founded on a business model of improving social or environmental circumstances. Many companies fall somewhere in between, with a focus on complying with new standards and surviving in a climate increasingly focused on public acceptance.[82] We encourage you to draw on current news events like this and your own experiences to understand social responsibility and the challenges and opportunities it poses for your career and the business world.

Summary

The term *social responsibility* came into widespread use during the last several decades, but there remains some confusion over the term's exact meaning. This text defines social responsibility as the adoption by a business of a strategic focus for fulfilling the economic, legal, ethical, and philanthropic responsibilities expected of it by its stakeholders.

All types of businesses can implement social responsibility initiatives to further their relationships with their customers, their employees, and the community at large. Although the efforts of large corporations usually receive the most attention, the actions of small businesses may have a greater impact on local communities.

The definition of social responsibility involves the extent to which a firm embraces the social responsibility philosophy and follows through with the implementation of initiatives. Social responsibility must be fully valued and championed by top managers and given the same planning time, priority, and management attention as is given to any other company initiative.

Many people believe that businesses should accept and abide by four types of responsibility—economic, legal, ethical, and philanthropic. Companies have a responsibility to be economically viable so that they can provide a return on investment for their owners, create jobs for the community, and contribute goods and services to the economy. They are also expected to obey laws and regulations that specify what is responsible business conduct. Business ethics refers to the principles and standards that guide behavior in the world of business. Philanthropic activities promote human welfare or goodwill. These responsibilities can be viewed holistically, with all four being related and integrated into a comprehensive approach. Social responsibility can also be expressed as a continuum.

Because customers, employees, investors and shareholders, suppliers, governments, communities, and others have a stake in or claim on some aspect of a company's products, operations, markets, industry, and outcomes, they are known as stakeholders. Adopting a stakeholder orientation is part of the social responsibility philosophy.

The influence of business has led many people to conclude that corporations should benefit their employees, their customers, their business partners, and their community, as well as their shareholders. However, these responsibilities and expectations have evolved over time. After World War II, many large U.S. firms dominated the global economy. Their power was largely mirrored by the autonomy of their top managers. Because of the relative lack of global competition and stockholder input during the 1950s and 1960s, there were few formal governance procedures to restrain management's actions. The stability experienced by mid-century firms dissolved in the economic turmoil of the 1970s and 1980s, leading companies to focus more on their core competencies and reduce their product diversity. The 1980s and 1990s brought a new focus on efficiency and productivity, which fostered a wave of downsizing and restructuring. Concern for corporate responsibilities was renewed in the 1990s. In the 1990s and beyond, the balance between the global market economy and an interest in social justice and cohesion best characterizes the intent and need for social responsibility. Despite major advances in the 1990s, the sheer number of corporate scandals in 2001 and 2002 prompted a new era of social responsibility.

The increasing globalization of business has made social responsibility an international concern. In most developed countries, social responsibility involves economic, legal, ethical, and philanthropic responsibilities to a variety of stakeholders. Global social responsibility also involves responsibilities to a confluence of governments, businesses, trade associations, and other groups. Progressive global businesses recognize the "shared bottom line" that results from the partnership among businesses, communities, governments, and other stakeholders.

The importance of social responsibility initiatives in enhancing stakeholder relationships, improving performance, and creating other benefits has been debated from many different perspectives. Many business managers view such programs as costly activities that provide rewards only to society at the expense of the bottom line. Others hold that some costs of social responsibility cannot be recovered through improved performance. Although it is true that some aspects of social responsibility may not accrue directly to the bottom line, we believe that organizations benefit indirectly over the long run from these activities. Moreover, ample research and anecdotal evidence demonstrate that there are many rewards for those companies that implement such programs.

The process of social responsibility begins with the social responsibility philosophy, includes the four responsibilities, involves many types of stakeholders, and ultimately results in both short- and long-term performance benefits. Once the social responsibility philosophy is accepted, the four types of responsibility are defined and implemented through programs that incorporate stakeholder input and feedback.

Key Terms

social responsibility (p. 4)
stakeholders (p. 11)

Discussion Questions

1. Define social responsibility. How does this view of the role of business differ from your previous perceptions? How is it consistent with your attitudes and beliefs about business?

2. If a company is named to one of the "best in social responsibility" lists, what positive effects can it potentially reap? What are the possible costs or negative outcomes that may be associated with being named to one of these lists?

3. What historical trends have affected the social responsibilities of business? In light of current trends and issues, what changes in these responsibilities and expectations do you predict over the next five years?

4. How would you respond to the statement that this chapter presents only the positive side of the argu-

ment that social responsibility results in improved organizational performance?

5. On the basis of the social responsibility model presented in Figure 1.5, describe the philosophy, responsibilities, and stakeholders that make up a company's approach to social responsibility. What are the short- and long-term outcomes of this effort?

6. Consider the role that various business disciplines, including marketing, finance, accounting, and human resources, have in social responsibility. What specific views and philosophies do these different disciplines bring to the implementation of social responsibility?

Experiential Exercise

Evaluate *Fortune* magazine's annual list of the most admired companies found on the magazine's web site (www.fortune.com) These companies as a group have superior financial performance compared to other firms. Go to each company's web site and try to assess its management commitment to the welfare of stakeholders. If any of the companies have experienced legal or ethical misconduct, explain how this may affect specific stakeholders. Rank the companies on the basis of the information available and your opinion on their fulfillment of social responsibility.

⁇ What Would You Do?

Jamie Ramos looked out her window at the early morning sky and gazed at the small crowd below. The words and pictures on their posters were pretty tame this time, she thought. The last protest group used pictures of tarred lungs, corpses, and other graphic photos to show the effects of smoking on a person's internal organs. Their words were also hateful, so much so, that employees at the Unified Tobacco headquarters were scared to walk in and out of the main building. Those who normally took smoking breaks on the back patio decided to skip the break and eat something instead at the company-subsidized cafeteria. By midday, Unified hired extra security to escort employees in and out of the building and to ensure the protestors followed the state guideline of staying at least 15 feet from the company's entrance. The media picked up on the story—and the photos—and it caused quite a stir in the national press.

At least this protest group seemed fairly reasonable. Late yesterday, a state court provided a reduced judgment to the family of a lifelong smoker, now deceased. This meant that Unified was going to owe millions less than originally expected. The length and stress of the lawsuit had taken its toll, especially on top management, although all employees were certainly affected. After two years of being battered in the media, learning of a huge settlement, and then continuing on with the appeals process, emotions were wearing thin with the continued criticism.

Jamie wondered what this day would bring. As the manager of community relations, her job was to represent Unified in the community, manage the employee volunteer program, create a quarterly newsletter, serve as a liaison to the company's philanthropic foundation, develop solid relationships, and serve on various boards related to social welfare and community needs. The company's foundation donated nearly $1.5 million a year to charities and causes. Over one-quarter of its employees volunteered ten hours a month in their communities.

Jamie reported to a vice president and was pleased with the career progress she had made since graduating from college eight years earlier. Although some of her friends wondered out loud how she could work for a tobacco company, Jamie was steadfast in her belief that even a tobacco firm could contribute something meaningful to society. She had the chance to effect some of those contributions in her community relations role.

Jamie's phone rang and she took a call from her vice president. The VP indicated that, although the protestors seemed relatively calm this time, he was not comfortable with their presence. Several employees had taped signs in office windows, telling the protestors to "Go away." Other VPs had dropped by his office to discuss the protest and thought that the responsibility for handling these issues fell to his group. He went on to say that he needed Jamie's help, and the assistance of a few others, in formulating a plan to (1) deal with the protest today and (2) strengthen the strategy for communicating the company's message and goodwill in the future. Their meeting would begin in one hour, so Jamie had some time to sketch out her recommendations on both issues. What would you do?

2

Strategic Management of Stakeholder Relationships

CHAPTER OBJECTIVES

- To define stakeholders and understand their importance
- To distinguish between primary and secondary stakeholders
- To discuss the global nature of stakeholder relationships
- To consider the impact of reputation and crisis situations on social responsibility performance
- To examine the development of stakeholder relationships
- To explore how stakeholder relationships are integral to social responsibility

CHAPTER OUTLINE

Stakeholders Defined

Stakeholder Identification and Importance

Performance with Stakeholders

Development of Stakeholder Relationships

Link Between Stakeholder Relationships and Social Responsibility

A recent report by the Federal Trade Commission (FTC) on violence in the media concluded that entertainment companies routinely target children under seventeen years of age when they market movies, music, and video games intended for adults. Among other things, the report indicated that 80 percent of R-rated movies were targeted at children under seventeen and that 50 percent of the thirteen- to sixteen-year-olds taking part in the study were allowed into R-rated movies. The report recommended that entertainment companies should not target children in their advertising, that enforcement of ratings should be strengthened at the retail level, and that more information about ratings should be made available to parents.

In a hearing before the Senate Commerce Committee, Jack Valenti, CEO of the Motion Picture Association of America (MPAA), admitted that the movie industry had made mistakes and agreed that targeting "very young children" with advertising for R-rated films is inappropriate. However, Valenti also attempted to rebut a number of allegations made by the FTC report. For example, although the FTC blasted advertising of R-rated movies during certain television programs that it claimed are most popular among children under seventeen, Valenti countered that, with one exception, the percentage of children watching the programs named is actually "quite small." Since the eighteen-and-over audience for these shows ranged from 79 percent to 63 percent of the total audience, they could not be considered children's shows and therefore were appropriate places for advertising R-rated movies. The MPAA president also defended the industry's effect on children by citing FBI statistics that showed a decrease in crime over the previous seven years and a decline in juvenile crime by 28 percent over the previous five years. Valenti argued that creative works involve subjective judgments and that what one person sees as reasonable may be viewed as unacceptable by another. Finally, Valenti reminded the senators that a movie's R rating does not mean that it is "for adults only," but rather that children viewing it must be accompanied by a parent or adult guardian. The movie rating system arms parents with a cautionary warning to help them to make their decisions about which movies their children should view. Parents have access to ratings advice in magazines, in newspapers, on television, and through a number of web sites (such as filmratings.com and MPAA.org).

After defending the industry, Valenti pledged that it would nonetheless examine its advertising and research practices and work with the National Association of Theater Owners to enforce ratings more effectively in order to honor its obligations to parents. The industry association launched a twelve-point plan to limit the marketing of adult-oriented films to children. Among other things, the plan calls for movie studios to ask theaters not to show advertisements for R-rated films during G-rated movies and not to include children younger than seventeen in focus groups for R-rated movies without a parent present. A number of film studios signed onto the plan, including Walt Disney Company, Dreamworks SKG, Metro-Goldwyn-Mayer, Paramount, Sony, Twentieth Century Fox, Universal, and Warner Bros. Although executives from these firms pledged to stop marketing inappropriate movies to children, they affirmed that preventing children from viewing R-rated films is ultimately the parents' responsibility. Some film studios have chosen to go beyond the industry plan to address their responsibilities. News Corporation, for instance, says that its Twentieth Century Fox film studio asks theater operators not to show advertisements for R-rated films during G- or PG-rated movies.

So far, self-regulation seems to be working for the movie industry. Follow-up FTC reports indicate that changes have been made, including movie ratings' becoming more prominent in advertisements and better explanations of movie ratings. Some critics contend, however, that the industry is suffering from "ratings creep," where increasingly violent or offensive material is making its way into the lucrative PG13 category. The effect of entertainment choices on crime and violence is not a new concern, as Gallup polls from the 1950s and the 1990s show markedly similar results. While Americans believe the entertainment industry carries some blame for exposing children to violence and sex, they also believe that parents are to blame for not closely monitoring their children's entertainment choices.[1]

As this example illustrates, most organizations have a number of constituents who, in turn, have other stakeholders to consider. In this case, the motion picture industry and its member companies are facing the complex task of balancing government, parent, theater, and corporate concerns. These stakeholders are increasingly expressing opinions that have an effect on the industry's time, operations, member relationships, and products. Today, many organizations are learning to anticipate such issues and to address them in their plans and actions long before they become the subject of media stories or negative attention.

In this chapter, we examine the concept of stakeholders and explore why these groups are important for today's businesses. First, we define stakeholders and examine primary, secondary, and global stakeholders. Next, we consider the impact of corporate reputation and crisis situations on stakeholder relationships. Finally, we examine the development of stakeholder relationships and the link between stakeholder relationships and social responsibility.

Stakeholders Defined

In Chapter 1, we defined stakeholders as those people and groups to whom an organization is responsible—including customers, investors and shareholders, employees, suppliers, governments, communities, and many others—because they have a "stake" or claim in some aspect of a company's products, operations, markets, industry, or outcomes. These groups not only are influenced by businesses, but they also have the ability to affect businesses. The relationship between organizations and their stakeholders is therefore a two-way street. Table 2.1 reviews the evolving definition of stakeholders. The definition from 1963, for example, indicates that organizations are dependent on external influences for their existence. The definition written in 1988 focuses on the effects companies have on others. Our definitions of social responsibility and stakeholders take these views, and others, into account.

The historical assumption that the foremost objective of business is profit maximization led to the belief that business is accountable primarily to investors and others involved in the market and economic aspects of an organization. Because stockholders and other investors provide the financial foundation for business and expect something in return, managers and executives naturally strive to maintain positive relationships with them. Customers, who provide a revenue stream, are also viewed as primary constituents by all types of organizations. Employees, too, are fundamental to the operations of any firm, although stories of downsizing, long work hours, and incompetent management raise questions about some organizations' treatment of employees.[2] Finally, suppliers and other business partners have a clear role in any business enterprise, as they provide goods and services (e.g., raw materials, component parts, distribution systems, advertising campaigns, and legal advice) that are necessary for an organization to function effectively and efficiently. Thus, investors, customers, employees, and suppliers are directly tied to a company's market prospects and success. In the late 1940s, the president of Johnson & Johnson developed a list of the company's "strictly business" stakeholders, which included customers, employees, managers, and shareholders. A few years later, Robert Wood, who captained Sears, Roebuck & Co. after World War II, discussed profit as a by-product of

TABLE 2.1	Historical Perspectives on Stakeholders

CHARACTERIZATION OF STAKEHOLDERS	
1963	"Those groups without whose support the organization would cease to exist"
1971	"Driven by their own interests and goals are participants in a firm, and thus depending on it and whom for its sake the firm is depending"
1983	"Can affect the achievement of an organization's objectives or who is affected by the achievement of an organization's objectives"
1988	"Benefit from or are harmed by, and whose rights are violated or respected by, corporate actions"
1991	"Have an interest in the actions of an organization and . . . the ability to influence it"
1994	"Interact with and give meaning and definition to the corporation"
1995	"Have, or claim, ownership, rights, or interests in a corporation and its activities"

Source: Ronald K. Mitchell, Bradley R. Agle, and Donna J. Wood, "Toward a Theory of Stakeholder Identification and Salience: Defining the Principle of Who and What Really Counts," *Academy of Management Review* 22 (October 1997): 853–886.

satisfying the needs and expectations of various parties, including customers, employees, investors, and the community.[3]

In the latter half of the twentieth century, perceptions of business accountability evolved toward an expanded model of the role and responsibilities of business in society. The expansion included questions about the normative role of business: "What is the appropriate role for business to play in society?" and "Should profit be the sole objective of business?"[4] Theodore Levitt, a renowned business professor, once wrote that although profits are required for business just like eating is required for living, profit is not the purpose of business any more than eating is the purpose of life.[5] Norman Bowie, a well-published philosopher, extended Levitt's sentiment by noting that a sole focus on profit can create an unfavorable paradox that causes a firm to fail to achieve its objective. Bowie contends that when a business also cares about the well-being of other constituencies, it earns trust and cooperation that ultimately reduce costs and increase productivity.[6] These perspectives take into account both market and nonmarket constituencies that may interact with a business and have some effect on the firm's policies and strategy.[7] Market constituencies are those that are directly involved and affected by the business purpose, including investors, employees, customers, and other business partners. Nonmarket groups include the general community, media, government, special-interest groups, and others that are not always directly tied to issues of profitability and performance.

input-output model
the philosophy that focuses on how investors, employees, and suppliers provide inputs for a company to transform into outputs that benefit customers; assumes a relatively mechanistic, simplistic, and nonstakeholder view of business

Two contrasting models illustrate the relationship between a business and its various stakeholders, as shown in Figures 2.1 and 2.2.[8] The **input-output model,** depicted in Figure 2.1, is based on the traditional profit-maximization approach to business, in which investors, employees, and suppliers provide inputs for a company to transform into outputs that benefit customers. In this model, the customer receives most of the value of the input-output process because investors, suppliers, and employees are compensated at a level that is normal or market competitive. The arrows in Figure 2.1 indicate a one-way relationship between the firm and these four

FIGURE 2.1 Input–Output Model

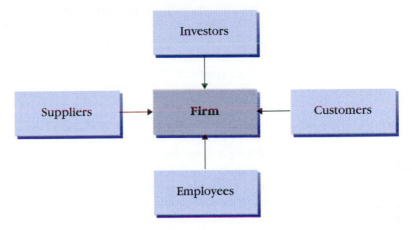

Source: Thomas Donaldson and Lee E. Preston, "The Stakeholder Theory of the Corporation: Concepts, Evidence and Implications," *Academy of Management Review* 29 (January 1995): 65–91. Republished with permission of the Academy of Management. Permission conveyed through Copyright Clearance Center.

constituents. It is important to note that in our definition of social responsibility, these groups are not really considered true stakeholders by the organization because there is no two-way directionality in the model.

At first glance, the input-output model may seem consistent with marketing strategies and advertising slogans that proclaim the "customer is always right." In

FIGURE 2.2 The Stakeholder Model

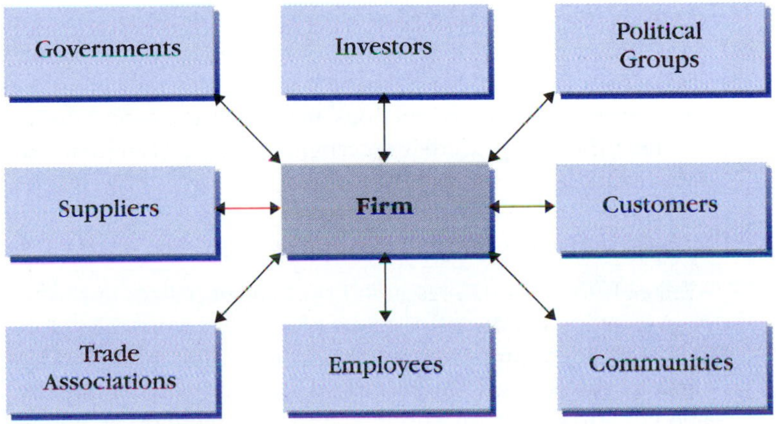

Source: Thomas Donaldson and Lee E. Preston, "The Stakeholder Theory of the Corporation: Concepts, Evidence and Implications," *Academy of Management Review* 29 (January 1995): 65–91. Republished with permission of the Academy of Management. Permission conveyed through Copyright Clearance Center.

reality, however, companies that focus on customer satisfaction are usually equally attuned to the integral role of employees, investors, and suppliers in the process of attracting and retaining customers. Indeed, consultant Frederick F. Reichheld argues in his book, *The Loyalty Effect*, that employee commitment and importance to an organization are necessary precursors to customer satisfaction. Thus, a firm must invest in employee training, retention, compensation, and other relationship factors before it can properly satisfy its customers. At Sears, the national retailer, employee satisfaction has been shown to account for 60 to 80 percent of customer satisfaction.[9] Because the input-output model does not account for two-way relationships between the firm and its investors, suppliers, and employees, it assumes a relatively mechanistic, simplistic, and nonstakeholder view of business.

Figure 2.2 represents a more current conceptualization of business that is better aligned with our definition of social responsibility. In the **stakeholder model,** there are two-way relationships between the firm and a host of stakeholders. In addition to the fundamental inputs of investors, employees, and suppliers, this approach recognizes other stakeholders and explicitly acknowledges the two-way dialog and effects that exist between a firm's internal and external environment. As our definition of social responsibility suggests, it is vital that all businesses consider a range of stakeholder relationships. Although the model seems to give relatively equal weight to all stakeholders, resource and time constraints mean that some type of hierarchy or prioritization is warranted. In the next section, we discuss the process of identifying the importance and salience of stakeholders to an organization.

> **stakeholder model**
> the model that assumes a two-way relationship between the firm and a host of stakeholders; acknowledges the two-way dialog and effects that exist between a firm's internal and external environment

Stakeholder Identification and Importance

The input-output and stakeholder models provide generic representations of business processes and relationships. However, in order to achieve strategic social responsibility, it is essential to understand specific stakeholders and their unique interests, claims, and relationships with an organization. In this section, we classify stakeholders as either primary or secondary, on the basis of their significance to a particular organization. We also consider the complexity of global stakeholders, because more and more firms have interactions and interests beyond domestic borders. Finally, we examine the attributes that determine the type of influence stakeholders can wield in their relationships with organizations.

Primary and Secondary Stakeholders

Walker Information, a research firm that specializes in stakeholder measurement and management, conducted a survey of 1,027 executives in global corporations to ascertain stakeholder importance to their firms. Survey respondents evaluated the importance of customers, financial analysts, government, community, shareholders, suppliers, and employees. Not surprisingly, customers, employees, and shareholders ranked highest (see Figure 2.3). Because such groups are fundamental to a company's operations and survival, they are considered primary stakeholders. Without these groups, a company would not be able to continue its fundamental operations. There is a high degree

| FIGURE 2.3 | Ranking of Stakeholder Importance |

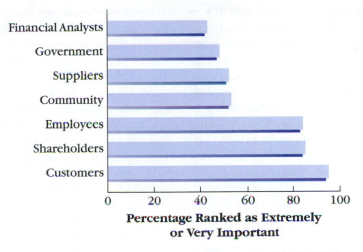

Source: Walker Information, *Stakeholder Management Around the World* (Indianapolis, IN: Walker Information Global Network, 1999). Reprinted by permission of Walker Information.

of interdependence among these groups, and any dissatisfaction or other serious disruption may threaten the very existence of the firm. Thus, shareholders and investors, employees, customers, and suppliers, as well as public stakeholders, such as government and the community, are **primary stakeholders.**[10] Balancing the needs and perspectives of primary stakeholders is a strategic imperative, as one group's dissatisfaction or withdrawal from the relationship can cause significant ramifications throughout the entire business. In the late 1990s, 185,000 union workers walked off their jobs at United Parcel Service (UPS) and staged the biggest labor strike of the decade. The strike lasted eighteen days, cost UPS nearly $775 million in lost revenue, created a wave of media reports, and caused a crisis of customer confidence in UPS.[11]

Secondary stakeholders, although they influence and/or are affected by the company, are neither engaged in economic exchanges with the firm nor fundamental to its daily survival. Media and special-interest groups are usually considered secondary stakeholders. These groups, however, can have a dramatic influence on a firm.[12] A series of class-action suits filed on behalf of family members of apartheid victims accuses more than thirty multinational firms of collaborating with the apartheid government of South Africa. For example, British Petroleum (BP) is charged with supplying oil and gas to the government while Barclay's Bank is alleged to have paid white employees more than black employees. The suit, which calls for a collective liability of up to $100 billion, may not significantly harm either company's balance sheet but could cast a shadow on the reputation and stock price of both.[13] In differentiating between primary and secondary stakeholders, it is important for managers to understand that although primary groups may present more day-to-day concerns, secondary groups cannot be ignored or consistently given less consideration in the social responsibility process.

primary stakeholders fundamental to a company's operations and survival and include shareholders and investors, employees, customers, suppliers, and public stakeholders, such as government and the community

secondary stakeholders influence and/or are affected by the company, but are neither engaged in transactions with the firm nor essential for its survival

Stakeholders Around the World

Stakeholder management has become a worldwide phenomenon on two levels. First, progressive companies in most economically developed nations have embraced the stakeholder model. Second, as more firms conduct business overseas, they encounter the complexity of stakeholder issues and relationships in tandem with other business operations and decisions. This section briefly explores both concerns.

In the Walker Information survey, 63 percent of the executives from around the world recognized the term *stakeholder* as it relates to business organizations (see Figure 2.4). Executives in South Africa, Canada, and the United States had the highest recognition levels, with Europe, Asia, the Middle East, and Latin America following. The study concluded that South Africa is the most "stakeholder savvy," as company executives there are more aware of the term, take stakeholders more into account for business planning, and link stakeholder measures and issues more to other business outcomes.[14]Although general awareness of stakeholders appears to be relatively high around the world, the importance of stakeholders varies from country to country. In the United States, Canada, and South Africa, employee and customer interests are considered to be nearly equal in importance. Government stakeholders receive greater attention in the Middle East and Latin America than in other parts of the world. In Japan, cultural and legal traditions mean that companies are tightly connected to a number of interrelated stakeholders, including customers, financial institutions, and suppliers. The law in Great Britain obliges British firms to include the interests of employees in strategic plans and decision making. Finally, publicly traded firms in Germany must have employees on second-tier boards of directors.[15]

International business transactions and investments have always entailed more risk and complexity than domestic activities. Although global economic conditions create incentives for market entry and expansion strategies, the environmental and stake-

| FIGURE 2.4 | Stakeholder Recognition Around the World |

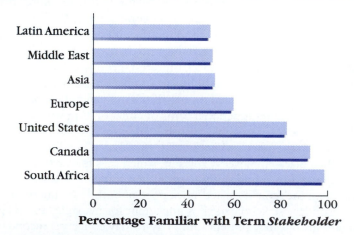

Percentage Familiar with Term *Stakeholder*

Source: Walker Information, *Stakeholder Management Around the World* (Indianapolis, IN: Walker Information Global Network, 1999). Reprinted by permission of Walker Information.

holder factors affecting these strategies must be fully considered. For example, a business expanding into another country will encounter unfamiliar laws, different consumer values, and other issues that create confusion and require adjustments in business philosophy and practice. Although businesses are cognizant of the economic opportunities available through international efforts, fewer firms may have invested resources to fully integrate stakeholder concerns into the business planning process. Other companies may become mired in the age-old dilemma of deciding between local values and customs and those of their country of origin. Companies with stakeholders in developing countries will have to consider unique cultural, political, and economic conditions and may have to make normative evaluations that do not occur in developed nations.[16]

Although decision makers bring experience and knowledge to the development and implementation of an international business strategy, there are always gaps in information that can lead to lapses in judgment, unintended consequences, and strategic errors. The decision to enter and remain in a region of the world can promote environmental uncertainty and instability, naturally leading managers to seek guidance on analysis and planning activities. This expertise may derive from sources either inside or outside the organization, such as industry and country reports, trade show conversations, government repositories, company history, and primary research studies.[17] Thus, understanding the attributes of various global stakeholders may require a more thorough and formal information search than what is conducted with domestic stakeholders.

Despite this complexity, global stakeholders may be granted less attention because of the geographic and often cultural distance between them and a company. However, managers must ensure that they are given due consideration. As some companies have learned, global constituents can have a dramatic influence on business. Monsanto, a manufacturer of pharmaceutical and agricultural products, experienced a flood of criticism in Europe after a British researcher claimed laboratory rats' growth was stunted after they ate the company's genetically modified potatoes. Although the research was later deemed misleading, it brought widespread attention to Monsanto's bioengineering research and genetically modified crops. The protests eventually crossed the Atlantic, where many stakeholders, including the U.S. federal government, called for tighter regulations on genetically altered crops and foods. At one point in the fray, a Wall Street analyst valued Monsanto's $5-billion-a-year agricultural business unit at less than zero dollars.[18]

Perhaps the most compelling case for building relationships with nondomestic stakeholders occurred in Bhopal, India. In 1984, a gas leak at a pesticide plant owned by Union Carbide killed 3,800 people and injured many more. The Bhopal leak is still considered one of the worst industrial tragedies in global history. Officials at Union Carbide may have thought the Bhopal accident was finally behind them when the company paid the Indian government $470 million to settle a civil lawsuit in 1989. In late 1999, however, victims of the contamination filed a class-action suit against Union Carbide and Warren Anderson, who was chairman of the board when the accident occurred. The suit, which claimed "depraved indifference to human life," was filed just as the company was finalizing merger plans with Dow Chemical. Anderson, who has retired to Florida, is not well known in the United States but still garners negative attention and notoriety in India. Every year since the disaster his

Legal and Regulatory Challenges

Satisfying Regulatory Stakeholders Around the World

Companies that operate in more than one country find that a secondary stakeholder, government, can have many effects on primary stakeholders and internal decision making. The complexity of meeting legal and regulatory statutes is very high and requires the expertise of attorneys and other knowledgeable consultants. For firms whose products or transactions cross borders, the process of adhering to differing legal and regulatory concerns can also be quite confusing. One case in point is the airline industry, where planes and passengers pass from one jurisdiction to another and thus pass from one set of regulations to another. In some cases, these rules are markedly different.

Several countries, including Australia, Panama, India, Jamaica, and New Zealand, require foreign airlines to spray their airplanes with insecticides to protect plants, animals, and people from various pests that could be carried on flights arriving from other countries. The process is called disinsection. While Australia, Jamaica, and New Zealand require planes to be sprayed after the passengers disembark, some countries, including India and Madagascar,

require planes to be sprayed while passengers are still on board.

There are two different methods of spraying the insecticides. Aerosol cans are used when passengers are on board or a blanketing technique is used when the plane is empty. With the first technique, airline personnel walk up and down the aisles spraying the pesticide. With the second technique, workers come on board the plane wearing protective gear and blanket the empty aircraft cabin with pesticides that leave a residue for nearly two months. As a result of consumer and airline employee concern, the U.S. Environmental Protection Agency (EPA) developed a campaign to stop the spraying while passengers were on board. Some countries changed their policy but still implement the blanketing technique.

The pesticides used contain permethrin and phenothrin, which are synthetic versions of a natural insecticide commonly found in chrysanthemums. The EPA classifies permethrin as a "moderately to practically nontoxic pesticide" that can cause eye or skin irritation. The EPA, however, no longer allows the use of these pesticides on aircraft in the United States. Thus, U.S.-based airlines that fly in and out of countries with quarantine and pesticide regulations must have the planes sprayed in the country

likeness has been burned in effigy, and graffiti in the city government building still calls for his execution. To some observers, this long-standing reaction seems extreme because Anderson flew to Bhopal immediately after the accident to take moral responsibility for it. At the time, this was an unusual step for such a high-ranking officer to take. However, a recent study found that groundwater surrounding the factory site is still contaminated. Two decades after the leak, environmental and human rights groups continue to call for action against Union Carbide and Anderson, including proper restitution to victims and their families.[19]

As the Bhopal example illustrates, a successful stakeholder is not only meaningful to the focal organization, but its claims must also pass scrutiny by the larger community, society, or relevant group. However, there may be stakeholders with the desire and means to influence a firm who have claims that are not legitimate or who use tactics that are not reasonable. For example, animal rights activists have thrown blood and paint on customers walking into department stores that sell furs. Although this type of activism clearly exerts power, its unreasonable and harmful tactics lessen

with the requirement. In satisfying its governmental stakeholders, however, the airlines have created issues with its employees and customers.

Both passengers and airline crew have felt the effects of the insecticides. Sharon Dorazio is one passenger who, on a United Airlines flight to the United States from Sydney, Australia, experienced stomach pain and burning eyes. Her two grandsons also suffered burning skin, itchy eyes, and loss of appetite. On the same flight, several other passengers reported feeling ill. Crew on the flight surmised that residue from the pesticides was causing the symptoms, which ranged from dizziness to rashes to breathing problems. Along with her husband, Ms. Dorazio filed a lawsuit against United Airlines, one of many lawsuits filed recently over the use of pesticides on airplanes. The Dorazios claim that United was not only evasive but also provided misinformation on the possible effects of the spraying.

In an article published in *USA Today,* two flight attendants reported they are no longer able to work because of their exposure to the pesticides. After being a flight attendant for six years, Diana Brown-Dodson is using an oxygen tank most of the day and suffering from loss of short-term memory and concentration. Six doctors have diagnosed the problem as being caused by exposure to pesticides.

Ms. Brown-Dodson estimates that she was exposed to pesticides approximately 150 times while working as a flight attendant. The Air Line Pilots Association is considering a campaign against using these pesticides on the planes. The California Department of Health is also examining approximately 100 cases of illnesses reportedly caused by pesticides on United flights. The U.S. State Department has asked the government of India to stop spraying while passengers are on board unless it is absolutely necessary.

While many groups are protesting the use of pesticides, government officials in countries requiring the insecticides on foreign planes stand by the practice. Officials maintain that the pesticides are not harmful and point out that the World Health Organization also considers the pesticides safe. One Australian spokesperson noted, "You've got more safety and health problems walking out into your garden than with what is sprayed on planes."

Sources:
"Aircraft Pesticide Spraying," http://www.kefir.net/spray/#AR, accessed December 21, 2002; "Class Action Over Plane Insect Spray," (Sydney) *Daily Telegraph,* August 24, 2001, p. 22; Diane Fairechild, *Jet Smarter: An Air Traveler's Rx,* (Hawaii: Flyana Rhyme Incorporated, 1999); "Pesticide Policy for International Flights Defended," (Wellington) *The Dominion,* May 17, 2001, p. 13; Chris Woodyard, "Fliers Fume Over Planes Treated with Pesticides," *USA Today,* September 10, 2001, pp. A11, A13.

the stores' willingness to create a dialog on the issues. The stakeholder process is negated because the stakeholder's attributes and tactics are not amenable to an effective and communicative relationship.

Stakeholder Attributes[20]

Traditionally, companies have had an easier time understanding the issues stakeholders raise than their attributes and the tactics they use to affect organizational decision making. It is therefore necessary to understand both the content (specific issues) and process (actions, tactics) of each stakeholder relationship. In the preceding example, the animal rights activists used an unreasonable process to communicate the content of their beliefs. Although they are controversial, animal rights issues do have solid support from a number of citizens. One mechanism for understanding stakeholders and their potential salience to a firm involves assessing three stakeholder attributes—power, legitimacy, and urgency. This assessment provides one analytical tool to help managers uncover the motivations and needs of stakeholders and how they relate to the company and its interests. In addition, stakeholder actions may also sensitize the firm to issues and viewpoints not previously considered.[21]

Power, legitimacy, and urgency are not constant, meaning stakeholder attributes can change over time and context. For example, there was a very strong "Buy American" sentiment in the United States in the 1980s, a time when Japanese manufacturers were making steady market share gains. Today, there is less consumer activism or retailer strategy on activism toward this nationalistic buying criterion. Thus, although these stakeholders may still have a legitimate claim for buying from U.S. firms, they are neither using their power nor creating a sense of urgency regarding this issue today. It seems that nationalism, as it relates to retail purchasing, is no longer a key buying criteria. The U.S. economy has been strong, so products from other countries were not seen as threatening. In polls post–September 11, 30 percent of Americans said they preferred to buy American-made goods while over 40 percent of Americans said they pay little attention to a good's origin.[22]

power
the extent to which a stakeholder can gain access to coercive, utilitarian, or symbolic means to impose or communicate its views to the organization; power may be coercive, utilitarian, or symbolic

Power A stakeholder has power to the extent that it can gain access to coercive, utilitarian, or symbolic means to impose or communicate its views to an organization.[23] *Coercive power* involves the use of physical force, violence, or some type of restraint. *Utilitarian power* involves financial or material control, such as boycotts that affect a company's bottom line. Finally, *symbolic power* relies on the use of symbols that connote social acceptance, prestige, or some other attribute. Symbolism contained in letter-writing campaigns, advertising messages, and web sites can be used to generate awareness and enthusiasm for more responsible business actions. In fact, the Internet has conferred tremendous power on stakeholder groups in recent years. A number of "hate sites" have been placed on the Internet by disgruntled stakeholders, especially customers and former employees, to share concerns about certain corporate behaviors. Richard B. Freeman, a Harvard labor economist, says, "With the Internet, information flows instantly, so even if we don't have more people concerned about companies, those who are can do more about it."[24] Symbolic power is the least threatening of the three types.

Utilitarian measures, including boycotts and lawsuits, are also fairly prevalent, although they often come about after symbolic strategies fail to yield the desired response. For example, the U.S. government, an important stakeholder for most firms, recently banned the importation of goods made by children under the age of fifteen through indentured or forced labor.[25] This action came about after the media and activist groups exposed widespread abuses in the apparel industry. This law carries financial—utilitarian—repercussions for firms that purchase products manufactured under unacceptable labor conditions.

Finally, some stakeholders use coercive power to communicate their message. During a rally to protest McDonald's as a symbol of global capitalism, worker exploitation, and environmental insensitivity, a handful of protesters stormed a McDonald's restaurant in London, eventually tearing down the hamburger chain's famous "golden arches." A company spokesperson said that although the company abhors violence and destruction, it planned to reopen the damaged restaurant and start a dialog with activists to counter false allegations and accusations. The spokesperson emphasized the local, not global, nature of McDonald's in the United Kingdom, where the company employs 70,000 people and does business with more than 6,000 suppliers.[26]

legitimacy
the perception or belief that a stakeholder's actions are proper, desirable, or appropriate within a given context

Legitimacy The second stakeholder attribute is legitimacy, which is the perception or belief that a stakeholder's actions are proper, desirable, or appropriate within a given context.[27] This definition suggests that stakeholder actions are considered legitimate when claims are judged to be reasonable by other stakeholders and by society in general. Legitimacy is gained through the stakeholder's ability and willingness to explore the issue from a variety of perspectives and then to communicate in an effective and respectful manner on the desire for change. Thus, extremist views are less likely to be considered legitimate because these groups often use covert and inflammatory measures that overshadow the issues and create animosity. For example, extreme groups have destroyed property, threatened customers, and committed other acts of violence that ultimately discredit their legitimacy.[28] McDonald's remained open to stakeholder dialog after the London restaurant was destroyed, although other companies might have shunned further communication with the protesters, citing their irrational and dangerous behavior. Although an issue may be legitimate, such as environmental sensitivity, it is difficult for the claim to be evaluated independently of the way the stakeholder group communicates on it.

urgency
the time sensitivity and the importance of the claim to the stakeholder

Urgency Stakeholders exercise greater pressures on managers and organizations when they stress the urgency of their claims. Urgency is based on two characteristics: time sensitivity and the importance of the claim to the stakeholder. Time sensitivity usually heightens the stakeholder's effort and may compress an organization's ability to research and react to a claim. For example, protesters in Thailand formed a human chain around a hotel hosting the Asian Development Bank's annual meeting. The protest was aimed at increasing the bank's efforts to revitalize the regional economy and create more economic equity for the working poor. The protest was timed to occur during the bank's annual meeting, when officials would be developing new policies. Although bank officials did not formally meet with the protesters, the Asian Development Bank committed monies and projects to reduce poverty and other socioeconomic ills.[29]

In another example, labor and human rights are widely recognized as critical issues because they are fundamental to the well-being of people around the world. These rights have become a focal point for college student associations that have relentlessly criticized Nike, the world's leading shoe company, for its failure to improve the working conditions of employees of suppliers and in not making information available to interested stakeholders. Student interest in these issues prompted several universities, including the University of Michigan, the University of Oregon, and Brown University, to join the Worker's Rights Consortium (WRC), an anti-sweatshop organization. The consortium has been critical of the corporate-sponsored Fair Labor Association's (FLA's) efforts on behalf of worker rights. Nike, a member of the FLA, decided to pull millions of dollars of contributions and contracts from these schools because of their affiliation with WRC. Nike's director of college sports marketing indicated that Nike prefers university partners with similar goals and aspirations.[30]

In this case, students, who represent a major stakeholder of universities, were able to make their claims known and actionable by at least three universities. Because of the students' pressure, one of Nike's key stakeholders and customers, the universities, decided to support workers' rights by joining a powerful interest group, the WRC. Because the WRC has voiced criticism of Nike and other manufacturers, Nike felt the association between the interest group and its university customers was not aligned with its own interests and objectives.[31] Overall, stakeholders are considered more important to an organization when their issues are legitimate, their claims are urgent, and they can make use of their power on the organization. These attributes assist the firm and employees in determining the relative importance of specific stakeholders and making resource allocations for developing and managing the stakeholder relationship.

Performance with Stakeholders

Managing stakeholder relationships effectively requires careful attention to a firm's reputation and the effective handling of crisis situations. Motorola, a large telecommunications company, was not aware that one of its European distributors sold Motorola semiconductor chips to a manufacturer of landmine component parts. When Motorola, the recipient of numerous social responsibility accolades, learned of the situation, it investigated, stopped selling to the distributor, and created better oversight for its distribution channels. In the process, Motorola was mindful of potential effects on its reputation with stakeholders. In a similar turn, De Beers, the world's largest diamond producer, announced it would stop buying diamonds from Angola, after a group of European organizations launched a campaign to alert the public to the fact that an Angolan rebel group, Unita, funded wars and casualties through diamond sales.[32]

Reputation Management

As our model of social responsibility suggests, there are short- and long-term outcomes associated with positive stakeholder relationships. One of the most significant of these is a positive reputation. Because a company's reputation has the power to attract or repel stakeholders, it can be either an asset or a liability in developing and implementing strategic plans and social responsibility initiatives.[33] Reputations take a long time to build or change, and it is far more important to monitor reputation than many companies believe. Whereas a strong reputation may take years to build, it can be destroyed seemingly overnight if a company does not handle crisis situations to the satisfaction of the various stakeholders involved. For example, Bridgestone/Firestone, Inc., a subsidiary of Japan's Bridgestone Corporation, saw its corporate reputation nosedive as a result of negative publicity surrounding the safety of some of its most popular tires. After the U.S. National Highway Traffic Safety Administration received more than 750 complaints and reports of 62 deaths linked to Firestone ATX and Wilderness AT tires, several retailers, including Sears, stopped selling the firm's tires. Bridgestone/Firestone recalled and offered to replace 6.5 million tires, but questions about the firm's handling of the recall—for example, not having enough replacement tires on hand to satisfy customers concerned about their safety—further eroded its reputation with consumers. By the end of 2002, the company's performance was rebounding from the crisis.[34] But once it is sullied, a reputation can take years to rebuild. Exxon still faces ill will and resentment over its handling of the *Exxon Valdez* oil spill in the late 1980s.[35]

Reputation management is the process of building and sustaining a company's good name and generating positive feedback from stakeholders. A company's reputation is affected by every contact with a stakeholder.[36] Various trends may affect how companies manage their reputations. These trends include market factors, such as increased consumer knowledge and community access to information, and workplace factors, including technological advances, closer vendor relationships, and more inquisitive employees. These factors make companies more cautious about their actions because increased scrutiny in this area requires more attention from management. A company needs to understand these factors and how to properly address them in order to achieve a strong reputation. These factors have also helped companies recognize a link between reputation and competitive advantage. If these trends are dealt with wisely and internal and external communication strategies are used effectively, a firm can position itself positively in stakeholders' minds, and thus create a competitive advantage. Intangible factors related to reputation can account for as much as 50 percent of a firm's market valuation.[37]

The importance of corporate reputation has created a need for accurate reputation measures. As indicated in Table 2.2, business publications, research firms, consultants, and public relations agencies have established a foothold in the new field of reputation management through research and lists of "the most reputable" firms. However, some questions have arisen as to who can best determine corporate

TABLE 2.2	Reputation Measures		
REPUTATION LIST	**CONDUCTED BY**	**GROUPS SURVEYED**	**PRIMARY PURPOSE**
100 Best Companies to Work for in America	Robert Lebering & Milton Moskowitz and Hewitt Associates	*Fortune* companies' employees and top managers	Publication
America's Most Admired Companies	*Fortune* magazine and Clark Martire & Bartolomeo	Company officers, directors, and analysts of *Fortune* 500 companies	Publication
Corporate Branding Index	Corporate Branding LLC	Vice president–level executives and above in the top 20 percent of U.S. businesses	Customized for clients
Corporate Reputation Index	Delahaye Medialink	Print and broadcast media	Sold as syndicated research
Maximizing Corporate Reputation	Burston-Marsteller	CEOs, executives, board members, financial community, government officials, business media, and consumers	Customized for clients
Reputation Quotient	Reputation Institute and Harris Interactive	General public	Customized for clients
World's Most-Respected Companies	Pricewaterhouse Coopers	CEOs from 75 countries	Publication

Sources: Christy Eidson and Melissa Master, "Who Makes the Call?" *Across the Board* 27 (March 2000): 16; Klein, "Measure What Matters," *Communication World* 16 (October/November 1999): 32; Prema Nakra, "Corporate Reputation Management: 'CRM' with a Strategic Twist," *Public Relations Quarterly* 45 (Summer 2000): 35.

FIGURE 2.5 Reputation Management Process

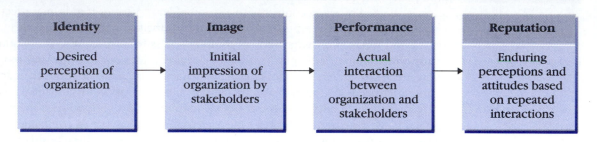

reputation. For example, some measures survey only chief executives, whereas others also elicit perceptions from the general public. Although executives may be biased toward a firm's financial performance, the general public may lack experience or data on which to evaluate a company's reputation. Regardless of how it is measured, reputation is the result of a process involving an organization and various constituents.[38]

The process of reputation management involves four components that work together: organizational identity, image, performance, and ultimately, reputation (see Figure 2.5).[39] Organizational identity refers to how an organization wants to be viewed by its stakeholders, whereas organizational image is how stakeholders interpret the various aspects of a company in order to form an overall impression of it. Organizational performance involves the actual interaction between the company and its stakeholders. The interaction of organizational image and performance results in organizational reputation, the collective view of all stakeholders after their image of the firm is shaped through interactions with the company.

In order to build and manage a good reputation, these four areas must be aligned. Companies must manage identity and culture by pinpointing those standards and responsibilities that will allow them to achieve their objectives, work with stakeholders effectively, and continuously monitor and change for effectiveness.[40] Ford Motor Company, for example, has embraced quality as a core value and highlighted this value in advertising to foster an identity associated with quality. Companies must also manage their image by communicating their identity to all stakeholders. This will help align the company's identity with stakeholders' images of the company and thus make it easier to live up to stakeholders' expectations. Because Ford was identified with the slogan "Quality is job #1," consumers and other stakeholders had a positive image of Ford and its automobiles. Performance must be managed by ensuring that organizational operations are consistent with the image that the company has built up in stakeholders' minds. At Ford, this effort involved consumers' actual use and evaluation of cars, their quality, and other performance indicators. Finally, stakeholders will reassess their views of the company on the basis of how the company has actually performed. This results in the enduring and collective attitudes that stakeholders have toward the company. For these reasons, Ford took dramatic steps to protect its reputation (and shield itself from liability lawsuits) after Bridgestone/Firestone recalled millions of truck tires due to concerns about their safety. Because these tires were installed as factory equipment on many Ford trucks and sport utility vehicles, including the best-selling Explorer, Ford executives feared growing publicity surrounding the crisis would affect the firm's sales and reputation for quality and safety. Ford began running advertisements reassuring customers that it would replace recalled tires on Ford vehicles, even suspending production at several plants in order to free up 70,000 replacement tires. The company also pressured Bridgestone/Firestone to resolve the crisis as quickly as possible, although the tire manufacturer suggested that the Explorer design was part of the problem.[41] Thus, all these elements must be continually implemented in order to ensure that the company's reputation is being maximized through community relations. However, most firms will, at one time or another, experience crisis situations that threaten or harm this reputation. How a company reacts, responds, and learns from the situation is indicative of its commitment and implementation of social responsibility.

Crisis Management[42]

Organizational crises are far-reaching events that can have dramatic effects on both the organization and its stakeholders. Along with the industrialization of society, companies and their products have become ever more complex and therefore more susceptible to crisis. As a result, disasters—like the gas leak in Bhopal—and crisis situations—like Firestone's tire safety issue and product contamination issues at Johnson & Johnson and Coca-Cola—are increasingly common events from which few organizations are exempt. For example, the size and geographic diversity of IBM's workforce and operations required the firm to develop a worldwide network of crisis management personnel. This group is trained to implement the company's crisis management team model in the event of natural disaster, product recall, major lawsuit, violence, or other misfortune. IBM put its plan into motion on September 11, 2001, and was able to restore core services within three days, lend its extra office space to house displaced customers and noncustomers, assist employees and communities affected by the tragedy, and use its technology and call centers to aid government agencies.[43]

Of course, many crises are not purposeful—meaning there was no intent to cause damage. On January 13, 1993, the Washington State Health Department was alerted that doctors at Children's Hospital in Seattle were treating an unusually high number of children with *E. coli* 0157:H7 infections. *E. coli* is a type of bacteria found in ground beef that can be life threatening to children and the elderly if it is not destroyed through sufficient cooking. Newspapers and television media soon carried shocking headlines that children were becoming ill after eating hamburgers at Jack in the Box. The *New York Times* described the crisis as Jack in the Box's worst nightmare. Within a month, three children in the Seattle area died of complications associated with *E. coli* poisoning. Overall, 400 people were infected in Washington, Idaho, and Nevada. In an early press release, the company focused stakeholder attention on the possibility that some of the children who became ill at Jack in the Box restaurants may have unwittingly spread the bacteria through physical contact with other children, thereby broadening the effects of the crisis. The company also noted that hundreds of cases of *E. coli* poisoning occur every year. Although Jack in the Box eventually recovered from the crisis, it suffered severe financial losses and a tarnished corporate image.[44]

It is critical for companies to manage crises effectively because research suggests that these events are a leading cause of organizational mortality. What follows are

crisis management
the process of handling a high-impact event characterized by ambiguity and the need for swift action

some key issues to consider in **crisis management,** the process of handling a high-impact event characterized by ambiguity and the need for swift action. In most cases, the crisis situation will not be handled in a completely effective or ineffective manner. Thus, a crisis usually leads to both success and failure outcomes for a business and its stakeholders and provides information for making improvements to future crisis management and social responsibility efforts.[45] Chapter 12 discusses the importance of social auditing in detecting and preventing crisis situations.

Organizational crises are characterized by a threat to a company's high-priority goals, surprise to its membership, and stakeholder demands for a short response time. The nature of crises requires a firm's leadership to communicate in an often stressful, emotional, uncertain, and demanding context. Crises are very difficult on a company's stakeholders as well. For this reason, the firm's stakeholders, especially its employees, shareholders, customers, government regulators, competitors, and creditors and the media, will closely scrutinize communication after a crisis. Hence, crises have widespread implications not only for the organization but also for each group affected by the crisis.

To better understand how crises develop and move toward resolution, some researchers use a medical analogy. Using the analogy, the organization proceeds through chronological stages much as a patient does from an illness. The prodromal stage is a precrisis period during which warning signs may exist. Next is the acute stage, in which the actual crisis occurs. During the third, or chronic, stage, the business is required to sufficiently explain its actions in order to move to the final stage, crisis resolution. Figure 2.6 illustrates these stages. Although the stages are conceptually distinct, some crises happen so quickly and without warning that the organization may move from the prodromal to acute stage within minutes. Many organizations faced this situation after terrorists hijacked airplanes and crashed into the World Trade Center and the Pentagon on September 11, 2001.

One of the fundamental difficulties that a company faces is how to communicate effectively to stakeholders during and after a disaster. Once a crisis strikes, the firm's stakeholders need a quick response in the midst of the duress and confusion. They need information about how the company plans to resolve the crisis, as well as what each constituent can do to mitigate its own negative effects. If a company is slow to respond, stakeholders may feel as though the company does not care about their needs or is not concerned or remorseful, if the company is at fault, about the crisis. Furthermore, a delayed response may in fact increase the suffering of particular

FIGURE 2.6 **Crisis Management Process**

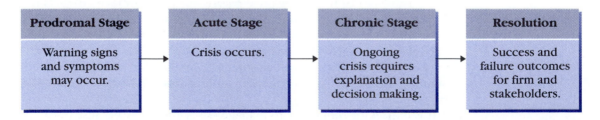

Prodromal Stage	Acute Stage	Chronic Stage	Resolution
Warning signs and symptoms may occur.	Crisis occurs.	Ongoing crisis requires explanation and decision making.	Success and failure outcomes for firm and stakeholders.

stakeholder groups. For instance, some stakeholders may take on considerable debt due to medical expenses as a result of the crisis. Therefore, a rapid response to stakeholders is central to any crisis resolution strategy so that these groups can plan their recovery.

Ironically, crisis events are often so chaotic that a company's leadership may not be certain of the cause of the situation before the media and other relevant groups demand a statement. Thus, it is not surprising for organizations to begin their crisis response with some degree of ambiguity in their statements. In fact, some crisis theorists advise companies to avoid too much detail in their initial response due to the embarrassment that results from changing positions later in the crisis when more information is available. Still, stakeholder groups want and, as a matter of safety in some cases, need access to whatever information the firm can share. Although tensions between the public's needs and the organization's fear of litigation can hamper an organization's willingness to communicate, the demand for information in such situations is unyielding.

Not only should the firm's leadership make a public statement quickly, but it is also necessary for the organization to communicate about specific issues to stakeholder groups. First, leadership should express concern and/or remorse for the event. Second, the organization should delineate guidelines regarding how it intends to address the crisis so that stakeholders can be confident that the situation will not escalate or recur. Finally, the company should provide explicit criteria to stakeholders regarding how each group will be compensated for any negative effects it experiences as a result of the crisis. Many companies, however, overlook these three essential conditions of crisis management. More often, they focus on minimizing harm to the organization's image, denying responsibility for the crisis, and shifting blame away from the organization and toward other stakeholder groups. Although this may be an appropriate strategy when the firm is not actually responsible, too often companies choose this course of action under the stress of the crisis when they are responsible or partially responsible for the crisis without expressing sufficient remorse for their involvement or concern for their stakeholders.

The varying communication needs and levels of concern of stakeholders during and after a crisis often hamper effective communication. The firm's leadership should try to communicate as much accurate information to these groups as possible to minimize their uncertainty. When a firm fails to do so, its credibility, legitimacy, and reputation in the eyes of stakeholders often suffer. Adding to the complexity of communication challenges, the needs of various stakeholder groups may conflict. For instance, the needs of customers who become ill as a result of a contaminated product and their desire to have medical bills paid may be at odds with the company's ability to bolster its stock price to satisfy shareholders. Some stakeholders will obviously have more opportunities than others to voice their concerns after a crisis. Victims and the general public rarely have an opportunity to meet with the organization's leadership after a crisis. Conversely, the organization's stockholders and employees will likely have a greater opportunity to express their views about the crisis and therefore may have their ideas accepted by management. Some researchers suggest that, due to this ability to communicate directly with leadership, internal stakeholder needs often take precedence over those of external

After the safety concerns with product tampering, Tylenol redesigned its products (producing caplets, tablets, and gelcaps instead of capsules) and triple-safety-sealed its packaging— (1) glued flaps on the outer box, (2) a tight plastic neck seal, and (3) a strong inner-foil seal over the mouth of the bottle. (Bettmann/Corbis)

stakeholders. Organizations have a responsibility to manage the competing interests of stakeholders to ensure that all stakeholder groups are treated fairly in the aftermath of a crisis. Responsible companies try to balance the needs of their stakeholders rather than favoring some groups over others. Organizations that fail to accomplish this communication function risk alienating stakeholder groups and intensifying the negative media attention toward the company. For many reasons, including effective crisis management, organizations need to understand and pursue solid and mutually beneficial relationships with stakeholders.

Development of Stakeholder Relationships

Relationships of any type, whether they involve family, friends, coworkers, or companies, are founded on principles of trust, commitment, and communication. They also are associated with a certain degree of time, interaction, and shared expectations. For instance, we do not normally speak of "having a relationship" with someone we have just met. We even differentiate between casual acquaintances, work colleagues, and close friends.

In business, the concept of relationships has gained much acceptance. Instead of just pursuing one-time transactions, companies are now searching for ways to develop long-term and collaborative relationships with their customers and business partners.[46] Throughout the 1990s, many companies focused on relationships with suppliers, buyers, employees, and others directly involved in economic exchange. These relationships involve investments of several types. Some investments are tangible, such as buildings, equipment, new tools, and other elements dedicated to a particular relationship. For example, Hormel Foods implemented an Internet-based procurement system that allowed its suppliers to view the firm's production schedules and revise their own business operations accordingly.[47] Other investments are less tangible, such as the time, effort, trust, and commitment required to develop a relationship. Although Hormel's suppliers need the electronic infrastructure and employee knowledge to use the new procurement process, these suppliers must also trust that their relationship with Hormel is solid and will be worth these investments. Some suppliers may have concerns that their investment in Hormel's system may not be transferable to other business opportunities and partnerships. They may also have concerns about information privacy.

Whereas tangible investments are often customized for a specific business relationship, intangible efforts have a more lucid and permeable quality. Although social responsibility involves tangible activities and other communication signals, the key to good stakeholder relationships resides in trust, communication quality, and mutual respect. As a company strives to develop a dialog and a solid relationship with one stakeholder, investments and lessons learned through the process should add value to other stakeholder relationships.

social capital
an asset that resides in relationships and is characterized by mutual goals and trust

These efforts result in **social capital,** an asset that resides in relationships and is characterized by mutual goals and trust.[48] Like financial and intellectual capital, social capital facilitates and smoothes internal and external transactions and processes. For example, social capital among companies in the chemical industry led to the development of Responsible Care, a progressive and voluntary program of environmental, health, and safety (EHS) standards in 1988. Several high-profile accidents, like the one in Bhopal, India, had eroded chemical companies' social capital with their communities, the government, and other stakeholder groups. The Chemical Manufacturers Association implemented the program to promote stronger EHS performance and to "improve the legislative, regulatory, market, and public interest climate for the industry." Thus, Responsible Care was aimed at advancing internal company operations as well as various stakeholder relationships. The industry continues to update and refine the initiative.[49] Unlike financial and intellectual capital, however, social capital is not tangible or the obvious property of one organization. In this same regard, social responsibility is not compartmentalized or reserved for a few issues or stakeholders, but should have the companywide strategic focus discussed in Chapter 1. This section and Table 2.3 discuss the best practices for developing mutually beneficial stakeholder relationships.[50]

The first step in developing stakeholder relationships involves acknowledging and actively monitoring the concerns of all legitimate stakeholders. Thus, a company must have a process for identifying and ordering the myriad of claims on and stakes in its business and, as appropriate, taking these interests into account in decision making, operations, and strategy. Although no company is obligated to act on every claim, all claims should be evaluated before a firm decides to ignore or pass judgment on them. In order to make accurate assumptions about stakeholders, managers need to listen to and openly communicate with stakeholders about their respective concerns and contributions. Getting to know stakeholders smoothes the communication process and eventually leads to more consistency in values and expectations between a company and each stakeholder.[51]

On the basis of an accurate understanding of interests and claims, a firm should adopt processes and modes of behavior that are sensitive to the concerns and

TABLE 2.3	Best Practices for Developing Stakeholder Relationships

STEP	PRACTICE
1.	Acknowledge and actively monitor the concerns of all legitimate stakeholders.
2.	As appropriate, take stakeholder interests in account in decision making, operations, and strategy.
3.	Listen to and openly communicate with stakeholders about their respective concerns and contributions and about any risks they assume because of involvement with the company.
4.	Adopt processes and modes of behavior that are sensitive to the concerns and capabilities of each stakeholder.
5.	Work cooperatively with other entities, both public and private, to insure that risks and harms arising from corporate activities are minimized and, where they cannot be avoided, appropriately compensated.
6.	Avoid activities that might jeopardize inalienable human rights (e.g., the right to life) or give rise to risks that, if clearly understood, would be patently unacceptable to relevant stakeholders.
7.	Acknowledge and openly address the potential conflicts between the company and its social responsibilities and stakeholder interests.
8.	Invest in education, training, and information that improve understanding and relationships with stakeholders.
9.	Periodically assess relationships with stakeholders and use the results for improving the corporate citizenship effort.

Sources: Adapted from "Principles of Stakeholder Management," Clarkson Centre for Business Ethics, http://www.rotman.utoronto.ca/ccbe/%7EStake/Principles.htm, (accessed) October 15, 2003; Malcolm McIntosh, Deborah Leipziger, Keith Jones, and Gill Coleman, *Corporate Citizenship: Successful Strategies for Responsible Companies* (London: Financial Times Management, 2000).

capabilities of each stakeholder. For example, although America Online (AOL) tracks and maintains records regarding the movements of subscribers throughout its system, it has chosen not to sell this data to third parties. Like many subscriber-based companies, AOL does sell subscriber names and addresses to other firms (a practice it discloses in its online privacy policy), but the firm's executives felt that going beyond this level would be inappropriate because of consumer concerns about privacy.[52] As discussed earlier, not all stakeholders are equal. For example, there are regulations and legal requirements that govern relationships with some stakeholders, such as holding shareholder meetings and disclosing financial outcomes to them. Business communications, such as advertising, press releases, and web sites, have the potential to reach many stakeholder groups, whereas formal proceedings may be the modus operandi for dealing with government officials. Regardless of the contact method, information should be communicated consistently across all stakeholders. This is especially salient when a company is facing a complex or crisis situation.

SAS Institute, a leading software manufacturer, enjoys strong relationships with its employees and their families because of its openness in resolving employee concerns through company benefits, including a high-quality, on-site daycare facility subsidized by the SAS. (Courtesy SAS Institute. Photo by Gregory Foster)

Another key aspect of strong relationships is the willingness to acknowledge and openly address potential conflicts. This is very important because it is likely that some degree of negotiation and conciliation will be needed to align the company with stakeholder interests. Sometimes, the firm will need to find a balance among competing stakeholder concerns and claims. A classic conflict arises between investors' needs for a return on their investment and other stakeholders' expectations. Investors may believe that closing an underperforming manufacturing plant is in the company's best financial interest. At the same time, however, the plant's employees may worry that such a closure will jeopardize their own financial stability, whereas members of the community may fear that it will threaten the community's economic health. Thus, the company will need to understand potential ramifications of the plant closure on other stakeholders, such as eliminating employee jobs, creating economic effects within the community, needing fewer suppliers, asking customers to find a new product provider, or answering to the media. In another type of potential conflict, managers and other decision makers must balance their personal and professional needs with those of their employer. Because they also belong to one primary stakeholder of the firm, responsible managers and executives ensure that their decisions and actions are transparent and subject to scrutiny in the best interest of all stakeholders. This special situation raises questions of corporate governance, which is discussed in Chapter 6.

Investments in education, training, and information will improve employees' understanding of and relationships with specific stakeholders. For example, several companies in the United Kingdom have invested in deaf awareness training for employees. Sainsbury's, a supermarket chain, offered courses in sign language to its employees.[53] Employee training related to stakeholder needs and concerns has the dual benefit of improving relationships with stakeholders while enhancing employee skills and knowledge. We discuss employees and social responsibility further in Chapter 8.

Finally, a company's relationships with stakeholders need to be periodically assessed. Informal methods can be used on an ongoing basis to gauge current relationship strengths and opportunities for improvement. Conversations between salespeople and customers and between purchasing agents and suppliers can serve as informal contact methods. Many companies currently use more formal methods, such as exit interviews, open-door policies, and confidential and toll-free telephone hot lines to get feedback from a primary stakeholder—employees. Questionnaires, focus groups, web sites, and other research tools can be used to gain feedback from customers, members of the local community, suppliers and business partners, investors, and other stakeholders. Royal Dutch/Shell, the global petroleum company, produces an annual report detailing its commitment to social responsibility. The report, which is available in printed form and on the firm's web site, employs a "Tell Shell" feedback mechanism for generating questions, criticisms, and other inquiries from its constituents. The report also discloses results of the Shell People Survey, which gathers opinions from employees on a range of issues, including the company's commitment to ethical values and environmental standards. Finally, the report includes an independent evaluation and verification of the company's claims.[54] As the Shell example demonstrates, the results of both formal and informal assessment should be made available to internal and external stakeholders for improving the social responsibility effort and stakeholder relationships. By sharing feedback, both positive and critical, a company is engaging in the two-way dialog that characterizes the stakeholder model discussed earlier in this chapter.

Link Between Stakeholder Relationships and Social Responsibility

You may be wondering what motivations companies have for pursuing stakeholder relationships. As Table 2.3 indicates, a great deal of time, effort, and commitment goes into the process of developing mutual understanding among so many groups. Some companies have been accused of "window dressing," or publicizing their stakeholder efforts without having a true commitment behind them. For example, The Body Shop, which has received much positive attention for its social responsibility efforts, has also been accused of selectively communicating information and hiding less-favorable company issues.[55] As was discussed in Chapter 1, social responsibility is a relational approach and involves the views and stakes of a number of groups. Stakeholders are engaged in the relationships that both challenge and support a company's efforts. Thus, without a solid understanding of stakeholders and their interests, a firm may miss important trends and changes in its environment and not achieve strategic social responsibility.

Rather than holding all companies to one standard, our approach to evaluating performance and effectiveness resides in the specific expectations and actual results that develop between each organization and its stakeholders. Max Clarkson, an influential contributor to our understanding of stakeholders, sums up this view:

> Performance is what counts. Performance can be measured and evaluated. Whether a corporation and its management are motivated by enlightened self-interest, common sense or high standards of ethical behavior cannot be determined by empirical methodologies available today. These are not questions that can be answered by economists, sociologists, psychologists, or any other kind of social scientist. They are interesting questions, but they are not relevant when it comes to evaluating a company's performance in managing its relationships with its stakeholder groups.[56]

TABLE 2.4	The Reactive-Defensive-Accommodative-Proactive Scale	
RATING	**STRATEGY**	**PERFORMANCE**
Reactive	Deny responsibility.	Doing less than required
Defensive	Admit responsibility, but fight it.	Doing the least that is required
Accommodative	Accept responsibility.	Doing all that is required
Proactive	Anticipate responsibility.	Doing more than is required

Source: Max B. E. Clarkson, "A Stakeholder Framework for Analyzing and Evaluating Corporate Social Performance," *Academy of Management Review* 20 (January 1995): 92–117.

Although critics and some researchers may seek answers and evidence as to the motivations of business for social responsibility, we are interested in what companies are actually doing that is positive, negative, or neutral for their stakeholders and their stakeholders' interests. The Reactive-Defensive-Accommodative-Proactive Scale (see Table 2.4) provides a method for assessing a company's strategy and performance with each stakeholder. This scale is based on a continuum of strategy options and performance outcomes with respect to stakeholders.[57] This evaluation can take place as stakeholder issues arise or are identified. Therefore, it is possible for one company to be rated at several different levels because of varying performance and transitions over time. For example, a poorly handled crisis situation may provide feedback for continuous improvement that creates more satisfactory performance in the future. Or, a company may demonstrate a proactive stance toward employees, yet be defensive with consumer activists.

The reactive approach involves denying responsibility and doing less than is required. This approach can be characterized as "fighting it all the way."[58] A firm that fails to invest in safety and health measures for employees is denying its responsibilities. An organization with a defensive strategy acknowledges reluctantly and partially the responsibility issues that may be raised by its stakeholders. A firm in this category fulfills basic legal obligations and demonstrates the minimal responsibility discussed in Chapter 1. With an accommodative strategy, a company attempts to satisfy stakeholder demands by doing all that is required and may be seen as progressive because it is obviously open to this expanded model of business relationships.[59] Today, many organizations are giving money and other resources to community organizations as a way of demonstrating social responsibility. Finally, the proactive approach not only accepts but also anticipates stakeholder interests. In this case, a company sincerely aligns legitimate stakeholder views with its responsibilities and will do more than is required to meet them.[60] Hoechst, a German life sciences company now part of Aventis, gradually assumed the proactive orientation with communities in which it operates. The initiation of a community discussion group led to information sharing and trust building and helped transform Hoechst into a society-driven company.[61]

The Reactive-Defensive-Accommodative-Proactive Scale is useful because it evaluates real practice and allows an organization to see its strengths and weaknesses

---

social audit

the process of assessing and reporting a firm's performance in adopting a strategic focus for fulfilling the economic, legal, ethical, and philanthropic social responsibilities expected of it by its stakeholders

---

within each stakeholder relationship. SABMiller, the second largest brewer in the world, uses a risk assessment program to understand the stakeholders and issues that may pose a potential risk to its reputation. These risks are prioritized, planned for, monitored, and if necessary, responded to if SABMiller cannot predict, preempt, or avoid the concern.[62] Results from a stakeholder assessment like the one at SABMiller should be included in the **social audit,** which assesses and reports a firm's performance in adopting a strategic focus for fulfilling the economic, legal, ethical, and philanthropic social responsibilities expected of it by its stakeholders. Chapter 12 takes an extensive look at this audit. Because stakeholders are so important to the concept of social responsibility, as well as to business success, Chapters 3–10 are devoted to exploring significant stakeholder relationships and issues.

S u m m a r y

Stakeholders refers to those people and groups who have a "stake" in some aspect of a company's products, operations, markets, industry, or outcomes. The relationship between organizations and their stakeholders is a two-way street.

The historical assumption that the key objective of business is profit maximization led to the belief that business is accountable primarily to investors and others involved in the market and economic aspects of the organization. In the latter half of the twentieth century, perceptions of business accountability evolved to include both market constituencies that are directly involved and affected by the business purpose (e.g., investors, employees, customers, and other business partners) and nonmarket constituencies that are not always directly tied to issues of profitability and performance (e.g., the general community, media, government, and special-interest groups).

In the input-output model of stakeholder relationships, investors, employees, and suppliers provide inputs for a company to transform into outputs that benefit customers. This approach assumes a relatively mechanistic, simplistic, and nonstakeholder view of business. The stakeholder model assumes a two-way relationship between the firm and a host of stakeholders. This approach recognizes additional stakeholders and acknowledges the two-way dialog and effects that exist with a firm's internal and external environment.

Primary stakeholders are fundamental to a company's operations and survival and include shareholders and investors, employees, customers, suppliers, and public stakeholders, such as government and the community. Secondary stakeholders influence and/or are affected by the company but are neither engaged in transactions with the firm nor essential for its survival.

As more firms conduct business overseas, they encounter the complexity of stakeholder issues and relationships in tandem with other business operations and decisions. Although general awareness of the concept of stakeholders is relatively high around the world, the importance of stakeholders varies from country to country.

A stakeholder has power to the extent that it can gain access to coercive, utilitarian, or symbolic means to impose or communicate its views to the organization. Such power may be coercive, utilitarian, or symbolic. Legitimacy is the perception or belief that a stakeholder's actions are proper, desirable, or appropriate within a given context. Stakeholders exercise greater pressures on managers and organizations when they stress the urgency of their claims. These attributes can change over time and context.

Reputation management is the process of building and sustaining a company's good name and generating positive feedback from stakeholders. The process of reputation management involves the interaction of organizational identity (how the firm wants to be viewed), organizational image (how stakeholders initially perceive the firm), organizational performance (actual interaction between the company and stakeholders), and organizational reputation (the collective view of stakeholders after interactions with the company). Stakeholders will reassess their views of the company on the basis of how the company has actually performed.

Crisis management is the process of handling a high-impact event characterized by ambiguity and the need for swift action. Some researchers describe an organization's progress through a prodromal, or precrisis, stage to the acute stage, chronic stage, and finally, crisis resolution. Stakeholders need a quick response with information about how the company plans to resolve the crisis, as well as what they can do to mitigate negative effects to themselves. It is also necessary to communicate specific issues to stakeholder groups, including remorse for the event, guidelines as to how the organization is going to address the crisis, and criteria regarding how stakeholder groups will be compensated for negative effects.

Companies are searching for ways to develop long-term, collaborative relationships with their stakeholders. These relationships involve both tangible and intangible investments. Investments and lessons learned through the process of developing a dialog and relationship with one stakeholder should add value to other stakeholder relationships. These efforts result in social capital, an asset that resides in relationships and is characterized by mutual goals and trust.

The first step in developing stakeholder relationships is to acknowledge and actively monitor the concerns of all legitimate stakeholders. A firm should adopt processes and modes of behavior that are sensitive to the concerns and capabilities of each stakeholder. Information should be communicated consistently across all stakeholders. A firm should be willing to acknowledge and openly address potential conflicts. Investments in education, training, and information will improve employees' understanding of and relationships with stakeholders. Relationships with stakeholders need to be periodically assessed through both formal and informal means. Sharing feedback with stakeholders helps establish the two-way dialog that characterizes the stakeholder model.

The Reactive-Defensive-Accommodative-Proactive Scale provides a method for assessing a company's strategy and performance with one stakeholder. The reactive approach involves denying responsibility and doing less than is required. The defensive approach acknowledges only reluctantly and partially the responsibility issues that may be raised by the firm's stakeholders. The accommodative strategy attempts to satisfy stakeholder demands. The proactive approach accepts and anticipates stakeholder interests. Results from this stakeholder assessment should be included in the social audit, which assesses and reports a firm's performance in fulfilling the economic, legal, ethical, and philanthropic social responsibilities expected of it by its stakeholders.

Key Terms

input-output model (p. 36)
stakeholder model (p. 38)
primary stakeholders (p. 39)
secondary stakeholders (p. 39)
power (p. 44)
legitimacy (p. 45)
urgency (p. 45)
reputation management (p. 47)
crisis management (p. 50)
social capital (p. 53)
social audit (p. 58)

Discussion Questions

1. Define *stakeholder* in your own terms. Compare your definition with the various conceptualizations presented in this chapter, including the historical perspectives in Table 2.1.
2. What is the difference between primary and secondary stakeholders? Why is it important for companies to make this distinction?
3. How do legitimacy, urgency, and power attributes positively and negatively affect a stakeholder's ability to develop relationships with organizations?
4. What is reputation management? Explain why companies are concerned about their reputation and its effects on stakeholders. What are the four elements of reputation management? Why is it important to manage these elements?
5. Define *crisis management*. What should a company facing a crisis do to satisfy its stakeholders and protect its reputation?
6. Describe the process of developing stakeholder relationships. What parts of the process seem most important? What parts seem most difficult?
7. What are the differences between the reactive, defensive, accommodative, and proactive approaches to stakeholder relationships? Using Table 2.4, assess Jack in the Box's response to the *E. coli* crisis. Is this scale a good assessment tool for companies pursuing strategic social responsibility? Why or why not?

Experiential Exercise

Choose two companies in different industries and visit their respective web sites. Peruse these sites for informa-

tion that is directed at three company stakeholders—employees, customers, and the media. For example, a company that places its annual reports online may be appealing primarily to the interests of investors. Make a list of the types of information that are on the site and indicate how the information might be used and perceived by these three stakeholder groups. What differences and similarities did you find between the two companies?

 ## What Would You Do?

Literally hundreds of buildings dotted the ground below and the thousands of cars on highways looked like ants on a mission. The jet airliner made its way to the Bangkok International Airport and eased into the humid afternoon. The group of four passed through customs control and looked for the limousine provided by Suvar Corporation, their Thai liaison in this new business venture. Representing Global Amusements were the vice president of corporate development, director of Asian operations, vice president of global relations, and director of governmental relations for Southeast Asia.

Global Amusements, headquartered in London, was considering the development of a Thai cultural amusement center on the island of Phuket. Phuket is a tourist destination known for its stunning beaches, fine resorts, and famous Thai hospitality. Both Global Amusements and Sukar Corporation believed Phuket was a great candidate for a new project. The amusement center would focus on the history of Thailand and include a variety of live performances, rides, exhibits, and restaurants. Domestic and international travelers who visited Phuket would be the primary target market.

Global Amusements had been in business for nearly twenty years and currently used a joint venture approach in establishing new properties. Suvar was its Thai partner and the two firms had been successful two years ago in developing a water amusement park outside of Bangkok. Phuket could hold much promise, but there were likely to be concerns about the potential destruction of its beauty and the exploitation of this well-preserved island and cultural reserve.

Following a day to adjust to the time zone and refine the strategy for the visit, the next three days would be spent in Bangkok, meeting with various company and governmental officials who had a stake in the proposed amusement facility. After a short flight to Phuket, the group would be the guest of the Southern Office of the Tourism Authority of Thailand for nearly a week. This part of the trip would involve visits to possible sites as well as meetings with island government officials and local interest groups.

After arriving at the hotel, the four employees of Global Amusement agreed to meet later that evening to discuss their strategy for the visit. One of their main concerns was the development of an effective stakeholder analysis. Each member of the group was asked to bring a list of primary and secondary stakeholders and indicate the various concerns or "stakes" that each might have with the proposed project. What would you do?

Legal, Regulatory, and Political Issues

CHAPTER OBJECTIVES

- To understand the rationale for government regulation of business
- To examine the key legislation that structures the legal environment for business
- To analyze the role of regulatory agencies in the enforcement of public policy
- To compare the costs and benefits of regulation
- To examine how business participates in and influences public policy
- To describe the government's approach for legal and ethical compliance

CHAPTER OUTLINE

Government's Influence on Business

Business's Influence on Government

The Government's Strategic Approach for Legal and Ethical Compliance

The Better Business Bureau (BBB) is one of the best-known self-regulatory associations in the United States. The BBB works to promote good business practices within communities and is supported by local member businesses. When a company violates bureau standards for good practice, the BBB warns consumers through the media. A recent nationwide alert was issued to advise college students, high school students, and other young people to beware of potentially fraudulent offers from modeling/talent agencies. Students are being approached on college campuses and targeted at sporting events and shopping venues. Some have responded to enticing ads that promise a glamorous career as a model or actor. The BBB is hoping to educate young people about the potential pitfalls of such offers.

Requests to local BBBs for reliability reports on various modeling/talent agencies have more than tripled during the past two years—an indication that more and more people are being approached by such agencies. Many of the 200,000 people who check with the BBB this year will find that the modeling/talent agency about which they are requesting information has an unsatisfactory record, and some of these will have already signed a contract or paid an upfront fee of $1,000 or more. The number of such complaints processed by the BBB rose by 50 percent in one year alone.

The BBB recommends that anyone considering an offer or advertisement to be a model or be in movies take the time to research the business, check its references, and come to a careful and well-examined decision. High-pressure sales tactics usually mean a scam artist is on the prowl. A reputable agency will give interested parties plenty of time to make an informed decision. Before paying any fees, the BBB suggests that potential signees (1) obtain all verbal promises, claims, and agency information in writing, (2) check the complaint history of the agency with the local BBB office, as well as the Consumer Protection Agency, and the state attorney general, (3) research state laws regarding such agencies and verify any licensing/bonding information, (4) ask for a blank copy of any contract to review before signing, (5) be wary of claims about high salaries, especially in smaller cities or towns, (6) use common sense, (7) do not give in to demands for cash, and (8) do not be swayed by promises that a deposit is totally refundable. BBB records show that fewer than half of all complaints against model/talent agencies are ever resolved to the customer's satisfaction, indicating that the industry has many bogus operators who rely on misleading claims and promises to entice unsuspecting consumers. According to the BBB, the quickest way to verify an agency's reliability is to ask for proof of its success. A reputable agency will be willing to provide contact information for models or actors who have secured successful work based on the agency's efforts, as well as information for companies that have hired models or actors trained by the agency. Use this information to research the agency and determine whether a successful experience is likely.[1]

Although self-regulatory associations such as the Better Business Bureau provide an important service, they generally lack the tools or authority to enforce their guidelines for good business practices. The government, however, has the power through laws and regulations to structure how businesses and individuals achieve their goals. The purpose of regulating firms is to create a fair competitive environment for businesses, consumers, and society. All stakeholders need to demonstrate a commitment to social responsibility through compliance with relevant laws and proactive consideration of social needs. Indeed, a recent study of 900 senior managers found that law ranks as one of the most important business subjects in terms of its effect on organizational practices and activities.[2] Thus, compliance with the law is an important foundation of social responsibility.

This chapter explores the complex relationship between business and government. First we discuss some of the laws that structure the environment for the regulation of business. Major legislation relating to competition and regulatory agencies is reviewed to provide an overview of the regulatory environment. Next we consider how businesses can participate in the public policy process through lobbying, political contributions, and political action committees. Finally, we offer a framework for a strategic approach to managing the legal and regulatory environment.

Government's Influence on Business

The government has a profound influence on business. In most Western countries, there is a history of elected representatives working through democratic institutions to provide the structure for the regulation of business conduct. For example, one of the differences that has long characterized the two major parties of the U.S. political system involves the government's role with respect to business. In general terms, the Republican Party favors less federal regulation of business whereas the Democratic Party is more open to such initiatives.[3] Third-party and independent candidates more often focus on specific business issues or proclaim their distance from the two major political parties. However, the power and freedom of big business have resulted in conflicts among private businesses, government, private interest groups, and even individuals.

In the United States, the role that society delegates to government is to provide laws that are logically deduced from the Constitution and the Bill of Rights and to enforce these laws through the judicial system. Individuals and businesses, therefore, live under a rule of law that protects society and supports an acceptable quality of life. Hopefully, by controlling the limitation of force by some parties, the overall welfare and freedom of all participants in the social system will be protected.

The provision of a court system to settle disputes and punish criminals, both organizational and individual, provides for justice and order in society. For example, Columbia/HCA, the world's largest hospital chain, was fined $745 million for defrauding Medicare through overbilling for home health care and laboratory services. In addition, the executives who were in charge when the violations occurred were initially convicted of fraud, but the convictions were later overturned.[4] This example illustrates how the judicial system can punish businesses that fail to comply with laws and regulatory requirements.

The legal system is not always accepted in some countries as insurance that business will be conducted in a legitimate way. A survey of Russian executives indicated that tax evasion methods, as well as other varieties of illegal corporate behavior, are presented in corporate training. Executives believe that business could not be successful in a completely legal way under Russia's existing conditions where illegal activities are viewed as socially acceptable.[5]

The existence of businesses, however, is based on laws permitting their creation, organization, and dissolution. From a social perspective, it is significant that a corporation has the same legal status as a "person" who can sue, be sued, and be held liable for debts. Laws may protect managers and stockholders from being personally liable for a company's debts, but individuals as well as organizations are still responsible for their conduct. Because corporations have a perpetual life, larger companies like Exxon, General Motors, and Sony take on an organizational culture, including social responsibility values, that extends beyond a specific time period or management team.

Most companies are owned by individual proprietors or operated as partnerships. However, large incorporated firms like Tyson Foods often receive the most attention because of their size, visibility, and impact on so many aspects of the economy and society. In a pluralistic society, many diverse stakeholder groups (business, labor, consumers, environmentalists, privacy advocates, and so on) attempt to influence the public officials who legislate, interpret laws, and regulate business. The public interest is served though open participation and debate that result in effective public policy. Because no system of government is perfect, legal and regulatory systems are constantly evolving and changing in response to social institutions, including the business environment. For example, increasing use of the Internet for information and business has created a need for legislation and regulations to protect the owners of creative materials from unauthorized use and consumers from fraud and invasions of privacy. The Better Business Bureau, for example, developed an online seal to certify reliability and privacy programs of organizations on the Internet. A recent survey indicates that 90 percent of the respondents had greater confidence when making a purchase from a company displaying the BBB's online seal.[6] The line between acceptable and illegal activity on the Internet is increasingly difficult to discern and is often determined by judges and juries. Companies that adopt a strategic approach to the legal and regulatory system develop proactive organizational values and compliance programs that identify areas of risks and include formal communication, training, and continuous improvement of responses to the legal and regulatory environment. Companies that apply for and receive the Better Business Bureau seal are examples of such companies.

In this section, we take a closer look at why and how the government affects businesses through laws and regulation, the costs and benefits of regulation, and how regulation may affect companies doing business in foreign countries.

The Rationale for Regulation

Although the United States was established as a capitalist system in which capitalist theory says "the invisible hand of competition" would regulate the economy, this system has not always worked effectively or in the best interest of consumers, business, or society as a whole. Since the days of Adam Smith, the federal and state governments have stepped in to enact legislation and create regulations to address particular issues and restrict the behavior of business in accordance with society's wishes. Many of these issues used to justify business regulation can be categorized as economic or social.

Economic and Competitive Reasons for Regulation A great number of regulations have been passed by legislatures over the last century in an effort "to level the playing field" on which businesses operate. When the United States became an independent nation in the eighteenth century, the business environment consisted of many small farms, manufacturers, and cottage industries operating on a primarily local scale. With the increasing industrialization of the United States after the Civil War, "captains of industry" like John D. Rockefeller (oil), Andrew Carnegie (railroads and steel), Andrew Mellon (aluminum), and J. P. Morgan (banking) began to consolidate their business holdings into large national trusts. **Trusts** are organizations generally established to gain control of a product market or industry by eliminating competition. Such organizations are often considered detrimental because, without serious competition, they can potentially charge higher prices and provide lower-quality products to consumers. Thus, as these firms grew in size and power, public distrust of them likewise grew because of often-legitimate concerns about unfair competition. This suspicion and the public's desire to require these increasingly powerful companies to act responsibly spurred the first antitrust legislation. If trusts are successful in eliminating competition, a monopoly can result.

A **monopoly** occurs when just one business provides a good or service in a given market. Utility companies that supply electricity, natural gas, water, or cable television are examples of monopolies. The government tolerates these monopolies because the cost of supplying the good or providing the service is so great that few companies would be willing to invest in new markets without some protection from competition. Monopolies may also be allowed by patent laws that grant the developer of a new technology a period of time (usually seventeen years) during which no

trust
organizations established to gain control of a product market or industry by eliminating competition

monopoly
the situation where one business provides a good or service in a given market

other firm can use the same technology without the patent holder's consent. These relatively short-term monopolies are permitted in order to encourage businesses to engage in riskier research and development by allowing them time to recoup their research, development, and production expenses and to earn a reasonable profit.

Because trusts and monopolies lack serious competition, there are concerns that they may either exploit their market dominance to restrict their output and raise prices or lower quality in order to gain greater profits. This concern is the primary rationalization for their regulation by the government. Public utilities, for example, are regulated by state public utility commissions and, where they involve interstate commerce, are subject to federal regulation as well. In recent years, some of these industries have been "deregulated" with the idea that greater competition will police the behavior of individual firms.

Related to the issue of regulation of trusts and monopolies is society's desire to restrict destructive or unfair competition. What is considered to be unfair varies with the standard practice of the industry, the impact of specific conduct, and the individual case. When one company dominates a particular industry, it may engage in destructive competition or employ anticompetitive tactics. For example, it may slash prices in an effort to drive competitors out of the market, and then later raise prices. It may conspire with other competitors to set or "fix" prices so that each firm can ensure a certain level of profit. Other examples of unfair competitive trade practices are stealing trade secrets or obtaining other confidential information from a competitor's employees, trademark and copyright infringement, false advertising, and deceptive selling methods such as "bait and switch" and false representation of products. Farber Blake Corporation paid fines of $300,000 and pled guilty to one criminal charge for misleading consumers in Canada and New Zealand with deceptive marketing tactics. Telemarketers contacted consumers, telling them they had won prizes such as cash or a cruise. In order to claim the prize, the consumers had to buy promotional products such as coin sets or artwork at inflated prices.[7]

Antitrust regulations also allow the government to punish firms that engage in anticompetitive practices. For example, two drug companies, Aventis SA and Andrx Corp., agreed to pay $80 million to settle allegations that they conspired to keep a cheaper, generic version of a blood-pressure medication off the market. Aventis paid Andrx almost $100 million not to market a generic form of Cardizem CD for 11 months. New York's attorney general said that consumers paid too much for Cardizem CD and its generic equivalents because the companies' conspiracy delayed the marketing of cheaper competitors.[8] We will take a closer look at specific antitrust regulations later in this chapter.

Social Reasons for Regulation Regulation may also occur when marketing activities result in undesirable consequences for society. Many manufacturing processes, for example, create air, water, or land pollution. Such consequences create "costs" in the form of contamination of natural resources, illness, and so on, that neither the manufacturer nor the consumer "pays" for directly. Because few companies are willing to shoulder these costs voluntarily, regulation is necessary to ensure that all firms within an industry do their part to minimize these costs and to pay their fair share. Likewise, regulations have proven necessary to protect natural (e.g., forests, fishing grounds, and other habitats) and social resources (e.g., historical and architecturally or archaeologically significant structures). We will take a closer look at some of these environmental protection regulations and related issues in Chapter 9.

Other regulations have come about in response to social demands for equality in the workplace, especially after the 1960s. Such laws and regulations require that companies ignore race, ethnicity, gender, religion, and disabilities in favor of qualifications that more accurately reflect an individual's capacity for performing a particular job. Likewise, deaths and injuries because of employer negligence resulted in regulations designed to ensure that people can enjoy a safe working environment. Lockheed was fined $1 million, the largest fine ever assessed against a contractor by the Energy Department, for violating such workplace safety regulations at a nuclear weapons plant in Oak Ridge, Tennessee.[9] We will take a closer look at laws and regulations related to the workplace in Chapter 8.

Still other regulations have resulted from special-interest group crusades for safer products. For example, Ralph Nader's *Unsafe at Any Speed,* published in 1965, criticized the automobile industry as a whole, and General Motors specifically, for putting profit and style ahead of lives and safety. Nader's consumer protection organization, popularly known as Nader's Raiders, successfully campaigned for legislation that required automobile makers to provide safety belts, padded dashboards, stronger door latches, head restraints, shatterproof windshields, and collapsible steering columns in automobiles. As we will see in Chapter 7, consumer activists also helped secure passage of several other consumer protection laws, such as the Wholesome Meat Act of 1967, the Clean Water Act of 1972, and the Toxic Substance Act of 1976.

Issues arising from the increasing use of the Internet have led to demands for new laws protecting consumers and business. According to a recent study, Internet users receive an average of 110 unwanted e-mails (spam) each week, and although 39 percent of online consumers use blocking software to avoid such unwanted e-mail, only about one-third of them are satisfied with the software's performance. Since spam-blocking technology is failing to keep up with unwanted electronic sales pitches for everything from lower interest rates to increased sexual drive, the two biggest Internet access services, America Online and Microsoft's MSN, have joined forces to press for tough federal legislation to stop illicit commercial e-mail. The two companies want stiff jail terms for spammers who commit fraud by mispresenting themselves online, the power to seek injunctions against the theft and use of proprietary e-mail addresses, and large fines to put spammers out of business. Legislation is needed that will block deceptive spammers without violating First Amendment rights.[10]

As we shall see in Chapter 10, the technology associated with the Internet has generated a number of issues related to privacy, fraud, and copyrights. For instance, creators of copyrighted works such as movies, books, and music are calling for new laws and regulations to safeguard their ownership of these works. In response to these concerns, Congress enacted the Digital Millennium Copyright Act in 1998, which extended existing copyright laws to better protect "digital" recordings of music, movies, and the like.[11] Concerns about the collection and use of personal information, especially regarding children, resulted in the passage of the Children's Online Privacy Protection Act of 2000 (COPPA). According to a recent study, many companies are not complying with COPPA. However, the Federal Trade Commission (FTC) enforces the act by levying fines against noncomplying web site operators. For example, the FTC imposed $100,000 in fines against girlslife.com, bigmail-box.com, and insidetheweb.com, finding that the sites collected more information than was necessary for the activities involved and encouraged age falsification.[12] Additional legislation addressing social concerns about privacy is likely. Consumers are also worried about becoming victims of online fraud. Online auction fraud resulted in an overall loss of $6.2 million in the first half of 2002 alone.[13] With online auctions generating an estimated $6.1 billion per year, consumers and businesses alike are exploring options, including regulation, to protect the security of online transactions.[14]

Laws And Regulations

As a result of business abuses and social demands for reform, the federal government began to pass legislation to regulate business conduct in the late nineteenth century. In this section, we will look at a few of the most significant of these laws. Table 3.1 summarizes many more laws that affect business operations.

Sherman Antitrust Act The Sherman Antitrust Act, passed in 1890, is the principal tool employed by the federal government to prevent businesses from restraining trade and monopolizing markets. Congress passed the law, almost unanimously, in response to public demands to curtail the growing power and abuses of trusts in the late nineteenth century. The law outlaws "every contract, combination in the form of trust or otherwise, or conspiracy, in restraint of trade or commerce."[15] It also makes a violation of the law a felony crime, punishable by a fine of up to $10 million for corporate violators and $350,000 and/or three years in prison for individual offenders.[16]

The Sherman Antitrust Act applies to all firms operating in interstate commerce as well as to U.S. firms engaged in foreign commerce. The law has been used to break up some of the most powerful companies in the United States, including the Standard Oil Company (1911), the American Tobacco Company (1911), and AT&T (1984), and there was an attempt to break up Microsoft. In the Microsoft case, a U.S. district court judge ruled that the software giant inhibited competition by using unlawful tactics to protect its Windows monopoly in computer operating systems and by illegally expanding its dominance into the market for Internet Web-browsing software. In ordering that the company be split into two independent firms, Judge Thomas Penfield Jackson said that Microsoft had placed "an oppressive thumb on the scale of competitive fortune" by targeting competitors that threatened its Windows software monopoly. However, the ruling to break up Microsoft was appealed and the order by Judge Jackson was overturned. The Supreme Court refused to hear an appeal by Microsoft that other aspects of its conviction should be overturned.[17] The Sherman Act remains the primary source of antitrust law in the United States, although it has been supplemented by several amendments and additional legislation.

Clayton Antitrust Act Because the provisions of the Sherman Antitrust Act were rather vague, the courts have not always interpreted the law as its creators intended. To rectify this situation, Congress enacted the Clayton Antitrust Act in 1914 to limit mergers and acquisitions that have the potential to stifle competition.[18] The Clayton

TABLE 3.1 Major Federal Legislation

ACT (DATE ENACTED)	PURPOSE
Sherman Antitrust Act (1890)	Prohibits contracts, combinations, or conspiracies to restrain trade; establishes as a misdemeanor monopolizing or attempting to monopolize
Clayton Act (1914)	Prohibits specific practices such as price discrimination, exclusive dealer arrangements, and stock acquisitions in which the effect may notably lessen competition or tend to create a monopoly
Federal Trade Commission Act (1914)	Created the Federal Trade Commission; also gives the FTC investigatory powers to be used in preventing unfair methods of competition
Robinson-Patman Act (1936)	Prohibits price discrimination that lessens competition among wholesalers or retailers; prohibits producers from giving disproportionate services of facilities to large buyers
Wheeler-Lea Act (1938)	Prohibits unfair and deceptive acts and practices regardless of whether competition is injured; places advertising of foods and drugs under the jurisdiction of the FTC
Lanham Act (1946)	Provides protections and regulation of brand names, brand marks, trade names, and trademarks
Celler-Kefauver Act (1950)	Prohibits any corporation engaged in commerce from acquiring the whole or any part of the stock or other share of the capital assets of another corporation when the effect substantially lessens competition or tends to create a monopoly
Fair Packaging and Labeling Act (1966)	Makes illegal the unfair or deceptive packaging or labeling of consumer products
Magnuson-Moss Warranty (FTC) Act (1975)	Provides for minimum disclosure standards for written consumer product warranties; defines minimum consent standards for written warranties; allows the FTC to prescribe interpretive rules in policy statements regarding unfair or deceptive practices
Consumer Goods Pricing Act (1975)	Prohibits the use of price maintenance agreements among manufacturers and resellers in interstate commerce
Antitrust Improvements Act (1976)	Requires large corporations to inform federal regulators of prospective mergers or acquisitions so that they can be studied for any possible violations of the law
Trademark Counterfeiting Act (1988)	Provides civil and criminal penalties against those who deal in counterfeit consumer goods or any counterfeit goods that can threaten health or safety
Trademark Law Revision Act (1988)	Amends the Lanham Act to allow brands not yet introduced to be protected through registration with the Patent and Trademark Office
Nutrition Labeling and Education Act (1990)	Prohibits exaggerated health claims and requires all processed foods to contain labels with nutritional information
Telephone Consumer Protection Act (1991)	Establishes procedures to avoid unwanted telephone solicitations; prohibits marketers from using automated telephone dialing system or an artificial or prerecorded voice to certain telephone lines
Federal Trademark Dilution Act (1995)	Provides trademark owners the right to protect trademarks and requires relinquishment of names that match or parallel existing trademarks
Digital Millenium Copyright Act (1998)	Refined copyright laws to protect digital versions of copyrighted materials, including music and movies
Children's Online Privacy Act (2000)	Regulates the collection of personally identifiable information (name, address, e-mail address, hobbies, interests, or information collected through cookies) online from children under age 13
Sarbanes-Oxley Act (2002)	Requires corporations to take responsibility to provide principles-based ethical leadership and holds CEOs and CFOs personally accountable for the credibility and accuracy of their company's financial statements

Act also specifically prohibits price discrimination, tying agreements (when a supplier furnishes a product to a buyer with the stipulation that the buyer must purchase other products as well), exclusive agreements (when a supplier forbids an intermediary to carry products of competing manufacturers), and the acquisition of stock in another corporation where the effect may be to substantially lessen competition or tend to create a monopoly. In addition, the Clayton Act prohibits members of one company's board of directors from holding seats on the boards of competing corporations. The law also exempts farm corporations and labor organizations from antitrust laws.

Federal Trade Commission Act In the same year the Clayton Act was passed, Congress also enacted the Federal Trade Commission Act to further strengthen the antitrust provisions of the Sherman Act. Unlike the Clayton Act, which prohibits specific practices, the Federal Trade Commission Act more broadly prohibits unfair methods of competition. More significantly, this law created the Federal Trade Commission (FTC) to protect consumers and businesses from unfair competition. Of all the federal regulatory agencies, the FTC has the greatest influence on business activities.

When the FTC receives a complaint about a business or finds reason to believe that a company is engaging in illegal conduct, it issues a formal complaint stating that the firm is in violation of the law. If the company continues the unlawful practice, the FTC can issue a cease-and-desist order, which requires the offender to stop the specified behavior. "Miss Cleo," the television persona who handled psychic hotlines, was

The Federal Trade Commission charged Miss Cleo, a professed psychic, with deceptive billing and collection practices as well as misleading advertising tactics. (David Young Wolff/PhotoEdit)

ordered by the FTC to forgive $500 million in outstanding consumer charges and to pay a fine of $5 million to the FTC. The charges included consumer billing for "psychic readings at no charge" as well as other deceptive billing, collection, and advertising tactics.[19]

Although a firm can appeal to the federal courts to have the order rescinded, the FTC can seek civil penalties in court, up to a maximum penalty of $10,000 a day for each infraction, if a cease-and-desist order is ignored. The commission can also require businesses to air corrective advertising to counter previous ads the commission considers misleading. For example, the maker of Doan's pills was required by the FTC to run corrective advertising to counter its unproven claim that its product is more effective than other pain relievers at alleviating back pain.[20]

In addition, the FTC helps to resolve disputes and makes rulings on business decisions, especially in emerging areas such as Internet privacy. For example, the commission approved a settlement that would permit the bankrupt Internet retailer Toysmart.com to sell its customer list as long as the buyer of the list agrees to abide by Toysmart's privacy guarantees.[21] Thus, in this case, the FTC helped to reinforce corporate guarantees of consumer privacy on the Internet.

Enforcement of the Laws Because violations of the Sherman Antitrust Act are felony crimes, the Antitrust Division of the U.S. Department of Justice enforces it. The FTC enforces antitrust regulations of a civil, rather than criminal, nature. There are many additional federal regulatory agencies (see Table 3.2) that oversee the enforcement of other laws and regulations. Most states also have regulatory agencies that make and enforce laws for individuals and businesses. In recent years, cooperation among state attorneys general and regulatory agencies and the federal government has increased, particularly in efforts related to the control of drugs, organized crime, and pollution. Such cooperation among state attorneys general and the FTC resulted in a $34 million settlement with Nine West Group, one of the nation's largest manufacturers of women's shoes, on price-fixing charges. Authorities said that Nine West violated federal and state antitrust laws by making agreements with retailers to fix the prices of its shoes and to limit sales promotion periods in order to maintain the prices of its shoes and restrict competition among retailers who sold Nine West brands. In addition to the $34 million payment, the settlement requires that Nine West not fix dealer prices, not pressure dealers to adopt any resale price, not threaten to limit supplies to dealers that adopt their own resale prices, and satisfy record-keeping provisions so the FTC can continue to monitor its compliance.[22]

In addition to enforcement by state and federal authorities, lawsuits by private citizens, competitors, and special-interest groups are used to enforce legal and regulatory policy. Through private civil actions, an individual or organization can file a lawsuit related to issues such as antitrust, price fixing, or unfair advertising. For example, the largest antitrust settlement to date occurred when several corporations brought a lawsuit against six of the world's largest manufacturers of vitamins. The suit accused the manufacturers, which accounted for 80 percent of the bulk sales of many popular vitamins, of colluding to fix prices with wholesale customers (large food and drug companies) over a nine-year period. The vitamin companies agreed to settle the case for $1.1 billion. Prior to this settlement, three of the manufacturers (F. Hoffman La Roche, BASF, and Rhone-Poulene) had been assessed a $750 million criminal fine

| TABLE 3.2 | Federal Regulatory Agencies |

AGENCY (DATE ESTABLISHED)	MAJOR AREAS OF RESPONSIBILITY
Food and Drug Administration (1906)	Enforces laws and regulations to prevent distribution of adulterated or misbranded foods, drugs, medical devices, cosmetics, veterinary products, and potentially hazardous consumer products
Federal Reserve Board (1913)	Regulates banking institutions; protects the credit rights of consumers; maintains the stability of the financial system; conducts the nation's monetary policy; and serves as the nation's central bank
Federal Trade Commission (1914)	Enforces laws and guidelines regarding business practices; takes action to stop false and deceptive advertising and labeling
Federal Communications Commission (1934)	Regulates communication by wire, radio, and television in interstate and foreign commerce
Securities and Exchange Commission (1934)	Regulates the offering and trading of securities, including stocks and bonds
National Labor Relations Board (1935)	Enforces the National Labor Relations Act; investigates and rectifies unfair labor practices by employers and unions
Equal Employment Opportunity Commission (1970)	Promotes equal opportunity in employment through administrative and judicial enforcement of civil rights laws and through education and technical assistance
Environmental Protection Agency (1970)	Develops and enforces environmental protection standards and conducts research into the adverse effects of pollution
Occupational Safety and Health Administration (1971)	Enforces the Occupational Safety and Health Act and other workplace health and safety laws and regulations; makes surprise inspections of facilities to ensure safe workplaces
Consumer Product Safety Commission (1972)	Ensures compliance with the Consumer Product Safety Act; protects the public from unreasonable risk of injury from any consumer product not covered by other regulatory agencies

for price fixing and market allocation.[23] An organization can also ask for assistance from a federal agency to address a concern. For example, American Express gained the assistance of the Department of Justice's Antitrust Division in accusing Visa and MasterCard of antitrust violations.[24]

Global Regulation

A company that engages in commerce beyond its own country's borders must contend with the potentially complex relationship among the laws of its own nation, international laws, and the laws of the nation in which it will be trading, as well as various trade restrictions imposed on international trade. International business activities are affected to varying degrees by each nation's laws, regulatory agencies, courts, the political environment, and special-interest groups. Some countries have established import barriers, including tariffs, quotas, minimum price levels, and port-of-entry taxes that affect the importation of products. The European Union and other countries, for example, banned cattle feed containing recycled cattle carcuses in order to prevent "mad cow" disease from which more than 100 people have died. France, for example, banned the importation of some cuts of beef and all livestock feed containing meat in order to curtail the spread of "mad cow" disease in that country.[25] Additionally, other laws may govern product quality and safety, distribution methods, and sales and advertising practices.

Although there is considerable variation and focus among different nations' laws, many countries have antitrust laws that are quite similar to those in the United States. Indeed, the Sherman Act has been copied throughout the world as the basis for regulating fair competition. German authorities, for example, accused Wal-Mart of exploiting its size to sell basic food items, such as milk, sugar, and flour, below cost on a regular basis, in violation of German antitrust laws. Authorities feared the practice would harm small- and medium-sized businesses that could not match the retail giant's lower prices.[26] Antitrust issues, such as price fixing and market allocation, have become a major area of international cooperation in the regulation of business.[27]

The North American Free Trade Agreement (NAFTA), which eliminates virtually all tariffs on goods produced and traded between the United States, Canada, and Mexico, makes it easier for businesses of each country to make investments in the other member countries. The agreement also provides some coordination of legal standards governing business transactions among the three countries. NAFTA promotes cooperation among various regulatory agencies to encourage effective law enforcement in the free trade area. Within the framework of NAFTA, the United States and Canada have developed many agreements to enforce each other's antitrust laws. The agreement provides for cooperation in investigations, including requests for information and the opportunity to visit the territory of the other nation in the course of conducting investigations.[28]

The European Union (EU) was established in 1958 to promote free trade among its members and now includes fifteen European nations, with ten more expected to be admitted over the next two years.[29] To facilitate trade among its members, the EU is working to standardize business laws and trade barriers, to eliminate customs checks among its members, and to create the use of a standard currency (the euro) for use by all members. Moreover, the Commission of the European Communities has entered into an agreement with the United States, similar to NAFTA, regarding joint antitrust laws.[30] A new offensive in the battle against Microsoft has been mounted by a coalition of computer, telephone, and Internet companies. The Computer and Communications Association filed a formal complaint with the European Commission, which enforces EU competition laws. The association has accused Microsoft of violating European antitrust law with its Windows XP operating system.[31] Another collaborative law enforcement effort, this one between the forty-one-nation Council of Europe and the United States, is the crafting of a treaty covering computer crimes.[32]

Costs and Benefits of Regulation

Costs of Regulation Regulation results in numerous costs for businesses, consumers, and society at large. According to one estimate, federal regulations cost the U.S.

| FIGURE 3.1 | Federal Regulatory Spending Activity, 1961–2003 (fiscal years, billions of dollars) |

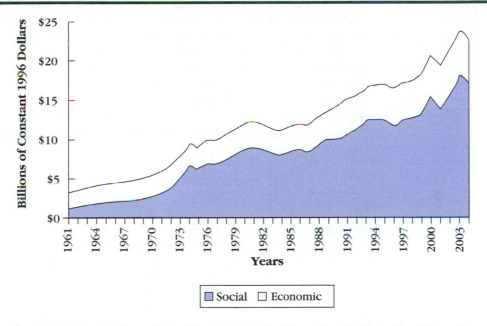

Source: "Administrative Costs of Federal Regulation," via http://wc.wustl.edu/RegBudgetNewsRelease.htm, accessed February 18, 2003. Susan Dudley and Melinda Warren, "Regulatory Response: An Analysis of the Shifting Priorities of the U.S. Budget for Fiscal Years 2002 and 2003," Regulatory Budget Report 24 (St. Louis, MO. and Washington, D.C.: Washington University's Weidenbaum Center and George Mason's Mercatus Center joint publication), June 2002. Reprinted with permission.

economy roughly $1 trillion a year.[33] Although many experts have attempted to quantify these costs, it is actually quite difficult to find an accurate measurement tool. To generate such measurements, economists often classify regulations as economic (applicable to specific industries or businesses) or social (broad regulations pertaining to health, safety, and the environment). One yardstick for the direct costs of regulation is the administrative spending patterns of federal regulatory agencies. In the United States, these expenditures have increased steadily over the years, culminating with a projected budget of $24.6 billion for federal regulatory spending in the year 2003, a slight decline from the all-time high of $25.1 billion in 2002, the highest level ever projected for the budgets of the fifty-four regulatory agencies (see Figure 3.1).[34] Another way to measure the direct cost of regulation is to look at the staffing levels of federal regulatory agencies. The expenditures and staffing of state and local regulatory agencies also generate direct costs to society.

Still another way to approach the measurement of the costs of regulation is to consider the burden that businesses incur in complying with regulations. Various federal regulations, for example, may require companies to make changes to their manufacturing processes or facilities (e.g., smokestack "scrubbers" to clean air, and wheelchair ramps to make facilities accessible to disabled customers and employees). Companies also must keep records to document their compliance and to obtain permits to implement plans that fall under the scope of specific regulatory agencies. Again, state regulatory agencies often add additional costs to this burden. Regulated firms may also spend large amounts of money and other resources to prevent additional legislation and to appear to be responsible. Philip Morris USA, for example, is spending more than $100 million a year to reduce underage smoking.[35]

Of course, businesses generally pass these regulatory costs on to their consumers in the form of higher prices, a cost that some label a "hidden tax" of government. Additionally, some businesses contend that the financial and time costs of complying with regulations stifle their ability to develop new products and make investments in facilities and equipment. Moreover, society must pay for the cost of staffing and operating regulatory agencies, and these costs may be reflected in federal income taxes.

Benefits of Regulation

Despite business complaints about the costs of regulation, it provides many benefits to business, consumers, and society as a whole. Among these benefits are greater equality in the workplace, safer workplaces, resources for disadvantaged members of society, safer products, more information about and greater choices among products, cleaner air and water, and the preservation of wildlife habitats to ensure that future generations can enjoy their beauty and diversity.

Antitrust laws and regulations strengthen competition by preventing monopolies. When markets are free and open to all, businesses must compete for consumers' dollars, and many try to differentiate their offerings by cutting prices or raising their quality. Companies that fail to respond to consumer desires or that employ inefficient processes are often forced out of the marketplace by savvier firms. Truly competitive markets also spur companies to invest in researching and developing product innovations as well as new, more efficient methods of production. These innovations benefit consumers through lower prices and improved goods and services.[36] For example, companies such as Apple, IBM, and Dell Computer continue to engineer smaller, faster, and more powerful computers that help individuals and businesses to be more productive.

Regulatory Reform Many businesses and individuals believe that the costs of regulation outweigh its benefits. They argue that removing regulation will allow Adam Smith's "invisible hand of competition" to more effectively and efficiently dictate business conduct. Some people desire complete **deregulation,** or removal of all regulatory authority. Proponents of deregulation believe that less government intervention allows business markets to work more effectively. For example, many businesses want their industries deregulated in order to decrease their costs of doing business. Many industries have been deregulated to a certain extent in recent years, including trucking, airlines, telecommunications (long-distance telephone and cable television), and, more recently, electric utilities. For example, the Federal Communications Commission (FCC) is diminishing its role in monitoring telephone equipment.[37] In many cases, this deregulation has resulted in lower prices for consumers as well as in greater product choice, particularly in the long-distance telephone industry. In the airline industry, for example, one of every four tickets sold is on a discount airline.[38]

deregulation
removal of all regulatory authority

Government regulation helps provide a competitive environment that encourages firms to produce smaller, more powerful notebook computers in order to assist both employees and companies in boosting productivity. (Digital Vision/Getty Images)

However, critics of deregulation point to higher prices, poor service, and decreased product quality that have plagued some deregulated industries. The year 2000 was considered one of the worst ever for air travel because of the prevalence of flight delays, high prices, and other issues. The September 11, 2001, airline terrorist attacks also pointed to problems of security in a deregulated environment. The federal government soon created the Homeland Security Act and instituted a national security effort for airports. However, there is still considerable debate on the relative merits and costs of regulation.

Self-Regulation Many companies attempt to regulate themselves in an effort to demonstrate social responsibility and to preclude further regulation by federal or state government. In addition to complying with all relevant laws and regulations, many firms choose to join trade associations that have self-regulatory programs. Although such programs are not a direct outgrowth of laws, many were established to stop or delay the development of laws and regulations that would restrict the associations' business practices. Some trade associations establish codes of conduct by which their members must abide or risk discipline or expulsion from the association.[39]

As noted in the opening vignette, perhaps the best-known self-regulatory association is the Better Business Bureau (BBB), a local organization supported by local member businesses. More than 145 local bureaus extending over 98 percent of the nation help resolve problems for nearly 24 million consumers and businesses each year.[40] Each bureau also works to champion good business practices within a community, although it usually does not have strong tools for enforcing its business conduct rules. When a company violates what the BBB believes to be good business practices, the bureau warns consumers through local newspapers or broadcast media.

If the offending organization is a member of the BBB, it may be expelled from the local bureau. For example, the membership of Priceline.com was revoked by a Connecticut Better Business Bureau after the online retailer failed to address numerous complaints related to misrepresentation of products, failure to provide promised refunds, and failure to correct billing problems.[41] The BBB has also developed a web site, BBB*OnLine*, to help consumers identify web sites that collect personal information in an ethical manner. BBB members that use the site agree to binding arbitration with regard to online privacy issues.

Self-regulatory programs like the Better Business Bureau have a number of advantages over government regulation. Establishment and implementation of such programs are usually less costly, and their guidelines or codes of conduct are generally more practical and realistic. Furthermore, effective self-regulatory programs reduce the need to expand government bureaucracy. However, self-regulation also has several limitations. Nonmember firms are under no obligation to abide by a trade association's industry guidelines or codes. Moreover, most associations lack the tools or authority to enforce their guidelines. Finally, these guidelines are often less strict than the regulations established by government agencies.[42]

Business's Influence on Government

Although the government has a profound effect on business activities, especially through its regulatory actions, business has an equal influence on government, and that influence has grown in recent years. Managing this relationship with government officials while navigating the dynamic world of politics is a major challenge for firms both large and small. In our pluralistic society, many participants are involved in the political process, and the economic stakes are high. Because government is a stakeholder of business (and vice versa), businesses and government can work together as both legitimately participate in the political process. For example, the Digital Electronic Signatures Act of 2000 was initiated by Internet businesses to improve efficiency and avoid the inconvenience and cost of written signatures. Contracts and documents electronically signed have the same legal status as those signed manually.[43] In promoting greater use of electronic signatures to authenticate transactions online, many businesses and consumers hope the bill will help reduce the incidence of fraud in e-commerce.

Obviously, many people believe that business should not be allowed to influence government because of its size, resources, and vested interests. Business participation can be either positive or negative for society's interest depending not only on the outcome but also on the perspective of various stakeholders. Before we look at specific tactics businesses use to influence government policy, it is useful to briefly examine the current political environment to understand how business influence has grown.

The Contemporary Political Environment

Beginning in the 1960s, a significant "antiestablishment" public, increasingly hostile to business, mounted protests to effect reform. Their increasingly vocal efforts spurred a fifteen-year wave of legislation and regulation to address a number of issues of the day, including product safety, employment discrimination, human rights, energy shortages, environmental degradation, and scandals related to bribery and payoffs. During the Republican-dominated 1980s, the pendulum swung back in favor of business. During the 1990s, economic prosperity driven by technological advances encouraged both the Republican and Democratic Parties to encourage the self-regulation of business while protecting competition and the natural environment. With the election of President George W. Bush in 2000, there is greater support of business. Environmental legislation passed under the previous Democratic leadership has been abandoned in recent years in favor of pro-business legislation. The balance between business interests and the environment may shift again. Critics have charged that Bush was too soft on business and environmental protection as governor of Texas and fear that this trend will continue, although after the terrorist attacks of September 11, 2001, national security emerged as the most important

President Bush shakes hands with Congressman Mike Oxley at the signing of the Sarbanes-Oxley Act in July 2002. (White House photo by Eric Draper)

issue, and the emphasis on environmental regulation diminished. Then the demise of Enron and WorldCom from corporate corruption created the need for the Bush administration to support major corporate reform legislation. Such changes in the political environment over the last forty years shaped the political environment in which businesses operate and created new avenues for businesses to participate in the political process. Among the most significant factors shaping the political environment were changes in Congress and the rise of special-interest groups.

Changes in Congress Among the calls for social reform in the 1960s were pressures for changes within the legislative process of the U.S. Congress itself. Bowing to this pressure, Congress enacted an amendment to the Legislative Reorganization Act in 1970, which effectively ushered in a new era of change for the political process. This legislation significantly revamped the procedures of congressional committees, most notably stripping committee chairpersons of much of their power, equalizing committee and chair assignments, and requiring committees to record and publish all roll-call votes taken in committee. By opening up the committee process to public scrutiny and reducing the power of senior members and committee leaders, the act reduced the level of secrecy surrounding the legislative process and effectively brought an end to an era of autonomous committee chairs and senior members.[44]

Another significant change occurred in 1974 when Congress amended the Federal Election Campaign Act to limit contributions from individuals, political parties, and special-interest groups organized to get specific candidates elected or policies enacted.[45] Around the same time, many states began to shift their electoral process from the traditional party caucus to primary elections, further eroding the influence of the party in the political process. These changes ultimately had the effect of reducing the importance of political parties by decreasing members' dependence on their parties. Many candidates for elected offices began to turn to special-interest groups to raise enough funds to mount serious campaigns.

Rise of Special-Interest Groups The success of activists' efforts in the 1960s and 1970s spawned the rise of special-interest groups. The movements to promote African American and women's rights and to protest the Vietnam War and environmental degradation of the day evolved into well-organized special-interest groups working to educate the public about significant social issues and to crusade for legislation and regulation of business conduct they deemed irresponsible. These progressive groups were soon joined on Capitol Hill by more conservative groups working to further their agendas on issues such as business deregulation, restriction of abortion and gun control, and promotion of prayer in schools. Businesses joined in by forming industry and trade associations. These increasingly powerful special-interest groups now focused on getting candidates elected who could further their own political agendas. Common Cause, for example, is a nonprofit, nonpartisan organization working to fight corrupt government and special interests backed by large sums of money. Since 1970, Common Cause, with over 200,000 members, has campaigned for greater openness and accountability in government. Some of its self-proclaimed "victories" include reform of presidential campaign finances, tax systems, congressional ethics, open meeting standards, and disclosure requirements for lobbyists.[46]

Corporate Approaches to Influencing Government

Although some businesses view regulatory and legal forces as beyond their control and simply react to conditions arising from those forces, other firms actively seek to influence the political process in order to achieve their goals. In some cases, companies publicly protest the actions of legislative bodies. More often, companies work for the election of political candidates who regard them positively. Lobbying, political action committees, and campaign contributions are some of the tools businesses employ to influence the political process.

Lobbying Among the most powerful tactics business can employ to participate in public policy decisions is direct representation through full-time staff that communicate with elected officials. **Lobbying** is the process of working to persuade public and/or government officials to favor a particular position in decision making. Organizations may lobby officials either directly or by combining their efforts with other organizations.

> **lobbying**
> the process of working to persuade public and/or government officials to favor a particular position in decision making

Many companies concerned about the threat of legislation or regulation that may negatively affect their operations employ lobbyists to communicate their concerns to officials on their behalf. Microsoft, for example, established a Washington office with a staff of fourteen lobbyists and spent $4.6 million to persuade federal officials that breaking up the company for antitrust violations would harm the computer industry and U.S. economy.[47] They were successful in preventing the breakup of the company.

Companies may attempt to influence the legislative or regulatory process more indirectly through trade associations and umbrella organizations that represent collective business interests of many firms. Virtually every industry has one or more trade associations that represent the interests of their members to federal officials and provide public education and other services for their members. Examples of such trade associations include the National Association of Home Builders, the Tobacco Institute, the American Booksellers Association, and the Pet Food Institute. The National Cable and Telecommunications Association (NCTA) responded to a lobbying campaign by Amazon.com, Apple Computers, Microsoft, eBay, and Yahoo, which asked the FCC to regulate high-speed Internet access to assure open availability to information products and services. The NCTA said that cable consumers had full access to Internet content and regulation would have had unintended negative consequences.[48] Additionally, there are often state trade associations, such as the Hawaii Coffee Association and the Michigan Beer and Wine Wholesalers Association, that work on state- and regional-level issues. Umbrella organizations such as the National Federation of Independent Businesses and the U.S. Chamber of Commerce also help to promote business interests to government officials. The U.S. Chamber of Commerce takes positions on many political, regulatory, and economic questions. With more than 200,000 member companies, its goal is to promote its members' views of the ideal free enterprise marketplace. There is growing interest and concern, however, about the relationship between corporations and the government. Lobbying by companies and their trade associations against social and environmental regulations or measures to help citizens in poorer countries has been identified as an emerging concern by Lifeworth.com in its recent Annual Review of Corporate Responsibility.[49]

The U.S. Chamber of Commerce provides information about improving business issues, and it works to minimize government interference. (http:// www.uschamber .org/government/ issues/econtax/bush plan.htm, accessed April 2003. Copyright © 2003 by the United States Chamber of Commerce. Reprinted with permission.)

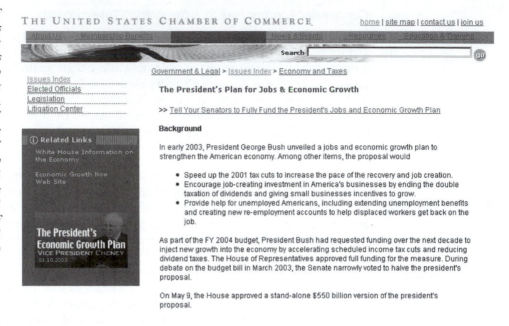

Political Action Committees Companies can also influence the political process through political action committees. **Political action committees (PACs)** are organizations that solicit donations from individuals and then contribute these funds to candidates running for political office. Companies are barred by federal law from donating directly to candidates for federal offices or to political action committees, and individuals are limited to relatively small donations. However, companies can organize PACS to which their executives, employees, and stockholders can make significant donations as individuals. PACs operate independently of business and are usually incorporated. Labor unions and other special-interest groups, such as teachers and medical doctors, can also establish PACs to promote their goals.

The Federal Election Committee has established rules to restrict PAC donations to $5,000 per candidate for each election. However, many PACs exploit loopholes in these regulations by donating so-called soft money to political parties that do not support a specific candidate for federal office. Under current rules, these contributors can make unlimited donations to political parties for general activities. Microsoft, for example, contributed $1 million to help underwrite both the Republican and Democratic Party conventions in 2000. In addition, the company gave $522,150 in soft money to the Republican Party and $341,250 to the Democratic Party. The Bill and Melinda Gates Foundation contributed another $10 million to the U.S. Capitol Visitors Center. All of this largesse occurred while the Justice Department was passing judgment on Microsoft for antitrust violations.[50] Some candidates form "leadership PACs" to avoid traditional PAC limitations since they are not specifically legislated by the FEC.[51]

Campaign Contributions Although federal laws restrict direct corporate contributions to electorion campaigns, corporate money may be channeled into candidates'

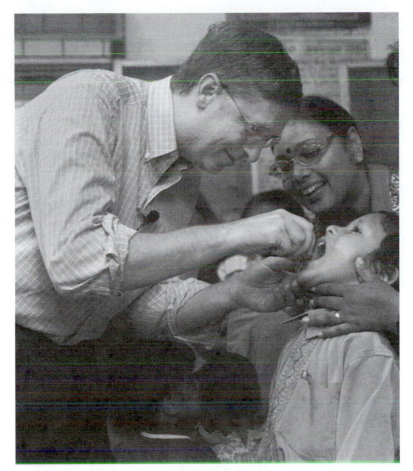

The Bill and Melinda Gates Foundation supports both health and human services. Bill Gates is shown here administering an oral polio vaccine in New Delhi. (Jeff Christensen/ Getty Images)

campaign coffers as corporate executives' or stockholders' personal contributions. Such donations can violate the spirit of corporate campaign laws. A sizable contribution to a candidate may carry with it an implied understanding that the elected official will perform some favor, such as voting in accordance with the contributor's desire on a particular law. Occasionally, some businesses find it so important to ensure favorable treatment that they make illegal corporate contributions to campaign funds. Former Louisiana governor Edwin Edwards not only accepted campaign contributions; he extorted contributions from some businesspeople who applied for riverboat casino licenses during Edwards's tenure as governor.[52]

Although laws limit corporate contributions to specific candidates, it is acceptable for businesses and other organizations to make donations to political parties. Table 3.3 lists selected organizations and their contributions to political parties. Note that labor unions typically donate to the Democratic Party, whereas the National Rifle Association contributes only to the Republican Party. Some companies, including SBC Communications (parent company of Southwestern Bell) and Citigroup, choose to give to both major political parties.

Global Initiatives

Royal Ahold Illustrates That Accounting Irregularities Are a Global Issue

Many people thought that problems that have plagued U.S. businesses and created huge scandals could not happen in Europe, but they were wrong. Royal Ahold, the giant Dutch-based grocer and food distributor, recently disclosed accounting irregularities that resulted in an overstatement of earnings by at least $500 million over the last two years. The company's top two executives, its chief executive and its chief financial officer, resigned. Cees van der Hoeven, Ahold's chief executive, had been instrumental in helping to transform a 116-year-old Dutch family grocer into one of the world's largest retailers. Ahold was popular with investors and trailed only Wal-Mart Stores, Inc., of the United States and Carrefour SA of France in global retailing. Under their own local

brand names, Ahold companies operate about 9,000 supermarkets, hypermarkets, and convenience stores in the United States, Europe, Latin America, and Asia. Ahold employs more than 450,000 people worldwide.

Thought to be a good corporate citizen, Ahold promoted many socially responsible activities. Giant Food Stores, a member of the Ahold family of retail food chains, was recognized as an "Outstanding Corporation" for its support of the Children's Miracle Network at Penn State Children's Hospital. Also, the Ahold organization raised more than $5 million to aid victims of the September 11 terrorist attacks.

The company's accounting problems were uncovered during an annual audit by Deloitte Touche Tohmatsu. Questions about Ahold's accounting practices were raised after company officials said that preparing its 2001 results under U.S. rather than Dutch accounting rules would have decreased

---

TABLE 3.3 Contributions from Selected Organizations in the 1999–2000 Election Cycle

ORGANIZATION	TOTAL CONTRIBUTION	TO DEMOCRATS	TO REPUBLICANS
AT&T	$3,452,540	$1,251,734	$2,200,806
Service Employees International Union	$2,380,650	$2,350,250	$30,400
Microsoft	$1,881,006	$799,292	$1,081,714
Philip Morris	$1,777,627	$256,641	$1,520,986
SBC Communications	$1,426,068	$718,650	$707,418
Enron Corp.	$1,384,915	$359,565	$1,025,350
United Food & Commercial Workers Union	$1,376,250	$1,376,250	
Citigroup	$1,337,140	$651,556	$685,584
National Rifle Association	$1,305,515		$1,305,515

Source: "Top Soft Money Donors: 2000 Election Cycle," Center for Responsive Politics, November 1, 2000. Reprinted by permission from the Center for Responsive Politics. www.opensecrets.org/parties/cgi-win/softtop_2000.exe?txtCycle=2000&txtSort=amnt.

its reported earnings by 90 percent. The problems centered mainly on promotional payments by manufacturers to an Ahold U.S. subsidiary. In some cases, the payments or allowances were booked too high. A standard practice in the food industry, promotional allowances frequently have been the subject of accounting inquiries and problems. Ahold, with operations in twenty-five countries, is also investigating possible irregularities at an Argentine subsidiary and has said the way results are reported from three other partly owned subsidiaries would be changed.

Effects of the disclosures were immediate. The company's credit rating was downgraded, and its banks insisted that a five-year unsecured credit line of 2 billion euros be replaced with less favorable financing. Scheduled to repay about $1.5 billion in debts this year, the company said it would try to raise cash by selling some operations and assets.

The disclosures by Ahold provide evidence that Europe is not immune to the accounting scandals that have plagued many of the United States's largest companies over the past few years. The developments have raised concerns that European accounting standards may be no better than U.S. standards at preventing such scandals. Whether in Europe, the United States, or another nation, failure to maintain integrity in financial reporting will result in problems.

Sources:
Deborah Ball, Ann Zimmerman, and Maaike Veen, "Supermarket Giant Ahold Ousts CEO in Big Accounting Scandal," *Wall Street Journal,* February 25, 2003; Gregory Crouch with Suzanne Kapner, "Dutch Grocer Overstated Earnings," *New York Times,* February 24, 2003, via http://www.nytimes.com; "Ahold USA: Our Vision," via http://www.aholdusa.com/, accessed February 25, 2003; and "Giant Food Stores Named 'Outstanding Corporation,'" Ahold USA Press Release, December 19, 2002, via http://www.aholdusa.com/press_display.cfm?press_ID=15, accessed February 25, 2003.

The Government's Approach for Legal and Ethical Compliance

Thus far, we have seen that although legal and regulatory forces have a strong influence on business operations, businesses can affect these forces through the political process. In addition, socially responsible firms strive to comply with society's wishes for responsible conduct through legal and ethical behavior. Indeed, the most effective way for businesses to manage the legal and regulatory environment is to establish values and policies that communicate and reward appropriate conduct. Most employees will try to comply with an organization's leadership and directions for responsible conduct. Therefore, top management must develop and implement a highly visible strategy for effective compliance. This means that top managers must take responsibility and be accountable for assessing legal risks and developing corporate programs that promote acceptable conduct.

Federal Sentencing Guidelines for Organizations (FSGO)
established in 1991 to streamline the sentencing and punishment for organizational crimes and to hold companies, as well as their employees, responsible for misconduct

Federal Sentencing Guidelines for Organizations

More and more companies are establishing organizational compliance programs to ensure that they operate legally and responsibly as well as to generate a competitive advantage based on a reputation for responsible citizenship. There are also strong legal incentives to establish such programs. The U.S. Sentencing Commission established the **Federal Sentencing Guidelines for Organizations (FSGO)** in 1991 not only to streamline the sentencing and punishment for organizational crimes but also to hold companies, as well as their employees, responsible for misconduct. Previously, the law punished only those employees responsible for an offense, not the company. Under the FSGO, if a court determines that a company's organizational culture rewarded or otherwise created opportunities that encouraged wrongdoing, the firm may be subject to stiff penalties in the event that one of its employees breaks the law. The guidelines apply to all felonies and Class A misdemeanors committed by employees in association with their work. Table 3.4 shows the percentage number of organizations receiving fines and/or ordered to make restitution for crimes sentenced in 2001. Of the 238 organizations sentenced under the guidelines, 90.8 percent were fined, ordered to make restitution, or both, and the average fine and/or restitution amounted to more than $9 million.[53]

The assumption underlying the FSGO is that good socially responsible organizations maintain compliance systems and internal governance controls that deter misconduct by their employees. Thus, the guidelines focus on crime prevention and detection by mitigating penalties for those firms that have implemented such compliance programs in the event that one of their employees commits a crime. To avoid or limit fines and other penalties as a result of wrongdoing by an employee, the employer must be able to demonstrate that it has implemented a reasonable program for deterring and preventing unlawful behavior.

The U.S. Sentencing Commission has delineated seven steps that companies must implement to demonstrate the existence of an effective compliance effort and thereby avoid penalties in the event of an employee's wrongdoing. These steps, which are listed in Table 3.5, are based on the commission's determination to emphasize compliance programs and to provide guidance for both organizations and courts regarding program effectiveness. The steps are not "a superficial checklist re-

TABLE 3.4 A Sample of Organizations Fined or Ordered to Make Restitution Under FSGO in 2001

OFFENSE	NO FINE OR RESTITUTION	RESTITUTION ONLY	FINE ONLY	BOTH FINE AND RESTITUTION
Antitrust	16	4	10	2
Bribery	2	0	0	2
Fraud	66	16	35	15
Import/export violation	13	0	11	2
Money laundering	11	4	5	2
Environmental water	30	1	19	10
Food & drugs	14	0	10	4

Source: *U.S. Sentencing Commission's Sourcebook of Federal Sentencing Statistics,* www.ussc.gov/ANNRPT/2001/table 51.pdf., accessed February 21, 2003.

TABLE 3.5	Seven Steps to Legal Compliance

1. Establish codes of conduct (identify key risk areas).
2. Appoint or hire high-level compliance manager (ethics officer).
3. Take care in delegating authority (background checks on employees).
4. Institute a training program and communication system (ethics training).
5. Monitor and audit for misconduct (reporting mechanisms).
6. Enforce and discipline (management implementation of policy).
7. Revise program as needed (feedback and action).

Source: U.S. Sentencing Commission, *Federal Sentencing Guidelines for Organizations,* 2001.

quiring little analysis or thought."[54] Rather, they help companies understand what is required of a compliance program that is capable of reducing employees' opportunities to engage in misconduct.

To develop an effective compliance program, an organization should first develop a code of conduct that communicates the standards it expects of its employees and identifies key risk areas for the firm. Next, oversight of the program should be assigned to high-ranking personnel in the organization (such as an ethics officer, a vice president of human resources, or a general counsel) who are known to abide by the legal and ethical standards of the industry. Authority should never be delegated to anyone with a known propensity to engage in misconduct. An effective compliance program also requires a meaningful communications system, often in the form of ethics training, to disseminate the company's standards and procedures. This system should provide for mechanisms, such as anonymous toll-free hot lines or company ombudsmen, through which employees can report wrongdoing without fear of retaliation. Monitoring and auditing systems designed to detect misconduct are also crucial ingredients for an effective compliance program. If a company does detect criminal behavior or other wrongdoing by an employee, it must take immediate, appropriate, and fair disciplinary action toward all individuals both directly and indirectly responsible for the offense. Finally, if a company discovers that a crime has occurred, it must take steps to prevent similar offenses in the future. This usually involves modifications to the compliance program, additional employee training, and communications about specific types of conduct. The government expects continuous improvement and refinement of these seven steps for compliance programs.[55]

A strong compliance program acts as a buffer to keep employees from committing crimes and to protect a company's reputation should wrongdoing occur despite its best efforts. If a firm can demonstrate that is has truly made an effort to communicate to its employees about their legal and ethical responsibilities, the public's response to any wrongdoing may be reduced along with any corporate punishment the courts mete out for the offense. It is important to point out, however, that executives who focus on strict legal compliance may be missing part of the picture when it comes to social responsibility. An effective compliance program must feature ethics and values as the driving force, as we shall see in the next chapter.

Sarbanes-Oxley Act

During probes into financial reporting fraud at Enron, WorldCom, and many other companies, investigators learned that hundreds of public corporations were not reporting their financial results accurately. Accounting firms, lawyers, top corporate officers, and boards of directors had developed a culture of deception to attempt to gain investor approval and competitive advantage. The downfall of many of these companies resulted in the loss to thousands of investors and employees lost much of their savings. In order to restore stakeholder confidence and provide a new standard of ethical behavior for U.S. business, the **Sarbanes-Oxley Act** was enacted. The act had almost unanimous support by Congress, government regulatory agencies, and the general public. When President Bush signed the act, he emphasized the need for the standards it provides, especially for top management and boards of directors responsible for company oversight. Table 3.6 details the requirements of the Act.

Sarbanes-Oxley Act legislation to protect investors by improving accuracy and reliability of corporate disclosures

Many company boards failed to provide the necessary oversight of the financial decisions of top officers and executives. At Adelphia Communications, for example, the Rigas family (Adelphia founders) collected more than $3 billion from the firm, using it as a kind of personal line of credit.[56] A former Kmart CEO, Charles Conaway, allegedly hired unqualified executives and consultants at fees that far exceeded the norm. There was also $24 million in board-approved loans just one month before Kmart filed for Chapter 11 bankruptcy.[57]

TABLE 3.6	Major Provisions of the Sarbanes-Oxley Act

1. Requires the establishment of an Independent Accounting Oversight Board in charge of regulations administered by the Securities and Exchange Commission.
2. Requires CEOs and CFOs to certify that their companies' financial statements are true and without misleading statements.
3. Requires that corporate board of directors' audit committees consist of independent members with no material interests in the company.
4. Prohibits corporations from making or offering loans to officers and board members
5. Requires codes of ethics for senior financial officers; code must be registered with the SEC.
6. Prohibits accounting firms from providing both auditing and consulting services to the same client.
7. Requires company attorneys to report wrongdoing to top managers and, if necessary, to the board of directors; if managers and directors fail to respond to reports of wrongdoing, the attorney should stop representing the company.
8. Mandates "whistle-blower protection" for persons who disclose wrongdoing to authorities.
9. Requires financial securities analysts to certify that their recommendations are based on objective reports.
10. Requires mutual fund managers to disclose how they vote shareholder proxies, giving investors information about how their shares influence decisions.
11. Establishes a ten-year penalty for mail/wire fraud.
12. Prohibits the two senior auditors from working on a corporation's account for more than five years; other auditors are prohibited from working on an account for more than seven years; in other words, accounting firms must rotate individual auditors from one account to another from time to time.

TABLE 3.7	Benefits of Sarbanes-Oxley

1. Greater accountability by top management and board of directors to employees, communities, and society. The goals of the business will be to provide stakeholders with a return on their investment, rather than providing a vehicle for management to reap excessive compensation and other benefits.

2. Renewed investor confidence providing managers and brokers with the information they need to make solid investment decisions, which will ultimately lead to a more stable and solid growth rate for investors.

3. Explanations by CEOs of why their compensation package is in the best interest of the company. It will also eliminate certain traditional senior management perks, including company loans, and require disclosures about stock trades, thus making executives more like other investors.

4. Greater protection of employee retirement plans. Employees can develop greater trust that they will not lose savings tied to such plans.

5. Greater penalties and accountability of senior management auditors and board members. The penalties now outweigh the rewards of purposeful manipulation and deception.

To address fraudulent occurrences such as these, the Sarbanes-Oxley Act provides for the creation of the Public Company Accounting Oversight Board, which provides oversight of the accounting firms that audit public companies and set standards and rules for the auditors in these firms. The board has investigatory and disciplinary power over accounting firm auditors and securities analysts who issue reports about companies. Conflicts of interest will be eliminated with auditing firms no longer able to act as both auditor and consultant without gaining special permission. Limitations on nonaudit services for clients have been imposed as have limitations on the amount of time lead auditors may serve a particular client.

The Sarbanes-Oxley Act requires corporations to take more responsibility and to provide principles-based ethical leadership. Enhanced financial disclosures are required including certification by top officers that audit reports are complete and that nothing material has been withheld from auditors. CEOs and CFOs will now be held personally accountable for the credibility and accuracy of their company's financial statements. A code of ethics for senior financial officers that addresses their specific areas of risk is now required. Other provisions of the act include whistle-blower protection and changes in the attorney-client relationship so that attorneys are now required to report wrongdoing to top managers or to the board of directors. Table 3.7 lists the benefits of the act.

There are some concerns with the act, however. While a law may help prevent misconduct, it will not stop executives who are determined to lie, steal, manipulate, or deceive for personal gain. The law requires that accountants and executives do the right thing, but a deep commitment by top company leadership is necessary to create an ethical corporate culture.

S u m m a r y

In a pluralistic society, many diverse stakeholder groups attempt to influence the public officials who legislate, interpret laws, and regulate business. Companies that adopt a strategic approach to the legal and regulatory system develop proactive organizational values and compliance programs that identify areas of risks and include formal communication, training, and continuous improvement of responses to the legal and regulatory environment.

Economic reasons for regulation often relate to efforts to level the playing field on which businesses operate. These efforts include regulating trusts, which are generally established to gain control of a product market or industry by eliminating competition, and eliminating monopolies, which occur when just one business provides a good or service in a given market. Another rationale for regulation is society's desire to restrict destructive or unfair competition. Social reasons for regulation address imperfections in the market that result in undesirable consequences, and the protection of natural and social resources. Other regulations are created in response to social demands for safety and equality in the workplace, safer products, and privacy issues.

The Sherman Antitrust Act is the principal tool used to prevent businesses from restraining trade and monopolizing markets. The Clayton Antitrust Act limits mergers and acquisitions that could stifle competition and prohibits specific activities that could substantially lessen competition or tend to create a monopoly. The Federal Trade Commission Act prohibits unfair methods of competition and created the Federal Trade Commission (FTC). Legal and regulatory policy is also enforced through lawsuits by private citizens, competitors, and special-interest groups.

A company that engages in commerce beyond its own country must contend with the complex relationship among the laws of its own nation, international laws, and the laws of the nation in which it will be trading. There is considerable variation and focus among different nations' laws, but many countries' antitrust laws are quite similar to those of the United States.

Regulation creates numerous costs for businesses, consumers, and society at large. Some measures of these costs include administrative spending patterns, staffing levels of federal regulatory agencies, and costs businesses incur in complying with regulations. The cost of regulation is passed on to consumers in the form of higher prices and may stifle product innovation and investments in new facilities and equipment. Regulation also provides many benefits, including greater equality in the workplace, safer workplaces, resources for disadvantaged members of society, safer products, more information about and greater choices among products, cleaner air and water, and the preservation of wildlife habitats. Antitrust laws and regulations strengthen competition and spur companies to invest in research and development. Many businesses and individuals believe that the costs of regulation outweigh its benefits. Some people desire complete deregulation, or removal of regulatory authority.

Because government is a stakeholder of business (and vice versa), businesses and government can work together as both legitimately participate in the political process. Business participation can be a positive or negative force in society's interest, depending not only on the outcome but also on the perspective of various stakeholders.

Changes over the last forty years have shaped the political environment in which businesses operate. Among the most significant of these changes were amendments to the Legislative Reorganization Act and the Federal Election Campaign Act, which had the effect of reducing the importance of political parties. Many candidates for elected offices turned to increasingly powerful special-interest groups to raise funds to campaign for elected office.

Some organizations view regulatory and legal forces as beyond their control and simply react to conditions arising from those forces; other firms seek to influence the political process in order to achieve their goals. One way they can do so is through lobbying, the process of working to persuade public and/or government officials to favor a particular position in decision making. Companies can also influence the political process through political action committees, which are organizations that solicit donations from individuals and then contribute these funds to candidates running for political office. Corporate funds may also be channeled into candidates' campaign coffers as corporate executives' or stockholders' personal contributions, although such donations can violate the spirit of corporate campaign laws. Although laws limit corporate contributions to specific candidates, it is acceptable for businesses and other organizations to make donations to political parties.

More companies are establishing organizational compliance programs to ensure that they operate legally and responsibly as well as to generate a competitive advantage based on a reputation for good citizenship. Under the *Federal Sentencing Guidelines for Organizations (FSGO)*, a company that wants to avoid or limit fines and other penalties as a result of an employee's crime must be able to demonstrate that it has implemented a reasonable program for deterring and preventing misconduct. To implement an effective compliance program, an organization should develop a code of conduct that communicates expected standards, assign oversight of the program to high-ranking personnel who abide by legal and ethical standards, communicate standards through training and other mechanisms, monitor and audit to detect wrongdoing, punish individuals responsible for misconduct, and take steps to continuously improve the program. A strong compliance program acts as a buffer to keep employees from committing crimes and to protect a company's reputation should wrongdoing occur despite its best efforts.

Enacted after many corporate financial fraud scandals, the Sarbanes-Oxley Act created the Public Company Accounting Oversight Board to provide oversight and set standards for the accounting firms that audit public companies. The board has investigatory and disciplinary power over accounting firm auditors and securities analysts. The act requires corporations to take responsibility to provide principles-based ethical leadership and holds CEOs and CFOs personally accountable for the credibility and accuracy of their company's financial statements. It is hoped that the act will provide for a new standard of ethical behavior for U.S. business, especially for top management and boards of directors responsible for company oversight.

Key Terms

trust (p. 66)
monopoly (p. 66)
deregulation (p. 76)
lobbying (p. 81)
political action committee (PAC) (p. 82)
Federal Sentencing Guidelines for Organizations (FSGO) (p. 85)
Sarbanes-Oxley Act (p. 88)

Discussion Questions

1. Discuss the existence of both cooperation and conflict between government and businesses concerning the regulation of business.

2. What is the rationale for government to regulate the activities of businesses? How is our economic and social existence shaped by government regulations?

3. What was the historical background that encouraged the government to enact legislation such as the Sherman Antitrust Act and the Clayton Act? Do these same conditions exist today?

4. What is the role and function of the Federal Trade Commission in the regulation of business? How does the FTC engage in proactive activities to avoid government regulation?

5. How do global regulations influence U.S. businesses operating internationally? What are the major obstacles to global regulation?

6. Compare the costs and benefits of regulation. In your opinion, do the benefits outweigh the costs or do the costs outweigh the benefits? What are the advantages and disadvantages of deregulation?

7. Name three tools that businesses can employ to influence government and public policy. Evaluate the strengths and weaknesses of each of these approaches.

8. How do political action committees influence society, and what is their appropriate role in a democratic society?

9. Why should an organization evaluate and possibly implement the Federal Sentencing Guidelines for Organizations (FSGO) as a strategic approach for legal compliance?

10. What are the seven steps for developing an effective ethical compliance program under the FSGO? What is the appropriate role of top management in developing effective compliance programs?

Experiential Exercise

Visit the web site of the Federal Trade Commission (FTC) (http://www.ftc.gov/). What is the FTC's current mission? What are the primary areas for which the FTC is responsible? Review the last two months of press releases from the FTC. On the basis of these releases, what appear to be major issues of concern at this time?

What Would You Do?

The election of a new governor brings many changes to any state capital, including the shuffling of a variety of appointed positions. In most cases, political appointees have contributed a great deal to the governor's election bid and have expertise in a specific area related to the appointed post. Joe Barritz was in that position when he became assistant agricultural commissioner in January 2003. He was instrumental in getting the governor elected, especially through his fundraising efforts. Joe's family owned thousands of acres in the state and had been farming and ranching since the 1930s. Joe earned a bachelor's degree in agricultural economics and policy and a law degree from one of the state's top institutions. He worked as an attorney in the state's capital city for over eighteen years and represented a range of clients, most of whom were involved in agriculture. Thus, he had many characteristics that made him a strong candidate for assistant commissioner. After about six months on the job, Joe had lunch with a couple of friends he had known for many years. During that June lunch, they had a casual conversation about the fact that Joe never did have a true "celebration" after being named assistant agricultural commissioner. His friends decided to talk with others about the possibility of holding that celebration in a few months. Before long, eight of Joe's friends were busy planning to hold a reception in his honor on October 5. Two of these friends were currently employed as lobbyists. One represented the beef industry association and the other worked for the cotton industry council. They asked Joe if they could hold the celebration at his lake home in the capital city. Joe talked with the commission's ethics officer about the party and learned that these types of parties, between close friends, were common for newly appointed and elected officials. The ethics officer told Joe that the reception and location were fine, but only if his lobbyist friends paid for the reception with personal funds. The state's ethics rules did not allow a standing government official to take any type of gift, including corporate dollars, that might influence his or her decision making. Joe communicated this information to his friends.

During the next few months, Joe was involved in a number of issues that could potentially help or harm agriculture-based industries. Various reports and policy statements within the Agricultural Commission were being used to tailor state legislation and regulatory proposals. The beef and cotton councils were actively supporting a proposal that would provide tax breaks to farmers and ranchers. Staff on the Agricultural Commission were mixed on the proposal, but Joe was expected to deliver a report to a legislative committee on the commission's preferences. His presentation was scheduled for October 17.

On October 5, nearly sixty of Joe's friends gathered at the catered reception to reminisce and congratulate him on his achievements. Most were good friends and acquaintances, so the mood and conversation were relatively light that evening. A college football game between two big rivals drew most people to the big-screen TV. By midnight, the guests were gone. Back at the office the following week, Joe began working on his presentation for the legislative committee. Through a series of economic analyses, long meetings, and electronic discussions, he decided to support the tax benefits for farmers and ranchers. News reports carried information from his presentation.

It was not long before some reporters made a "connection" between the reception in Joe's honor and his stand on the tax breaks for agriculture industries. An investigation quickly ensued, including reports that the beef and cotton industry associations had not only been present but also financially supported the reception on October 5. The small company used to plan and cater the party indicated that checks from the cotton industry council and beef industry association were used to cover some of the expenses. A relationship between the "gift" of the reception and Joe's presentation to the legislative committee would be a breach of his oath of office and state ethics rules. If you were Joe, what would you do?

Chapter 4

Business Ethics and Ethical Decision Making

CHAPTER OBJECTIVES

- To define and describe the importance of business ethics
- To understand the diverse and complex nature of existing and emerging ethical issues
- To discuss the individual factors that influence ethical or unethical decisions
- To explore the effect of organizational relationships on ethical decision making
- To evaluate the role of opportunity in ethical or unethical decisions

CHAPTER OUTLINE

The Nature of Business Ethics

Foundations of Business Ethics

Ethical Issues in Business

Understanding the Ethical Decision-Making Process

Like many automakers around the world, Mitsubishi Motors, Japan's number four automaker, faces intense competition in markets both at home in Japan and abroad. The company was losing hundreds of millions of dollars in the early 2000s with decreasing sales, whereas rival Toyota Motor and Honda Motor were experiencing increased sales. Mitsubishi's poor performance led it to make alliances with Volvo and Daimler-Chrysler, the latter acquiring a 34 percent stake in the Japanese firm. However, the bad news for Mitsubishi worsened into a scandal after a twenty-year practice of hiding consumer complaints came to light.

Mitsubishi admitted that for more than twenty years, it had systematically covered up customer complaints about tens of thousands of defective automobiles. During this period, when customers brought their cars in for repairs, Mitsubishi employees fixed the defects but pigeonholed the complaints in a file known as "H," for a Japanese word for conceal or defer. When rumors of the secret file began to circulate in the summer of 2000, the company president Katsuhiko Kawasoe at first denied the allegations. Soon after, Japan Transportation Ministry officials, acting on an anonymous tip, found the complaints in the company locker room during an inspection.

By not reporting customer complaints about defects to the government, as required by both Japanese and U.S. law, Mitsubishi headed off the threat of expensive recalls and negative publicity. Although none of the defects resulted in any serious or fatal accidents, Japan's Transportation Ministry made charges. In the United States, the National Highway Safety Administration investigated to determine the extent of violations of U.S. law.

After the secret files came to light, Mitsubishi admitted to hiding complaints and agreed to recall a total of 620,000 vehicles, including 50,000 that had been exported to the United States, to repair faulty fuel tanks, fuel tank caps, clutches, crankshafts, and brakes. The recalls were expected to cost the company about $69 million. The practice of concealing evidence of defects that could precipitate a recall is not so unusual in Japan. In Japanese culture, product recalls are judged an enormous humiliation, especially for Japan's acclaimed automotive manufacturers.

After the scandal was publicized, the Mitsubishi president Katsuhiko Kawasoe apologized to the minister of transportation, Hajime Morita, with a deep bow, as well as to Mitsubishi vehicle owners. Kawasoe also promised that the company would punish those directly responsible. "The whole state of affairs is, in a word, the result of a lack of respect for rules and regulations on the part of the company officers and employees involved," he said. Moreover, Kawasoe, along with other top Mitsubishi executives, agreed to take a salary cut to acknowledge his accountability in the cover-up, even though Kawasoe continued to deny prior knowledge of it. Kawasoe added, "My job is to work to regain the public's trust in this company.[1]

As illustrated by the Mitsubishi scandal, key business ethics concerns relate to questions about whether various stakeholders consider specific business practices acceptable. Wal-Mart, for example, has been accused of paying its female employees less than its male employees for the same jobs even after seniority, store location, and other factors have been considered. The retailer has also been accused of failing to advance women into higher-level jobs at a rate comparable to that for men. If the accusations prove to be true, Wal-Mart could face penalties in the hundreds of millions of dollars and could be forced to overhaul its entire pay and promotion system.[2] The Minnesota attorney general sued U.S. Bank for allegedly releasing customers' private information—including social security numbers, account numbers and balances, and credit-card numbers—to a telemarketing company.[3] Regardless of the legality of the actions of these companies, others have judged the conduct as unacceptable.

By its very nature, the field of business ethics is controversial, and no universally accepted approach has emerged for resolving its questions. Nonetheless, most businesses are establishing initiatives that include the development and implementation of ethics programs designed to deter conduct that some stakeholders might consider objectionable. Unisys, for example, provides ethics training for 34,000 employees working in 100 countries worldwide. It reaches about 90 percent of them annually through videos, an internal web site, newsletters, and other ethics training.[4] This training helps Unisys communicate its values and policies to ensure that employees understand what the company expects of them, as well as what will happen if they violate the company's policies or the law.

The definition of social responsibility that appears in Chapter 1 incorporates society's expectations and includes four levels of concern: economic, legal, ethical, and philanthropic. Because ethics is becoming an increasingly important issue in business today, this chapter and Chapter 5 are devoted to exploring this dimension of social responsibility. First, we define business ethics, examine its importance from an organizational perspective, and review its foundations. Next, we define ethical issues in business to help understand areas of risk. We then look at the individual, organizational, and opportunity factors that influence ethical decision making in the workplace.

The Nature of Business Ethics

To support business decisions that are both acceptable and beneficial to society, it is necessary to examine business ethics from an organizational perspective. The term *ethics* relates to choices and judgments about acceptable standards of conduct that guide the behavior of individuals and groups. These standards require both organizations and individuals to accept responsibility for their actions and to comply with established value systems. As Figure 4.1 indicates, most employees perceive that the values of honesty, respect, and trust are applied frequently in the workplace. Without a shared view of what values and conduct are appropriate and acceptable, companies may fail to balance their desires for profits against the wishes and needs of society. Maintaining this balance often demands compromises or trade-offs. For example, the controversy surrounding the promotion of cigarettes to children and teenagers has put pressure on tobacco manufacturers to stop advertising in magazines in which 15 percent or more of the readers are teenagers. In response, leading companies such as Philip Morris have pledged to pull ads from magazines with substantial numbers of young readers, including *Rolling Stone* and *Sports Illustrated*.[5] This example illustrates the legal and social pressures to act appropriately in order to protect children from the dangers of smoking. Society has developed rules—both legal and implied—to guide companies in their efforts to earn profits through means that do not bring harm to individuals or to society at large.

business ethics
the principles and standards that guide the behavior of individuals and groups in the world of business

Business ethics comprises the principles and standards that guide the behavior of individuals and groups in the world of business. Managers, employees, consumers, industry associations, government regulators, business partners, and special-interest

| FIGURE 4.1 | Values Applied in the Workplace |

At least 70 percent of employees say that trust, respect, and honesty are applied frequently in their organizations.

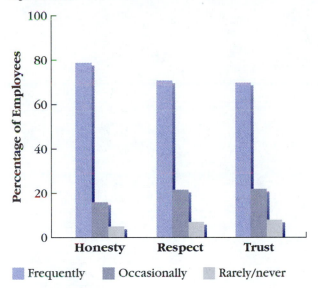

Source: Ethics Resource Center, *The Ethics Resource Center's 2000 National Business Ethics Survey: How Employees Perceive Ethics at Work* (Washington DC: Ethics Resource Center, 2000), p. 55. Reprinted by permission from Ethics Resource Center.

groups all contribute to these conventions, and they may change over time. The most basic of these standards have been codified as laws and regulations to encourage companies to conform to society's expectations of business conduct. As we said in Chapter 3, public concerns about accounting fraud and conflicts of interest in the securities industry led to the passage of the Sarbanes-Oxley Act to restore the public's trust in the stock market. The chair of the Securities and Exchange Commission, who enforces many aspects of the act, issued the challenge for "American organizations to behave more ethically than the law requires to help restore investors' trust."[6]

It is vital to recognize that business ethics goes beyond legal issues. Ethical business decisions foster trust in business relationships, and, as we discussed in Chapter 1, trust is a key factor in improving productivity and achieving success in most organizations. When companies deviate from the prevailing standards of industry and society, the result is customer dissatisfaction, lack of trust, and lawsuits. Indeed, 78 percent of U.S. consumers say they avoid certain businesses or products because of negative perceptions about them.[7] Consumers in other countries also avoid businesses or products because of negative perceptions. According to a recent survey, two-thirds of consumers in their thirties and forties in the United Kingdom boycotted brands because of "unethical behavior" by the manufacturers. Ninety-five percent of the 1,000 consumers surveyed indicated they would never purchase the brands.[8]

Some businesspeople choose to behave ethically because of enlightened self-interest, or the expectation that "ethics pays." They want to act responsibly and assume that

Andrea Jung, Avon chairwoman and CEO, balances business performance and ethical values at Avon. (Mario Tama/Getty Images)

the public and customers will reward the company for its ethical actions. Avon, for example, is a company that achieves success, contributes to society, and has ethical management. The CEO Andrea Jung and the chief operating officer Susan Kropf work in the high-risk area of direct selling without scandals or major ethical issues. *Business Week* ranked them among the best business managers and noted that 2002 was Avon's third consecutive year of double-digit earnings per share growth.[9]

Foundations of Business Ethics

Because all individuals and groups within a company may not have embraced the same set of values, there is always the possibility of ethical conflict. Most ethical issues in an organizational context are addressed openly whenever a policy, code, or rule is questioned. Even then it may be hard to distinguish between the ethical issue and the legal means used to resolve it. Because it is difficult to draw a boundary between legal and ethical issues, all questionable issues need an organizational mechanism for resolution.

The legal ramifications of some issues and situations may be obvious, but questionable decisions and actions more often result in disputes that must be resolved through some type of negotiation or even litigation. For example, a number of franchisees of The Body Shop filed lawsuits against the cosmetics firm, alleging fraud, fraudulent inducement, inequitable treatment, and retaliatory practices. The British firm settled lawsuits with franchisees in Canada, Singapore, Norway, France, and Israel, in some cases, by buying out franchisees. The lawsuits have involved millions of dollars and years of court proceedings.[10] When ethical disputes wind up in court, the costs and distractions associated with litigation can be crippling to a business. In addition to the compensatory or nominal damages actually incurred, punitive damages may be imposed on a company that is judged to have acted improperly in order to punish the firm and to send an intimidating message to others. The legal system, therefore, provides a formal venue for businesspeople to resolve ethical disputes as well as legal ones; in fact, many of the examples we cite in this chapter had to be resolved through the courts. To avoid the costs of litigation, companies should develop systems to monitor complaints, suggestions, and other feedback from stakeholders. In many cases, issues can be negotiated or resolved without legal intervention. Strategic responsibility entails systems for listening to, understanding, and effectively managing stakeholder concerns.[11]

A high level of personal morality may not be sufficient to prevent an individual from violating the law in an organizational context in which even experienced attorneys debate the exact meaning of the law. Because it is impossible to train all the members of an organization as lawyers, the identification of ethical issues and the implementation of standards of conduct that incorporate both legal and ethical concerns are the best approach to preventing crime and avoiding civil litigation. Codifying ethical standards into meaningful policies that spell out what is and is not acceptable gives businesspeople an opportunity to reduce the probability of behavior that could create legal problems. Without proper ethical training and guidance, it is impossible for the average business manager to understand the exact boundaries for illegal behavior in the areas of price fixing, fraud, export/import violations, copyright violations, insider trading, and so on. Even top executives have been accused of violations such as insider trading. Sam Waksal, former CEO of ImClone, was arrested and charged with selling stock and sharing information with family members that ImClone's promising cancer drug Erbitux would not receive FDA approval. Waksal was sentenced to seven years and three months in prison, fined $3 million, and ordered to pay $1.26 million in restitution for insider trading that ensnared friends and family, including Martha Stewart.[12]

Although the values of honesty, respect, and trust are often assumed to be self-evident and universally accepted, business decisions involve complex and detailed discussions in which correctness may not be so clear-cut. Both employees and managers need experience within their specific industry to understand how to operate in gray areas or to handle close calls in evolving areas, such as Internet privacy. For example, how much personal information should be stored on customers who visit a firm's web site without their permission? Selling or renting mailing lists is prohibited in Europe under the European Union Directive on Data Protection—consumers' data cannot be used without their permission.[13] In the United States, companies have more freedom to decide how to collect and use customers' personal data, but advancing technology raises new questions every day. For example, the ability of firms such as Fair, Isaac & Co. to generate sophisticated consumer profiles has generated much concern among privacy advocates. The company devised a formula to create a mathematically generated guess at why consumers buy, what they are likely to buy in the future, and how much of a credit risk they are. One application of the process is being offered to credit-card companies in order to highlight risky credit users. The process pinpoints repeated cash advances, large-balance transfers, and frequent trips to liquor stores or online gambling sites. Fair, Isaac argues that it is doing consumers a favor; privacy advocates disagree.[14]

Many people who have limited business experience suddenly find themselves required to make decisions about product quality, advertising, pricing, sales tech-

Zirtek Allergy Solution uses puffery in its advertising by exaggerating the medication's ability to impact children's health and activity levels. (Advertising Archive Ltd/The Picture Desk)

niques, hiring practices, privacy, and pollution control. For example, how do advertisers know when they are making misleading statements in advertising versus "puffery"? Bayer is "the world's best aspirin," Hush Puppies, "the earth's most comfortable shoes," and Firestone (before recalling 6.5 million tires) promised "quality you can trust."[15] The personal values learned through nonwork socialization from family, religion, and school may not provide specific guidelines for these complex business decisions. In other words, a person's experiences and decisions at home, in school, and in the community may be quite different from the experiences and the decisions he or she has to make at work. Moreover, the interests and values of individual employees may differ from those of the company in which they work, from industry standards, and from society in general. When personal values are inconsistent with the configuration of values held by the work group, ethical conflict may ensue. It is important that a shared vision of acceptable behavior develop from an organizational perspective to cultivate consistent and reliable relationships with all concerned stakeholders. A shared vision of ethics that is part of an organization's culture can be questioned, analyzed, and modified as new issues develop. However, business ethics should relate to work environment decisions and should not control or influence personal ethical issues.

Ethical Issues in Business

Classification of Ethical Issues

An **ethical issue** is a problem, situation, or opportunity requiring an individual, group, or organization to choose among several actions that must be evaluated as right or wrong, ethical or unethical. Surveys can render a useful overview of the many unsettled ethical issues in business. A constructive next step toward identifying and resolving ethical issues is to classify the issues relevant to most business organizations. In this section we classify ethical issues in relation to honesty and fairness, conflict of interest, fraud, and discrimination. Ethical issues related to information technology are addressed in Chapter 10. Although not all-inclusive or mutually exclusive, these classifications provide an overview of some major ethical issues that business decision makers face. Table 4.1 shows how the increased awareness of ethical dilemmas in organizations has caused deterioration in consumer trust of U.S. businesses. More than two-thirds of Americans are skeptical and cynical about U.S. business.

> **ethical issue**
> a problem, situation, or opportunity requiring an individual, group, or organization to choose among several actions that must be evaluated as right or wrong, ethical or unethical

Honesty and Fairness

Honesty refers to truthfulness, integrity, and trustworthiness; **fairness** is the quality of being just, equitable, and impartial. Honesty and fairness relate to the general moral attributes of decision makers. At a minimum, businesspeople are expected to follow all applicable laws and regulations. In addition, they should not knowingly harm customers, clients, employees, or even other competitors through deception, misrepresentation, or coercion. The Justice Department and state officials in Louisiana investigated complaints filed by a New Orleans doctor. The doctor alleged that pharmaceutical giant Merck & Co. sold Pepcid, its popular heartburn and ulcer

> **honesty**
> truthfulness, integrity, and trustworthiness

> **fairness**
> the quality of being just, equitable, and impartial

TABLE 4.1	Deterioration of Trust in U.S. Business

LEAST-TRUSTED BUSINESSES	MOST-TRUSTED BUSINESSES
Oil & gas	Groceries/supermarkets
Insurance	Major retail chains
Brokerage/Wall Street	Drug stores
Utilities	Computer hardware/software
Airlines/travel	Health & beauty
Accounting	Fast-food restaurants
Chemical	Food product manufacturers
Telecom	Entertainment/sports
Advertising/marketing	Automotive
Media companies	Banks/savings & loans

Source: "Golin/Harris Trust Survey Finds 69% of Americans Say 'I Don't Know Who to Trust Anymore,'" www.prnewswire.com, February 26, 2002.

medicine, to hospitals and other health care institutions for about $.10 per tablet, while charging as much as $1.65 per tablet to Medicaid and other government health care programs. Merck disputed the allegations, and the investigation continues.[16] Although people in business often act in their own economic self-interest, ethical business relations should be grounded on fairness, justice, and trust. Buyers should be able to trust sellers; lenders should be able to trust borrowers. Failure to live up to these expectations or to abide by laws and standards destroys trust and makes it difficult, if not impossible, to continue business exchanges.[17]

Ideas of fairness are sometimes shaped by vested interests. One or both parties in the relationship may view an action as unfair or unethical because the outcome was less beneficial than expected. For example, Fuji and Kodak have waged a long legal battle against Jazz Photo Corp. and other firms that recycle disposable cameras by patching them with electrical tape, inserting new film, putting new sleeves on them, and reselling them for much less than the new disposable cameras marketed by the two film and camera giants. In addition to the fact that many consumers do not realize these "single-use" cameras have been previously used as many as seven times, Fuji contends that these disposable camera reloaders are violating its patents on disposable cameras. A federal jury recently sided with Fuji and ordered Jazz Photo to pay the Japanese firm $25 million in damages for lost profits and royalties.[18]

Issues related to fairness and honesty also arise because business is sometimes regarded as a "game" governed by its own rules rather than those of society. Author Eric Beversluis suggests that unfairness is a problem because people often reason along these lines:

1. Business relationships are a subset of human relationships that are governed by their own rules, which, in a market society, involve competition, profit maximization, and personal advancement within the organization.

2. Business can therefore be considered a game people play, comparable in certain respects to competitive sports such as basketball or boxing.

3. Ordinary rules and morality do not hold in games like basketball or boxing. (What if a basketball player did unto others as he would have them do unto him? What if a boxer decided it was wrong to try to injure another person?)

4. Logically, then, if business is a game like basketball or boxing, ordinary ethical rules do not apply.[19]

This type of reasoning leads many people to conclude that anything is fair in sports, war, and business. Indeed, several books have compared business to warfare—for example, Harvey Mackay's *Swim with the Sharks* and Jay Conrad Levinson's *Guerrilla Marketing*. The common theme is that surprise attacks, guerrilla warfare, and other warlike tactics are necessary to win the battle for consumers' dollars. This business-as-war mentality may foster the idea that fairness and honesty are not necessary in business.

Many argue, however, that business is not a game like basketball or boxing. Because people are not economically self-sufficient, they cannot withdraw from the game of business. Therefore, business ethics must not only make clear what rules apply in the game of business but must also develop rules appropriate to the nonvoluntary character of participation in the game.[20] Table 4.2 reveals how damaging ethical and legal misconduct has been on the reputation of many professions.

Conflict of Interest

conflict of interest
the situation of an individual who must choose whether to advance his or her own interests, those of his or her organization, or those of some other group

A **conflict of interest** exists when an individual must choose whether to advance his or her own interests, those of his or her organization, or those of some other group. For example, federal investigators are considering whether a $1 million donation by Citigroup to the 92nd St. Y nursery school represents a conflict of interest. Jack Grubman, an analyst for Salomon Smith Barney, upgraded his rating for AT&T stock after Sanford Weill, the CEO of Citigroup (the parent company of Salomon Smith Barney), agreed to use his influence to help Grubman's twins gain admission to the elite Manhattan nursery school. Grubman has denied elevating his rating for AT&T's stock to gain admission to the school, but his children were enrolled.[21] To avoid conflicts of interest, employees must be able to separate their private interests from their business dealings.

TABLE 4.2	Lowest-Rated Professions in Honesty and Ethics
Telemarketers	Labor union leaders
Car salespeople	Lawyers
Advertising practitioners	Business executives
Stockbrokers	Building contractors
Real estate agents	Congresspeople

Source: Jeffrey M. Jones, "Effects of Year's Scandals Evident in Honesty and Ethics Ratings," www.gallup.com/poll/releases/pr021204.asp, December 5, 2002.

Organizations, too, must avoid potential conflicts of interest in providing goods or services. For example, Arthur Andersen LLP served as outside auditor for Waste Management, Inc., while providing consulting services to the firm—a situation that led the Securities and Exchange Commission to investigate charges that the consulting fees received by Arthur Andersen may have compromised the independence of its auditing of Waste Management's books. The accounting firm eventually agreed to pay $7 million to settle the case. Arthur Andersen later paid $100 million to settle a lawsuit brought against the firm by Waste Management shareholders. Within a year, Arthur Andersen found itself stuck in a pattern, paying out millions of dollars to settle similar federal charges and shareholder lawsuits surrounding accounting irregularities at Sunbeam and Qwest Communications, while investigations of its auditing of WorldCom, Enron, Global Crossing, and other firms continued.[22]

In many developed countries, it is generally recognized that employees should not accept bribes, personal payments, gifts, or special favors from people who hope to influence the outcome of a decision. However, as discussed later in this text, bribery is an accepted way of doing business in many countries. One source estimates that some $80 billion is paid out worldwide in the form of bribes or some other payoff every year.[23] According to a recent survey, four out of ten companies say they have lost business in the last five years because a competitor paid a bribe. Companies in the United States were ranked fifth behind those in Canada, Germany, the Netherlands, and the United Kingdom in terms of complying with anti-corruption laws.[24] Bribes also have been associated with the downfall of many managers, legislators, and government officials. When a government official accepts a

The United States Senate has conducted many hearings to review Enron's accounting irregularities and ethical breaches. (Alex Wong/Getty Images)

bribe, it is usually from a business that seeks some favor, perhaps a chance to influence legislation that affects it. Giving bribes to legislators or public officials, then, is a business ethics issue.

Fraud

When an individual engages in deceptive practices to advance his or her own interests over those of the organization or some other group, charges of illegal fraud may result. In general, **fraud** is any false communication that deceives, manipulates, or conceals facts in order to create a false impression when others are damaged or denied a benefit. It is considered a crime and convictions may result in fines, imprisonment, or both. Fraud costs U.S. organizations more than $600 billion a year; the average company loses about 6 percent of total revenues to fraud and abuses committed by its own employees.[25] Among the most common fraudulent activities reported by employees about their coworkers are stealing office supplies and shoplifting, claiming to have worked extra hours, and stealing money or products.[26] In recent years, accounting fraud has become a major ethical issue, but fraud may also relate to marketing and consumer issues (covered in Chapter 7).

Accounting Fraud The field of accounting has changed dramatically over the last decade. The profession used to have a club-type mentality: those who became certified public accountants (CPAs) were not concerned about competition. Now CPAs advertise their skills or short-term results in an environment in which competition has increased and overall billable hours have significantly decreased because of technological innovations. Pressures on accountants include time, reduced fees, client requests for altered opinions concerning financial conditions or for lower tax payments, and increased competition. Because of such pressures, and the ethical predicaments they spawn, some accounting firms have had problems. Accounting firms have a responsibility to report a true and accurate picture of the financial condition of the companies for which they work. Failure to do so may result in charges and fines for both the accounting firm and the employing company. For example, Xerox settled charges by the Securities and Exchange Commission that it had improperly booked $6.4 billion in revenue over four years, while the accounting firm of KPMG LLP faced charges of civil fraud for its role in auditing Xerox. Although KPMG objected to Xerox's accounting, it allowed its implementation anyway.[27] Such scrutiny of financial reporting increased dramatically in the wake of the accounting scandals in the early 2000s. As a result of the negative publicity surrounding the allegations of accounting fraud at a number of companies, many firms were forced to take a second look at their financial documents, and a record 330 companies chose to restate their earnings to avoid being drawn into the scandal in 2002.[28]

Other issues that accountants face daily involve complex rules and regulations that must be followed, data overload, contingent fees, and commissions. An accountant's life is filled with rules and data that have to be interpreted correctly. As a result, accountants must abide by a strict code of ethics, which defines their responsibilities to their clients and the public interest. The code also discusses the concepts of integrity, objectivity, independence, and due care. Finally, the code delineates an accountant's

---

fraud
any false communication that deceives, manipulates, or conceals facts in order to create a false impression and damage others

Legal and Regulatory Challenges

Qwest Struggles with Both Accounting and Marketing Ethics

Qwest Communications is the local phone company for fourteen states extending from Minnesota west to Washington and southwest to Arizona and New Mexico. Recently, four former executives of the company were indicted on criminal charges of fraud. The four, including the chief financial officer, a senior vice president, the assistant controller, and a vice president, were accused of devising a scheme to create more than $33 million in revenue, violating Securities and Exchange Commission rules by wrongly reporting a purchase order with the Arizona School Facilities Board. According to the government, Qwest sold equipment to the statewide school computer network, billed the customer, and then held the merchandise for later delivery. According to government officials, the executives took the action to help Qwest meet its numbers

during a difficult time for the company. "Simply put, the defendants couldn't make the numbers work, so they cheated," said the chairman of the SEC. The Justice Department said the company knowingly filed false documents to hide its actions. The SEC also sought civil penalties against a total of eight former employees, including the loss of salaries and bonuses during the time of the alleged misdeed. This was not the first time the company has been in trouble.

In 2002, the Qwest chief executive Joseph Nacchio resigned under pressure. In his public testimony, Nacchio said that he talked with the founder and director Philip Anschutz about all major decisions. On the other hand, divisional managers thought they were hearing orders to make the numbers. Congressional investigators then interviewed Anschutz about his role in the company's day-to-day affairs. Qwest had been investigated by the Justice Department and the Securities and Exchange Commission and was the subject of con-

scope and the nature of services that ethically should be provided. In this last portion of the code, contingent fees and commissions are indirectly addressed. Despite the standards provided by the code, the accounting industry has been the source of numerous fraud investigations in recent years. Table 4.3 shows major firms under investigation for accounting fraud. At some companies, fraud is rewarded. A recent report indicated that CEOs at twenty-three large companies under investigation for accounting irregularities earned an average of $62 million over a three-year period compared to $36 million for all CEOs.[29]

TABLE 4.3	Major Firms Under Investigation for Accounting Fraud	
Enron	El Paso Corp.	Bristol-Myers Squibb
WorldCom	Halliburton	Adelphia
Qwest	Williams Co.	Rite-Aid Corp.
Tyco	AOL Time Warner	Dynergy
Citigroup	CMS Energy	J. P. Morgan Chase

Source: CNN/Money, http://money.cnn.com/news/specials/corruption, accessed January 31, 2003.

gressional hearings into its financial practices. The investigations probed whether Qwest artificially inflated its revenues by swapping network capacity with another scandal-plagued company, Global Crossing Ltd. The company restated its financial reports for 1999 to 2001 because of accounting errors and said it would erase $950 million from improperly booked swaps. Still attempting to clean up its image and its books, Qwest announced in February 2003 that $531 million in revenue that was booked prematurely in the last two years would be deferred. Qwest eventually restated the figure to $2.2 billion in improperly booked revenue.

In 2003, Qwest was fined $20.3 million by California regulators for switching customers' long-distance accounts without permission (known as "slamming") and adding unauthorized charges to their bills (known as "cramming"). At that time, it was the largest fine ever levied against Qwest by a regulatory agency, but Minnesota officials were considering an even larger one. The administrative judge in California cited 3,583 cases of slamming and 4,871 cases of cramming. Qwest said it had disciplined sales agencies that committed the unlawful practices and had introduced new procedures to prevent them in the future. California utilities commissioners took Qwest's efforts into consideration before levying the fine, but the commission president said, "This company fixed its systems only after regulators began investigating." The commission also required the company to provide refunds to the affected customers within ninety days.

Sources:
"Qwest's Anschutz to face second questioning-WSJ," Reuters, October 8, 2002; Kris Hudson, "Qwest Assessed $20 Million Fine," *Denver Post*, October 25, 2002; Andrew Backover, "Write-down by Qwest grows to $40.8 billion," *USA Today*, October 29, 2002, p. B1; Andrew Backover, "Blame Spreads Far in Telecom's Fall," *USA Today*, August 18, 2003, p. B1; "Feds indict four ex-Qwest executives," MSNBC, February 25, 2003, via www.msnbc.com/news/876997.asp, accessed February 26, 2003; "Ex-Qwest execs indicted," CNN/Money, February 25, 2003, via http://money.cnn.com/2003/02/25/technology/qwest/index.htm, accessed February 25, 2003; Andrew Backover and Greg Farrell, "Qwest Execs Charged With Fraud," *USA Today*, February 26, 2003, p. B1.

Marketing Fraud Communications that are false or misleading can destroy customers' trust in an organization. Lying, a major ethical issue within communications, may be a significant problem. It causes ethical predicaments in both external and internal communications because it destroys trust. For example, Bell Labs fired a scientist for falsifying experiments on superconductivity and molecular electronics and misrepresenting data in scientific publications. Jan Hendrik Schon's work on creating tiny, powerful microprocessors seemed poised to significantly advance microprocessor technology and potentially bring yet another Nobel Prize in physics to the award-winning laboratory, a subsidiary of Lucent Technologies.[30]

False and deceptive advertising is a key issue in communications. Abuses in advertising can range from exaggerated claims and concealed facts to outright lying. Exaggerated claims are those that cannot be substantiated, as when a commercial states that a certain product is superior to any other on the market. For example, Papa John's International, Inc., invested years and millions of dollars into its "Better Ingredients, Better Pizza" advertising campaign to promote its pizza quality and taste. However, a Texas jury found that the slogan constituted deceptive advertising because the company could not prove this claim and the judge ordered the company to stop using the claim in future advertising.[31]

Another form of advertising abuse involves making ambiguous statements, whose words are so weak that the viewer, reader, or listener must infer the advertiser's intended message. These "weasel" words are inherently vague and enable the advertiser to deny any intent to deceive. The verb *help* is a good example (as in expressions such as "helps prevent," "helps fight," "helps make you feel").[32] Consumers may view such advertisements as unethical because they fail to communicate all the information needed to make a good purchasing decision or because they deceive the consumer outright.

The Federal Trade Commission and other agencies are monitoring more closely the advertisements for work-at-home business ventures. Consumers are losing millions of dollars each year responding to ads for phony business opportunities, such as those promising $50,000 a year for doing medical billing from a home computer.[33] Sometimes differing interpretations of advertising messages create ethical issues that must be resolved in court. For example, the television ads for HMO Kaiser Permanente state that Kaiser is a place where "no one but you and your doctor decides what's right for you" and "there are no financial pressures to prevent your physician from giving you the medical care you need." According to a lawsuit filed by a California consumer group, however, Kaiser drastically reduced its medical budget as it added hundreds of thousands of new members. The consumer group also alleged that Kaiser set quotas for doctors to reduce the number of patients hospitalized, while tying a significant portion of physician pay to meeting the quotas.[34]

Labeling issues are even murkier. For example, Mott's, Inc., the nation's leading producer of applesauce and apple juice, agreed to revise the labels of some of its fruit products after New York's attorney general claimed they were misleading consumers. The products—often made by blending apple juice with enough grape juice or cherry juice to make the designated flavor—had labels with the phrase "100% Juice" and a picture of grapes or cherries and the fruits' names in large lettering underneath. The attorney general argued that placing the fruit's name under "100% Juice" could lead consumers to assume that the products were 100 percent grape juice or cherry juice. Mott's admitted no wrongdoing but agreed to pay $177,500 to cover the investigation costs and to institute a minor change to the labels in question.[35]

In the telephone industry, AT&T sued Business Discount Plan (BDP), accusing it of using fraud and deception to routinely slam customers to its telecommunication service. Slamming refers to changing a customer's telephone service without authorization. AT&T charged that BDP gave the impression that it was affiliated with AT&T. As part of the settlement, BDP had to send letters to consumers telling them that BDP was not affiliated with AT&T.[36] Such misleading behavior creates ethical issues because the communicated messages do not include all the information consumers need to make good purchasing decisions. They frustrate and anger customers, who feel that they have been deceived. In addition, they damage the seller's credibility and reputation.

Advertising and direct sales communication can also mislead by concealing facts within a message. For instance, a salesperson anxious to sell a medical insurance policy might list a large number of illnesses covered by the policy but fail to mention that it does not cover some commonly covered illnesses. Indeed, the fastest growth of fraudulent activity is in the area of direct marketing, which employs the telephone and nonpersonal media to communicate information to customers, who then purchase products via mail, telephone, or the Internet. In 2000, consumers reported losses of $138 million resulting from fraud to the Federal Trade Commission. In

2001, the FTC received an estimated 25,000 complaints about Internet fraud alone.[37]

Discrimination

Another important ethics issue in business today is discrimination. Once dominated by white men, the U.S. workforce today includes significantly more women, African Americans, Hispanics, and other minorities, as well as disabled and older workers. Experts project that within the next fifty years, Hispanics will represent 24 percent of the population, while African Americans and Asians/Pacific Islanders will make up 15 percent and 9 percent, respectively.[38] These groups have traditionally faced discrimination and higher unemployment rates and have been denied opportunities to assume leadership roles in corporate America.[39]

Discrimination remains a significant ethical issue in business despite nearly forty years of legislation to outlaw it. The most significant piece of legislation is Title VII of the Civil Rights Act of 1964, which prohibits employment discrimination on the basis of race, national origin, color, religion, and gender. This law is fundamental to employees' rights to join and advance in an organization according to merit, not one of the characteristics listed above. As a result of racial discrimination class-action settlements, some companies, such as Coca-Cola and Texaco, are being required to establish independent task forces to monitor and modify company practices to combat racial discrimination. A racial discrimination lawsuit filed by 1,000 salaried minority employees seeks permanent structural changes in corporate practices by health care products manufacturer Johnson & Johnson.[40]

Additional laws passed in the 1970s, 1980s, and 1990s were also designed to prohibit discrimination related to pregnancy, disabilities, age, and other factors. The Americans with Disabilities Act, for example, prohibits companies from discriminating on the basis of physical or mental disability in all employment practices and requires them to make facilities accessible to and usable by persons with disabilities.[41] The Age Discrimination in Employment Act specifically outlaws hiring practices that discriminate against people between the ages of forty-nine and sixty-nine, but it also bans policies that require employees to retire before the age of seventy. Despite this legislation, charges of age discrimination persist in the workplace.[42] For example, Woolworth's, now known as Foot Locker Specialty, paid $3.5 million to settle charges that it systematically laid off workers over forty in order to reduce costs, although the company denied any wrongdoing.[43] A survey by the American Association for Retired Persons (AARP), an advocacy organization for people fifty and older, highlighted how little most companies value older workers. When AARP mailed invitations to 10,000 companies for a chance to compete for a listing in *Modern Maturity* magazine as one of the "best employers for workers over 50," it received just fourteen applications. Given that nearly 20 percent of the nation's workers will be fifty-five years old or over by 2015, many companies need to change their approach toward older workers.[44]

To help build workforces that reflect their customer base, many companies have initiated **affirmative action programs,** which involve efforts to recruit, hire, train, and promote qualified individuals from groups that have traditionally been discriminated

affirmative action programs
programs that involve efforts to recruit, hire, train, and promote qualified individuals from groups that have traditionally been discriminated against on the basis of race, gender, or other characteristics

against on the basis of race, gender, or other characteristics. Such initiatives may be imposed on an employer by federal law on federal government contractors and subcontractors; as part of a settlement agreement with a state or federal agency; or by a court order.[45] Many companies voluntarily implement affirmative action plans in order to build a more diverse workforce.[46] For example, a Chicago real estate developer launched the Female Employment Initiative, an outreach program designed to create opportunities for women in the construction industry through training programs, counseling and information services, and referral listings to help employers identify available women workers.[47]

Although many people believe that affirmative action requires the use of quotas to govern employment decisions, it is important to note that two decades of Supreme Court rulings have made it clear that affirmative action does *not* require or permit quotas, reverse discrimination, or favorable treatment of unqualified women or minorities. To ensure that affirmative action programs are fair, the Supreme Court has established a number of standards to guide their implementation: (1) there must be a strong reason for developing an affirmative action program, (2) affirmative action programs must apply only to qualified candidates, and (3) affirmative action programs must be limited and temporary and therefore cannot include "rigid and inflexible quotas."[48]

The Equal Employment Opportunity Commission (EEOC) monitors compliance with Title VII, with a mission to "promote equal opportunity in employment through administrative and judicial enforcement of the federal civil rights laws and

The NAACP protests against discrimination of employees of color and guests of color at Adam's Mark Hotels. (Ronald J. Colleran/ The Buffalo News)

through education and technical assistance."[49] For example, the EEOC won a lawsuit against the Chuck E. Cheese pizza chain for firing a mentally disabled janitor because of his disability; the jury in the case awarded the victim $13 million in compensatory and punitive damages.[50] A special type of discrimination, sexual harassment, is also prohibited through Title VII. As part of its settlement in a sexual discrimination lawsuit, Mitsubishi Motors of America promised to adopt a companywide, zero-tolerance program against harassment. The agreement also included a court-appointed panel to monitor company efforts.[51]

Discrimination also occurs against some groups of consumers. For example, a study by a Vanderbilt professor found that African American customers paid up to $800 more than white customers for car loans through Nissan dealers. Citing the study, a class-action lawsuit was filed against the Nissan loan unit. Similar cases have been filed against the financing units of Ford, Daimler-Chrysler, and Toyota.[52] This issue is discussed in detail in Chapter 8.

Information Technology

The final category of ethical issues relates to technology and the numerous advances made in the Internet and other forms of electronic communications in the last few years. As the number of people who use the Internet increases, the areas of concern related to its use increase as well. Some issues that must be addressed by businesses include monitoring of employee use of available technology, consumer privacy, site development and online marketing, and legal protection of intellectual properties, such as music, books, and movies. This issue is discussed in detail in Chapter 10.

Recognizing an Ethical Issue

Although we have described a number of relationships and situations that may generate ethical issues, it can be difficult to recognize specific ethical issues in practice. Failure to acknowledge ethical issues is a great danger in any organization, particularly if business is treated as a game in which ordinary rules of fairness do not apply. Sometimes people who take this view do things that are not only unethical but also illegal in order to maximize their own position or boost the profits or goals of the organization. However, just because an unsettled situation or activity is an ethical issue does not mean the behavior is necessarily unethical. An ethical issue is simply a situation, a problem, or even an opportunity that requires thought, discussion, or investigation to determine the moral impact of the decision. Because the business world is dynamic, new ethical issues are emerging all the time.

One way to determine whether a specific behavior or situation has an ethical component is to ask other individuals in the business how they feel about it and whether they approve. Table 4.4 provides questions to ask when considering solutions to an ethical dilemma. Another way is to determine whether the organization has adopted specific policies on the activity. An activity approved of by most members of an organization, if it is also customary in the industry, is probably ethical. An issue, activity, or situation that can withstand open discussion between many stakeholders, both in and outside the organization, and survive untarnished probably does not pose ethical problems. For instance, when engineers and designers at Ford Motor Co. discussed what type of gas-tank protection should be used in its Pinto automobile, they

TABLE 4.4	Criteria Useful in Achieving Ethical Business Decision Making

1. What are the business consequences of an action or decision?
2. What impact will this action or decision have on others or my relationship with them?
3. What is the right thing to do—as defined by the values and principles that apply to this situation?
4. What will happen to me as a consequence of this action?

Source: "Opinion Poll: What Criteria Do You Use When Making Business Decisions?" *Ethics Today* 1, no. 5, January 2003.

reached consensus within the organization, but they did not take into account the interests of various external stakeholders, such as the public's desire for maximum safety. Consequently, even though they might have believed the issue had no ethical dimension, Ford erred in not opening up the issue to public scrutiny. (As it turned out, the type of gas-tank protection in the Pinto resulted in several fires and deaths when the cars were involved in rear-end collisions.)

Understanding the Ethical Decision-Making Process

To grasp the significance of ethics in business decision making, it is important to understand how ethical decisions are made within the context of an organization. Understanding the ethical decision-making process can help individuals and businesses design strategies to deter misconduct. Our descriptive approach to understanding ethical decision making does not prescribe what to do but, rather, provides a framework for managing ethical behavior in the workplace. Figure 4.2 depicts this framework, which shows how individual factors, organizational relationships, and opportunity interact to determine ethical decisions in business.

FIGURE 4.2	Factors That Influence the Ethical Decision-Making Process

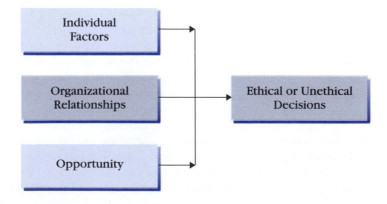

Individual Factors

Individuals make ethical choices on the basis of their own concepts of right or wrong, and they act accordingly in their daily lives. Studies suggest that individual ethics are reaching a new low. For example, a recent survey found that one out of four Americans says it is acceptable to cheat on their taxes,[53] and according to *Golf Digest*, CEOs cheat at golf at four times the rate of average golfers.[54] A Gallup poll found that only 23 percent of those surveyed felt that "most CEOs of large corporations can be trusted."[55] Significant factors that affect the ethical decision-making process include an individual's personal moral philosophy, stage of moral development, motivation, and other personal factors such as gender, age, and experience.

Moral Philosophy[56] Many people have justified difficult decisions by citing the Golden Rule ("Do unto others as you would have them do unto you") or some other principle. Such principles, or rules, which individuals apply in deciding what is right or wrong, are often referred to as **moral philosophies.** These philosophies are learned through socialization by family members, social groups, religion, and formal education. Most moral philosophies can be classified as consequentialism, ethical formalism, or justice.

Consequentialism is a class of moral philosophy that considers a decision right or acceptable if it accomplishes a desired result such as pleasure, knowledge, career growth, the realization of self-interest, or utility. For example, the nation's largest disability insurer, Unum Provident Insurance Co., has been accused by former employees of terminating legitimate policies and cheating disabled people out of money to which they were entitled in an effort to increase company profits. The employees allege that the company had an incentive structure that rewarded workers for cheating customers while saving money for the company.[57] Egoism and utilitarianism are two important consequentialist philosophies that often guide decision making in business.

Egoism is a philosophy that defines right or acceptable conduct in terms of the consequences for the individual. Egoists believe they should make decisions that maximize their own self-interest, which, depending on the individual, may be defined as physical well-being, power, pleasure, fame, a satisfying career, a good family life, wealth, or something else. In a decision-making situation, the egoist will probably choose the alternative that most benefits his or her self-interest. Many people feel that egoists are inherently unethical, that they focus on the short term, and that they will take advantage of any opportunity to exploit consumers or employees. An example of egoism in the business world might be telemarketers who prey on elderly consumers who may be vulnerable because of loneliness or fear of losing their financial independence. Tens of thousands of senior citizens fall victim to telemarketing fraud every year. In Tucson, Arizona, for example, police uncovered a telemarketing scam in which elderly people received calls telling them they had won a lottery or sweepstakes contest. However, the victims were also told that they needed to pay a "tax" in order to receive the contest winnings. In one case, the tax was $10,000.[58]

Utilitarianism is another consequentialist philosophy that is concerned with seeking the greatest good for the greatest number of people. Using a cost-benefit analysis, a utilitarian decision maker calculates the utility of the consequences of all possible

---

moral philosophies
principles, or rules, that individuals apply in deciding what is right or wrong

consequentialism
a class of moral philosophy that considers a decision right or acceptable if it accomplishes a desired result such as pleasure, knowledge, career growth, the realization of self-interest, or utility

egoism
a philosophy that defines right or acceptable conduct in terms of the consequences for the individual

utilitarianism
a consequentialist philosophy that is concerned with seeking to find the greatest good for the greatest number of people

alternatives and then chooses the one that achieves the greatest utility. For example, the Occupational Safety and Health Administration (OSHA) recently proposed new standards for ensuring health and safety in the workplace. Thus, the federal agency has concluded that the greatest utility and benefits to society and employees will result from greater corporate efforts and leadership on safety and health issues on the job.[59]

ethical formalism
a class of moral philosophy that focuses on the rights of individuals and on the intentions associated with a particular behavior rather than on its consequences

In contrast with consequentialism, **ethical formalism** is a class of moral philosophy that focuses on the rights of individuals and on the intentions associated with a particular behavior rather than on its consequences. Ethical formalists regard certain behaviors as inherently right, and their determination of rightness focuses on the individual actor, not on society. Thus, these perspectives are sometimes referred to as nonconsequentialism and the ethics of respect for persons. A recent survey by the Institute of Ethics, an independent research arm of the American Medical Association, found that some doctors are manipulating insurance reimbursement rules to ensure treatment for their patients. For instance, a doctor might code a patient's illness as a sleep disorder, which is usually covered by insurance, rather than depression, which is not covered by most insurance plans, so that the insurance company would reimburse the patient for prescribed medications. According to the survey, 39 percent of the physicians reported sometimes or often exaggerating to insurance companies, and 10 percent admitted to outright lies.[60] These doctors may be applying ethical formalism in their decisions to flout the rules for their patients' benefit. But the application of formalism in this context could be illegal if it violated the doctor's requirement to report accurately to the insurance company.

Contemporary ethical formalism has been greatly influenced by the German philosopher Immanuel Kant, who developed the so-called categorical imperative: "Act as if the maxim of thy action were to become by thy will a universal law of nature."[61] Unlike utilitarians, ethical formalists contend that there are some things that people should not do, even to maximize utility. For example, an ethical formalist would consider it unacceptable for a coal mine to continue to operate if some workers became ill and died of black lung disease. A utilitarian, however, might consider some disease or death an acceptable consequence of a decision that resulted in large-scale employment and economic prosperity.

justice theory
a class of moral philosophy that relates to evaluations of fairness, or the disposition to deal with perceived injustices of others

Justice theory is a class of moral philosophy that relates to evaluations of fairness, or the disposition to deal with perceived injustices of others. Justice demands fair treatment and due reward in accordance with ethical or legal standards. In business, this requires that the rules an individual uses to determine justice be based on the perceived rights of individuals and on the intentions associated with a business interaction. Justice, therefore, is more likely to be based on nonconsequentialist moral philosophies than on consequentialist ones. Justice primarily addresses the issue of what individuals feel they are due based on their rights and performance in the workplace. For example, the U.S. Equal Employment Opportunity Commission exists to help employees who suspect the injustice of discrimination in the workplace.

There are three types of justice that can be used to assess fairness in different situations. Distributive justice evaluates the outcomes or results of a business relationship. For example, if an employee feels that she is being paid less than her coworkers for the same work, she has concerns about distributive justice. Procedural justice assesses the processes and activities employed to produce an outcome or results. Procedural justice concerns about compensation would relate to the perception that salary and benefit decisions were consistent and fair to all categories of employees. A recent study found that procedural justice is associated with group cohesiveness and helping behaviors.[62] Interactional justice evaluates the communication processes used in the business relationship. Being untruthful about the reasons for missing work is an example of an interactional justice issue.[63]

It is important to recognize that there is no one "correct" moral philosophy to apply in resolving ethical and legal issues in the workplace. It is also important to acknowledge that each philosophy presents an ideal perspective and that most people seem to adapt a number of moral philosophies as they interpret the context of different decision-making situations.[64] Moreover, research suggests that individuals may apply different moral philosophies in different decision situations.[65] Each philosophy could result in a different decision in a situation requiring an ethical judgment. And, depending on the situation, people may even change their value structure or moral philosophy when making decisions.[66]

Stage of Moral Development[67]   One reason that different people make different decisions when confronted with similar ethical situations may be that they are in different stages of moral development. Psychologist Lawrence Kohlberg proposed that people progress through stages in their development of moral reasoning or, as he called it, cognitive moral development.[68] He believes that people progress through the following six stages:

1. The stage of punishment and obedience. An individual in this stage of development defines right as literal obedience to rules and authority and responds to rules in terms of the physical power of those who determine such rules. Individuals in this stage do not associate right and wrong with any higher-order or moral philosophy but instead with a person who has power. For example, a plant supervisor may choose to go along with a superior's order to release untreated wastewater into a nearby stream, even though she knows that would be illegal, because she fears the superior's power to fire her if she does not comply.

2. The stage of individual instrumental purpose and exchange. A person in this stage defines right as that which serves his or her own needs. In this stage, people evaluate behavior on the basis of its fairness to themselves rather than solely on the basis of specific rules or authority figures. For example, a corporate buyer may choose to accept an expensive gift from a salesperson despite the presence of a company rule prohibiting the acceptance of gifts because the gift is something he needs or wants. This stage is sometimes labeled the stage of reciprocity, because from a practical standpoint, ethical decisions are based on "you-scratch-my-back-and-I'll-scratch-yours" agreements instead of on principles such as loyalty or justice.

3. The stage of mutual interpersonal expectation, relationships, and conformity. An individual in this stage emphasizes others over himself or herself. Although these individuals still derive motivation from obedience to rules, they also consider the well-being of others. For example, a production manager might choose to obey an order from upper management to speed up an assembly line because she believes this action will generate more profit for the company and thereby preserve her employees' jobs.

4. The stage of social justice and conscience maintenance. A person in this stage determines what is right by considering duty to society, as well as to other specific people. Duty, respect for authority, and maintaining social order become fundamental goals in decision making. For example, Jeffrey Wigand, a former executive at Brown & Williamson Tobacco Corporation, believed that the company was hiding from the public the truth that cigarettes are addictive and dangerous. He chose to "blow the whistle" by testifying against his former employer after he was fired.[69] Wigand's story was later dramatized in the movie *The Insider*.

5. The stage of prior rights, social contract, or utility. In this stage, an individual is concerned with upholding the basic rights, values, and legal contracts of society. Such individuals feel a sense of obligation or "social contract" to other groups and recognize that legal and moral points of view may conflict in some instances. To minimize conflict, persons in this stage base decisions on a rational calculation of overall utilities. For example, a business owner may choose to establish an organizational compliance program because it will serve as a buffer to prevent legal problems and to protect the company's good name.

6. The stage of universal ethical principles. A person in this stage believes that right is determined by universal ethical principles that everyone should follow. Such individuals believe that there are inalienable rights that are universal in nature and consequence. Justice and equality are examples of such universal rights. Thus, a businessperson in this stage may be more concerned with social ethical issues and rely less on the company for direction in situations with an ethical component.[70] For example, a marketing manager may argue for the termination of a toy that has resulted in injury and death because she believes the product threatens the universal value of right to life.

Because there is some spillover effect among these stages, cognitive moral development can be viewed as a continuum. Kohlberg's theory suggests that people may change their moral beliefs and behavior as they gain education and experience in resolving conflicts and this helps accelerate their progress along the moral development continuum. A survey by the Ethics Resource Center provides some confirmation that this occurs. Nearly half (49 percent) of 4,000 individuals surveyed believed that their business ethics had improved over the course of their careers. One-third (34 percent) thought their business ethics had improved because of their personal ethics. Surprisingly, nearly one in eight (13 percent) believed that their personal ethics had improved because of their business ethics.[71]

Kohlberg's model also suggests that there are universal values by which people in the highest level of moral development abide. These rights are considered valid not because of a particular society's laws or customs, but because they rest on the premise of universality. Many organizations and researchers have attempted to identify a set of global or universal ethical standards that every individual should follow, regardless of where they live or work. One result of these efforts is the Caux Round Table Business Principles of Ethics, developed in collaboration with business leaders in Europe, Japan, and the United States (see Table 4.5). These principles encourage decisions that further fairness and respect for others in promoting free trade, environmental and cultural integrity, and the prevention of corruption in global business.[72]

	TABLE 4.5	The Caux Round Table Business Principles of Ethics

	GENERAL PRINCIPLES
Principle 1	The responsibilities of businesses: beyond shareholders toward stakeholders
Principle 2	The economic and social impact of business: toward innovation, justice, and world community
Principle 3	Business behavior: beyond the letter of law toward a spirit of trust
Principle 4	Respect for rules
Principle 5	Support for multilateral trade
Principle 6	Respect for the environment
Principle 7	Avoidance of illicit operations

Stakeholder Principles
(customers, employees, owners /investors, suppliers, competitors, communities)

The value of a business to society is the wealth and employment it creates and the marketable products and services it provides to consumers at a reasonable price commensurate with quality. To create such value, a business must maintain its own economic health and viability, but survival is not a sufficient goal.

Businesses have a role to play in improving the lives of all their customers, employees, and shareholders by sharing with them the wealth they have created. Suppliers and competitors as well should expect businesses to honor their obligations in a spirit of honesty and fairness. As responsible citizens of the local, national, regional, and global communities in which they operate, businesses share a part in shaping the future of those communities.

Businesses established in foreign countries to develop, produce, or sell should also contribute to the social advancement of those countries by creating productive employment and helping to raise the purchasing power of their citizens. Businesses also should contribute to human rights, education, welfare, and vitalization of the countries in which they operate.

Businesses should contribute to economic and social development not only in the countries in which they operate, but also in the world community at large, through effective and prudent use of resources, free and fair competition, and emphasis on innovation in technology, production methods, marketing, and communications.

While accepting the legitimacy of trade secrets, businesses should recognize that sincerity, candor, truthfulness, the keeping of promises, and transparency contribute not only to their own credibility and stability but also to the smoothness and efficiency of business transactions, particularly on the international level.

To avoid trade frictions and to promote freer trade, equal conditions for competition, and fair and equitable treatment for all participants, businesses should respect international and domestic rules. In addition, they should recognize that some behavior, although legal, may still have adverse consequences.

Businesses should support the multilateral trade systems of the GATT/World Trade Organization and similar international agreements. They should cooperate in efforts to promote the progressive and judicious liberalization of trade and to relax those domestic measures that unreasonably hinder global commerce, while giving due respect to national policy objectives.

A business should protect and, where possible, improve the environment, promote sustainable development, and prevent the wasteful use of natural resources.

A business should not participate in or condone bribery, money laundering, or other corrupt practices; indeed, it should seek cooperation with others to eliminate them. It should not trade in arms or other materials used for terrorist activities, drug traffic, or other organized crime.

(continued on next page)

> **TABLE 4.5** *(Continued)*

We believe in treating all customers with dignity, irrespective of whether they purchase our products and services directly from us or otherwise acquire them in the market. We therefore have a responsibility to:

- Treat our customers fairly in all aspects of our business transactions, including a high level of service and remedies for their dissatisfaction
- Make every effort to ensure that the health and safety of our customers, as well as the quality of their environment, will be sustained or enhanced by our products and services
- Assure respect for human dignity in products offered, marketing, and advertising; and respect the integrity of the culture of our customers

We believe in the dignity of every employee and in taking employee interests seriously. We therefore have a responsibility to:

- Provide jobs and compensation that improve workers' living conditions
- Provide working conditions that respect each employee's health and dignity
- Be honest in communications with employees and open in sharing information, limited only by legal and competitive constraints
- Listen to and, where possible, act on employee suggestions, ideas, requests, and complaints
- Engage in good faith negotiations when conflict arises
- Avoid discriminatory practices and guarantee equal treatment and opportunity in areas such as gender, age, race, and religion
- Promote in the business itself the employment of differently abled people in places of work where they can be genuinely useful
- Protect employees from avoidable injury and illness in the workplace
- Encourage and assist employees in developing relevant and transferable skills and knowledge
- Be sensitive to the serious unemployment problems frequently associated with business decisions, and work with governments, employee groups, other agencies, and each other in addressing these dislocations

We believe in honoring the trust our investors place in us. We therefore have a responsibility to:

- Apply professional and diligent management in order to secure a fair and competitive return on our owners' investment
- Disclose relevant information to owners/investors subject to legal requirements and competitive constraints
- Conserve, protect, and increase the owners'/investors' assets
- Respect owners'/investors' requests, suggestions, complaints, and formal resolutions

Our relationship with suppliers and subcontractors must be based on mutual respect. We therefore have a responsibility to:

- Seek fairness and truthfulness in all our activities, including pricing, licensing, and rights to sell
- Ensure that our business activities are free from coercion and unnecessary litigation
- Foster long-term stability in the supplier relationship in return for value, quality, competitiveness, and reliability
- Share information with suppliers and integrate them into our planning processes
- Pay suppliers on time and in accordance with agreed terms of trade
- Seek, encourage, and prefer suppliers and subcontractors whose employment practices respect human dignity

| TABLE 4.5 | *(Continued)* |

We believe that fair economic competition is one of the basic requirements for increasing the wealth of nations and ultimately for making possible the just distribution of goods and services. We therefore have a responsibility to:

- Foster open markets for trade and investment
- Promote competitive behavior that is socially and environmentally beneficial and demonstrates mutual respect among competitors
- Refrain from either seeking or participating in questionable payments or favors to secure competitive advantages
- Respect both tangible and intellectual property rights
- Refuse to acquire commercial information by dishonest or unethical means, such as industrial espionage

We believe that as global corporate citizens we can contribute to such forces of reform and human rights as are at work in the communities in which we operate. We therefore have a responsibility in those communities to:

- Respect human rights and democratic institutions and promote them wherever practicable
- Recognize government's legitimate obligation to the society at large and support public policies and practices that promote human development through harmonious relations between business and other segments of society
- Collaborate with those forces in the community dedicated to raising standards of health, education, workplace safety, and economic well-being
- Promote and stimulate sustainable development and play a leading role in preserving and enhancing the physical environment and conserving the earth's resources
- Support peace, security, diversity, and social integration
- Respect the integrity of local cultures
- Be a good corporate citizen through charitable donations, educational and cultural contributions, and employee participation in community and civic affairs

Gordon Bethune, Chairman of Continental Airlines is building trust with union members by telling them the truth and promising only what he can deliver. He is trying to build a corporate culture based on trust.

Source: "Principles for Business English Translation," Caux Round Table, www.cauxroundtable.org/ ENGLISH.HTM, accessed October 21, 2001. Reprinted by permission from Caux Round Table.

Motivation Another significant factor in the ethical decision-making process is an individual's motivation. The psychologist David McClelland identified three different social needs that may motivate an individual in an ethical decision-making situation—achievement, affiliation, and power.[73]

The need for achievement refers to an individual's preference for goals that are well defined and moderately challenging, include employee participation, and provide for feedback. People with a high need for achievement tend to be motivated, show great initiative, and work hard to accomplish common shared goals. McClelland's theory suggests that if employees are given role models that have high ethical standards, they will then emulate these values. At Home Depot, for example, community service is viewed as an important part of social responsibility. Therefore, volunteering to build a playground would show initiative toward Home Depot's shared goals.

The need for affiliation relates to an individual's inclination to work with others in the organization rather than alone. Individuals with a high need for affiliation prefer to interact with others, guide others, and learn from those with whom they work.

They are, therefore, more effective working in an environment with peers rather than working at home alone. Such employees will be easier to socialize into the core values of the organization compared to those who telecommute from home. Peers and coworkers have been found to have more influence on ethical decision making in an organizational context than any other factor.[74]

The need for power refers to an individual's desire to have influence and control over others. Business environments often limit or constrain what people are able to contribute. To exercise power successfully within an organization, an individual must be accepted, assertive, and capable. The greater the need for power, the greater is the probability that an individual or group may engage in questionable or unethical behavior. Although the need for power does not always lead to negative effects, it is important for employees to balance this need with organizational goals and standards. The emergence of team-and project-based organizational structures often means that power and control are decentralized. Such structures require a great deal of trust, communication, and relationship building, all key factors in both social responsibility and business performance.

Organizational Relationships

Although individuals can and do make ethical decisions, they do not operate in a vacuum.[75] Ethical choices in business are most often made jointly in committees and work groups or in conversations with coworkers. Moreover, people learn to settle ethical issues not only from their individual backgrounds, but also from others with whom they associate in the business environment. The outcome of this learning process depends on the strength of each individual's personal values, opportunity for unethical behavior, and exposure to others who behave ethically or unethically. Consequently, the culture of the organization, as well as superiors, peers, and subordinates, can have a significant impact on the ethical decision-making process.

organizational, or corporate, culture
a set of values, beliefs, goals, norms, and rituals shared by members or employees of an organization

Organizational Culture **Organizational,** or **corporate, culture** can be defined as a set of values, beliefs, goals, norms, and rituals shared by members or employees of an organization. It answers questions such as "What is important?" "How do we treat each other?" and "How do we do things around here?" Culture may be conveyed formally in employee handbooks, codes of conduct, memos, and ceremonies, but it is also expressed informally through dress codes, extracurricular activities, and anecdotes. A firm's culture gives its members meaning and offers direction as to how to behave and deal with problems within the organization. The corporate culture at American Express, for example, includes numerous anecdotes about employees who have gone beyond the call of duty to help customers out of difficult situations. This strong tradition of customer service might encourage an American Express employee to take extra steps to help a customer who encounters a problem while traveling overseas.

On the other hand, an organization's culture may also encourage employees to make decisions that others may judge as unethical, or it may not discourage actions that may be viewed as unethical. For example, at Hypercom Corp., Jairo Gonzalez has opened new overseas markets that have resulted in huge sales growth and market shares of up to 80 percent. Gonzalez's successes helped build Hypercom into the world's second-largest vendor of card swipes for checkout counters. Twenty months ago, he was promoted to president of Hypercom's biggest division, and now he is in line to become chief executive. But Hypercom's star has a problem. He has been accused of rape by his former secretary, who was paid almost $100,000 by Hypercom to keep quiet about the matter, and of sexual harassment or verbal abuse by three other women at Hypercom, one of whom also was given a $100,000 payoff. This alleged behavior was not enough to derail Gonzalez's career, however. George Wallner, Hypercom's chairman, said, "He was bringing in $70 million a year. Do you fire your top rock star because he's difficult?" In settling the rape charge, Wallner said, "The $100,000 we spent was well worth the [sales] he was bringing in." He also said, "On a moral level this is confusing. But if you think of only the business decision, it was dead right."[76]

Whereas a firm's overall culture establishes ideals that guide a wide range of behaviors for members of the organization, its **ethical climate** focuses specifically on issues of right and wrong. We think of ethical climate as that part of a corporate culture that relates to an organization's expectations about appropriate conduct. To some extent, ethical climate is the character component of an organization. Corporate policies and codes, the conduct of top managers, the values and moral philosophies of coworkers, and opportunity for misconduct all contribute to a firm's ethical climate. When top managers strive to establish an ethical climate based on responsibility and citizenship, they set the tone for ethical decisions.

Such is the case at the White Dog Café in Philadelphia. Owner Judy Wicks pays a living wage to all restaurant employees, including dishwashers, with a minimum of $8.75 an hour after three months' employment. Wicks also keeps a five-to-one ratio between the highest- and lowest-paid employees. The restaurant is run using 100 percent wind-powered electricity, and 20 percent of all profits are donated to charity.

ethical climate
part of a corporate culture that relates to an organization's expectations about appropriate conduct that focuses specifically on issues of right and wrong

The White Dog Café pays a fair wage to all employees and 20 percent of all profits are donated to charity. (http://www.whitedogcafe.com/, downloaded April 2003. Copyright © 2003 www.whitedog.com. Reprinted with permission)

White Dog Cafe
Fun

The White Dog Cafe is located in three adjacent Victorian brownstones in the University City section of Philadelphia. Known for our unusual blend of award-winning cuisine and social activism, the cafe presents numerous events throughout the year which please palates while raising consciousness. Find out how we derived our name, read our tail-wagging menus, learn about our Sister Restaurants in the Philadelphia area and around the world, join a community service project, take a stand on a social issue, or take a tour of The Black Cat, our eclectic gift shop.

White Dog Cafe Newsletter
Our Summer 2003 newsletter is in the mail, full of tours, talks, block parties, movies, and community service days

Click here for a complete listing of events.

(Download the complete newsletter in PDF (acrobat) format)

History of the White Dog Cafe
Menus
Community Activities
Events
The White Dog Cafe Cookbook
Hours & Directions
Private Parties
The Black Cat Gift Shop
Newsletter

Wicks purchases only organic produce and humanely raised meats. She says, "Business is about relationships more than money."[77] Thus, the White Dog Café management has established an ethical climate that promotes responsible conduct. Ethical climate also determines whether an individual perceives an issue as having an ethical component. Recognizing ethical issues and generating alternatives to address them are manifestations of ethical climate.

significant others
superiors, peers, and subordinates in the organization who influence the ethical decision-making process

Significant Others **Significant others** include superiors, peers, and subordinates in the organization who influence the ethical decision-making process. Although people outside the firm, such as family members and friends, also influence decision makers, organizational structure and culture operate through significant others to influence ethical decisions.

Most experts agree that the chief executive officer establishes the ethical tone for the entire firm. Lower-level managers obtain their cues from top managers, and then, in turn, impose some of their personal values on the company. This interaction between corporate culture and executive leadership helps determine the ethical value system of the firm. However, obedience to authority can also explain why many people resolve workplace issues by following the directives of a superior. An employee may feel obligated to carry out the orders of a superior, even if those orders conflict with the employee's values of right and wrong. If that decision is later judged to have been wrong, the employee may justify it by saying, "I was only carrying out orders" or "My boss told me to do it this way."

Coworkers' influence on ethical decision making depends on the person's exposure to unethical behavior in making ethical decisions. The more a person is exposed to unethical activity by others in the organization, the more likely it is that he or she will behave unethically, especially in ethically "gray" areas. Thus, a decision maker who associates with others who act unethically is more likely to behave unethically as well. Within work groups, employees may be subject to the phenomenon of "groupthink," going along with group decisions even when those decisions run counter to their own values. They may rationalize the decision with "safety in numbers" when everyone else appears to back a particular decision. Most businesspeople take their cues or learn from coworkers how to solve problems—including ethical dilemmas.[78] According to Michael R. Cunningham of the University of Louisville, "We evaluate other people based upon their behavior; we evaluate ourselves based upon our intentions."[79] Close friends at work exert the most influence on ethical decisions that relate to roles associated with a particular job.

Superiors and coworkers can create organizational pressure, which plays a key role in creating ethical issues. For example, Mitsubishi employees kept silent for eight years about potential defects in large-screen televisions the firm manufactured between 1987 and 1990. Despite ten major cases of TV sets overheating, six of which caused extensive home fires, employees choose not to disclose the liability until recently, when the firm announced a major recall.[80] Remember from the opening vignette that in Japan, concealing evidence of defects that could result in a recall is not uncommon in a culture that views product recalls as a source of great humiliation. In such a culture, pressure from superiors and coworkers to remain silent may be enormous.

Nearly all businesspeople face difficult issues where solutions are not obvious or where organizational objectives and personal ethical values may conflict. For exam-

FIGURE 4.3 Sources of Pressure to Compromise Ethics Standards

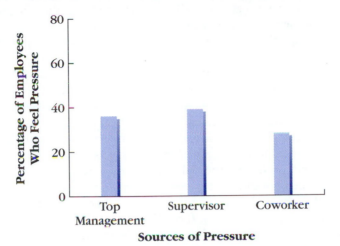

Source: Ethics Resource Center, *The Ethics Resource Center's 2000 National Business Ethics Survey: How Employees Perceive Ethics at Work* (Washington, DC: Ethics Resource Center, 2000), p. 38. Reprinted by permission from Ethics Resource Center.

ple, a salesperson for a Web-based retailer may be asked by a superior to lie to a customer over the telephone about a late product shipment. In one survey, 47 percent of human resources managers said they had felt pressured by other employees or managers to compromise their firm's standards of business conduct in order to attain business objectives.[81] A study by the Ethics Resource Center found that 60 percent of those surveyed said they had experienced pressure from superiors or coworkers to compromise ethics standards in order to achieve business objectives.[82] Figure 4.3 shows the sources of pressure reported by employees.

Opportunity

opportunity
a set of conditions that limit barriers or provide rewards

Together, organizational culture and the influence of coworkers may foster conditions that either hinder or permit misconduct. **Opportunity** is a set of conditions that limit barriers or provide rewards. When these conditions provide rewards—be it financial gain, recognition, promotion, or simply the good feeling from a job well done—the opportunity for unethical conduct may be encouraged or discouraged. For example, a company policy that fails to specify the punishment for employees who violate the rules provides an opportunity for unethical behavior because it allows individuals to engage in such behavior without fear of consequences. Thus, company policies, processes, and other factors may create opportunities to act unethically. Advancing technology associated with the Internet is challenging companies working to limit opportunities to engage in unethical and illegal behavior. In a survey of online retailers, 83 percent reported that fraud is a problem in online transactions, and 61 percent indicated that they were taking precautions to limit the opportunity to engage in fraud.[83] Individual factors as well as organizational relationships may influence whether an individual becomes opportunistic and takes advantage of situations in an unethical or even illegal manner.

Opportunity usually relates to employees' immediate job context—where they work, with whom they work, and the nature of the work. This context includes the motivational "carrots and sticks," or rewards and punishments, that superiors can use to influence employee behavior. Rewards, or positive reinforcers, include pay raises, bonuses, and public recognition, whereas reprimands, pay penalties, demotions, and even firings act as negative reinforcers. For example, a manager who decides to sell customers' personal data may be confident that such behavior is an easy way to boost revenue because other companies sell customer account information. Even if this activity violates the employee's personal value system, it may be viewed as acceptable within the organization's culture. This manager may be motivated by opportunities to increase company revenue and his or her performance standing within the organization. A natural gas trader for Dynegy Inc. was indicated for allegedly manipulating gas price indexes during the California energy crisis in order to increase prices. The trader pleaded not guilty when arrested on federal criminal fraud charges. While it is alleged that the trader sent fictitious trade information, the deception may have had rewards if it increased profits. If convicted, the trader faces a fine of up to $2.75 million and a prison sentence of up to thirty-five years.[84]

If an employee takes advantage of an opportunity to act unethically and is rewarded or suffers no penalty, he or she may repeat such acts as other opportunities arise. For example, about 1,500 coal miners died of black lung disease in 1994, but experts believe that almost no deaths would have occurred if mining companies had obeyed thirty-year-old federal regulations. Miners say that companies routinely falsify air-quality reports and run sample pumps less than the required time or place them in clean air away from working areas.[85] Because monitoring and enforcement of federal regulations was inadequate, the opportunity to falsify reports existed. When company managers got away with the illegal conduct, their behavior was reinforced. Indeed, opportunity to engage in unethical conduct is often a better predictor of unethical activities than personal values.[86]

In addition to rewards and the absence of punishment, other elements in the business environment tend to create opportunities. Professional codes of conduct and ethics-related corporate policies also influence opportunity by prescribing what behaviors are acceptable. The larger the rewards and the milder the punishment for unethical behavior, the greater is the probability that unethical behavior will be practiced.

Summary

Business ethics comprises principles and standards that guide individual and work group behavior in the world of business. Stakeholders determine these conventions, and they may change over time. The most basic of these standards have been codified as laws and regulations. Business ethics goes beyond legal issues.

Because individuals and groups within a company may not have embraced the same set of values, ethical conflict may occur. Questionable decisions and actions may result in disputes that must be resolved through some type of negotiation or even litigation. Codifying ethical standards into meaningful policies that spell out what is and is not acceptable gives businesspeople an opportunity to reduce the possibility of behavior that could create legal problems. Business decisions involve complex and detailed discussions in which correctness may not be clear-cut. It is important that a shared vision of acceptable behavior develop from an organizational perspective to develop consistent and reliable relationships with all concerned stakeholders.

Understanding the ethical decision-making process can help individuals and businesses design strategies to prevent misconduct. Three of the important components of ethical decision making are individual factors, organizational relationships, and opportunity.

Significant individual factors that affect the ethical decision-making process include personal moral philosophy, stage of moral development, motivation, and other personal factors such as gender, age, and experience. Moral philosophies are the principles or rules that individuals apply in deciding what is right or wrong. Most moral philosophies can be classified as consequentialism, ethical formalism, or justice. Consequentialist philosophies consider a decision to be right or acceptable if it accomplishes a desired result such as pleasure, knowledge, career growth, the realization of self-interest, or utility. Consequentialism may be further classified as egoism and utilitarianism. Ethical formalism focuses on the rights of individuals and on the intentions associated with a particular behavior rather than on its consequences. Justice theory relates to evaluations of fairness, or the disposition to deal with perceived injustices of others. Kohlberg proposed that people progress through six stages in their development of cognitive moral development. McClelland identified three different social needs that may motivate an individual in an ethical decision-making situation—achievement, affiliation, and power.

The culture of the organization, as well as superiors, peers, and subordinates, can have a significant impact on the ethical decision-making process. Organizational, or corporate, culture can be defined as a set of values, beliefs, goals, norms, and rituals shared by members or employees of an organization. Whereas a firm's overall culture establishes ideals that guide a wide range of behaviors for members of the organization, its ethical climate focuses specifically on issues of right and wrong. Significant others include superiors, peers, and subordinates in the organization who influence the ethical decision-making process. Interaction between corporate culture and executive leadership helps determine the ethical value system of the firm, but obedience to authority can also explain why many people resolve workplace issues by following the directives of a superior. The more a person is exposed to unethical activity by others in the organization, the more likely it is that he or she will behave unethically. Superiors and coworkers can create organizational pressure, which plays a key role in creating ethical issues.

Opportunity is a set of conditions that limit barriers or provide rewards. If an individual takes advantage of an opportunity to act unethically and escapes punishment or gains a reward, that person may repeat such acts when circumstances favor them.

Key Terms

business ethics (p. 96)
ethical issue (p. 101)

honesty (p. 101)
fairness (p. 101)
conflict of interest (p. 103)
fraud (p. 105)

affirmative action programs (p. 109)
moral philosophies (p. 113)
consequentialism (p. 113)
egoism (p. 113)
utilitarianism (p. 113)
ethical formalism (p. 114)
justice theory (p. 114)
organizational, or corporate, culture (p. 120)
ethical climate (p. 121)
significant others (p. 122)
opportunity (p. 123)

Discussion Questions

1. Why is business ethics a strategic consideration in organizational decisions?
2. How do individual, organizational, and opportunity factors interact to influence ethical or unethical decisions?
3. How do moral philosophies influence the individual factor in organizational ethical decision making?
4. How can ethical formalism be used in organizational ethics programs and still respect diversity and the right for individual values?
5. What are the potential benefits of an emphasis on procedural justice?
6. How can knowledge of Kohlberg's stages of moral development be useful in developing an organizational ethics program?
7. How do organizations create an ethical climate?
8. Why are we seeing more evidence of widespread ethical dilemmas within organizations?

Experiential Exercise

Visit www.bbb.org, the home page for the Better Business Bureau. Locate the International Marketplace Ethics award criteria. Find recent winners of the award and summarize what they did to achieve this recognition. Describe the role of the BBB in supporting self-regulatory activities and business ethics.

What Would You Do?

On Sunday, Armando went to work to pick up a report he needed to review before an early Monday meeting. While at work, he noticed a colleague's light on and went over to her cubicle for a short visit. Monica was one of the newest systems designers on the department's staff.

She was hired six weeks ago to assist with a series of human resources (HR) projects for the company. Before joining the firm, she worked as an independent consultant to organizations trying to upgrade their human resources systems that track payroll, benefits, compliance, and other issues. Monica was very well qualified, detail oriented, and hard working. She was the only female on the systems staff.

In his brief conversation with Monica, Armando felt that he was not getting the full story of her reason for being at work on a Sunday. After all, the systems team completed the first HR systems proposal on Thursday and was prepared to present its report and recommendations on Monday. Monica said she was "working on a few parts" of the project but did not get more specific. Her face turned red when Armando joked, "With the beautiful sunshine outside, only someone hoping to earn a little extra money would be at work today."

Armando and another coworker, David, presented the systems team's report to the HR staff on Monday. HR was generally pleased with the recommendations but wanted a number of specifications changes. This was normal and the systems designers were prepared for the changes. Everyone on the team met that afternoon and Tuesday morning to develop a plan for revamping the HR system. By Tuesday afternoon, each member was working on his or her part of the project again.

On Friday afternoon, David went up and down the hall, encouraging everyone to go to happy hour at the pub down the street. About ten people, including Monica and Armando, went to the pub. The conversation was mainly about work and the new HR project. On several occasions, Monica offered ideas about other systems and companies with which she was familiar. Most of the systems designers listened, but a few were quick to question her suggestions. Armando assumed her suggestions were the result of work with previous clients. Over the weekend, however, Armando began to wonder whether Monica was talking about current clients. He remembered their conversation on Sunday and decided to look into the matter.

On Monday, Armando asked Monica directly whether she still had clients. Monica said yes and that she was finishing up on projects with two of them. She went on to say that she worked late hours and on the weekends and was not skimping on her company responsibilities. Armando agreed that she was a good colleague but was not comfortable with her use of company resources on personal, money-making projects. He was also concerned that the team's intellectual capital was being used. What would you do?

5

Strategic Approaches to Improving Ethical Behavior

CHAPTER OBJECTIVES

- To provide an overview of the need for an organizational ethics program
- To consider crucial keys to development of an effective ethics program
- To examine effective implementation of an ethics program

CHAPTER OUTLINE

The Need for Organizational Ethics Programs

Codes of Conduct

Ethics Officers

Ethics Training and Communication

Establishing Systems to Monitor and Enforce Ethical Standards

Continuous Improvement of the Ethics Program

Implementing Organizational Ethics Programs

Due to recent corporate scandals and the tough corporate governance rules they inspired, companies are finding they need changes in their boards of directors. Legislation requires a greater number of independent directors who do not work for or do business with a company or its executives. At least one financial expert must be on the board's audit committee, while the full panel must review financial statements every quarter after certification by the CEO and finance chief. Under the Sarbanes-Oxley Act, CEOs and chief financial officers may be criminally prosecuted if they knowingly certify misleading financial statements. For this reason, they are under pressure to hire board members, and particularly audit committee members, who will make sure that things are done correctly.

In the past, board positions typically were filled with CEOs from other companies, people with high-profile resumes, and even notable names in government or sports. No longer can board audit committees passively monitor their company's outside auditors. New SEC rules have increased the pressure to safeguard the integrity of a company's financial controls and disclosures by requiring that board audit committees (1) help prepare the audits, (2) ratify internal accounting controls, (3) resolve disputes over accounting rules, (4) document compliance with those rules, and (5) monitor disclosures.

In order to comply with the legislation and new rules, including a seventy-five-page definition of who qualifies as a "financial expert," corporations are changing the way they compensate their boards. A survey of 200 large U.S. companies found that, on average, directors received a little more than $152,000 for their services in 2001 as well as a variety of different stock option plans. In an effort to recruit and retain higher-caliber directors, many companies are increasing board members' cash payments and changing stock options. Many companies are placing strict limits on the sale of board members' stock shares or eliminating stock options altogether. Sara Lee Corp. dropped directors' options last year, while Nuevo Energy Co. plans to do so this year. Starbucks Corp. is considering a board compensation plan that includes a mix of cash and equity, instead of options. Many corporations are increasing the annual stipends paid to their boards and compensating them for certain committee leadership roles that require more time and accountability. Proponents of the increased compensation packages say that higher board pay "will translate into more-experienced people coming into the board market and probably will improve corporate governance." Critics, however, contend that compensation for the part-time work, typically about 200 hours a year, is already too high.

Although most directors bring diverse business experience to their boards, few have any special education or training for the role. Many corporations now are offering training to board members on everything from how to read a company's books to how to set ethics guidelines for executives. The New York Stock Exchange has started its own director-training courses, and the exchange's chair plans to encourage the chairs of all companies listed on the exchange to send their directors through one of them.[1]

A strategic approach to ethical decisions will contribute to both business and society. This chapter provides a framework that is consistent with research, best practices, and regulatory requirements. Business ethics programs have not been implemented effectively by many companies, and there is still much debate concerning the usefulness and effectiveness of such programs in preventing misconduct. Our framework for developing effective ethics programs is consistent with the ethical decision-making process described in Chapter 4. In addition, the strategic approach to an ethics program presented here is consistent with the Federal Sentencing Guidelines for Organizations and the Sarbanes-Oxley Act described in Chapter 3. These legislative reforms require managers to assume responsibility and ensure that ethical standards are implemented properly on a daily basis. Ethics programs include not only the need for top executive oversight but also responsibility by boards of directors for corporate governance. The courts and recent reform legislation indicate that boards have an obligation "to manage the corporation for the best interests of the corporation."[2] This means that an action that is in the best interest of the organization for ethical reasons but does not necessarily maximize profits is required as the best ethical decision for all stakeholders.

Such an approach is not without controversy, as much unethical and illegal business conduct continues to occur, including in organizations that have ethics programs. For example, although Enron had a code of ethics and was a member of the Better Business Bureau, the company was devastated by unethical activities and corporate scandal. Many business leaders believe that personal moral development and character are all that is needed for corporate responsibility. There are those who feel that ethics initiatives should arise inherently from a company's culture and that hiring good employees will limit unethical behavior within the organization. Many executives and board members do not understand how organizational ethical decisions are made and how to develop an ethical corporate culture. We believe, however, that a prescribed, customized ethical program may help many organizations provide guidance in order for employees from diverse backgrounds to gain an understanding of acceptable behavior within the organization. Many ethical issues in business are complex and include considerations that require organizational agreement regarding appropriate action. Top executives and boards of directors must provide the leadership and a system to resolve these issues.

In this chapter, we provide an overview of why businesses need to develop an organizational ethics program. Next, we consider the factors that are crucial for the development of such a program: a code of conduct, an ethics officer and appropriate delegation of authority, an effective ethics training program, a system to monitor and support ethical compliance, and continual efforts to improve the ethics program. Finally, we discuss implementation of an organizational ethics program, including the roles of leadership and corporate culture.

The Need for Organizational Ethics Programs

Great care must be taken to avoid infringing on employees' personal freedoms and ethical beliefs. In cases where an individual's personal beliefs and activities are inconsistent with company policies on ethics, conflict may develop. If the individual feels that ethical systems in the organization are deficient or directed in an inappropriate manner, some type of open conflict resolution may be needed to deal with the differences. Usually an organization is held accountable for the conduct of its employees. Companies must assess their ethical risks and develop values and compliance systems to avoid legal and ethical mistakes that could damage the organization.

Understanding the factors that influence how individuals make decisions to resolve ethical issues, as discussed in Chapter 4, can help companies encourage ethical behavior and discourage undesirable conduct. Fostering ethical decisions within an organization requires eliminating unethical persons and improving the firm's ethical standards. Consider the "bad apple–bad barrel" analogy. Some people are "bad apples" who will always do things in their own self-interest regardless of organizational goals or accepted standards of conduct. For example, ClearOne Communications Inc. relieved its CEO and CFO after they were named as defendants in a complaint from the Securities and Exchange Commission. A civil complaint alleged that they directed sales personnel to push extra products to customers beyond their orders to inflate sales and earnings.[3] Eliminating such bad apples through screening techniques and enforcement of the firm's ethical standards can help improve the firm's overall ethical conduct. In this case, it is alleged that the CEO and CFO were not only individuals who directed unethical actions but who also contributed to an unethical corporate culture.

Organizations can create unethical corporate cultures, not because individuals within them are bad, but because the pressures to succeed create opportunities that reward unethical decisions. In the case of an unethical corporate culture, the organization must redesign its ethical standards to conform to industry and stakeholder standards of acceptable behavior. Most businesses attempt to improve ethical decision making by establishing and implementing a strategic approach to improving organizational ethics. Companies such as Texas Instruments, Starbucks, Ford Motor Company, and Johnson & Johnson take a strategic approach to organizational ethics but monitor their programs on a continuous basis and make improvements when problems occur.

To be socially responsible and promote legal and ethical conduct, an organization should develop an organizational ethics program by establishing, communicating, and monitoring ethical values and legal requirements that characterize its history, culture, industry, and operating environment. Without such programs and uniform standards and policies of conduct, it is difficult for employees to determine what behaviors are acceptable within a company. As discussed in Chapter 4, in the absence of such programs and standards, employees generally will make decisions based on their observations of how their coworkers and managers behave. A strong ethics program

The Institute for Global Ethics develops ethics training programs and recently launched a new series for training executives, staff, and board members of nonprofit organizations. (www.globalethics.org/corp/default.html, downloaded July 8, 2003. The Institute for Global Ethics, with operations in the U.S., U.K., and Canada, is an independent, nonsectarian, nonpartisan, nonprofit organization working in educational, corporate, and public settings to advance ethical action worldwide. Reprinted with permission.)

Institute for **Global Ethics**

CAMDEN LONDON TORONTO

Mission: To promote ethical behavior in individuals, institutions, and nations through research, public discourse, and practical action.

INSTITUTE HOME
EDUCATION
ORGANIZATIONAL SERVICES
PUBLIC POLICY

ABOUT IGE
DILEMMA: RIGHT vs. RIGHT
ETHICAL FITNESS® SEMINARS
IGE PUBLICATIONS
JOIN IGE
NEWS RELEASES

SEARCH IGE SITE:
[ ] Go

Organizational Services

Institute for Global Ethics Kicks Off Nonprofit Ethics Training
The Institute has launched a comprehensive ethics training and consulting project based on CD-ROM for executives, staff, and board members of the nation's nonprofit organizations. IGE is working together with Independent Sector, The National Council of Nonprofit Associations, The Alliance for Nonprofit Management, and The National Center for Nonprofit Boards to deliver services aimed at helping nonprofits use the lens of ethics to increase their effectiveness. Funding for the project is being provided by The Rockefeller Brothers Fund and the David and Lucile Packard Foundation. Read the press release here, or see more about the CD-ROM here.

Navigating the Waters, Ethics Training on CD-ROM for the Insurance Industry
Our computer-based training module, customized for the insurance industry, is now available. The CD-ROM is accompanied by a book of

includes a written code of conduct, an ethics officer to oversee the program, care in the delegation of authority, formal ethics training, and auditing, monitoring, enforcement, and revision of program standards. Without a strong program, problems likely will develop.

Such is the case in Latin America where Argentine businesses have the greatest number of ethical problems, according to a recent survey by the most prestigious and comprehensive Latin American business magazine. In Latin America there is no method, rule, or corporate internal policy that controls in absolute terms what business managers plan or do, and only 26 percent of all executives follow the values of the founder or owner of the business in which they are employed.[4]

Recent corporate ethics crises in the United States have destroyed trust in top management and significantly lowered the public's trust of business. A *Wall Street Journal*–NBC poll of the general public indicated that 57 percent of the general public felt that "standards and values of corporate leaders and executives had dropped in the last 20 years."[5] A Golin/Harris trust survey found that 82 percent of the public believes the crisis of trust in the United States will stay the same or get worse, and two-thirds hold CEOs personally accountable for restoring trust and confidence in U.S. business.[6] Consumers are looking for clear, creative, and constructive leadership from CEOs that demonstrates trust is a priority. Survey respondents were asked to make recommendations they considered essential or important to establishing and maintaining trust. Table 5.1 shows the top survey responses.

While there are no universal standards that can be applied to organizational ethics programs, most companies develop codes, values, or policies for guidance about business behavior. It would be very naive to think that simply having a code of ethics would solve ethical dilemmas the company might face.[7] The majority of companies that have been in ethical or legal trouble usually have stated ethics codes and programs. Often, the problem is that top management, as well as the overall corporate culture, has not integrated these codes, values, and standards into daily decision making. For example, Tyco had an ethics program and was one of the members of the Ethics Officer Association. It was never active in that organization, and top management was involved in misconduct that resulted in a complete loss of public confidence in the company. CEO Dennis Kozlowski took millions of dollars of company funds for personal use and was indicted for criminal tax avoidance schemes. If the

TABLE 5.1   Top Recommendations for CEOs to Rebuild Trust and Confidence

Make customers the top priority.	91%
Assume personal responsibility and accountability.	90%
Communicate openly and frequently.	89%
Handle crises better and more honestly.	87%
Stick to code of business ethics no matter what.	85%

Source: Golin/Harris Trust Survey Results from Golin/Harris News Release, June 20, 2002, from http://www.golinharris.com/news/releases.asp?ID=3788, accessed January 31, 2003.

leadership of a company does not provide the vision and support for ethical conduct, then an ethics program will not be effective. Ethics is not something to be delegated to lower-level employees while top management is empowered to break all the rules.

To meet the public's escalating demands for ethical decision making, companies need to develop plans and structures for addressing ethical considerations. Some directions for the improvement of ethics have been mandated through regulations, but companies must be willing to have in place a values and ethics implementation system that exceeds the minimum regulatory requirements.

Codes of Conduct

codes of conduct
formal statements that describe what an organization expects of its employees

Because people come from diverse family, educational, and business backgrounds, it cannot be assumed that they know how to behave appropriately when they enter a new organization or job. Most companies begin the process of establishing organizational ethics programs by developing **codes of conduct** (also called codes of ethics), which are formal statements that describe what an organization expects of its employees. According to an Ethics Resource Center survey, 79 percent of respondents (employees) reported that their firm has written standards of ethical business conduct—such as codes of ethics, policy statements on ethics, or guidelines on proper business conduct.[8] These codes may address a variety of situations from internal operations to sales presentations and financial disclosure practices.

A code of ethics has to reflect the board of directors' and senior management's desire for organizational compliance with the values, rules, and policies that support an ethical climate. Development of a code of ethics should involve the board of directors, president, and senior managers who will be implementing the code. Legal staff should be called on to ensure that the code has correctly assessed key areas of risk and that potential legal problems are buffered by standards in the code. A code of ethics that does not address specific high-risk activities within the scope of daily operations is inadequate for maintaining standards that can prevent misconduct. Table 5.2 shows considerations in developing and implementing a code of ethics.

A large multinational firm, Texas Instruments manufactures computers, calculators, and other high-technology products. Its code of ethics resembles that of many other organizations. The code addresses issues relating to policies and procedures; government laws and regulations; relationships with customers, suppliers, and com-

TABLE 5.2	Developing and Implementing a Code of Ethics

1. Consider areas of risk and state values as well as conduct necessary to comply with laws and regulations. Values are an important buffer in preventing serious misconduct.

2. Identify values that specifically address current ethical issues.

3. Consider values that link the organization to a stakeholder orientation. Attempt to find overlaps in organizational and stakeholder values.

4. Make the code understandable by providing examples that reflect values.

5. Communicate the code frequently and in language that employees can understand.

6. Revise the code every year with input from organizational members and stakeholders.

petitors; acceptance of gifts, travel, and entertainment; political contributions; expense reporting; business payments; conflicts of interest; investment in TI stock; handling of proprietary information and trade secrets; use of TI employees and assets to perform personal work; relationships with government officials and agencies; and enforcement of the code. TI's code emphasizes that ethical behavior is critical to maintaining long-term success and that each individual is responsible for upholding the integrity of the company.

> Our reputation at TI depends upon all of the decisions we make and all the actions we take personally each day. Our values define how we will evaluate our decisions and actions . . . and how we will conduct our business. We are working in a difficult and demanding, ever-changing business environment. Together we are building a work environment on the foundation of integrity, innovation, and commitment. Together we are moving our company into a new century . . . one good decision at a time. We are prepared to make the tough decisions or take the critical actions . . . and do it right. Our high standards have rewarded us with an enviable reputation in today's marketplace . . . a reputation of integrity, honesty, and trustworthiness. That strong ethical reputation is a vital asset . . . and each of us shares a personal responsibility to protect, to preserve, and to enhance it. Our reputation is a strong but silent partner in all business relationships. By understanding and applying the values presented on the following pages, each of us can say to ourselves and to others, "TI is a good company, and one reason is that I am part of it." Know what's right. Value what's right. Do what's right.[9]

Like most codes of ethics, TI's requires employees to obey the law. In many instances, moreover, TI expects its employees to adhere to ethical standards more demanding than the law. For example, although some local laws permit companies to contribute to political candidates or elected officials, TI's code states that "no company funds may be used for making political contributions of any kind to any political candidate or holder of any office of any government—national, state or local. This is so even where permitted by local law." TI also goes beyond the federal law prohibiting discrimination against minorities and expects its employees to treat all fellow workers with dignity and respect. "The hours we spend at work are more satisfying and rewarding when we demonstrate respect for all associates regardless of gender, age, creed, racial background, religion, disability, national origin, sexual orientation, marital status, veteran status, or status in TI's organization."

This code of ethics is not just lip service paid to societal concerns about business ethics; the company enforces the code through audits and disciplinary action where necessary. TI's corporate internal audit function measures several aspects of business ethics, including compliance with policies, procedures, and regulations; the economical and efficient use of resources; and the internal controls of management systems. In addition, the code states that "any employee who violates TI's ethical standards is subject to disciplinary action which can include oral reprimand, written reprimand, probation, suspension, or immediate termination." Established in 1987, the TI Ethics Committee oversees all the activities of the ethics office. The committee consists of five high-level TI managers, who review and approve policy, procedures, and publications; monitor compliance initiatives; review any major ethical issues; and approve appropriate corrective actions.

To ensure that its employees understand the nature of business ethics and the ethical standards they are expected to follow, TI has three key publications: (1) *Standard Policies and Procedures,* (2) *The TI Commitment,* and (3) *The Values and Ethics of TI.* Employees are also provided with a minipamphlet containing an "ethics quick test" to help them when they have doubts about the ethics of specific situations and behaviors:

Is the action legal?

Does it comply with our values?

If you do it, will you feel bad?

How will it look in the newspaper?

If you know it's wrong, don't do it!

If you're not sure, ask.

Keep asking until you get an answer.

TI provides a toll-free number (1-800-33-ETHIC) for employees to call, anonymously, to report incidents of unethical behavior or simply to ask questions.[10]

The extent of TI's commitment to its employees is evidenced by the programs and support it offers them:

"Open door" policy for all managers (any level)

No retaliation, retribution, discrimination, or harassment

Required sexual harassment training

Required ethics training

Educational support from external sources

Promotion from within

Community involvement support

Career development networks

Texas Instruments explicitly states what it expects of its employees and what behaviors are unacceptable. By enforcing the codes wholeheartedly, TI has taken logical steps to safeguard its excellent reputation for ethical and responsible behavior. When such standards of behavior are not made explicit, employees sometimes base ethical decisions on their observations of the behavior of peers and management. The use of rewards and punishments to enforce codes and policies controls the opportunity to behave unethically and increases employees' acceptance of ethical standards.

As we stated, codes of conduct may address a variety of situations, from internal operations to sales presentations and financial disclosure practices. Figure 5.1 presents Fidelity Investments's codes of ethics. Note that Fidelity's code focuses on ensuring that employees do not have a conflict of interest that could create problems for the company's mutual funds.

Research has found that corporate codes of ethics often have five to seven core values or principles in addition to more-detailed descriptions and examples of appropriate conduct.[11] The six values that have been suggested as desirable to appearing in the codes of ethics include: (1) trustworthiness, (2) respect, (3) responsibility,

| FIGURE 5.1 | Fidelity Investments' Code of Ethics |

Code of Ethics Summary

Fidelity Investments understands the importance of trust and integrity to its customers and emphasizes these principles in the policies governing the conduct of Fidelity's employees. Fidelity's Code of Ethics is designed to ensure that employees of Fidelity understand and honor their duty to place the interests of Fidelity's customers ahead of their own. This summary of the Code of Ethics is intended to provide a general overview and is not comprehensive in nature.

What is Fidelity's Code of Ethics?

The Code of Ethics applies to all Fidelity employees and provides guidance for personal investment activity and other activities that have the potential to create actual or apparent conflicts of interest between employees and the funds managed by Fidelity. The Code of Ethics is based on the principle that officers, directors, partners, and employees of Fidelity have a fiduciary duty to place the interests of Fidelity's customers above their own. The Code of Ethics provides guidelines for personal trading and other activities, which employees and their immediate family members are required to follow. Instituted in the late 1960's and updated annually, the Code of Ethics incorporates a variety of internal, regulatory, and industry standards.

How does the Code of Ethics apply to Fidelity's Employees?

Upon hire, new employees are briefed on the Code of Ethics, provided with a copy of it, and required to acknowledge in writing that they have read it and will abide by it. All employees are required to review the Code of Ethics annually and to acknowledge in writing that their personal investing has been conducted in compliance with it.

While certain provisions of the Code of Ethics apply to all employees, the application of other provisions is dependent upon an employee's access to information related to day-to-day fund activities and investment recommendations regarding Fidelity funds. Employees with access to this type of information are referred to as "Access Persons" under the Code of Ethics.

Among other requirements, the Code of Ethics requires that all employees must: report personal securities transactions in any account in which they have a beneficial interest; adhere to the Code's rules for buying and selling securities; and conduct their personal investing through a Fidelity brokerage account. The latter requirement facilitates the monitoring of employee compliance with the Code of Ethics by providing the Ethics Office with the means to review the personal account activity of employees on an ongoing basis.

Employees who are Access Persons must receive permission from Fidelity's Ethics Office before making a personal transaction in most securities. Employee transactions are restricted when they create an actual or apparent conflict of interest with trades of Fidelity funds. This requirement does not apply to transactions in open-end mutual funds, certificates of deposit, short-term government obligations and certain other types of securities for which the potential for conflicts of interest is minimal.

"Investment Professionals" and "Senior Executives" are Access Persons who are subject to even more requirements because of the greater access they have to

(continued)

FIGURE 5.1 *(Continued)*

information about the trading activities of Fidelity funds. Among other requirements, these employees must: recommend suitable securities for the benefit of the Fidelity funds prior to personally transacting in them; surrender profits made from transactions in the same or equivalent securities if the transactions are made within 60 calendar days of each other; wait two business days following the issuance of a research note on a company before trading in the securities of that company for their personal accounts; and obtain pre-approval from the Ethics Office before serving on a board of directors or participating in a private placement. In addition, the Code of Ethics provides that Investment Professionals who are Portfolio Managers may not buy or sell a security that their fund has traded within seven calendar days on either side of the fund's trade date.

Monitoring and Enforcement

Fidelity's Ethics Office has primary responsibility for monitoring employee trading activity to ensure that employees are complying with the Code of Ethics.

When there is reason to believe that an employee has violated the Code of Ethics, the Ethics Office investigates the matter. Depending on the severity of the infraction, sanctions may include a warning, a fine, a personal trading ban, termination of employment, or referral to civil or criminal authorities.

Code of Ethics on File with SEC

Fidelity is required to file its Code of Ethics as an exhibit to the annual reports of its registered investment companies, which are filed with the Securities and Exchange Commission. The full text of the Code of Ethics may be obtained by viewing the public records of the SEC.

Fidelity Distributors Corporation
82 Devonshire Street, Boston, MA 02109

Fidelity Brokerage Services, Member NYSE, SIPC
100 Summer Street, Boston, MA 02110

(4) fairness, (5) caring, and (6) citizenship.[12] These values will not be effective without distribution, training, and the support of top management in making these values a part of the corporate culture. Employees need specific examples of how the values can be implemented.

Codes of conduct will not resolve every ethical issue encountered in daily operations, but they help employees and managers deal with ethical dilemmas by prescribing or limiting specific activities. Many companies have a code of ethics, but it is not communicated effectively. A code that is placed on a web site or in a training manual is useless if it is not reinforced on a daily basis. By communicating to employees both what is expected of them and what punishments they face if they violate the rules, codes of conduct curtail opportunities for unethical behavior and thereby improve ethical decision making. Fidelity's code, for example, specifies that sanctions for violating it range from cautions and warnings to dismissal and criminal prosecution.[13]

Codes of conduct do not have to be so detailed that they take into account every situation, but they should provide guidelines and principles that are capable of helping employees achieve organizational ethical objectives and address risks in an accepted manner.

Ethics Officers

> **ethics officer**
> usually a high-ranking person known to respect legal and ethical standards who is responsible for assessing the needs and risks to be addressed in an organizationwide ethics program, developing and distributing a code of conduct or ethics, conducting training programs for employees, establishing and maintaining a confidential service to answer questions about ethical issues, making sure that the company is in compliance with government regulation, monitoring and auditing ethical conduct, taking action on possible violations of the company's code, and reviewing and updating the code

Organizational ethics programs also must have oversight by a high-ranking person known to respect legal and ethical standards. This person often is referred to as an **ethics officer.** An ethics officer is usually responsible for assessing the needs and risks to be addressed in an organizationwide ethics program, developing and distributing a code of conduct or ethics, conducting training programs for employees, establishing and maintaining a confidential service to answer questions about ethical issues, making sure that the company is in compliance with government regulation, monitoring and auditing ethical conduct, taking action on possible violations of the company's code, and reviewing and updating the code. According to the Ethics Resource Center Survey, 50 percent of respondents reported that their firm has a designated office, person, or telephone line where they can get advice about ethical issues.[14]

The Ethics Officer Association has approximately 900 members. These ethics officers are responsible for oversight of their organization's ethics and legal compliance programs and demonstrate professional commitment by being a member of an organization that shares best practices and provides programs to assist members. Ethics officers are in the front lines of managing ethics programs and now have the attention of top managers and boards of directors.[15] The ethics officer position has existed for over fifteen years, but its role increased tremendously when the Federal Sentencing Guidelines for Organizations (FSGO) were passed in 1991. The guidelines gave companies that faced federal charges for misconduct the incentive of fine reductions up to 95 percent if they had an effective comprehensive ethics program in place. In 1996, a Delaware court ruled that individual board members would be liable for a company's ethical lapses unless they had an effective ethics program to prevent misconduct.[16]

Often ethics officers move from other jobs in their company rather than having formal ethics training. One-third have law degrees, one-fourth have financial backgrounds, and in some cases, the ethics officer has moved through the company ranks and was selected because of his or her knowledge of the company and his or her ability to communicate and develop training programs. The financial reporting requirements of the Sarbanes-Oxley Act put more pressure on ethics officers to monitor financial reporting, as well as reporting of sales and inventory movements, to prevent fraud in reporting revenue and profits.[17]

In most firms, ethics officers do not report directly to the board of directors. Sun Microsystems is one of the exceptions, and in the next few years, most ethics officers probably will report to the company's board. At Sun, employees can report concerns to someone outside the firm, and if there is merit, the outside help center can report directly to the appropriate board committee. Then the board committee can request an investigation. A Conference Board survey of 100 senior ethics officers revealed that 60 percent indicated that their own board of directors is not engaged enough in ethics issues. Fifty-seven percent say they have never engaged their board of directors in ethics training.[18]

The Ethics Officer Association exists for members to share best practices in managing ethics and organizing compliance programs. (http://www.eoa.org/home.asp, downloaded April 30, 2003. Reprinted with permission of the Ethics Officer Association.)

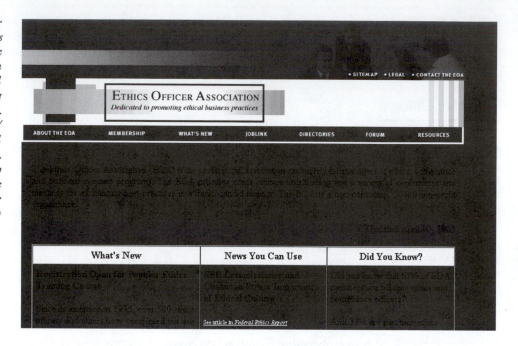

The European equivalent of the U.S. Ethics Officer Association has been set up as a debating and training forum for those responsible for managing company ethics. Named the Ethics Practitioner Forum, the group has attracted interest from Spain, France, Germany, the Netherlands, Belgium, Denmark, Norway, Italy, and the United Kingdom. Initially, the forum will consist of a series of small national groups that will share information and best practices on a web site and meet annually.[19]

Building an ethics program and hiring an ethics officer to avoid fines will not be effective alone. Only with the involvement of top management and the board can an ethics officer earn the trust and cooperation of all key decision makers. Ethics officers are responsible for knowing about thousands of pages of regulations as well as communicating and reinforcing values that build an ethical organizational culture.

Ethics Training and Communication

Instituting a training program and communication system to communicate and educate about the firm's ethical standards is a major step in developing an effective ethics program. Such training can educate employees about the firm's policies and expectations, relevant laws and regulations, and general social standards. Training programs can make employees aware of available resources, support systems, and designated personnel who can assist them with ethical and legal advice. Training also can help empower employees to ask tough questions and make ethical decisions. According to the Ethics Resource Center survey, 55 percent of respondents employed by for-profit organizations reported that their firm provides ethics training.[20] Figure 5.2 indicates that a significant number of employees report that they frequently find such training useful. Many companies are now incorporating ethics training into their employee and management development training efforts. For example, at HCA-The Healthcare Company, two hours of orientation training on the company's code of conduct is required for each employee within thirty days of employment, and a code of conduct refresher course is conducted for all employees each year.[21]

Ethics officers provide the oversight and management of most ethics training. While training and communication should reinforce values and provide learning opportunities about rules, it is only one part of an effective ethics program. The employee's capacity to exercise judgments that result in ethical decisions must be reinforced and developed. Ethics training that is just done because it is required or because ethics involvement is considered to be something that other companies do will not be effective.

The majority of ethics officers surveyed by the Conference Board said that even ethics training would not have prevented the collapse of Enron. Even if Enron's senior management had extensive ethics training, it would have made little or no difference in preventing misconduct.[22] This is because Enron knew that it had the support of Arthur Andersen, its auditing and accounting consulting partner, as well as that of law firms, investment analysts, and in some cases, government regulators. Enron's top management thought they would not be caught in their fraud and manipulation.

The Conference Board survey indicated that 56 percent of ethics officers responded that they do not survey their employees to assess the effectiveness of their

| FIGURE 5.2 | Usefulness of Ethics Training |

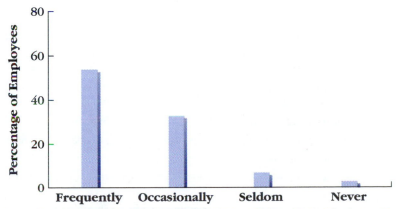

"How often have you found ethics training to be useful in guiding your decisions and conduct at work?"

Source: From the Ethics Resource Center's 2000 National Business Ethics Survey: How Employees Perceive Ethics at Work, p. 38 © 2000. Reprinted by permission from Ethics Resource Center.

ethics programs, and 54 percent do not have ethics measurements in their performance appraisal systems.[23] Both of these could help in determining the effectiveness of ethics training in an organization. If ethical performance is not a part of regular performance appraisals, the message is that ethics is not an important component of decision making. For ethics training to make a difference, employees must understand why it is conducted, how it fits into the organization, and their own role in implementing it.

Top corporate executives must communicate with managers at the operations level (in production, sales, and finance, for instance) and enforce overall ethical standards within the organization. Table 5.3 lists the factors crucial to successful ethics training. It is most important to help employees identify ethical issues and give them the means to address and resolve such issues in ambiguous situations. In addition, employees must be offered direction on seeking assistance from managers or other designated personnel in resolving ethical problems. An effective ethics program can reduce criminal, civil, and administrative consequences, including fines, penalties, judgments, debarment from government contracts, and court control of the organization. An ineffective ethics program that results in many unethical acts may cause negative publicity and a decrease in organizational financial performance. An ethical disaster can do as much damage (or more) to a company than a natural disaster.

Companies can implement ethical principles in their organizations through training programs. Discussions conducted in ethical training programs sometimes break down into personal opinions about what should or should not be done in particular situations. To be successful, business ethics programs need to educate employees about formal ethical frameworks and models for analyzing business ethics issues. Then employees are able to base ethical decisions on their knowledge of choices rather than on emotions.

TABLE 5.3	**Keys to Successful Ethics Training**

1. Help employees identify the ethical dimensions of a business decision.
2. Give employees a means to address ethical issues.
3. Help employees understand the ambiguity inherent in ethical situations.
4. Make employees aware that their actions define the company's ethical posture both internally and externally.
5. Provide direction for finding managers or others who can assist in ethical conflict resolution.
6. Eliminate the belief that unethical behavior is ever justifiable by stressing that
   - Stretching the ethical boundaries results in unethical behavior.
   - Whether discovered or not, an unethical act is just that.
   - An unethical act is *never* in the best interests of the company.
   - The firm is held responsible for the misconduct of its members.

Source: Adapted from Walter W. Manley II, *The Handbook of Good Business Practice* (Stamford, CT: International Thomson Publishing, 1992), p. 87. Reprinted by permission of International Thomson Publishing Ltd.

Training and communication initiatives should reflect the unique characteristics of an organization: its size, culture, values, management style, and employee base. It is important for the ethics program to differentiate between personal and organizational ethics. If ethics training is to be effective, it must start with a foundation, a code of ethics, an ethical concerns procedure, line and staff involvements, and executive priorities on ethics that are communicated to employees. Managers from every department must be involved in the development of an ethics training program.

Most experts on training agree that one of the most effective methods of ethics training is involvement in resolving ethical dilemmas that relate to actual situations that employees experience in carrying out their responsibilities. For example, Lockheed Martin developed a training game called *Gray Matters*. This training device is available on your textbook web site and includes dilemmas that can be resolved in teams. Each member of the team can offer their perspective and understand the ramifications of the decision for coworkers and the organization. Figure 5.3 gives an example of the type of issue covered in the game.

A relatively new training device is the behavorial simulation or role-play exercise in which participants are given a short, hypothetical ethical issue situation to review. The participants are assigned roles within the hypothetical organization and are provided with varying levels of information about the issue. They then must interact to provide recommended courses of action representing short-term, midrange, and long-term considerations. The simulation recreates the complexities of organizational relationships and of having to address a situation without complete information. Learning objectives of the simulation exercise include (1) increased awareness by participants of the ethical, legal, and social dimensions of business decision making, (2) development of analytical skills for resolving ethical issues, and (3) exposure to the complexity of ethical decision making in organizations. According to recent research, "the simulation not only instructs on the importance of ethics but on the processes for managing ethical concerns and conflict."[24]

Some of the goals of an ethics training program might be to improve employee understanding of ethical issues and the ability to identify them, to inform employees of related procedures and rules, and to identify the contact person who could help in resolving ethical problems. In accordance with these goals, the purpose of the Boeing Ethics and Business Conduct program is to:

- Communicate the Boeing values and standards of ethical business conduct to employees.
- Inform employees of company policies and procedures regarding ethical business conduct.
- Establish companywide processes to assist employees in obtaining guidance and resolving questions regarding compliance with the company's standards of conduct and the Boeing values.
- Establish companywide criteria for ethics education and awareness programs and to coordinate compliance oversight activities.[25]

To help ensure employees' continuing business ethics expertise, the company asks them to take ethics refresher training each year. On the company's "Ethics

Gray Matters

MINI-CASE

For several months now, one of your colleagues has been slacking off, and you are getting stuck doing the work. You think this is unfair. What do you do?

POTENTIAL ANSWERS

A. Recognize this as an opportunity for you to demonstrate how capable you are.

B. Go to your supervisor and complain about this unfair workload.

C. Discuss the problem with your colleague in an attempt to solve the problem without involving others.

D. Discuss the problem with the human resources department.

MINI-CASE

Your coworker is copying company-purchased software and taking it home. You know a certain program costs $400, and you have been saving for a while to buy it. What do you do?

POTENTIAL ANSWERS

A. You figure you can copy it too since nothing had ever happened to your coworker.

B. You tell your coworker he can't legally do this.

C. You report the matter to the ethics office.

D. You mention this to your boss.

MINI-CASE

You are aware that a fellow employee uses drugs on the job. Another friend encourages you to confront the person instead of informing the supervisor. What do you do?

POTENTIAL ANSWERS

A. You speak to the alleged user and encourage him to get help.

B. You elect to tell your supervisor that you suspect an employee is using drugs on the job.

C. You confront the alleged user and tell him to quit using drugs or you'll "turn him in."

D. You report the matter to employee assistance.

Source: Sammet, Jr., George, Gray Matters: The Ethics Game. Mr. Sammet published the game while serving as Vice President of Ethics for Martin Marietta. Copyright © 1992. Reprinted with permission.

Challenge" Web pages, employees (as well as the general public) can select from a variety of ethical dilemma scenarios, discuss them with their peers, and select from several potential answers. After clicking on the answer they think is most ethically correct, employees get feedback with the company's opinion and a rationale for each answer.

Ethical decision making is influenced by organizational culture, by coworkers and supervisors, and by the opportunity to engage in unethical behavior.[26] All three types of influence can be affected by ethics training. Full awareness of the philosophy of management, rules, and procedures can strengthen both the organizational culture and the ethical stance of peers and supervisors. Such awareness, too, arms employees against opportunities for unethical behavior and lessens the likelihood of misconduct. Thus, the existence and enforcement of company rules and procedures limit unethical practices in the organization. If adequately and thoughtfully designed, ethics training can ensure that everyone in the organization (1) recognizes situations that might involve ethical decision making, (2) understands the values and culture of the organization, and (3) is able to evaluate the impact of ethical decisions on the company in the light of its value structure.[27]

Establishing Systems to Monitor and Enforce Ethical Standards

Ethical compliance involves comparing employee ethical performance with the organization's ethical standards. Ethical compliance can be measured through employee observation, internal audits, surveys, reporting systems, and investigations. An effective ethical program uses a variety of resources to effectively monitor ethical conduct. Sometimes external auditing and review of company activities are helpful in developing benchmarks of compliance.

The existence of an internal system for employees to report misconduct is especially useful in monitoring and evaluating ethical performance. A number of firms have set up ethics assistance lines, often called help lines, or help desks to offer support and give employees an opportunity to register ethical concerns. Although there is always some worry that people may misreport a situation or misuse a help line to retaliate against another employee, help lines have become widespread, and employees do utilize them. The ethics line at Boeing is available not only to all Boeing employees, including those in subsidiaries, but also to concerned individuals outside the company.[28]

Help or Assistance Lines

A survey of *Fortune* 500 companies indicates that 90 percent offer toll-free help lines to report and request assistance when there are ethical concerns. It is interesting that Kenneth Lay, who was often a featured ethics speaker at conferences, did not offer employees at Enron a help line when he was Enron's CEO. His supportive auditor, Arthur Andersen, did not have a help line either.[29] About half of the issues raised on help lines relate to human resource issues and complaints such as coworker abuse, failure of management to intervene in such abuse, and inappropriate language. Lubrizol, a company of 4,500 employees, offers a help line, conducts employee surveys, and has employees rate their managers on ethical performance. Ethical issues have ranged from an employee who used the corporation to advance a personal business to human-resource-related issues such as sexual harassment.[30]

Sears offers a help line to its 330,000 employees and deals with questions about how to interpret company policy as well as specific work-related issues. The company received 17,000 calls per year to its two assist lines, and about 11,000 of those were directed to a human resources manager and five associates who were trained in negotiation, conflict resolution, and investigation.[31] Organizations need a help or assistance line or place where employees and managers can report suspected cases of

The irony related to ethics training materials is illustrated in this cartoon. (A. Bacall/Cartoon Resource)

A. BACALL

"Stan, are you walking off with my 'Ethics in the Workplace' book?"

unethical conduct. Critical comments, dilemmas, and advice can be handled at a central contact point where the most appropriate person can deal with a specific case.[32] A help line or desk is characterized by ease of accessibility and simple procedures and serves as a safety net that facilitates monitoring and reporting. Outside companies, such as The Network, can provide help line services that enable employees and consumers to voice concerns twenty-four hours a day, seven days a week.[33] This reporting approach increases the chance of detecting unethical conduct and enables responsible management to take adequate and timely measures to maintain compliance with standards.[34]

Observation and Feedback

To determine whether a person is performing his or her job adequately and ethically, observation might focus on how the person handles an ethically charged situation. For example, many businesses use role-playing in the training of salespeople and managers. Ethical issues can be introduced into the discussion, and the results can be videotaped so that both the participant and the superior can evaluate the results of the ethical dilemma.

Questionnaires that survey employees' ethical perceptions of their company, their superiors, their coworkers, and themselves, as well as ratings of ethical or unethical practices within the firm and industry, can serve as benchmarks in an ongoing assessment of ethical performance. Then, if unethical behavior is perceived to increase, management will have a better understanding of what types of unethical practices may be occurring and why. A change in the ethics training within the company may be necessary.

Corrective action involves rewarding employees who comply with company policies and standards and punishing those who do not. When employees comply with organizational standards, their efforts may be acknowledged and rewarded through public recognition, bonuses, raises, or some other means. Conversely, when employees deviate from organizational standards, they may be reprimanded, transferred, docked, suspended, or even fired.

Whistle-blowing

Efforts to deter unethical behavior are important to companies' long-term relationships with their employees, customers, and community. If corrective action is not taken against behavior that is organizationally or socially defined as unethical, such behavior will continue. In the Ethics Resource Center Survey, two in five employees who reported misconduct were dissatisfied with their organization's response, indicating that such corrective action is often not taken.[35]

whistle-blowers
people who expose an employer's wrongdoing to outsiders, such as the media or government regulatory agencies

If employees conclude that they cannot discuss current or potential unethical activities with coworkers or superiors, they may go outside the organization for help. **Whistle-blowers** expose an employer's wrongdoing to outsiders, such as the media or government regulatory agencies. Historically, the outcome for whistle-blowers has not been very positive. A University of Pennsylvania study indicates that 69 percent of the 300 whistle-blowers surveyed lost their jobs or were forced to retire as a result of trying to flush out corporate wrongdoing.[36] After being passed over for a promotion, the Dynegy management trainee Ted Beatty resigned, taking with him documents that revealed complex energy trades that used questionable accounting methods to exaggerate cash flows and cut taxes. Beatty moved to Colorado and provided the media, an investment fund's executives, and then the SEC with the documents, which led to the resignation of some top Dynegy officers. The company agreed to a fine for securities fraud but did not deny or admit the allegations. Beatty, however, has been unable to find another job. He claims that his house was burglarized and that he has received threats.[37]

More recently, whistle-blowers have provided evidence to indicate organizational wrongdoing. In 2002, Cynthia Cooper of WorldCom, Coleen Rowley of the FBI, and Sherron Watkins of Enron were named as *Time's* "Persons of the Year." Sherron Watkins, an Enron vice president, wrote a letter to Kenneth Lay in Summer 2001 warning that the company's accounting methods were improper. When Congress investigated Enron, Watkins's letter was released. Coleen Rowley wrote a memo charging that the FBI glossed over how much they knew about the September 11, 2001, terrorist attacks on the United States. Cynthia Cooper told the audit committee of WorldCom's board of directors that the company was using improper accounting in reporting earnings. She was told by her superior, CFO Scott Sullivan (later indicted for fraud), to back off, but she kept digging and reporting what she found. She still works at WorldCom, where earnings had been inflated by over $9 billion and 23,000 employees lost their jobs.[38]

If whistle-blowers present an accurate picture of organizational wrongdoing, they should not lose their job. Table 5.4 provides a checklist of questions that a potential whistle-blower should ask before acting. The Sarbanes-Oxley Act requires publicly traded companies to have an anonymous reporting mechanism for employees to

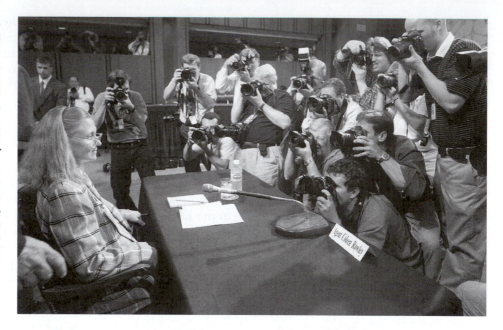

Three women, Cynthia Cooper, Sherron Watkins, and Coleen Rowley, independently and courageously exposed ethical issues at Enron, WorldCom, and the Federal Bureau of Investigation (FBI) in 2002, prompting Time *magazine to name them "Persons of the Year." (Mark Wilson/ Getty Images)*

question issues related to securities fraud. In addition, the act makes it unlawful to "discharge, demote, suspend, threaten, harass, or in any manner discriminate against" a whistle-blower and establishes penalties of up to ten years in jail for executives who retaliate against whistle-blowers.[39] In some cases, the company is required to report substantiated misconduct to a designated government or regulatory agent in order to receive credit that can reduce fines under the Federal Sentencing Guidelines for Organizations for having an effective compliance program.[40] The FSGO includes rewards for companies that detect and address unethical or illegal activities on a systematic basis. Failure to report misconduct that is discovered indicates an effort to conceal wrongdoing from regulators. If this occurs, all involved parties will be subject to additional regulatory enforcement actions. We discuss more about whistle-blowing in Chapter 8.

Consistent enforcement and necessary disciplinary action are essential to a functional ethical compliance program. The ethics or compliance officer is usually respon-

TABLE 5.4	**Questions to Ask Before Whistle-blowing**

1. Is this the only method to resolve my concerns?
2. Do I have the appropriate documentation and evidence to prove my case?
3. What is my motivation for expressing concern over employee/company activities?
4. Am I prepared to deal with the matter on a personal and professional level?

Source: Adapted from Paula Dwyer, Dan Carney, Amy Borrus, Lorraine Woellert, and Christopher Palmeri, "Year of the Whistleblower," *Business Week,* December 16, 2002, p. 108.

sible for companywide disciplinary systems, implementing all disciplinary actions the company takes for violations of its ethical standards. Many companies are including ethical compliance in employee performance appraisals. During performance appraisals, employees may be asked to sign an acknowledgment that they have read the company's current guidelines on its ethical policies. The company must also promptly investigate any known or suspected misconduct. The appropriate company official, often the ethics officer, needs to make a recommendation to senior management on how to deal with a particular ethical infraction.

Continuous Improvement of the Ethics Program

Improving the system that encourages employees to make more ethical decisions is not very different from implementing other types of business strategies. Implementation means putting strategies into action. Implementation in ethical compliance means the design of activities to achieve organizational objectives, using available resources and given existing constraints. Implementation translates a plan for action into operational terms and establishes a means by which organizational ethical performance will be monitored, controlled, and improved.

A firm's ability to plan and implement ethical business standards depends in part on the organization's structuring resources and activities to achieve its ethical objectives in an effective and efficient manner. For example, ever since its merger, and independently before the merger, ChevronTexaco has communicated company values—what it stands for and what its people believe in, as well as its tradition of always treating people fairly and caring about their welfare.[41] The firm's Values Statement (see Table 5.5) is its foundation. It guides the company in all of its actions. People's attitudes and behavior must be guided by a shared commitment to the business instead of by obedience to traditional managerial authority. Encouraging diversity of perspectives, disagreement, and the empowerment of people within the organization helps to align the company's leadership with its employees.

If a company determines that its performance has not been satisfactory in ethical terms, that company's management may want to reorganize the way certain kinds of ethical decisions are made. For example, a decentralized organization may need to centralize key decisions, if only for a time, so that top-level managers can ensure that the decisions are ethical. Centralization may reduce the opportunity for lower-level managers and employees to make unethical decisions. Top management can then focus on improving the corporate culture and infusing more ethical values throughout the organization by providing rewards for positive behavior and sanctions for negative behavior. General Motors and Dell Computer are examples of centralized organizations possibly because of their focus on manufacturing processes. In other companies, decentralization of important decisions may be a better way to attack ethical problems, so that lower-level managers, familiar with the forces of the local business environment and local culture and values, can make more decisions. Coca-Cola is a more decentralized company due to its use of independent distributors and unique localized cultures. Whether the ethics function is centralized or decentralized, the key need is to delegate authority in such a way that the organization can achieve ethical performance.

TABLE 5.5	The ChevronTexaco Way

VALUES

Our Company's foundation is built on our Values, which distinguish us and guide our actions. We conduct our business in a socially responsible and ethical manner. We respect the law, support universal human rights, protect the environment, and benefit the communities where we work.

- **Integrity.** We are honest with others and ourselves. We meet the highest ethical standards in all business dealings. We do what we say we will do.
- **Trust.** We trust, respect and support each other, and we strive to earn the trust of our colleagues and partners.
- **Diversity.** We learn from and respect the cultures in which we work. We value and demonstrate respect for the uniqueness of individuals and the varied perspectives and talents they provide. We have an inclusive work environment and actively embrace a diversity of people, ideas, talents and experiences.
- **Partnership.** We have an unwavering commitment to being a good partner, focused on building productive, collaborative, trusting and beneficial relationships with governments, other companies, our customers, our communities and each other.
- **High Performance.** We are committed to excellence in everything we do, and we strive to continually improve. We are passionate about achieving results that exceed expectations—our own and those of others.
- **Responsibility.** We take responsibility—as individuals and as teams—for our work and our actions, and we are recognized for doing so. We welcome scrutiny, and we hold ourselves accountable.
- **Growth.** We embrace change and encourage innovation. We seek out and pursue smart, challenging opportunities that contribute to personal and business growth.

Protecting People and the Environment We protect the safety and health of people and the environment. Our goal is to be recognized and admired worldwide for safety, health and environmental excellence. The following principles and expectations guide our behavior.

- **Leadership.** Strive for world-class performance by institutionalizing a rigorous system (Operational Excellence Management System) for managing safety, health and environmental affairs. Assess and manage risks to our employees, contractors, the public and the environment from our operations and products.
- **Safety & Incident-Free Operations.** Design, construct, operate, maintain and ultimately decommission our assets to prevent injury, illness and incidents.
- **Advocacy.** Work ethically and constructively to influence proposed laws and regulations, and debate on emerging issues.
- **Compliance Assurance.** Verify conformity with company policy and government regulations. Ensure that employees and contractors understand their safety, health and environmental responsibilities.
- **Conservation.** Conserve company and natural resources by continually improving our processes and measuring our progress.
- **Product Stewardship.** Manage potential risks of our products with everyone involved throughout the products' life cycles.
- **Pollution Prevention.** Continually improve our processes to minimize pollution and waste.
- **Property Transfer.** Assess and manage our environmental liabilities prior to any property transaction.
- **Community Outreach.** Reach out to the community and engage in open dialogue to build trust.
- **Emergency Management.** Prevention is a first priority, but be prepared for any emergency and mitigate any incident quickly and effectively.

Source: http://www.chevrontexaco.com/about/chevtex_way/values.asp. Reprinted with permission of ChevronTexaco Corporation.

Implementing Organizational Ethics Programs

There is increasing support that it is good business for an organization to be ethical and that ethical cultures emerge from strong leadership. Many agree that the character and success of the most-admired companies emanates from their leader. John Kotter noted that there are five things that a leader must do. First, leaders should create a common goal or vision for the company. Leaders are also good at getting "buy in" or support from significant partners. Great leaders are also great motivators and know how to use the resources that are available to them. The last character is the spirit of great leaders who enjoy their jobs and approach them with an almost contagious tenacity, passion, and commitment.[42]

If a company is to maintain ethical behavior, its policies and standards must be modeled by top management. Maintaining an ethical culture can be difficult if top management does not support such behavior. In an effort to keep earnings high and boost stock prices, many firms have engaged in falsifying revenue reports. Top executives in these firms encouraged the behavior because they held stock options—and could receive bonus packages—tied to the company's performance. Thus, higher reported revenues meant larger executive payoffs.

Along with strong ethical leadership, a strong corporate culture in support of ethical behavior can also play a key role in guiding employee behavior. A study of 330,000 employees at seventy-two U.S. companies indicated that "ethical lapses" are often caused by problems in corporate belief and value systems more than by individual unethical behavior.[43] In the following sections we will discuss the roles of leadership and culture in shaping organizational ethics.

The Role of Leadership

Leadership influences many aspects of organizational behavior including employees' acceptance of and adherence to organizational norms and values. Leadership that focuses on building strong organizational values among employees creates agreement on norms of conduct. Leaders in highly visible positions in the organization play a key role in transmitting values and diffusing values, norms, and codes of ethics.[44] Two dominant leadership styles are transactional and transformational leadership. Transactional leadership attempts to create employee satisfaction through negotiating for levels of performance or "bartering" for desired behaviors. Transformational leaders, in contrast, try to raise the level of commitment of employees and create greater trust and motivation.[45] Transformational leaders attempt to promote activities and behavior through a shared vision and common learning experience. Both transformational and transactional leaders can positively influence the organizational climate.

Transformational Leadership Transformational leaders communicate a sense of mission, stimulate new ways of thinking, and enhance as well as generate new learning experiences. Transformational leadership considers the employees' needs and aspirations in conjunction with organizational needs. Therefore, transformational leaders have a stronger influence on coworker support and building of an ethical culture than transactional leaders. Transformational leaders also build a commitment and

Legal and Regulatory Challenges

Unethical Leadership at Kmart?

Kmart, the Michigan-based retailer, filed for bankruptcy in January 2002 citing stiff competition from Wal-Mart Stores Inc. and Target Corp. Shortly thereafter, an anonymous letter claiming to be from Kmart employees was received by the company's board of directors, the U.S. attorney's office for Michigan, the FBI in Detroit, and the Securities and Exchange Commission. The letter detailed internal company problems, including alleged accounting irregularities, and led to investigations that still continue. Charles Conaway, then Kmart CEO, left the company in March 2002. Other top executives soon followed.

On the basis of information in the letter, Kmart's board of directors immediately began an internal probe into the allegations. After interviews with Kmart employees and reviews of 1.5 million pages of documents, the board, in January 2003, accused Conaway and his management team of being "grossly derelict." The probe found that Conaway and other former executives had engaged in financial abuses that hastened the company's collapse while allowing some managers to improperly profit. Under Conaway, Kmart allegedly hired "unquali-

fied" executives and consultants and compensated them at rates that "far exceeded" company norms. One specified instance involved an alleged kickback between a former top executive and a retail consulting firm. Also, some managers were accused of using company planes for personal travel.

The most-damaging disclosure from the internal probe was Kmart's acknowledgment that its executives had in place an abusive returns policy involving supposedly faulty merchandise. The company claimed more than $92 million in "questionable returns" in the first three quarters of 2001. Doing so enabled Kmart to cut costs and increase margins, which then-CEO Conaway cited as "evidence" he was reversing the retailer's downward spiral. Investigators also say that executives inflated profit forecasts in order to obtain board-approved executive loans for $24 million just one month before the company filed for bankruptcy. Other allegations include that some employees were demoted or transferred if they objected to the irregularities and that inaccurate documents were placed in company files "after the fact."

A court in February 2003 detailed all of the allegations against Conaway. The effort by the trust that represents the company's creditors could force Conaway to repay millions of dollars in severance pay and a $5 million loan that was forgiven. Ac-

---

respect for values that provide agreement on how to deal with ethical issues. Transformational ethical leadership is best suited for higher levels of ethical commitment among employees and strong stakeholder support for an ethical climate. A number of industry trade associations, including the American Institute of Certified Public Accountants, Defense Initiative on Business Ethics and Conduct, Ethics Officer Association, and Mortgage Bankers Association of America, are helping companies provide transformational leadership.[46]

Transactional Leadership Transactional leadership focuses on making certain that the required conduct and procedures are implemented. The "barter" aspects of negotiation to achieve the desired outcomes result in a dynamic relationship between leaders and employees where reactions, conflict, and crisis influence the relationship more than ethical concerns. Transactional leaders produce employees who achieve a negotiated level of required ethical performance or compliance. As long as employ-

cording to the filing, Conaway "permitted company executives to receive millions of dollars in retention loans and other payments that they would not have received had all material information been disclosed." All of the employees who received these loans have either left the company or been fired.

Also in February 2003, the first two federal indictments were handed down by authorities. After an exhaustive investigation, two former Kmart executives who ran the drugstore division until they were dismissed in May 2003 were indicted on federal charges of fraud, conspiracy, and making false statements that led to an overstatement of Kmart's financial results. Enio Montini, former senior vice president and general merchandise manager, and Joseph Hofmeister, former vice president of merchandising, also were charged with fraud by the SEC in a separate civil lawsuit. The suit seeks to bar either from serving as an officer of any public company and to recover a $750,000 loan given to Montini by Kmart. If convicted of the criminal charges, Montini and Hofmeister face a maximum of ten years in prison, a $1 million fine for securities fraud, and five years and $250,000 each for conspiracy and false statements. Immediately after the indictments were publicized, Montini resigned from his current job as head of merchandising for the Rite-Aid chain.

Federal officials emphasized that their investigations are continuing and that more indictments are likely. One retail expert predicted that the SEC would almost certainly call for an overhaul of retail accounting rules soon. A retail analyst said, "The temptation is too great to abuse the accounting so you can deliver what the Street wants you to deliver." In early March 2003, Kmart officials, led by Julian Day, new president and CEO, pledged to emerge from bankruptcy as a business "culturally" changed. Day said that Kmart is no longer operating "by the seat of its pants" but is "grounded in financial reality." With more financial controls in place, the retailer is attempting to rebuild itself around a vastly reduced number of stores and a management focused on honesty, integrity, discipline, and leadership—a "four cornerstone approach."

Sources:
Elliot Blair Smith, "Probe: Former Kmart CEO 'grossly derelict,'" *USA Today*, January 27, 2003, p. B1; "Kmart board faults ex-CEO Conaway," CNN Money, February 25, 2003, via http://money.cnn.com/2003/02/25/news/kmart.reut/index.htm, accessed February 25, 2003; Constance L. Hays, "Two Ex-Officials at Kmart Face Fraud Charges," *New York Times*, February 27, 2003, via www.nytimes.com/2003/02/27/business/27SHOP. html?th, accessed February 27, 2003; Lorrie Grant, "Former Kmart executives face 3-count federal indictment," *USA Today*, February 27, 2003, p. B1; "Today's Briefing," *Commercial Appeal*, March 5, 2003, p. C1.

ees and leaders find the exchange mutually rewarding, the compliance relationship is likely to be successful. However, transactional leadership is best suited to quickly changing ethical climates or reacting to ethical problems or issues. Michael Capellas used transactional leadership to change the firm's culture and ethical conduct when he took over as CEO and chair after an accounting scandal forced the company into bankruptcy proceedings. Capellas sought to restore WorldCom's—now called MCI—credibility in the marketplace by bringing in a new board of directors, creating a corporate ethics office, enhancing the code of ethics, and launching new employee financial reporting and ethics training initiatives.[47]

The Role of an Ethical Corporate Culture

Top management provides a plan for the corporate culture. If executives and CEOs do not explicitly address these issues, a culture may emerge where unethical behavior is sanctioned and rewarded. To be most successful, ethical standards and expected behaviors should be integrated throughout every organizational process from hiring, training, compensating, and rewarding to firing. An ethics program overlaid on an existing weak or unethical organizational culture is destined to fail, according to Steve Priest, founder of the Ethical Leadership Group.[48] Many employees who view unethical conduct do not report it because they fear inaction, they are afraid they will not remain anonymous, or they believe their organization is not concerned about the activity. Frank Navran, a consultant to the Ethics Resource Center, has identified seven steps to changing the ethical culture of an organization (see Table 5.6).

Organizational ethical culture is important to employees. A fair, open, and trusting organizational climate supports an ethical culture and can be attributed to lower turnover and higher employee satisfaction. Starbucks offers excellent health benefits to its employees as well as a stock ownership plan called "Bean Stock." These benefits are available to the entire employee workforce, which is mostly part-time. Turnover at Starbucks has historically been one-seventh of the industry standard, while its sales and profits continue to soar. Starbucks was noted as one of the 100 Best Companies to Work For in *Fortune*'s annual survey in 1998, 1999, 2000, and 2002. Howard Schultz, founder and CEO, was voted one of the "Top 25 Managers" by *Business Week*.[49] In 2003, Starbucks was named in the top ten of America's most admired companies.[50]

Some leaders assume that hiring or promoting good, ethical managers will automatically produce an ethical organizational climate. This ignores the fact that an individual may have limited opportunity to enforce their own personal ethics on management systems and informal decision making that occurs in the organization. The greatest influence on employee behavior is that of peers and coworkers.[51] Many times workers do not know what constitutes specific ethical violations such as price fixing, deceptive advertising, consumer fraud, and copyright violations. The more ethical the culture of the organization is perceived to be, the less likely it is that unethical decision making will occur. Over time, an organization's failure to monitor or manage its culture may foster questionable behavior. FedEx maintains a strong ethical culture and has woven its values and expectations throughout the company. FedEx's

TABLE 5.6	Steps for Changing the Ethical Culture of an Organization

1. State your position, philosophy, or belief.
2. Create formal organizational systems.
3. Communicate expectations through informal (leadership) systems.
4. Reinforce the policy through measurements and rewards.
5. Implement communications and education strategies.
6. Use responses to critical events to underscore commitment.
7. Avoid the perception of hidden agendas.

Source: Financial Executives Research Foundation, February 13, 2003, http://www.fei.org. 1998 Ethics Resource Center. Used with permission of the Ethics Resource Center, 1747 Pennsylvania Avenue NW, Suite 400, Washington, DC. 20006, www.ethics.org.

Many companies facilitate ethical corporate cultures by managing open and accessible work environments. (Amy Etra/ PhotoEdit)

open-door policy specifies that employees may bring up any work issue or problem with any manager in the organization.[52]

Reducing unethical behavior is a business goal no different from increasing profits. If progress is not being made toward creating and maintaining an ethical culture, the company needs to determine why and take corrective action, either by enforcing current standards more strictly or by setting higher standards. If the code of ethics is aggressively enforced and becomes part of the corporate culture, it can be effective in improving ethical behavior within the organization. If a code is merely window-dressing and not genuinely part of the corporate culture, it will accomplish very little.

Summary

A strategic approach to ethical decisions will contribute to both business and society. To be socially responsible and promote legal and ethical conduct, an organization should develop an organizational ethics program by establishing, communicating, and monitoring ethical values and legal requirements that characterize its history, culture, industry, and operating environment. Most companies begin the process of establishing an organizational ethics program by developing a code of conduct, a formal statement that describes what the organization expects of its employees. A code should reflect senior management's desire for organizational compliance with values, rules, and policies that support an ethical climate. Codes of conduct help employees and managers address ethical dilemmas by prescribing or limiting specific activities.

Organizational ethics programs must have oversight by high-ranking persons known to respect legal and ethical standards. Often referred to as ethics officers, these persons are responsible for assessing the needs and risks to be addressed in an organizationwide ethics program, developing and distributing a code of conduct, conducting training programs for employees, establishing and maintaining a confidential service to answer questions about ethical issues, making sure the company is in compliance with government regulations, monitoring and auditing ethical conduct, taking action on possible violations of the organization's code, and reviewing and updating the code. Instituting a training program and a system to communicate and educate employees about the firm's ethical standards is a major step in developing an effective ethics program.

Ethical compliance involves comparing employee ethical performance with the organization's ethical standards. Ethical compliance can be measured through employee observation, internal audits, reporting systems, and investigations. An internal system for reporting misconduct is especially useful. Employees who conclude that they cannot discuss current or potential unethical activities with coworkers or superiors and go outside the organization for help are known as whistle-blowers.

Consistent enforcement and necessary disciplinary action are essential to a functional ethical compliance program. Continuous improvement of the ethics program is necessary. Ethical leadership and a strong corporate culture in support of ethical behavior are necessary to the implementation of an effective organizational ethics program.

Key Terms

codes of conduct (p. 132)
ethics officer (p. 137)
whistle-blowers (p. 145)

Discussion Questions

1. How can an organization be socially responsible and promote legal and ethical conduct?
2. What are the elements that should be included in a strong ethics program?
3. What is a code of conduct and how can a code be communicated effectively to employees?
4. How and why are a training program and a communications system important in developing an effective ethics program?
5. What does ethical compliance involve and how can it be measured?
6. What role does leadership play in influencing organizational behavior?
7. Compare transformational leadership and transactional leadership.

Experiential Exercise

Visit the web site of the Ethics Officer Association (http://www.eoa.org). What is the association's current mission and membership composition? Review the web site to determine the issues and concerns that comprise the EOA's most recent programs, publications, and research. What trends do you find? What topics seem to be most important to ethics officers today?

What Would You Do?

Robert Rubine flipped through his messages and wondered which call he should return first. It was only 3:30 P.M., but he felt as though he had been through a week's worth of decisions and worries. Mondays were normally busy, but this one was anything but normal. Robert's employer, Medic-All, is in the business of selling a wide array of medical supplies and equipment. The company's products range from relatively inexpensive items, like bandages, gloves, and syringes, to more costly items such as microscopes, incubators, and examination tables. Although the product line is broad, it represents the "basics" required in most health care settings. Medic-All utilizes an inside sales force to market its products to private hospitals, elder care facilities, government health care institutions, and other similar organizations. The company employs 275 people and is considered a small business under government rules.

The inside sales force has the authority to negotiate on price, which works well in the highly competitive market of medical supplies and equipment. The salespeople are compensated primarily on a commission basis. The sales force and other employees receive legal training on an annual basis. All employees are required to sign Medic-All's code of ethics each year and attend an ethics training session. Despite the importance of the inside sales force, Medic-All has experienced a good deal of turnover in its sales management team. A new lead manager was hired about four months ago. Robert oversees the sales division in his role as vice president of marketing and operations.

Late Friday afternoon last week, Robert received word that two employees in the company's headquarters were selling products to the government at a higher price than they were selling them to other organizations. Both employees have been on the job for over two years and seem to be good performers. A few of their sales colleagues have complained to the lead sales manager about the high quarterly commissions that the two employees recently received. They insinuated that these commissions were earned unfairly by charging government-run hospitals high prices. A cursory review of their accounts showed that, in many instances, the government is paying more than other organizations. Under procurement rules, the government is supposed to pay a fair price, one that other cost-conscious customers would pay. When asked about the situation, the two employees said that the price offered was based on volume, so the pricing always varied from customer to customer.

Robert took the information to his boss, the company president. The president and Robert discussed how these employees received legal and ethics training, signed the company code of ethics, and should have been knowledgeable about rules related to government procurement. The president said that these two salespeople sounded liked "rogue employees," who committed acts without management approval in order to increase their commissions. Robert and the president discussed many issues and scenarios, such as how to deal with the two salespeople, whether to continue the investigation and inform the government, strategies for preventing the problem in the future, how to protect the firm's good name, whether the company could face suspension from lucrative government business, and others. What would you do?

Corporate Governance

CHAPTER OBJECTIVES

- Define corporate governance
- Describe the history and practice of corporate governance
- Examine key issues to consider in designing corporate governance systems
- Describe the application of corporate governance principles around the world
- Provide information on the future of corporate governance

CHAPTER OUTLINE

Corporate Governance Defined

Corporate Governance and Social Responsibility

History of Corporate Governance

Issues in Corporate Governance Systems

Corporate Governance Around the World

Future of Corporate Governance

In the early 2000s, Adelphia Communications Corporation was the sixth largest cable television company in the country. It was the dominant cable provider for southern Florida, western New York, and Los Angeles. In addition to cable entertainment, Adelphia offered digital cable, high-speed Internet access, long-distance telephone service, home security, and paging. Adelphia was founded by the brothers John and Gus Rigas in 1952 and was part of the pioneering effort to encourage customers to throw away the "rabbit ears" on their televisions sets. In 2001, John was inducted into the Cable Television Hall of Fame. John's sons, Michael, Tim, and James, were executives at Adelphia and, along with their father, sat on the board of directors. The company was admired for its aggressive growth.

Adelphia filed for Chapter 11 of the U.S. Bankruptcy Code in June 2002. The events leading to the bankruptcy highlight the misconduct that can occur when a firm's corporate governance system is weak or barely existent. Consider these actions and their effect on stakeholders, such as employees, shareholders, and others: A relative was paid nearly $13 million for furniture and design services in 2001. In addition to the use of corporate jets for personal business, off-balance-sheet loans were made to family members. For example, Adelphia helped fund the family purchase of a golf course and the Buffalo Sabres. The hockey team filed for bankruptcy in 2003 after the National Hockey League assumed control of the franchise amid the Adelphia downfall. The cable company was listed as one of the Sabres's largest creditors, as Adelphia attempted to reclaim $130 million that the Rigas family illegally used to purchase and run the sports team. John Rigas's daughter, Ellen, and her husband lived rent-free in a Manhattan apartment owned by Adelphia. Ellen's husband served on Adelphia's board of directors. A Rigas-owned farm made most of its revenue by performing snow removal, landscaping, and related services for Adelphia.

In late 2002, John Rigas, Michael Rigas, Tim Rigas, the former vice president of finance James R. Brown, and the former assistant treasurer Michael Mulcahey were indicted on twenty-four counts of conspiracy, bank fraud, securities fraud, and wire fraud. All executives originally pleaded innocent, but Brown later pleaded guilty to three charges in exchange for his testimony against the Rigases. Adelphia is pursuing its own lawsuit in federal court that charges Rigas family members and twenty companies controlled by the family with violation of the Racketeer Influenced and Corrupt Organizations Act (RICO), including a breach of fiduciary duty, abuse of control, waste of corporate assets, and substantial self-dealing.

Adelphia sued its external auditor, Deloitte & Touche, for fraud and negligence in failing to uncover the personal gain afforded to the Rigas family. The auditing firm countered that Adelphia's board of directors knew of and approved some of the transactions under complaint. At the time, the board was stacked with family and insiders and there were few internal control systems in place. Adelphia's new board revoked the $4.2 million severance package offered to the former chief executive John Rigas. Three insurers that provided liability coverage for Adelphia's directors and officers of the firm sued to rescind the contract on the basis that these leaders were aware of the fraud when they applied for coverage.

Other stakeholders potentially harmed by Adelphia's bankruptcy are Scientific-Atlanta Inc., Fox News, In Demand, FX, and other channels. These companies are waiting for collections from Adelphia. Scientific-Atlanta advanced $83.8 million to Adelphia to promote a box to help market digital service; however, Adelphia used that money to pay off reported expenses. Not only were the suppliers affected but also rival cable companies and the entire industry. Share prices of leading cable firms fell as a result of the Adelphia scandal. The cable industry became wary of the misconduct's effect on its reputation and worried that investors might lose faith or confidence because of situations at Adelphia and other companies like WorldCom. Investors were guarded because there are still founding families operating cable companies. The central problem is that several executives acted in their own self-interest at a company with an ineffectual control, risk, and governance system to detect and prevent such misconduct.[1]

The Adelphia story spotlights the increasing accountability that accompanies business decisions today, especially those made by high-level personnel in publicly held corporations. Stakeholders are demanding greater transparency in business, meaning that company motives and actions must be clear, open for discussion, and subject to scrutiny. Although some organizations have operated fairly independently in the past, recent scandals and the associated focus on the role of business in society have highlighted a need for systems that take into account the goals and expectations of various stakeholders. To respond to these pressures, businesses must effectively implement policies that provide strategic guidance on appropriate courses of action. This focus is part of corporate governance, the system of checks and balances that ensures that organizations are fulfilling the goals of social responsibility.

Governance procedures and policies are typically discussed in the context of publicly traded firms, especially as they relate to corporations' responsibilities to investors.[2] However, the trend is toward discussing governance within many industry sectors, including nonprofits, small businesses, and family-owned enterprises. We believe governance deserves broader consideration because there is evidence of a link between good governance and strong social responsibility. Before the governance crises of Enron, Tyco, and other firms, James McRitchie, editor of Corporate Governance.Net, commented on corporate governance: "Despite its still relatively low profile, it's where much of the real action is going on when it comes to positively changing corporate behavior."[3] A prophetic report issued by the Institute of Chartered Accountants in Great Britain in early 2001 concurred, citing corporate governance and accountability as one of the key drivers of change for business in the twenty-first century.[4] By 2002 and 2003, however, it was abundantly clear, to experts and nonexperts alike, that corporate governance was in need of immediate attention by a wide range of firms and stakeholders. The corporate scandals at Adelphia, WorldCom, Tyco, Global Crossing, and other firms in the early 2000s represented a fundamental breakdown in basic principles of the capitalistic system. Investors and other stakeholders must be able to trust management while boards of directors oversee managerial decisions. The egregious oversights that left thousands without jobs or retirement savings saw executives' being led away to court, prompted federal legislation, and sparked major reform in the accounting and auditing fields challenged the tenets of our economic system.[5]

In this chapter, we define corporate governance and integrate the concept with the other elements of social responsibility. Next, we trace the evolution of corporate governance and provide information on the status of corporate governance systems in several countries. We also examine primary issues that should be considered in the development and improvement of corporate governance systems, including the roles of boards of directors, shareholders and investors, internal control and risk management, and executive compensation. Finally, we consider the future of corporate governance and indicate how strong governance is tied to corporate performance and economic growth. Our approach in this chapter is to demonstrate that corporate governance is a fundamental aspect of social responsibility.

Corporate Governance Defined

In a general sense, the term *governance* relates to the exercise of control and authority. For example, most institutions, governments, and businesses are organized so that control and authority are clearly delineated. These organizations usually have an owner, president, chief executive officer, or board of directors that serves as the ultimate authority on decisions and actions. A clear delineation of power and accountability helps employees, customers, investors, government authorities, and other stakeholders understand why and how the organization chooses and achieves its goals. This delineation also demonstrates who bears the ultimate risk for organizational decisions. Although many companies have adopted decentralized decision making, empowerment, team projects, and less hierarchical structures, governance remains important as a mechanism for ensuring continued growth, change, and accountability for organizational resources and strategy. Even if a company has adopted a consensus approach for its operations, there has to be authority for delegating tasks, making tough and controversial decisions, and balancing power throughout the organization. Governance also provides oversight to uncover and address mistakes, problems, and risks.

corporate governance
the formal system of accountability and control for organizational decisions and resources

We define **corporate governance** as the formal system of accountability and control for organizational decisions and resources. Accountability relates to how well the content of workplace decisions is aligned with a firm's stated strategic direction. Control involves the process of auditing and improving organizational decisions and actions. The philosophy that a board or firm holds regarding accountability and control directly affects how corporate governance works.

Table 6.1 lists examples of the major categories to consider in corporate governance discussions. As you can see, these issues normally involve strategic-level decisions and actions taken by boards of directors, business owners, executives, and other people with high levels of authority and accountability. Although these groups have often been relatively free from scrutiny in the past, the wave of scandals, changes in technology, consumer activism, government attention, and other factors have raised questions about such issues as executive pay, risk and control, resource accountability, strategic direction, shareholder rights, and other decisions made for the organization.

From a control perspective, companies want to develop, reinforce, and refine policies in order to achieve consistency across organizational decisions and actions. This consistency may relate to a range of business practices, including product quality, financial reporting, human resources, and selection of vendors and business partners. Accountability for organizational decisions and resources begins with a strategic mission and vision that informs all levels of employees and stakeholders. From this

TABLE 6.1	Corporate Governance Issues
Strategic planning	Performance assessment
Corporate culture and ethical climate	Auditing and control
Shareholder rights	Risk management
Executive compensation	Disclosure and transparency
Mergers and acquisitions	CEO selection and executive succession plans
Composition and structure of the board of directors	

strategic directive, it is possible to account for and assess decisions made on behalf of the organization. Thus, corporate governance is about the process and content of decision making in business organizations.

For example, a common board-level decision that relates to corporate governance is in the area of mergers and acquisitions. When a corporation seeks to merge with or purchase another firm, complex questions must be answered. Among these is whether the action makes sense from a strategic perspective. A number of mergers and acquisitions occurred throughout the 1960s, 1970s, and 1980s that seemed to benefit executives and some shareholders yet made little sense from a strategic and long-term point of view. Another issue that often emerges is conflict in corporate culture, policies, and operating standards that must be remedied through the merger process.[6] Although top executives may recognize the importance of maintaining traditions from premerger organizations, it is also important to resolve conflicts that may present legal risks, perceptions of inequity, differences in quality standards, problems in strategic direction, and ultimately, performance trouble. For example, the 2000 merger of AOL with Time Warner was heralded as the largest in U.S. history, but the companies found much difficulty in developing synergy in operations and culture. Three years later, several top executives including Steve Case, founder of AOL and chair of the board, and Ted Turner, vice chair of the board, resigned amidst staggering losses.[7] Other firms have found similar difficulties.

In January 2003, Ted Turner resigned from AOL Time Warner amidst growing discontent from the conglomerate's stakeholders. (Spencer Platt/Getty Images)

When Daimler Benz and Chrysler merged in 1998, it was obvious that the integration of the two automakers' operations, policies, standards, and cultures was going to be a long and complex process. The companies not only had distinct histories and corporate cultures, but they were also headquartered on different sides of the Atlantic Ocean. A year into the merger, Thomas T. Stallkamp, president of DaimlerChrysler's North American division and the person charged with handling the details of the merger, resigned. Stallkamp, who had been a key executive during Chrysler's financial turnaround in the early 1990s, was widely regarded as the merged automaker's "spiritual leader." In this role, Stallkamp had sought to integrate the two firms in many areas, ranging from trust to organizational values to supplier relationships. However, analysts say that his outspoken manner may have led to conflict with DaimlerChrysler's German cochairman of the board, Jurgen E. Schrempp. When discussing his brief time within the merged company, Stallkamp noted a number of areas in which it was difficult to reach agreement or consensus. For example, because of Daimler Benz's luxury image and status, its employees were accustomed to flying first class, whereas only top officers at Chrysler were allowed to do so under company travel policy. Labor relations, steel specifications, and emission-control policies also created problems. At the time of Stallkamp's resignation, DaimlerChrysler's cochairs had agreed to put a hold on the integration of the company's three automotive units. Business analysts wondered how long it would take for the merged firm to realize its goal of global integration and the $3 billion in cost savings promised through the deal. In addition, other analysts questioned Daimler's due diligence process and whether it uncovered Chrysler's poor timing of model changes, brand erosion in the United States, and excessive inventories.[8] Two years later, DaimlerChrysler acquired one-third of the stock of Mitsubishi, and within six months of that purchase, Chairperson Schrempp had effectively assumed control of that Japanese automaker. Analysts also questioned this move, citing strategic problems and even greater differences between the initial German-American deal and this additional Asian venture.[9] These questions were ultimately focused on the costs and benefits of these decisions and how well management and the board had assumed responsibility for their actions.

Corporate Governance and Social Responsibility

Although most executives and board members do not deal with issues as complex as mergers on a daily basis, they are accountable for strategic-level decisions and their effects throughout the organization and society. However, there is variability in how individuals, industries, and even nations approach business accountability and control. In order to understand the role of corporate governance in business today, it is also important to consider how it relates to fundamental beliefs about the purpose of business organizations. Some people believe that as long as a company is maximizing shareholder wealth and profitability, it is fulfilling its core responsibility. Although this must be accomplished in accordance with legal and ethical standards, the primary focus is on the economic dimension of social responsibility. Thus, this belief places the philanthropic dimension beyond the scope of business. Other people, however, take the view that a business is an important member, or citizen, of society and must assume broad responsibilities. This view assumes that business performance is reflexive, meaning it both affects and is influenced by internal and external factors. In this case, performance is often considered from a financial, social, and ethical perspective. From these assumptions, we can derive two major conceptualizations of corporate governance—the shareholder model and the stakeholder model.[10]

shareholder model of corporate governance

model that bases management decisions toward what is in the best interests of investors; founded in classic economic precepts, including the maximization of wealth for investors and owners

The **shareholder model of corporate governance** is founded in classic economic precepts, including the maximization of wealth for investors and owners. For publicly traded firms, corporate governance focuses on developing and improving the formal system of performance accountability between top management and the firms' shareholders.[11] Thus, the shareholder orientation should drive management decisions toward what is in the best interests of investors. Underlying these decisions is a classic agency problem, where ownership (i.e., investors) and control (i.e., managers) are separate. Managers act as agents for investors, whose primary goal is shareholder value. However, investors and managers are distinct parties with unique insights, goals, and values with respect to the business. Managers, for example, may have motivations beyond shareholder value, such as market share, personal compensation, or attachment to particular products and projects. Because of these potential differences, corporate governance mechanisms are needed to ensure an alignment between investor and management interests. Although the shareholder orientation is primarily relevant to publicly held businesses, it also has implications for private firms. The shareholder model has been criticized for its somewhat singular purpose and focus, because there are other ways of "investing" in a business. Suppliers, creditors, customers, employees, business partners, the community, and other groups also invest resources into the success of the firm.[12]

stakeholder model of corporate governance

model that sees management as having a responsibility to its stakeholders in addition to its responsibility for economic success; based on a collaborative and relational approach to business and its constituents

In the **stakeholder model of corporate governance,** the purpose of business is conceived in a broader fashion. Although a company has a responsibility for economic success and viability, it must also answer to other parties, including employees, suppliers, government agencies, communities, and groups with which it interacts. This model presumes a collaborative and relational approach to business and its constituents. Because management time and resources are limited, a key decision within the stakeholder model is to determine which stakeholders are primary. Once primary groups have been identified, appropriate corporate governance mechanisms are implemented to promote the development of long-term relationships.[13] As we discussed in Chapter 2, primary stakeholders include stockholders, suppliers, customers, employees, the government, and the community. Governance systems that consider stakeholder welfare in tandem with corporate needs and interests characterize this approach. Occidental Petroleum Corporation experienced the complexity of the stakeholder model when it began drilling for oil in Colombia. The Colombian government hired Occidental, but the native tribe of U'wa opposed the drilling on religious and historical grounds. The clash of interests placed Occidental in the difficult position of balancing consumer, investor, government, and other stakeholder concerns. Occidental eventually exited Columbia.

Although these two approaches seem to represent both ends of a continuum, the reality is that the shareholder model is a more restrictive precursor to the stakeholder model. Many businesses have evolved into the stakeholder model as a result of government initiatives, consumer activism, industry activity, and other external forces. In the aftermath of corporate scandals, the polarity between the two views was narrowed, as it became clear how even the economic accountability of corporations could not be detached from other responsibilities and stakeholder concerns. While this trend began with large, publicly held firms, its aftereffects are being felt in many types of organizations and industries. Public hospitals, for example, have recently experienced a transition to the more holistic approach to corporate governance. Although public hospitals serve as a "safety net" for local governments' ability to provide health care, some experts object to the influence of government officials on these hospitals' boards of directors and operations. A new model of governance has emerged that calls for fewer government controls, more management autonomy and accountability, formal CEO and board evaluation systems, and more effective community involvement.[14]

The shareholder model focuses on a primary stakeholder—the investor—whereas the stakeholder model incorporates a broader philosophy toward internal and external constituents. According to the World Bank, a development institution whose goal is to reduce poverty by promoting sustainable economic growth around the world, corporate governance is defined by both internal (i.e., long-term value and efficient operations) and external (i.e., public policy and economic development) factors.[15] We are concerned with the broader conceptualization of corporate governance in this chapter.

In the social responsibility model that we propose, governance is the organizing dimension for keeping a firm focused on continuous improvement and accountability, and engagement with stakeholders. Although financial return, or economic viability, is an important measure of success for all firms, the legal dimension of social responsibility is also a compulsory consideration. The ethical and philanthropic dimensions, however, have not been traditionally mandated through regulation or contracts. This represents a critical divide in our social responsibility model and associated governance goals and systems, because there are some critics who challenge the use of organizational resources for concerns beyond financial performance and legalities. This view was summarized in a 1999 editorial in *National Journal,* a nonpartisan magazine on politics and government: "Corporations are not governments. In the everyday course of their business, they are not accountable to society or to the citizenry at large. . . . Corporations are bound by the law, and by the rules of what you might call ordinary decency. Beyond this, however, they have no duty to pursue the collective goals of society."[16] This type of philosophy, long associated with the shareholder model of corporate governance, was prevalent throughout the twentieth century, as we shall see in the next section. However, the revolution in corporate governance in the twenty-first century somewhat quieted proponents of this editorial's perspective.

History of Corporate Governance

In the United States, a discussion of corporate governance draws on many parallels with the goals and values held by the United States's founding fathers.[17] As we mentioned earlier in the chapter, governance involves a system of checks and balances, a concept associated with the distribution of power within the executive, judiciary, and legislative branches of the U.S. government. The U.S. Constitution and other documents have a strong focus on accountability, individual rights, and the representation of broad interests in decision making and resource allocation.

In the late 1800s and early 1900s, corporations were headed by such familiar names as Carnegie, DuPont, and Rockefeller. These "captains of industry" had ownership investment and managerial control over their businesses. Thus, there was less reason to talk about corporate governance because the owner of the firm was also the same individual who made strategic decisions about the business. The owner primarily bore the consequences—positive or negative—of decisions made. During the twentieth century, however, an increasing number of public companies and investors brought about a gradual shift in the separation of ownership and control. By the 1930s, corporate ownership was dispersed across a large number of individuals. This raised new questions about control and accountability for organizational resources and decisions.

One of the first known anecdotes that helped shape our current understanding of accountability and control in business occurred in the 1930s. In 1932, Lewis Gilbert, a stockholder in New York's Consolidated Gas Company, found his questions repeatedly ignored at the firm's annual shareholders' meeting. With his brother, Gilbert pushed for reform, which led the brand-new U.S. Securities and Exchange Commission (SEC) to require corporations to allow shareholder resolutions to be brought to a vote of all stockholders. Because of the Gilbert brothers' activism, the SEC formalized the process by which executives and boards of directors respond to the concerns and questions of investors.[18]

Since the mid-1900s, the approach to corporate governance has involved a legal discussion of principals and agents to the business relationship. Essentially, owners are "principals" who hire "agents," the executives, to run the business. A key goal of businesses is to align the interests of principals and agents so that organizational value and viability are maintained. Achieving this balance has been difficult, as evidenced by these terms coined about business in the media—*junk bonds, empire building, golden parachute,* and *merger madness.* In these cases, the long-term value and competitive stance of organizations were traded for short-term financial gains or rewards. The results of this short-term view included workforce reduction, closed manufacturing plants, struggling communities, and a generally negative perception of corporate leadership. In our philosophy of social responsibility, these long-term effects should be considered alongside decisions designed to generate short-run gains in financial performance.

The Sarbanes-Oxley Act of 2002, which we introduced in Chapter 3, provided the most significant piece of corporate governance reform in over sixty years. Under these rules, both CEOs and CFOs are required to certify that their quarterly and annual reports accurately reflect performance and comply with requirements of the SEC. Among other changes, the act also requires more independence of boards of directors, protects whistle-blowers, and establishes a Public Company Accounting Oversight Board. The New York Stock Exchange (NYSE) and NASDAQ overhauled the governance standards required for listed firms and submitted the changes for review, comment, and approval by the SEC. Business ethics, director qualifications, unique concerns of foreign firms, loans to officers and directors, internal auditing, and many other issues are part of the NYSE and NASDAQ reforms.[19]

Thus, the lack of effective control and accountability mechanisms has prompted the current interest in corporate governance. Beyond the legal issues associated with governance, there has also been interest in the board's role in corporate strategy and stakeholder engagement. A Conference Board survey of eighty-two companies in Europe and the United States in the mid-1990s indicated that boards of directors were playing a greater role in strategy formulation than they did in the early 1990s. In addition, survey results also showed some movement toward corporate governance committees that would allow for greater participation and dialog between directors and other stakeholders.[20] From these results, it is apparent that some boards have been assuming greater responsibility for strategic decisions and have decided to focus on building more effective stakeholder relationships.

Issues in Corporate Governance Systems

Organizations that strive to develop effective corporate governance systems consider a number of internal and external issues. In this section, we look at four areas that need to be addressed in the design and improvement of governance mechanisms. We begin with boards of directors, which have the ultimate responsibility for ensuring a governance focus. Then, we discuss the role of shareholders and investors, internal control and risk management, and executive compensation within the governance system. These issues affect most organizations, although individual businesses may face unique factors that create additional governance questions. For example, a company operating in several countries will need to resolve issues related to international governance policy.

Boards of Directors

Members of a company's board of directors assume legal responsibility for the firm's resources and decisions, and they appoint its top executive officers. This is also true of a university's board of trustees, and there are similar arrangements in the nonprofit sector. In each of these cases, board members have fiduciary duty, meaning they have assumed a position of trust and confidence that entails certain requisite responsibilities. These responsibilities include acting in the best interests of those they serve. Thus, board membership is not designed as a vehicle for personal financial gain; rather, it provides the intangible benefit of ensuring the success of the organization and the stakeholders affected and involved in the fiduciary arrangement.

The traditional approach to directorship assumed that board members managed the corporation's business. Research and practical observation have shown that boards of directors rarely, if ever, perform the management function.[21] Because boards meet only a few times a year, there is no way that time allocation would allow for effective management. In addition, the complexity of organizations requires full attention on a daily basis. Today, boards of directors are concerned primarily with monitoring the decisions made by managers on behalf of the company. This includes choosing top executives, assessing their performance, helping to set strategic direction, evaluating company performance, developing CEO succession plans, communicating with stakeholders, maintaining legal and ethical practices, ensuring that control and accountability mechanisms are in place, and evaluating the board's own performance. In sum, board members assume the ultimate authority for organizational effectiveness and subsequent performance.

Independence Just as social responsibility objectives require more of employees and executives, boards of directors are also experiencing increasing accountability and disclosure mandates. The desire for independence is one reason that a few firms have chosen to split the powerful roles of chair of the board and CEO. While the practice is common in the United Kingdom and activists have called for this move for years, the idea has only recently been considered by U.S. and Canadian firms. Chubb Corporation, Midas, Pathmark Stores, Toronto Dominion Bank, and Closure Medical have already made the transition. In addition to independence concerns, it is unlikely that one person can devote the time and energy it takes to be effective in both roles. The National Association of Corporate Directors is in favor of splitting the roles, whereas other experts suggest that a "presiding" chair take over most of the chair's and CEO's duties with respect to the board. Finally, opponents believe the new rules and practices emerging from governance reform may negate the role split debate by improving other aspects of the board's membership and impact.[22]

Traditionally, board members were often retired company executives or friends of current executives, but the trend throughout the 1990s was toward "outside directors," who had valuable expertise yet little vested interest in the firm before assuming the director role. Thus, directors today are chosen for their competence, motivation, and ability to bring enlightened and diverse perspectives to strategic discussions. Outside directors are thought to bring more independence to the monitoring function because they are not bound by past allegiances, friendships, a current role in the company, or some other matter that may create a conflict of interest. However, independent directors who sit on a board for a long time may eventually lose some of the outsider perspective.

Although insiders traditionally represented approximately 20 percent of members on most boards of directors, many dot-com high-technology companies filled their boards with insiders who were heavily invested in the firm. In addition to higher percentages of inside directors, these boards were often smaller than those found in large, traditional businesses. Yahoo!, for example, once had a board of six, including three company executives. Directors of new high-tech firms were usually brought in to add management and strategic expertise to the business, whereas traditional firms tended to choose board members who understood governance, succession planning, and other oversight roles. The dot-com crash brought complaints that many new technology companies had not adequately or carefully considered the importance of strong governance to their long-term success. As legal expert Charles M. Elson notes, "It's really not until something goes wrong that people focus on [governance]."[23]

Quality Finding board members who have some expertise in the firm's industry or who have served as chief executives at similar-sized organizations is a good strategy for improving the board's overall quality. Directors with competence and experiences that reflect some of the firm's core issues should bring valuable insights to bear on discussions and decisions. Directors without direct industry or comparable executive experience may bring expertise on important issues, like auditing, executive compensation, succession planning, and risk management, to improve decision making. Board members must understand the company's strategy and operations; this suggests that members should limit the number of boards on which they serve. Directors need time to read reports, attend board and committee meetings, and participate in continuing education that promotes strong understanding and quality guidance. For example, directors on the board's audit committee may need to be educated on new accounting and auditing standards. Experts recommend that fully employed board members sit on no more than four boards, whereas retired members should limit their memberships to seven boards. Directors should be able to attend at least 75 percent of the meetings. Thus, many of the factors that promote board quality are within the control of directors.[24]

Performance An effective board of directors can serve as a type of insurance against the business cycle and the natural highs and lows of the economy. A study by *Business Week* showed that during robust economic times the stocks of firms with strong governance and boards outperformed companies with weaker governance by a two-to-one margin. During the economic slowdown in 2000 and 2001, however, the stocks of companies with strong governance bested weakly governed firms by four to one. A similar study by GovernanceMetrics International demonstrated that firms with strong governance greatly outperform Standard & Poor's 500-stock index, while those with weak governance significantly underperform the index.[25] Strong boards ask the tough, yet strategic, questions of management to ensure long-term performance. For example, many Internet businesses found that customer acquisition costs were as much as four times higher online than offline. Other firms soon learned that brand recognition is a long way from brand loyalty and the financial benefits of repeat customers. In hindsight, the high cash burn rate and other problems in dot-com businesses that failed may have been noticed and remedied under more robust governance structures.

Board independence, along with board quality, stock ownership, and corporate performance, are often used to assess the quality of corporate boards of directors. Table 6.2 shows the best and worst boards, as recently evaluated by *Business Week* magazine. Several factors stand out about the best boards of directors. These boards are generally more independent and have greater accountability to shareholders than

| TABLE 6.2 | Best and Worst Boards of Directors |

BEST BOARDS	WORST BOARDS
3M	Apple
Apria Healthcare	Conesco
Colgate-Palmolive	Dillard's
General Electric	Gap
Home Depot	Kmart
Intel	Qwest
Johnson & Johnson	Tyson Foods
Medtronic	Xerox
Pfizer	
Texas Instruments	

Source: Louis Lavelle, "The Best and Worst Boards," *Business Week*, October 7, 2002, p. 104. Reproduced by special permission, copyright © 2002 by The McGraw-Hill Companies, Inc.

other corporations. Their directors own company stock; this makes them more sympathetic to shareholder concerns. Moreover, these directors encourage innovative practices and take a more active role than directors of other firms. Apria Healthcare's board includes three shareholder activists and a separate chair and CEO. At 3M, all investors receive user-friendly communications regarding the rights and responsibilities of shareholders, along with an explanation of basic board processes and rules. The head of 3M's audit committee is the former chief financial officer of a leading retailer. Home Depot's ten outside directors visit twenty stores every year; this gives them a stronger sense of what is going on within the company, as well as the opportunity to address issues before they become problems. Medtronic's board has been praised for its strong evaluation system, where board members are evaluated on their ability to hold management accountable and on their meaningful participation in meetings.[26]

Rules promulgated by the Sarbanes-Oxley Act and various stock exchanges now require a majority of independent directors on the board; regular meetings between nonmanagement board members; audit, compensation, governance, and nominating committees either fully made up of or with a majority of independent directors; and a financial expert on the audit committee. The governance area will continue to evolve as the corporate scandals are resolved and the government and companies begin to implement and test new policies and practices. Regardless of the size and type of business for which boards are responsible, a system of governance is needed to ensure effective control and accountability. As a corporation grows, matures, enters international markets, and takes other strategic directions, it is likely that the board of directors will evolve and change to meet its new demands. Sir Adrian Cadbury, president of the Centre for Board Effectiveness in the United Kingdom and an architect of corporate governance changes around the world, has detailed responsibilities of boards in the future:

- Boards will be responsible for developing company purpose statements that cover a range of aims and stakeholder concerns.
- Annual reports and other documents will include more nonfinancial information.
- Boards will be required to define their role and implement self-assessment processes better.
- Selection of board members will become increasingly formalized, with less emphasis on personal networks and word of mouth.
- Boards will need to work more effectively as teams.
- Serving on boards will require more time and commitment than in the past.[27]

These trends are consistent with our previous discussion of social responsibility. In all facets of organizational life, greater demands are being placed on business decisions and people. Many of these expectations emanate from those who provide substantial resources in the organization, namely shareholders and other investors.

Shareholders and Investors

Because they have allocated scarce resources to the organization, shareholders and investors expect to grow and reap rewards from their investments. This type of financial exchange represents a formal contractual arrangement and provides the capital necessary to fund all types of organizational initiatives, such as new product development and facilities construction. A shareholder is concerned with his or her ownership investment in publicly traded firms, whereas *investor* is a more general term for any individual or organization that provides capital to a firm. Investments include financial, human, and intellectual capital.

Shareholder Activism Shareholders, including large institutional ones, have become more active in articulating their positions with respect to company strategy and executive decision making. *Activism* is a broad term that can encompass engaging in dialog with management, attending annual meetings, submitting shareholder resolutions, bringing lawsuits, and other mechanisms designed to communicate shareholder interests to the corporation. Table 6.3 lists characteristics of effective shareholder activism campaigns.

Shareholder resolutions are nonbinding, yet important, statements about shareholder concerns. A shareholder that meets certain guidelines may bring one resolution per year to a proxy vote of all shareholders at a corporation's annual meeting. Recent resolutions brought forward relate to auditor independence, executive compensation, independent directors, environmental impact, human rights, and other social responsibility issues. In some cases, the company will modify its policies or practices before the resolution is ever brought to a vote. In other situations, a resolution will receive less than a majority vote, but the media attention, educational value, and other stakeholder effects will cause a firm to reconsider, if not change, its original position to meet the resolution's proposal. The accounting scandals prompted many resolutions about executive compensation among shareholders who believe that improper compensation structures are often a precursor to accounting mismanagement.[28] The resolution process is regulated by the SEC in the United States and by complementary offices in other countries; some claim this is more favorable to the corporation than to shareholders.

TABLE 6.3	**Characteristics of a Successful Shareholder Activism Campaign**

- Alliances with social movements or public interest groups, where shareholder concerns and activity mesh with and play a part in a larger, multifaceted campaign

- Grass-roots pressure, such as letter writings or phone-ins to public investors to generate support for the resolution

- Communications: media outreach, public and shareholder education, etc.

- High-level negotiations with senior decision makers

- Support and active involvement from large institutional investors

- A climate that makes it difficult for the company not to make the "right decision." For example, if you have plainly compelling financial argument, you have a better chance of getting company management and other shareholders on board with your proposal.

- Persistence. Shareholders don't go away. They own the company and have a right to be heard. Often shareholder activists stick with issues for years.

Source: "Characteristics of a Successful Shareholder Activism Campaign," Friends of the Earth, http://www.foe.org/international/shareholder/characteristics.html, accessed August 7, 2003. Courtesy Friends of the Earth © 2003.

Legal and Regulatory Challenges

Governance Reform at Cendant

Most people view accounting as a routine but necessary business practice, but for Henry R. Silverman, it now has far greater significance than most other business practices. Accounting irregularities almost brought down Silverman's company after it merged with the direct-marketing firm CUC International Inc. to form Cendant in 1997. The accounting improprieties in CUC's books came to light only after the merger occurred, and thus began years of turmoil for Henry Silverman.

Henry Silverman built his company, HFS, into a giant franchiser of well-known hotel and real estate brands, including Days Inn, Ramada Inn, Howard Johnson, Century 21, and Coldwell Banker, through strategic acquisitions. Silverman took HFS public in 1992 and was rewarded by a stock increase of 1,836 percent over the next five years. In 1997, he merged HFS with CUC International, which sold memberships in discount buying clubs, to form Cendant. Under the merger agreement, Silverman became Cendant's CEO, and CUC's chief executive, Walter A. Forbes, became its chair. The agreement also stipulated that the two men would switch jobs in 2000, at which time Silverman planned to slow down and relax more.

However, in July 1998, Cendant executives discovered accounting irregularities in CUC's books, which, when compounded with errors, had allowed CUC to overstate its earnings by $700 million between 1995 and 1997. When an investigation by Cendant's board of directors audit committee confirmed the improprieties, the company announced that it would have to restate earnings for 1997 and perhaps earlier. Cendant's stock plummeted 46 percent in one day. Forbes and nine of his allies on the company's board of directors soon resigned, although Forbes received a severance package of $35 million and stock options worth about $12.5 million. Forbes was eventually indicted on securities fraud and insider trading.

In 1999 Cendant sued Ernst & Young, CUC's auditors, for "gross negligence." The company also settled a class-action shareholder suit for $2.8 billion. Settling the shareholder suit minimized one of Cendant's greatest threats after the scandal was revealed: If shareholders had been able to convince the judge that the damages were equal to the market decline, then Cendant would have been forced to liquidate. The settlement required Cendant to give a majority of its board seats to independent directors in an attempt to provide stronger corporate governance. Before the scandal emerged, Cendant's twenty-eight-member board had included equal

Other shareholder concerns reach the legal realm. For example, the California Public Employees' Retirement System (CalPERS) led a suit against W. R. Grace & Co. after officers and directors paid a $20 million severance package to a chief executive officer (CEO) who resigned amid sexual harassment allegations in 1995. Known as an aggressive institutional investor, CalPERS bolstered the lawsuit effort because it demanded stronger corporate governance mechanisms, including a sexual harassment policy. The lawsuit was finally settled in 1999 and included a recovery of nearly $4 million, to be divided among all company stockholders. The insurer that covers the company's board of directors paid the $4 million. In addition, the company agreed to develop a progressive policy against sexual harassment and to appoint more independent, outside directors on the board of directors' auditing, nominating, and compensation committees.[29]

One of the first and most-celebrated acts of shareholder activism occurred when the Episcopal Church, a member of the Interfaith Center on Corporate Responsibil-

representation from CUC and HFS and some board members had close ties to at least one of the firms.

The pain still kept coming, however, for in 2000, *Business Week* ranked Cendant as having one of the worst boards of directors. Although the company's board members were entirely new by that time, some people still wondered, "Where was the board of directors during the CUC accounting scandal?" Some people see Henry Silverman as a victim, but others thought the whole fiasco was his own fault and that he should have been more thorough in examining CUC before the merger. Some experts questioned the due diligence process used in the premerger analysis. Regardless of fault, Silverman had to rebuild his credibility. Although most analysts believed that Cendant would eventually fully recover, Silverman's own credibility was a different story. Always a Wall Street "darling," Henry Silverman's reputation and stock were built on his "wheeling and dealing." The irony is that the strategy and tactics he used to build his empire helped to shatter his credibility.

Now several years after the scandal, Cendant has continued its acquisition strategy, even though some investors are not pleased since the firm's large number of businesses make it difficult to assess performance. Some of Cendant's acquisitions have proved troublesome, including its purchase of CheapTickets.com, a firm facing a class-action lawsuit for allowing a sexually hostile environment in its now-closed Los Angeles office. Amidst the wave of governance reform in 2002, Cendant's board reduced Silverman's pay package and decided to expense stock options. The board announced more changes in corporate governance including barring its auditors from performing nonauditing services, curtailing senior executives' ability to trade company stock, allowing shareholders to vote on stock option plans for executives, and restricting severance packages for executives. This time in *Business Week*'s review of the best and worst boards, Cendant was named to the Most Improved Boards list.

Sources:
"Cendant Cuts CEO's Pay, Will Expense Stock Options Starting Next Year," *National Mortgage News,* September 9, 2002, p. 6; "Henry Silverman on Fraud and Recovery," *Business Week Online,* July 31, 2002, available at LexisNexis; Amy Barrett, "Henry Silverman's Long Road Back," *Business Week,* February 28, 2000, pp. 126–136; John A. Byrne, "The Best and Worst Boards," *Business Week,* January 24, 2000, pp. 142–152; Louis Lavelle, "The Best and Worst Boards," *Business Week,* October 7, 2002, p. 104; Andy Serwer, "Are Investors Ready to Check Back into Cendant?" *Fortune,* January 24, 2000, pp. 183–184; Dennis Schaal, "CheapTickets, Cendant Hit with Sexual Harassment Lawsuit," *Travel Weekly,* September 23, 2002, p. 16.

ity, filed a resolution in 1971 calling on General Motors to withdraw from South Africa because of that nation's policy of apartheid. Apartheid was an official policy of racial segregation practiced in South Africa, involving political, legal, and economic discrimination against nonwhites. Many organizations and individuals supported the Episcopal Church's condemnation of South Africa's policy and urged other companies to suspend doing business there until racial equality was restored.[30] Examples like these illustrate that although shareholders and investors want their resources used efficiently and effectively, they are increasingly willing to take a stand to encourage companies to change for reasons beyond financial return.

Social Investing Many investors assume the stakeholder model of corporate governance, which carries into a strategy of social investing, "the integration of social and ethical criteria into the investment decision-making process."[31] Roughly three-quarters of U.S. investors take social responsibility issues into account when choosing investment opportunities. Twelve percent indicate they are willing to take a lower rate of return if the company is a strong performer in the social responsibility area.[32] However, most social investors do not have to worry about a poor return on their investments. Socially conscious firms are strong performers for many of the reasons we discussed in Chapter 1. For example, over the past decade, the Domini 400 Social Index, the benchmark for social investing, had an average annualized 14.02 percent return versus a 13.27 percent return for the Standard & Poor's 500-stock index. While social investing has traditionally been conducted through managed mutual funds, like those with Domini Social Investments, TIAA-CREF, Vanguard, and Calvert Group, some individual investors are using Web-based research to venture on their own. Web sites such as FOLIOfn, SocialFunds.com, Morningstar, Inc., and others provide information and services to help the socially conscious investor in decision making.[33] Thus, there are a number of opportunities for individuals to demonstrate an active strategy with respect to investing and social responsibility. Whereas a passive investor

Domini Social Investments produces a semiannual report detailing the performance and social impact of its investments. (Domini Social Investments®, Domini Social Equity Fund®, Domini Social Bond Fund®, and "the way you invest matters"® are registered service marks of Domini Social Investments LLC and are used by permission. © 2003 Domini Social Investments LLC. All rights reserved.)

Semi-Annual Report

Domini Social Equity Fund®
Domini Social Bond Fund®

is mainly concerned with buying and selling stock and receiving dividends, social investors are taking a variety of stakeholder issues into account when making investment decisions. A social investor takes the social responsibility of "ownership" seriously since a firm in which he or she invests implements plans and tactics on behalf of its owners. It could be argued that the dishonest actions of a firm were carried out on behalf of shareholders; thus, an investor in the firm would also be responsible. Conversely, it could be argued that a firm implementing a strong social responsibility strategy and agenda is doing so on behalf of its owners.[34] Shareholder activism is the strategy for ensuring that owners' perspectives on social responsibility are included on the corporate agenda.

Although social investing has received strong media attention over the last few years, the Quakers, a religious group, applied social investment criteria in the seventeenth century when they refused to invest, patronize, or partner with any business involved in the slave trade or military concerns.[35] Investors today use similar screening criteria in determining where to place their funds and resources. Table 6.4 provides an example of the screening criteria used to exclude or include companies in the social investment funds at Calvert Group, Ltd. Several other

---

TABLE 6.4   Social Analysis Criteria

---

1. *Environment*

   Maintain at least an average record in industry.

   Develop products or processes that reduce or minimize environmental impact.

   Implement innovative pollution prevention programs.

2. *Workplace*

   Actively hire and promote minorities/women.

   Provide safe and healthy workplace.

   Provide work-family programs.

3. *Product safety and impact*

   Do not allow major manufacturers of alcohol or tobacco or business in gambling establishments.

   Produce or market products that enhance health or quality of life.

   Respond promptly to product problems.

4. *International operations and human rights*

   Have adopted specific human rights standards to govern international operations.

   Use more stringent environmental and workplace standards than required by local law.

5. *Indigenous peoples' rights*

   Respect land, sovereignty, and natural resource of indigenous communities.

   Contribute to community-drive development and environmental management plans.

6. *Community Relations*

   Develop programs that target neglected communities, including low-income and minority populations.

   Have a strong working relationship with local and community development organizations.

Source: "Social Analysis Criteria," adapted from Calvert Group, Ltd, www.calvertgroup.com/sri_647.html, accessed August 7, 2003.

mutual funds and investors have similar standards. These criteria are used to screen for elimination or inclusion into a particular investment strategy. For example, one strategy may focus on the environmental records of firms, whereas another strategy may examine several social responsibility issues in tandem when including and excluding companies. The process used to evaluate a firm's record is another consideration for investors. For example, Calvert assesses policies and performance, whereas the Oekom Research primarily reviews policies and company disclosure. Although Oekom considers performance, it can be difficult for a firm to be rated highly if it does not publish the information. Whereas Calvert takes the stance that a firm can perform well without disclosing its outcomes, Oekom focuses on the possibility for reputation problems if the company is not fully transparent in its activities.[36] Despite its subjective nature, professionally managed social investments total more than $2 trillion in the United States.[37] Not only do these social investments help individuals and institutions meet their social responsibility goals, they also provide strong financial returns.

Shareholder activism and social investing are especially prevalent in the United States and United Kingdom, two countries that score relatively high on various corporate governance indexes. Several other European countries are also experiencing increasing rates of activism and social investing. Most activism and investing take place on an organizational level through mutual funds and other institutional arrangements, but some individual investors have affected company strategy and policy. Robert Monks, a leading corporate governance activist, once described Warren Buffett, the legendary investor from Omaha, Nebraska, as "epitomizing the kind of monitoring shareholder whose involvement enhances the value of the whole enterprise. Mr. Buffett personally salvaged the rogue Salomon Brothers [now Salomon Smith Barney] from the bankrupting implications of its illegal activities."[38] Although few investors have Buffett's financial clout and respect, he serves as a role model by paying attention to the control and accountability mechanisms of the companies in which he invests. After the series of crises in the early 2000s, investors started to become more interested, educated, and vigilant about companies in which they invest.

Colleges and universities are also becoming active in social investing. For example, most colleges have endowment funds, or monies that are invested for the long-term future of the university. Because of these investments, stakeholders of higher-education institutions are drawing attention to social responsibility issues. Harvard University, with an estimated endowment of nearly $13 billion, solicits input from the university community when deciding how to vote in a socially responsible manner on shareholder resolutions. A committee of faculty, students, and alumni advises the endowment fund's governing board, which ultimately votes on the resolutions. In 1999, the governing board voted with the advisory group's recommendation in fifty out of eighty cases. In the remaining thirty votes, the board abstained in twenty-six votes and went against the advisory group in only four cases.[39]

The Student Alliance to Reform Corporations (STARC) has student contacts at 120 colleges and universities who are dedicated to implementing socially responsible investment policies.[40] Such student pressure has led colleges to sell stocks that are deemed counter to socially responsible investment goals. For example, the University of Wisconsin and the University of Minnesota divested shares of corporations with operations that support the military regime in Burma. Stanford, Tufts, Haverford, and the University of Washington no longer invest in tobacco companies.

STARC campaigns are committed to the following principles for investor responsibility at universities and colleges:

- Challenge corporate conduct that harms humans, animals, and the environment.

- Disclose to the university community all actions affecting corporate conduct that the institution takes as an investor or shareholder, including votes on shareholder resolutions.

- Empower a democratically selected committee to review the social implications of institutional investment decisions and policy.

- Commit to following the recommendations of this investor responsibility advisory committee in order to fulfill the institution's aim of advancing the public interest.

- Adopt guidelines for investment and shareholder activity that support responsible corporate conduct promoting human rights, indigenous rights, equity and diversity, animal rights, environmental quality, labor rights, and the production of safe and beneficial products; guidelines should also include requirements for corporate disclosure of records of corporate performance in these areas.[41]

Investor Confidence Shareholders and other investors must have assurance that their money is being placed in the care of capable and trustworthy organizations. These

Since 1984, the International Center for Finance at the Yale School of Management has conducted research on investor behavior and attitudes, including their confidence in the stock market. (http://icf.som.yale .edu/confidence .index/, downloaded December 16, 2003. Reprinted by permission of the Yale University School of Management.)

primary stakeholders are expecting a solid return for their investment but, as illustrated earlier, have additional concerns about social responsibility. When these fundamental expectations are not met, the confidence that investors and shareholders have in corporations, market analysts, investment houses, stockbrokers, mutual fund managers, financial planners, and other economic players and institutions can be severely tested. In Chapter 1, we discussed the importance of investor trust and loyalty to organizational and societal performance. Part of this trust relates to the perceived efficacy of corporate governance. Figures 6.1 and 6.2 demonstrate the extent to which strong governance is now considered an investment criterion and reason for premium price.

Bankruptcies and financial misconduct in the early 2000s shook investor confidence. In the days after each major scandal broke, volatile, intraday market swings of 200 to 300 points were common. Mutual fund managers with sizable investments in firms accused of misconduct were questioned about their aptitude in choosing and selling stocks. Consumers, becoming financially uneasy and more cautious about spending, saw their portfolios and retirement accounts dwindle. At Charles Schwab, the largest discount brokerage in the United States, annual trades

---

| FIGURE 6.1 | Corporate Governance as an Investment Criterion |

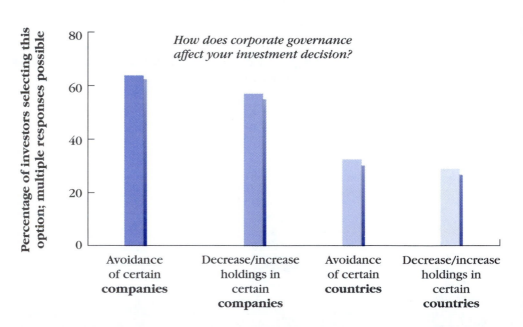

Source: McKinsey & Company, *McKinsey Global Investor Opinion Survey on Corporate Governance*, 2002, http://www.mckinsey.com/practices/corporategovernance/PDF/GlobalInvestorOpinionSurvey2002.pdf, accessed November 10, 2003. Copyright © 2002 by McKinsey & Company. Reprinted with permission.

| FIGURE 6.2 | Investor Willingness to Pay a Premium for Well-Governed Firms |

A significant majority of investors say they are willing to pay a premium for a well-governed company.

Percentage of Investors

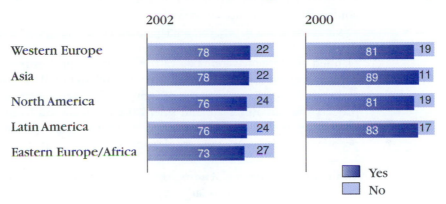

	2002	2000
Western Europe	78 / 22	81 / 19
Asia	78 / 22	89 / 11
North America	76 / 24	81 / 19
Latin America	76 / 24	83 / 17
Eastern Europe/Africa	73 / 27	

■ Yes
☐ No

Source: McKinsey & Company, *McKinsey Global Investor Opinion Survey on Corporate Governance*, 2002, http://www.mckinsey.com/practices/corporategovernance/PDF/GlobalInvestorOpinionSurvey2002.pdf, accessed November 10, 2003. Copyright © 2002 by McKinsey & Company. Reprinted with permission.

per account dropped to an average 3.6, compared to more than 8 per account the previous year. A group of finance ministers from twenty-four countries, known as G24, asked the United States to take quick action to restore investor confidence and ensure the continuation of global growth. The malfeasance at Global Crossing, Tyco, and other firms had effects throughout the global economic system. Essentially, stakeholders were calling for boards of directors and others with access to financial records and the power to demand accountability to tighten the control and risk environment in companies today.[42]

Internal Control and Risk Management

Throughout the 1990s, the National Baptist Convention (NBC USA), the oldest and one of the largest African American religious organizations, became a respected and influential member of the religious community. However, the actions of a recent president, along with a lack of solid corporate governance mechanisms, have raised questions about the strength and role of the organization. Reverend Henry J. Lyons was elected NBC USA's president in 1994, becoming only the second president in the convention's nearly two decades of existence. Lyons adopted a theme of "Raise a Standard!" for his presidency, but his conduct throughout the mid-1990s seemed to contradict the theme. Lyons's legal troubles stemmed from accusations that he swindled about $250,000 from NBC USA, where record keeping was lax. According to a prosecutor, Lyons took money that had been designated for rebuilding churches destroyed by arson. The prosecution further charged that Lyons had deceived a number of corporations and the Anti-Defamation League (ADL) of B'nai B'rith through a series of broken promises and false claims. Money entrusted for the purpose of rebuilding burned churches never reached those churches until Lyons's legal trial began. His actions tested public expectations about leadership and governance in nonprofit and religious organizations. These actions eventually brought him to criminal trial, created embarrassment and anger among the organization's stakeholders, prompted Lyons's resignation, and created a need for the board to examine its control and governance environment.[43]

Controls and a strong risk management system are fundamental to effective operations, as they allow for comparisons between the actual performance and the planned performance and goals of the organization. Controls are used to safeguard corporate assets and resources, protect the reliability of organizational information, and ensure compliance with regulations, laws, and contracts. Risk management is the process used to anticipate and shield the organization from unnecessary or overwhelming circumstances, while ensuring that executive leadership is taking the appropriate steps to move the organization and its strategy forward.

Internal and External Audits Auditing, both internal and external, is the linchpin between risk and controls and corporate governance. Boards of directors must ensure that the internal auditing function of the company is provided with adequate funding, up-to-date technology, unrestricted access, independence, and authority to carry out its audit plan. To ensure these characteristics, the internal audit executive should report to the board's audit committee and, in most cases, the chief executive officer.[44]

The external auditor should be chosen by the board and must clearly identify its client as the board, not the company's chief financial officer. Under Sarbanes-Oxley, the board audit committee should be directly responsible for the selection, payment, and supervision of the company's external auditor. The act also prohibits an external auditing firm from performing some nonaudit work for the same public company, including bookkeeping, human resources, actuarial services, valuation services, legal services, and investment banking. The friendly relationship that can develop between an external auditor and the firm's financial team may affect the auditor's ability to maintain independence in the auditing process and report. For example, in more than half of the largest bankruptcies since 1996, the external audit report provided no hint of the pending financial downfall. The external audits conducted on Kmart, Global Crossing, and Enron issued clean audit perspectives just months before their respective bankruptcies. Part of the problem relates to the sheer size and complexity of organizations, but these factors do not negate the tremendous responsibility that external auditors assume.

Control Systems The area of internal control covers a wide range of company decisions and actions, not just the accuracy of financial statements and accounting records. Controls also foster understanding when discrepancies exist between corporate expectations and stakeholder interests and issues. Internal controls effectively limit employee or management opportunism, or the use of corporate assets for individualistic or nonstrategic purposes. Controls also ensure the board of directors has access to timely and quality information that can be used to determine strategic options and effectiveness. For these reasons, the board of directors should have ultimate oversight for the integrity of the internal control system.[45] Although board members do not develop or administer the control system, they are responsible for ensuring that an effective system exists. The need for internal controls is rarely disputed, but implementation can vary. Thus, internal control represents a set of tasks and resource commitments that require high-level attention.

Although most large corporations have designed internal controls, smaller companies and nonprofit organizations are less likely to have invested in a complete system. For example, a small computer shop in Columbus, Ohio, lost thousands of dollars due to embezzlement by the accounts receivable clerk. Because of the clerk's position and role in the company, she was able to post credit-card payments due her employer to her own account and then later withdraw the income. Although she faced felony theft charges, her previous employer admitted feeling ashamed and did not want his business associated with a story on employee theft.[46] Such crime is common in small businesses because they often lack effective internal controls. Simple, yet proven, control mechanisms that can be used in all types of organizations are listed in Table 6.5. These techniques are not always costly and they conform to best practices in the prevention of ethical and legal problems that threaten the efficacy of governance mechanisms.

Risk Management A strong internal control system should alert decision makers to possible problems, or risks, that may threaten business operations, including worker safety, company solvency, vendor relationships, proprietary information, environmental impact, and other concerns. As we discussed in Chapter 2, having a strong crisis management plan is part of the process for managing risk. The term *risk management* is normally used in a narrow sense to indicate responsibilities associated with

---

TABLE 6.5	Internal Control Mechanisms for Small Businesses and Nonprofits

- Develop and disseminate a code of conduct that explicitly addresses ethical and legal issues in the workplace.
- Rotate and segregate job functions to reduce the opportunity for opportunism (i.e., the person reconciling bank statements does not make deposits or pay invoices).
- Screen employment applicants thoroughly, especially those who would assume much responsibility if hired.
- Watch new employees especially carefully until they have gained knowledge and your trust.
- Require all employees to take at least one week of vacation on an annual basis.
- Limit access to valuable inventory and financial records. Use technology to track inventory, costs, human resources, finances, and other valuable business processes.
- Implement unannounced inspections, spot checks, or "tests" of departments, systems, and outcomes.
- Keep keys and pass codes secure and limit their duplication and distribution.
- Insist that operating statements are produced on at least a monthly basis.
- Ask questions about confusing financial statements and other records.

Sources: *Curtailing Crime: Inside and Out,* Crime Prevention Series, U.S. Small Business Administration, http://www.sba.gov/library/pubs/cp-2.doc, accessed August 7, 2003; "Protecting Against Employee Fraud," *Business First–Western New York,* June 14, 1999, p. 31; Kathy Hoke, "Eyes Wide Open," *Business First–Columbus,* August 27, 1999, pp. 27–28.

insurance, liability, financial decisions, and related issues. Kraft General Foods, for example, has a risk management policy for understanding how prices of commodities, such as coffee, sugar, wheat, and cocoa, will affect its relationships throughout the supply chain.[47]

Risk is always present within organizations, so executives must develop processes for remedying or managing its effects. A board of directors will expect the top management team to have risk management skills and plans in place. There are at least three ways to consider how risk poses either a potentially negative or positive concern for organizations.[48] First, risk can be categorized as a hazard. In this view, risk management is focused on minimizing negative situations, such as fraud, injury, or financial loss. Second, risk may be considered an uncertainty that needs to be hedged through quantitative plans and models. This type of risk is best associated with the term *risk management,* which is used in financial and business literature. Third, risk also creates the opportunity for innovation and entrepreneurship. Just as management can be criticized for taking too much risk, it can also be subject to concerns about not taking enough risk. For example, the merger between Daimler Benz and Chrysler represented risk taking for the potential benefit of both firms and their stakeholders. All three types of risk are implicitly covered by our definition of corporate governance, because there are risks for both control (i.e., preventing fraud and ensuring accuracy of financial statements) and accountability (i.e., innovation to develop new products and markets). For example, the Internet and electronic commerce capabilities have introduced new risks of all types for organizations. Privacy, as we discuss in Chapter 10, is a major concern for many stakeholders and has created the need for policies and certification procedures. A board of directors may ensure that the company has established privacy policies that are not only effective but can also be properly monitored and improved as new technology risks and opportunities emerge in the business environment.[49]

Executive Compensation

How executives are compensated for their leadership, organizational service, and performance has become an extremely troublesome topic. Leading business publications, including the *Harvard Business Review* and *The Economist,* have weighed in on problems with compensation, perhaps the most controversial aspect of corporate governance in recent memory.[50] Indeed, 73 percent of respondents in a *Business Week*–Harris poll indicated they believe that top officers of large U.S. companies receive too much compensation.[51] Many people believe that no executive is worth millions of dollars in annual salary and stock options, even if he or she has brought great financial returns to investors. The reality, however, is that some executives continue to receive extremely high pay packages while their companies fall into ruin. A study by United for a Fair Economy and the Institute for Policy Studies found that CEOs in twenty-three firms under federal investigation received compensation averaging $62 million over three years. These firms laid off 162,000 employees and their combined stock values plunged $530 billion in the same period.[52]

Unease over executive compensation often centers on the relationship between the highest-paid executives and median employee wages in the company. If this ratio is perceived as too large, then critics believe that either rank-and-file employees are not being compensated fairly or high executive salaries represent an improper use of company resources. The average executive now earns nearly 600 times the average worker's salary, up from 40 times the average salary in the 1960s. Critics have asked whether business executives are generating such strong performance that they deserve this striking movement in pay over the last thirty or forty years. The usual answer is a resounding no.[53] Because of the enormous difference between CEO and employee pay, the business press is careful to support high levels of executive compensation only when it is directly linked to strong company performance. Most of the business press has criticized compensation packages over the last few years. Although the issue of executive compensation has received much attention in the media of late, some business owners have long recognized its potentially ill effects. In the early twentieth century, for example, the capitalist J. P. Morgan implemented a policy that limited the pay of top managers in businesses he owned to no more than twenty times the pay of any other employee.[54]

Other people argue that because executives assume so much risk on behalf of the company, they deserve the rewards that follow from strong company performance. In addition, many executives' personal and professional lives meld to the point that they are "on call" twenty-four hours a day. Because not everyone has the skill, experience, and desire to become an executive and assume so much pressure and responsibility, market forces dictate a high level of compensation. When the pool of qualified individuals is limited, many corporate board members feel that offering a large compensation package is the only way to attract and retain a top executive to ensure their firm is not left without strong leadership. In an era where top executives are increasingly willing to "jump ship" to other firms that offer higher pay, potentially lucrative stock options, bonuses, and other benefits, such thinking is not without merit.[55] Table 6.6 lists the median total compensation of chief executives in U.S. industries.

John Lauer, CEO of Cleveland-based Oglebay Norton, decided to modify his own compensation package after he completed a doctoral dissertation on executive compensation. His research suggested that most top managers were overcompensated, with their pay's having very little to do with company performance.[56] In another situation, when AMR Corp., the corporate parent of American Airlines, was experiencing financial difficulties, CEO Robert Crandall asked the company's board of directors not to grant him a bonus or stock options. Because he was asking airline employees to take pay cuts at the time, he felt he could not justify being treated differently than the rest of the workforce. Moreover, he did not want to create more tension within the organization at a time when spirits were already low. However, a successor of Crandall's at AMR was quickly terminated once it was learned that he tried to hide executive pay perks in the midst of a massive employee layoff.[57] The ETrade Group CEO Christos M. Cotsakos returned $21 million in pay after shareholder complaints about his $80 million pay package. Cal Turner Jr., the CEO of Dollar General, gave back $6.8 million after the firm's financial results were restated.[58]

These examples show that executive compensation is an important, yet potentially explosive, issue for boards of directors and other stakeholders to consider. Under new NYSE rules, the compensation committee must be entirely made up of independent directors and must establish goals and responsibilities, member qualifications, and a process of self-evaluation. The NASDAQ revisions require independent directors' approval of CEO compensation, either through an independent compensation

TABLE 6.6	Total Median Compensation of Chief Executive Officers (including salary, bonus, and value of other long-term incentives)

INDUSTRY	MEDIAN COMPENSATION
Financial services	$3,754,000
Computer services	$2,756,000
Construction	$2,123, 000
Communications	$2,000,000
Insurance	$1,856,000
Energy	$1,851,000
Utilities	$1,788,000
Manufacturing	$1,736,000
Retail trade	$1,722,000
Commercial banking	$1,706,000
Diversified service	$1,551,000
Transportation	$1,515,000
Wholesale trade	$1,325,000

Source: "Conference Board Reports Outside Director Pay Drops, CEO Pay Rises," *Report on Salary Surveys* 2 (February 2002): 3. Reprinted by permission of IOMA (the Institute of Management & Administration) © 2003 RSS 212-44-0360. http://www.ioma.com.

committee or through a majority of independent directors meeting in a closed session. Regardless of the structure, an integral matter for boards and compensation committees to consider is the extent to which executive compensation is linked to long-term company performance. Plans that base compensation on the achievement of several performance goals are intended to align the interests of owners with management. However, many executives are rewarded through stock options and other programs that provide an incentive for managing stock price and short-run gains. When executive wealth is heavily tied to the short-term performance of the company's stock, it can drive aggressive and mispresentative accounting and related practices revealed in recent corporate scandals. Other points for review include the evaluation criteria for executive performance, use of compensation consultants to help determine appropriate pay, disclosure of executive compensation, industry standards for remuneration, the ability to attract top talent, and incentives for superior performance.[59] Questions like these are being asked around the world, with many constituents calling for more formalization and professionalism in corporate control systems and accountability to stakeholders.[60]

Corporate Governance Around the World

Increased globalization, enhanced electronic communications, economic agreements and zones, and the reduction of trade barriers have created opportunities for firms around the world to conduct business with both consumers and industrial partners.

These factors are propelling the need for greater homogenization in corporate governance principles. Standard & Poor's recently launched a new service, Corporate Governance Scores, which analyzes four macro forces that affect the general governance climate of a country, including legal infrastructure, regulation, information infrastructure, and market infrastructure. On the basis of these factors, a country can be categorized as having strong, moderate, or weak support for effective governance practices at the company level. Institutional investors are very interested in this measure, as it helps determine possible risk.[61] As financial, human, and intellectual capital cross borders, a number of business, social, and cultural concerns arise.

In response to this business climate, the Organisation for Economic Cooperation and Development (OECD), a forum for governments to discuss, develop, and enhance economic and social policy, issued a set of principles intended to serve as a global model for corporate governance.[62] After years of discussion and debate among institutional investors, business executives, government representatives, trade unions, and nongovernmental organizations, thirty OECD member governments signaled their agreement with the principles by signing a declaration to integrate them within their countries' economic systems and institutions. The purpose of the OECD Corporate Governance Principles (see Table 6.7) is to formulate minimum standards of fairness, transparency, accountability, disclosure, and responsibility for business practice. The principles focus on the board of directors, which the OECD says should recognize the impact of governance on the firm's competitiveness. In addition, the OECD charges boards, executives, and corporations with maximizing shareholder value while responding to the demands and expectations of their key stakeholders.

TABLE 6.7	**OECD Principles of Corporate Governance**
PRINCIPLE	**EXPLANATION**
1. The rights of shareholders	The corporate governance framework should protect shareholders' rights.
2. The equitable treatment of shareholders	The corporate governance framework should ensure the equitable treatment of all shareholders, including minority and foreign shareholders. All shareholders should have the opportunity to obtain effective redress for violation of their rights.
3. The role of stakeholders in corporate governance	The corporate governance framework should recognize the rights of stakeholders as established by law and encourage active cooperation between corporations and stakeholders in creating wealth, jobs, and the sustainability of financially sound enterprises.
4. Disclosure and transparency	The corporate governance framework should ensure that timely and accurate disclosure is made on all material matters regarding the corporation, including the financial situation, performance, ownership, and governance of the company.
5. The responsibilities of the board	The corporate governance framework should ensure the strategic guidance of the company, the effective monitoring of management by the board, and the board's accountability to the company and the shareholders.

Source: "OECD Principles for Corporate Governance," Organisation for Economic Cooperation and Development, http://www.oecd.org/EN/document/0,,EN-document-77-nodirectorate-no-15-8293-28,00.html, accessed November 10, 2003.

The OECD Corporate Governance Principles cover many specific best practices, including (1) rights of shareholders to vote and influence corporate strategy; (2) greater numbers of skilled, independent members on boards of directors; (3) fewer techniques to protect failing management and strategy; (4) wider use of international accounting standards; and (5) better disclosure of executive pay and remuneration. Although member governments of the OECD are expected to uphold the governance principles, there is some room for cultural adaptation.

Best practices may vary slightly from country to country because of unique factors such as market structure, governmental control, role of banks and lending institutions, labor unions, and other economic, legal, and historical factors. Table 6.8 provides information on the relative strengths and weaknesses of developed markets with respect to the OECD principles and other established best practices. As you can see, the United Kingdom has made the greatest progress with respect to corporate governance, whereas Portugal and Japan lag behind other nations on these dimensions. Both industry groups and government regulators moved quickly in the United Kingdom after the Enron crisis was revealed. Several British reforms are under way, including annual shareowners' votes on board remuneration policies and greater supervision of investment analysts and the accounting profession. Portugal is at the beginning stages of its capitalist market, with many companies still family controlled. The country's government issued a best practices code modeled after the OECD principles, but most companies are not yet in compliance. For example, 96 percent of listed companies do not offer proxy voting, which is one of the seventeen best practices.[63] Reasons for the financial crisis that occurred in Southeast Asia in the late 1990s partly involved corporate governance. For example, the government structure of some Asian countries created greater opportunities for corruption and nepotism.

TABLE 6.8	Comparing Corporate Governance Mechanisms Around the World

INDICATOR	BELGIUM	FRANCE	GERMANY	JAPAN	NETHERLANDS	PORTUGAL	U.K.	U.S.
1.1 Best Practice codes	5	9	6	3	4	4	9	9
1.2 Nonexecutive directors	8	9	5	1	10	3	6	8
1.3 Board independence	2	3	2	0	1	0	4	7
1.4 Split chair/CEO	6	2	5	0	5	2	6	1
1.5 Board committees	3	4	1	0	3	3	6	8
2.1 Voting rights	10	6	9	10	6	6	10	9
2.2 Voting issues	8	8	5	4	5	7	7	3
3.1 Accounting standards	2	3	7	0	6	2	9	10
3.2 Executive pay	3	10	2	2	8	2	10	10
4.1 Takeover barriers	3	4	3	0	1	2	10	7
Overall score	**5.0**	**5.8**	**4.5**	**2.0**	**4.9**	**3.1**	**7.7**	**7.2**

Source: Davis Global Advisors, *Leading Corporate Governance Indicators™ 2002: An International Comparison,* November 2002, Newton, MA. Reprinted by permission from Davis Global Advisors, www.davisglobal.com.

Banks were encouraged to extend credit to companies favored by the government. In many cases, these companies were in the export business, which created an imbalance in financing for other types of businesses. The concentration of business power within a few families and tycoons reduced overall competitiveness and transparency. Many of these businesses were more focused on size and expanded operations than profitability. Foreign investors recognized the weakening economies and pulled their money out of investments. The U.S. dollar appreciated sharply and Asian currencies were largely devalued. Finally, the crisis brought to light the necessity of stronger governance mechanisms and regulatory reform in the region.[64]

Future of Corporate Governance

As the issues discussed in the previous section demonstrate, corporate governance is primarily focused on strategic-level concerns for accountability and control. Although many discussions of corporate governance still revolve around responsibility in investor-owned companies, good governance is fundamental to effective performance in all types of organizations. As you have gleaned from history and government classes, a system of checks and balances is important for ensuring a focus on multiple perspectives and constituencies; proper distribution of resources, power, and decision authority; and the responsibility for making changes and setting direction.

In order to pursue social responsibility successfully, organizations must consider issues of control and accountability. As we learned earlier, the concept of corporate governance is in transition from the shareholder model to one that considers broader stakeholder concerns and inputs to financial performance. A number of market and

Callaway Golf demonstrates its commitment to strong corporate governance by placing information on its web site. (www.callawaygolf. com/corporate /corp_gov.asp. Copyright © 2003. Reprinted with permission.)

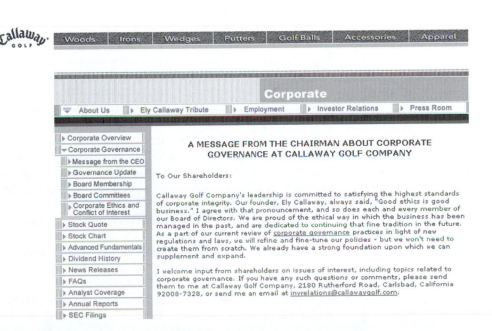

environmental forces, such as the OECD and shareholder activism, have created pressures in this direction. This evolution is consistent with our view of social responsibility. Although some critics deride this expanded focus, a number of external and internal forces are driving business toward the stakeholder orientation and the formalization of governance mechanisms. One concern centers on the cost of governance. For example, the combined cost of meeting regulations for safety, health, labor standards, employee benefits, and civil rights is estimated at $91.9 million for all companies operating in the United States.[65]

Most businesspeople and academicians agree that the benefits of a strong approach to corporate governance outweigh its costs. However, the positive return on governance goes beyond organizational performance to benefit the industrial competitiveness of entire nations, something we discussed in Chapter 1. For example, corrupt organizations often fail to develop competitiveness on a global scale and can leave behind financial ruin, thus negating the overall economic growth of the entire region or nation. At the same time, corrupt governments usually have difficulty sustaining and supporting the types of organizations that can succeed in global markets. Thus, a lack of good governance can lead to insular and selfish motives because there is no effective system of checks and balances. In today's interactive and interdependent business environment, most organizations are learning the benefits of a more cooperative approach to commerce. It is possible for a company to retain its competitive nature while seeking a "win-win" solution for all parties to the exchange.[66] Further, as nations with large economies embrace responsible governance principles, it becomes even more difficult for nations and organizations that do not abide by such principles to compete in these lucrative and rich markets. There is a contagion effect toward corporate governance among members of the global economy, much like peer pressure influences the actions and decisions of individuals. Portugal is a good example of this effect.

Because governance is concerned with the decisions made by boards of directors and executives, it has the potential for far-reaching positive—and negative—effects. A recent study by the OECD found that stronger financial performance is the result of several governance factors and practices, including (1) large institutional shareholders that are active monitors of company decisions and boards, (2) owner-controlled firms, (3) fewer mergers, especially between firms with disparate corporate values and business lines, and (4) shareholders' decisions on executive remuneration, not boards of directors.[67] The authors of the study note that these practices may not hold true for strong performance in all countries and economic systems. However, they also point out that a consensus view is emerging, with fewer differences among OECD countries than among all other nations. Similarities in organizational-level accountability and control should lead to smoother operations between different companies and countries, thereby bolstering competitiveness on many levels.

The future of corporate governance is directly linked to the future of social responsibility. Because governance is the control and accountability process for achieving social responsibility, it is important to consider who should be involved in the future. First and most obviously, business leaders and managers will need to embrace governance as an essential part of effective performance. Some of the elements of corporate governance, particularly executive pay, board composition, and shareholder rights, are likely to stir debate for many years. However, business leaders must recognize the forces that have brought governance to the forefront as a precondition of management responsibility. Thus, they may need to accept the "creative tension" that exists between managers, owners, and other primary stakeholders as the preferable route to mutual success.[68]

Second, governments have a key role to play in corporate governance. National competitiveness depends on the strength of various institutions, with primacy on the effective performance of business and capital markets. Strong corporate governance is essential to this performance, and thus, governments will need to be actively engaged in affording both protection and accountability for corporate power and decisions. Just like the corporate crises in the United States, the Asian economic crisis discussed earlier prompted companies and governments around the world to consider tighter governance procedures. Finally, other stakeholders may become more willing to use governance mechanisms to influence corporate strategy or decision making. Investors, whether shareholders, employees, or business partners, have a stake in decisions and should be willing to take steps to align various interests for long-term benefits. There are many investors and stakeholders willing to exert great influence on underperforming companies.

Until 2001 and 2002, governance was one area in the business literature that had not received the same level of attention as other issues, such as environmental impact, diversity, and sexual harassment. Over the next few years, however, corporate governance will emerge as the operational centerpiece to the social responsibility effort. The future will require that business leaders have a different set of skills and attitudes, including the ability to balance multiple interests, handle ambiguity, manage complex systems and networks, create trust among stakeholders, and improve processes so leadership is pervasive throughout the organization.[69]

In the past, the primary emphasis of governance systems and theory was on the conflict of interests between management and investors.[70] Governance today holds people at the highest organizational levels accountable and responsible to a broad and diverse set of stakeholders. Although top managers and boards of directors have always assumed responsibility, their actions are now subject to greater accountability and transparency. A *Wall Street Journal* writer put the shift succinctly, indicating, "Boards of directors have been put on notice." An article on the need for change in corporate governance in *The Economist* provided an equally concise rationale, stating, "Too many boards are stuffed with yes men who question little that their chief executive suggests." In the aftermath of crises in 2001 and 2002, both publications devoted significant space to various reform mechanisms and their likelihood of success. Perhaps the greatest challenge is the power shift taking place between executives and board members. A key issue going forward will be the board's ability to align corporate decisions with various stakeholder interests.[71] Robert Monks, the activist money manager and leader on corporate governance issues, wrote that effective corporate governance requires understanding that the "indispensable link between the corporate constituents is the creation of a credible structure (with incentives and disincentives) that enables people with overlapping but not entirely congruent interests to have a sufficient level of confidence in each other and the viability of the enterprise as a whole."[72] We will take a closer look at some of these constituents and their concerns in the next few chapters.

Summary

To respond to stakeholder pressures to answer for organizational decisions and policies, organizations must effectively implement policies that provide strategic guidance on appropriate courses of action. Such policies are often known as corporate governance, the formal system of accountability and control for organizational decisions and resources. Accountability relates to how well the content of workplace decisions is aligned with the firm's stated strategic direction, whereas control involves the process of auditing and improving organizational decisions and actions.

There are two major conceptualizations of corporate governance. The shareholder model of corporate governance focuses on developing and improving the formal system of performance accountability between top management and the firms' shareholders. The stakeholder model of corporate governance views the purpose of business in a broader fashion, in which the organization not only has a responsibility for economic success and viability but also must answer to other stakeholders. The shareholder model focuses on a primary stakeholder—the investor—whereas the stakeholder model incorporates a broader philosophy that focuses on internal and external constituents.

In the late 1800s and early 1900s, corporate governance was not a major issue because company owners made strategic decisions about their businesses. By the 1930s, ownership was dispersed across many individuals, raising questions about control and accountability. In response to shareholder activism, the Securities and Exchange Commission required corporations to allow shareholder resolutions to be brought to a vote of all shareholders. Since the mid-1900s, the approach to corporate governance has involved a legal discussion of principals (owners) and agents (managers) in the business relationship. The lack of effective control and accountability mechanisms in years past has prompted a current trend toward boards of directors' playing a greater role in strategy formulation than they did in the early 1990s. Members of a company's board of directors assume legal responsibility and fiduciary duty for organizational resources and decisions. Boards today are concerned primarily with monitoring the decisions made by managers on behalf of the company. The trend today is toward boards composed of outside directors who have little vested interest in the firm.

Shareholders have become more active in articulating their positions with respect to company strategy and executive decision making. Many investors assume the stakeholder model of corporate governance, which implies a strategy of integrating social and ethical criteria into the investment decision-making process. Although most activism and investing take place on an organizational level through mutual funds and other institutional arrangements, some individual investors have affected company strategy and policy.

Another significant governance issue is internal control and risk management. Controls allow for comparisons between actual performance and the planned performance and goals of the organization and are used to safeguard corporate assets and resources, protect the reliability of organizational information, and ensure compliance with regulations, laws, and contracts. Controls foster understanding when discrepancies exist between corporate expectations and stakeholder interests and issues. A strong internal control system should alert decision makers to possible problems or risks that may threaten business operations. Risk can be categorized (1) as a hazard, in which case risk management focuses on minimizing negative situations, such as fraud, injury, or financial loss; (2) as an uncertainty that needs to be hedged through quantitative plans and models; or (3) as an opportunity for innovation and entrepreneurship.

How executives are compensated for their leadership, service, and performance is another governance issue. Many people believe the ratio between the highest-paid executives and median employee wages in the company should be reasonable. Others argue that because executives assume so much risk on behalf of the organization, they deserve the rewards that follow from strong company performance. One area for board members to consider is the extent to which executive compensation is linked to company performance.

The Organisation for Economic Cooperation and Development has issued a set of principles from which to formulate minimum standards of fairness, transparency, accountability, disclosure, and responsibility for business practice. These principles help guide companies around the world and are part of the convergence that is occurring with respect to corporate governance.

Most businesspeople and academicians agree that the benefits of a strong approach to corporate governance outweigh its costs. Because governance is concerned with the decisions taken by boards of directors and executives, it has the potential for far-reaching positive, and negative, effects. The future of corporate governance is directly linked to the future of social responsibility. Business leaders and managers will need to embrace governance as an essential part of effective performance. Governments also have a role to play in corporate governance. National competitiveness depends on the strength of various institutions, with primacy on the effective performance of business and capital markets. Other stakeholders may become more willing to use governance mechanisms to affect corporate strategy or decision making.

Key Terms

corporate governance (p. 159)
shareholder model of corporate governance (p. 162)
stakeholder model of corporate governance (p. 162)

Discussion Questions

1. What is corporate governance? Why is corporate governance an important concern for companies that are pursuing the social responsibility approach? How does it improve or change the nature of executive and managerial decision making?

2. Compare the shareholder and stakeholder models of corporate governance. Which one seems to predominate today? What implications does this have for businesses in today's complex environment?

3. How have economic circumstances contributed to the growing trend toward increasing corporate governance? Why are accountability and control so important in the twenty-first century?

4. What is the role of the board of directors in corporate governance? What responsibilities does the board have?

5. What role do shareholders and other investors play in corporate governance? How can investors effect change?

6. Why are internal control and risk management important in corporate governance? Describe three approaches organizations may take to managing risk.

7. Why is the issue of executive compensation controversial? Are today's corporate executives worth the compensation packages they receive?

8. In what ways are corporate governance practices becoming standardized around the world? What differences exist?

9. As corporate governance becomes a more important aspect of social responsibility, what new skills and characteristics will managers and executives need?

Consider how pressures for governance require managers and executives to relate and interact with stakeholders in new ways.

Experiential Exercise

Visit the web site of the Organisation for Economic Co-operation and Development (http://www.oecd.org). Examine the origins of the organization and its unique role in the global economy. After visiting the site, answer the following questions:

1. What are the primary reasons that OECD exists?
2. How would you describe OECD's current areas of concern and focus?
3. What role do you think OECD will play in the future with respect to corporate governance and related issues?

What Would You Do?

The statewide news carried a story about Core-Tex that evening. There were rumors swirling that one of the largest manufacturers in the state was facing serious questions about its social responsibility. A former accountant for Core-Tex, whose identity was not revealed, made allegations about aggressive accounting methods and practices that overstated company earnings. He said he left Core-Tex after his supervisor and colleagues did not take his concerns seriously. The former accountant hinted that the company's relationship with its external auditor was quite close, since Core-Tex's new CFO had once been on the external auditing team. Core-Tex had recently laid off 270 employees—a move that was not unexpected in these turbulent financial times. However, the layoff hit some parts of the site's community pretty hard. Finally, inspectors from the state environmental protection agency had just issued a serious of citations to Core-Tex for improper disposal and high emissions at one of its larger manufacturing plants. A television station had run an exposé on the environmental citations a week ago.

CEO Kelly Buscio clicked off the television set and thought about the company's next steps. Core-Tex's attorney had cautioned the executive group earlier that week about communicating too much with the media and other constituents. The firm's vice president for marketing countered the attorney by insisting that Core-Tex needed to stay ahead of the rumors and assumptions that were being made about the company. The marketing VP said that suppliers and business partners were starting to question Core-Tex's financial viability. The vice president for information technology and the vice president for operations were undecided on the proper next steps. The vice president of manufacturing had not been at the meeting. Buscio rubbed her eyes and wondered what tomorrow could bring.

To her surprise, the newspapers were pretty gentle on Core-Tex the next day. There had been a major oil spill, the retirement of a *Fortune* 500 CEO, and a major-league baseball championship game the night before, so the reporters were focused on those stories. The company's stock price, which averaged around $11.15, was down $.35 by midmorning. Her VP of marketing suggested that employees needed to hear from the CEO and to be reassured about Core-Tex's strong future. Her first call after lunch came from a member of the firm's board of directors. The director asked Buscio what the board could do to help the situation. What would you do?

Consumer and Community Relations

CHAPTER OBJECTIVES

- To describe customers as stakeholders
- To investigate consumer protection laws
- To examine six consumer rights
- To describe the community as a stakeholder
- To discuss the community relations function
- To describe a neighbor of choice

CHAPTER OUTLINE

Consumer Stakeholders

Responsibilities to Consumers

Community Stakeholders

Responsibilities to the Community

Strategic Implementation of Responsibilities to Consumers and the Community

Like many corporations today, salesforce.com is striving to implement its social responsibility philosophy. Unlike some firms, however, the company's chairperson and CEO, Marc Benioff, has experience in managing large philanthropic efforts to benefit consumers and the community. Before starting salesforce.com, Benioff oversaw Oracle Corporation's donation of over $100 million worth of computers to schools. The program, called Oracle's Promise, was largely successful and eventually caused Benioff to rethink his understanding and views of corporate social responsibility.

Salesforce.com delivers online sales force automation, account management, customer relationship management, and related sales and marketing tools to companies of all sizes, including Daiwa Securities, *USA Today,* and Autodesk. While salesforce.com is a business-to-business marketer, its products ultimately affect a wide range of customers and consumers of the businesses that use its management systems. Some analysts view its innovative approach, which centers on a Web-based model for delivery, as ahead of some corporations' capabilities. However, the company is generally well regarded by industry experts and boasts a client list of over 5,000. Salesforce.com has received awards from *Fortune* magazine, Morgan Stanley, *PC Magazine,* and other respected sources.

What may be less known about the firm is its dedication to an integrated model of social responsibility. As Benioff describes it, a company that adopts this philosophy "creates value for its shareholders and its stakeholders alike. Its size and the location of its headquarters don't dictate a centralized return of its value; rather, its value is fully distributed not only to its leadership, but to the communities in which it operates, and the global community as a whole." On founding salesforce.com, Benioff ensured that the company's success would also benefit its stakeholders through a nonprofit foundation. The salesforce.com foundation is funded through private sources and company stock. The foundation's mission is to use "technology to build stronger communities through relationships between youth, employees, and the public and private sectors."

The foundation uses a seemingly simple approach: 1 percent of the company's stock will be held by the foundation when salesforce.com goes public, 1 percent of the company's profits are donated to the community, and 1 percent of employees' time is given to charitable causes. In just a few years, the foundation has built nearly forty technology centers in the United States and other countries. Employees volunteer their time and skills to the centers, which are housed in after-school programs from San Francisco to County Kildare, Ireland, to Israel. The centers teach technology skills and lessen the digital divide that exists in many areas. Since mid-2000, employees have donated over 3,700 hours to the centers and related causes. Salesforce.com seems on the path of achieving Benioff's dream: "As the company grows, the foundation grows proportionately and is fully integrated into the company that powers it."[1]

This vignette illustrates that organizations with strong profitability, operations expertise, and other core competencies can also be focused on implementing social responsibility and satisfying stakeholder groups. From a social responsibility perspective, the key challenge is how an organization assesses its stakeholders' needs, integrates them with company strategy, reconciles differences between stakeholders' needs, strives for better relationships with stakeholders, achieves mutual understandings with them, and finds solutions for problems. In this chapter, therefore, we explore relationships with two important stakeholders—consumers and the community. Although these constituencies are different by definition, they often have similar expectations of the economic, legal, ethical, and philanthropic responsibilities that must be addressed by business.

Consumer Stakeholders

Throughout the 1980s and much of the 1990s, "green marketing," the promotion of more environmentally friendly products, became a much-discussed strategy in the package goods industry. Both Energizer and Rayovac, for example, marketed environmentally friendly batteries. Today, those products have disappeared from most store shelves, replaced by the alkaline batteries needed to run electronic devices that have become so common for both children and adults. Around the same time, Procter & Gamble (P&G), the venerable manufacturer of soap, paper goods, and other household products, feared that increasing environmental consciousness among consumers would lead to a resurgence in the use of cloth diapers, which would have had a negative effect on its disposable diaper business. P&G launched a marketing campaign touting the benefits of disposables, including the fact that their use does not require hot water for laundering or fuel for diaper service trucks. P&G also initiated a pilot project for composting disposable diapers. Today, the debate over cloth versus disposables has largely faded, and the P&G marketing campaign and composting sites have disappeared.

The dawn of the twenty-first century brought many new products, including disposable tableware, food containers that can be used repeatedly or thrown away, and electrostatic mops with cloths that are disposed of after one use. Although these product introductions suggest a decline in environmental consciousness among consumers, other initiatives counter this assumption. Whole Foods Markets, a grocery chain that specializes in organic and environmentally friendly items, reports $689 sales per square foot versus the $400 sales per square foot earned by most supermarkets. The company is the world's largest retailer of natural and organic goods and recently underwrote a thirteen-part PBS special, "Chefs A'Field," to expose consumers to sustainable practices, from the field to the table.[2] Indeed, environmental initiatives have become a global phenomenon. One goal of the annual Buy Nothing Day, sponsored by consumer associations around the world, is to encourage consumers to consider the environmental consequences of their buying habits. The event's organizers remind consumers that the richest 20 percent of people consume 80 percent of the world's resources.[3]

Although the future of green marketing can be debated, the real test of its effectiveness lies in the expectations, attitudes, and buying patterns of consumers. The preceding examples illustrate that there is no true consensus around issues such as environmental responsibility, and companies therefore face complex decisions about how to respond to them. This is true for all types of expectations, including the ones we explore in this chapter. In this section, we examine the economic, legal, ethical, and philanthropic responsibilities that businesses have to **consumers,** those individuals who purchase, use, and dispose of products for themselves and their homes.

consumers
individuals who purchase, use, and dispose of products for themselves and their homes

Responsibilities to Consumers

Consumers International, a London-based nonprofit federation of more than 250 consumer organizations in 115 countries, is dedicated to protecting and promoting consumers' interests and rights and implementing campaigns and research programs to aid governments, businesses, and nonprofit groups in decision making.[4] For example, the federation sponsors an annual World Consumer Rights Day every March 15 to further solidarity among the global consumer movement by promoting consumer rights, demanding the protection of these rights, and protesting abuses and injustices. Each observance has a particular theme—a pressing issue that is likely to affect a majority of consumers around the world. Issues over the last few years have included genetically modified foods, the natural environment, food safety, and consumer representation in government decision making. Another recent project evaluated the credibility and integrity of information found on the Internet. Consumers International worked with researchers in thirteen consumer organizations around the world and concluded that most consumers have difficulty evaluating the credibility of information sources on the Web.[5] The association's many efforts have led to the development of the Consumer Charter for Global Business, which offers guidance on a variety of business practices, including product standards, advertising, guarantees, consumer complaint procedures, and competitive tactics. At a minimum, the charter asks companies to consider their economic relationship with consumers through all stages of the production, distribution, and marketing process; to obey all relevant laws; and to establish clear ethical standards for business practice.[6] The charter therefore covers three of the four responsibilities we have discussed throughout this book.

Economic Issues

As we saw in Chapter 2, consumers are primary stakeholders because their awareness, purchase, use, and repurchase of products are vital to a company's existence. Fundamentally, therefore, consumers and businesses are connected by an economic relationship. This relationship begins with an exchange, usually of a good or service for money, which often leads to deeper attachments or affiliation. An advertising campaign slogan, "You are what you drive," typifies the close relationship that some consumers develop with the products they purchase. Other consumers may choose to shun particular brands or opt for the environmentally sensitive products described earlier. In all of these cases, however, consumers expect the products they purchase to perform as guaranteed by their sellers. Thus, a firm's economic responsibilities include following through on promises made in the exchange process. Although this responsibility seems basic today, business practices have not always been directed in this way. In the early part of the 1900s, the caveat "Let the buyer beware" typified the power that business—not consumers—wielded in most exchange relationships.[7]

Fulfillment of economic responsibilities depends on interactions with the consumer. However, there are situations where the consumer does not act as a fair participant in the exchange.[8] **Consumer fraud** involves intentional deception to derive an unfair economic advantage over an organization. Examples of fraudulent activities include shoplifting, collusion or duplicity, and guile. Collusion typically involves an employee who assists the consumer in fraud. For example, a cashier may not ring up all merchandise or may give an unwarranted discount. Duplicity may involve a consumer staging an accident in a grocery store and then seeking damages against the store for its lack of attention to safety. A consumer may purchase, wear, and then return an item of clothing for a full refund. In other situations, the consumer may ask

consumer fraud
intentional deception to derive an unfair economic advantage over an organization

for a refund by claiming a defect that either is nonexistent or was caused by consumer misuse.[9] Although some of these acts warrant legal prosecution, they can be very difficult to prove, and many companies are reluctant to accuse patrons of a crime when there is no way of verifying it. Businesses that operate with the "customer is always right" philosophy have found that some consumers will take advantage of this promise and have therefore modified return policies to curb unfair use. Because of the vague nature of some types of consumer fraud, its full financial toll has been difficult to tally. However, rough estimates indicate that inventory shrinkage costs U.S. businesses more than $30 billion per year. Companies in many countries have problems with excessive shrinkage rates. For example, Figure 7.1 lists the average retail

| **FIGURE 7.1** | Retail Shrinkage in Europe |

RANDOM SAMPLING

Customer Not King, but Thief

Napoleon, with his lifelong dislike for the English, would have been delighted to know that the country he deprecatingly called a "nation of shopkeepers" nearly two centuries ago has become a nation of shoplifters instead.

According to a survey conducted by the Centre of Retail Research based in Nottingham, England, of 476 major European retailers in 16 countries, the United Kingdom (England being the largest contributor) took top honors for the highest amount of retail shrinkage, mainly attributed to theft by customers. Employees were second in line as a cause of retail shrinkage.

In 2001, European retailers apprehended nearly 1.23 million people for theft, primarily customers. Shrinkage is expected to cost European retailers £19.2 billion (more than $30 billion) in 2002, compared with £18.7 billion (more than $29 billion) last year.

Retail Shrinkage
(as % of annual sales including value-added tax in 2001—2002)

United Kingdom	1.77
Norway	1.59
Greece	1.53
France	1.49
The Netherlands	1.48
Finland	1.48
Spain	1.47
Portugal	1.42
Italy	1.41
Sweden	1.37
Ireland	1.34
Denmark	1.32
Belgium/Luxembourg	1.28
Germany	1.19
Austria	0.97
Switzerland	0.85

Source: "Random Sampling: Customer Not King, but Thief," *Marketing News*, December 9, 2002, p. 4. Copyright © 2002 by the American Marketing Association. Reprinted with permission.

shrinkage rates in sixteen European countries. Shoplifting represents about one-third of all inventory shrinkage experienced by retail companies. Retailers of cards, gifts, apparel, shoes, and household furnishing products experience higher-than-average shrinkage rates.[10]

Most consumers, of course, do not engage in such activities. However, there are cases where buyers and sellers disagree on whether or how well companies have satisfied their economic responsibilities. Thus, a consumer may believe that a product is not worth the price paid for one reason or another, perhaps because he or she believes the product's benefits have been exaggerated by the seller. For example, although some marketers claim that their creams, pills, special massages, and other techniques can reduce or even eliminate cellulite, most medical experts and dermatologists believe that only exercise and weight loss can reduce the appearance of this undesirable condition. Most of the products for reducing cellulite remain on the market, but many consumers have returned these products and complained about the lack of results.[11] If consumers believe that a firm has not fulfilled its basic economic responsibilities, they may ask for a refund, tell others about their bad experience, discontinue their patronage, contact a consumer agency, and even seek legal redress. Many consumer and government agencies keep track of consumer complaints. For example, district attorneys in California recently reported the top ten consumer complaints received by their offices. Identity theft, Internet fraud, negative option contracts, phone company fraud, contractor and auto repair fraud, and auto purchasing and leasing issues topped the list.[12] To protect consumers and provide businesses with guidance, a number of laws and regulations have been enacted to ensure that economic responsibility is met in accordance with institutionalized standards.

Legal Issues

As we discussed in Chapter 3, legal issues with respect to consumers in the United States primarily fall under the domain of the Federal Trade Commission (FTC), which enforces federal antitrust and consumer protection laws. Within this agency, the Bureau of Consumer Protection works to protect consumers against unfair, deceptive, and fraudulent practices.[13] For example, consumer complaints about problems receiving merchandise ordered online prompted the FTC to launch Project TooLate.com to investigate whether Internet retailers had violated the Mail and Telephone Order Rule during the 1999 holiday season. Seven online retailers eventually settled with the FTC over charges that they did not provide consumers with adequate notice of shipping delays or they promised specific delivery dates that they knew were impossible to meet. The companies, which included CDnow, Macy's, the Original Honey Baked Ham Company, and Toys 'R' Us, agreed to modify their procedures and paid civil fines totaling $1.5 million. In a follow-up campaign, dubbed HolidaySmarts2.com, FTC staff visited sixty-three web sites and issued fifty-one letters reminding the e-tailers about FTC statutes and regulations.[14] In this case, the companies' inability to honor the economic exchange agreement resulted in legal action and continuing oversight on behalf of consumers. The lessons learned in the 1999 holiday shopping season prompted online retailers to intensify their focus on customer service and associated expectations, and many chose to modify procedures and resources accordingly.[15]

In addition to the FTC, several other federal agencies regulate specific goods, services, or business practices to protect consumers. The Food and Drug Administration, for example, enforces laws and regulations enacted to prevent distribution of adulterated or misbranded foods, drugs, medical devices, cosmetics, veterinary products, and potentially hazardous consumer products. The Consumer Product Safety Commission enforces laws and regulations designed to protect the public from unreasonable risk of injury from consumer products. Many states also have regulatory agencies that enforce laws and regulations regarding business practices within their states. Most federal agencies and states also have consumer affairs or information offices to help consumers. The Federal Communications Commission's Consumer Information Bureau educates consumers on issues related to cable service, telecommunications, and other areas under the FCC's domain.[16] In Iowa, the attorney general's Consumer Protection Division publishes brochures to assist consumers in complaining effectively, buying a new or used car, recognizing scams, and avoiding identity theft.[17]

In this section, we focus on U.S. laws related to exchanges and relationships with consumers. Table 7.1 summarizes some of the laws that are likely to affect a wide range of companies and consumers. State and local laws can be more stringent than federal statutes, so it is important that businesses fully investigate the laws applicable to all markets in which they operate. In Texas, for example, the Deceptive Trade Practices Act prohibits a business from selling anything to a consumer that he or she does not need or cannot afford.[18]

Health and Safety   One of the first consumer protection laws in the United States came about in response to public outrage over a novel. In *The Jungle,* Upton Sinclair exposed atrocities, including unsanitary conditions and inhuman labor practices, by the meatpacking industry in turn-of-the-century Chicago. Appalled by the unwholesome practices described in the book, the public demanded reform. Congress responded by passing the Pure Food and Drug Act in 1906, just six months after *The Jungle* was widely published.[19] In addition to prohibiting the adulteration and mislabeling of food and drug products, the new law also established one of the nation's first federal regulatory agencies, the Food and Drug Administration.

Since the passage of the Pure Food and Drug Act, public health and safety have been major targets of federal and state regulation. For example, the Consumer Product Safety Act established the Consumer Product Safety Commission (CPSC), whereas the Flammable Fabrics Act set standards for the flammability of clothing, children's sleepwear, carpets and rugs, and mattresses. The Standard Mattress Co. paid $60,000 to settle charges that it violated the Flammable Fabrics Act by making and selling futons that failed to meet flammability standards. Despite its agreement with the CPSC, the company denies that it violated any consumer product safety laws.[20] Other laws attempt to protect children from harm, including the Child Protection and Toy Safety Act and the Children's Online Privacy Protection Act.

Credit and Ownership   Abuses and inequities associated with loans and credit have resulted in the passage of laws designed to protect consumers' rights and public interests. The most significant of these laws prohibit discrimination in the extension of credit, require creditors to disclose all finance charges and related aspects of credit transactions, give consumers the right to dispute and correct inaccurate information on their credit reports, and regulate the activities of debt collectors. For example, the Home Ownership and Equity Protection Act requires home equity

| TABLE 7.1 | Major Consumer Laws |

ACT (DATE ENACTED)	PURPOSE
Pure Food and Drug Act (1906)	Established the Food and Drug Administration; outlaws the adulteration or mislabeling of food and drug products sold in interstate commerce.
Cigarette Labeling and Advertising Act (1965)	Requires manufacturers to add to package labels warnings about the possible health hazards associated with smoking cigarettes.
Fair Packaging and Labeling Act (1966)	Outlaws unfair or deceptive packaging or labeling of consumer products.
Truth in Lending Act (1968)	Requires creditors to disclose in writing all finance charges and related aspects of credit transactions.
Child Protection and Toy Safety Act (1969)	Requires childproof devices and special labeling.
Fair Credit Reporting Act (1970)	Promotes accuracy, fairness, and privacy of credit information; gives consumers the right to see their personal credit reports and to dispute any inaccurate information therein.
Consumer Product Safety Act (1972)	Established the Consumer Product Safety Commission to regulate potentially hazardous consumer products.
Odometer Act (1972)	Provides protections for consumers against odometer fraud in used-car sales.
Equal Credit Opportunity Act (1974)	Outlaws denial of credit on the basis of race, color, religion, national origin, sex, marital status, age, or receipt of public assistance, and requires creditors to provide applicants, on request, with the reasons for credit denial.
Magnuson-Moss Warranty (FTC) Act (1975)	Establishes rules for consumer product warranties, including minimum content and disclosure standards; allows the FTC to prescribe interpretive rules in policy statements regarding unfair or deceptive practices.
Consumer Goods Pricing Act (1975)	Prohibits the use of price maintenance agreements among manufacturers and resellers in interstate commerce.
Fair Debt Collection Practices Act (1977)	Prohibits third-party debt collectors from engaging in deceptive or abusive conduct when collecting consumer debts incurred for personal, family, or household purposes.
Toy Safety Act (1984)	Authorizes the Consumer Product Safety Commission to recall products intended for use by children when they present substantial risk of injury.
Nutrition Labeling and Education Act (1990)	Prohibits exaggerated health claims and requires all processed foods to contain standardized labels with nutritional information.
Telephone Consumer Protection Act (1991)	Establishes procedures to avoid unwanted telephone solicitations; prohibits marketers from using automated telephone dialing systems or an artificial or prerecorded voice to certain telephone lines.
Home Ownership and Equity Protection Act (1994)	Requires home equity lenders to disclose to borrowers in writing the payment amounts, the consequences of default, and the borrowers' right to cancel the loan within a certain time period.

(continued)

TABLE 7.1	Major Consumer Laws *(continued)*
ACT (DATE ENACTED)	**PURPOSE**
Telemarketing and Consumer Fraud and Abuse Prevention Act (1994)	Authorized the FTC to establish regulations for telemarketing, including prohibiting deceptive, coercive, or privacy-invading telemarketing practices; restricting the time during which unsolicited telephone calls may be made to consumers; and requiring telemarketers to disclose the nature of the call at the beginning of an unsolicited sales call.

Sources: "Statutes Relating to Consumer Protection Mission," Federal Trade Commission, www.ftc.gov/ogc/stat3.htm, accessed November 12, 2003; O. C. Ferrell, John Fraedrich, and Linda Ferrell, *Business Ethics: Ethical Decision Making and Cases,* 5th ed. (Boston: Houghton Mifflin, 2005), p. 56; Roger L. Miller and Gaylord A. Jentz, *Business Law Today* (Cincinnati, OH: West Legal Studies in Business, 2000).

lenders to disclose, in writing, the borrower's rights, payment amounts, and the consequences of defaulting on the loan. Together, the U.S. Department of Justice and Department of Housing and Urban Development enforce laws that ensure equal access to sale and rental housing. Every April, the government sponsors Fair Housing Month to educate property owners, agents, and consumers on rights with respect to housing.[21]

Marketing, Advertising, and Packaging Legal issues in marketing often relate to sales and advertising communications and information about product content and safety. Abuses in promotion can range from exaggerated claims, concealed facts, and deception to outright lying. Such misleading information creates ethical issues because the communicated messages do not include all the information consumers need to make sound purchasing decisions. Figure 7.2 discloses the top practices that consumers believe dominate the advertising industry, only two of which are positive.

Publishers Clearing House recently settled charges brought by twenty-six states and the District of Columbia that it used deceptive sweepstakes promotions in order to get consumers to buy magazines. The settlement required the company to pay $34 million to the states to give refunds to customers, especially the elderly, who bought magazines under the belief that such purchases would boost their chances of winning the oft-touted million-dollar sweepstakes. Although Publishers Clearing House did not admit to any wrongdoing, it agreed to stop using the phrase "You are a winner," unless adequately balanced with statements specifying the conditions necessary to win, and to clearly indicate the odds of winning in sweepstakes promotions. In the same year, United States Sales Corporation and Time Inc. agreed to similar settlements over allegations of deceptive sweepstakes promotions with forty-eight states and the District of Columbia.[22]

Although a certain amount of exaggeration and hyperbole is tolerated, deceptive claims or claims that cannot be substantiated are likely to invite legal action from the FTC. For example, the FTC levied a $3 million fine against the marketers of Blue Stuff pain relievers for marketing campaigns that used unsupported claims. The FTC also sued Body Solutions over ads that declared consumers could eat pizza, tacos, and other fatty foods and burn away the fat while sleeping. Cases such as these prompted the FTC to develop a list of false phrases that should alert both consumers and marketers to unsubstantiated or false claims.[23]

| FIGURE 7.2 | Consumer's Ranking of the Ten Most Widely Prevalent Practices in Advertising |

❶ Unrealistic standards of beauty

❷ Exploiting children by convincing them to buy things that are bad for them or unnecessary

❸ Being creative or entertaining with advertising

❹ Reducing amount of product and charging the same price

❺ Targeting specific groups and convincing them to buy things that are bad for them or unnecessary

❻ Misleading claims about or exaggerating health benefits

❼ Misleading claims about or exaggerating environmental benefits

❽ Subliminal advertising

❾ Making unfair or misleading comparisons

❿ Using online services to provide more-detailed information

Source: "You Have an Image Problem," *Marketing News*, December 9, 2002, p. 3. Copyright © 2002 by the American Marketing Association. Reprinted with permission

Since the Federal Trade Commission Act of 1914 outlawed all deceptive and unfair trade practices, additional legislation has further delineated which activities are permissible and which are illegal. For example, the Telemarketing and Consumer Fraud and Abuse Prevention Act requires telemarketers to disclose the nature of the call at the beginning of an unsolicited sales call and restricts the times during which such calls may be made to consumers. Another legal issue in marketing has to do with the promotion of products that involve health or safety. Numerous laws regulate the promotion of alcohol and tobacco products, including the Public Health Cigarette Smoking Act (1970) and the Cigarette Labeling and Advertising Act (1965). The Eighteenth Amendment to the U.S. Constitution prohibited the manufacture and sale of alcoholic beverages in 1919; the prohibition was repealed in 1933 by the Twenty-first Amendment. However, this amendment gave to the states the power to regulate the transportation of alcoholic beverages across state lines. Today, each state has unique regulations, some of which require the use of wholesalers and retailers to limit direct sales of alcoholic beverages to final consumers in other states. In this case, a law aimed at protecting consumers by promoting temperance in alcohol consumption now affects wine sellers' ability to implement e-commerce and subsequent interstate sales.[24]

Sales and Warranties Another area of law that affects business relationships with consumers has to do with warranties. Many consumers consider the warranty behind a product when making a purchase decision, especially for expensive durable goods such as automobiles and appliances. One of the most significant laws affecting warranties is the Magnuson-Moss Warranty (FTC) Act, which established rules for

Global Initiatives

Consumer Credit in Mexico

Banco Azteca, Mexico's first bank aimed at the country's middle and working class, opened its doors in late 2002. For a security guard and father of four like Humberto Vidal, Banco Azteca is a welcomed sight. He received a personal loan of $350 and commented, "Now I have a place where I can go if I need support." Before the bank opened, most Mexican consumers had little access to credit unless they chose to pay exorbitant interest rates. Banco Azteca is targeting the 73 million people in Mexico who live in households with combined incomes of $250 to $4,000 a month. This mass market has been neglected by Mexico's traditional banking system. Not only is the bank going after a new market, it is bucking the trend of bank closures or mergers with foreign banks. Banco Azteca is the first and only purely Mexican-owned bank to be licensed by the Finance Ministry since 1994. Company executives also speak of a greater mission: improving the personal financial situation of millions of Mexican citizens.

Most of the new bank's 800 branches are located inside the retail stores of Elektra, Salinas & Rocha, and Bodega de Ramates, all owned by Grupo Elektra S.A. de C.V., Latin America's leading specialty retailer and consumer finance company. The retail stores have offered consumer credit options for some time and claim several million active accounts. Many Mexican consumers purchased refrigerators, furniture, television sets, and appliances on the popular fifty-three-week financing plan, often paying nearly double the original price. For example, 65 percent of Elektra's sales are made on the installment plan. The retail stores will eventually close down their consumer financing operation as they drive business to Banco Azteca. Unlike the retail financing operation, the bank has access to interbank borrowing rates, which average around 8 percent annually. This status opens new doors for consumer credit in Mexico.

In its first few months of operation, Banco Azteca opened nearly 250,000 savings accounts. One customer, Stephanie Diaz, started a savings account with only $5, but plans to have her employer deposit her paycheck with Banco Azteca, some of which will go into the savings account. Consumers who work in the informal business sector, such as taxi drivers, street merchants, and electricians, will now have access to loans. In the past, these workers could not receive loans because they could not meet lending requirements, including the proof of income. Small business owners and would-be entrepreneurs will also benefit from Banco Azteca.

In addition to savings accounts and personal loans, Banco Azteca will offer car loans, mortgage loans, installment plans, debit cards, and other services. Databases from the retail accounts will enable bank staff to make credit decisions and develop marketing campaigns. Elektra is taking its understanding of these underserved consumers from the retail store into the banking operations. The company is fervent in its belief that low and middle income is not necessarily synonymous with loan defaults and high risk, as long as the right control mechanisms are in place. The bank's business model and potential for the ordinary Mexican consumer is consistent with Grupo Elektra's vision: *The success of our business rests on an optimistic view of the huge possibilities that exist in Mexico and Latin America, as well as on a talented and creative work team.*

Sources:
"Grupo Elektra Announces 3Q02 EBITDA of US $66 Million, Up 11% YoY," *PR Newswire*, October 25, 2002; Grupo Elektra, http://www.grupoelektra.com.mx/elektra/english/default.asp, accessed August 19, 2003; Lucy Conger, "A Bank for Mexico's Working Families," *New York Times*, December 31, 2002, p. W1; Jenalia Moreno, "Small Loans Add Up In Untapped Market; Mexican Chain Serves High-Risk Customers," *Houston Chronicle*, December 6, 2002, p. Business1.

consumer product warranties, including minimum content and standards for disclosure. All fifty states have enacted "lemon laws" to ensure that automobile sales are accompanied by appropriate warranties and remedies for defects that impair the safety, use, or value of the vehicle.[25]

Product Liability One area of law that has a profound effect on business and its relations with consumers is **product liability,** which refers to a business's legal responsibility for the performance of its products. This responsibility, which has evolved through both legislation and court interpretation (common law), may include a legal obligation to provide financial compensation to a consumer who has been harmed by a defective product. To receive compensation, a consumer who files suit in the United States must prove that the product was defective, that the defect caused an injury, and that the defect made the product unreasonably dangerous. Under the concept of *strict liability,* an injured consumer can apply this legal responsibility to any firm in the supply chain of a defective product, including contractors, suppliers of component parts, wholesalers, and retailers. Companies with operations in other countries must understand the various forms of product liability law that exist. For example, South Korea recently passed a new law making it easier for consumers to win product liability cases. In response to the law, many South Korean firms developed product liability teams for assessing risk and safety issues, reviewing insurance coverage, and educating employees on the importance of product safety.[26]

Because the law typically holds businesses liable for their products' performance, many companies choose to recall potentially harmful products; such recalls may be required by legal or regulatory authorities as well. Warner-Lambert, for example, was asked by the Food and Drug Administration to recall Rezulin, a diabetes drug, after thirty-five cases of liver damage occurred in patients using the drug during its first year on the market.[27]

Kraft Foods recalled Taco Bell taco shells after it learned the shells were made with genetically modified corn not yet approved for human consumption. (Jeff Kan Lee © The Press Democrat, Santa Rosa, CA)

Product liability lawsuits have increased dramatically in recent years, and many suits have resulted in huge damage awards to injured consumers or their families. In a much-publicized case, a jury awarded a McDonald's customer $2.9 million after she was scalded when she spilled hot McDonald's coffee in her lap. Although that award was eventually reduced on appeal, McDonald's and other fast-food restaurants now display warning signs that their coffee is hot in order to eliminate both further injury and liability. Because of multimillion-dollar judgments like that against McDonald's, companies sometimes pass on the costs of damage awards to their customers in the form of higher prices. Most companies have taken steps to minimize their liability, and some firms—such as pharmaceutical firms making serum for the DPT (diphtheria-pertussis-tetanus) vaccine and manufacturers of small planes—have stopped making products or withdrawn completely from problematic markets because of the high risk of expensive liability lawsuits.[28] Although some states have limited damage awards and legislative reform is often on the agenda, the issue of product liability remains politically controversial.[29]

International Issues Concerns about protecting consumers' legal rights are not limited to the United States. Most developed nations have laws and offices devoted to this goal. In the European Union (EU), the health and consumer protection directorate general oversees efforts to increase consumer confidence in the unified market. Its initiatives center on health, safety, economic, and public-health interests. One recently passed EU directive establishes minimum levels of consumer protection in member states. For example, EU consumers now have a legal guarantee of two years on all consumer goods. If they find a defective product, they may choose repair or replacement or, in special circumstances, ask for a price reduction or rescind the contract altogether.[30]

In Japan, unlike in the United States, product liability lawsuits are much less common. In the early 1990s, Chikara Minami filed one of the first such lawsuits against Japanese automaker Mitsubishi. Minami's suit alleged a defect in the Mitsubishi Pajero. Although the court sided with the automaker in that case, ten years later Mitsubishi was accused of deliberately covering up consumer complaints. Despite this revelation and an enhanced product liability law in 1995, consumer rights are often subverted in order to preserve the power and structure of big business in Japan.[31] China's consumer rights movement is also relatively new and resulted from economic policy changes away from isolationism and central planning. The China Consumers' Association was established in 1984 and has helped create consumer expectations and company responses that are starting to resemble those found in Western economies.[32]

As we have discussed in this section, there are many laws that influence business practices with respect to consumers all over the world. Every year, new laws are enacted and existing rules are modified in response to the changing business environment. For example, the EU recently implemented new standards for labeling beef products after the "mad cow disease" scare of tainted beef.[33] Although companies must monitor and obey all laws and regulations, they also have to keep abreast of the ethical obligations and standards that exist in the marketplace.

Ethical Issues

In 1962, President John F. Kennedy proclaimed a Consumer Bill of Rights that includes the rights to choose, to safety, to be informed, and to be heard. Kennedy also established the Consumer Advisory Council to integrate consumer concerns into government regulations and processes. These four rights established a philosophical basis on which state and local consumer protection rules were later developed.[34] Around the same time, Ralph Nader's investigations of auto safety and his publication of *Unsafe at Any Speed* in 1965 alerted citizens to the dangers of a common consumer product. Nader's activism and Kennedy's speech provided support for **consumerism,** the movement to protect consumers from an imbalance of power on the side of business and to maximize consumer welfare in the marketplace.[35] When Nader ran for the U.S. presidency in 2000, his platform included many of the same concerns about consumers and business that were being discussed thirty-five years earlier.[36] As we have pointed out, the consumer movement is a global phenomenon, including the World Consumer Rights Day celebrated every year.

> **consumerism**
> movement to protect consumers from an imbalance of power on the side of business and to maximize consumer welfare in the marketplace

Over the last four decades, consumerism has affected public policy through a variety of mechanisms. Early efforts were aimed primarily at advocating for legislation and regulation, whereas more recent efforts have shifted to education and protection programs directed at consumers.[37] The Consumers Union (CU), for example, works with regional and federal legislators and international groups to protect consumer interests, sponsors conferences and research projects, tests consumer products, and publishes the results in its *Consumer Reports* magazine. A recent issue of the magazine detailed business practices that CU deems unfair to consumers, including predatory lending, the poor value of some life insurance products, and advertisements aimed at vulnerable people, like children.[38] The Internet has also created new vehicles for consumer education and protection. Visitors to the National Consumers League web site at http://www.nclnet.org/ or www.consumerworld.org find publications on many consumer issues, research and campaign reports, product reviews, retailer rankings, updates on legal matters, ways to track used-car histories, and many other types of services. Thus, consumer groups and information services have shifted the balance of power between consumer and business because consumers are able to compare prices, read independent rankings, communicate with other buyers, and, in general, have greater knowledge about products, companies, and competitors.[39] Despite the opportunities to exert more power, some researchers question whether most consumers actually take the time and energy to do so. For example, although the Internet provides a great deal of information and choices, access to the Internet partly depends on educational level and income. In addition, the volume of information available online may actually make it more difficult to analyze and assimilate.

All U.S. presidents since Kennedy have confirmed the four basic consumer rights and added new ones in response to changing business conditions. President William J. Clinton, for example, appointed a commission to study the changing health care environment and its implications for consumer rights. The result was the proposal of a Patient's Bill of Rights and Responsibilities to ensure rights to confidentiality of patient information, to participate in health care decisions, to access to emergency services, and other needs.[40] During the same period, a Financial Consumer's Bill of Rights Act was proposed in the U.S. House of Representatives to curb high bank fees, automated teller machine surcharges, and other practices that have angered consumers.[41]

Although consumer rights were first formalized through a presidential speech and subsequent affirmations, they have not yet reached the legal domain of social respon-

TABLE 7.2	Basic Consumer Rights

RIGHT	GENERAL ISSUES
To choose	Access to a variety of products at competitive and reasonable prices
To safety	Protection of health, safety, and financial well-being in the marketplace
To be informed	Opportunity to have accurate and adequate information on which to base decisions and protection from misleading or deceptive information
To be heard	Consideration given to consumer interests in government processes
To redress	Opportunity to express dissatisfaction and to have the complaint resolved effectively
To privacy	Protection of consumer information and its use

Source: Adapted from E. Thomas Garman, *Consumer Economic Issues in America* (Houston, TX: Dame Publications, 1997).

sibility. Some specific elements of these rights have been mandated through law, but the relatively broad nature of the rights means they must be interpreted and implemented on a company-by-company basis. Table 7.2 lists six consumer rights that have become part of the ethical expectations of business. Although these rights are not necessarily provided by all organizations, our social responsibility philosophy requires attention and implementation of them.

Right to Choose The right to choose implies that, to the extent possible, consumers have the opportunity to select from a variety of products at competitive prices. This right is based on the philosophy of the competitive nature of markets, which should lead to high-quality products at reasonable prices. Antitrust activities that reduce competition may jeopardize this right. This right has been called into question with respect to the safety of some parts of the United States. Domino's Pizza, for example, was accused of discriminating against African American customers through a delivery policy that seemed to be based on a neighborhood's racial composition rather than the legitimate threat of danger to drivers delivering in those neighborhoods. In effect, consumers in these neighborhoods were denied access to pizza delivery service. Although no lawsuit was filed, Domino's worked with the U.S. Justice Department to revise the delivery policy to narrowly define delivery limitations on the basis of real safety threats and to reevaluate the status of excluded areas on a yearly basis.[42]

Right to Safety The right to safety means that businesses have an obligation not to knowingly market a product that could harm consumers. Some consumer advocates believe that this right means that the manufacture and sale of firearms should be outlawed in the United States. Although organizations like the National Rifle Association have vehemently opposed this view, questions about gun safety, especially around children, have prompted a number of state laws to regulate the manufacture and sale of guns. For example, Massachusetts recently required that all guns sold in that state meet stringent standards and carry internal identification numbers. Maryland requires that all guns be equipped with trigger locks.[43]

The right to safety also implies that all products should be safe for their intended use, include instructions for proper and safe use, and have been sufficiently tested to ensure reliability. Companies must take great care in designing warning messages about products with potentially dangerous or unsafe effects. These messages should take into account consumers' ability to understand and respond to the information. Warnings should be relevant and meaningful to every potential user of the product. Some warnings use symbols or pictures to communicate. Companies that fail to honor the right to safety risk expensive product liability lawsuits. In 1998, the five largest tobacco manufacturers in the United States reached a landmark $246 billion settlement with the attorneys general of forty-six states. The master settlement agreement (MSA) required the companies to give billions of dollars to the state governments every year to help relieve the burden that smoking-related illnesses put on state health care systems and to fund campaigns designed to discourage smoking, especially among children. Under the settlement, the companies agreed to stop using cartoon characters, like R. J. Reynolds's Joe Camel. The MSA barred companies from a number of traditional marketing strategies, such as using billboards or direct-mail advertising or passing out samples at shopping malls to tout their products. To help pay for the costs of the settlement, the companies raised prices. Thus, the settlement was designed to force the tobacco firms to bear more of the costs of illnesses caused by their product and to make them act more responsibly. Although corporate executives point to declining teen smoking rates as evidence of their responsibility, many antismoking activists believe that the responsible thing to do is to stop selling a product that causes illness and death.[44]

Right to Be Informed Consumers also have the right to be informed. Any information, whether written or verbal, should be accurate, adequate, and free of deception so that consumers can make a sound decision. This general assertion has also led to specific legislation, such as the Nutrition Labeling and Education Act of 1990, which requires certain nutrition facts on food labels and limits the use of terms such as *low fat*. This right can be associated with safety issues if consumers do not have sufficient information to purchase or use a product effectively. For example, a woman in New York leveled a $50 million lawsuit against Robert's American Gourmet Food, Inc., for mislabeling its snack products and causing her "weight gain . . . mental anguish, outrage and indignation." The snacks, branded Pirate's Booty, Veggie Booty, and Fruity Booty, were sold in packages that claimed to have 120 calories and 2.5 grams of fat. When independently tested, however, the Good Housekeeping Institute published numbers that came as a shock to many dieters; the snack actually contained 147 calories and 8.5 grams of fat. Bags that claimed to have 1 ounce of product actually had 1.25 ounces of the product. Robert's recalled the snacks prior to the *Good Housekeeping* magazine report and blamed new manufacturing equipment on the mislabeling and fat content problem. The snack, once so popular that it made the pages of *Vanity Fair*, reminded consumers that "if something tastes too good to be true, it probably is too good to be true."[45]

In an age of rapid technological advances and globalization, the degree of complexity in product marketing is another concern related to consumers' right to information. This complexity may relate to the ways in which product features and benefits are discussed in advertising, how effective salespeople are in answering consumer questions, the expertise needed to operate or use the product, and the ease of returning or exchanging the product. To help consumers make decisions based on adequate and timely information, some organizations sponsor consumer education programs. For example, pharmaceutical companies and health maintenance organizations sponsor free seminars, health screenings, web sites, and other programs to educate consumers about their health and treatment options. The proliferation of web sites devoted to consumer health information prompted the American Accreditation Healthcare Commission to develop a Health Web Site Accreditation program. The program's "seal of approval" should let consumers know that the web site's content is trustworthy and reliable.[46] In Russia, consumer advocacy organizations have established a telephone hot line to educate consumers about their rights and to advise them when they encounter poor-quality products marketed as leading consumer brands. According to the hot line director Yelena Poluektova, "Although there has been a law on consumer rights since 1992 it turns out very many people have no knowledge of their rights."[47]

Right to Be Heard The right to be heard relates to opportunities for consumers to communicate or voice their concerns in the public policy process. This also implies that governments have the responsibility to listen and take consumer issues into account. One mechanism for fulfilling this responsibility is through the FTC and state consumer affairs offices. Another vehicle includes congressional hearings held to educate elected officials about specific issues of concern to consumers. At the same time, consumers are expected to be full participants in the process, meaning they must be informed and willing to take action against wrongs in the marketplace.

Right to Seek Redress In addition to the rights described by Kennedy, consumers also have the right to express dissatisfaction and seek restitution from a business when a good or service does not meet their expectations. However, consumers need to be educated in the process for seeking redress and to recognize that the first course of action in such cases should be with the seller. At the same time, companies need to have explicit and formal processes for dealing with customer dissatisfaction. Although some product problems lead to third-party intervention or legal recourse, the majority of issues should be resolvable between the consumer and the business. One third party that consumers may consult in such cases is the Better Business Bureau (BBB), which promotes self-regulation of business. In order to gain and maintain membership, a firm must agree to abide by the ethical standards established by the BBB. This organization collects complaints on businesses and makes this information, along with other reports, available for consumer decision making. The BBB also operates the dispute resolution division to assist in out-of-court settlements between consumers and businesses. For example, this division has a program, BBB Auto Line, to handle disputes between consumers and twenty-five automobile manufacturers.[48] This self-regulatory approach not only provides differentiation in the market but can also stave off new laws and regulations.

Right to Privacy The advent of new information technology and the Internet have prompted increasing concerns about consumer privacy. This right relates to consumers' awareness of how personal data are collected and used, and it places a burden on firms to protect this information. How information is used can create concerns for consumers. Although some e-commerce firms have joined together to develop privacy standards for the Internet, many web sites do not meet the FTC's criteria for fair information practices, including notice, choice, access, and security.[49] We will take a closer look at the debate surrounding privacy rights in Chapter 10.

A firm's ability to address these consumer rights can serve as a competitive advantage. CMC Properties, a recent recipient of the National Torch Award for Marketplace Ethics given by the Better Business Bureau, is regarded for the ethical approach to consumers of its real estate and property management services. Instead of viewing its business as "bricks and mortar," the company is focused on "bodies and souls." As the company's mission states, CMC strives to simplify the lives of its customers.[50] Another example is in the highly competitive market for air travel. Many airlines have developed a strong focus on customer service and satisfaction. Together with the air transport association, several airlines launched the airline customer service commitment to demonstrate an industry focus on alleviating passenger frustrations and complaints. Delta Airlines established the Delta Customer Commitment, a twelve-point plan that details the airline's practices before, during, and after a customer flight (see Figure 7.3).[51]

When consumers believe a firm is operating outside ethical or legal standards, they may be motivated to take some type of action. As we discussed earlier, there are a number of strategies consumers can employ to communicate their dissatisfaction, such as complaining or discontinuing the exchange relationship. For example, some people believe Wal-Mart's presence has contributed to the demise of locally owned pharmacies and variety stores in many small towns. The chain's buying power ensures lower prices and wider product variety for consumers but also makes it difficult for smaller retailers to compete. Other consumers and community leaders worry about traffic congestion and urban sprawl that accompany new retail sites. Some Wal-Mart critics have taken their discontent with the retailer to the Internet. One disgruntled customer developed a web site as a forum for sharing complaints about the retail chain. The site, http://www.walmartsucks.com, includes sections for rating local stores, updates on legal action against Wal-Mart, and customer and employee complaints. Another web site, http://www.walmartsurvivor.com, details court rulings against Wal-Mart and lists attorneys who have been successful in opposing the retail giant.[52] Stakeholders may use the three types of power—symbolic, utilitarian, and coercive—that were discussed in Chapter 2 to create organizational awareness on an important issue. For example, some Chinese consumers feel that Japanese people believe they are racially superior to the Chinese. This sentiment stems from Japan's occupation of China in the 1940s. More recently, Toshiba has been accused of racism for not compensating Chinese users of potentially faulty Toshiba laptop computers. This perceived slight, along with feelings of nationalism, have prompted Chinese consumers to dismiss Toshiba and other Japanese manufacturers. Chinese retailers have pulled Japanese products off their shelves as well.[53] These consumers are engaging in another form of consumer action, a **boycott,** by abstaining from using, purchasing, or dealing with an organization. The World Jewish Congress encouraged its members to boycott the insurance company Transamerica after its parent company, Aegon NV, refused to join the international commission on Holocaust-era insurance claims. The commission was established to resolve insurance claims that resulted from the Holocaust and World War II.[54]

boycott
consumer action of abstaining from using, purchasing, or dealing with an organization

FIGURE 7.3   Delta Customer Commitment (12-Point Plan)

Before You Fly

1. Delta Air Lines® will offer on our telephone reservation system, airport ticket counters, and city ticket offices the lowest published fare for which the customer is eligible for the date, flight, and class of service requested.

2. Delta Air Lines® will give you time to compare our fares with those of other airlines by holding your telephone reservation without payment until midnight one day after the reservation is made, and guaranteeing the fare if you buy your ticket with Delta®.

3. Delta Air Lines® will issue refunds for eligible domestic tickets within seven business days for credit card purchases and 20 business days for purchases made by cash or check.

4. Delta Air Lines® will inform you, upon your request by telephone, if the flight on which you are ticketed is overbooked. We also will provide information at airports about our policies and procedures for handling situations when all ticketed customers cannot be accommodated on a flight.

5. Delta Air Lines® will provide you with timely and complete information about policies and procedures that affect your travel, including: changing aircraft on a flight that has a single flight number.

6. Delta Air Lines® will ensure our domestic codeshare partners commit to providing comparable consumer plans and policies. Our partners are regional airlines that connect small- and medium-sized markets with Delta's network.

At the Airport

7. Delta Air Lines® will provide you with information about our policies and procedures for accommodating disabled and special needs customers, and unaccompanied minors.

8. Delta Air Lines® will provide full and timely information on the status of delayed and canceled flights.

9. Delta Air Lines® will provide full and timely information regarding the status of a flight if there is an extreme delay after you have boarded or after the plane has landed, and we will provide for your essential needs such as food, water, heat, air conditioning, and restroom facilities while onboard.

After Landing

10. Delta Air Lines® will strive to return your misplaced baggage within 24 hours, and we will attempt to contact owners of unclaimed baggage when a name and address or telephone number is available.

11. Delta Air Lines® supported a proposal by the U.S. Department of Transportation to increase the per passenger domestic baggage liability limitation. The limitation was increased from $1,250 to $2,500. At the urging of Delta® and other member carriers, the ATA filed comments with the Department of Transportation August 27, 1999, supporting the increase for the per passenger baggage liability limitation from $1,250 to $2,500. The amount will include periodic adjustments for inflation.

12. Delta Air Lines® will respond to written customer complaints within 30 days exceeding the 60-day response standard adopted by ATA member airlines.

Source: "12-Point Plan: Airline Customer Service Commitment," www.delta-air.com/care/service_plan/index.jsp, accessed November 12, 2003. Reprinted courtesy of Delta Airlines © 2003.

Consumers around the globe are sometimes weary of big business and its power to influence culture and consumption. (AP Photo/Bullit Marquez)

Philanthropic Issues

Although relationships with consumers are fundamentally grounded in economic exchanges, the previous sections demonstrate that additional levels of expectations exist. As we discussed in Chapter 1, a national survey by Cone/Roper reported that 70 percent of consumers would be likely to switch to brands associated with a good cause, as long as price and quality were equal. These results suggest that today's consumers take it for granted that they can obtain high-quality products at reasonable prices, so businesses need to do something to differentiate themselves from the competition.[55] More firms are therefore investigating ways to link their philanthropic efforts with consumer interests. Eastman Kodak, for example, has funded environmental literacy programs of the World Wildlife Fund. These programs not only link between the company's possible effects and its interest in the natural environment but also provide a service to its customers and other stakeholders.[56]

From a strategic perspective, a firm's ability to link consumer interests to philanthropy should lead to stronger economic relationships. As we shall see in Chapter 11, philanthropic responsibilities to consumers usually entail broader benefits, including those that affect the community. For example, large pharmaceutical and health insurance firms provide financial support to the Foundation for Accountability (FACCT), a nonprofit organization that assists health care consumers in making better decisions. FACCT initiated an online system for patients to evaluate their physician on several quality indicators.[57]

Community Stakeholders

Whereas customers of all types, including consumers, are considered key constituents in the input-output and stakeholder models presented in Chapter 2, the community does not always receive the same level of acceptance as other stakeholders. One reason for this may be that *community* can be an amorphous concept, making it difficult to define and delineate.[58] Some people even wonder how a company determines who is in the community. Is a community determined by city or county boundaries? What if the firm operates in multiple locations? Or is a community prescribed by the interactions a firm has with various constituents who do not fit neatly into other stakeholder categories? The definition and scope of community seemed to expand in the aftermath of the September 11, 2001, terrorist attack on the World Trade Center and the Pentagon. People and organizations from around the world rallied to provide financial and emotional support to those affected by the tragedy. For a small restaurant in a large city, the owner may define the community as the immediate neighborhood where most of his or her patrons live. The restaurant may demonstrate social responsibility by hiring people from the neighborhood, participating in the neighborhood crime watch program, donating food to the elementary school's annual parent-teacher meetings, or sponsoring a neighborhood Little League team. For example, Merlino's Steak House in North Conway, New Hampshire, sponsors an annual golf tournament that benefits the Center for Hope, an organization that provides transportation for local individuals with disabilities.[59] For a corporation with facilities in North and South America, Europe, and Africa, the community may be viewed as virtually the entire world. To focus its social responsibility efforts, the multinational corporation might employ a community relations officer in each facility who reports to and coordinates with the company's head office.

Under our social responsibility philosophy, the term *community* should be viewed from a global perspective, beyond the immediate town, city, or state where a business is located. Thus, we define **community** as those members of society who are aware, concerned, or in some way affected by the operations and output of an organization. With information technology, high-speed travel, and the emergence of global business interests, the community as a constituency can be quite geographically, culturally, and attitudinally diverse. Issues that could become important include pollution of the environment, land use, economic advantages to the region, and discrimination within the community, as well as exploitation of workers or consumers.

From a positive perspective, an organization can significantly improve the quality of life through employment opportunities, economic development, and financial contributions for educational, health, the arts, and recreational activities. Through such efforts, a firm may become a **neighbor of choice,** an organization that builds and sustains trust with the community.[60] To become a neighbor of choice, a company should strive for positive and sustainable relationships with key individuals, groups, and organizations; demonstrate sensitivity to community concerns and issues; and design and implement programs that improve the quality of community life while promoting the company's long-term business strategies and goals.[61] Churchill Downs, Incorporated, a company with interests in racetracks and betting facilities, implements its community relations effort using the neighbor of choice strategy. Provisions of its strategy include developing a social vision, identifying pressing issues, building trusting relationships with stakeholders, and implementing the strategy effectively. The company employs community relations staff at its headquarters and major facilities and produces an annual report on its three-pronged approach to community relations, including volunteerism, financial contributions, and industry-specific campaigns.[62]

community
those members of society who are aware, concerned, or in some way affected by the operations and output of an organization

neighbor of choice
an organization that builds and sustains trust with the community

UPS encourages its employees to volunteer in the community. (UPS Photo)

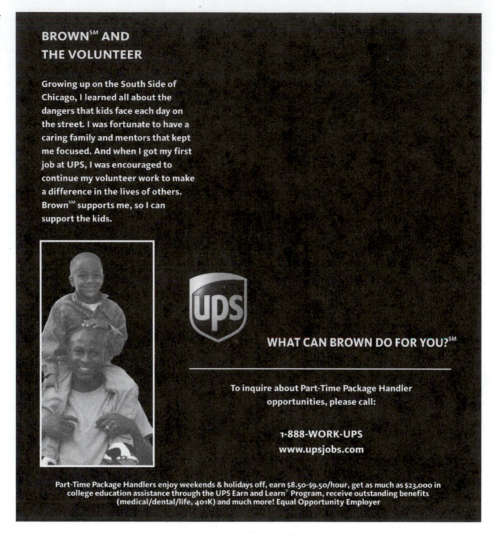

Similar to other areas of life, the relationship between a business and the community should be symbiotic. A business may support educational opportunities in the community because the owners feel it is the right thing to do, but it also helps develop the human resources and consumer skills necessary to operate the business. Customers and employees are also community members who benefit from contributions supporting recreational activities, environmental initiatives, safety, and education. Many firms rely on universities and community colleges to provide support for ongoing education of their employees. Sykes Enterprises, for example, often locates its customer call and support centers in towns where the local community college is willing to develop courses that educate employees in the skills and aptitude needed to effectively operate a call center.

community relations
the organizational function dedicated to building and maintaining relationships and trust with the community

In order to build and support these initiatives, companies may invest in **community relations,** the organizational function dedicated to building and maintaining relationships and trust with the community. In the past, most businesses have not viewed community relations as strategically important or associated them with the firm's ultimate performance. Although the community relations department interacted with the community and often doled out large sums of money to charities, it essentially served as a buffer between the organization and its immediate community. Today, community relations activities have achieved greater prominence and responsibility within most companies, especially due to the rise of stakeholder power and global business interests. The function has gained strategic importance through linking to overall business goals, professionalizing its staff and their knowledge of business and community issues, assessing its performance in quantitative and qualitative terms, and recognizing the breadth of stakeholders to which the organization is accountable.[63] For example, as director of community relations for Universal Studios Florida, Jan Stratton was instrumental in the firm's community projects, including the Universal Studios Escape Foundation, which raises funds for four-year college scholarships, the Universal Studios Employee Volunteer Program, the Children's Advocacy Center at the Howard Phillips Center for Children and Families, and the company's internal United Way campaign.[64] Community relations also assist in short-term and crisis situations, such as the product liability situations discussed earlier in the chapter.[65]

In a survey of more than 250 top executives, the majority of whose firms employed less than 500 people, nearly 45 percent indicated that they manage formal community programs and allocate resources to these initiatives. According to the survey results, the top five social responsibilities that companies have include supporting environmental issues, demonstrating ethical behavior in business operations, earning profits, employing local residents, and paying taxes. The top five issues with the greatest impact on business include education, job training and development, health care, crime, and substance abuse.[66]

In a diverse society, however, there is no general agreement as to what constitutes the ideal model of responsibility to the community. Businesses are likely to experience conflicts among stakeholders as to what constitutes a real commitment to the community. Therefore, the community relations function should cooperate with various internal and external constituents to develop community mission statements and assess opportunities and develop priorities for the types of contributions it will make to the community. Table 7.3 provides several examples of company missions and programs with respect to community involvement. As you can see, these missions are specific to the needs of the people and areas in which the companies operate and are usually aligned with the competencies of the organizations involved and their employees.

Community mission statements are likely to change as needs are met and new issues emerge. For example, when Delphi Automotive opened a manufacturing site in Mexico, it worked with the Mexican government to build subsidized housing for Delphi employees. The project helped more than 2,000 employees find better housing and was recently extended to serve nonemployees through a partnership with Habitat for Humanity.[67] This effort addressed a basic need in life, and now that it has been largely met, Delphi may consider investments in other community areas, such as edu-

TABLE 7.3	Community Mission Statements

ORGANIZATION	COMMUNITY MISSION
MTV Network's REACH Out (Responsible Employees Acting Caring and Helping Out)	Connects the company to the community and demonstrates its commitment to meeting the needs and interests of employees and the community. Initiated in 1995, the program is managed through the networks' Public Responsibility Department.
Portland Trail Blazers	Encourages employees to volunteer in health, education, and sports programs for youngsters living in communities near the Rose Garden Arena, the team's home.
Petroleos de Venezuela	As the only state-owned Venezuelan firm with an employee volunteer program, this energy corporation's goal for the program is to involve all workers, retirees, and their families as members of an organized and enthusiastic team, actively participating in volunteer activities and recognizing it for its contributions to the community.
Johnson Controls, Inc.	Focuses on community projects aligned with the company's mission of delivering quality indoor environments. For example, the company recently secured most of the funding to install heating, air conditioning, fire protection, security, and lighting controls in a new school in Milwaukee, Wisconsin, where the firm is headquartered.
Colgate-Palmolive Company	Sponsors an oral health education program that has reached 5 million children, and recruits volunteers to provide dental health services to children with Medicaid or no insurance.
Alibris	Since its inception in the late 1990s, social responsibility has been part of this California-based online supplier of rare and hard-to-find books. An employee volunteer program was written into the start-up's strategic plan and is utilized by 75 percent of employees. Most of its social responsibility efforts involve literacy and link back to the company's core mission.
LensCrafters	Created the Give the Gift of Sight program that has helped more than 2 million underprivileged people in the United States and in 25 developing countries. Employees work with the Lions Club International and other civic groups to collect and distribute glasses around the world.

Sources: "Awards for Excellence in Corporate Community Service," Points of Light Foundation, http://www.pointsoflight.org/awards/corporate.cfm#honorees, accessed August 19, 2003; "Progress Report," America's Promise, www.americaspromise. org/OurPartners/ViewCommitments.cfm, accessed December 6, 2000; "Give the Gift of Sight," LensCrafters, www.lenscrafters.com/gos.html, accessed August 15, 2003; Gret Mazurkiewicz, "HVAC Manufacturers Show Their Good Samaritan Side," *Air Conditioning, Heating & Refrigeration News,* February 7, 2000, p. 122.

cation or health care. Thus, as stakeholder needs and concerns change, the organization will need to adapt its community relations efforts. In order to determine key areas that require support and to refine the mission statement, a company should periodically conduct a community needs assessment like the one presented in Table 7.4.[68]

Responsibilities to the Community

It is important for a company to view community stakeholders in a trusting manner, recognizing the potential mutual benefit to each party. In a networked world,

TABLE 7.4	**Community Needs Assessment**

Please check yes or no for each of the following areas that may need support from business to improve quality of life in this community:

YES	NO	COMMUNITY ISSUES
❏	❏	Parks
❏	❏	Recreational facilities
❏	❏	Air quality
❏	❏	Pollution control
❏	❏	Water quality
❏	❏	Arts and cultural activities
❏	❏	Police and law enforcement
❏	❏	Drug enforcement
❏	❏	Gang control
❏	❏	Domestic violence
❏	❏	Child abuse
❏	❏	Traffic and safety
❏	❏	Fire department
❏	❏	Open spaces and planned use
❏	❏	Education
❏	❏	Affordable housing
❏	❏	Economic development
❏	❏	City planning for growth
❏	❏	Zoning
❏	❏	Beautification and landscaping
❏	❏	Health care and medical services
❏	❏	Volunteerism

much about a company can be learned with a few clicks of a mouse. Activists and disgruntled individuals have used web sites to publicize the questionable activities of some companies. McDonald's Corporation, like Wal-Mart, has been the target of numerous "hate" web sites that broadcast concerns about the company's products, pricing strategies, and marketing to children. Because of the visibility of business activities and the desire for strategic social responsibility, successful companies strive to build long-term mutually beneficial relationships with relevant communities. Achieving these relationships may involve some trial and error. Table 7.5 illustrates some of the common mistakes that organizations make in planning for and implementing community responsibilities. In contrast, Eli Lilly Pharmaceuticals, headquartered in Indianapolis, Indiana, is a strong supporter of the Indianapolis Symphony Orchestra. In return, the orchestra stages private concerts for Eli Lilly employees. Dell Computer has a similar relationship with the Round Rock Express, a minor-league (Texas League) baseball team. A community focus can be integrated with concerns for employees and consumers. Chapter 1 provided evidence that satisfied customers and employees are correlated with improved organizational performance.

TABLE 7.5	Ten Common Myths and Mistakes About Community Relations

WE WON'T NEED CONSENT OR SUPPORT FROM OUR LOCAL GOVERNMENT OFFICIALS OR LOCAL COMMUNITY.

Many organizations have learned the importance of community relations the hard way when they have tried to clean up sites; get permits; and site, expand and operate facilities. It is difficult to put a dollar value on community relations until negative relations threaten or jeopardize a company's goals or operations. Organizations often do not allocate sufficient resources to community relations until it is too late. Unresolved conflicts which result from inadequate communication or poor relations can result in ugly and expensive ramifications for companies including injunctions from localities, permit denials, delays in projects, negative press, cease and desist orders, law suits, new legislation, etc. Community relations is much more rewarding and well received than crisis management.

WE WILL BE STIRRING UP TROUBLE IF WE TALK TO THE COMMUNITY.

Many project managers are afraid to talk with the community because they are afraid that they will make things worse by stirring up issues that might not already exist. It generally works the opposite. In fact, they are usually flattered and disarmed (and maybe a tad suspicious) when organizations care enough to talk with them. If you have never initiated dialogue before, you can expect the first few times to be contentious as negative comments, complaints and fears are expressed. But if you are committed to establishing and maintaining good relations, you have the opportunity to turn those negative comments into positive, or at least neutral and balanced, ones. That is, if your organization's plans are solid. Proactive community relations efforts are very rewarding and can actually make your job much easier in the future. You can even establish yourself as a leader in the community.

WE CAN IMPROVE RELATIONS WITH ONE-WAY COMMUNICATIONS EFFORTS (WITHOUT INTERACTION WITH INTERESTED PARTIES).

If your company or facility is experiencing negative press or strained relations with the community, controlled one-way communication is not the answer. Human nature causes us to want to play it close to the chest. Productive (and perhaps facilitated) interaction is necessary to allow both parties to work through and resolve the issues. Many conflicts are caused by a lack of information, misinformation, different interpretations, stereotypes, repetitive negative behavior, a perception of different interests. Many of these conflicts can only be resolved through improved, effective communication and joint problem solving which can only occur through interaction and dialogue.

THE COMMUNITY CANNOT ADD ANYTHING MEANINGFUL TO THIS PROCESS BECAUSE IT IS TOO TECHNICALLY COMPLEX.

I am consistently amazed at the level of contribution communities have made to a number of very complex projects that we have been involved with. When given the opportunity and sufficient time to review technical information, it is amazing how much local residents can grasp and contribute to projects. Local involvement and buy-in on engineering projects may even reduce the liability of technical decisions in the future.

COMMUNITY LEADERS WILL REQUEST THE MOST UNREASONABLE OR COSTLY SOLUTIONS.

We usually approach issues based on the way we define them. As a community relations firm, we often find that the way our clients define community relations issues and the way the community defines them is quite different. We can't truly know how people will react until we talk with them. We often find that community leaders are sympathetic to companies and facilities in terms of the cost associated with regulatory compliances and environmental cleanup and are much more practical (e.g., when it comes to cleanup levels, etc.) than one might imagine.

(continued)

| TABLE 7.5 | **Ten Common Myths and Mistakes About Community Relations** *(continued)* |

WE SHOULDN'T TALK TO THE COMMUNITY UNTIL WE HAVE ALL THE ANSWERS.

Actually, you gain more credibility by being open enough to allow the community to be involved throughout the process. There is a comfort in knowing all the layers, steps, models, assumptions, and coordination that organizations are undertaking to develop and implement cleanup and other engineering projects. The more the community knows about this effort the more credible the information will be.

CONSULTING WITH ELECTED OFFICIALS IS ENOUGH COMMUNITY RELATIONS.

The old-fashioned public affairs approach focused on covering your bases with the media and with elected officials. The truth is that elected officials and the media usually tend to their constituents when issues stir up. Your efforts are better spent on improving relations with the local community. This is not to suggest that you shouldn't have relations with the local media and elected officials, but be careful of relying too heavily (or exclusively) on them when an issue escalates.

IF OUR RELATIONS ARE CURRENTLY STRAINED, WE WILL MAKE RELATIONS WORSE BY COMMUNICATING WITH THE COMMUNITY NOW.

The first step is to find out why relations are strained (which may require an independent reliable source to uncover). If your intentions are sound and mutually beneficial in some way, how can communication make relations worse? How can relationships get better if you don't communicate?

IT WILL BE EASIER TO IMPLEMENT OUR PROJECT WITHOUT COMMUNITY RELATIONS.

Reactive communication efforts resulting from unexpected community concern or media interest always seem to cause more upheaval, require more time and money, and are more disruptive to my clients than planned communication efforts.

WE NEED TO DO A BETTER JOB COMMUNICATING THE TECHNICAL ISSUES.

Don't underestimate the value of the trust and credibility factors that are less technically based: caring and empathy, commitment, openness and honesty. Messages that communicate these are much more powerful in relations building than technical knowledge.

Source: "10 Common Myths About Community Relations," Chaloux Environmental Communications, Inc., www.ce-com.com/10commonmyths.htm, accessed November 12, 2003. ©2000 Chaloux Environmental Communications, Inc. All Rights Reserved.

Economic Issues

From an economic perspective, business is absolutely vital to a community. Companies play a major role in community economic development by bringing jobs to the community and allowing employees to support themselves and their families. These companies also buy supplies, raw materials, utilities, advertising services, and other goods and services from area firms; this in turn produces more economic effects. In communities with few employers, an organization that expands in or moves to the area can reduce some of the burden on community services and other subsidized support. Even in large cities with many employers, some companies choose to address social problems that tax the community. In California, for example, a coalition of insurance companies has invested more than $40 million in affordable housing projects throughout the state. By increasing the capital available for low-income housing, the coalition aims to help satisfy the state's escalating demand for affordable housing.[69] In countries with developing economies, a business or industry can also provide many benefits. A new company brings not only jobs but also new technology, related businesses, improvements to infrastructure, and other positive factors. Conversely, the "McDonaldization" of developing countries is a common criticism regarding the effects of U.S. businesses on other parts of the world. For example, although Coca-Cola has been criticized for selling sugared water and exploiting consumers in developing countries, the firm's market expansion strategy often involves creating a network of distributors that improves both employment and entrepreneurship opportunities in a given area.[70]

Interactions with suppliers and other vendors also stimulate the economy. Some companies are even dedicated to finding local or regional business partners in an effort to enhance their economic responsibility. For example, the VisionLand Theme Park, located near Birmingham, Alabama, relies on local vendors for all of its food products and services. The theme park's food service equipment and restaurant design was contracted to a Birmingham company, and park guests enjoy hot dogs manufactured by Bryan, a food marketer with a southern heritage.[71] Furthermore, there is often a contagion effect when one business moves into an area: By virtue of its prestige or business relationships, such a move can signal to other firms that the area is a viable and attractive place for others to locate. In the United States, there are parts of the country that are highly concentrated with automotive manufacturing, financial services, or technology. Local chambers of commerce and economic development organizations often entice new firms to a region because of the positive reputation and economic contagion it brings. Finally, business contributions to local health, education, and recreation projects not only benefit local residents and employees but also may bring additional revenue into the community from tourism and other businesses that appreciate the region's quality of life. John Deere, for example, sponsors the John Deere Classic golf tournament and contributed to the Quad Cities Graduate Studies Center and the John Deere Commons Project, a multiuse development on the Mississippi River.[72]

Just as a business brings positive economic effects by expanding in or relocating to an area, it can also cause financial repercussions when it exits a particular market or geographic location. Thus, workforce reduction, or downsizing—a topic that we will revisit in Chapter 8—is a key issue with respect to economic responsibility. The impact of layoffs due to plant closings and corporate restructuring often extends well beyond the financial well-being of affected employees. Laid-off employees typically limit their spending to basic necessities while they look for new employment, and many may ultimately leave the area altogether. Even employees who retain their jobs in such a downsizing may suffer from poor morale, distrust, guilt, and continued anxiety over their own job security, further stifling spending in a community.

Because companies have such a profound impact on the economic viability of the communities in which they operate, firms that value social responsibility consider both the short- and long-term effects on the community of changes in their workforce. Today, many companies that must reduce their workforce—regardless of the reasons why—strive to give both employees and the community advance notice and offer placement services to help the community absorb those employees who lose their jobs. For example, when Service Merchandise Co. closed 150 stores and laid off more than 10,000 employees, the company offered those employees placement services that included coaching on interviewing and resume writing and lists of other job opportunities available in the area.[73] Other companies may choose to offer extra compensation commensurate with an employee's length of employment that gives laid-off employees a financial cushion while they find new work.

Legal Issues

In order to do business, a company must be granted a "license to operate." For many firms, a series of legal and regulatory matters must be resolved before the first employee is hired or the first customer served. If you open a restaurant, for example, most states require a business license and sales tax number. These documents require basic information, such as business type, ownership structure, owner information, number of expected employees, and other data.

On a fundamental level, society has the ability to dictate what types of organizations are allowed to operate. In exchange for the license to operate, organizations are expected to uphold all legal obligations and standards. We have discussed many of these laws throughout this book, although individual cities, counties, and municipalities will have additional laws and regulations that firms must obey. For example, the city of Baltimore, Maryland, enacted an ordinance that requires companies with municipal contracts to pay their employees a "living wage" to keep them above the area's poverty level. Today, over ninety cities and counties, including Los Angeles, Chicago, Detroit, and San Francisco, have passed similar laws. Critics of these ordinances believe living wages, because they exceed the federal minimum wage, harm communities through job losses and other negative effects. However, recent studies comparing cities with and without living-wage laws found no significant differences in job losses, tax rates, and corporate defections.[74]

Other communities have concerns about whether and how businesses fit into existing communities, especially those threatened by urban sprawl and small towns working to preserve a traditional way of life. Some states, cities, and counties have enacted legislation that limits the square footage of stores in an effort to deter "big-box stores," such as Wal-Mart and Home Depot, unless local voters specifically approve their being allowed to build. In most cases, these communities have called for such legislation to combat the noise and traffic congestion that may be associated with such stores, to protect neighborhoods, and to preserve the viability of local small businesses.[75] Thus, although living wages and store location may be ethical issues for business, some local governments have chosen to move them into the legal realm.

Ethical Issues

As more companies view themselves as responsible to the community, they will contemplate their role and the impact of their decisions on communities from an ethical perspective. Consider Clyde Oatis, who is renovating an abandoned rice mill in Houston's Fifth Ward to house a business that he hopes will address both environmental and economic issues in the low-income neighborhood. Oatis's U.S. Custom Feed will process food waste once destined for landfills into nutritious food pellets customized for the needs of different species of animals. The company will also employ and pay a living wage to workers in an area that desperately needs the jobs. Says Oatis, "You've got to have some social responsibility. . . . I think I should do my part."[76]

Business leaders are increasingly recognizing the significance of the role their firms play in the community and the need for their leadership in tackling community problems. Pizza Corner India, a pizza restaurant chain headquartered in Chennai, India, was founded with the vision of giving back to the community what the consumers' patronage and loyalty had brought to the firm's success. Since its primary target market is children, Pizza Corner decided to focus its community efforts on enhancing the status and welfare of underprivileged Indian children. One innovative program secured bank deposits of roughly $4,000, each designated for twenty street children in the city of Bangalore. Another initiative created the Citizen of the Year Awards, most of which are granted to citizens whose work benefited children. Although Pizza Corner India competes against global giants like Domino's and Pizza Hut, the company is financially successful and recently announced plans to grow to 100 outlets.[77]

These examples demonstrate that the ethical dimension of community responsibility can be multifaceted. This dimension and related programs are not legally mandated, but emanate from the particular philosophy of a company and its top managers. For example, since many cities have not mandated a living wage, Clyde Oatis's actions in Houston are based on an ethical obligation that he feels to employees and the community. There are many ways that a company can demonstrate its ethical commitment to the community. We examine many of these issues, such as effects on the natural environment. As the Pizza Corner example illustrates, a common extension of "doing the right thing" ethically is for companies to begin to allocate funds and other resources to assist community groups and others in need.

Pizza Corner India believes in giving back to the communities it serves. Most of its philanthropic programs benefit children. (www.pizzacorner.com/storelocator/bangalore.htm, downloaded April 2003. Copyright © 2003 by Pizza Corner India (P) Ltd. Reprinted with permission.)

MENU

STORE LOCATOR

ABOUT US

CAREERS

FRANCHISE ENQUIRY

HISTORY OF PIZZA

RESOURCES

DOWNLOAD

WHAT'S HOT

BACK

Name : Domlur Store
Category : Delivery Restaurant
Services offered : Take Away, Delivery
Street : 721, Airport Road, Domlur
City : Bangalore
Code : 560 071
Phone : 091 80 344 6111

Name : Koramangala Restaurant
Category : Medium Restaurant
Services offered : Dine In, Take Away, Delivery
Street : 121, Money Estate, Koramangala Industrial Layout City
City : Bangalore
Code : 560 034
Phone : 091 80 344 6111

Name : Brigade Road Store
Category : Super Restaurant
Services offered : Dine In, Take Away, Delivery
Street : 185, 1st floor Brigade Road
City : Bangalore
Code : 560 001
Phone : 091 80 344 6111

Philanthropic Issues

The community relations function has always been associated with philanthropy, as one of the main historical roles of community relations was to provide gifts, grants, and other resources to worthy causes. Today, that thinking has shifted. Although businesses have the potential to help solve social issues, the success of a business can be enhanced from the publicity generated by and through stakeholder acceptance of community activities. For example, Colorado-based New Belgium Brewing Company donates $1 for every barrel of beer brewed the prior year to charities within the markets it serves. The brewery tries to divide the funds among states in proportion to interests and needs, considering environmental, social, drug and alcohol awareness, and cultural issues. Donation decisions are made by the firm's philanthropy committee, which is a volunteer group of diverse employees and one or two of the owners; employees are encouraged to bring philanthropy suggestions to the committee.[78] However, New Belgium belongs to an industry that some members of society believe contributes to social problems. Thus, regardless of the positive contributions such a firm makes to the community, some members will always have a negative view of the business.

One of the most significant ways that organizations are exercising their philanthropic responsibilities is through volunteer programs. **Volunteerism** in the workplace, when employees spend company-supported time in support of social causes, has been increasing among companies of all sizes. The number of companies with memberships on volunteer councils has increased from 600 in the mid-1980s to more than 1,500. Benefits of volunteering accrue to both the individual, in terms of greater motivation, enjoyment, and satisfaction, and to the organization through employee retention and productivity increases.[79] Communities benefit from the application of new skills and initiative toward problems, better relations with business, a greater supply of volunteers, assistance to stretch limited resources, and social and economic regeneration.[80]

In the mid-1990s, Americans spent nearly 15.7 million hours supporting formal volunteer activities. At Toyota, for example, the Volunteers in Place (VIP) program offers incentives to encourage employees to volunteer at least thirty hours per year. The top volunteers win recognition and additional cash contributions to the charity of their choice. A spokesperson for Toyota Motor Manufacturing states, "Employee morale, productivity, and turnover have all improved since the VIP program was implemented four years ago."[81] IBM contributes $1,500 to the charity of any employee who donates more than 100 hours of volunteer time to a community school each year.[82]

There are several considerations in deciding how to structure a volunteer program. Attention must be paid to employee values and beliefs; therefore, political or religious organizations should be supported on the basis of individual employee initiative and interest. Warner Brothers, the motion picture company, allows its employees to select from a menu outlining volunteer opportunities. One very successful program for Time Warner Communications is Time to Read, which pairs tutors with children throughout the company's 300 sites.[83] Another issue is what to do when some employees do not wish to volunteer. If the company is not paying for the employees' time to volunteer, and volunteering is not a condition of employment or an aspect of the job description, it may be difficult to convince a certain percentage of

volunteerism
the time companies urge employees to volunteer to social causes

the workforce to participate. If the organization is paying for one day a month, for example, to allow the employee exposure to volunteerism, then individual compliance is usually expected.

Strategic Implementation of Responsibilities to Consumers and the Community

As this chapter has demonstrated, social responsibility entails relationships with many stakeholders—including consumers and the community—and many firms are finding creative ways to meet these responsibilities. Although consumers are commonly recognized as key stakeholders, the inclusion of community views and beliefs into corporate planning is a more recent and progressive phenomenon. Just as in other aspects of social responsibility, these relationships must be managed, nurtured, and continuously assessed. Resources devoted to this effort may include programs for educating and listening to consumers, surveys to discover strengths and weaknesses in stakeholder relationships, hiring consumer affairs professionals, the development of a community relations office, and other initiatives. Understanding stakeholder issues can be especially complex in the global environment. For example, a group of 150 Nigerian women led a peaceful protest that shut down most of ChevronTexaco's Nigerian oil operations for a week. These women, who live in the Niger Delta, are among the poorest in Nigeria although they live on oil-rich land. The women demanded that ChevronTexaco hire their sons and provide electricity in their villages. The company viewed the women's complaints as unjustified and pointed to its local hires and contributions to development projects in the area. Because the government has failed to develop good roads, schools, and utility systems in the area, these activists turned to a multinational corporation for some resolution.[84]

The utility industry represents an interesting case study in its resource investments and relationships with both consumers and the community. There is much public interest in issues related to utility prices, environmental impact, plant closures, plant location, and more. In the late 1980s and early 1990s, larger utilities held "town hall" meetings and other sessions to obtain stakeholder views and feedback. This approach, along with sophisticated and directed programs, is making a comeback. Kansas City Power & Light (KCPL), for example, held an open house that attracted more than 1,000 people. Employees of KCPL served as babysitters while parents learned more about electric and magnetic fields and other emerging topics. The open house not only addressed the information needs of customers but also provided for their family needs by utilizing employee time and talent.[85] KCPL understands the importance of integrating all stakeholders in its social responsibility effort, including employees, as we will discover in the next chapter.

Summary

Companies face complex decisions about how to respond to the expectations, attitudes, and buying patterns of consumers, those individuals who purchase, use, and dispose of products for personal and household use. Consumers are primary stakeholders because their awareness, purchase, use, and repurchase of products are vital to a company's existence.

Consumers and businesses are fundamentally connected by an economic relationship. Economic responsibilities include following through on promises made in the exchange process. Consumer fraud involves intentional deception to derive an unfair economic advantage over an organization. If consumers believe that a firm has not fulfilled its economic responsibility, they may ask for a refund, tell others about the bad experience, discontinue their patronage, contact a consumer agency, or seek legal redress.

In the United States, legal issues with respect to consumers fall under the jurisdiction of the Federal Trade Commission (FTC), which enforces federal antitrust and consumer protection laws. Other federal and state regulatory agencies regulate specific goods, services, or business practices. Among the issues that may have been addressed through specific state or federal laws and regulations are consumer health and safety, credit and ownership, marketing and advertising, sales and warranties, and product liability. Product liability refers to a business's legal responsibility for the performance of its products. Concerns about protecting consumers' legal rights are not limited to the United States.

Ethical issues related to consumers include the rights enumerated by President Kennedy. Consumerism refers to the movement to protect consumers from an imbalance of power with business and to maximize consumer welfare in the marketplace. Some specific elements of consumer rights have been mandated by law, but the relatively broad nature of the rights means they must be interpreted and implemented on a company-by-company basis. Consumer rights have evolved to include the right to choose, the right to safety, the right to be informed, the right to be heard, the right to seek redress, and the right to privacy. When consumers believe a firm is operating outside ethical or legal standards, they may be motivated to take action, including boycotting—abstaining from using, purchasing, or dealing with an organization.

More firms are investigating ways to link their philanthropic efforts with consumer interests. From a strategic perspective, a firm's ability to link consumer interests to philanthropy should lead to stronger economic relationships.

The community—those members of society who are aware, concerned, or in some way affected by the operations and output of the organization—does not always receive the same level of acceptance as other stakeholder groups. Community relations are the organizational function dedicated to building and maintaining relationships and trust with the community. In order to determine the key areas that require support and to refine the mission statement, a company should periodically conduct a community needs assessment.

Companies play a major role in community economic development by bringing jobs to the community, interacting with other businesses, and making contributions to local health, education, and recreation projects that benefit local residents and employees. When a company leaves an area, financial repercussions may be devastating. Because they have such a profound impact on the economic viability of their communities, firms that value social responsibility consider both the short- and long-term effects of changes in their workforce on the community.

For many firms, a series of legal and regulatory matters must be resolved before launching a business. On a basic level, society has the ability to dictate what types of organizations are allowed to operate. As more companies view themselves as responsible to the community, they consider their role and the impact of their decisions on communities from an ethical perspective.

The success of a business can be enhanced from the publicity generated by and through stakeholder acceptance of community activities. One way that organizations are exercising their philanthropic responsibilities is through volunteerism, the donation of employee time by companies in support of social causes. In structuring volunteer programs, attention must be paid to employee values and beliefs.

Many companies are finding creative ways to satisfy their responsibilities to consumers and the community. These relationships must be managed, nurtured, and continuously assessed. Resources devoted to this effort may include programs for educating and listening to consumers, surveys to discover strengths and weaknesses in stakeholder relationships, hiring consumer affairs professionals, the development of a community relations office, and other initiatives.

Key Terms

consumers (p. 193)
consumer fraud (p. 194)
product liability (p. 202)
consumerism (p. 204)
boycott (p. 208)
community (p. 211)
neighbor of choice (p. 211)
community relations (p. 213)
volunteerism (p. 221)

Discussion Questions

1. List and describe the consumer rights that have become social expectations of business. Why have some of these rights been formalized through legislation? Should these rights be considered ethical standards?
2. Review Delta's Twelve-Point Plan for customer service in Figure 7.3. Create a chart to link each of the twelve points to a specific economic, legal, ethical, or philanthropic responsibility that Delta has to its customers.
3. What is the purpose of a boycott? Describe the characteristics of companies and consumers that are likely to be involved in a boycott situation. What circumstances would cause you to consider participating in a boycott?
4. Define community as a business stakeholder. Is it better to define community in a narrow or broad fashion? Explain.
5. Why would an organization want to develop an employee volunteer program? Explain the costs and benefits associated with this type of program. How would a volunteer program affect your interest in a potential employer?

Experiential Exercise

Visit the web site of IdealsWork (http://www.ideals work.com/). What is the purpose of this web site? Use the site's "Compare brands in any category" feature to examine companies in a particular industry for ratings on various social responsibility issues. Using the basic form, choose five issues on which to evaluate the companies. Print out at least one page of the ratings results and then examine the detail for a few company ratings. How useful is this information to you? What information could a business derive from this site to improve its reputation for social responsibility?

What Would You Do?

Justin Thompson was excited. He really enjoyed his job at the Kingston's department store downtown. This location housed Kingston's first store and still had many of its original features. As he rode the subway into the city center, Justin thought about the money he would earn this summer and the great car he hoped to buy before school started. He was lucky to have secured this type of job, since many of his friends were working early or late hours at fast-food chains or out in the summer heat. The management team at Kingston's had initiated a program with his high school counselors, hoping to attract top high school seniors into retail management throughout their college career and beyond. Justin was a strong student from a single-parent background, and his counselor was highly complimentary of his work ethic and prospects for professional employment.

Justin's first week was consumed with various training sessions. There were eight students in the special high school program. They watched a company video that discussed Kingston's history, current operations, and customer service philosophy. They met with staff from Human Resources to fill out paperwork. They learned how to scan merchandise and operate the computer software and cash register. They toured the store's three levels and visited with each department manager. Justin was especially excited about working in the electronics department, but he was assigned to men's clothing.

Justin worked alongside several employees during the first few weeks on the store floor. He watched the experienced employees approach customers, help them, and ring up the sale. He noticed that some employees took personal telephone calls and that others did not clean up the dressing rooms or restock items very quickly. On slower days, he eventually worked alone in the department. Several times when he came to work in the afternoon, he had to clean up the mess left behind by the morning shift. When he spoke to various colleagues about it in the break room, they told him it was best to keep quiet. After all, he was a high school student earning money for a car, not a "real employee" with kids to feed and bills to pay. Justin assumed that retail work was much like team projects in school—not everyone pulled their weight but it was hard to be the tattletale.

One Saturday morning was extremely busy, as Kingston's was running a big sale. People were swarming to the sales racks and Justin was amazed at how fast the time was passing. In the late afternoon, several friends of one of his coworkers dropped by the men's section. Before long, their hands were full with merchandise. The crowd was starting to wane, so Justin took a few minutes to clean up the dressing room. When he came out of the dressing room, his coworker was ringing up the friends' merchandise. Justin saw two ties go into the bag, but only one was scanned into the system. He saw an extra discount provided on an expensive shirt. Justin was shocked to see that not every item was scanned or that improper discounts were applied, and his mind was racing. Should he stop his coworker? Should he "take a break" and get security? Was there another alternative? What would you do?

Chapter 8

Employee Relations

CHAPTER OBJECTIVES

- To discuss employees as stakeholders
- To examine the economic, legal, ethical, and philanthropic responsibilities related to employees
- To describe an employer of choice and the employer of choice's relationship to social responsibility

CHAPTER OUTLINE

Employee Stakeholders

Responsibilities to Employees

Strategic Implementation of Responsibilities to Employees

For the employees of SAS Institute, the world's largest private software company, the workplace resembles a modern-day utopia. Although the North Carolina company competes with Silicon Valley firms, its workplace bears little resemblance to the fast-paced and demanding atmosphere that often characterizes other high-tech firms. James Goodnight, SAS's founder, believes that dinnertime should be spent with family and friends, not in the office. Most employees leave by 5:00 P.M. and others participate in flextime or job-sharing arrangements that allow for work/life balance. Other perks, such as on-site day care and a health center staffed with dentists and physicians, also contribute to the company's high ranking on *Fortune* magazine's annual list of the 100 Best Companies to Work For. For over a decade, the company has also been named to *Working Mother* magazine's 100 Best Companies for Working Mothers.

Beyond these perks, piano melodies entertain employees at lunch, which many of them share with their children. Meals are subsidized, so employees rarely spend more than $3 for lunch. Take-out dinners are also available. Shiatsu, Swedish, and deep-tissue massages are available on-site, as is a 55,000-square-foot athletic facility supporting yoga, tennis, walking, golf, Frisbee, and a host of other sports. Once an employee has finished exercising, gym clothes are laundered and returned the next day. Other timesaving benefits, such as free car washes and a farmers' market on the SAS campus, are available. Ergonomically designed work spaces ensure employees are inspired and physically comfortable in their daily tasks.

Cynics may question the lengthy list of unusual benefits that SAS provides its employees. A key concern is the link between the expenditures for these perks and the private firm's performance. For example, annual employee turnover rate is 4 percent, compared to a 20 percent rate in the computer software industry as a whole. In 1999, SAS's sales grew 17 percent, reaching more than $1 billion. Employees earned $16 million in bonuses and $30 million in profit sharing in that same year. Even in the tumultuous year of 2001, SAS posted sales of $1.13 billion, continued its aggressive research and development efforts, and nearly doubled its sales force.

Although many firms say they are dedicated to providing work/life balance for their employees, SAS's efforts led one employee to say, "We're spoiled rotten." When Goodnight founded SAS, he vowed to create a work atmosphere in stark contrast to that of his first employer, NASA. He believes that treating people as if they make a difference will foster employee loyalty, performance, and innovation. Like employees, clients and business partners, who include 90 percent of the *Fortune* 100 companies, experience low-pressure and cooperative tactics that inspire mutual goals and commitment. Thus, the social responsibility philosophy that began with Goodnight's vision has a major focus on employees and extends to a variety of stakeholders.[1]

This vignette illustrates the extent to which some firms consider the needs, wants, and characteristics of employees in designing various business processes and practices. Although proponents of both the input-output and stakeholder models presented in Chapter 2 recognize the importance of employees, beliefs about the extent and types of responsibilities that organizations should assume toward employees are likely to vary. For example, the input-output model is more consistent with the economic and legal responsibilities, whereas the stakeholder model entails a broader perspective. As this chapter will show, a delicate balance of power, responsibility, and accountability resides in the relationships a company develops with its employees.

Because employee stakeholders are so important to the success of any company, this chapter is devoted to the employer-employee relationship. We explore the many issues related to the social responsibilities employers have to their employees, including the employee-employer contract, workforce reduction, wages and benefits, labor unions, health and safety, equal opportunity, sexual harassment, whistle-blowing, diversity, and work/life balance. Along the way, we discuss a number of significant laws that affect companies' human resources programs. Finally, we look at the concept of employer of choice and what it takes to earn that designation.

Employee Stakeholders

Think for a minute about the first job or volunteer position you held. What information were you given about the organization's strategic direction? How were you managed and treated by supervisors? Did you feel empowered to make decisions? How much training did you receive? The answers to these questions may reveal the types of responsibilities that employers have toward employees. If you worked in a restaurant, for example, training should have covered safety, cleanliness, and other health issues that are mandated by law. If you volunteered at a hospital, you may have learned about the ethical and economic considerations in providing health care for the uninsured or poor and the philanthropic efforts used to support the hospital financially. Although such issues may have seemed subtle or even unimportant at the time, they are related to the responsibilities that employees, government, and other stakeholders expect of employing organizations.

Responsibilities to Employees

In her book, *The Working Life: The Promise and Betrayal of Modern Work*, the business professor Joanne B. Ciulla writes about the different types of work, the history of work, the value of work to a person's self-concept, the relationship between work and

Teens work in all kinds of businesses to earn extra spending money, help support their families, and save for college. (David Young Wolff/PhotoEdit)

freedom, and, as the title implies, the rewards and pitfalls that exist in the employee-employer relationship. Ciulla contends that two common phrases, "Get a job!" and "Get a life!" are antithetical in today's society, meaning they seem to be diametrically opposed goals or values.[2] For the ancient Greeks, work was seen as the gods' way of punishing humans. Centuries later, Benedictine monks, who built farms, church abbeys, and villages, were considered the lowest order of monks because they labored. By the eighteenth century, the Protestant work ethic had emerged to imply that work was a method for discovering and creating a person.[3] Today, psychologists, families, and friends lament how work has become the primary source of many individuals' fulfillment, status, and happiness. Just as in the complicated history of work, the responsibilities, obligations, and expectations between employees and employers are also fraught with challenges and debates. In this section, we review the four levels of corporate social responsibilities as they relate to employees. Although we focus primarily on the responsibilities of employers to employees, we also acknowledge the role that employees have in achieving strategic social responsibility.

Economic

Perhaps no story in recent memory underscores the economic realm of employment more vividly than the saga of Malden Mills Industries. In 1995, 750,000 square feet of factory and office space at Malden Mills burned to the ground. It was just a few weeks before the winter holidays, and in addition, workers were injured. In an unusual move, CEO Aaron Feuerstein paid end-of-year bonuses and employees' full wages and benefits while the buildings were reconstructed. Human resource managers set up a temporary job-training center, collected Christmas gifts for employees' children, and worked with community agencies to support employees and their families.[4] Even after injured employees filed a workers' compensation claim against Malden Mills, Feuerstein said, "The welfare of our employees has always been and continues to be a priority of Malden Mills."[5] When economic factors forced Malden Mills through several employee layoffs in the late 1990s, employees were offered jobs at another plant and received career transition assistance. Essentially, Feuerstein believes in an unwritten contract that considers the economic prospects of both employer and employees. Several years later, Malden Mills filed for bankruptcy protection, part of which was blamed on losses from the fire. Lenders provided funding for the company to continue operations and develop a reorganization strategy to emerge from bankruptcy. The company emerged from bankruptcy, but the plan took the CEO's responsibility from Feuerstein and placed it with lenders and creditors. Feuerstein vowed to fight the plan, citing concerns about the future of his employees.[6]

Employee-Employer Contract As we discussed in Chapter 1, the recent history of social responsibility has brought many changes to bear on stakeholder relationships. One of the more dramatic shifts has been in the "contract" that exists between employee and employer. At the beginning of the twenty-first century, many companies had to learn and accept new rules for recruiting, retaining, and compensating employees. For example, although employers held the position of power for many years, the new century brought record employment rates and the tightest job market in years. Huge salaries, signing bonuses, multiple offers, and flexible, not seniority-based, compensation plans became commonplace throughout the late 1990s. The economic downturn, September 11, 2001 attacks, and series of business scandals in the early 2000s brought a sharp halt to lucrative employment opportunities and forced many firms to implement layoffs and other cost-cutting measures. Pay raises, health care benefits, mental health coverage, retirement funding, paid maternity leave, and other employee benefits were sharply reduced.[7]

psychological contract
the beliefs, perceptions, expectations, and obligations that make up the agreement between individuals and the organizations that employ them

Regardless of salary, perks, and specific position, a **psychological contract** exists between an employee and his or her employer. This contract is largely unwritten and includes the beliefs, perceptions, expectations, and obligations that make up the agreement between individuals and the organizations that employ them.[8] Details of the contract develop through interactions with managers and coworkers and through perceptions of the corporate culture.[9] This contract, though informal, has a significant influence on the way employees act. When promises and expectations are not met, a psychological contract breach occurs, and employees may become less loyal, less trusting, inattentive to work, or otherwise dissatisfied with their employment situation.[10] On the other hand, when employers present information in a credible, competent, and trustworthy manner, employees are more likely to be supportive of and committed to the organization. This commitment is revealed through employee interactions with important stakeholders and ultimately has a positive influence on shareholder value, as we discussed in Chapter 1.[11] Just as in other stakeholder relationships, expectations in the employment psychological contract are subject to a variety of influences. This section discusses how the contract has evolved over the last 100 years. Table 8.1 profiles six characteristics that have evolved over time in employees' psychological contract with employers.

Until the early 1900s, the relationship between employer and employee was best characterized as a master-servant relationship.[12] In this view, there was a natural imbalance in power that meant employment was viewed as a privilege that included few rights and many obligations. Employees were expected to work for the best interests of the organization, even at the expense of personal and family welfare. At this time, most psychologists and management scholars believed that good leadership required aggressive and domineering behavior.[13] Images from Upton Sinclair's novel, *The Jungle,* which we discussed briefly in Chapter 7, characterized the extreme negative effects of this employment contract.[14]

TABLE 8.1   Changes in Employees' Psychological Contract with Employers

CHARACTERISTIC	OLD	NEW
Attachment to employer	Long-term	Near-term
Readiness to change jobs	Not interested	Not looking, but will listen
Priorities on the job	Company and its goals	Personal life and career
Devotion to employer goals	Follows orders	Usually buys in
Effort on the job	100 percent	110 percent
Motto	Semper fidelis "Always faithful"	Carpe diem "Seize the day"

Source: Jennifer Laabs, "The New Loyalty: Grasp It, Earn It, Keep It," *Workforce* 77 (November 1998): 34–39.

In the 1920s and 1930s, employees assumed a relationship with an employer that was more balanced in terms of power, responsibilities, and obligations. This shift meant that employees and employers were coequals, and in legal terms, employees had many more rights than under the master-servant model.[15] Much of the employment law in the United States was enacted in the 1930s, when legislators passed laws related to child labor, wages, working hours, and labor unions.[16] Throughout the twentieth century, the employee-employer contract evolved along the coequals model, although social critics began to question the influence large companies had on employees.

In the 1950s, the political commentator and sociologist C. Wright Mills criticized white-collar work as draining on employees' time, energy, and even personalities. He also believed that those individuals with business power were apt to keep employees happy in an attempt to ward off the development of stronger labor unions and unfavorable government regulations.[17] A few years later, the classic book *The Organization Man* by William H. Whyte was published. This book examined the social nature of work, including the inherent conflict between belonging and contributing to a group on the job while maintaining a sense of independence and identity.[18] Organizational researchers and managers in the 1960s began to question authoritarian behavior and consider participatory management styles that assumed employees were motivated and eager to assume responsibility for work. A study by the U.S. Department of Health, Education, and Welfare in the early 1970s confirmed that employees wanted interesting work and a chance to demonstrate their skills. The report also recommended job redesign and managerial approaches that increased participation, freedom, and democracy at work.[19] By the 1980s, a family analogy was being used to describe the workplace. This implied strong attention to employee welfare and prompted the focus on business ethics that we explored in Chapters 4 and 5. At the same time, corporate mission statements touted the importance of customers and employees, and *In Search of Excellence,* a best-selling book by the distinguished professor Thomas J. Peters and the business consultant Robert H. Waterman, Jr., profiled companies with strong corporate cultures that inspired employees toward better work, products, and customer satisfaction.[20] The total quality management (TQM) movement increased empowerment and teamwork on the job throughout the 1990s and led the charge toward workplaces simultaneously devoted to employee achievement at work and home.[21]

Although there were many positive initiatives for employees in the 1990s, the confluence of economic progress with demands for global competitiveness convinced many executives of the need for cost cutting. For individuals accustomed to messages about the importance of employees to organizational success, workforce reduction was both unexpected and traumatic. These experiences effectively ended the loyalty- and commitment-based contract that employees had developed with employers. A study of Generation X employees showed that their greatest psychological need in the workplace is security but that they viewed many employers as "terminators."[22]

Workforce Reduction[23]   At different points in a company's history there are likely to be factors that beg the question, "What can we do to decrease our overall costs?" In a highly competitive business environment, where new companies, customers, and products emerge and disappear every day, there is a continuous push for greater organizational efficiency and effectiveness. This pressure often leads to difficult decisions, including ones that require careful balance and consideration for the short-run survival and long-term vision of the company. This situation can create the need for **workforce reduction,** the process of eliminating employment positions. This process places considerable pressure on top management, causes speculation and tension among employees, and raises public ire about the role of business in society.[24]

workforce reduction the process of eliminating employment positions

There are several strategies that companies use to reduce overall costs and expenditures. For example, organizations may choose to reduce the number of employees, simplify products and processes, decrease quality and promises in service delivery, or develop some other mechanism for eliminating resources or nonperforming assets. Managers may find it difficult to communicate about cost reductions, as this message carries both emotional and social risk. Employees may wonder, "What value do I bring to the company?" and "Does anyone really care about my years of service?" Customers may inquire, "Can we expect the same level of service and product quality?" Governments and the community may ask, "Is this really necessary? How will it affect our economy?" For all of these questions, company leadership must have a clear answer. This response should be based on a thorough analysis of costs within the organizational system and how any changes are likely to affect business processes and outcomes.

In the last two decades, many firms chose to adopt the strategy that also creates the most anxiety and criticism—the reduction of the workforce. Throughout the 1990s, the numbers were staggering, as Sears eliminated 50,000 jobs, Kodak terminated nearly 17,000 people, and IBM laid off 63,000 employees. The scandals in the early 2000s also created a wave of layoffs. These actions effectively signaled the "end of the old contract" that employees had with employers.[25] This strategy, sometimes called "downsizing" or "rightsizing," usually entails employee layoffs and terminations. In other cases, a company freezes new hiring, hopes for natural workforce attrition, offers incentives for early retirement, or encourages job sharing among existing employees. With a reduction strategy, the reality is that some employees will lose their current positions one way or another. Thus, although workforce reduction may be the strategy chosen to control and reduce costs, it may have profound implications for the welfare of employees, their families, and the economic prospects of a geographic region and other constituents, as well as for the corporation itself.

As with other aspects of business, it is difficult to separate financial considerations for costs from other obligations and expectations that develop between a company and its stakeholders. Depending on a firm's resource base and current financial situation, the psychological contract that exists between an employer and employee is likely to be broken through layoffs, and the social contract between employers, communities, and other groups may also be threatened. Downsizing makes the private relationship between employee and employer a public issue that affects many stakeholders and subsequently draws heavy criticism.[26]

The impact of the workforce reduction process depends on a host of factors, including corporate culture, long-term plans, and creative calculations on both quantitative and qualitative aspects of the workplace. Because few human resource directors and other managers have extensive experience in restructuring the workforce, there are several issues to consider before embarking on the process.[27] First, a comprehensive plan must be developed that takes into account the financial implications and qualitative and emotional toll of the reduction strategy. This plan may include a systematic analysis of workflow so that management understands how tasks are currently completed and how they will be completed after restructuring. Second, the organization should commit to assisting employees who must make a career transition as a result of the reduction process. To make the transition productive for employees, this assistance should begin as soon as management is aware of possible reductions. Through the Worker Adjustment and Retraining Notification Act (WARN), U.S. employers are required to give at least sixty days' advance notice if a layoff will affect fifty or more workers or more than one-third of the workforce. Offering career assistance is beneficial over the long term, as it demonstrates a firm's commitment to social responsibility.

External factors also play a role in how quickly employees find new work and affect perceptions of a firm's decision to downsize. When the Opryland Hotel in Nashville, Tennessee, laid off 160 employees, other hotels in the area quickly hired them. With the unemployment rate in Nashville below 2.7 percent at the time, the other hotels appreciated the service training and competency of the former Opryland employees.[28] Thus, the Opryland Hotel probably did not suffer the types of reputation problems that other firms may have experienced in less favorable labor markets. Individuals who are reemployed quickly, whether through company efforts or market circumstances, experience fewer negative economic and emotional repercussions.[29]

Companies must be willing to accept the consequences of terminating employees. Although workforce reduction can improve a firm's financial performance, especially in the short run, there are costs to consider, including the loss of intellectual capital.[30] The years of knowledge, skills, relationships, and commitment that employees develop cannot be easily replaced or substituted, and the loss of one employee can cost a firm between $50,000 and $100,000.[31] Skandia Assurance and Financial Services, based in Stockholm, Sweden, is one of a few firms to measure and report its intellectual capital to investors, a move that illuminates an intangible asset for better decision making. Skandia has been recognized by *Fortune* magazine as one of ten great companies in Europe.[32] Although workforce reduction lowers costs, it often results in lost intellectual capital, strained customer relationships, negative media attention, and other issues that drain company resources. Employees who retain their jobs may suffer guilt, depression, or stress as a result of the reduction in force. Thus, a long-term understanding of the qualitative and quantitative costs and benefits should guide downsizing decisions.[33]

Although workforce reduction is a corporate decision, it is also important to recognize the potential role of employees in these decisions. Whereas hiring and job growth reached a frantic pace by the late 1990s, a wave of downsizings in the early 1990s and 2000s meant that some individuals had embraced the reality of having little job security. Instead of becoming cynical or angry, employees may have reversed roles and began asking, "What is this company doing for me?" and "Am I getting what I need from my employer?" Employees of all types began taking more responsibility for career growth, demanding balance in work and personal responsibilities, and seeking opportunities in upstart firms and emerging industries. Thus, although workforce reduction has negative effects, it has also shifted the psychological contract and power between employee and employer. The following suggestions examine how individuals can potentially mitigate the onset and effects of downsizing.

First, all employees should understand how their skills and competencies affect business performance. Not recognizing and improving this relationship makes it more difficult to prove their worth to managers faced with workforce reduction decisions. Second, employees should strive for cost-cutting and conservation strategies regardless of the employer's current financial condition. This is a workforce's first line of defense against layoffs—assisting the organization in reducing its costs before drastic measures are necessary. Third, today's work environment requires that most employees fulfill diverse and varying roles. For example, manufacturing managers must understand the whole product development and introduction process, ranging from engineering to marketing and distribution activities. Thus, another way of ensuring worth to the company, and to potential employers, is through an employee's ability to navigate different customer environments and organizational systems. It is now necessary to "cross train," show flexibility, and learn the entire business, even if a company does not offer a formal program for gaining this type of experience and exposure. Although this advice may not prevent workforce reduction, it does empower employees against some of its harmful effects. Through laws and regulations, the government has also created a system for ensuring that employees are treated properly on the job. The next section covers the myriad of laws that all employers and employees should consider in daily and strategic decisions.

Legal

Employment law is a very complex and evolving area. In fact, most large companies employ human resource managers and legal specialists who are trained in the detail and implementation of specific statutes related to employee hiring, compensation, benefits, safety, and other areas. Smaller organizations often send human resource managers to workshops and conferences in order to keep abreast of legal imperatives in the workplace. Table 8.2 lists the major federal laws that cover employer responsibilities with respect to wages, labor unions, benefits, health and safety, equal opportunity, and other areas. Until the early 1900s, employment was primarily governed by the concept of **employment at will,** a common-law doctrine that allows either the employer or the employee to terminate the relationship at any time as long as it does not violate an employment contract. Today, many states still use the employment-at-will philosophy, but laws and statutes may limit total discretion in this regard.[34] The following discussion highlights employment laws and their fundamental contribution to social responsibilty.[35]

employment at will a common-law doctrine that allows either the employer or the employee to terminate the relationship at any time as long as it does not violate an employment contract

Wages and Benefits After the Great Depression, the U.S. Congress enacted a number of laws to protect employee rights and extend employer responsibilities. The Fair Labor Standards Act (FLSA) of 1938 prescribed minimum wage and overtime pay, record keeping, and child labor standards for most private and public employers. The minimum wage is set by the federal government and is periodically revised, although states have the option to adopt a higher standard. For example, the federal minimum wage was raised from $4.45 per hour to $5.15 per hour in September 1997. The majority of states abide by the federal standard, although Alaska, California, Oregon, Vermont, Washington, and four others have adopted a higher minimum wage. Most employees who work more than forty hours per week are entitled to overtime pay in the amount of one and a half times their regular pay. There are exemptions to the overtime pay provisions for four classes of employees: executives, outside salespeople, administrators, and professionals.[36]

TABLE 8.2	Major Employment Laws

ACT (DATE ENACTED)	PURPOSE
National Labor Relations Act (1935)	Established the rights of employees to engage in collective bargaining and to strike.
Fair Labor Standards Act (1938)	Established minimum wage and overtime pay standards, record keeping, and child labor standards for most private and public employers.
Equal Pay Act (1963)	Protects women and men who perform substantially equal work in the same establishment from gender-based wage discrimination.
Civil Rights Act, Title VII (1964)	Prohibits employment discrimination on the basis of race, national origin, color, religion, and gender.
Age Discrimination in Employment Act (1967)	Protects individuals age forty or older from age-based discrimination.
Occupational Safety and Health Act (1970)	Ensures safe and healthy working conditions for all employees by providing specific standards that employers must meet.
Employee Retirement Income Security Act (1974)	Sets uniform minimum standards to assure that employee benefit plans are established and maintained in a fair and financially sound manner.
Americans with Disabilities Act (1990)	Prohibits discrimination on the basis of physical or mental disability in all employment practices and requires employers to make reasonable accommodation to make facilities accessible to and usable by persons with disabilities.
Family and Medical Leave Act (1993)	Requires certain employers to provide up to twelve weeks of unpaid, job-protected leave to eligible employees for certain family and medical reasons.

Sources: "Federal Laws Prohibiting Job Discrimination Questions and Answers," Equal Employment Opportunity Commission, http://www.eeoc.gov/facts/qanda.html, accessed November 12, 2003; Gillian Flynn, "Looking Back on 100 Years of Employment Law," *Workforce* 78 (November 1999): 74–77; Roger LeRoy Miller and Gaylord A. Jentz, *Business Law Today* (Cincinnati: West Legal Studies in Business, 2000); U.S. Department of Labor, Employment Law Guide, http://www.dol.gov/asp/programs/handbook/main2.htm, accessed January 9, 2003.

The FLSA also affected child labor, including the provision that individuals under the age of fourteen are allowed to do only certain types of work, such as delivering newspapers and working in their parents' businesses. Children under age sixteen are often required to get a work permit, and their work hours are restricted so that they can attend school. Persons between the ages of sixteen and eighteen are not restricted in terms of number of work hours, but cannot be employed in hazardous or dangerous positions. Although passage of the FLSA was necessary to eliminate abusive child labor practices, its restrictions became somewhat problematic during the booming economy of the late 1990s, when unemployment rates were extremely low in the United States. Some business owners may have even considered lobbying for relaxed standards in very restrictive states so that they could hire more teens. In addition, general FLSA restrictions have created problems in implementing job-sharing and flextime arrangements with employees who are paid on an hourly basis.[37]

Two other pieces of legislation relate to employer responsibilities for benefits and job security. The Employee Retirement Income Security Act (ERISA) of 1974 set uniform minimum standards to assure that employee benefit plans are established and maintained in a fair and financially sound manner. ERISA does not require companies to establish retirement pension plans; instead, it developed standards for the administration of plans that management chooses to offer employees. A key provision relates to **vesting,** the legal right to pension plan benefits. In general, contributions an employee makes to the plan are vested immediately, whereas company contributions are vested after five years of employment. ERISA is a very complicated aspect of employer responsibilities because it involves tax law, financial investments, and plan participants and beneficiaries.[38]

vesting
the legal right to
pension plan benefits

The Family and Medical Leave Act (FMLA) of 1993 requires certain employers to provide up to twelve weeks of unpaid, job-protected leave to eligible employees for certain family and medical reasons. However, if the employee is paid in the top 10 percent of the entire workforce, the employer does not have to reinstate him or her in the same or comparable position.[39] Typical reasons for this type of leave include the birth or adoption of a child, personal illness, or the serious health condition of a close relative. The FMLA applies to employers with fifty or more employees, which means that its provisions do not cover a large number of U.S. employees. In addition, employees must have worked at least one year for the firm and at least twenty-five hours per week during the past year before the FMLA is required.

Labor Unions In one of the earliest pieces of employment legislation, the National Labor Relations Act (NLRA) of 1935 legitimized the rights of employees to engage in collective bargaining and to strike. This law was originally passed to protect employee rights, but subsequent legislation gave more rights to employers and restricted the power of unions. Before the NLRA, many companies attempted to prohibit their employees from creating or joining labor organizations. Employees who were members of unions were often discriminated against in terms of hiring and retention decisions. This act sought to eliminate the perceived imbalance of power between employers and employees. Through unions, employees gained a collective bargaining mechanism that enabled greater power on several fronts, including wages and safety.[40] For example, after a weeks-long strike against Verizon Communications, members of the Communications Workers of America (CWA) and International Brotherhood of Electrical Workers (IBEW) negotiated a deal that gave workers of the telecommunications firm a 12 percent pay raise (over three years), a cap on overtime hours, and other provisions, including the elimination of the threat of layoffs for the period of the labor contract. Verizon also upgraded its web site for delivering information and services to its employees.[41]

Health and Safety In 1970, the Occupational Safety and Health Act (OSHA) sought to ensure safe and healthy working conditions for all employees by providing specific standards that employers must meet. This act led to the development of the Occupational Safety and Health Administration, also known as OSHA, the agency that oversees the regulations intended to make workplaces in the United States the safest in the world. In its more than thirty years of existence, OSHA has made great strides to improve and maintain the health and safety of employees. For example, since the 1970s, the workplace death rate in the United States has been reduced by 50 percent, and the agency's initiatives in cotton dust and lead standards have reduced disease in several industries. The agency continues to innovate and uses feedback systems for improving its services and standards. For example, OSHA recently translated a variety of its documents into Spanish and posted them to a prominent place on its web site. OSHA officials were concerned about Spanish-speaking workers' understanding of the agency and their rights in the workplace.[42] OSHA has the authority to enter and make inspections of most employers. Because of its far-reaching power and unwarranted inspections made in the 1970s, the agency's relationship with business has not always been positive. For example, OSHA recently proposed rules to increase employer responsibility for **ergonomics,** the design, arrangement, and use of equipment to maximize productivity and minimize fatigue and physical discomfort. Without proper attention to ergonomics, employees may suffer injuries and long-term health issues as a result of work motion and tasks. Many business and industry associations have opposed the proposal, citing enormous costs and unsubstantiated claims. A federal ergonomics rule was established under the Clinton presidency, but was repealed by President George W. Bush. However, the issue continues to be raised on the regulatory agenda. OSHA is currently focusing its ergonomics efforts on one industry at a time, while individual states, such as Alaska, Washington, and California, are forging ahead with their own ergonomics rules.[43] Despite differences between this federal agency and some states and companies on a number of regulations, most employers are required to display the poster shown in Figure 8.1 or one required by their state safety and health agency.

> **ergonomics**
> the design, arrangement, and use of equipment to maximize productivity and minimize fatigue and physical discomfort

An emerging issue in the area of health and safety is the increasing rate of violence in the workplace. According to OSHA, 1.5 million workers are assaulted and nearly 1,000 are murdered in the workplace every year.[44] A recent survey of *Fortune* 1000 companies indicates that workplace violence is one of the most important security issues they face, costs them $36 billion annually, and results in three deaths daily and thousands of injuries each year. The third leading cause of all occupational fatalities is homicide.[45] Surveys in the insurance industry show that nearly 25 percent of insurance employees have been threatened, harassed, or attacked in job-related circumstances.[46]

The state of California's Occupational Safety and Health Agency has identified three types of workplace violence: (1) crimes committed by strangers and intruders in the workplace; (2) acts committed by nonemployees, such as customers, patients, students, and clients, who have expected or normal contact with employees; and (3) violence committed by coworkers.[47] Taxi drivers and clerks working late-night shifts at convenience stores are often subject to the first type of violence. Airline attendants are increasingly experiencing the second category of workplace violence when passengers become unruly, drunk, or otherwise violent while in flight. Airline employees across the United States, Australia, and Switzerland staged a campaign to combat "air rage," the uncivil and dangerous acts of passengers that are not only punishable by large fines but can also threaten the safety of everyone aboard the aircraft. The groups asked government officials to toughen penalties and control of air rage perpetrators. The terrorist attacks on the World Trade Center and the Pentagon further highlighted workplace risks and violence, including the steps that many organizations are taking to protect employees and other stakeholders. Some organizations with employees who travel a great deal are hiring training firms to educate employees on aircraft evacuation, air rage, how to respond to hijackers, and other safety measures.[48]

FIGURE 8.1 Job Safety and Health Protection Poster

You Have a Right to a Safe and Healthful Workplace.

IT'S THE LAW!

- You have the right to notify your employer or OSHA about workplace hazards. You may ask OSHA to keep your name confidential.

- You have the right to request an OSHA inspection if you believe that there are unsafe and unhealthful conditions in your workplace. You or your representative may participate in the inspection.

- You can file a complaint with OSHA within 30 days of discrimination by your employer for making safety and health complaints or for exercising your rights under the *OSH Act*.

- You have a right to see OSHA citations issued to your employer. Your employer must post the citations at or near the place of the alleged violation.

- Your employer must correct workplace hazards by the date indicated on the citation and must certify that these hazards have been reduced or eliminated.

- You have the right to copies of your medical records or records of your exposure to toxic and harmful substances or conditions.

- Your employer must post this notice in your workplace.

The *Occupational Safety and Health Act of 1970 (OSH Act)*, P.L. 91-596, assures safe and healthful working conditions for working men and women throughout the Nation. The Occupational Safety and Health Administration, in the U.S. Department of Labor, has the primary responsibility for administering the *OSH Act*. The rights listed here may vary depending on the particular circumstances. To file a complaint, report an emergency, or seek OSHA advice, assistance, or products, call 1-800-321-OSHA or your nearest OSHA office: • Atlanta (404) 562-2300 • Boston (617) 565-9860 • Chicago (312) 353-2220 • Dallas (214) 767-4731 • Denver (303) 844-1600 • Kansas City (816) 426-5861 • New York (212) 337-2378 • Philadelphia (215) 861-4900 • San Francisco (415) 975-4310 • Seattle (206) 553-5930. Teletypewriter (TTY) number is 1-877-889-5627. To file a complaint online or obtain more information on OSHA federal and state programs, visit OSHA's website at **www.osha.gov**. If your workplace is in a state operating under an OSHA-approved plan, your employer must post the required state equivalent of this poster.

1-800-321-OSHA
www.osha.gov

U.S. Department of Labor • **Occupational Safety and Health Administration** • **OSHA 3165**

© U.S. GOVERNMENT PRINTING OFFICE: 2000-467-945

Source: "New OSHA Workplace Poster," Occupational Safety and Health Administration, http://www.osha.gov/Publications/poster.html, accessed November 15, 2003.

Finally, disagreements and stress in the workplace may escalate into employee-on-employee violence. For example, a Xerox Corporation warehouse employee opened fire during a team meeting at a facility in Honolulu, killing seven coworkers. The employee, Bryan Uyesugi, was eventually convicted of murder and sentenced to life in prison without parole for the shooting, which Xerox officials described as the "worst tragedy" in the company's history. The Hawaii Occupational Safety and Health Division later cited Xerox for failing to enforce workplace-violence policies that might have prevented the deaths.[49] In many of these cases, the perpetrator has been recently reprimanded, dismissed, or received other negative feedback that prompted the violent attack. Although crimes reflect general problems in society, employers have a responsibility to assess risks and provide security, training, and safeguards to protect employees and other stakeholders from such acts. Experts estimate that 50 percent of all companies have no workplace violence prevention program, whereas 40 percent have a program "in name only."[50] Companies often purchase insurance policies to cover the costs of workplace violence, including business interruption, psychological counseling, informant rewards, and medical claims related to injuries.[51]

Equal Opportunity Title VII of the Civil Rights Act of 1964 prohibits employment discrimination on the basis of race, national origin, color, religion, and gender. This law is fundamental to employees' rights to join and advance in an organization according to merit, not one of the characteristics in the preceding list. For example, employers are not permitted to categorize jobs as just for men or women, unless there is a reason gender is fundamental to the tasks and responsibilities. Additional laws passed in the 1970s, 1980s, and 1990s were also designed to prohibit discrimination related to pregnancy, disabilities, age, and other factors. For example, the Americans with Disabilities Act prohibits companies from discriminating on the basis of physical or mental disability in all employment practices and requires them to make facilities accessible to and usable by persons with disabilities. These legal imperatives require that companies formalize employment practices to ensure that no discrimination is occurring. Thus, managers must be fully aware of the types of practices that constitute discrimination and work to ensure that hiring, promotion, annual evaluation, and other procedures are fair and based on merit. The spread of HIV and AIDS has prompted multinational firms with operations in Africa to distribute educational literature and launch prevention programs. Some companies work with internal and external stakeholders and even fund medical facilities that help prevent the disease and treat HIV/AIDS patients. Another component to their initiatives involves education on fair treatment of employees with the disease.[52]

To ensure that they build balanced workforces, many companies have initiated affirmative action programs, which involve efforts to recruit, hire, train, and promote qualified individuals from groups that have traditionally been discriminated against on the basis of race, sex, or other characteristics. We discussed these programs in Chapter 4. Safeway, a chain of supermarkets, established a program to expand opportunities for women in middle- and upper-level management after settling a sex-discrimination lawsuit.[53] However, many companies voluntarily implement affirmative action plans in order to build a more diverse workforce.[54] A key goal of these programs is to reduce any bias that may exist in hiring, evaluating, and promoting employees. A special type of discrimination, sexual harassment, is also prohibited through Title VII.

Sexual Harassment The flood of women into the workplace during the last half of the twentieth century brought new challenges and opportunities for organizations. Although harassment has probably always existed in the workplace, the presence of both genders in roughly equal numbers changed norms of behavior. When men dominated the workplace, it may have been acceptable to have photos of partially nude women or sexually suggestive materials posted on walls or in lockers. Today, such materials could be viewed as illegal if they contribute to a work environment that is intimidating, offensive, or otherwise interferes with an employee's work performance. The U.S. government indicates the nature of this illegal activity:

Unwelcome sexual advances, requests for sexual favors, and other verbal or physical conduct of a sexual nature constitutes **sexual harassment** when submission to or rejection of this conduct explicitly or implicitly affects an individual's employment, unreasonably interferes with an individual's work performance, or creates an intimidating, hostile, or offensive work environment.[55]

Prior to 1986, sexual harassment was not a specific violation of federal law in the United States. In *Meritor Savings Bank v. Vinson*, the U.S. Supreme Court ruled that sexual harassment creates a "hostile environment" that violates Title VII of the Civil Rights Act, even in the absence of economic harm or demand for sexual favors in exchange for promotions, raises, or related work incentives.[56] In other countries, sexual harassment in the workplace is considered an illegal act, although the specific conditions may vary by legal and social culture. In Mexico, the law protects employees only if their jobs are jeopardized on the basis of the exchange of sexual favors or relations. Employees of Mexican public entities, such as government offices, will be fired if found guilty of the offending behavior.[57] In the European Union (EU), sexual harassment legislation focuses on the liability that employers carry when they fail to promote a workplace culture free of harassment and other forms of discrimination. The EU recently strengthened its rules on sexual harassment, including definitions of direct and indirect harassment, the removal of an upper limit on victim compensation, and the requirement that businesses develop and make "equality reports" available to employees.[58]

There are two general categories of sexual harassment: quid pro quo and hostile work environment.[59] **Quid pro quo sexual harassment** is a type of sexual extortion, where there is a proposed or explicit exchange of job benefits for sexual favors. For example, telling an employee, "You will be fired if you do not have sex with me," is a direct form of sexual harassment. Usually, the person making such a statement is in a position of authority over the harassed employee, and thus, the threat of job loss is real. One incident of quid pro quo harassment may create a justifiable legal claim. **Hostile work environment sexual harassment** is less direct than quid pro quo harassment and can involve epithets, slurs, negative stereotyping, intimidating acts, graphic materials that show hostility toward an individual or group, and other types of conduct that affect the employment situation. For example, an e-mail message containing sexually explicit jokes that is broadcast to employees could be viewed as contributing to a hostile work environment. Some hostile work environment harassment is nonsexual, meaning the harassing conduct is based on gender without explicit reference to sexual acts. For example, in *Campbell v. Kansas State University* (1991), the courts found repeated remarks about women "being intellectually inferior to men" to be part of a hostile environment. Unlike quid pro quo cases, one in-

---

sexual harassment
unwelcome sexual advances, requests for sexual favors, and other verbal or physical conduct of a sexual nature when submission to or rejection of this conduct explicitly or implicitly affects an individual's employment, unreasonably interferes with an individual's work performance, or creates an intimidating, hostile, or offensive work environment

quid pro quo sexual harassment
a type of sexual extortion, where there is a proposed or explicit exchange of job benefits for sexual favors

hostile work environment sexual harassment
conduct that shows hostility toward an individual or group in a work environment. It can involve epithets, slurs, negative stereotyping, intimidating acts, and graphic materials; less direct than quid pro quo harassment.

cident may not justify a legal claim. Instead, the courts will examine a range of acts and circumstances to determine if the work environment was intolerable and the victim's job performance was impaired.[60] From a social responsibility perspective, a key issue in both types of sexual harassment is the employing organization's knowledge and tolerance for these types of behaviors. A number of court cases have shed more light on the issues that constitute sexual harassment and organizations' responsibility in this regard.

In *Harris v. Forklift Systems* (1993), Teresa Harris claimed that her boss at Forklift Systems made suggestive sexual remarks, asked her to retrieve coins from his pants pocket, and joked that they should go to a motel to "negotiate her raise." Courts at the state level threw out her case because she did not suffer major psychological injury. The U.S. Supreme Court overturned these decisions and ruled that employers can be forced to pay damages even if the worker suffered no proven psychological harm. This case brought about the "reasonable person" standard in evaluating what conduct constitutes sexual harassment. From this case, juries now evaluate the alleged conduct with respect to commonly held beliefs and expectations.[61]

Several global firms have been embroiled in sexual harassment suits. For example, Ford Motor Company settled a class-action lawsuit for $7.75 million in the late 1990s, the fourth-largest sexual harassment settlement in the Equal Employment Opportunity Commission's history, after more than 500 female employees claimed they were groped and sexually harassed at two different Ford plants. The settlement also required that the company spend an additional $10 million on sensitivity training programs.[62] Mitsubishi Motors agreed in 1998 to pay $34 million in a settlement with 350 women who made serious allegations of harassment and brought lawsuits against the company. Their allegations of sexual harassment included the distribution of lewd videos and photos, inappropriate conversations and jokes, and general tolerance by management for these actions and overtones. As part of the settlement, the company also agreed to periodic monitoring by a three-member panel and implementing an effective sexual harassment policy.[63]

Recent U.S. Supreme Court decisions on sexual harassment cases indicate that (1) employers are liable for the acts of supervisors; (2) employers are liable for sexual harassment by supervisors that culminates in a tangible employment action (loss of job, demotion, etc.); (3) employers are liable for a hostile environment created by a supervisor, but may escape liability if they demonstrate that they exercised reasonable care to prevent and promptly correct any sexually harassing behavior and that the plaintiff employee unreasonably failed to take advantage of any preventive or corrective measures offered by the employer; and (4) claims of hostile environment sexual harassment must be severe and pervasive in order to be viewed as actionable by the courts.[64]

Much like the underlying philosophy of the Federal Sentencing Guidelines for Organizations that we discussed in earlier chapters, these decisions require top managers in organizations to take the detection and prevention of sexual harassment seriously. To this end, many firms have implemented programs on sexual harassment. In order to satisfy current legal standards and set a higher standard for social responsibility, employees, supervisors, and other close business partners should be educated on the company's zero-tolerance policy against harassment. Employees must be educated on the policy prohibiting harassment, including the types of behaviors that constitute harassment, how offenders will be punished, and what employees should do if they experience harassment. Just like an organizational compliance program, employees must be assured of confidentiality and no retaliation for reporting harassment. Training on sexual harassment should be balanced in terms of legal definitions and practical tips and tools. Although employees need to be aware of the legal issues and ramifications, they also may need assistance in learning to recognize and avoid behaviors that may constitute quid pro quo or hostile environment harassment. Finally, employees should be aware that same-sex conduct may also constitute sexual harassment.[65] Table 8.3 lists facts about sexual harassment that should be used in company communication and training on this workplace issue.

Whistle-blowing[66] As we discussed in Chapter 5, an employee who reports individual or company wrongdoing to either internal or external sources is considered a **whistle-blower.**[67] Whistle-blowers usually focus on issues or behaviors that need corrective action, although managers and other employees may not appreciate reports that expose company weaknesses, raise embarrassing questions, or otherwise detract from

TABLE 8.3	Sexual Harassment in the Workplace

FACTS

Sexual harassment is a form of sex discrimination that violates Title VII of the Civil Rights Act of 1964.

Unwelcome sexual advances, requests for sexual favors, and other verbal or physical conduct of a sexual nature constitute sexual harassment when submission to or rejection of this conduct explicitly or implicitly affects an individual's employment, unreasonably interferes with an individual's work performance, or creates an intimidating, hostile, or offensive work environment.

Sexual harassment can occur in a variety of circumstances, including but not limited to the following:
- The victim as well as the harasser may be a woman or a man. The victim does not have to be of the opposite sex.
- The harasser can be the victim's supervisor, an agent of the employer, a supervisor in another area, a coworker, or a nonemployee.
- The victim does not have to be the person harassed but could be anyone affected by the offensive conduct.
- Unlawful sexual harassment may occur without economic injury to or discharge of the victim.
- The harasser's conduct must be unwelcome.

It is helpful for the victim to inform the harasser directly that the conduct is unwelcome and must stop. The victim should use any employer complaint mechanism or grievance system available.

When investigating allegations of sexual harassment, the Equal Employment Opportunity Commission looks at the whole record: the circumstances, such as the nature of the sexual advances, and the context in which the alleged incidents occurred. A determination of the allegations is made from the facts on a case-by-case basis.

Source: "Facts About Sexual Harassment," U.S. Equal Employment Opportunity Commission, www.eeoc.gov/facts/fs-sex.html, accessed November 12, 2003.

organizational tasks. Although not all whistle-blowing activity leads to an extreme reaction, whistle-blowers have been retaliated against, demoted, fired, and even worse as a result of their actions. For example, Jacob F. Horton, senior vice president at Gulf Power, was on his way to talk with company officials about alleged thefts, payoffs, and cover-ups at the utility when he died in a plane crash in 1989. Allegations that his death was related to whistle-blowing still linger.[68]

Partly as a result of business and industry scandals in the 1980s, most large corporations have formal organizational ethics and compliance programs, including toll-free hot lines and other anonymous means for employees to ask questions, gain clarification, or report suspicious behavior. These programs are designed to facilitate internal whistle-blowing, as they engender a more ethical organizational culture and provide mechanisms for monitoring and supporting appropriate behavior. Thus, an effective ethics and legal compliance program should provide employees and other stakeholders with opportunities to make possible transgressions known (e.g., ethics hot line, open-door policy, and strong ethical climate).

The federal government and most state governments in the United States have enacted measures to protect whistle-blowers from retaliation. For example, the Whistle-blower Protection Act of 1986 protects federal employees from retaliatory behavior. The Sarbanes-Oxley Act provides solid protection to whistle-blowers and strong penalties for those who retaliate against them. Other legislation actually rewards whistle-blowers for revealing illegal behavior. Under the False Claims Act of 1986, an individual who reports fraud perpetrated against the federal government may receive between 15 and 25 percent of the proceeds if a suit is brought against the perpetrator.

Ethical

Laws are imperative for social responsibility. The ethical climate of the workplace, however, is more subjective and dependent on top management leadership and corporate culture. In this section, we examine several trends in employment practices that have not fully reached the legal realm. Company initiatives in these areas indicate a corporate philosophy or culture that respects and promotes certain ethical values.

Training and Development   As discussed in Chapter 4, organizational culture and the associated values, beliefs, and norms operate on many levels and affect a number of workplace practices. Some organizations value employees as individuals, not just "cogs in a wheel." Firms with this ethical stance fund initiatives to develop employees' skills, knowledge, and other personal characteristics. Although this development is linked to business strategy and aids the employer, it also demonstrates a commitment to the future of the employee and his or her interests. Employees of the Taco Cabana restaurant chain, for example, receive training in Spanish along with cross-training of skills needed in various parts of restaurant operations. At each workstation, employees find reminders and instructions in both English and Spanish to promote greater retention. Employees also rotate through the workstations; this not only reinforces and extends their skill sets but also reduces their boredom and fatigue.[69]

Professionals also appreciate and respect a training and development focus from their employers. For example, the Los Angeles–based law firm of Latham & Watkins

Legal and Regulatory Challenges

The Whistle-blower Phenomenon

When *Time* magazine named three women, all whistle-blowers, as its celebratory "persons of the year," the selection was another hallmark in the disastrous tales of Enron, Worldcom, and the September 11 attacks. Cynthia Cooper disclosed the $3.8 billion accounting fraud at Worldcom through her role as head of internal auditing. Sherron Watkins warned Enron chief Ken Lay of an accounting hoax, a message that went unheeded. Colleen Rowley exposed bureaucracy and missteps at the Federal Bureau of Investigation that may have aided the terrorists' success on September 11, 2001. Their stories are relatively well known by now. But what about the whistle-blower who reported people gaining unauthorized bargains at a military commissary? Have you read much about the interim chief financial officer who disclosed errors in Rite-Aid's accounting records? Did you know that several whistle-blowers have levied severe claims about the marketing and business practices of large phar-

maceutical companies? Finally, have you read that whistle-blowing is not isolated to the United States?

To be certain, the public's awareness of whistle-blowing has been sharpened in the twenty-first century. The examples listed above highlight just a few of the many cases where an employee bravely comes forward to disclose misconduct. Companies and the government are also preparing for the whistle-blower phenomenon. One of the most important steps is to develop a forum or mechanism where employees can bring forth concerns without fear. The mechanism, sometimes a toll-free hot line to the firm's ethics officer, must also allow for assurance that action will be taken when warranted. The widespread implementation of these mechanisms has prompted employees to become more comfortable in reporting violations, but many choose not to when they believe their facts are not in order or they are not sure how the organization will respond.

Much like the sexual harassment training that became so popular in the 1990s, many executives

launched a series of initiatives, including "Latham & Watkins University," for first- and fourth-year associates. This training program covers legal updates, professional skill development, and information on career management and planning. Other law firms have upgraded their development opportunities, including mentoring programs, sabbaticals, and feedback sessions for commenting on firm policies and procedures.[70] These firms are finding many benefits of employee training and development, including stronger employee recruitment and retention strategies. Indeed, there is a link between investments in employees and the amount of commitment, job satisfaction, and productivity demonstrated by them. Happier employees tend to stay with their employer and to better serve coworkers, customers, and other constituents, which has direct bearing on the quality of relationships and financial prospects of a firm. Management training is also critical, as the top reason employees leave a company is because of poor or unskilled managers, not salary, benefits, or other organizational factors.[71]

Employees recognize when a company is diligently investing in programs that not only improve operations but also give them and coworkers increased empowerment and new opportunities to improve knowledge and grow professionally. Through formal training and development classes, workers get a better sense of where they fit and

are seeking guidance on whistle-blowing, including the legal ramifications of the Sarbanes-Oxley Act of 2002. Company officials who retaliate against whistle-blowers may receive up to ten years of jail time. The audit committees of boards of directors are now required to implement a process for hearing whistle-blowers' complaints. Attorneys who find wrongdoing must report it to top management. If executives fail to take action, the attorney must go to the board of directors. Whistle-blowers also have the right to a jury trial and can bypass lengthy and arduous administrative hearings. Finally, the U.S. Secretary of Labor can order a firm to rehire a terminated whistle-blower without any legal hearings. However, the Sarbanes-Oxley Act does not provide any financial incentives for whistle-blowers to speak up. United States federal employees have this incentive through the Whistleblower Protection Act of 1986. Some critics claim that this provision would add even more strength to the ramifications of Sarbanes-Oxley.

A burning question, however, is what makes an employee blow the whistle? In some cases, the whistle-blower is a member of a recognized profession, such as accounting or engineering, and is unwavering in how the profession is practiced or perceived. In other situations, the whistle-blower may have unintentionally or knowingly contributed to the problems and comes clean as a way of clearing his or her conscience and aiding an investigation. Other whistle-blowers have either come across the wrongdoing outside of their normal responsibilities or are essentially outsiders in the corporate culture. Unfortunately, whistle-blowers may have to be prepared for rejection, social repercussions, and even retaliation.

Sources:
Integrity in the Workplace: 2001 National Employee Benchmark Study, (Chicago: Walker Information, 2001); Amy Barrett and Lorraine Woellert, "Can Big Pharma Cure Its Legal Migraines?" *Business Week,* July 22, 2002, pp.76–77; Geoffrey Colvin, "Wonder Women of Whistleblowing," *Fortune,* August 12, 2002, p. 56; Paula Dwyer, Dan Carney, Amy Borrus, Lorraine Woellert, and Christopher Palmeri, "Year of the Whistleblower," *Business Week,* December 16, 2002, pp. 106–110; Andrew Peaple, "Catalysts for Change," *Accountancy* 130 (November 2002): 58–59, Amanda Ripley, "The Night Detective," *Time,* December 30, 2002, pp. 44–49; Bruce Rubenstein, "Sarbanes-Oxley Shields Whistle-Blowers From Retaliation," *Corporate Legal Times* (November 2002): 24–25.

how they contribute to the overall organization. This understanding empowers them to become more responsive, accurate, and confident in workplace decisions. Training also increases conflict resolution skills, accountability and responsibility, a situation most employees prefer to micromanaging or "hand-holding." All these effects contribute to the financial and cultural health of an organization.[72] Thus, a firm can enhance its organizational capacity to fulfill stakeholder expectations.

Training and development activities require resources and the commitment of all managers to be successful. For example, a departmental manager must be supportive of an employee using part of the workday to attend a training session on a new software package. At the same time, the organization must pay for the training, regardless of whether it uses inside or outside trainers and develops in-house materials or purchases them from educational providers. A study by the American Society for Training and Development indicates that, on average, employers in developed countries spend about $630 per employee on training every year. Survey respondents in Latin America reported spending the least per employee ($311), whereas their Middle Eastern counterparts reported the highest rate per employee ($783). Companies in all regions indicated they were training more employees than ever before, with an average of 76.7 percent of employees being trained in a given year. Australia and

New Zealand had the highest figures, with over 90 percent of all employees receiving training in those surveyed companies. Despite the differences in training expenditures, the types of training programs and workplace practices in effect in these regions are remarkably similar. Managerial skills, supervisory strategies, information technology skills, occupational safety and compliance, and customer relations are the topic of training programs in all countries.[73] Another area that has received much attention in the United States but less focus in other countries involves the diverse nature of today's workforce.

Diversity Whereas Title VII of the Civil Rights Act grants legal protection to different types of employees, initiatives in **workplace diversity** focus on recruiting and retaining a diverse workforce as a business imperative.[74] With diversity programs, companies assume an ethical obligation to employ and empower individuals, regardless of age, gender, physical or mental ability, or other characteristics. These firms go beyond compliance with government guidelines to develop cultures that not only tolerate but also embrace the unique skills and contributions of all types of people. Thus, legal statutes focus on removing discrimination, whereas diversity represents a management approach for harnessing and cultivating employee talent.[75] Firms with an effective diversity effort link their diversity mission statement with the corporate strategic plan, implement plans to recruit and retain a diverse talent pool, support community programs of diverse cultural groups, hold management accountable for various types of diversity performance, and have tangible outcomes of the diversity strategy.[76]

> **workplace diversity**
> initiatives focused on recruiting and retaining a diverse workforce as a business imperative

Many firms embrace employee diversity to deal with supplier and customer diversity. Their assumption is that in order to effectively design, market, and support products for different target groups, a company must employ individuals who reflect its customers' characteristics.[77] Organizations and industries with a populationwide customer base may use national demographics for assessing their diversity effort. For example, the Newspaper Association of America implemented a minority recruitment and diversity strategy in the early 1990s to help the industry better align staff demographics to community demographics. A study in the newspaper industry found that although racial and ethnic minorities make up nearly 30 percent of the U.S. population, less than 12 percent of all news reporters fall into that category. This finding prompted the National Association of Black Journalists to call for greater attention to diversity in the newsroom. Several years later, the Scripps Howard Foundation, associated with the Cincinnati media conglomerate, funded a media school at Hampton University, a historically African American school in Virginia. Although specific newspapers and media firms have made significant progress in recent years, the entire industry is not yet fully aligned with demographic trends.[78] After the 2000 U.S. census data were released, some companies began to reconsider marketing strategy, including the link between employee and customer characteristics. For example, census data revealed sharp growth in the Hispanic population and, for some firms, prompted hiring of Hispanic employees and consultants.[79]

As we discussed in Chapter 1, there are opportunities to link social responsibility objectives with business performance, and many firms are learning the benefits of employing individuals with different backgrounds and perspectives. For example,

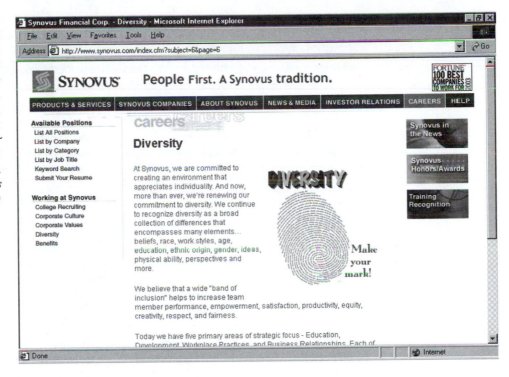

executives at Ernst & Young believe diversity brings a competitive advantage to the consulting firm through multiple perspectives.[80] Even small businesses are discovering these advantages. The Wilson Street Grill, an upscale restaurant in Madison, Wisconsin, makes a point of hiring mentally disabled workers. Owners Nancy Christy and Andrea Craig have established a flexible workplace that designs jobs around workers' abilities instead of trying to fit the person into a job description. Their efforts have been richly rewarded with loyal, creative, hard-working employees who stay for years, a rare occurrence in an industry known for its high turnover, as well as a National Restaurant Association's Restaurant Neighbors Award and an Americans with Disabilities Act award.[81] Verizon, a global provider of wireless communication services, is also committed to including people with disabilities into the workplace. Along with other businesses and nonprofit organizations, Verizon helped establish several initiatives to educate businesses on the unique opportunities and challenges with this employment category.[82]

Conflicting views and voices of different generations abound in the workplace, and this is the first time in history that the workforce has been composed of so many generations at one time. Generations have worked together in the past, but these groups were usually divided by organizational stratification. Many workplaces now include members of multiple generations sitting side by side and working shoulder to shoulder. The result may be greater dissension among the age groups than when they were stratified by the organizational hierarchy. Because employees serve an important role in the social responsibility framework, managers need to be aware of generational differences and their potential effects on teamwork, conflict, and other

TABLE 8.4		Profiles of Generations at Work
GENERATION NAME	**BIRTH YEARS**	**KEY CHARACTERISTICS**
Veterans	1922–1943	Hard-working, detail-oriented, uncomfortable with conflict
Baby boomers	1943–1960	Service-oriented, good team players, sensitive to feedback
Generation X	1960–1980	Adaptable, independent, impatient
Nexters	1980–2000	Optimistic, technologically savvy, need supervision

Source: Ron Zemke, Claire Raines, and Bob Filipczak, *Generations at Work: Managing the Clash of Veterans, Boomers, Xers, and Nexters in Your Workplace* (New York: AMACOM, 2000).

workplace behaviors. Table 8.4 lists the four generations in today's workplace as well as their key characteristics.

Veterans tend to bring stability and loyalty to the workplace. Although veterans are very hard-working and detail-oriented, they are often uncomfortable with conflict and ambiguity and reluctant to buck the system. The baby boomers are service-oriented, are good team players, and want to please. However, they are also known for being self-centered, overly sensitive to feedback, and not budget-minded. People in Generation X are adaptable, technologically literate, independent, and not intimidated by authority. However, their liabilities include impatience, cynicism, and inexperience. The latest generation to enter the workforce, the Nexters, is technologically savvy. They also bring the assets of collective action, optimism, and tenacity to the workplace. However, they bring the liabilities of inexperience, especially with difficult people issues, and a need for supervision and structure.

Although generational issues existed in the workforce in the 1920s and the 1960s, there are some new twists today. The older generations no longer have all the money and power. Times of anxiety and uncertainty can aggravate differences and generational conflict, and these conflicts need to be handled correctly when they occur. Understanding the different generations and how they see things is a crucial part of handling this conflict. The authors of *Generations at Work: Managing the Clash of Veterans, Boomers, Xers, and Nexters in Your Workplace* developed the ACORN acronym to describe five principles that managers can use to deal with generational issues. **A**ccommodating employee differences entails treating employees as customers and giving them the best service that the company can give. **C**reating workplace choices as to what and how employees work can allow for change and satisfaction. **O**perating from a sophisticated management style requires that management be direct but tactful. **R**especting competence and initiative assumes the best from the different generations and responds accordingly. **N**ourishing retention means keeping the best employees. When combined with effective communication efforts, the ACORN principles can help managers mend generational conflicts for the benefit of everyone in the company.[83]

Although workplace diversity reaps benefits for both employees and employers, it also brings challenges that must be addressed. For example, diverse employees may

Today's workplace is filled with people from several different generations. Employees must learn to respect and value these generational differences. (Stephen Agricola/ The Image Works)

have more difficulty communicating and working with each other. Although differences can breed innovation and creativity, they can also create an atmosphere of distrust or lack of cooperation. Many companies found a way to turn general anger, fear, and confusion over the September 11, 2001, terrorist strikes into an opportunity for discussing diversity and creating stronger bonds between employees of different ethnicities, religions, beliefs, and experiences related to the strikes.

Finally, the diversity message will not be taken seriously unless top management and organizational systems fully support a diverse workforce. After Home Depot settled a sex-discrimination lawsuit, it developed an automated hiring and promotion computer program. Although the Job Preference Program (JPP) was originally intended as insurance against discrimination, the system opens all jobs and applicants to the companywide network, eliminates unqualified applications, and enables managers to learn employee aspirations and skills in a more effective manner. JPP has also brought positive change to the number of female and minority managers within Home Depot.[84] In contrast to this success story, some employees of companies with diversity training programs have viewed such training as intended to blame or change white men only. Other training has focused on the reasons diversity should be important, not the actual changes in attitudes, work styles, expectations, and business processes that are needed for diversity to work.[85]

Work/Life Balance A recent in-depth study focused on two women and their career and family progression over sixteen years. Both women had great work achievements in their twenties and later decided to marry, have children, and devote more time to family than career. From this study and many others, the authors note the inherent trade-offs between work and family life. They conclude that most working women are typically forced to make tough trade-offs among career goals, child rearing, household management, and economic realities. These are not easy decisions for everyone, thus giving rise to potential stress and conflict at home and work.[86] Just as increasing numbers of women in the workplace have changed the norms of behavior at work and prompted attention to sexual harassment, they have also brought challenges in work/life balance. This balance is not just an issue for women, as men also have multiple roles that can create the same types of stress and conflict.[87]

Because employees have roles within and outside the organization, there is increasing corporate focus on the types of support that employees have in balancing these obligations. Deloitte & Touche (now Deloitte Touche Tohmatsu), an international professional services firm, recently came to grips with issues of work/life balance when it discovered the alarming rate at which women were leaving the firm. In the early 1990s, only four of the fifty employees being considered for partner status were women, despite the company's heavy recruitment of women from business schools. A closer examination of the company's turnover rate also illuminated the gender issue, although many executives assumed the women had left to have and raise children. The company convened the Initiative for the Retention and Advancement of Women task force and soon uncovered cultural beliefs and practices that needed modification. The task force found that younger employees—both male and female—wanted a balanced life, were willing to forgo some pay for more time with family and less stress, and had similar career goals. Thus, Deloitte & Touche set out to change its culture and operating practices so that all employees were given similar opportunities and to ensure that concerns and issues were open for discussion. A major initiative included reduced travel schedules and flexible work arrangements to benefit both men and women employees of the firm.[88]

work/life programs
programs to assist employees in balancing work responsibilities with personal and family responsibilities

Such **work/life programs** assist employees in balancing work responsibilities with personal and family responsibilities. A central feature of these programs is flexibility, so that employees of all types are able to achieve their own definition of balance. For example, a single parent may want child care and consistent work hours, whereas another employee may need assistance in finding elder care or support for a parent with Alzheimer's disease. A working mother may need access to "just-in-time" care when a child is sick or school is out of session. Employees of all types appreciate flextime arrangements, which allow them to work forty hours per week on a schedule they develop within a range of hours specified by the company. Other employees work some hours at home or in a location more conducive to their personal obligations. DuPont, for example, has been recognized by *Working Mother* magazine for its exceptional flexibility to support work/life balance. At nearly all of its eighty-five locations, DuPont's employees enjoy compressed scheduling, telecommuting, job-sharing, and other arrangements. The company has installed roughly 12,000 data lines to support employee telecommuting, which benefits nearly one-third of its workforce.[89]

More than 65 million Americans suffer from symptoms of stress at work, including headaches, sleeplessness, and other physical ailments. To remedy these concerns, Americans spend more than $370 million per year on stress-reducing products, services, and strategies. Compared to Japanese workers, however, the U.S. figures are moderate. A study by the Japanese Ministry of Health and Welfare found that nearly 60 percent of Japanese employees feel fairly fatigued from work, whereas only 15 to 30 percent of U.S. workers feel the same way. The work ethic in both countries is among the strongest in the world. However, 10,000 Japanese men die every year as a result of job-related stressors, physical problems, and associated psychological ramifications.[90]

There is no generic work/life program. Instead, companies need to consider their employee base and the types of support their employees are likely to need and appreciate. Successful work/life programs, like that developed by the SAS Institute, are an extension of the diversity philosophy, so that employees are respected as individuals in the process of contributing to company goals. Thus, connecting employees' personal needs, lives, and goals to strategic business issues can be fruitful for both parties. This perspective is in contrast to the "employee goals vs. business goals" trade-off mentality that has been pervasive for decades.[91]

A recent study by jobtrack.com found that nearly 50 percent of all applicants consider work/life balance the most important consideration in identifying potential employers and considering job offers.[92] For this reason, companies have become quite innovative in their approach to work/life balance. DaimlerChrysler, for example, developed the work/family account, where employees allocate $4,000 for child care, adoption costs, elder care, education costs, or retirement. The allocation was gradually increased to $8,000.[93] Cisco Systems opened a $10 million child-care facility at its San Jose, California, headquarters with Internet cameras that enable parents to log on to check on their children even while they are at work.[94] Such efforts are able to accommodate diverse interests and employee needs.

Philanthropic

In Chapter 11, we examine the philanthropic efforts of companies and the important role that employees play in the process of selecting and implementing projects that contribute time, resources, and human activity to worthy causes. In social responsibility, philanthropic responsibilities are primarily directed outside the organization, so they are not that focused on employees. However, as discussed in Chapter 7, employees benefit from participating in volunteerism and other philanthropic projects. A recent study by the Points of Light Foundation asked corporate executives about the effect of employee volunteerism on organizational competitiveness and success. The surveyed executives reported that this aspect of philanthropy increases employee productivity and builds teamwork skills. In a tight job market, employees may even view philanthropic activity, such as volunteer opportunities, as one criterion in evaluating potential employers. Thus, the benefits of corporate philanthropy in the community reflect back on the organization.[95] McDonald's recently launched a series of web sites intended to serve both employment needs and community relations goals. On a state-by-state basis, the venerable fast-food chain set up sites, such as www.McWisconsin.com and www.McMinnesota.com, to aid both corporate and local franchisees' ability to hire new employees, educate consumers, deliver promotional materials, and reach other business goals.[96]

McMinnesota.com is an online source of information on employment, community outreach, and other opportunities sponsored by participating McDonald's in the state of Minnesota. (www.mcminnesota .com. Used with permission from McDonald's Corporation.)

Strategic Implementation of Responsibilities to Employees

As this chapter has demonstrated, responsibilities toward employees are varied and complex. Legal issues alone require full-time attention from lawyers and human resource specialists. These issues are also emotional, because corporate decisions have ramifications on families and communities, as well as employees. In light of this complexity, many companies have chosen to embrace these obligations to benefit both employee and organizational goals. This philosophy stands in stark contrast to the master-servant model popular more than 100 years ago. Today, companies are using distinctive programs and initiatives to set themselves apart and to become known as desirable employers. Low unemployment levels in the late 1990s, along with diversity, work/life balance, and generational differences, prompted companies to use marketing strategy and business insight normally applied to customer development in the employee recruitment and retention realm. Even in a time of economic downturn, employers will need to be mindful of keeping top talent and maintaining employee satisfaction. For example, Small Dog Electronics, a small Vermont computer retailer, recently began offering a rather unusual perk in order to satisfy and retain its fourteen employees: dog insurance. The firm, which already allows employees to bring their dogs to work, picks up 80 percent of employees' veterinarians' bills, minus a deductible.[97]

An **employer of choice** is an organization of any size in any industry that is able to attract, optimize, and retain the best employee talent over the long term.[98] Advertising, web sites, and other company communications often use the term to describe and market the organization to current and potential employees. These messages

employer of choice
an organization of any size in any industry that is able to attract, optimize, and retain the best employee talent over the long term

center on the various practices that companies have implemented to create employee satisfaction. Firms with this distinction value the human component of business, not just financial considerations, ensure that employees are engaged in meaningful work, and stimulate the intellectual curiosity of employees. These businesses have strong training practices, delegate authority, and recognize the link between employee satisfaction and customer satisfaction.[99] Thus, becoming an employer of choice is an important manifestation of strategic social responsibility.

From employees' perspectives, one traditional way to strengthen trust is through employee stock ownership plans (ESOPs), which provide the opportunity both to contribute to and gain from organizational success. Such programs confer not only ownership but also opportunities for employees to participate in management planning, which foster an environment that many organizations believe increases profits. Several studies of companies with ESOPs cast a positive light on these plans. ESOPs appear to increase sales by about 2.3 to 2.4 percent over what would have been expected absent an ESOP. ESOP companies were also found to pay better benefits, higher wages, and provide nearly twice the retirement income for employees than their non-ESOP counterparts. Under these plans, employees must take on an ownership perspective, work as a team in an environment that forges trust, and provide excellent interactions and service to customers. ESOPs are also thought to improve employee loyalty and lower employee turnover rates. Some of the 10,000 "employee-owned" firms include Lowe's, Acadian Ambulance, Publix Supermarkets, Procter & Gamble, Hallmark Cards, and Ferrellgas.[100] Despite the advantages of ESOPs, experts also warn that some plans are potentially risky for employees, as in the case of Enron.[101] Becoming an employer of choice has many benefits, including an enhanced ability to hire and retain the best people. The expectations of such businesses are very high because employee stakeholders have specific criteria in mind when assessing the attractiveness of a particular employer. Although top managers must decide on how the firm will achieve strategic social responsibility with employees, Table 8.5 provides general guidance on some of the best practices that are implemented by employers of choice.

Finally, the global dimensions of today's workplace shape an organization's ability to effectively work with employee stakeholders and to become an employer of choice. Firms with offices and sites around the world must deal with a complexity of norms and expectations, all of which can have an affect on its reputation at home. For example, when Nike was first accused of dealing with suppliers that used child labor in the mid-1990s, the company claimed that it was not in the business of manufacturing shoes and that it could therefore not be blamed for the practices of Asian manufacturers. Following media criticism, Nike publicized a report claiming that the employees of its Indonesian and Vietnamese suppliers were living quite well. The veracity of this report was tarnished by contradictory evidence produced by activists. Next, Nike started introducing workers' rights and environmental guidelines for its suppliers. Yet some company representatives explained that any additional social responsibility initiative would damage the competitive position of the firm. In the late 1990s, Nike designed a suppliers' auditing process that invited student representatives along with other activists to visit manufacturing plants and provide recommendations for better practice. Before the company's shift, many media reports discussed

TABLE 8.5	Best Practices of Employers of Choice
PRACTICE	**EXPLANATION**
Foster openness.	Give all employees full access to company information.
Foster community.	Instill in employees a concern for coworkers and society at large.
Foster creativity.	Allow workers to create their own work environments.
Foster loyalty.	Train workers extensively, then pay them generously for greater productivity.
Foster responsibility.	Put new workers in charge and move them quickly through the ranks.
Foster individuality.	Allow workers to do their own thing, no matter how wacky their thing is.
Foster teamwork.	Throw out the old management hierarchy and encourage group over individual success.

Sources: "Main Page," Employer of Choice.net, http://www.employerofchoice.net/, accessed August 21, 2003; Roger E. Herman and Joyce L. Gioia, *How to Become an Employer of Choice* (Winchester, VA: Oakhill Press, 2000); Mark Mazetti, "Managing, Texas-Style," *Texas Monthly* 28 (December 2000): 64–78.

Nike's manufacturing practices and it is likely that some consumers and potential employees turned their attention away from Nike. In this case, Nike's relationships with its manufacturing suppliers and their employees affected its ability to achieve strategic social responsibility.[102]

S u m m a r y

Throughout history, peoples' perceptions of work and employment have evolved from necessary evil to source of fulfillment. The relationship between employer and employee involves responsibilities, obligations, and expectations as well as challenges.

On an economic level, many believe there is an unwritten, informal psychological contract that includes the beliefs, perceptions, expectations, and obligations that make up the agreement between individuals and their employers. This contract has evolved from a primarily master-servant relationship, in which employers held the power, to one in which employees assume a more-balanced relationship with employers. Workforce reduction, the process of eliminating employment positions, breaches the psychological contract that exists between an employer and employee and threatens the social contract between employers, communities, and other groups. Although workforce reduction lowers costs, it often results in lost intellectual capital, strained customer relationships, negative media attention, and other issues that drain company resources.

Employment law is a complex and evolving area. In the past, employment was primarily governed by employment at will, a common-law doctrine that allows either the employer or employee to terminate the relationship at any time as long as it does not violate an employment contract. Many laws have been enacted to regulate business conduct with regard to wages and benefits, labor unions, health and safety, equal employment opportunity, sexual harassment, and whistle-blowing. Title VII of the Civil

Rights Act, which prohibits employment discrimination on the basis of race, national origin, color, religion, and gender, is fundamental to employees' rights to join and advance in an organization according to merit. Sexual harassment is defined as unwelcome sexual advances, requests for sexual favors, and other verbal or physical conduct of a sexual nature when submission to or rejection of this conduct explicitly or implicitly affects an individual's employment, unreasonably interferes with an individual's work performance, or creates an intimidating, hostile, or offensive work environment. Sexual harassment may take the form of either quid pro quo harassment or hostile work environment harassment. An employee who reports individual or corporate wrongdoing to either internal or external sources is considered a whistle-blower.

Although legal compliance is imperative for social responsibility, the ethical climate of the workplace is more subjective and dependent on top management support and corporate culture. Companies with a strong ethical stance fund initiatives to develop employees' skills, knowledge, and other personal characteristics. With diversity programs, companies assume an ethical obligation to employ and empower individuals, regardless of age, gender, physical and mental ability, and other characteristics. Work/life programs assist employees in balancing work responsibilities with personal and family responsibilities.

Employees may play an important role in a firm's philanthropic efforts. Employees benefit from such initiatives through participation in volunteerism and other projects.

In light of the complexity of and emotions involved with responsibilities toward employees, many companies have chosen to embrace these obligations to benefit both employee and organizational goals. An employer of choice is an organization of any size in any industry that is able to attract, optimize, and retain the best employee talent over the long term. One traditional way to strengthen trust is through ESOPs, which provide the opportunity both to contribute to and gain from organizational success. Finally, the global dimensions of today's workplace shape an organization's ability to effectively work with employee stakeholders and to become an employer of choice.

Key Terms

psychological contract (p. 230)
workforce reduction (p. 232)
employment at will (p. 234)
vesting (p. 236)
ergonomics (p. 237)
sexual harassment (p. 240)
quid pro quo sexual harassment (p. 240)
hostile work environment sexual harassment (p. 240)
workplace diversity (p. 246)
work/life programs (p. 250)
employer of choice (p. 252)

Discussion Questions

1. Review Table 8.1, Changes in Employees' Psychological Contract with Employers. Create additional columns to indicate the positive and negative effects associated with the "old" and "new" contract characteristics. For example, what is positive and negative about the belief that employees should follow orders? What is positive and negative about giving 110 percent effort on the job?

2. What is workforce reduction? How does it affect employees, consumers, and the local community? What steps should a company take to address these effects?

3. What responsibilities do companies have with respect to workplace violence? Using the three categories of violence presented in the chapter, describe the responsibilities and actions that you believe are necessary for an organization to demonstrate social responsibility in this area.

4. Describe the differences between workplace diversity and equal employment opportunity. How do these differences affect managerial responsibilities

and the development of social responsibility programs?

5. Why it is important to understand the profiles of different generations at work? How can managers use the ACORN principles to develop a strong sense of community and solidarity among all employee groups?

6. Why are organizations developing work/life programs? What trends have contributed to these programs?

7. What is an employer of choice? Describe how a firm could use traditional marketing concepts and strategies to appeal to current and potential employees.

8. Review the seven suggestions in Table 8.5 for becoming an employer of choice. What are some potential drawbacks to each tactic? Rank the seven suggestions in terms of their importance to you.

Experiential Exercise

Develop a list of five criteria that describe your employer of choice. Then visit the web sites of three companies in which you have some employment interest. Peruse each firm's web site to find evidence on how it fulfills your criteria. On the basis of this evidence, develop a chart to show how well each firm meets your description and criteria of your employer of choice. Finally, provide three recommendations on how these companies can better communicate their commitment to employees and the employer-of-choice criteria.

What Would You Do?

Dawn Burke, director of employee relations, glanced at her online calendar and remembered her appointment at 3:00 P.M. today. She quickly found the file labeled "McCullen and Aranda" and started preparing for the meeting. She recalled that this was essentially an employee-supervisor case, where the employee had been unwilling or unable to meet the supervisor's requests. The employee claimed that the supervisor was too demanding and impatient. Their conflict had escalated to the point that both were unhappy and uncomfortable in the work environment. Other employees had noticed, and overheard, some of the conflict.

In her role, Dawn was responsible for many programs, including a new mediation initiative to resolve workplace conflict. The program was designed to help employees develop stronger communication and conflict resolution

skills. In this case, the program was also providing an intermediary step between informal and formal discipline. Today, she was meeting with both parties to discuss mediation guidelines, a time line, their goal, and their general points of conflict.

John McCullen, 51, a buyer in the facilities department, and Terry Aranda, the director of facilities procurement, arrived separately. John had been with the company for thirty-two years and had started his career with the company right out of high school. Terry, 31, was hired from another firm to oversee the procurement area a year ago and was recently graduated from a prestigious M.B.A. program. Dawn started the meeting by reviewing the mediation guidelines and time line. She reminded John and Terry that their goal was to develop a workable and agreeable solution to the current situation. Dawn then asked for each party to explain his or her position on the conflict.

John began, "Ms. Aranda is a very smart lady. She seems to know the buying and procurement area, but she knows less about the company and its history. I am not sure she has taken the time to learn our ways and values. Ms. Aranda is impatient with our use of the new software and computer system. Some of us don't have college degrees, and we haven't been using computers since we were young. I started working at this company about the time she was born, and I am not sure that her management style is good for our department. Everything was going pretty well until we starting changing our systems."

Terry commented, "John is a valuable member of the department, as he knows everyone at this company. I appreciate his knowledge and loyalty. On the other hand, he has not completed several tasks in a timely manner, nor has he asked for an extension. I feel that I must check up on his schedule and proof all of his work. John has attended several training classes, and I asked that he use an electronic calendar so that projects are completed on time. He continues to ignore my advice and deadlines. We've had several conversations, but John's work has not substantially improved. We have many goals to achieve in the department, and I need everyone's best work in order to make that happen."

Dawn thanked them for their candor and told them she would meet with them next week to start the mediation process. As she contemplated the discussion, she remembered an article that discussed how people born in different generations often have contrasting perceptions about work. Dawn started to jot a few notes about the next steps in resolving their conflict. What would you do?

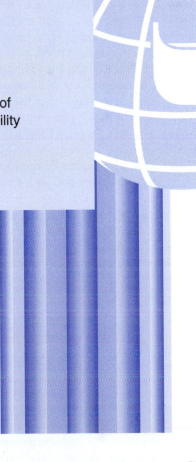

Chapter 9

Environment Issues

CHAPTER OBJECTIVES

- To define the nature of the natural environment as it relates to social responsibility
- To explore a variety of environmental issues faced by business and society
- To examine the impact of environmental policy and regulations
- To discuss a strategic approach to respond to environmental issues

CHAPTER OUTLINE

Global Environmental Issues

Environmental Policy and Regulation

Business Response to Environmental Issues

Strategic Implementation of Environmental Responsibility

Many companies today face a dilemma: Should they invest resources in creating, supporting, and maintaining organizational initiatives that protect the natural environment? By striving to be one of the most environmentally conscious companies, Herman Miller, Inc., has answered that question with a resounding yes. The ergonomic furniture maker has implemented a comprehensive strategy to protect the environment. Today, Miller's environmental responsibility initiatives encompass every element of its product supply chain, from the acquisition of raw materials through production and design, to the end user who ultimately purchases its furniture.

Herman Miller has committed to designing and manufacturing environmentally friendly furniture that has minimal impact on the environment. The strategy begins with an analysis of the "life cycle" of raw materials and finished goods to identify opportunities to reduce, reuse, and recycle. For example, the company is increasingly replacing its paint and lacquer finishes with a powder coat technology that uses fewer volatile organic compounds (VOCs). Toxic glues used in foam application have been replaced with water-based ones that are less harmful to the environment. The company also chooses woods carefully to ensure that they come from renewable sources. In fact, one of Herman Miller's most famous designs, the Eames lounge chair, is no longer made of rosewood due to diminishing renewable supplies of that wood. Some furniture requires simple assembly to compress space and box requirements, thereby reducing waste. The company also seeks ways to combine outgoing delivery shipments with incoming raw material pickups to move products with the greatest efficiency possible. Miller is also establishing an Internet presence to sell directly to the consumer, eliminating the waste of "double shipping" to stores and then to customers as well as other expenses. The company requires its suppliers to replace single-use packaging materials with packaging that can be reused. It also gives preferential treatment to suppliers that use recycled materials in their products.

Although many companies have become more environmentally responsible by improving their products, Herman Miller has gone a step further by designing and managing production facilities that function as efficiently as possible, thereby reducing waste and energy use. The buildings employ natural light whenever possible. Awnings have been installed over factory and office windows to reduce cooling costs in the summer, but can be retracted to take advantage of the sun's energy for wintertime heating. Landscaping on the company site incorporates local natural prairies and meadows that require no additional energy for maintenance. Miller's "Energy Center" converts material waste into heat to boil water to generate energy that can be used for manufacturing processes.

Miller's environmental initiatives not only have supported its founder's and managers' own personal beliefs of environmental stewardship and self-actualization but also have proven effective in reducing costs and building shareholder value. While Herman Miller has invested in the environment, it has also reduced waste and improved overall operating efficiency. For example, the Energy Plant has reduced landfill and fuel costs by $750,000 a year. In addition, the firm saves $250,000 a year in shipping and packaging materials. Herman Miller has embraced a strategic approach to making the natural environment an important concern in achieving long-run success.[1]

As Herman Miller's efforts illustrate, public and business support for environmental causes has increased since the first Earth Day was held in 1970. Four out of five respondents in a Gallup poll reported that they agree with the goals of the environmental movement, and another 80 percent indicated that they have participated in environmentally conscious activities such as recycling, avoiding products that harm the environment, trying to use less water, and reducing household consumption of energy.[2] Another survey found that 83.5 percent of *Fortune* 500 respondents have a written environmental policy, 74.7 percent recycle, and 69.7 percent have made investments in waste-reduction efforts.[3]

In this chapter, we explore the concept of the natural environment in the context of social responsibility in today's complex business environment. First, we define the natural environment and explore some of the significant environmental issues that businesses and society face. Next we consider the impact of government environmental policy and regulation on business and examine how some companies are going beyond the scope of these laws to address environmental issues and act in an environmentally responsible manner. Finally, we highlight a strategic approach to environmental issues, including risk management and strategic audits.

Global Environmental Issues

Most people probably associate the term *environment* with nature, including wildlife, trees, oceans, rivers, mountains, and prairies. Until the twentieth century, people generally thought of the environment solely in terms of how these resources could be harnessed to satisfy their needs for food, shelter, transportation, and recreation. As the Earth's population swelled throughout the twentieth century, however, humans began to use more and more of these resources, and, with technological advancements, to do so with ever-greater efficiency. Although these conditions have resulted in a much-improved standard of living, they come with a cost. Plant and animal species, along with wildlife habitats, are disappearing at an accelerated rate; water use has become a critical issue in some parts of the globe; and pollution has rendered the atmosphere of some cities a gloomy haze. How to deal with these issues has become a major concern for business and society in the twenty-first century.

Although the scope of the natural environment is quite broad—including plants, animals, human beings, oceans and other waterways, land, and the atmosphere—in this book, we discuss the term from a strategic business perspective. Thus, we define the **natural environment** as the physical world, including all biological entities, as well as the interaction among nature and individuals, organizations, and business strategies. In recent years, business has played a significant role in adapting, using, and maintaining the quality of the natural environment.

natural environment
the physical world, including all biological entities, as well as the interaction among nature and individuals, organizations, and business strategies

The protection of air, water, land, biodiversity, and renewable natural resources emerged as a major issue in the twentieth century in the face of increasing evidence that pollution, uncontrolled use of natural resources, and population growth were putting increasing pressure on the long-term sustainability of these resources. As the environmental movement sounded the alarm over these issues, governments around the globe responded with environmental protection laws during the 1970s. In recent years, companies have been increasingly incorporating these issues into their overall business strategies. Most of these issues have been the focus of concerned citizens as well as government and corporate efforts. Some nonprofit organizations have stepped forward to provide leadership in gaining the cooperation of diverse groups in responsible environmental activities. For example, the Coalition for Environmentally Responsible Economies (CERES), a union of businesses, consumer groups, environmentalists, and other stakeholders, has established a set of goals for environmental performance.

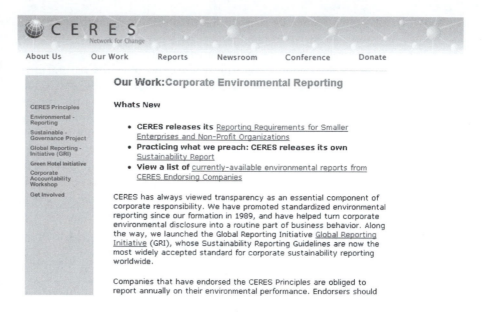

In this section, we examine some of the most significant environmental issues facing business and society today, including air pollution, acid rain, global warming, water pollution and water quantity, land pollution, waste management, deforestation, urban sprawl, biodiversity, and genetically modified foods.

Atmospheric Issues

Among the most far-reaching, and controversial, environmental issues are those that relate to the air we breathe. These include air pollution, acid rain, and global warming.

Air Pollution Air pollution typically arises from three different sources: stationary sources such as factories and power plants; mobile sources such as cars, trucks, planes, and trains; and natural sources such as windblown dust and volcanic eruptions.[4] These sources discharge gases, as well as particulates, that can be carried long distances by surface winds or linger on the surface for days if lack of winds or geographic conditions permit. Mexico City, for example, is surrounded by mountains, which trap the emissions from automobiles and industry and leave that city with the poorest air quality in the world. Such conditions can cause respiratory problems (e.g., asthma, bronchitis, and allergies) in humans and animals, especially in the elderly and the very young. Some of the chemicals associated with air pollution may contribute to birth defects, cancer, and brain, nerve, and respiratory system damage. Air pollution can also harm plants, animals, and water bodies. Haze caused by air pollution can reduce visibility, interfering with aviation, driving, and recreation.[5]

Acid Rain In addition to the health risks posed by air pollution, when nitrous oxides and sulfur dioxides emitted from manufacturing facilities react with air and rain, the result is acid rain. This phenomenon has contributed to the deaths of many valuable forests and lakes in North America as well as in Europe. Acid rain can also corrode paint and deteriorate stone, leaving automobiles, buildings, and cultural resources such as architecture and outside art vulnerable unless they are protected from its effects.[6]

Global Warming When carbon dioxide and other gases collect in the Earth's atmosphere, they trap the sun's heat like a greenhouse and prevent the Earth's surface from cooling. Without this process, the planet would become too cold to sustain life. However, during the twentieth century, the burning of fossil fuels—gasoline, natural gas, oil, and coal—accelerated dramatically, increasing the concentration of "greenhouse" gases like carbon dioxide and methane in the Earth's atmosphere. Chlorofluorocarbons—from refrigerants, coolants, and aerosol cans—also harm the Earth's ozone layer, which filters out the sun's harmful ultraviolet light. The United States produces almost 20 percent of all the greenhouse gases emitted (see Figure 9.1).[7] The United States plans to reduce greenhouse gases through incentives to businesses over the next ten years. Within the plan, they hope to set mandatory targets to reduce power plant emissions by 70 percent by the year 2018.[8]

Many scientists believe that increasing concentrations of greenhouse gases like methane and carbon dioxide in the atmosphere are warming the planet. In fact, accumulations of greenhouse gases have increased dramatically since preindustrial times.[9] However, a new study conducted and funded by NASA says the growth of so-called

FIGURE 9.1   Leading Emitters of Greenhouse Gases (by percentage)

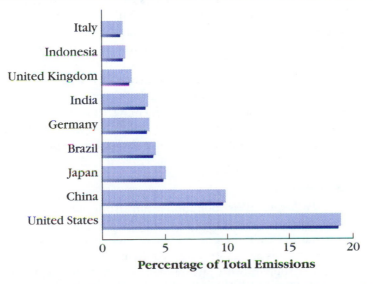

Source: Miles O'Brien, "Causes of Global Warming: Messing with the Thermostat Can Be Devastating," CNN, www.cnn.com/SPECIALS/1997/global.warming/causes/, accessed January 31, 2003.

greenhouse gas emissions in the atmosphere continues, but the growth rate peaked in 1980 and has slowed ever since.[10] The accumulation of these gases does appear to have increased average temperatures by an estimated 1 degree Fahrenheit over the last century. The year 2000—with many cities breaking records for the longest period without rain since the Dust Bowl of the 1930s and for the highest number of days over 100 degrees Fahrenheit—was the hottest year on record. Although 1 degree doesn't sound like much of a change, it is sufficient to increase the rate of polar ice sheet melting, which has already started to occur. Additionally, larger-than-normal icebergs are breaking away from the Antarctic ice shelf and drifting into shipping lanes. If this global warming continues, scientists warn that the planet's polar ice caps will begin to melt, potentially raising the sea level and perhaps flooding some of the world's most-populated areas. With less snow and ice cover to reflect the sun's rays, the Earth absorbs even more of the sun's heat, accelerating the warming process. Some scientists also think that global warming may alter long-term weather patterns, causing drought in some parts of the world while bringing floods to others.[11]

The theory of global warming has been rather controversial, and some scientists continue to dispute its existence. Critics of global warming argue that apparent temperature increases are part of a natural cycle of temperature variation that the planet has experienced over millions of years. Many companies and organizations have also maligned the theory. Indeed, one of the most aggressive critics has been the Global Climate Coalition, an alliance of electric utilities, coal and oil companies, petrochemical manufacturers, automakers, and related trade associations. The coalition has sponsored scientific research, public speaking tours, and advertising campaigns in an effort to thwart the **Kyoto Protocol,** a treaty proposed among industrialized nations to slow global warming. In the face of mounting evidence in support of global warming, however, many member firms have left the organization in recent years, including BP Amoco, Royal Dutch/Shell, Dow Chemical, Ford, DaimlerChrysler, and Texaco.[12] The Kyoto treaty continues to be a controversial and contentious issue in global politics. The United States has balked at signing the treaty, which would require slashing its level of greenhouse gas emissions to 6 percent that of 1990 by 2012, because leaders fear that compliance would jeopardize U.S. businesses and economy.[13] As of 2002, Canada has ratified the agreement and makes the protocol 17 percent closer to becoming mandatory for all countries within the United Nations. Russia is seriously considering joining within the next year, putting the number of signatories above the 55 percent agreed-on level of all UN members for the protocol to become mandatory. President George W. Bush is trying to come up with alternative incentives for businesses in fear of loss of profits.[14]

> **Kyoto Protocol**
> a treaty proposed among industrialized nations to slow global warming

Water Issues

Water Pollution   Water pollution results from the dumping of raw sewage and toxic chemicals into rivers and oceans, from oil and gasoline spills, and from the burial of industrial wastes in the ground where they may filter into underground water supplies. Fertilizers and pesticides used in farming and grounds maintenance also drain into water supplies with each rainfall. When these chemicals reach the oceans, they encourage the growth of algae that use up all the nearby oxygen, thus killing the sea life. According to the Environmental Protection Agency (EPA), more than a third of the nation's rivers, lakes, and coastal waters are not safe for swimming or fishing as a result of contaminated runoff. Lake Champlain and the Great Lakes, for example, have been polluted by mercury-contaminated rain caused by air pollution from coal-burning power plants, making the waters' fish unsafe to eat.[15] Water pollution problems are especially notable in heavily industrialized areas.

Water pollution can affect drinking water quality, whether a community obtains its water from surface reservoirs (rivers and lakes) or underground aquifers. In central Texas, for example, local citizens concerned about gasoline leaks contaminating drinking water supplies have vehemently protested a project to refit a fifty-year-old pipeline to carry gasoline across the state, directly over one major aquifer. One out of five drinking water systems in the United States is in violation of federal safety standards, and nearly one million Americans get sick every year because of contaminated water, according to a report by the EPA.[16] Two hundred eighteen million Americans live within ten miles of a polluted lake, river, stream, or coastal area, and over one-third of the nation's assessed waters are still unsafe for fishing, swimming, or supporting aquatic life.[17] One source of water contamination may be somewhat surprising. Researchers have found traces of antibiotics and other pharmaceuticals in streams, rivers, and municipal water supplies in the United States and Europe. Scientists worry that the presence of antibiotics in water supplies may encourage the development of "superbugs," infection-causing bacteria that are immune to currently available antibiotics.[18] The U.S. Environmental Protection Agency stated that millions of pounds of antibiotics and steroids used by U.S. agriculture are seeping into waterways, their effects still unknown. Animal-feeding operations are a significant part of the water pollution caused by U.S. agriculture, the leading source of pollution of the nation's lakes and rivers. Across the Great Plains, many communities are fighting increasingly vast animal-feeding operations. Some worry about the health effects from breathing the dust and gases produced by animal waste and from being exposed to chemicals that might get into the water or air.[19]

Mark Van Putton, president of the National Wildlife Foundation, believes that many states are ignoring federal legislation and regulations that would improve water quality. Many states have not aggressively enforced federal requirements, and many sources of pollution—agribusiness, logging, and power plants—often have strong political power to resist efforts to regulate their operations in ways that would reduce discharges that contaminate water supplies.[20] As an example, researchers issued an alarming report stating that virtually every sample of tap water they tested contained large quantities of hydrogen, which is a type of atom believed to have caused the Hindenburg dirigible disaster.[21] Special interests make it even more difficult to regulate water pollution in other parts of the world. Tougher regulations are needed globally to address pollution from activities such as dumping wastes into the ocean, large animal-feeding operations, logging sites, public roads, parking lots, and industrial waste created by production operations. The Sierra Club noted that 2002 marked the twenty-fifth anniversary of the Clean Water Act, one of the most successful environmental laws in our nation's history. Since the act was passed, nearly two-thirds of our lakes and rivers have become safe for swimming, compared to just 36 percent in 1970. However, the Sierra Club notes, we have not yet achieved the act's goal to make all waters safe for fishing and swimming; nor have we eliminated the discharge of all pollutants into the nation's lakes, rivers, and coastal waters.[22]

The National Fish and Wildlife Foundation provides grants to support conservation education, habitat protection and restoration, and natural resource management. (www.nfwf.org, downloaded April 2003.)

National Fish and Wildlife Foundation

Home Who We Are Grant Programs Contact Us Give Partners Careers Site Map

The National Fish and Wildlife Foundation conserves healthy populations of fish, wildlife and plants, on land and in the sea, through creative and respectful partnerships, sustainable solutions, and better education.

The Foundation meets these goals by awarding challenge grants to projects benefiting conservation education, habitat protection and restoration, and natural resource management.

Water Quantity In addition to concerns about the quality of water, some parts of the globe are increasingly worried about its quantity. There has been a sixfold increase in water use worldwide since 1990, and as a result, one-fifth of the world's population now has no access to safe drinking water. Since 1960, irrigation has jumped by 60 percent, with serious consequences for the global water supply. After several years of scorching summer months and below-average precipitation across most of the nation, as much as 49 percent of the United States is in the grips of a drought, according to the National Climatic Data Center. By summer 2003, long-term moisture deficits persisted, especially in Western states and parts of the Great Lakes to Northeast regions. These conditions put added pressure on facility managers to conserve water. The world's supply of accessible fresh water is decreasing drastically, in no small part because of U.S. consumption. The average American uses 86.2 gallons of fresh water per day—40 percent of which is flushed down toilets. New low-consumption toilets have proved they can assist in reducing water use.[23]

In other areas, poor weather conditions in conjunction with growing demand for water by booming populations has outpaced nature's ability to replenish surface and underground water sources, especially during periods of prolonged drought. A severe drought hit Colorado, Texas, New Mexico, and Mexico, but increased snow and rain the following year provided some replenishment of water supply. Nearly 500 emergency drilling permits were issued for farms and residences where groundwater wells, some 150 years old, went dry.[24] Concerns about water quantity have led to intense political and legal wrangling in a number of states. Indeed, Mark Twain (Samuel Clemens) once said, "Whiskey is for drinking, water is for fighting over."

Land Issues

Land Pollution Land pollution results from the dumping of residential and industrial wastes, strip mining, and poor forest conservation. Such pollution jeopardizes wildlife habitats, causes erosion, alters watercourses (leading to flooding), poisons groundwater supplies, and can contribute to illnesses in humans and animals. For example, the dumping of toxic industrial wastes into Love Canal, near Niagara Falls, New York, caused residents who moved to the area years later to experience high rates of birth defects and cancer.

Waste Management Another aspect of the land pollution problem is the issue of how to dispose of waste in an environmentally responsible manner. Consumers contribute an average of 1,500 pounds of garbage per person each year to landfills, and landfill space is declining. Within a few years, 70 percent of the nation's landfills will be full. Also compounding the waste-disposal problem is the fact that more than 50 percent of all garbage is made out of plastic, most of which does not decompose. Some communities have passed laws that prohibit the use of plastics such as Styrofoam for this reason.

Deforestation With a global population that exceeds 6 billion, human beings are squeezing other life from the planet. In Brazil and other South American countries, rain forests are being destroyed—at a rate of 1 acre per minute—to make way for farms and ranches, at a cost of the extinction of the many plants and animals (including some endangered species) that call the rain forest home. Nearly 60 percent of the world's rain forests have been lost to agricultural or timber interests.[25] Many of Africa's tropical forests and jungles are threatened by deforestation and development by humans. Large-scale deforestation also depletes the oxygen supply available to humans and other animals. Deforestation may also contribute to flooding when it destroys erosion-controlling plants. The causes of deforestation are very complex. A competitive global economy drives the need for money in economically challenged tropical countries. At the national level, governments sell logging concessions to raise money for projects, to pay international debt, or to develop industry. For example, Brazil has billions of dollars in international debt, on which it must make payments each year. The logging companies seek to harvest the forest and make profit from the sales of pulp and valuable hardwoods such as mahogany.[26]

Urban Sprawl One cause of deforestation in the United States is urban sprawl. The author James Howard Kunstler has defined urban sprawl as "a degenerate urban form that is too congested to be efficient, too chaotic to be beautiful, and too dispersed to possess the diversity and vitality of a great city."[27] Urban sprawl began with the post–World War II building boom that transformed the nation from primarily low-density communities designed to accommodate one-car households, bicyclists, and pedestrians to large-scale suburban developments at the edges of established towns and cities. Downtowns and inner cities deteriorated as strip and shopping malls, office parks, corporate campuses, and residential developments sprang up on what was once forest, prairie, or farm and ranch land. As the places where people live,

Environmentalists protest the destruction of the Redwood Forest by Old Navy and Gap. (Robert Brenner/ PhotoEdit)

work, and shop grew further apart, people began spending more time in automobiles, driving ever-greater distances.[28] According to the Surface Transportation Policy Project (STPP), almost 70 percent of the increase in driving between 1983 and 1990 was due to the effects of such sprawl.[29] Urban sprawl has not only consumed wildlife habitat, wetlands, and farmland, but it has also contributed to land, water, and especially air pollution. Table 9.1 lists the U.S. cities most threatened by sprawl.

TABLE 9.1	U.S. Cities Threatened by Urban Sprawl

LARGE CITIES (POPULATION ONE MILLION OR MORE)	MEDIUM CITIES (POPULATION 500,000 TO ONE MILLION)	SMALL CITIES (POPULATION 200,000–500,000)
1. Atlanta, GA	1. Orlando, FL	1. McAllen, TX
2. St. Louis, MO	2. Austin, TX	2. Raleigh, NC
3. Washington, DC	3. Las Vegas, NV	3. Pensacola, FL
4. Cincinnati, OH	4. West Palm Beach, FL	4. Daytona Beach, FL
5. Kansas City, MO	5. Akron, OH	5. Little Rock, AR
6. Denver, CO		
7. Seattle, WA		
8. Minneapolis-St. Paul, MN		
9. Ft. Lauderdale, FL		
10. Chicago, IL		

Source: "Thirty Most Sprawl-Threatened Cities," *The Dark Side of the American Dream: The Costs and Consequences of Suburban Sprawl,* Sierra Club, 1998, available at www.sierraclub.org/sprawl/report98/map.html. Reprinted by permission from Sierra Club.

Because of the problems associated with urban sprawl, some communities have taken drastic steps to limit it. Oregon, for example, has established an Urban Growth Boundary around the city of Portland to restrict growth and preserve open space and farm and ranch land around the city. In Texas, the city of Austin implemented a Smart Growth initiative that directs development away from environmentally sensitive areas. A number of Colorado cities, including Boulder and Fort Collins, require as much as 80 percent of new residential housing developments to be devoted to agriculture, wetlands, or open spaces for wildlife.

Biodiversity

Deforestation, pollution, development, and urban sprawl have put increasing pressure on wildlife, plants, and their habitats. Many plants and animals have become extinct, and thousands more are threatened. In the Florida Everglades, for example, channeling, damming, and diverting water for urban and agricultural uses have dramatically altered the sensitive ecosystem. As a result, 68 percent of the Everglades's native resident species, including the manatee and the panther, are now endangered.[30]

The world's tropical forests, which cover just 7 percent of the Earth's land surface, account for more than half of the planet's biological species.[31] The importance of these ecosystems is highlighted by the fact that 25 percent of the world's prescription drugs are extracted from plants primarily growing in tropical rain forests. Seventy percent of the 3,000 plants identified as sources of cancer-fighting drugs come from tropical forests, and scientists suspect that many more tropical plants may have pharmaceutical benefits. However, these forests are being depleted at alarming rates because of commercial logging, mining, and drilling and to make way for roads, farms, and ranches. More than half of the world's tropical forests have disappeared in the last century, and with them, many plant and animal species.[32] The most recent extinction: the Miss Waldron's red colobus monkey, a primate that once frequented the tropical forests of West Africa. With experts predicting that West Africa will lose 70 percent of its remaining forests, scientists fear that many more primates will become extinct during the twenty-first century.[33]

Many ecologists believe that the loss of such species threatens the success of entire ecosystems, which require a diversity of organisms in order to function properly. Recent global research indicates that declining numbers of available plant species result in lower ecosystem productivity, whereas increasing the number of species raises productivity.[34] Because each biological species plays a unique role in its ecosystem, the loss of any one of them may threaten the entire ecosystem. Pollinators, for example, play a significant role in any ecosystem. However, increasing development and widespread use of pesticides have reduced the populations of bees, insects, and bats that help plants reproduce. Among honeybees, the primary pollinators of food-producing plants, populations of domestic honeybees have declined by one-third, whereas many wild honeybees have become virtually extinct in many places around the world. Declines in pollinating species not only threaten the success of their relevant ecosystems but also may harm long-term global food production because one-third of all food products require pollinators to reproduce.[35]

Despite evidence of the importance of biodiversity in ecosystems, many people argue that human beings are more important than any single plant or animal species.

This argument lies at the heart of environmental battles over endangered species habitats throughout the United States and around the globe. In the Pacific Northwest, for example, old-growth forests are prime habitat for the endangered northern spotted owl, but their valuable timber provides jobs for hundreds of families as well as lumber to house a multiplying society. Although statistical evidence suggests that timber-related job losses in the Pacific Northwest are due as much to decades of overcutting of timberlands as to conservation measures to protect the owl, the battle of people's needs versus endangered species' needs continues there and elsewhere around the globe.[36]

Genetically Modified Foods

New technologies are also creating environmental issues, especially with regard to manipulating genes in plants and animals. Genetic engineering involves transferring one or more genes from one organism to another to create a new life form that has unique traits. Many of these genetically modified organisms have been developed to provide natural immunity against insects and viruses. Companies like Monsanto and DuPont marketed the idea that genetically modified (GMO) corn, soybeans, potatoes, canola oil seeds, and cotton plants are more pest resistant, require fewer chemicals to produce, and have higher yields.[37] Indeed, one of the primary goals of using these GMO plants is the reduction in the use of pesticides and other farming practices that harm the environment. Moreover, the resulting increase in crop yields can reduce costs, thereby making potentially more food available for world consumption.

On the other hand, the long-term impact of this genetic tinkering is not known. A study sponsored by the National Academy of Sciences reported that the GMO varieties developed so far do not pose allergy problems. However, the report called for further research to determine how to prevent GMO crops from killing beneficial and harmless insects, such as the monarch butterfly, and to deter herbicide-resistant genes from spreading into weeds.[38] Health, safety, and environmental concerns have prompted consumers around the world, particularly in Europe and Japan, to boycott products made from GMO crops.

Even while a backlash against GMO products builds, biotech companies are extending genetic engineering by experimenting with inserting artificial chromosomes into the cells of animals. For example, genetically engineered animal milk can be used as a culture for producing a vast range of drugs. However, many consumers are finding this technology as unpalatable as GMO plants. Regulators in Germany and France have already banned its use, and the U.S. Food and Drug Administration will not approve the testing of artificial chromosomes in people as therapies for genetic diseases. As with GMO plants, the problem with genetic engineering of animal cells is that the long-run effects cannot currently be predicted. Large numbers of genetically altered animals could upset the balance in relationships among various species with undetermined effects, such as the ability to reproduce or fight diseases and pests.[39] Until further research addresses public concerns about the safety and long-term environmental effects of these technologies, their success in the marketplace is uncertain. We will take a further look at some of the issues associated with the technology of GMO foods in Chapter 10.

Environmental Policy and Regulation

The United States, like most other nations, has passed numerous laws and established regulatory agencies to address environmental issues. Most of these efforts have focused on the activities of businesses, government agencies, and other organizations that use natural resources in providing goods and services.

Environmental Protection Agency

The most influential regulatory agency that deals with environmental issues and enforces environmental legislation in the United States is the Environmental Protection Agency (EPA). The EPA's founding in 1970 was the culmination of a decade of growing protests over the deterioration of the natural environment. This movement reached a significant climax with the publication of Rachel Carson's *Silent Spring,* an attack on the indiscriminate use of pesticides, which rallied scientists, activists, and citizens from around the country to crusade to protect the environment from abuses of the time. Twenty million Americans joined together on April 22, 1970, for Earth Day, a nationwide demonstration for environmental reforms. President Richard Nixon responded to these events by establishing the EPA as an independent agency to establish and enforce environmental protection standards, conduct environmental research, provide assistance in fighting pollution, and assist in developing and recommending new policies for environmental protection.[40] The agency is also charged with ensuring that

- All Americans are protected from significant risks to their health and to the environment in which they live and work.
- National efforts to manage environmental risk are based on the best scientific information available.
- Federal laws protecting human health and the environment are enforced fairly and effectively.
- Environmental protection is an integral consideration in U.S. policies concerning natural resources, human health, economic growth, energy, transportation, agriculture, industry, and international trade and these factors are considered in establishing environmental policy.
- All parts of society have access to accurate information sufficient to participate effectively in managing human health and environmental risks.
- Environmental protection contributes to diverse, sustainable, and economically productive communities and ecosystems.
- The United States plays a leadership role in working with other nations to protect the environment.[41]

With these charges, the EPA has become one of the most powerful regulatory forces in the United States. For example, the agency recently reached an agreement with Syngenta, the leading manufacturer of diazinon, to phase out home and garden use of the commonly used pesticide and permit only limited commercial use of the product, which belongs to a class of pesticides that have been linked to neurological disorders and other health problems in children. Although diazinon is considered less risky than other organophosphates, Syngenta executives said the company could not justify paying for the research needed to prove the pesticide's safety for consumer use and therefore agreed to the phaseout.[42]

To fulfill its primary mission to protect human health and the natural environment into the next century, the EPA recently established ten long-term strategic goals to define its planning, budgeting, analysis, and accountability processes (see Table 9.2). To determine these goals, the agency solicited and evaluated significant stakeholder input on priority areas related to human health and environmental protection activities. Thus, these goals reflect public priorities as voiced by Congress in the form of statutes and regulations designed to achieve clean air and water, proper waste management, and other important concerns.[43]

To achieve these goals and carry out its public mission, the EPA may also file civil charges against companies that violate the law. For example, the EPA, along with the U.S. Department of Justice and the state of Texas, settled two lawsuits against Koch Industries over more than 300 oil spills from the Kansas-based firm's pipelines and facilities in six states. The settlement imposed $30 million in civil penalties—the largest ever in the history of federal environmental law—against Koch and required the firm to hire an independent auditor to oversee repairs on 2,500 miles of pipeline, to improve its maintenance and training programs, and to spend $5 million on environmental projects in Kansas, Oklahoma, and Texas.[44] In comparison, Exxon's settlement with state and federal governments amounted to nearly $6 billion in compensatory and punitive damages after its tanker, the *Exxon Valdez,* ran aground and leaked 11 million gallons of oil into Alaska's Prince William Sound. The company also paid more than $2 billion to clean up damage from the ecological disaster and

---

TABLE 9.2	Goals of the Environmental Protection Agency

GOAL	LONG-TERM OUTCOME
1	Clean air
2	Clean and safe water
3	Safe food
4	Preventing pollution and reducing risk in communities, homes, workplaces, and ecosystems
5	Better waste management, restoration of contaminated waste sites, and emergency response
6	Reduction of global and cross-border environmental risks
7	Quality environmental information
8	Sound science, improved understanding of environmental risk, and greater innovation to address environmental problems
9	A credible deterrent to pollution and greater compliance with the law
10	Effective management

Source: "Strategic Plan," Office of the Chief Financial Officer, Environmental Protection Agency, www.epa.gov/ocfo/plan/plan.htm., accessed January 31, 2003.

to reimburse government agencies for their expenses in response to the spill. Although the Exxon oil spill occurred more than a decade ago, the legal, political, and social implications of this event are still evolving.[45]

Environmental Legislation

A significant number of laws have been passed to address both general and specific environmental issues, including public health, threatened species, toxic substances, clean air and water, and natural resources. Table 9.3 summarizes some of the most significant laws related to environmental protection.

Clean Air Act The Clean Air Act, passed in 1970, is a comprehensive federal law that regulates atmospheric emissions from a variety of sources.[46] Among its most significant provisions is the requirement that the Environmental Protection Agency establish national air quality standards as well as standards for significant new pollution sources and for all facilities emitting hazardous substances. These maximum pollutant standards, called National Ambient Air Quality Standards (NAAQS), were mandated for every state in order to protect public health and the environment. The states were further directed to develop state implementation plans (SIPs) pertinent to the industries in each state. The law also established deadlines for reducing automobile emission levels—90 percent reductions in hydrocarbon and carbon monoxide levels by 1975 and a 90 percent reduction in nitrogen oxides by 1976. Because many areas of the country failed to meet these deadlines, the Clean Air Act was amended in 1977 to set new dates for attainment of the NAAQS.[47] The Clean Air Act was revised again as the Clean Air Act Amendments of 1990 to address lingering problems or issues that were not acknowledged in the original law, such as acid rain, ground-level ozone, stratospheric ozone depletion, and air toxins. The amended act also increased the number of regulated pollutants from fewer than 20 to more than 380.[48]

Federal Insecticide, Fungicide, and Rodenticide Act The primary focus of the Federal Insecticide, Fungicide, and Rodenticide Act of 1972 was to place the distribution, sale, and use of pesticides under federal control. The law granted the EPA the authority to study the consequences of pesticide use and to require all users to register when purchasing pesticides. All pesticides used in the United States must be registered (licensed) with the EPA to assure that they will be properly labeled and so that, if used according to specifications, they will not cause unreasonable harm to the environment. Later amendments to the law also require users to take exams in order to be certified as applicators of pesticides.[49]

Endangered Species Act The Endangered Species Act of 1973 established a program to protect threatened and endangered species as well as the habitats in which they are found.[50] An endangered species is one that is in danger of extinction, whereas a threatened species is one that may become endangered without protection. The U.S. Fish and Wildlife Service of the Department of the Interior maintains the list of endangered and threatened species, which currently includes 632 endangered species (326 are plants) and 190 threatened species (78 are plants). The Endangered Species

| TABLE 9.3 | Major Environmental Laws |

ACT (DATE ENACTED)	PURPOSE
National Environmental Policy Act (1969)	Established national environmental policy, set goals, and provided a means for implementing the policy; promotes efforts to prevent damage to the biosphere and to stimulate human health and welfare, established a Council on Environmental Quality.
Occupational Safety and Health Act (1970)	Ensures worker and workplace safety by requiring employers to provide a place of employment free from health and safety hazards.
Clean Air Act (1970)	Regulates emissions from natural, stationary, and mobile sources; authorized the EPA to establish National Ambient Air Quality Standards (NAAQS) to protect public health and the environment.
Federal Insecticide, Fungicide, and Rodenticide Act (1972)	Provides for federal control of pesticide distribution, sale, and use; requires users to register when purchasing pesticides.
Endangered Species Act (1973)	Established a conservation program for threatened and endangered plants and animals and their habitats; prohibits the import, export, interstate, and foreign commerce or any action that results in a "taking" of a listed species or that adversely affects habitat.
Safe Drinking Water Act (1974)	Protects the quality of drinking water in the United States; authorized the EPA to establish water purity standards and required public water systems to comply with health-related standards.
Toxic Substances Control Act (1976)	Empowered the EPA to track industrial chemicals currently produced or imported into the United States; authorized the EPA to require reporting or testing of chemicals and to ban the manufacture and import of chemicals that pose an unreasonable risk.
Resource Conservation Recovery Act (1976)	Empowered the EPA to control the generation, and transportation, treatment, storage, and disposal of hazardous waste.
Clean Water Act (1977)	Authorized the EPA to set effluent standards on an industrywide basis and to continue to set water quality standards for all contaminants in surface waters; made it unlawful for any person to discharge any pollutant from a point source into navigable waters without a permit.
Comprehensive Environmental Response, Compensation, and Liability Act (1980)	Established prohibitions and requirements concerning closed and abandoned hazardous waste sites; authorized a tax on the chemical and petroleum industries to establish a "superfund" to provide for cleanup when no responsible party could be identified.
Superfund Amendments Reauthorization Act (1986)	Amended the Comprehensive Environmental and Response, Compensation, and Liability Act to increase the size of the superfund; required superfund actions to consider the standards and requirements found in other state and federal environmental laws and regulations; provided new enforcement authorities and tools.
Emergency Planning and Community Right-to-Know Act (1986)	Enacted to help local communities protect public health and safety and the environment from chemical hazards; requires each state to appoint a State Emergency Response Commission (SERC) and to establish Emergency Planning Districts.

(continued on next page)

TABLE 9.3	Major Environmental Laws *(continued)*
Oil Pollution Act (1990)	Requires oil storage facilities and vessels to submit plans detailing how they will respond to large spills; requires the development of area contingency plans to prepare and plan for responses to oil spills on a regional scale.
Pollution Prevention Act (1990)	Promotes pollution reduction through cost-effective changes in production, operation, and use of raw materials and practices that increase efficiency and conserve natural resources, such as recycling, source reduction, and sustainable agriculture.
Food Quality Protection Act (1996)	Amended the Federal Insecticide, Fungicide, and Rodenticide Act and the Federal Food, Drug, and Cosmetic Act to change the way the EPA regulates pesticides; applies a new safety standard—reasonable certainty of no harm—to all pesticides used on foods.

Source: "Major Environmental Laws," Environmental Protection Agency, www.epa.gov/epahome/laws.htm, accessed January 31, 2003.

Act prohibits any action that results in the harm to or death of a listed species or that adversely affects endangered species habitat. It also makes the import, export, and interstate and foreign commerce of listed species illegal. Protected species may include birds, insects, fish, reptiles, mammals, crustaceans, flowers, grasses, cacti, and trees.[51]

The Endangered Species Act has become one of the most controversial environmental laws passed in the United States. Some environmentalists fear the law may backfire if landowners who find endangered or threatened species on their property fail to notify authorities in order to avoid the expense and hassle of complying with the law; in some cases, threatened or endangered species have been harmed by landowners seeking to avoid the law. Concerns about the restrictions and costs associated with the law are not entirely unfounded. Consider the case of Brandt Child, who purchased 500 acres in Utah with the intention of building a campground and golf course. However, the U.S. Fish and Wildlife Service ordered Child not to use the land because 200,000 federally protected Kanab ambersnails inhabited three lakes on the premises. The federal government not only refused to compensate Child for his loss of the use of the property, it also threatened to fine him $50,000 per snail if geese that wandered onto the property had eaten any of the snails (the geese were later found to be snail free).[52] Such anecdotes have angered many property rights activists who believe that the Endangered Species Act goes too far in protecting threatened species at the expense of human rights.

Toxic Substances Control Act Congress passed the Toxic Substances Control Act in 1976 to empower the Environmental Protection Agency with the ability to track the 75,000 industrial chemicals currently produced or imported into the United States. The agency repeatedly screens these chemicals and can require reporting or testing of those which may pose an environmental or human-health hazard. It can also ban the manufacture and import of those chemicals which pose an unreasonable risk. The EPA has the ability to track the thousands of new chemicals developed by industry each year with either unknown or dangerous characteristics. It then can control these chemicals as necessary to protect human health and the environment.[53]

Clean Water Act In 1977, Congress amended the Federal Water Pollution Control Act of 1972 as the Clean Water Act. This law granted the EPA the authority to establish effluent standards on an industry basis and continued the earlier law's requirements to set water quality limits for all contaminants in surface waters. The Clean Water Act makes it illegal for anyone to discharge any pollutant from a point source into navigable waters without a permit.[54]

Emergency Planning and Community Right-to-Know Act The Emergency Planning and Community Right-to-Know Act was enacted in 1986 to help local communities identify and protect public health, safety, and the environment from chemical hazards. To achieve this goal, the law requires that businesses report the locations and quantities of stored chemicals to state and local governments to help them respond to chemical spills and similar emergencies. Additionally, the law mandates that most manufacturers file a **Toxics Release Inventory (TRI)** of all releases of specified chemicals into the air, water, or land, as well as transfers of chemicals for treatment or disposal. TRIs must also be filed with the U.S. EPA, which compiles the reports in a publicly accessible online database. As such, the TRI program serves as a "public report card" of chemical pollution from U.S. manufacturing facilities. It also creates a powerful incentive for manufacturers to reduce their emissions and wastes.[55]

Toxics Release Inventory (TRI)
"public report card" filed with the U.S. EPA that contains all releases of specified chemicals into the air, water, or land, as well as transfers by manufacturers of chemicals for treatment or disposal

Pollution Prevention Act The Pollution Prevention Act of 1990 focused industry, government, and public attention on reducing pollution through cost-effective changes in production, operation, and raw materials use. Practices include recycling, source reduction, sustainable agriculture, and other practices that increase efficiency in the use of energy, water, or other natural resources and protect resources through conservation.[56]

Food Quality Protection Act In 1996, the Food Quality Protection Act amended the Federal Insecticide, Fungicide, and Rodenticide Act and the Federal Food, Drug, and Cosmetic Act to fundamentally change the way the EPA regulates pesticides. The law included a new safety standard—reasonable certainty of no harm—that must be applied to all pesticides used on foods.[57] The legislation establishes a more consistent, science-based regulatory environment and mandates a single, health-based standard for all pesticides in all foods. The law also provides special protections for infants and children, expedites approval of safer pesticides, provides incentives for the development and maintenance of effective crop protection tools for farmers, and requires periodic reevaluation of pesticide registrations and tolerances to ensure that they are up-to-date and based on good science.[58]

Business Response to Environmental Issues

Partly in response to federal legislation such as the National Environmental Policy Act of 1969 and partly due to stakeholder concerns, businesses are applying creativity, technology, and business resources to respond to environmental issues. In many cases, these firms not only have improved their reputations with interested stakeholders but also have seen dramatic cost savings by making their operations more efficient. Moreover, many companies, including Walt Disney, Chevron, and Scott Paper, have created a new executive position, vice president of environmental affairs. This position is designed to help these companies achieve their business goals in an environmentally responsible manner. In an effort to protect our resources, AT&T supports and helps publish the *Green Business Letter,* a hands-on journal for environmentally conscious companies. Corporate efforts to respond to environmental issues focus on green marketing, recycling, emissions reductions, and socially responsible buying.

Green Marketing

green marketing
the specific development, pricing, promotion, and distribution of products that do less harm to the environment

Green marketing refers to the specific development, pricing, promotion, and distribution of products that do less harm to the environment. General Motors, for example, is developing new "hybrid" pickup trucks and buses that employ electric motors to augment their internal-combustion engines, improving the vehicles' fuel economy without a loss in power. The full-size trucks, for example, will get nearly 15 percent better gas mileage than a conventional pickup.[59]

One truly "green" firm is the Parks Company, which donates 5 percent of the gross profit from its catalog sales to U.S. national parks to help bridge their $9 billion budget shortfall. Since the company was founded in 1995, the mailing list for its catalog of parks-related gift items has grown to 60,000, and the firm donated $20,000 in its first twenty-eight months of business. The company also established a grass-roots campaign, One for the Parks, to crusade for using 1 percent of the federal budget surplus to help meet the parks' budget needs.[60]

General Motors responds to environmental concerns by producing environmentally friendly hybrid cars. (General Motors Corporation)

Even some real estate developers are attempting to integrate environmental concerns into new communities to protect the land. One example, in Colorado, is Meadow Ranch. The developer of Meadow Ranch deliberately designed a community that spares wildlife habitat to ensure that new homeowners do not evict the hawks and red foxes that have long roamed the land. Homes in Meadow Ranch sit on land once zoned light industrial, which, had it been developed as such, would have destroyed thirty of the forty wetland acres preserved on the site today. The developers also consulted the Colorado National Plant Society, the Army Corps of Engineers, and the Soil Conservation District to ensure that new landscaping harmonized with the native plants. The firm even prints its brochures on recycled paper.[61]

Many products are certified as "green" by environmental organizations such as Green Seal and carry a special logo identifying them as such. In Europe, companies can voluntarily apply for an Eco-label (see Figure 9.2) to indicate that their product is less harmful to the environment than competing products, based on scientifically determined criteria. About 250 products have been awarded an Eco-label.[62] Lumber products at Home Depot and the U.K.-based B&Q may carry a seal from the Forest Stewardship Council to indicate that they were harvested from sustainable forests using environmentally friendly methods.[63] Likewise, most Chiquita bananas are certified through the Better Banana Project as having been grown with more environmental- and labor-friendly practices.[64]

However, a recent study by Consumers International suggests that consumers are being confused and even misled by green marketing claims. Researchers compared claims on products sold in ten countries, including the United States, to labeling guidelines established by the International Standards Organization (ISO), which prohibit vague and misleading claims as well as unverifiable ones such as "environmentally friendly" and "nonpolluting." The study found that many products' claims are too vague or misleading to meet ISO standards. For example, one brand of flour claimed to be "nonpolluting," and a German compost was described as "earthworm friendly." Among the products with the highest number of misleading or unverifiable claims were laundry detergents, household cleaners, and paints. Anna Fielder, the director of Consumers International, contends that the study shows that although there are many useful claims made about the environmental responsibility of products, there is still a long way to go to ensure that shoppers are adequately informed about the environmental impact of the products they buy.[65]

Although the demand for legal and practical solutions to environmental issues is widespread, the environmental movement includes many diverse groups, whose val-

---

FIGURE 9.2   The European Eco-label

Source: "European Union Eco-label Logo," *Europa,* European Union, europa.eu.int/comm/environment/ecolabel/, accessed March 4, 2003.

ues and goals often conflict. There is growing agreement among environmentalists and businesses, however, that companies should work to protect and preserve the natural environment by implementing a number of goals. First, companies should strive to eliminate the concept of waste. Because pollution and waste usually stem from inefficiency, the issue should not be what to do with waste but, rather, how to make things more efficiently so that no waste is produced. Second, companies should rethink the concept of a product. Products can be classified as consumables, which are eaten or biodegradable; durable goods, such as cars, televisions, computers, and refrigerators; and unsalables, including such undesirable by-products as radioactive materials, heavy metals, and toxins. The design of durable goods should utilize a closed loop system of manufacture and use, and a return to the manufacturing process that allows products and resources to be disassembled and recycled and minimizes the disposal of unsalables. Third, the price of products should reflect their true costs, including the costs of replenishing natural resources that are utilized or damaged during the production process. Finally, businesses should seek ways to make their commitment to the environment profitable.[66]

recycling
the reprocessing of materials, especially steel, aluminum, paper, glass, rubber, and some plastics, for reuse

Recycling Initiatives

Many organizations engage in **recycling,** the reprocessing of materials, especially steel, aluminum, paper, glass, rubber, and some plastics, for reuse (see Figure 9.3). Procter & Gamble, for example, uses recycled materials in some of its packaging and

FIGURE 9.3   **Recycling Steel Cans**

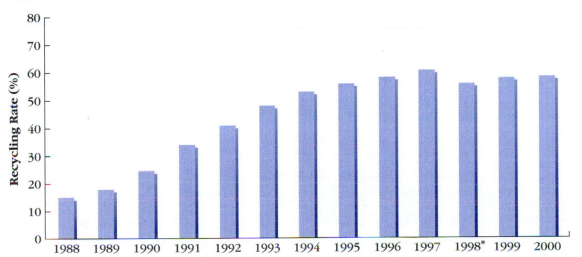

*Drop in 1998 recycling rates can be attributed to U.S. steel industry production cutbacks caused by record increases in unfairly traded foreign steel imports.

Source: "A Few Facts About Steel—North America's #1 Recycled Material," Steel Recycling Institute, www.recycle-steel.org/index2.html, accessed January 31, 2003. Reprinted by permission from the Steel Recycling Institute.

markets refills for some products, which reduce packaging waste. Sonoma County (California) Stable and Livestock markets rubber mats recycled from used tires for use in horse stalls.[67] More than 50 percent of all products sold in stores are packed in 100 percent recycled paperboard. Other markets using 100 percent recycled paperboard include book covers, jigsaw puzzles, board games, greeting cards, and video and CD covers.[68] Starbucks makes coffee grounds available free to those who wish to use them for compost to add nutrition to their gardens. Ben Pachard, Starbucks's environmental affairs manager, says, "Recycling the grounds back into the garden is a better alternative then throwing them away into the trash."[69]

A number of beverage companies have formed an alliance called WasteWise to represent and share industry goals and best practices with respect to recycling and waste management. Anheuser-Busch Companies, for example, reduced its total solid waste by 15 percent, or 19 million pounds, in one year through waste prevention and recycling. Coca-Cola purchases more than $2 billion in recycled content materials in the United States alone. Pepsi-Cola switched to reusable plastic shipping cases and saved $44 million. Coors, by using a lighter-weight bottle, saved more than one million pounds of glass.[70] Table 9.4 shows some of the goals and techniques the beverage industry maintains in managing waste.

Future Solutions, Inc., distributes recycled products ranging from automated teller machine (ATM) supplies and toilet bowl brushes to recycled mouse pads and

---

TABLE 9.4   A Sampling of Beverage Industry Waste Management Initiatives

INITIATIVE

Utilize lightweight plastic and glass bottles.

Switch from corrugated shippers to reusable plastic cases.

Institute a glove-reuse program in manufacturing facilities.

Develop a waste tracking system for syrup production facilities that measures and tracks the amount of waste generated on a per-unit basis.

Refurbish, rather than replace, vending equipment.

Implement a six-pack ring-recycling program.

Collect and bale corrugated shipping containers from the public.

Establish a facility to buy back used beverage containers from the public.

Increase recycled content in glass bottles.

Increase recycled content in corrugated shipping containers.

COMPANIES SUPPORTING THE BEVERAGE INDUSTRY WASTEWISE INITIATIVES

7UP/RC Bottling	Anheuser-Busch Companies
Coors Brewing Companies	Pepsi-Cola Company
Coca-Cola Company	Poland Spring Natural Spring Water
Very Fine Products	

Source: "Doing What It Takes to Be Wastewise," Environmental Protection Agency, April 1999, www.epa.gov/wastewise/about/id-bev.htm, accessed January 28, 2003.

vacuum cleaners from more than 300 manufacturers. Among the firm's clients are the U.S. Department of Energy and the states of Colorado, California, and Arizona. Plans for Future Solutions include constructing a new office headquarters out of 100 percent recycled materials that utilizes both energy-efficient and water-conserving products.[71]

Companies are finding ways to recycle water to avoid discharging chemicals into rivers and streams and to preserve diminishing water supplies. DaimlerChrysler, for example, has three manufacturing plants that operate wastewater-recycling facilities. The company's facility in Toluca, Mexico, which manufactures the PT Cruiser, operates a comprehensive recycling system that treats more than 610,000 gallons of wastewater—enough to fill up ten medium-sized baseball stadiums—each day from both manufacturing operations and sanitary operations (like restrooms, showers, and cafeterias). Because the plant totally recycles all the water used, it draws less from the area's receding aquifer and minimizes the potential for polluted water to reach a nearby river system. Moreover, the system allows DaimlerChrysler's water quality standards to be stricter than those set by Mexico or the United States.[72]

Emissions Reduction Initiatives

To combat air pollution and the threat of global warming, many companies have begun to take steps to reduce the emissions of greenhouse gases from their facilities. Many firms, such as Herman Miller, Inc., which designs and manages production facilities to function as efficiently as possible, are finding new ways to light and heat their buildings and factories to improve efficiency, thereby reducing waste and energy use. Making improvements in energy efficiency can save a company approximately $1 per square foot of office or factory space per year.[73] There is even a new term coined, **green power.** It is defined as energy sources that are commonly accepted as having relatively low impact on human, animal, and ecosystem health. Renewable energy sources including solar, wind, biomass, landfill gas, and geothermal qualify as green power. Companies such as General Motors, IBM, and Johnson & Johnson are helping pave the way for the creation of cost-competitive clean power options. A few of the benefits of using this type of energy are that it provides on-site electricity generation, helps stabilize corporate energy costs, and provides a hedge against the uncertainty of future environmental regulations.[74]

> **green power**
> energy sources that are commonly accepted as having relatively low impact on human, animal, and ecosystem health

Many companies are going beyond the emission reductions called for by the 1997 Kyoto Protocol, which set a goal of reducing greenhouse emissions by signing countries by 7 percent from their 2000 levels. DuPont, for example, is slashing its greenhouse gas emissions to 58 million tons, or 40 percent of their 1991 levels. Royal Dutch/Shell is working to reduce greenhouse gas emissions from its plants to 100 million tons, or 25 percent below 1990 levels. To achieve an equivalent reduction, every car in New England would have to be taken off the road for five years.[75] Those companies that achieve reductions in excess of that called for by the Kyoto Protocol earn credits that may then be "traded" to other firms that have not yet achieved their targets. Nations may also trade credits earned from reducing emissions to other nations that have yet to do so. Russia, for example, plans to use the revenue from the sale of these credits to fund clean-energy projects.[76]

Legal and Regulatory Challenges

Single-Use Camera Recycling Issues

Disposable cameras are increasingly popular because of their size and convenience. They account for 40 percent of worldwide film sales, which equates to about $2 billion annually. Fujifilm (Fuji), the world's number two film maker, holds the key patent for disposable cameras. Eastman Kodak obtained licensing rights from Fuji to produce and manufacture single-use cameras. No matter how convenient these disposable cameras are, they tend to be thrown away and added to the ever-growing amount of waste.

As landfills continue to bulge with waste and the increasing scarcity of natural resources jeopardizes our delicate ecosystem, companies are responding to the challenge of protecting and preserving our environment in a socially responsible manner. To accomplish this, Fuji decided to conduct a recycling program for the QuickSnap camera in 1990. They added it as an essential attribute to their corporate philosophy, in part because of their sensitivity and commitment to worldwide environmental concerns. Part of their challenge with this new initiative

was to get people to stop thinking "disposable" and start thinking recyclable.

Kodak has also taken an environmentally concerned approach by starting a recycling program as part of their design-for-the-environment initiative. Both companies are proud to be manufacturers of one of the most-recycled and most recyclable products in the world. Globally, the percentage of cameras returned is about 60 percent and growing. In the United States, single-use camera (74 percent) recycling rates surpass those of corrugated containers (73 percent), aluminum cans (63 percent), steel cans (58 percent), and bottles (33 percent). Since the program began, hundreds of millions of cameras have been recycled, diverting 70 million pounds of waste from landfills. By almost any benchmark, this type of recycling achievement is unparalleled. Another added benefit of reusing instead of disposing is that the cameras can be recycled more than three times on average.

As an incentive to recycle, the large camera corporations offer a base price for all one-time-use cameras returned, around 25 cents. They also pay for the pickup and delivery charges. However, somewhere along the way a company by the name

Socially Responsible Buying

Socially responsible buying initiatives are another way that companies are finding to incorporate environmental responsibility into their business strategies. Minette Drumwright has defined socially responsible buying (SRB) as "that which attempts to take into account the public consequences of organizational buying or bring about positive social change through organizational buying behavior."[77] DaimlerChrysler, for example, required its plastic parts suppliers to include 30 percent recycled parts by 2002. Staples, Inc., recently committed to reducing its consumption of paper products from endangered forests.[78]

A company that takes a proactive approach to socially responsible buying is likely to (1) be actively involved in the development of SRB principles and practices both inside and outside of its own operations, (2) routinely and objectively evaluate its suppliers' achievements with respect to the social responsibilities involved, and (3) communicate its achievements and failures to its primary stakeholders. How companies implement SRB strategies ranges from terminating relations with suppliers who will not abide by the firm's environmental goals to seeking out partners who can

of Jazz Photo Corporation decided to shave profits from the giant, eco-friendly companies. Jazz was created in the late 1990s by latching on to the phenomenal growth of disposable cameras. They had the idea to take the used Fuji and Kodak camera cases discarded by film processors, place new film in them, color out the label, and market them to retailers such as Wal-Mart Stores, Inc. The reloaded cameras sold for a dollar or two less than the name brands, and sales skyrocketed.

After this had gone on for awhile, it caught the attention of Fuji because they noticed that Jazz was eating into the market. The "reloaders" had about 10 percent of the market in 1999 when Fuji and Kodak decided to file suit against them for patent infringement and use of stolen technology. Jazz's strategy was to go into the backdoors of photo labs and offer more for a base price than the camera companies were offering. Then they would use the camera shell and fill it with cheap, generic, low-priced film and batteries to make it appear to be legit. In fact, it was very different. In a study conducted on behalf of the lawsuit, of almost 500 reloaded cameras that were tested, close to 50 percent were found to have at least one observable defect. Kodak warns that

photo retailers should use caution in selling and promoting these reloads because of the risk that consumers who buy and use these cameras may be dissatisfied with the quality of their prints.

Finally after four years of deliberations, a jury agreed with Fuji and awarded them $22.9 million in damages for the relabeling of 41 million rebuilt cameras between 1995 and 2001. The International Trade Commission has since barred Jazz and similar firms from refurbishing single-use cameras. The ruling may help Fuji and Kodak eliminate at least one competitor in the market, which is gaining in popularity.

Sources:
These facts came from "Kodak: HSE Annual Report, 2000—Single-Use Cameras," Kodak.com/US/en/corp/environment/00CoprEnviroRpt/HSEsingle-use.shtml, accessed March 6, 2003; "Explore the World of Fujifilm–Recycling," www.fujifilm.com/JSP/fuji/epartners/recycling.jsp?nav=3, accessed March 6, 2003; "Nonmetallics," *Recycling Today*, March 2001, www.recyclingtoday.com/articles/article.asp?ID=442&CatID=&SubCatID=/, accessed March 6, 2003; "Picture This: Disposable Camera Could Spoil Memories," NBC5.com, November 25, 2002, www.nbc5.com/print/1806438/detail.html?use=print, accessed March 6, 2003; "Fuji Wins Disposable-Camera Suit," *Wall Street Journal Online*, March 3, 2003, online.wsj.com/article, accessed March 6, 2003; Susan Decker, "Disposable Camera Firm Ordered to Pay," *CanWest Global Communications*, March 4, 2003; "Judge: Firm Must Pay for Taking Fuji's One-Use Camera Technology," *Miami Herald*, March 3, 2003.

supply environmentally friendly parts and supplies to forming industrywide agreements. In the United Kingdom, for example, Co-operative Bank, after discovering that one of its furniture suppliers was unknowingly using endangered tropical hardwoods, introduced the manufacturer to a firm that could supply it with more sustainable resources.[79]

Strategic Implementation of Environmental Responsibility

Businesses have responded to the opportunities and threats created by environmental issues with varying levels of commitment. The World Resources Institute states that the "principle of environmental governance is decision-making that is 'accessible,'" that is, decisions that are transparent and open to public input and oversight.[80] As Figure 9.4 indicates, a low-commitment business attempts to avoid dealing with environmental issues and hopes that nothing bad will happen or that no one will ever find out about an environmental accident or abuse. Such firms may try to protect themselves against lawsuits. Hooker Chemical, for example, disposed of its chemical

FIGURE 9.4	Strategic Approaches to Environmental Issues

Low Commitment	Medium Commitment	High Commitment
Deals only with existing problems	Attempts to comply with environmental laws	Has strategic programs to address environmental issues
Plans limitedly anticipated issues	Deals with issues that could cause public relations issues	Views environment as an opportunity to advance the business strategy
Fails to consider stakeholder environmental issues	Views environmental issues from a tactical, not a strategic, perspective	Consults with stakeholders about their environmental concerns
Operates without concern for long-term environmental impact	Views environment as more of a threat than an opportunity	Conducts an environmental audit to assess performance issues and adopts international standards

wastes in and around Love Canal near Niagara Falls, New York, because the area was sparsely populated. When the area was developed years later, new residents were surprised when toxic fumes were detected in some basements. Many families were ultimately forced to abandon their homes. Many people felt that Hooker had failed by not being actively involved in preventing this tragedy. On the other hand, some companies take a high-commitment approach toward natural environment issues. Such firms develop strategic management programs, which view the environment as an opportunity for advancing organizational interests. These companies respond to stakeholder interests, assess risks, and develop a comprehensive environmental strategy. Home Depot, for example, has established a set of environmental principles that include selling responsibly marketed products, eliminating unnecessary packaging, recycling and encouraging the use of products with recycled content, and conserving natural resources by using them wisely. The company also makes contributions to many environmental organizations, including Keep America Beautiful, the Tampa Audubon Society, and the World Wildlife Fund.[81]

Stakeholder Assessment

Stakeholder analysis, as discussed in Chapter 2, is an important part of a high-commitment approach to environmental issues. This process requires acknowledging and actively monitoring the environmental concerns of all legitimate stakeholders. Thus, a company must have a process in place for identifying and prioritizing the many claims and stakes on its business and for dealing with trade-offs related to the impact on different stakeholders. Although no company can satisfy every claim, all risk-related claims should be evaluated before a firm decides to take action on or ignore a particular issue. In order to make accurate assumptions about stakeholder interests, managers need to conduct research, assess risks, and communicate with stakeholders about their respective concerns.

As we discussed in Chapter 2, not all stakeholders are equal. There are specific regulations and legal requirements that govern some aspects of stakeholder relationships, such as air and water quality. Additionally, some special interest groups take extreme positions that, if adopted, would undermine the economic base of many other stakeholders (e.g., fishing rights, logging, and hunting). Regardless of the final decision a company makes with regard to particular environmental issues, information should be communicated consistently across all stakeholders. This is especially important when a company faces a crisis or negative publicity about a decision. Another aspect of strong relationships is the willingness to acknowledge and openly address potential conflicts. Some degree of negotiation and conciliation will be necessary to align a company's decisions and strategies with stakeholder interests.

Risk Analysis

The next step in a high-commitment response to environmental concerns is assessing risk. Through industry and government research, an organization can usually identify environmental issues that relate to manufacturing, marketing, and consumption and use patterns associated with its products. Through risk analysis, it is possible to assess the environmental risks associated with business decisions. The real difficulty is measuring the costs and benefits of environmental decisions, especially in the eyes of interested stakeholders. Research studies often conflict. For example, a well-respected researcher reported in a leading journal that a certain type of genetically modified corn kills significant numbers of monarch butterflies. However, twenty other studies and the EPA have found that genetically modified corn does not pose a significant risk to the monarch butterfly. In fact, in the year before the study was reported, Monarch Watch found a 30 percent increase in the monarch butterfly population when 40 percent more genetically modified corn was planted.[82]

Debate surrounding environmental issues will force corporate decision makers to weigh the evidence and take some risks in final decisions. The important thing for high-commitment organizations is to continue to evaluate the latest information and to maintain communication with all stakeholders. For example, if the 68 million sport utility vehicles (SUVs) on U.S. roads today were replaced with fuel-efficient electric-powered cars and trucks, there would be a tremendous reduction of greenhouse gas emissions.[83] However, the cooperation and commitment needed to gain the support of government, manufacturers, consumers, and other stakeholders to accomplish this would be next to impossible. Although SUVs may harm the environment, many of their owners believe they provide greater protection in an accident.

The issue of environmental responsibility versus safety in SUVs illustrates that many environmental decisions involve trade-offs for various stakeholders' risks. Through risk management, it is possible to quantify these trade-offs in determining whether to accept or reject environmentally related activities and programs. Usually, the key decision is between the amount of investment required to reduce the risk of damage and the amount of risk acceptable in stakeholder relationships. A company should assess these relationships on an ongoing basis. Both formal and informal

Sport utility vehicles (SUVs) became very popular in recent years but were heavily criticized for poor fuel efficiency, propensity to roll over, and safety risks because of their height and weight advantage over smaller vehicles. (© 2003 John Klossner, www. masondarrow.com)

methods are needed to get feedback from stakeholders. For example, the employees of a firm can use formal methods such as exit interviews, an open-door policy, and toll-free telephone hot lines. Conversations between employees could provide informal feedback. But it is ultimately the responsibility of the business to make the best decision possible after processing all available research and information. Then, if it is later discovered that a mistake has been made, change is still possible through open disclosure and thoughtful reasoning. Finally, a high-commitment organization will incorporate new information and insights into the strategic planning process.

The Strategic Environmental Audit

Organizations that are highly committed to environmental responsibility may conduct an audit of their efforts and report the results to all interested stakeholders. Table 9.5 provides a starting point for examining environmental sensitivity. Such organizations may also wish to use globally accepted standards, such as ISO 14000, as benchmarks in a strategic environmental audit. The International Standards Organization developed **ISO 14000** as a comprehensive set of environmental standards that encourage a cleaner, safer, and healthier world. There is currently considerable variation among the environmental laws and regulations of nations and regions, making it difficult for high-commitment organizations to find acceptable solutions on a global scale. The goal of the ISO 14000 standards is to promote a common approach to environmental management and to help companies attain and measure improvements in environmental performance.[84] Companies that choose to abide by the ISO standards may receive a certificate to indicate their compliance; some companies, including DaimlerChrysler, Ford Motor Company, and General Motors, require their suppliers to be ISO 14000 certified.[85] Other performance benchmarks available for use in environmental audits come from nonprofit organizations such as CERES, which has also developed standards for reporting information about environmental performance to interested stakeholders.

As this chapter has demonstrated, social responsibility entails responding to stakeholder concerns about the environment, and many firms are finding creative ways to address environmental challenges. Although many of the companies mentioned in this chapter have chosen to implement strategic environmental initiatives in order to capitalize on opportunities and achieve greater efficiency and cost savings, most also

ISO 14000
a comprehensive set of environmental standards that encourage a cleaner, safer, and healthier world

TABLE 9.5	Strategic Natural Environment Audit

YES	NO	CHECKLIST
○	○	Does the organization show a high commitment to a strategic environmental policy?
○	○	Do employees know the environmental compliance policies of the organization?
○	○	Do suppliers and customers recognize the organization's stand on environmental issues?
○	○	Are managers familiar with the environmental strategies of other organizations in the industry?
○	○	Has the organization compared its environmental initiatives with those of other firms?
○	○	Is the company aware of the best practices in environmental management regardless of industry?
○	○	Has the organization developed measurable performance standards for environmental compliance?
○	○	Does the firm reconcile the need for consistent responsible values with the needs of various stakeholders?
○	○	Do the organization's philanthropic efforts consider environmental issues?
○	○	Does the organization comply with all laws and regulations that relate to environmental impact?

believe that responding to stakeholders' concerns about environmental issues will both improve relationships with stakeholders and make the world a better place.

Summary

Although the scope of the natural environment is quite broad, we define the term as the physical world, including all biological entities, as well as the interaction among nature and individuals, organizations, and business strategies. In recent years, companies have been increasingly incorporating environmental issues into their business strategies.

Air pollution arises from stationary sources such as factories and power plants; mobile sources such as cars, trucks, planes, and trains; and natural sources such as wind-blown dust and volcanic eruptions. Acid rain results when nitrous oxides and sulfur dioxides emitted from manufacturing facilities react with air and rain. Scientists believe that increasing concentrations of greenhouse gases in the atmosphere are warming the planet, although this theory is still controversial. The Kyoto Protocol is a treaty proposed among industrialized nations to slow global warming.

Water pollution results from the dumping of raw sewage and toxic chemicals into rivers and oceans, from oil and gasoline spills, from the burial of industrial waste in the ground where it may filter into underground water supplies, and from the runoff of fertilizers and pesticides used in farming and grounds maintenance. The amount of water available is also a concern and the topic of political disputes.

Land pollution results from the dumping of residential and industrial waste, strip mining, and poor forest conservation. How to dispose of waste in an environmentally responsible manner is another issue. Deforestation to make way for agriculture and development threatens animal and plant species. Urban sprawl, the result of changing human development patterns, consumes wildlife habitat, wetlands, and farmland.

Deforestation, pollution, and urban sprawl threaten wildlife, plants, and their habitats and have caused many species to become extinct or endangered. Genetic engineering involves transferring one or more genes from one organism to another to create a new life form that has unique traits. However, the long-term impact of this technology is not known, and many people fear its use.

The U.S. Environmental Protection Agency (EPA) is an independent regulatory agency that establishes and enforces environmental protection standards, conducts environmental research, provides assistance in fighting pollution, and assists in developing and recommending new policies for environmental protection. The Clean Air Act regulates atmospheric emissions from a variety of sources, whereas the Federal Insecticide, Fungicide, and Rodenticide Act regulates the distribution, sale, and use of pesticides. The Endangered Species Act protects threatened and endangered species as well as the habitats in which they are found. The Toxic Substances Control Act empowered the EPA to track, test, and ban industrial chemicals. The Clean Water Act authorized the EPA to establish effluent standards and to set water quality limits for all contaminants in surface waters. The Emergency Planning and Community Right-to-Know Act required most manufacturers to file Toxics Release Inventories detailing their releases of chemicals into the air, water, and land. The Pollution Prevention Act focused industry, government, and public attention on pollution reduction efforts. The Food Quality Protection Act changed the way the EPA regulates pesticides by applying the same standard to all pesticides used in food products.

Businesses are applying creativity, technology, and business resources to respond to environmental issues. Some firms have created a new executive position, vice president of environmental affairs, to help them achieve their business goals in an environmentally responsible manner. Green marketing refers to the specific development, pricing, promotion, and distribution of products that do less harm to the environment. There is growing agreement among environmentalists and businesses, however, that companies should work to protect and preserve the natural environment by implementing a number of goals: (1) eliminate the concept of waste, (2) rethink the concept of a product, (3) make the price of products reflect their true costs, and (4) seek ways to make business's commitment to the environment profitable. Many organizations engage in recycling, the reprocessing of materials—especially steel, aluminum, paper, glass, rubber, and some plastics—for reuse. To combat air pollution and the threat of global warming, many companies are striving for greater efficiency, waste reduction, and the reduction of greenhouse-gas emissions. Socially responsible buying initiatives are another way that companies are finding to incorporate environmental responsibility into their business strategies.

Businesses have responded to the opportunities and threats created by environmental issues with varying levels of commitment. A high-commitment business develops strategic management programs, which view the environment as an opportunity for advancing organizational interests. Stakeholder analysis requires a process for identifying and prioritizing the many claims and stakes on its business and for dealing with trade-offs related to the impact on different stakeholders. Risk analysis tries to assess the environmental risks and trade-offs associated with business decisions. Organizations that are highly committed to environmental responsibility may conduct an audit of their efforts and report the results to all interested stakeholders. Such organizations may use globally accepted standards, such as ISO 14000, as benchmarks in a strategic environmental audit.

Key Terms

natural environment (p. 259)
Kyoto Protocol (p. 262)
Toxics Release Inventory (TRI) (p. 274)
green marketing (p. 275)
recycling (p. 277)
green power (p. 279)
ISO 14000 (p. 284)

Discussion Questions

1. Define the natural environment in the context of social responsibility. How does this definition differ from your definition of the environment?
2. Identify how some of the environmental issues discussed in this chapter are affecting your community. What steps have local businesses taken to address these issues?
3. How serious is the issue of global warming? Discuss the need for global cooperation in addressing this issue.
4. Discuss some of the potential problems associated with attempts to manage biodiversity and endangered species.
5. What is the role of the EPA in U.S. environmental policy? What impact does this agency have on businesses?
6. What federal laws seem to have the greatest impact on business efforts to be environmentally responsible?
7. What role do stakeholders play in a strategic approach to environmental issues? How can businesses satisfy the interests of diverse stakeholders?
8. What is environmental risk analysis? Why is it important for an environmentally conscious company?
9. What is ISO 14000? What is its potential impact on key stakeholders, community, businesses, and global organizations concerned about environmental issues?

10. How can businesses plan for and manage environmental responsibility?

Experiential Exercise

Visit the web site of the U.S. EPA (http://www.epa.gov/). What topics and issues fall under the authority of the EPA? Peruse the agency's most recent news releases. What themes, issues, regulations, and other areas is the EPA most concerned with today? How can this site be useful to consumers and businesses?

What Would You Do?

The Sustainability Committee's first meeting was scheduled for Thursday afternoon. Although it was only Tuesday, several people had already dropped by committee members' offices to express their opinions and concerns about the company's new focus on sustainability. Some colleagues had trouble with the broad definition of sustainability—"to balance the economic, environmental, and social needs of today's world while planning for future generations." Others worried the sustainability project was just another passing fad. A small group of colleagues believed the company should be most concerned with performance and should forget about trying to become a leader in the social responsibility movement. In general, however, most employees were either supportive or neutral on the initiative.

As the committee's meeting started, the committee chair reminded the group that the company's CEO was very committed to sustainability for several reasons. First, the company was engaged in product development and manufacturing processes that had environmental effects. Second, most companies in the industry were starting initiatives on sustainable development. Third, recent scandals had negatively affected public opinion about business in general. Finally, the company was exploring markets in

Europe where environmental activism and rules were often more stringent. With these reasons in mind, the committee set out to develop plans for the next year.

For an hour, the committee discussed the general scope of sustainability in the company. They agreed that sustainability was concerned with increasing positive results while reducing negative effects on a variety of stakeholders. They also agreed that sustainability focused on the "triple bottom line" of financial, social, and environmental performance. For example, a company dedicated to sustainability could design and build a new facility that used alternative energy sources, minimized impact on environmentally sensitive surrounding areas, and encouraged recycling and composting. Another firm might implement its sustainability objectives by requiring suppliers to meet certain standards for environmental impact, business ethics, economic efficiency, community involvement, and others.

After this discussion, the committee made a list of current and potential projects that were likely to be affected by the company's new sustainability focus. These projects included

Energy consumption	Philanthropy
Manufacturing emissions and waste	Product development
Employee diversity	Technology
Community relations	Supplier selection
Supplier selection	Corporate governance
Employee health and safety	Regulations and compliance
Volunteerism	

After much discussion, the committee agreed that each member would take one of these thirteen projects and prepare a brief report on its link to the environmental component of sustainability. This report should review the ways environmental issues can be discussed, changed, improved, or implemented within that area to demonstrate a commitment to sustainability. What would you do?

Chapter 10

Technology Issues

CHAPTER OBJECTIVES

- To examine the nature and characteristics of technology
- To explore the economic impact of technology
- To examine technology's influence on society
- To provide a framework for the strategic management of technology issues

CHAPTER OUTLINE

The Nature of Technology

Technology's Influence on the Economy

Technology's Influence on Society

Strategic Implementation of Responsibility for Technology

The ailing music industry is poised to make a new push to copy-proof its music CDs, in hopes of slowing the epidemic of Internet piracy. Microsoft, meanwhile, is making its entry into encrypted music CDs with the introduction of its Windows Media Data Session Toolkit, which it plans to give away to the recording labels. The music CDs contain two tracks of music, one that's in standard CD format, known as "redbook audio," and an encrypted data session for computers. The ease and availability to share files is even interrupting employees at work using corporate computers to copy songs for free. The use of file-sharing services to copy music appears to be an important ethical and legal issue for employees, companies, and the music industry. What companies should be concerned about is viruses and other security attacks, as well as loss of productivity from their employees. They could also face additional legal issues if allowing employees to use their network for file sharing.

Record labels facing sharp drops in sales, tied to unauthorized digital song swapping and widespread CD burning, have begun to take action toward suing individuals who are aggressive distributors of their songs. Companies may need to stop worrying because of a recent court decision. The Recording Industry Association of America (RIAA) demanded the name of an individual subscriber from Verizon Communications, Inc. Verizon's defense was that the customer did not store the songs on their server; instead, the customer saved them on his hard drive. In a written opinion, under copyright laws, Verizon was responsible for identifying the user.

This decision is similar to the one made against Napster. Napster was an online service provider based in California that provided an index of all the songs available on the computers of members currently logged on to the service. In a little over one year, Napster became one of the most popular Internet sites, claiming some 15 million users. Indeed, so many students were downloading songs from Napster that many universities were forced to block the site from their systems in order to regain bandwidth.

After just as much controversy as popularity, Napster started getting sued. The RIAA claimed that Napster violated copyright laws by allowing users to swap music for free. Napster argued that because it does not directly provide the copyrighted music, the Digital Millennium Copyright Act protects its actions. The firm's attorneys asserted that Napster is merely a conduit because it does not copy music and has no way of knowing whether its members have paid for recordings they offer for trade.

Despite its claims, Napster was found guilty of direct infringement of the RIAA's musical recordings, and the ruling was upheld on appeal. The District Court of Appeals refuted all of Napster's defense tactics and ordered the company to stop allowing its millions of users to download and share copyrighted material without properly compensating the owners of the material.

With failed attempts to reach a suitable compromise and litigation expenses mounting, the company filed for Chapter 7 liquidation bankruptcy in September of 2002. Shortly after that, Napster laid off all forty-two of its employees and closed its doors. Napster reemerged under new ownership in 2003 as a fee-based music provider.

The RIAA filed 261 lawsuits against individuals it says illegally used file-sharing software to distribute copyrighted music as the first of a wave of thousands of copyright infringement lawsuits. Unit shipments of CDs fell 26 percent from 1999 to 2002. Universal Music slashed CD prices in late 2003 to reinvigorate sales.[1]

The technology behind music file sharing is just one example of the many advances that have enriched our lives in recent decades. Technology brings to mind scientific advances as well as concerns about the impact of technology on society. Although we enjoy the benefits of communicating through the Internet, we are increasingly concerned about protecting our privacy and our intellectual property. Although health and medical research creates new drugs that save lives, cloning and genetically modified foods have become controversial issues to many segments of society. In various ways and to varying degrees, home environments, health care, leisure, and work performance are all influenced by both current technology and advances in technology.

In this chapter, we explore the nature of technology and its positive and negative effects on society. Technology's influence on the economy is very powerful, especially with regard to growth, employment, and working environments. This influence on society includes issues related to the Internet, privacy, intellectual property, health, and the general quality of life. The strategic direction for technology depends on government, as well as on business's ability to plan, implement, and audit the influence of technology on society.

The Nature of Technology

technology
the application of knowledge, including the processes and applications to solve problems, perform tasks, and create new methods to obtain desired outcomes

Technology relates to the application of knowledge, including the processes and applications to solve problems, perform tasks, and create new methods to obtain desired outcomes. It includes intellectual knowledge as well as the physical systems devised to achieve business and personal objectives. The evolution of civilization is tied to developments in technology. Through technological advances, humans have moved from a hunter-gatherer existence to a stable agricultural economy to the Industrial Revolution. Today, our economy is based more on information technology and services than on manufacturing. This technology is changing the way we take vacations, have dinner, do homework, track criminals, know where we are, and maintain friendships. Technology has made it possible to go to work or meetings without leaving the house. Our new economy is based on these dynamic technological changes in our society.

Characteristics of Technology

Some of the characteristics of technology include the dynamics, reach, and self-sustaining nature of technological progress. The dynamics of technology relate to the constant change that often challenges the structure of social institutions. The automobile, airplane, and personal computer all created major changes and influenced government, the family, social relationships, education, military, and leisure. These changes can come so fast that they require significant adjustments in the political, religious, and economic structures of society. Some societies have difficulty adjusting to this rate of change to the point that they even attempt to legislate against new technologies in order to isolate themselves. In the past, China tried to isolate its citizens from innovations such as the Internet and social trends that result from the application of new technology to products such as music and movies on compact discs and digital video discs. But even China has responded to the new Internet technology by issuing trial online advertising licenses in a country where advertising has not been widely accepted.[2] Since then, Internet use in China is growing, with the number of people logging on regularly, totaling 45.8 million users. Today, China ranks number three in the world, with only the United States and Japan having more Internet users.[3]

The future dynamics of technology are challenging many traditional products, including books. E Ink and Xerox, for example, are developing thin paper and plastic films that can function as screens with digital ink. Users of the technology would still be able to turn the pages as with a traditional book or newspaper, but the pages could be reloaded with a new article or bestseller through wireless transmission. The flat sheet of enhanced paper could even be used to receive a movie. E Ink has joined Lucent Technologies to get the rights to use plastic transistors developed by Lucent needed to show color.[4] The challenges to traditional ways of receiving information are accelerating change in every aspect of life. In many cases, a new technology may become obsolete in a very short period after introduction. Thus, the dynamic characteristic of technology keeps challenging society to adjust.

Reach relates to the broad nature of technology as it moves through society. For instance, every community in both developed and developing countries has been influenced by cellular and wireless telephones. The ability to make a call from almost any location has many positive effects, but negative side effects include increases in traffic accidents and noise pollution as well as fears about potential health risks. Through telecommunications, businesses, families, and governments have been linked from far distances. Satellites allow instant visual and voice electronic connections almost anywhere in the world. These technologies have reduced the need for business travel, as shown in Figure 10.1.

The self-sustaining nature of technology relates to the fact that technology acts as a catalyst to spur even faster development. As new innovations are introduced, they stimulate the need for more technology to facilitate further development. For example, the Internet has created the need for broadband transmission of electric signals through phone lines (DSL), satellites, and cable. Broadband allows connections to the Internet to be fifty times faster than through a traditional telephone modem, allows users to download large files, and creates the opportunity for a rich multimedia experience. As broadband becomes available to more businesses and households,

---

FIGURE 10.1   Technology Decreases the Need for Business Travel

Sixty-three percent of executives surveyed indicated that technology has decreased their business travel.

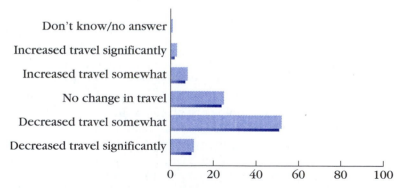

Source: Darryl Haralson and Marcy E. Mullins, "More Technology, Less Business Travel," *USA Today,* December 6, 2000, p. 1B. Copyright December 6, 2000. Reprinted with permission.

other technologies will have to advance to keep up with the ability to access so much data quickly.[5] In the future, it could be possible to have broadband transmission to computers through electric lines. This means that users could have a broadband connection anywhere that a computer can be plugged in. The invention of the personal computer resulted in changes in personal financial management related to banking, insurance, taxes, and stock trading. Technology starts a change process that creates new opportunities for new technologies in every industry segment or personal life experience that it touches. At some point, there is even a multiplier effect that causes an even greater demand for more change to improve performance. In the marketing sense, technology is not really fulfilling any new need; it is simply filling an old need more efficiently and effectively.

Effects of Technology

Civilizations must harness and adapt to changes in technology in order to maintain a desired quality of life. The cell phone, for example, has dramatically altered communication patterns, particularly in developing countries where there are few telephone lines. New innovations can also change entire industries. Companies like IBM are creating supercomputers that will be 2 million times more powerful than today's PCs. These computers will be used to load biopsies, which will analyze the genes of cancer cells. They will then help researchers find the most effective drug or treatment for exploiting a tumor's weaknesses.[6]

Such examples illustrate how technology can provide new methods to accomplish tasks that were once thought impossible. These advancements create new processes, new products, and economic progress and ultimately have profound effects on society.

The global economy experienced the greatest acceleration of technological advancement that ever occurred, propelling increased productivity, output, corporate profits, and stock prices over the last decade.[7] Among the positive contributions of these advances were reductions in the number of worker hours required to generate

Companies like IBM are creating super-computers that are 2 million times more powerful than today's personal computers. (AP Photo/Bob Jordan)

the nation's output. At the same time, the economic conditions that accompanied this period of technical innovation resulted in increased job opportunities. But in the early 2000s, with the fall of the dot-coms and the integrity meltdown of major U.S. corporations, the economy had taken a downturn, along with the stock market. However, advances in information technology have continued to drive productivity and economic growth. The U.S. unemployment rate rose in 2001 and 2002. The economy lost more than 1.2 million jobs by the end of 2002.[8] Many information technology firms expanded too rapidly and misreported revenue and earnings to hold onto stock prices and please executives and investors. The result was incidences of massive accounting fraud that damaged confidence and the economy. The traditional work environment has changed because telecommunications (e.g., e-mail and videoconferencing) reduce the need for face-to-face interaction. Through online shopping, the Internet can also reduce the need for trips to a shopping center and has increased the amount of business done by UPS and FedEx. Also, the ease and amount of business-to-business transactions has expanded.

However, there are concerns that dramatic shifts in the acceleration and innovations derived from technology may be spurring imbalances not only in the economy but also in our social existence. The flow of technology into developing countries can serve as a method to jump-start economic development. On the other hand, a failure to share technology or provide methods to disseminate technology could cause a major divide in the quality of life. It is in the best interest of the United States to be supportive of technology development throughout the world. Limited resources in underdeveloped countries and the lack of a technology infrastructure will lead to many social, political, and economic problems in the future. In addition, trade with the United States will be impacted by these problems.

World's first equine clone, Moscow, Idaho, May 29, 2003. (AP Photo/Kevin German)

In the United States, the federal government is stepping in with plans to spend $50 million to subsidize computers and Internet access for 300,000 low-income households across the nation. Although this initiative is somewhat controversial, proponents believe it has the potential to raise the standard of living for low-income families much as the Rural Electrification Administration (REA) did in the 1930s, after President Franklin Delano Roosevelt established it to extend electrical power and telephone services to remote communities and rural areas.[9] Some companies are also trying to help bridge the technology gap that is developing between those who can afford technology and those who are on the other side of the so-called digital divide. Gateway, Inc., in partnership with the Association of Equal Opportunity in Higher Education, is working to provide discounted computers to 118 predominately African American colleges and universities.[10] Gateway is an example of a corporate attempt to keep the positive effects of the reach of technology available to all segments of society. Unfortunately, Gateway's market share has dropped as Dell, HP, IBM, and NEC dominate the PC market.

There are concerns about the way information technology can improve the quality of life for society. In addition, there are concerns about the negative consequences of the reduction of privacy and the emergence of cybercrime. At some point, abrupt adjustment could occur from changes in our economy, and members of society could become unhappy about changes in their lifestyles or the role of business and government in their lives. Public advocacy organizations are helping by participating in charting the future of computer networks to integrate these technological innovations into the way we live.[11] Berners-Lee, the crafter of the Internet, has a new futuristic scenario. The Semantic Web, a sequel to the first, offers controlled access to U.S. health care data, plus databases charting the location and status of rivers, underground water, and forests and local vegetation, along with economic data on local industries and what they produce—all marked up in special vocabularies. Those allow scientists to run global queries across the Web, fishing randomly for correlations that might exist between where sick people live, worked, and played, such as a polluted stream or industrial dump. He is trying to create a tool that might replace our aging Web browsers, letting us display data by color codes, by geographic maps, or by types of sources searched.[12]

Technology's Influence on the Economy

Technological advancements have had a profound impact on economic growth and employment, but they raise concerns as well.

Economic Growth and Employment

Over the past fifty years, technology has been a major factor in the economic growth in the United States. Investments in educational technologies, increased support for basic government research, and continued commitment to the mission of research and development (R&D) in both the public and private sectors have become major drivers of economic growth. Through deficit reduction, lower interest rates, tax credits, and liberalization of export controls, the government established the economic infrastructure for using technology to drive economic development. The expansion of industry-led technology partnerships between corporations, governments, and nonprofit organizations has also been a key component of growth. Table 10.1 shows the industries that have received the highest federal support for research and development.

Investments in research and development are among the highest-return investments a nation can make. A report by the Council of Economic Advisors notes that over the past fifty years, technological innovation has been responsible for half or more of the nation's growth in productivity.[13] For example, the ability to access information in real time through the electronic data interface between retailers, wholesalers, and manufacturers has reduced delivery lead times as well as the hours required to produce and deliver products. Likewise, product design times and costs have declined because computer modeling has minimized the need for architectural drafters and some engineers required for building projects. Medical diagnoses have become faster, more thorough, and more accurate, thanks to access to information and records over the Internet, hastening treatment and eliminating unnecessary procedures.[14]

The relationship between businesses and consumers already is being changed by the expanding opportunities for e-commerce, the sharing of business information, maintaining business relationships, and conducting business transactions by means of telecommunications networks. Business-to-business (B2B) e-commerce involving

TABLE 10.1	Industries with the Highest Federal Support for Research and Development
INDUSTRY	**PAYOFF**
Computers and communications	Defense-related research and development to provide for communications in the event of war led to what has become the Internet.
Semiconductors	The U.S. semiconductor industry developed as a direct result of federal R&D investments and procurement activities.
Biotechnology	Federally funded discoveries in biology, food science, agriculture, genetics, and drugs on which the private sector has been able to build and expand a world-class industry.
Aerospace	The federal government traditionally has funded the lion's share of aerospace R&D, and this support has made U.S. aerospace companies the world's most advanced.
Environmental technologies	The federal government provides nearly $2 billion a year in support of R&D related to environmental technologies.
Energy efficiency	Many of the products sold and installed by this industry are the product of partnerships between the federal government and private industry.
Lasers	Refined though government, industry, and university research, lasers are now one of the most powerful, versatile, and pervasive technologies in our lives.
Magnetic resonance imaging	Nuclear physicists and chemists worked out the fundamental technique of using radio beams and magnetic fields to analyze the chemical structure of biomedical and other materials.

Source: *Technology and Economic Growth: Producing Real Results for the American People,* The White House, November 8, 1995.

companies buying from and selling to each other online is the fastest-growing segment of e-commerce. It has facilitated supply chain management as more companies outsource purchasing over the Internet.[15]

More and more people are turning to the Internet to purchase computers and related peripherals, software, books, music, and even furniture; consumers are increasingly using the Internet to book travel reservations, transact banking business, and trade securities. The forces unleashed by the Internet are particularly important in business-to-business relationships, where the improved quantity, reliability, and timeliness of information have reduced uncertainties. This is the case in companies such as General Motors, IBM, and Procter & Gamble, which are learning to consolidate and rationalize their supply chains using the Internet.[16] Consider the Covisint alliance between Ford, General Motors, DaimlerChrysler, Renault, Nissan, Oracle, and Commerce One, which makes parts from suppliers available through a competitive online auction, reducing months of negotiations into a single day. The goal of the alliance is to reduce the time it takes to bring a new vehicle to market from fifty-four months to eighteen.[17] In many cases, companies are moving toward making most of their purchases online.[18] The downturn in the economy hasn't stopped the momentum of the Contract Division of office supplies retailer Staples Inc., the company's main business-to-business arm. The unit had annual sales of $1 billion and managed double-digit quarterly growth for more than three years.[19]

Economic growth means more jobs and improved living standards. Americans hold millions of jobs in industries that have grown as a result of public and private investment in R&D. These include biotechnology, computers, communications, software, aerospace, and semiconductors; even retailing, wholesaling, and other commercial institutions have been transformed by technology. Average pay for workers in these high-technology industries is about 60 percent higher than the average wage for all U.S. workers.

Science and technology are powerful drivers of economic growth and improvements in the quality of life in the United States. Advances in technology have created not only millions of new jobs but also better health and longer lives, new opportunities, and enrichment of our lives in ways we could not have imagined half a century ago. For example, electric plugs and outlets are becoming a thing of the past. Because of improved battery technologies and better utilization of radio frequencies (RFs), we are becoming a wireless society. Wireless devices in use today include almost everything, PDAs laptop Internet connections, radios, cell phones, TVs, pagers, and car keys. In the future, most long-distance communication will likely be through fiber optics, and short-distance communication will be wireless. The *Wireless News Factor* has a special report that says free wireless broadband may be coming in the future. But the article says that while some people enjoy free wireless broadband now, the day when it is free to all is still a ways off for a variety of reasons, including "shifting business models and a lack of public commitment."[20] There is also concern about "wacking," or tapping onto other peoples' wireless connection.

Demand for wireless technology is accelerating, with 50 percent of *Fortune* 1000 companies expected to commit 15 percent of all network spending to wireless voice and data technology. *Computerworld*'s Mark Hall stated that by 2012, every new digital device in the enterprise will be wirelessly connected.[21] In the future, refrigerators, medicine cabinets, and even product packaging may contain wireless microdevices that broadcast product characteristics, features, expiration dates, and other information. Wireless LANs are being installed on navy warships to free up manpower, reduce crew sizes, and improve monitoring of a range of mechanical and electrical systems.[22]

Economic Concerns About the Use of Technology

Despite the staggering economic growth fostered by technological advancements, there are economic downsides to technology. Small businesses in particular may have difficulty taking advantage of the opportunities surrounding the Internet. Consider the case of Joseph Serna, who thought the Internet could be a powerful tool to attract more customers to his seven-employee print shop in Denver. However, like millions of other small businesspeople and thousands of communities, Serna now fears the new medium will crush his small business instead. Serna's customers want to send art, photos, and layouts to him via e-mail, but his conventional computer modem requires a laborious twenty minutes to send or receive a simple eight-page brochure. A new high-speed Internet connection could slash that time to seconds if it was available in his area. Telephone companies are now offering high-speed service in other, often more upscale, Denver areas, but they have no immediate plans to bring service to Serna's neighborhood. His choice: Pay more than $1,000 a month for a dedicated T-1 telephone line or stand by and watch while competitors with greater resources steal his customers. High-speed connections, also known as broadband, are becoming a must-have for businesses of any size.[23] Nearly one-third (31 percent) of U.S. Internet users have broadband access at home, work, or school.[24]

The study "Broadband Revolution 2: The Media World of Speedies" found that 64 percent of Internet users who have broadband access (identified as "speedies" in the report) are connected through their workplace and 37 percent have access at home. In addition, there is little overlap between those with broadband at work and at home, the study found. Of consumers with access to broadband at home and/or work, 58 percent have access only at work; 27 percent have access only at home. Only 15 percent have access at both locations. More importantly for those with a stake in widespread broadband access, the study found that college students with broadband access are likely to get residential broadband service in the future. More than one-third (38 percent) of college "speedies" say they are either very likely or somewhat likely to get broadband at home if they were no longer in school. Nearly one-quarter (22 percent) use broadband as a source of entertainment. On average, broadband households pay nearly twice what dial-up households do each month for their Web connection ($35.40 versus $18.05).[25] Without greater access to the latest technology, especially high-speed Internet services, economic development could suffer in underserved communities, especially poor suburban neighborhoods, inner cities, and rural areas. The ability to purchase other types of technology may affect the nature of competition and the success of various types of businesses.

There are several ways to address these problems that are the inevitable consequences of accelerating change in the technology drivers of the new economy. One way is to examine the outcomes associated with the attempts to use technology. For example, the small town of Glasgow, Kentucky, thanks to the foresight of local leaders, was hard-wired for high-speed Internet access years before the technology was available in many larger urban areas. Community leaders thought the technology would not only benefit citizens but also lead to a high-tech boom for the town of 14,000. The city exploits the high-speed wiring to control traffic lights, share computerized maps to coordinate utility repairs, and monitor electric meters, and a number of businesses have incorporated Internet access into their business strategies. However, only two-thirds of the community's businesses and one-quarter of its residences have signed up for the service, and the high-tech boom has yet to begin. Nonetheless, many other small communities are installing similar high-speed links in preparation for the future.[26] Another way to address the negative consequences of accelerating new techology is to assess problems related to its impact on competition. Restraining competition, domestic or international, to suppress competitive turmoil is a major concern of governments. Allowing anticompetitive practices, price fixing, or other unfair methods of competition would be counterproductive to rising standards of living.[27] Online shoppers may get a tax break, as members of Congress move to ban taxes on Internet access, taxes on Internet transactions involving several jurisdictions, and discriminatory taxes that treat Internet purchases differently from other types of commerce.[28]

Technology's Influence on Society

Information and telecommunications technology minimizes the borders between countries, businesses, and people and allows people to overcome the physical limitations of time and space. Technological advances also enable people to acquire customized goods and services that cost less and are of higher quality than ever imagined.[29] For example, parents can give their children robotic pets and dolls, which often cost less than $50, that can be programmed to respond to their child's voice.[30] Airline passengers can purchase tickets online and print out boarding passes on their home or office printers so that they can go straight to their plane on arrival at the airport after clearing security.[31] Cartographers and geologists can create custom maps— even in three dimensions—that may help experts manage water supplies, find oil, and pinpoint future earthquakes.[32] In this section, we explore four broad issues related to technology and its impact on society, including the Internet, privacy, intellectual property, and health and biotechnology. Although there are many other pressing issues related to technology, these seem to be the most widely debated at this time. As technology advances, there will probably be more issues by the time you read this book.

The Internet

The Internet, the global information system that links many computer networks together, has profoundly altered the way people communicate, learn, do business, and find entertainment. Although many people believe the Internet began in the early 1990s, its origins can actually be traced to the late 1950s (see Table 10.2). Over the last four decades, the network evolved from a system for government and university researchers into an information and entertainment tool used by millions around the globe. With the development of the World Wide Web, which organizes the information on the Internet into interconnected "pages" of text, graphics, audio, and video, use of the Internet exploded in the early 1990s.

TABLE 10.2	History of the Internet	

YEAR	EVENT	SIGNIFICANCE
1836	Telegraph	The telegraph revolutionized human (tele)communications with Morse Code, a series of dots and dashes used to communicate between humans.
1858–1866	Transatlantic cable	Transatlantic cable allowed direct instantaneous communication across the Atlantic Ocean.
1876	Telephone	The telephone created voice communication, and telephone exchanges provided the backbone of Internet connections today.
1957	USSR launched *Sputnik*.	*Sputnik* was the first artificial Earth satellite and the start of global communications.
1962–1968	Packet switching	The Internet relies on packet-switching networks, networks that split data into tiny packets that may take different routes to a destination.
1971	Beginning of the Internet	People communicate over the Internet with a program to send messages across a distributed network.
1973	Global networking becomes a reality.	Ethernet outlined—this is how local networks are basically connected today, and gateways define how large networks (maybe of different architecture) can be connected together.
1991	World Wide Web with text-based, menu-driven interface to access Internet resources	User-friendly interface to World Wide Web established.
1992	Multimedia changes the face of the Internet.	The term *surfing the Internet* is coined.
1993	World Wide Web revolution begins.	Mosaic, a user-friendly Graphical Front End to the World Wide Web, makes the Web more accessible and evolves into Netscape.
1995	Internet service providers advance.	Online dial-up systems (CompuServe, America Online, and Prodigy) begin to provide Internet access.
2000	Broadband emerges.	Provides fast access to multimedia and large text files.
2002	Wireless expands.	Devices for wireless linkage to the Internet grow rapidly.

Source: Adapted from "History of the Internet," Internet Valley, www.internetvalley.com/archives/mirrors/davemarsh-timeline-1.htm, accessed November 2, 2001.

Today, nearly half a billion people around the world tap into the Internet. In the United States alone, about 168 million Americans access the Internet at home or at work. Internet use by consumers in other countries, especially Japan (26.9 million users), the United Kingdom (33 million), Germany (26 million), China (22.5 million), and Canada (14 million), is escalating rapidly.[33] To keep up with the growing demand for new e-mail and web site addresses, the Internet Corporation for Assigned Names and Numbers has added seven new domain name suffixes to allow for the creation of millions of new addresses. Now, in addition to .com (for companies), .edu (schools and universities), .gov (government agencies and offices), .mil (military use), .net (networks), and hundreds of country codes, computer users will see addresses followed by .zero (air-transport industry), .biz (businesses), .coop (nonprofit cooperatives), .info (unrestricted), .museum (museums), .name (personal names), and .pro (professionals such as doctors and accountants).[34]

The interactive nature of the Internet has created tremendous opportunities for businesses to forge relationships with consumers and business customers, target markets more precisely, and even reach previously inaccessible markets. The Internet also facilitates supply-chain management, allowing companies to network with manufacturers, wholesalers, retailers, suppliers, and outsource firms to serve customers more efficiently.[35] Despite the growing importance and popularity of the Internet, fraud has become a major issue for businesses and consumers. Because shopping via the Internet does not require a signature to verify transactions, credit-card fraud online is more than three and a half times greater than credit-card fraud through mail-order catalogs and almost nine times greater than for traditional storefront retailers.[36] More than $700 million in online sales were lost to fraud in 2001, representing 1.14 percent of total annual online sales of $61.8 billion. Some are attempting to fight fraud by embracing two new credit-card protection systems: Visa's Verified by Visa and MasterCard's Universal Cardholder Authentication Field (UCAF) standard and Secure Payment Application (SPA).[37]

Consumers are also increasingly worried about becoming victims of fraud online. For example, complaints about fraud in online auctions have risen dramatically over the last five years.[38] A survey, conducted by Harris Interactive, found that 31 percent of Americans who go online, or approximately 35 million people, participate in online auctions. However, online auctions made up 78 percent of Internet fraud complaints last year, with an average loss of $326 per victim, the survey found. Still, a whopping 94 percent of respondents who have participated as bidders said they are somewhat or very confident that as the winning bidder in an online auction, they will get what they pay for from a seller.[39] One online auction site, eBay, has more than 16 million regular customers exchanging $14 million every day. The company received 10,700 fraud complaints in one year. Among the complaints are accusations of "shill bidding," which involves sellers bidding on their own items to heighten interest, and competitive bidding. Another problem is sellers not delivering promised items after receiving the buyers' funds. The formula for fraud is enhanced by anonymity, quick access, low overhead, satellite access, and little regulation.[40] Corporations are buying industrial-strength IT gear via online auctions. Todd Lutwak, director of San Jose–based eBay Inc.'s Technology Marketplace, says that in fiscal 2001, $1.8 billion worth of equipment was sold in that division (which includes consumer electronics and computers in addition to enterprise IT equipment). This fiscal year, the Technology Marketplace is projecting $2.6 billion in sales.[41] Increasing complaints about online auctions have made them one of the Federal Trade Commission's top ten "dot cons" (see Figure 10.2). With online auctions generating an estimated $6.1 billion, consumers and merchants alike are exploring options, including regulation, to protect the security of online transactions.[42]

FIGURE 10.2   The Top Ten "Dot Cons"

1 Internet Auctions

The Bait: Shop in a "virtual marketplace" that offers a huge selection of products at great deals.

The Catch: After sending their money, consumers say they've received an item that is less valuable than promised or, worse yet, nothing at all.

The Safety Net: When bidding through an Internet auction, particularly for a valuable item, check out the seller and insist on paying with a credit card or using an escrow service.

2 Internet Access Services

The Bait: Free money, simply for cashing a check.

The Catch: Consumers say they've been "trapped" into long-term contracts for Internet access or another Web service, with big penalties for cancellation or early termination.

The Safety Net: If a check arrives at your home or business, read both sides carefully and look inside the envelope to find the conditions you're agreeing to if you cash the check. Read your telephone bill carefully for unexpected or unauthorized charges.

3 Credit-Card Fraud

The Bait: Surf the Internet and view adult images online for free, just for sharing your credit-card number to prove you're over eighteen.

The Catch: Consumers say that fraudulent promoters have used their credit-card numbers to run up charges on their cards.

The Safety Net: Share credit-card information only when buying from a company you trust. Dispute unauthorized charges on your credit-card bill by complaining to the bank that issued the card. Federal law limits your liability to $50 in charges if your card is misused.

4 International Modem Dialing

The Bait: Get free access to adult material and pornography by downloading a "viewer" or "dialer" computer program.

The Catch: Consumers complain about exorbitant long-distance charges on their telephone bill. Through the program, their modem is disconnected, then reconnected to the Internet through an international long-distance number.

The Safety Net: Don't download any program to access a so-called free service without reading all the disclosures carefully for cost information. Just as important, read your telephone bill carefully and challenge any charges you didn't authorize or don't understand.

5 Web Cramming

The Bait: Get a free custom-designed web site for a thirty-day trial period, with no obligation to continue.

The Catch: Consumers say they've been charged on their telephone bills or received a separate invoice, even if they never accepted the offer or agreed to continue the service after the trial period.

The Safety Net: Review your telephone bills and challenge any charges you don't recognize.

(continued on next page)

FIGURE 10.2 *(Continued)*

6 Multilevel Marketing Plans/Pyramids

The Bait: Make money through the products and services you sell as well as those sold by the people you recruit into the program.

The Catch: Consumers say that they've bought into plans and programs, but their customers are other distributors, not the general public. Some multilevel marketing programs are actually illegal pyramid schemes. When products or services are sold only to distributors like yourself, there's no way to make money.

The Safety Net: Avoid plans that require you to recruit distributors, buy expensive inventory, or commit to a minimum sales volume.

7 Travel and Vacation

The Bait: Get a luxurious trip with lots of "extras" at a bargain-basement price.

The Catch: Consumers say some companies deliver lower-quality accommodations and services than they've advertised or no trip at all. Others have been hit with hidden charges or additional requirements after they've paid.

The Safety Net: Get references on any travel company you're planning to do business with. Then, get details of the trip in writing, including the cancellation policy, before signing on.

8 Business Opportunities

The Bait: Be your own boss and earn big bucks.

The Catch: Taken in by promises about potential earnings, many consumers have invested in a "biz op" that turned out to be a "biz flop." There was no evidence to back up the earnings claims.

The Safety Net: Talk to other people who started businesses through the same company, get all the promises in writing, and study the proposed contract carefully before signing. Get an attorney or an accountant to take a look at it, too.

9 Investments

The Bait: Make an initial investment in a day trading system or service and you'll quickly realize huge returns.

The Catch: Big profits always mean big risk. Consumers have lost money to programs that claim to be able to predict the market with 100 percent accuracy.

The Safety Net: Check out the promoter with state and federal securities and commodities regulators, and talk to other people who invested through the program to find out what level of risk you're assuming.

10 Health Care Products/Services

The Bait: Items not sold through traditional suppliers are "proven" to cure serious and even fatal health problems.

The Catch: Claims for "miracle" products and treatments convince consumers that their health problems can be cured. But people with serious illnesses who put their hopes in these offers might delay getting the health care they need.

The Safety Net: Consult a health care professional before buying any "cure-all" that claims to treat a wide range of ailments or offers quick cures and easy solutions to serious illnesses.

Source: "Dot Con? Dot Con," Federal Trade Commission, www.ftc.gov/bcp/conline/edcams/dotcon, accessed March 4, 2003.

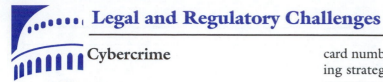

Legal and Regulatory Challenges

Cybercrime

Increases in cybercrime, widespread worm and virus outbreaks, and regulatory requirements such as Gramm Leach Bliley have boosted the profile of computer security. It has become a regular agenda item at board meetings. Every day, it seems the media reports on new viruses or attacks by hackers. Although many of these crimes are relatively harmless, others do billions of dollars in damage, defraud innocent people, and frighten potential online shoppers away. CEOs have to justify spending that has been allocated to security initiatives. Shareholders need to see that this expense is delivering value by ensuring that the company isn't vandalized by hackers or shut down by damaging viruses.

The term *hacker* has evolved over the years to mean a person who breaks into a computer system or network to explore, steal, or wreak havoc. The more secure the system, the more desirable a target it becomes. Hackers often use specialized software that can enter millions of possible passwords until one is accepted by the system. Once inside a system, they may use other specialized programs to search for sensitive information. Although many hackers simply explore the contents of a computer network and later brag about their exploits to other hackers, others have much more malicious intent. Some hackers deface web sites to express political or personal opinions or to damage the site's reputation. Hackers may sell the information they find, such as customers' credit-card numbers, telephone calling-card numbers, or plans for new products or marketing strategies. A credit-card transaction processing company confirmed that 8 million credit-card numbers were stolen when someone hacked into its computers. Computer-savvy hackers use text messages on wireless telephones to crash cell phones.

Other hackers may damage systems by altering or deleting files, unleashing "denial-of-service attacks," mail bombs, or computer viruses. Denial-of-service attacks inundate a computer system with fake requests for access to Web pages in order to slow its performance. Mail bombs are similar but involve attacks to mail servers. No matter what form hackers choose, companies need to be on the lookout. These occurrences have forced companies to spend extra for "network risk insurance," which costs about $5,000 to $30,000 a year for $1 million in coverage. Insurers are delivering an ultimatum: Invest in stand-alone hacker policies or go unprotected. Losses from computer crime are expected to soar 25 percent to $2.8 billion in the United States in 2003. Successful web site attacks nearly doubled to 600 a day. Hacker insurance is expected to jump from a $100 million market today to $900 million by 2005. That may result in higher costs for consumers as the cost of doing business goes up. Some predict that hacker insurance will be ubiquitous in a few years. Companies cannot budget for the next computer worm, but insurance is a fixed cost that reduces risk.

The threat of computer worms such as Slammer, which clogged global Internet traffic, underscores Corporate America's growing dependence on the

Privacy

The extraordinary growth of the Internet has generated issues related to privacy. Businesses have long tracked consumers' shopping habits with little controversy. However, observing the contents of a consumer's shopping cart or the process a consumer goes through when choosing a box of cereal generally involves the collection of aggregate data, rather than specific personally identifying data. And, although some consumers' use of credit cards, shopping cards, and coupons involves giving up

Internet and the vulnerability of its computer networks. The Code Red worm in 2001 caused an estimated $2 billion in damages and cleanup costs. Such security breaches prompted the government to urge companies to insure against losses and for insurance companies to offer more cyber-risk policies as part of its "National Strategy to Secure Cyberspace" plan. However, security experts warn that hacker insurance is not entirely foolproof.

Hackers may also unleash viruses, which are self-replicating programs. A virus may attach itself to a file, such as an e-mail message or a word-processing macro. Some viruses are relatively harmless, leaving behind nothing more than simple "hello" messages. Others may crash the affected computer by using up all its resources, attacking and corrupting critical files, or erasing the hard drive. History has shown that during a time of increased international tension, illegal cyber activity often escalates. Attacks may have several motivations. Two of the most common are political activism by self-described "patriot" hackers and criminal activity to further personal goals.

Regardless of the motivation, the National Infrastructure Protection Center reiterates that such activity is illegal and punishable as a felony. During times of potentially increased cyber disruption, owners/operators of computers and networked systems should review their defensive postures and procedures and stress the importance of increased vigilance in system monitoring. Computer users and system administrators can limit potential problems through the use of "security best practices." Some

of the most basic and effective measures that can be taken are:

Increase user awareness.

Update antivirus software.

Stop potentially hostile/suspicious attachments at the e-mail server.

Utilize filtering to maximize security.

Establish policies and procedures for responding and recovery.

To combat cybercrime, companies are spending millions of dollars to hire security consultants and purchase specialized software to deter or detect unauthorized entry. Even so, cybercrime is detected only about 40 percent of the time. The problem is further compounded by the fact that companies are reluctant to report such crimes, often because it makes both customers and shareholders uncomfortable and damages the companies' reputations. As the Internet grows ever more popular, the threat of losses from cybercrime will only grow.

Sources:
These facts are from Lucas Mearian, "System Break-in Nets Hackers 8 Million Credit Card Numbers," *ComputerWorld,* February 24, 2003, www.computerworld.com/securitytopics/security/story/0, 10801,78747,00.html, accessed March 6, 2003; "Security Company Says Nokia 6210 Vulnerable to Hackers," *RCR Wireless News,* February 27, 2003, rcrnews.com/cgi-bin/news.pl?newsId=7359, accessed March 6, 2003; Jon Swartz, "Firms' hacking-related insurance costs soar," *USA Today,* February 9, 2003; "Encourages Heightened Cyber Security as Iraq—US Tensions Increase," February 11, 2003, www.nipc.gov/warnings/advisories/2003/03-002.htm, accessed March 6, 2003; Andrew Conry-Murray, "Strategies & Issues: Security Spending," *Network Magazine,* March 1, 2003.

a certain degree of anonymity in the shopping process, consumers could still choose to remain anonymous by paying cash. Shopping on the Internet, however, allows businesses to track consumers on a far more personal level, from their online purchases to the web sites they favor.[43] More than 71 percent of respondents surveyed in a UCLA study indicated they will probably make more purchases online in the future, up from 66 percent in 2001 and 54 percent in 2000. Privacy concerns, while still high, have declined slightly, and the most experienced users show lower levels of concern about credit-card security than do new users.[44] Indeed, current technology has made it possible to amass vast quantities of personal information, often without consumers' knowledge. The Internet allows for the collection, sharing, and selling of this information to interested third parties. The web site peoplesearch.com, for example, permits anyone to do asset verification checks and criminal background checks on any individual for a fee of $39 to $125. Another web site, whowhere.com, supplies background information, including property ownership, civil judgments, driver's license, physical description, and summary of assets, on any individual in its database for only $39.95.[45] In all, 88.8 percent of respondents in the UCLA survey—users and nonusers alike—expressed some concern about the privacy of their personal information when or if they buy on the Internet, down from 94.6 percent in 2001.[46]

On the positive side, today's technology makes it easier for law enforcement agents to catch criminals, for banks to detect fraud, and for consumers to learn about goods and services and to communicate directly with businesses about their needs. Because of the ease of access to personal information, however, unauthorized use of this information may occur.[47] Spam has reached an epidemic level, affecting hundreds of millions of e-mail users worldwide, impairing productivity and sapping network resources. Estimates now claim about 50 percent of e-mail consists of spam. A real need has emerged for spam-blocking software to revitalize productivity and to stop unwanted e-mails.[48]

Information can be collected on the Internet with or without a person's knowledge. Many web sites follow users' tracks through their site by storing a "cookie," or identifying string of text, on their computers. These cookies permit web site operators to track how often a user visits the site, what he or she looks at while there, and in what sequence. Cookies also allow web site visitors to customize services, such as virtual shopping carts, as well as the particular content they see when they log on to a Web page. However, if a web site operator can exploit cookies to link a visitor's interests to a name and address, that information could be sold to advertisers and other parties without the visitor's consent or even knowledge. The potential for misuse has left many consumers rather uncomfortable with this technology.[49] Identity theft is one of the fastest-growing crimes in the nation, hitting nearly 1.1 million people a year for an average of $6,767 each. In 2002, Federal authorities broke up what they called the biggest identity-theft case in U.S. history and charged three men with stealing credit information via the Internet from more than 30,000 people, draining bank accounts, and ruining credit ratings.[50]

Cookies aren't the only way that businesses can track consumers online. Companies such as DoubleClick, Digital Envoy, and Quova are developing technology that can match Internet addresses with geographical locations. This technology involves bouncing homing bits to a browser's computer from multiple locations and then analyzing the data to triangulate the computer's actual location. Quova says that it can provide its customers with a web site visitor's city in a fiftieth of a second with 90 percent accuracy. These companies claim that they are not collecting specific customer names and addresses, only their city of origin so that web site operators can tailor their content—and advertisements—to different users. The technology also gets around the problem of savvier users who block Web pages from storing cookies on their computers.[51]

A growing number of Internet web sites require visitors to register and provide information about themselves in order to access some or all of their content. How this information will be used is also generating concern. For example, 75 percent of users of health-related web sites worry that the information they supply when they register for access to the site or respond to surveys may be sold to third parties without their permission.[52] Some people are concerned that personal information about their health may be sold to insurance companies that may deny them coverage on the basis of that information. Although many health-oriented and other web sites post privacy policies that specify whether and how they will use any personal information they gather, some consumers still worry that such policies are just "lip service." Amazon.com received complaints through the Federal Trade Commission (FTC) after it modified its privacy policy, which allows it to disclose personal information to third parties and to sell customer information in the event it goes out of business or sells assets.[53] According to the FTC, about two-thirds of commercial web sites post information on their privacy policies. However, about 93 percent of these sites collect at least one type of personally identifying information from visitors, and 57 percent gather some type of demographic information.[54] Moreover, only 20 percent of sites have voluntarily implemented adequate privacy-protection standards.[55] Even the Federal Trade Commission's own web site fails to meet its privacy standards.[56]

Privacy issues related to children are generating even more debate, as well as laws to protect children's interests. Concerns about protecting children's privacy were highlighted in a recent study by the Annenberg Public Policy Center, which reported that two-thirds of children ages ten to seventeen would divulge their favorite online stores in order to receive a free gift, whereas more than half would reveal their parents' favorite stores, and another quarter would disclose details about their parents' activities on the weekend. The study also found that many children would share information about the family car and the amount of their allowance. It should be noted that this survey was conducted before the U.S. Children's Online Privacy Protection Act (COPPA) went into effect in 2000. That law prohibits web sites and Internet providers from seeking personal information from children under age thirteen without parental consent.[57] Recent Census Bureau statistics bear out the increasing use of computers and the Internet among children. That's provoking a lot of worries and assorted attempts to tame the Internet. The government has waded in with the Children's Internet Protection Act, which requires schools and libraries that receive federal funds to block access to inappropriate content. The measure as it applies to libraries was struck down on First Amendment grounds, and is on appeal to the U.S. Supreme Court.[58]

Another area of growing concern is "identity theft," which occurs when criminals obtain personal information that allows them to impersonate someone else and use their credit to obtain financial accounts and make purchases. Because of the Internet's relative anonymity and speed, it fosters legal and illegal access to databases containing social security numbers, drivers' license numbers, dates of birth, mothers' maiden names, and other information that can be used to establish a credit card or bank account in another person's name in order to make transactions. According to the National Fraud Center, arrests for identity theft fraud have increased to nearly 10,000 a year, with losses from such fraud reaching $745 million. The Federal Trade Commission said complaints about identity theft doubled in 2002, with victims' reporting hijacked credit cards, drained bank accounts, and tarnished reputations.[59] To deter identity theft, the National Fraud Center wants financial institutions to implement new technologies, such as digital certificates, digital signatures, and biometrics—the use of fingerprinting or retina scanning.[60] Legislation was introduced to protect people from identity theft, with a focus on cases involving the Internet. The bill would require social security numbers to be removed from public records published on the Web; it would also prohibit the sale of social security numbers to the general public and remove such numbers from government checks and driver's licenses. The measure would permit legitimate business and government use of the numbers. Identity theft topped the Federal Trade Commission's annual report on consumer complaints in 2002, accounting for 43 percent of the complaints lodged with the FTC and losses for consumers of about $343 million.[61]

Some measure of protection for personal privacy is already provided by the U.S. Constitution, as well as Supreme Court rulings and federal laws (see Table 10.3). The U.S. Federal Trade Commission (FTC) also regulates and enforces privacy standards and monitors web sites to ensure compliance. A recent study commissioned by the FTC reported that 98 percent of the 100 top web sites collect at least one type of personal information, and 93 percent have posted at least one type of disclosure (privacy policy notice or the site practices).[62] The 2002 Online Customer Respect Study of *Fortune* 100 Companies rated Verizon as sixth best overall, third in online privacy and first in how well it explains online policies to customers, called "transparency" in the survey.[63] As the FTC chair Robert Pitofsky told a Senate panel, "Companies say self-regulation will work, but it's becoming clear that companies on the Net are not protecting the privacy of consumers."[64] For example, the FTC accused GeoCities, a popular entertainment web site, of misrepresenting the purposes for which it was harvesting personal information from both children and adults. GeoCities did not disclose the information collected, the purpose for which it was collected, or to whom it would be disclosed. The company settled the charges, agreeing to post an explicit privacy policy detailing what information it collects, for what purpose, to whom it will be disclosed, and how consumers can access and remove the information.[65]

International Initiatives on Privacy Privacy concerns are not limited to the United States. The European Union (EU) has made great strides in protecting the privacy of its citizens. The 1998 European Union Directive on Data Protection specifically requires companies that want to collect personal information to explain how the information will be used and to obtain the individual's permission. Companies must make customer data files available on request, just as U.S. credit-reporting firms must grant customers access to their personal credit histories. The law also bars web site operators from selling e-mail addresses and using cookies to track visitors' movements and preferences without first obtaining permission. Because of this legislation, no company may deliver personal information about EU citizens to countries whose privacy laws do not meet EU standards.[66] Some European countries have taken further steps to protect their citizens. Italy, for example, established an Italian Data Protection Commission to enforce its stringent privacy laws. Such agencies highlight the differences in how Europeans and Americans approach the online privacy issue.[67]

TABLE 10.3 Privacy Laws

ACT (DATE ENACTED)	PURPOSE
Privacy Act (1974)	Requires federal agencies to adopt minimum standards for collecting and processing personal information; limits the disclosure of such records to other public or private parties; requires agencies to make records on individuals available to them on request, subject to certain conditions.
Right to Financial Privacy Act (1978)	Protects the rights of financial institution customers to keep their financial records private and free from unjust government investigation.
Computer Security Act (1987)	Brought greater confidentiality and integrity to the regulation of information in the public realm by assigning responsibility for the standardization of communication protocols, data structures, and interfaces in telecommunications and computer systems to the National Institute of Standards and Technology (NIST), which also announced security and privacy guidelines for federal computer systems.
Computer Matching and Privacy Protection Act (1988)	Amended the Privacy Act by adding provisions regulating the use of computer matching, the computerized comparison of individual information for purposes of determining eligibility for federal benefits programs.
Video Privacy Protection Act (1988)	Specifies the circumstances under which a business that rents or sells videos can disclose personally identifiable information about a consumer or reveal an individual's video rental or sales records.
Telephone Consumer Protection Act (1991)	Regulates the activities of telemarketers by limiting the hours during which they can solicit residential subscribers, outlawing the use of artificial or prerecorded voice messages to residences without prior consent, prohibiting unsolicited advertisements by telephone facsimile machines, and requiring telemarketers to maintain a "do not call list" of any consumers who request not to receive further solicitation.
Driver Privacy Protection Act (1993)	Restricts the circumstances under which state departments of motor vehicles may disclose personal information about any individual obtained by the department in connection with a motor vehicle record.
Fair Credit Reporting Act (amended in 1997)	Promotes accuracy, fairness, and privacy of information in the files of consumer reporting agencies (e.g., credit bureaus); grants consumers the right to see their personal credit reports, to find out who has requested access to their reports, to dispute any inaccurate information with the consumer reporting agency, and to have inaccurate information corrected or deleted.
Children's Online Privacy Protection Act (2000)	Regulates the online collection of personally identifiable information (name, address, e-mail address, hobbies, interests, or information collected through cookies) from children under age thirteen by specifying what a web site operator must include in a privacy policy, when and how to seek consent from a parent, and what responsibilities an operator has to protect children's privacy and safety online.

Sources: "Privacy Act of 1974," U.S. Bureau of Reclamation, www.usbr.gov/laws/privacy.html, accessed December 27, 2000; "Right to Financial Privacy Act (RFPA) Summary," Right Data, www.rightdata.com/graphics/info_d.htm, accessed December 27, 2000; "Statement of Customer Rights Under the Right to Financial Privacy Act of 1978," Associated Mortgage Professionals, Inc., http://cyber-mortgage.com/amp_disclosureofprivacy.htm, accessed December 27, 2000; E. Maria Grace, "Privacy vs. Convenience: The Benefits and Drawbacks of Tax System Modernization," *Federal Communications Law Journal* 47 (December 1994), www.law.indiana.edu/fclj/pubs/v47/no2/grace.html; "A Citizen's Guide on Using the Freedom of Information Act and the Privacy Act of 1974 to Request Records," Tennessee Criminal Law Defense Resources, http://tncrimlaw.com/foia/VII_B. html, accessed December 27, 2000; "Sec. 2710. Wrongful Disclosure of Video Tape Rental or Sale Records," Legal Information Institute, www4.law.cornell.edu/uscode/18/2710.text.html, accessed December 27, 2000; "Summary and Analysis of Rules Implementing the Telephone Consumer Protection Act of 1991," Arent Fox Kintner Plotkin & Kahn, PLLC, www.arentfox. com/publications/alerts/cpa1991/cpa1991.html, accessed December 27, 2000; "Sec. 2721. Prohibition on Release and Use of Certain Personal Information from State Motor Vehicle Records," Legal Information Institute, www4.law.cornell.edu/uscode/18/2721.text. html, accessed December 27, 2000; "A Summary of Your Rights Under the Fair Credit Reporting Act," Federal Trade Commission, www. ftc.gov/bcp/conline/edcams/fcra/summary.htm, accessed December 27, 2000; "How to Comply With the Children's Online Privacy Protection Rule According to the Federal Trade Commission," COPPA, November 1999, http://coppa.org/ftc_how_to.htm.

In Canada, private industry has taken the lead in creating and developing privacy policies through the Direct Marketing Association of Canada (DMAC). The DMAC's policies resulted in the proposal of legislation to protect personal privacy. The Personal Information Protection and Electronic Documents Act, which went into effect on January 1, 2001, established a right of personal privacy for information collected by Canadian businesses and organizations. The new law instituted rules governing the collection, use, and disclosure of personal information in the private sector. The law also works in conjunction with other legislation that protects personal information collected by federal and/or provincial governments. The Canadian Standards Association (CSA) was also instrumental in bringing about privacy protection guidelines in Canada. The CSA 1996 Model Code for the Protection of Personal Information requires organizations to protect personal information and to allow individuals access to their own personal information, allowing for correction if necessary.[68]

In Japan, the Ministry of International Trade and Industry established the Electronic Network Consortium (ENC) to resolve issues associated with the Internet. The ENC (which comprises ninety-two corporate members, fifty-one local community organizations, and fifteen special members) has prepared guidelines for protecting personal data gathered by Japanese online service providers. These guidelines require web sites to obtain an individual's consent before collecting personal data or using or transferring such data to a third party. The guidelines also call for organizations to appoint managers who understand the ENC guidelines to oversee the collection and use of personal data and to utilize privacy information management systems such as the Platform for Privacy Protection (P3P).[69] P3P is a set of standards under development by the World Wide Web Consortium that would permit web sites to translate their privacy statements and standards into a uniform format that Web browsing software could access in order to supply users with relevant information about a particular firm's policies. Web site visitors could then decide what information, if any, they are willing to share with web sites.[70]

Protection of citizens' privacy on the Internet is not a major public concern in Russia. Few Russian web sites have privacy policy or disclosure statements explaining how collected information will be used. International companies conducting business in Russia or managing Russian subsidiaries maintain online privacy information for their U.S. customers but not for Russian customers.[71] The country is not currently looking to a tightening of its information privacy laws. Corporate databases as well as comprehensive files on customers of retail product and service providers are readily available across Russia. It is common practice in Russia to sell databases.[72] Until recently, Russian law gave authorities the right to monitor private e-mail. However, Nail Murzakhanov, the founder of a small Internet service provider in Volgograd, challenged this right when he refused to purchase the equipment that would have permitted Russian security agencies to eavesdrop on his customers' e-mail. Murzakhanov stood firm in his belief that complying with the law would jeopardize his guarantee of privacy to his customers, even after the Ministry of Communications threatened to revoke his license to operate. Eventually, the Ministry of Communications dropped all charges against Murzakhanov's company, setting a precedent for other Internet service providers who wish to protect their customers' privacy.[73] Russian antitrust regulators are going after the last space where Russian vodka makers can still advertise: the Internet. An official of the antitrust service said that advertising for alcohol was allowed neither on television nor in the street, and therefore it was not allowed on the Internet either.[74]

Privacy Officers and Certification Businesses are beginning to recognize that the only way to circumvent further government regulation with respect to privacy is to develop systems and policies to protect consumers' interests. In addition to creating and posting policies regarding the gathering and use of personal information, more companies—including American Express, AT&T, Citigroup, and Prudential Insurance—are beginning to hire chief privacy officers (CPOs). New laws requiring companies to protect consumer privacy will create 30,000 jobs. Most health-care-related businesses must appoint a privacy official to safeguard patient data. About 20 percent of the new jobs will be for executives, such as at Ford, where privacy officers typically earn between $100,000 and $350,000 a year and report either to a company's general counsel or its chief operating officer.[75] These high-level executives are typically given broad powers to establish policies to protect consumer privacy and, in so doing, to protect their companies from negative publicity and legal scrutiny.

Several nonprofit organizations have also stepped in to help companies develop privacy policies. Among the best known of these are TRUSTe and the BBBOnLine. TRUSTe is a nonprofit organization devoted to promoting global trust in Internet technology by providing a standardized, third-party oversight program that addresses the privacy concerns of consumers, web site operators, and government regulators. Companies that agree to abide by TRUSTe's privacy standards may display a "trustmark" on their web sites. These firms must disclose their personal information collection and privacy policies in a straightforward privacy statement. TRUSTe is supported by a network of corporate, industry, and nonprofit sponsors including the Electronic Frontier Foundation, CommerceNet, America Online, Compaq, Ernst & Young, Excite, IBM, MatchLogic, Microsoft, Netcom, and Netscape.[76] For example, eBay's web site is TRUSTe certified, which means that its online privacy practices fulfill TRUSTe's requirements. The online auction company's privacy policy promises that eBay will not share any personal information gathered from customers with any third parties and specifies how it will use the information it obtains. TRUSTe maintains the largest privacy seal program with more than 1,500 web sites certified throughout the world.[77]

The mission of BBBOnLine is to promote trust and confidence in the Internet by promoting ethical business practices. The BBBOnLine program provides verification, monitoring and review, consumer dispute resolution, a compliance seal, enforcement mechanisms, and an educational component. It is managed by the Council of Better Business Bureaus, an organization with considerable experience in conducting self-regulation and dispute-resolution programs, and it employs guidelines and requirements outlined by the Federal Trade Commission and the U.S. Department of Commerce.[78] Over 12,000 web sites have qualified to display the BBBOnLine trustmarks. Together with PlanetFeedback.com, whose 400,000 registered users make it one of the largest online consumer feedback services, have created consumer feedback solutions for some of the nation's top companies, including Procter & Gamble, Nokia, HealthNow New York, and others. This venture will help companies meet whistle-blower provisions of the recent corporate reform legislation.[79]

TRUSTe is a non-profit, independent group dedicated to protecting privacy on the Internet, building users' confidence and trust in the Internet, and helping to accelerate Web-based economic growth. (www.TRUSTe.org, downloaded April 2003. Copyright © 2003. Reprinted with permission.)

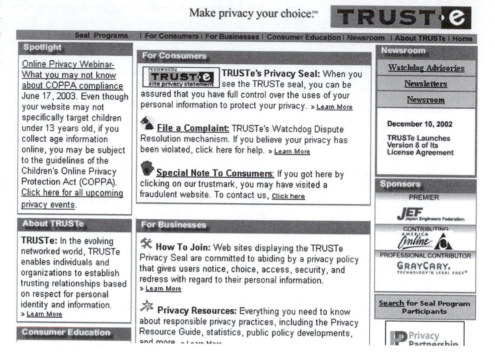

Intellectual Property

In addition to protecting personal privacy, Internet users and others are concerned about protecting their rights to property they create, including songs, movies, books, and software. Such **intellectual property** consists of the ideas and creative materials developed to solve problems, carry out applications, educate, and entertain others. It is the result or end product of the creative process. Intellectual property is generally protected via patents and copyrights. However, technological advancements are increasingly challenging the ownership of such property. For example, the FTC sued to block Internet retailer Toysmart.com from selling the names, addresses, billing information, family profiles, and buying habits of customers who have visited its web site. The company, which filed for bankruptcy, had posted a privacy policy specifying that it would not share such personal information with third parties and had once been certified by TRUSTe. The FTC's suit may open the door for litigation against other failing Internet companies that attempt to sell their only significant assets—their databases.[80]

Intellectual property losses in the United States total more than $11 billion a year in lost revenue from the illegal copying of computer programs, movies, compact discs, and books. This issue has become a global concern because of disparities in enforcement of laws throughout the world. For example, according to the trade association International Intellectual Property Alliance, more than half of the business software used in Israel is pirated, costing U.S. companies roughly $170 million in one year.[81] The Business Software Alliance says business software producers, including alliance members such as Microsoft Corp., Adobe Systems Inc., and Apple Computer

intellectual property
the ideas and creative material developed to solve problems, carry out applications, educate, and entertain others; the end product of the creative process

Inc., are losing $12 billion a year to piracy worldwide. The price of software lost to piracy ranges from $40 for desktop utilities to $13,000 for computer-aided design programs. Thirty-seven percent of all commercial software is pirated, said trade group officials. Illegal use of software downloaded from the Internet is a growing concern for the trade group. By 2005, the BSA predicted, two-thirds of all software will be delivered online, up from just more than 10 percent in 2000.[82] Russia and China are the two worst countries in terms of piracy violations. It is predicted that the trade-related aspects of intellectual property rights disputes will make countries more accountable for adhering to copyright standards.[83] Cisco Systems Inc. announced that it has filed a lawsuit against Chinese network equipment maker Huawei Technologies and its subsidiaries, claiming unlawful copying of its intellectual property. Cisco claims that Huawei copied extensively from Cisco's copyrighted technical documentation and portions of the Cisco IOS source code and included the technology in its operating system.[84]

Microsoft has been particularly aggressive in battling software piracy. The company has initiated legal action against 7,500 Internet listings in thirty-three countries for products it says are pirated. The company's efforts to stamp out piracy have been facilitated by software that searches the Internet for offers to sell counterfeit or illegally copied software.[85] If Microsoft is successful in its attempts, by showing courage, foresight, and leadership on this issue, it could transform the economics of the software business, allowing cheaper, more innovative software to be available for legitimate, paying customers.[86] Microsoft has even opened up a howtotell.com web site for people to consult when loading software onto their computers. The web site helps educate customers on how to tell if their software is genuine. Microsoft is also employing a new Office Registration Wizard that authorizes purchasers of its software to load the programs onto only one desktop and one portable computer. If a purchaser attempts to register the software on more than two computers, the program will abort.[87] Can you think of another industry that would tolerate 40 percent of its products being stolen?

United States copyright laws protect original works in text form, pictures, movies, computer software, musical multimedia, and audiovisual work. Owners of copyrights have the right to reproduce, derive from, distribute, and publicly display and perform the copyrighted works. Copyright infringement is the unauthorized execution of the rights reserved by a copyright holder. Congress passed the Digital Millennium Copyright Act (DMCA) in 1998 to protect copyrighted materials on the Internet and to limit the liability of online service providers (OSPs). The DMCA provides a "safe harbor" provision that limits judgments that can be levied against OSPs for copyright infringement by their customers. In order to limit their liability, service providers must pay a nominal fee and comply with the act's reporting requirements.[88] In a lawsuit brought by Ticketmaster against Tickets.com under the DMCA, a judge ruled that Tickets.com could legally place a hypertext link to Ticketmaster on its web site. Although Ticketmaster claimed that the link infringed its copyrights, Tickets.com contended that it placed the Ticketmaster and other similar hot links on its web site so that its customers could access those sites to obtain tickets not available through Tickets.com. Because the link automatically directed potential customers to Ticketmaster's actual web site, the court ruled no copyright violation occurred.[89] Table 10.4 provides additional facts about copyrights.

TABLE 10.4	Facts About Copyrights

- A copyright notice is not necessary to protect private and original work created after April 1, 1989.
- Granting work to the public domain relinquishes all of the copyright holder's rights.
- The "fair use" exemption to copyright law allows for commentary, parody, news reporting, as well as research and education without seeking the copyright holder's permission, but giving appropriate acknowledgment.
- Legal defense of a copyright is not necessary for maintaining the copyright—unlike trademarks, which may be damaged if not defended.
- Derivative works, based on another copyrighted work, come under the control of the original copyright holder. A notable exception is parody—making fun of an original work.
- Most copyright litigation is civil versus criminal in nature, but criminal litigation is possible with more than ten copies of an original work and a valuation of over $2,500 (representing a commercial copyright violation).

Source: Brad Templeton, "10 Big Myths About Copyrights Explained," Brad Templeton's Home Page, www.templetons.com/brad/copymyths.html, accessed March 4, 2003.

The Internet has created other copyright issues for some organizations that have found that the Web addresses (URLs) of other online firms either match or are very similar to their own trademarks. In some cases, "cybersquatters" have deliberately registered Web addresses that match or relate to other firms' trademarks and then have attempted to sell the registration to the trademark owners. A number of companies, including Taco Bell, MTC, and KFC, have paid thousands of dollars to gain control of names that match or parallel company trademarks.[90] Registering a domain name is currently done on the honor system; a registrant simply fills out an online form, and his domain name is automatically reserved for him. As such, the process is ideal for cybersquatters or other scammers looking to defraud businesses and consumers. On November 11, 2002, a scammer who set up a spoof eBay web site that has since been taken down was allowed to register the domain name Ebaylogin.com with VeriSign using 555-555-5555 as his fax number.[91] The Federal Trademark Dilution Act of 1995 was enacted to help companies resolve this conflict. The law gives trademark owners the right to protect their trademarks, prevents the use of trademark-protected entities by others, and requires cybersquatters to relinquish trademarked names.[92]

The Internet Corporation for Assigned Names and Numbers (ICANN), a nonprofit group charged with overseeing basic technical matters related to addressing on the Internet, has had success, including the introduction of a competitive domain registrar and registration market, the Uniform Dispute Resolution Policy (UDRP), and the creation of seven new top-level domains.[93] Many trademark holders immediately turn to the Internet Corporation for Assigned Names and Numbers' Uniform Dispute Resolution Policy as a vehicle for combating cybersquatters. However, remedies available in federal court under the Anti-Cybersquatting Consumer Production Act may better protect the rights of trademark holders. All ICANN-authorized registrars of domain names in the .com, .net, and .org top-level domains must agree to abide by the UDRP. Under the terms of the UDRP, a domain name will be trans-

The Internet Corporation for Assigned Names and Numbers

About ICANN   Supporting Organizations   Committees, Task Forces, Etc.   Organizational Chart   Site Search

ICANN Resources

- Announcements
- At Large Advisory Committee
- Calendar of Events
- Contact ICANN
- Country-Code Top-Level Domain Resource Materials
- Correspondence
- Domain-Name Dispute Resolution (UDRP)
- Frequently Asked Questions (FAQ)
- Links

New and Noteworthy:

NEW: Whois Data Reminder Policy Posted (16 June 2003)

NEW: Nominating Committee Announces Nominees to Be Seated at Montréal Meeting (16 June 2003)

UPDATED: ICANN Meeting in Montréal.
Background papers:

- Formation of At-Large Groups (15 June 2003)
- Proposed Budget for 2003-2004 (13 June 2003)

ferred between parties only by agreement between them or by order of a court of competent jurisdiction or a UDRP-authorized dispute resolution provider.[94]

Health and Biotechnology

The advance of life-supporting technologies has raised a number of medical and health issues related to technology. **Bioethics** refers to the study of ethical issues in the fields of medical treatment and research, including medicine, nursing, law, philosophy, and theology, though today medical ethics is also recognized as a separate discipline.[95] All of these fields have been influenced by rapid changes in technology that require new approaches for solving issues. New genetic technologies promise to give medical ethics an even greater role in social decision making. For example, the Human Genome Project, a fifteen-year, $3 billion federally funded program to decode the entire human genetic map, has already identified a number of genes that may contribute to particular diseases or traits.[96]

Because so many of our resources are spent on health care, the role of the private sector in determining the quality of health care is an important consideration to society. The pharmaceutical industry, for example, has been sharply criticized by politicians, health care organizations, and consumers because of escalating drug costs. Investigators from federal and state agencies have threatened legal action over allegations that Medicare and Medicaid overpaid for drugs by $1 billion or more a year.[97] In the beginning of 2003, Merck & Co. was alleged of overcharging the government on its popular Pepcid heartburn and ulcer medication, potentially costing the Medicaid program hundreds of millions of dollars. Merck was alleged to have sold Pepcid to hospitals and other health care institutions for about $.10 a tablet, while charging as much as $1.65 a tablet to Medicaid and other government health care programs.[98] Merck denied that it had engaged in illegal pricing.

bioethics
the study of ethical issues in the fields of medical treatment and research, including medicine, nursing, law, philosophy, and theology, though today medical ethics is also recognized as a separate discipline

In another example, Pfizer Inc. agreed to pay $49 million to settle a whistle-blower case that lawyers predict will be followed by many like it. The case involved claims that Pfizer had bilked the federal government out of millions when selling the anticholesterol drug Lipitor. This case, in essence, signifies a new niche of cases against the drug industry that fall under the federal False Claims Act. Under federal law, it is illegal for a drug company to pay a doctor or an organization, such as an HMO, as an inducement for that company to give a drug preferred status.[99] On the other hand, pharmaceutical companies claim that the development of new lifesaving drugs and tests requires huge expenditures in research and development. Figure 10.3 provides evidence that large amounts of money are spent in this process. The pharmaceutical industry is among the most profitable U.S. industries and spends nearly $14 billion a year in promotion, including drug samples provided to doctors.[100]

Biotechnology Driven by human genome projects, the value of biotech firms is three and a half times greater than it was two years ago.[101] According to a recent world study by KPMG, for the third consecutive year, Canada is the fastest-growing country in biomedical research and development. A Statistics Canada report states that the Canadian biotechnology sector, which is second only to the United States's, saw revenues increase by 53 percent over the past four years.[102] The remarkable feat of mapping the human genome has spurred a rush to cash in on the booming business of genetic research. In fact, genetic research is one of the fastest-growing areas of

---

FIGURE 10.3   **Research and Development Expenditures by Pharmaceutical Companies (billions of dollars)**

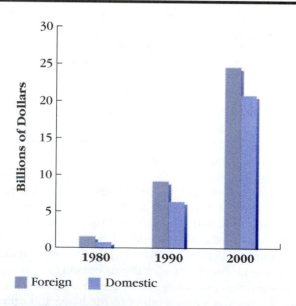

Source: Republished with permission of Dow Jones & Company from *The Wall Street Journal*, "Drug Companies Face Assault on Prices" by Shailagh Murrah and Lucette Lagnado, May 11, 2000, p. B1. Permission conveyed through Copyright Clearance Center, Inc.

high technology. Patent applications from biotechnology companies are flooding into the U.S. Patent Office at a rate of 400 a week, and there are some 20,000 applications pending for gene-related discoveries. There are 1,283 biotechnology companies with 153,000 employees and a stock worth of almost $100 billion.[103] More than 500,000 patents have been applied for on genes or gene sequences worldwide, according to the activist group GeneWatch UK. The U.S. Patent and Trademark Office alone has issued approximately 20,000 patents on genes or gene-related molecules and 25,000 more applications are pending.[104]

The government and the private sector often partner with academic researchers and nonprofit institutes to develop new technologies in health and biotechnology. Research ranges from mapping the human genetic code to finding drugs that cure cancer to genetically modifying food products. Many of these collaborative efforts to improve health involve scientists, funded globally by a variety of sources. For example, the Avon Foundation granted nearly $30 million through the Avon Kiss Goodbye to Breast Cancer Crusade, which supports virtually every facet of the cause by funding five critical areas: breast cancer biomedical research, clinical care, support services, education, and early detection programs.[105] National Institutes of Health scientists created great excitement when they reported that embryonic stem cells had been coaxed to form pancreatic cells that make insulin, a potential treatment for diabetes. But a new study suggests that the cells didn't really make insulin and instead just absorbed it from the culture medium they were grown in and later released it.[106] Using cell-engineering techniques, scientists may have found a way to generate unlimited supplies of brain cells for transplanting into Parkinson's disease patients. These examples illustrate technology advances that could result in commercially viable products that save and/or prolong life.

Cloning, the replication of organisms that are genetically identical to their parent, has become a highly controversial topic in biotechnology and bioethics. Human cloning has raised unanswered questions about the future of human reproduction. Only six years have passed since Scottish scientists first cloned Dolly the sheep. Since that time, scientists have also successfully cloned mice, cows, pigs, goats, and cats but with mixed reports about the health of the cloned progeny. While cloning humans would appear to be the final step of scientific reproduction, indisputable proof of the first human clone will actually serve as a starting point for many years of research. Like in vitro fertilization, human clones will need to grow up before scientists know the effects that this process will have on a person's physical, mental, and emotional states.[107] Cloning has the potential to revolutionize the treatment of diseases and conditions such as Parkinson's disease and cancer. Cloning technology might also allow doctors to create replacement organs, thereby lengthening human lives. Some scientists believe that cloning could be used to recreate extinct or endangered species in a last-ditch conservation effort. The ability to create and modify life processes is often generated through business and government collaborative research; the results of such research may contribute to life-altering products of tomorrow.

Despite the potential of this technology, many people have negative views about cloning. Some contend that it is unethical to "meddle with nature," whereas others believe that cloning is wrong because every time it is used to treat a patient, a cloned human embryo is destroyed, one that might otherwise have been capable of life.[108] The cloning of a miniature pig, named Goldie, lacking both copies of a gene involved in immediate immune rejection has brought the prospect of transplanting pig organs into people a little closer. The small pig's organs are similar in size to those of humans and the missing genes make the organs less likely to be rejected. But while Goldie's creation may have solved the problem of immediate transplant rejection, there is a slower rejection in which the transplant is attacked by the recipient's white blood cells.[109] Some people argue that cloning of human beings should be banned, and several bills have been introduced in Congress and various state legislatures to do just that. Additionally, nineteen European nations have signed an agreement prohibiting the genetic replication of humans. Harvesting stem cells from surplus in vitro fertilization (IVF) embryos was given the go-ahead by the Australian Senate by a vote of nearly two to one in favor of a bill legalizing the procedure. The new Australian law lies between those in the United Kingdom and the United States. In the United Kingdom, the law already allows researchers to harvest stem cells from surplus IVF embryos and to conduct therapeutic cloning. But in the United States, federally funded researchers cannot pursue therapeutic cloning or harvest stem cells from discarded embryos, although private companies can.[110]

Genetic research holds the promise to revolutionize how many diseases are diagnosed and treated. However, consumer advocates have urged the World Trade Organization (WTO) to place limits on gene patents, which they claim are tantamount to "ownership of life." Patents dealing with human DNA have increased dramatically in the last decade as researchers have identified more genes that play a role in a number of diseases. The WTO rules governing patents on intellectual property currently permit patents to be owned for twenty years and allow patent holders to prevent other firms from profiting from a particular technology during that period. But some consumer groups, including Ralph Nader's Public Citizen, fear that these patents have the potential to permit a company to "corner the market" on the diagnosis and treatment of specific diseases for years. These groups worry that such long-term protection could prohibit other companies from developing alternative tests and treatments that might result in improved care at lower prices.[111] The fact that genes are both material molecules and informational systems helps explain the difficulty that the patent system is going to continue to have.[112]

Genetically Modified Foods As many as 800 million people around the world don't have enough to eat. Increasing food production to satisfy growing demand for food without increasing land use will require farmers to achieve significant increases in productivity. Genetically modified foods (GM foods or GMF) offer a way to quickly improve crop characteristics such as yield, pest resistance, or herbicide tolerance, often to a degree not possible with traditional methods. Further, GM crops can be manipulated to produce completely artificial substances, from the precursors to plastics to consumable vaccines.[113] As we discussed in Chapter 9, genetically modified, or transgenic, crops are created when scientists introduce a gene from one organism to another. Scientists believe that genetically engineered crops could raise overall crop production in developing countries as much as 25 percent.[114] According to a report by seven independent academies from both developed and developing countries, in order to combat world hunger, developed countries must boost funding for research into genetically modified crops, and poor farmers must be protected from corporate control of the technology.[115] The European public calls GM products "Frankenstein" food for fear it could pose a health threat or create an environmental disaster where genes jump from GM crops to wild plants and reduce biodiversity or create superweeds. For four years, Europe has held up new approvals of U.S. exports of "Frankenfood." Europe's parliament voted to require extensive labeling and traceability of food containing genetically modified organisms, even if no remnants of genetic modification are detectable. With European public confidence in food safety badly shaken by foot-and-mouth and mad-cow disease, no new GM products have been authorized for use in Europe since 1998. European Union officials admit this is likely illegal under WTO rules and hurts largely U.S. farm exporters. In an effort to restart the approval process by addressing public concerns over consumer choice and environmental protection, the EU proposed burdensome new rules for biotech food and animal feed labeling and for "farm-to-fork" traceability measures on products.[116] Table 10.5 lists some examples of genetically modified (GM) foods. Genetic modification has raised numerous health, ethical, and environmental questions. We looked at some of the environmental issues in Chapter 9.

Many people do not realize that some of the foods they eat were made from genetically engineered crops. Consumer groups are increasingly concerned that these foods could be unhealthy and/or harmful to the environment. Concerns about the safety of genetically altered crops have led to a backlash in Europe and, more recently, in the United States and Japan. For example, Campbell Soup, the first firm to license a genetically modified food—the FlavSavr tomato, which was engineered for a longer shelf life—has been the target of a massive letter-writing campaign by

TABLE 10.5 Genetically Modified Foods

PRODUCT	GENETIC MODIFICATION	PURPOSE
Tomatoes, peas, peppers, tropical fruit, broccoli, raspberries, melons	Controlled ripening	Allows shipping of vine-ripened tomatoes; improves shelf life, quality
Tomatoes, potatoes, corn, lettuce, coffee, cabbage family, apples	Insect resistance	Reduces insecticide use
Peppers, tomatoes, cucumbers	Fungal resistance	Reduces fungicide use
Potatoes, tomatoes, cantaloupe, squash, cucumbers, corn, oilseed rape (canola), soybeans, grapes	Viral resistance	Reduces diseases caused by plant viruses and, because insects carry viruses, reduces use of insecticides
Soybeans, tomatoes, corn, oilseed rape (canola), wheat	Herbicide tolerance	Improves weed control
Corn, sunflowers, soybeans, and other plants	Improved nutrition	Increases amount of essential amino acids, vitamins, or other nutrients in the host plants
Oilseed rape (canola), peanuts	Heat stability	Improves the processing quality, permits new food uses for healthier oils

Source: Food Marketing Institute, The Hale Group/Decision Resources, Inc., Food Processing and BIO/technology magazines, as reported in "Weighing the Future of Biotech Food," MSNBC, www.msnbc.com, accessed July 18, 2000. Courtesy of Food Marketing Institute.

consumers worried about the lack of safety testing and labels on foods containing gene-altered crops.[117] The power of genetic modification techniques raises the possibility of human health, environmental, and economic problems, including unanticipated allergic responses to novel substances in foods, the spread of pest resistance or herbicide tolerance to wild plants, inadvertent toxicity to benign wildlife, and increasing control of agriculture by biotechnology corporations.[118] Many consumers are boycotting so-called Frankenfoods, products made from genetically modified materials. Several countries have opposed trade in GM foods through the World Trade Organization, and Japan has asked U.S. corn producers not to include genetically modified corn in animal feed exported to Japan. The European Parliament has called for all GM foods to be labeled.[119] Insects and birds transport seeds from one field to the next, allowing cross-pollination geneticists never intended. Unlike chemical or nuclear contamination, gene pollution can never be cleaned up.[120]

A number of companies have responded to public concerns about genetically modified food products by limiting or avoiding their use altogether. Major European supermarkets are considering banning GM foods, and Nestlé UK and Unilever have stopped using them in their food products. In the United States, Archer Daniels Midland, the largest buyer of genetically modified crops in the United States, has asked farmers and grain merchants to segregate GM crops from traditionally grown plants. The company may discard a load of grain when tests detect even a tiny amount of altered genes. In fact, large agribusiness purchasers of farm crops are paying less per bushel for genetically altered products.[121] Genetically engineered food crops, virtually unknown ten years ago, now occupy over 100 million acres of U.S. farmland. This is an astonishing 167,000 square miles, an area larger than the entire state of California. Over half of the soybeans grown in the United States last year were genetically engineered, and over a third of the entire U.S. corn crop.[122] McDonald's and Frito-Lay have asked their suppliers to stop using GM potatoes developed by Monsanto.[123] Gerber and Heinz both announced that they will not permit genetically engineered corn or soybeans in their baby food products. Corn growers in the United States say they are losing $300 million annually because their GM crops are barred—along with many other modified products—from the European market. About 70 percent of soybeans and more than 25 percent of corn in the United States is grown from GM seeds. Biotech company Monsanto wants to bring biotech wheat to market.[124]

Ethical questions about the use of some types of genetically modified products have also been raised. For example, Monsanto and other companies are developing so-called terminator technology to create plants that are genetically engineered to produce sterile seeds. Dr. Jane Rissler, a scientist with the Union of Concerned Scientists, says, "The fact that terminator technology will work to the disadvantage of the subsistence farmer who depends on harvesting seeds for the next year's crops illustrates the intent of the companies, which is to get the maximum return on their investment." Other plants in development will require spraying with chemicals supplied by the seed companies in order to produce desired traits, such as resistance to certain pests or disease. Farmers say the issue isn't the technology itself, but rather, who controls the technology—in most cases, the multinational seed companies. In response to global concerns about this issue, Monsanto announced that it would halt commercial development of the terminator technology, although it plans to continue researching it.[125]

Defenders of biotechnology say consumer fears about genetically modified foods have not been substantiated by research.[126] India froze food-aid shipments of corn and soy from the United States, and Zambia turned away 18,000 tons of U.S. corn, even though 3 million of its citizens teeter on the brink of starvation. So far, genetic technologies haven't led to drastically lowered prices, but as supplies increase, some experts think 30 percent drops are likely. In 2001, GM crops worldwide covered 53 million hectares, 15 percent more than the year before. As the U.S. agriculture industry is eager to point out, the technology has been a big success: It has reduced the amount of pesticides farmers have had to spray on their cornfields, with happy consequences for the environment and human health. U.S. health regulators have not been able to find anything wrong with eating Bt corn. It is now found in roughly two-thirds of all corn products on U.S. store shelves.[127]

Strategic Implementation of Responsibility for Technology

In order to accrue the maximum benefits from the technologies driving the New Economy, many parties within society have important roles to play. While the media and public continue to debate the issues associated with technology, the government must take steps to provide support for continued technological advancements and establish regulations, as needed, to ensure that the benefits of technology apply to as many people as possible while minimizing any potential for harm, especially to competition, the environment, and human welfare. Various stakeholders, including employees, customers, and special-interest groups, as well as the general public, can influence the use and control of technology through the public policy process. Businesses also have a significant role to play in supporting technology. New technologies are developed, refined, and introduced to the market through the research and development and marketing activities of business. Businesses that aspire to be socially responsible must monitor the impact of technology and harness it for the good of all.

The Role of Government

With an economy that is increasingly driven by technology, the government must maintain the basic infrastructure and support for technology in our society. The Defense Department, for example, explores ways that technology can improve the quality of life. The government also serves as a watchdog to ensure that technology benefits society, not criminals. However, as the pace of technology continues to escalate, law enforcement agencies ranging from the FBI to local police forces are struggling to recruit and retain officers and prosecutors who are knowledgeable about the latest technology and the ways criminals can exploit it. The nation currently has only a few hundred high-caliber forensic computer experts, but many of these officers are being lured to technology firms and private security outfits by salaries more than twice their government paychecks. Only a handful of police and sheriffs' departments across the country have enough money to support squads of high-tech investigators, and many top detectives leap to the corporate realm anyway.[128] Computer crimes currently share sentencing guidelines with larceny, embezzlement, and theft, where the most significant sentencing factor is the amount of financial loss inflicted, and additional points are awarded for using false ID or ripping off more than ten victims. But in a congressional session that heard much talk about "cyberterrorism," lawmakers became convinced that computer outlaws had more in common with al Qaeda than common thieves. The USSC's Federal Sentencing Guidelines set the range of sentences a court can choose from in a given case, on the basis of a point system that sets a starting value for a particular crime, and then adds or subtracts points for specific aggravating or mitigating circumstances.[129]

In addition to cybercriminals, many commercial users of the Internet are implementing new technologies in ways that our existing legal system could not have conceived of when our laws were framed. Hollywood film studios, for example, are concerned that new technology will allow computer users to copy and trade entire videos on the Internet, much like they traded music recordings via Napster and other peer-to-peer file-sharing services. The recording and movie industry saw the threat of this technology when Shawn Fanning, the creator of the peer-to-peer file-swapping service, was a child.

Indeed, the road to the controversial Digital Millennium Copyright Act (DMCA) probably began in 1975, when Sony Corp. introduced the Betamax VCR. That was the start of a long series of court battles and legislative fights over electronic duplication of copyrighted material. But it wasn't until PCs were in wide use that Congress acted in a broad way to extend copyright protections to the digital domain. President Clinton signed the DMCA in October 1998. Five years later, copyright holders are using the DMCA to successfully fight Napster-like services and protect their anti-copying technology. But the law has many critics and challengers, who say it impinges on the right of consumers to copy content and creates a predicament for scientists conducting certain kinds of security research.[130]

Shawn Fanning created peer-to-peer file sharing, raising numerous ethical and legal copyright issues. (Justin Sullivan/ Getty Images)

Both the Napster and RIAA lawsuits illustrate a significant difference in opinion in the interpretation of existing laws when exploiting the evolving multimedia potential of the Internet. Although the government's strategy thus far has been not to interfere with the commercial use of technology, disputes and differing interpretations of current laws increasingly bring technology into the domain of the legal system. New laws related to breakthrough technologies that change the nature of competition are constantly being considered. Usually, the issues of privacy, ownership of intellectual property, health and safety, environmental impact, competition, or consumer welfare are the legislative platforms for changing the legal and regulatory system.

The Role of Business

Business, like government, is involved in both reactive and proactive attempts to market and make effective use of technology. Reactive concerns relate to issues that have legal and/or ethical implications as well as to issues of productivity, customer welfare, or other stakeholder issues. One example of a reactive response to the consequences of new technologies relates to employee access to and use of the World Wide Web. Websense is the worldwide leader of employee Internet management (EIM) solutions. Websense Enterprise software enables businesses to manage how their employees use the Internet, improving productivity, conserving network bandwidth and storage costs, and mitigating legal liability. Founded in 1994, Websense serves more than 18,100 worldwide customers, ranging in size from 100-person firms to global corporations.[131] At any given time, about 20 percent of employee PCs are surfing non-business-related sites, such as ESPN.com or pornographic web sites. This includes both staff and executives, including the CIO, chief technology officer, and even the CEO.[132] Many large firms have suffered public embarrassment, legal bills, compensation claims, and clear-up costs when employees seek out inappropriate material online, send e-mail to people they shouldn't, accidentally circulate confidential information outside a business, or spread a computer virus. The annual Department of Trade and Industry security survey revealed that 44 percent of businesses have suffered an e-mail breach.[133]

About 40 percent of companies are now using such software, and the International Data Corporation projects that 80 percent of companies are monitoring online behavior. The American Management Association reports that three-quarters of major U.S. companies are now monitoring employee communications, including telephone calls, e-mail, and Internet connections, and that figure has doubled since 1997.[134] The courts have ruled that because communications occurring on company-provided equipment are not private under current law, such monitoring is legal.[135] However, established high-tech companies like Microsoft and Oracle, and many startups like MP3.com, often choose not to monitor or limit employees' Web usage or e-mail.[136]

Concerns about undesirable employee use of telecommunications equipment represent reactions to changes in information technology that affect the workplace. Even though companies may be legally within their right to monitor and control the use of certain web sites by employees, such control raises strategic issues related to trust and the type of long-run relationships that firms want to have with their employees.

On the other hand, a strategic, proactive approach to technology will consider the impact on social responsibility. Proactive management of technology requires developing a plan for utilizing resources to take advantage of competitive opportunities. For example, there is great demand for high-speed Internet connections, including cable modems, DSL, and other broadband connections, because computing speed and power have moved beyond current bandwidth capacity. Many telecommunications firms are racing to install and market the infrastructure for broadband connections to satisfy this demand. In a few years, however, new technologies, probably wireless connections, will more than likely provide even greater connection speeds, and the opportunity for new companies to provide broadband service will vanish.

With competition increasing, companies are spending more time and resources to establish technology-based competitive advantages. The strategic approach to technology requires an overall mission, strategy, and coordination of all functional activities, including a concern for social responsibility, to have an effective program. To promote the responsible use of technology, a firm's policies, rules, and standards must be integrated into its corporate culture. Reducing undesirable behavior in this area is a goal that is no different from reducing costs, increasing profits, or improving quality that is aggressively enforced and integrated into the corporate culture to be effective in improving appropriate behavior within the organization.

Top managers must consider the social consequences of technology in the strategic planning process. When all stakeholders are involved in the process, everyone can better understand the need for and requirements of responsible development and use of technology. There will always be conflicts in making the right choices, but through participation in decision making, the best solutions can be found. Individual participants in this process should not abdicate their personal responsibility as concerned members of society. Organizations that are concerned about the consequences of their decisions create an environment for different opinions on important issues. As Richard Purcell, Microsoft's chief privacy officer, says, "No matter what legislation is enacted, it is the responsibility of the leaders in the online industry to provide and implement technologies that help consumers feel safer and more comfortable online."[137]

Strategic Technology Assessment

technology assessment
a procedure that companies can use to foresee the effects new products and processes will have on their operation, on other business organizations, and on society in general

In order to calculate the effects of new technologies, companies can employ a procedure known as **technology assessment** to foresee the effects new products and processes will have on their firm's operation, on other business organizations, and on society in general. This assessment is a tool that managers can use to evaluate their firm's performance and to chart strategic courses of action to respond to new technologies. With information obtained through a technology assessment or audit, managers can estimate whether the benefits of adopting a specific technology outweigh costs to the firm and to society at large. The assessment process can also help companies ensure compliance with government regulations related to technology. Remember that one of the four components of social responsibility is legal compliance. Because technology is evolving so rapidly, even lawyers are struggling to keep up with the legal implications of these advances. Social institutions, including reli-

TABLE 10.6		Strategic Technology Assessment Issues
YES	**NO**	**CHECKLIST**
○	○	Are top managers in your organization aware of the federal, state, and local laws related to technology decisions?
○	○	Does your organization have an effective system for monitoring changes in the federal, state, and local laws related to technology?
○	○	Is there an individual, committee, or department in your organization responsible for overseeing government technology issues?
○	○	Does your organization do checks on technology brought into the organization by employees?
○	○	Are there communications and training programs in your organization to create an effective culture to protect employees and organizational interests related to technology?
○	○	Does your organization have monitoring and auditing systems to determine the impact of technology on key stakeholders?
○	○	Does your organization have a method for reporting concerns about the use or impact of technology?
○	○	Is there a system to determine ethical risks and appropriate ethical conduct to deal with technology issues?
○	○	Do top managers in your organization understand the ramifications of using technology to communicate with employees and customers?
○	○	Is there an individual or department in your organization responsible for maintaining compliance standards to protect the organization in the areas of privacy and intellectual property?

gion, education, the law, and business, have to respond to changing technology by adapting or developing new approaches to address the evolving issues. A strategic technology assessment or audit can help organizations understand these issues and to develop appropriate and responsible responses to them.

If the assessment process indicates that the company has not been effective at utilizing technologies or is using them in a way that raises questions, changes may be necessary. Companies may need to consider setting higher standards, improving reporting processes, and improving communication of standards and training programs, as well as participating in aboveboard discussions with other organizations. If performance has not been satisfactory, management may want to reorganize the way certain kinds of decisions are made. Table 10.6 contains some issues to assess for proactive and reactive technology responsibility issues. Some social concerns might relate to a technology's impact on the environment, employee health and working conditions, consumer safety, and community values.

Finally, the organization should focus on the positive aspects of technology to determine how it can be used to improve the work environment, its products, and the general welfare of society. Technology can be used to reduce pollution, encourage recycling, and save energy. Also, information can be made available to customers to help them maximize the benefits of products. Technology has been and will continue to be a major force that can improve society.

Summary

Technology relates to the application of knowledge, including the processes and applications to solve problems, perform tasks, and create new methods to obtain desired outcomes. The dynamics of technology relate to the constant change that requires significant adjustments in the political, religious, and economic structures of society. Reach relates to the far-reaching nature of technology as it moves through society. The self-sustaining nature of technology relates to the fact that technology acts as a catalyst to spur even faster development. Civilizations must harness and adapt to changes in technology in order to maintain a desired quality of life. Although technological advances have improved our quality of life, they have also raised ethical, legal, and social concerns.

Advances in technology have created millions of new jobs, better health and longer lives, new opportunities, and the enrichment of lives. Without greater access to the latest technology, however, economic development could suffer in underserved areas. The ability to purchase technology may affect the nature of competition and business success. Information and telecommunications technology minimizes borders, allows people to overcome the physical limitations of time and space, and enables people to acquire customized goods and services that cost less and are of higher quality.

The Internet, a global information system that links many computer networks together, has altered the way people communicate, learn, do business, and find entertainment. The growth of the Internet has generated issues never before encountered and that social institutions, including the legal system, have been slow to address.

Because current technology has made it possible to collect, share, and sell vast quantities of personal information, often without consumers' knowledge, privacy has become a major concern associated with technology. Many web sites follow users' tracks through their site by storing a cookie, or identifying string of text, on the users' computers. What companies do with the information about consumers they collect through cookies and other technologies is generating concern. Privacy issues related to children are generating even more debate and laws to protect children's interests. Identity theft occurs when criminals obtain personal information that allows them to impersonate someone else in order to use that individual's credit to obtain financial accounts and to make purchases. Some measure of protection of personal privacy is provided by the U.S. Constitution, as well as by Supreme Court rulings and federal laws. Europe and other regions of the world are also addressing privacy concerns. In addition to creating and posting policies regarding the gathering and use of personal information, more companies are beginning to hire chief privacy officers.

Intellectual property consists of the ideas and creative materials developed to solve problems, carry out applications, educate, and entertain others. Copyright infringement is the unauthorized execution of the rights reserved by a copyright holder. Technological advancements are challenging the ownership of intellectual property. Other issues relate to "cybersquatters" who deliberately register Web addresses that match or relate to other firms' trademarks and then attempt to sell the registration to the trademark owners.

Bioethics refers to the study of ethical issues in the fields of medical treatment and research, including medicine, nursing, law, philosophy, and theology. Genetic research, including cloning, may revolutionize how diseases are diagnosed and treated. Genetically modified crops are created when scientists introduce a gene from one organism to another. However, these technologies are controversial because some people believe they are immoral, unsafe, or harmful to the environment.

To accrue the maximum benefits from the technology driving the New Economy, many parties within society have important roles to play. With an economy that is increasingly driven by technology, the government must maintain the basic infrastructure and support for technology in our society. The government also serves as a watchdog to ensure that technology benefits society, not criminals.

Business is involved in both reactive and proactive attempts to make effective use of technology. Reactive concerns relate to issues that have legal or ethical implications as well as to productivity, customer welfare, or other stakeholder issues. Proactive management of technology requires developing a plan for utilizing resources to take advantage of competitive opportunities. The strategic approach to technology requires an overall mission, strategy, and coordination of all functional activities, including a concern for social responsibility, to produce an effective program. To calculate the effects of new technologies, companies can employ a procedure known as technology assessment to foresee the effects of new products and processes on their firm's operation, on other business organizations, and on society in general.

Key Terms

technology (p. 291)
intellectual property (p. 312)
bioethics (p. 315)
technology assessment (p. 324)

Discussion Questions

1. Define technology and describe three characteristics that can be used to assess it.
2. What effect has technology had on the U.S. and global economies? Have these effects been positive or negative?
3. Many people believe that the government should regulate business with respect to privacy online, but companies say self-regulation is more appropriate. Which approach would benefit consumers most? Business?

4. What is intellectual property? How can owners of intellectual property protect their rights?
5. What is bioethics? What are some of the consequences of biomedical research?
6. Should genetically modified foods be labeled? Why or why not?
7. How can a strategic technology assessment help a company?

Experiential Exercise

Visit three web sites that are primarily designed for children or that focus on products of interest to children under age thirteen. For example, visit the web sites for new movies, games, action figures, candy, cereal, or beverages. While visiting these sites, put yourself in the role and mindset of a child. What type of language and persuasion is used? Is there a privacy statement on the site that can be understood by children? Are there any parts of the site that might be offensive or worrisome to parents? Provide a brief evaluation of how well these sites attend to the provisions of the Children's Online Privacy Protection Act.

What Would You Do?

James Kitling thought about his conversation with Ira Romero earlier that day. He was not really surprised that the Human Resources (HR) Department was concerned about the time employees were spending on personal issues during the workday. Several departments were known for their rather loose management approach. Internet access for personal tasks, like shopping, using Instant Messaging services, and answering nonwork e-mails, had been a concern for several months. Recent news reports indicated that over 50 percent of large companies now filter or monitor e-mail. Companies are also monitoring Web browsing, file downloads, chat room use, and group postings. A survey published in the media reported that workers spend an average of eight hours a week looking at nonwork Internet sites.

As the director of information technology, James was very dedicated to the effective use of technology to enhance business productivity. Although he was knowledgeable about technology, James was equally attuned to the ways in which technology can be abused in a work setting. He knew that some employees were probably using too much Internet time on personal tasks.

On the other hand, his company mainly employed professionals, administrative staff, and customer service personnel. All 310 employees were expected to use the computer a great deal throughout the day. At present, the company had a skeleton code of ethics and policy on the use of company resources, including the Internet.

A couple of managers and now HR had spoken with James about the prospects of monitoring employee computer and Internet use. Ira's inquiry about the software, however, was a bit more serious. An employee had recently been formally reprimanded for downloading and printing nonwork documents from the Internet. These documents were designed to help the employee's spouse in a new business venture. Although the employee did most of the searching and downloading during lunch, the supervisor felt this was an improper use of company resources. Other employees had been informally spoken with about their use of the Internet for personal matters. Ira believed this was a growing problem that definitely affected productivity. He had read the news reports and believed that monitoring software was becoming a necessary tool in today's workplace.

So far, James had been hesitant to purchase and implement one of these systems. The employee Internet management software was somewhat expensive, running approximately $25 per computer. He felt that the software could cause employee trust to sharply decline, resulting in even greater problems than currently existed. After all, employees engage in some personal tasks during work hours, including making telephone calls home, getting coffee, chatting with coworkers, going to the doctor, and so forth. James wondered if the Internet was that much different from these other personal activities. He recalled a discussion in a management class in his M.B.A. program, where they learned that employees in the early 1900s were only allowed to use the telephone to call the police. Thus, the telephone was once thought of as a great distractor, much like the Internet today.

Ira and a few other managers were pretty firm in their beliefs about the Internet monitoring system. James was still not convinced that it was the best route to curbing the problem. In his role, however, he was expected to provide leadership in developing a solution. What would you do?

Chapter 11

Strategic Philanthropy

CHAPTER OBJECTIVES

- Describe the history of corporate philanthropy in the United States
- Distinguish between strategic philanthropy and cause-related marketing
- Provide examples of strategic philanthropy
- Identify the benefits of strategic philanthropy
- Explain the key factors in implementing strategic philanthropy

CHAPTER OUTLINE

Strategic Philanthropy Defined

Strategic Philanthropy and Social Responsibility

Stakeholders in Strategic Philanthropy

Benefits of Strategic Philanthropy

Implementation of Strategic Philanthropy

Grupo de Institutos Fundacoes E Empresas, or Group of Institutes, Foundations, and Enterprises (GIFE), is a Brazilian-based organization devoted to enhancing the use of private resources to promote democracy and national welfare. The organization grew out of increased efforts to reduce the social inequities that exist in Brazil, a country that began to develop strong political awareness and civil and nonprofit organizations in the mid-1980s. The GIFE's Code of Ethics focuses on the ties between business and other organizations that fund projects to support citizenship activities and the common good in Brazil. GIFE is designed to improve the role and efficacy of private funding and corporate giving to aid social problems. In order to become a member of GIFE, an organization must provide funds and other support to education, health, community development, culture, and/or science and technology projects. Thus, GIFE is made up of businesses and private foundations that work on and contribute to social causes. In its first few years, members of GIFE invested $300 million in social programs in Brazil. The amount has climbed every year since that time. While these numbers are strong, especially amid the Brazilian economic situation, GIFE leaders know they are far less than investments made in the United States and Europe.

GIFE was formally founded in 1995, but several years of dialog and activity preceded this formality. In 1988, representatives in the Brazilian offices of Alcoa and the Kellogg Foundation asked the American Chamber of Commerce to sponsor a workshop on philanthropy. The seminar took place in 1989 and included representatives from many large companies in Brazil. This activity, and others that emanated from the workshop, built the foundation of GIFE. Philosophically, GIFE members believe that government and market forces can be complementary in the struggle against social imbalances and poverty. However, scandals in Brazil have made citizens wary of groups seeking donations or those dedicated to social change. This is one reason that early participants wanted to formalize GIFE's mission and organizational structure and develop a code of ethics in 1995. GIFE only partners with organizations that submit to external auditing. Today, the organization's main objective is to "contribute towards the sustainable development of Brazil through political and institutional strengthening of institutes and foundations of business origin, and to support the activities of these organizations and other private organizations that carry out systematic and voluntary social investment for the social good."

An intriguing aspect of GIFE's work is the technical assistance it provides to members and others who are interested in formalizing and institutionalizing their philanthropic efforts. This assistance includes training on how to establish a corporate foundation, develop guidelines for giving programs, monitor effectiveness, evaluate programs, and improve staff skills and professionalism. The organization also sponsors conferences, including one on Private Social Investment, that draw participants from business, nongovernmental organizations, private foundations, the media, and other sectors. This conference, as well as other GIFE events, focuses on new ideas and strong models in social investment and how they can be replicated in other parts of the country and world. GIFE's educational approach to philanthropy has helped stem the tide of public distrust while it has improved the efficacy of corporate giving and volunteerism. By focusing on best practices in corporate philanthropy, GIFE is aiding its members and other groups as they become more strategic in planning, implementing, and evaluating their financial and intangible support for social change in Brazil.[1]

Like the members of GIFE, companies around the world are considering how to integrate their philanthropic efforts with their organizational objectives and core competencies. Research by the American Productivity and Quality Center (APQC) indicates that the definition of corporate success is slowly evolving to include four equal and complementary goals: Corporations are seeking to become the (1) supplier and provider of choice, (2) employer of choice, (3) investment of choice, and (4) neighbor of choice. Progressive businesses are investigating ways to tie their corporate objectives to community relations activities, especially through the development of citizen advisory panels, public hearings, meetings with community service organizations, and participation in community events. Such practices are intended to create "corporate equity with communities and stakeholders."[2] These activities are also aligned with our concept of strategic social responsibility.

In this chapter, we define strategic philanthropy and integrate this concept with other elements of social responsibility. Next, we trace the evolution of corporate philanthropy and distinguish the concept from cause-related marketing. We also provide examples of best practices of addressing stakeholders' interests that meet our definition of strategic philanthropy. From there, we consider the benefits of investing in strategic philanthropy to satisfy both stakeholders and corporate objectives. Finally, we examine the process of implementing strategic philanthropy in business. Our approach in this chapter is to demonstrate how companies can link strategic philanthropy with economic, legal, and ethical concerns for the benefit of all stakeholders.

Strategic Philanthropy Defined

In a general sense, philanthropy involves any acts of benevolence and goodwill, such as making gifts to charities, volunteering for community projects, and taking action to benefit others. For example, your parents may have spent time on nonwork projects that directly benefited the community or a special population. Perhaps you have participated in similar activities through work, school groups, or associations. Have you ever served Thanksgiving dinner at a homeless shelter? Have you ever raised money for a neighborhood school? Have you ever joined a social club that volunteered member services to local charities? Most religious organizations, educational institutions, and arts programs rely heavily on philanthropic donations from both individuals and organizations. Philanthropy is a major driver of the nonprofit sector of the economy, as these organizations rely on the time, money, and talents of both individuals and organizations to operate and fund their programs. Consider the Sakharov Museum in Moscow. The museum, named for the Nobel Peace Prize winner and human rights activist Andrei Sakharov, recently faced a severe financial crisis because Russia lacks a culture of corporate philanthropy and the associated funding of nongovernment museums. The museum's political bent, along with Russian laws prohibiting tax benefits on charitable donations, caused museum managers to look outside their country for funding. For example, the Moscow office of the U.S.-based Ford Foundation has partnered with the museum.[3]

Figure 11.1 displays the major recipients of the more than $240 billion in philanthropic donations made in 2002. Religious organizations received 35 percent of all contributions, with educational causes collecting 13 percent of the funds. As Figure 11.2 indicates, individuals made 76 percent of these donations, with corporations contributing 5 percent, or just over $12 billion. Corporate donations fell by over 10 percent between 2000 and 2001, but rebounded in 2002.[4]

In addition to financial resources, companies also contribute goods and services. Apple Computer, for example, was one of the first companies to make major inroads in education with donated and deeply discounted computers after it recognized that

FIGURE 11.1   Focus of Philanthropic Development

2002 Contributions: $240.92 Billion by Type of Recipient Organization

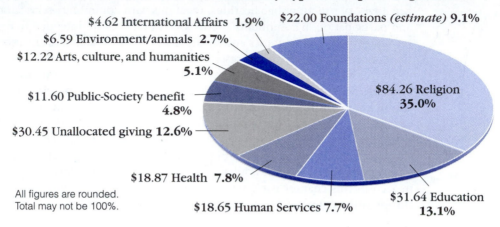

$4.62 International Affairs **1.9%**

$6.59 Environment/animals **2.7%**

$12.22 Arts, culture, and humanities **5.1%**

$11.60 Public-Society benefit **4.8%**

$30.45 Unallocated giving **12.6%**

$18.87 Health **7.8%**

$18.65 Human Services 7.7%

$22.00 Foundations *(estimate)* **9.1%**

$84.26 Religion **35.0%**

$31.64 Education **13.1%**

All figures are rounded.
Total may not be 100%.

Source: "2002 Contributions: $240.92 Billion by Type of Recipient Organization," AAFRC Trust for Philanthropy/Giving USA 2003, http://www.aafrc.org/bytypeof.html, accessed August 22, 2003.

student loyalty to a computer system would extend beyond the educational environment. Johnson & Johnson donates medical products to hospitals and similar facilities; this enhances its relationships with a key stakeholder group. A consortium of private computer companies provided Dalhousie University in Canada with $61 million in computers and software to aid the university's engineering program. These in-kind donations, while not providing direct funds, are important to nonprofit groups that need technology, office supplies, equipment, building supplies, soft goods, consulting, and other services. Gifts in Kind International is in the field of "product philanthropy," as it helps manufacturers and retailers to provide in-kind donations around

FIGURE 11.2   Sources of Philanthropic Donations

2002 Contributions: $240.92 Billion by Source of Contributions

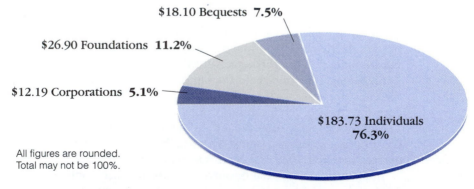

$18.10 Bequests **7.5%**

$26.90 Foundations **11.2%**

$12.19 Corporations **5.1%**

$183.73 Individuals **76.3%**

All figures are rounded.
Total may not be 100%.

Source: "2002 Contributions: $240.92 Billion by Source of Contributions," AAFRC Trust for Philanthropy/Giving USA 2003, http://www.aafrc.org/bysourceof.html, accessed August 22, 2003.

the world. In one year, Gifts in Kind International and its 350 global affiliates distributed more than $675 million in products to 50,000 charitable organizations. The nonprofit product philanthropy group recently expanded its services to include the Gift in Time program, where well-trained corporate volunteers donate their expertise to nonprofit groups.[5]

Our concept of corporate philanthropy extends beyond financial contributions and explicitly links company missions, organizational competencies, and various stakeholders. Thus, we define **strategic philanthropy** as the synergistic use of an organization's core competencies and resources to address key stakeholders' interests and to achieve both organizational and social benefits. Strategic philanthropy goes well beyond the traditional benevolent philanthropy of donating a percentage of sales to social causes by involving employees (utilizing their core skills); organizational resources and expertise (equipment, knowledge, and money); and the ability to link employees, customers, suppliers, and social needs with these key assets. Strategic philanthropy involves both financial and nonfinancial contributions to stakeholders (employee time, goods and services, and company technology and equipment, as well as facilities), but it also benefits the company.

John Damonti, president of the Bristol-Myers Squibb Foundation, reflected, "When you align your contributions with your business focus, you then can draw on the greater wealth of the corporation's people, information, and resources."[6] Organizations are best suited to deal with social or stakeholder issues in areas with which they have some experience, knowledge, or expertise. From a business perspective, companies want to refine their intellectual capital, reinforce their core competencies, and develop synergies between business and philanthropic activities. The process of addressing stakeholder concerns through philanthropy should be strategic to a company's ongoing development and improvement. For example, American Express, a global financial and travel company, contributed funds and know-how to initiate the development of the Academy of Travel and Tourism in Hungary. This project benefited the Hungarian economy, tested the entrepreneurial spirit and skills of American Express employees, and reinforced the company's understanding of the Hungarian market.[7] Some critics would argue that this was not true philanthropy because American Express received business benefits. Because social responsibility takes place on many levels, effective philanthropy depends on the synergy between stakeholder needs and business competencies and goals. Thus, the fact that each partner to the Academy of Travel and Tourism had different goals and earned unique benefits does not diminish the overall good that resulted from the project. As global competition escalates, companies are increasingly responsible to stakeholders in justifying their philanthropic endeavors. This ultimately requires greater planning and alignment of philanthropic efforts with overall strategic goals. Table 11.1 provides additional examples of philanthropic activities.

Strategic Philanthropy and Social Responsibility

It is important to place strategic philanthropy in the context of organizational responsibilities at the economic, legal, ethical, and philanthropic levels. Most companies understand the need to be economically successful for the benefit of all stakeholders and to comply with the laws required within our society and others in which they do

strategic philanthropy the synergistic use of an organization's core competencies and resources to address key stakeholders' interests and to achieve both organizational and social benefit

TABLE 11.1	Examples of Corporate Philanthropy

- After British Petroleum (now BP Amoco) was criticized by Greenpeace for its environmental practices, the company created a $1 billion business and many new jobs in solar power, a renewable and nonpolluting source of energy.

- Dayton-Hudson Corporation regularly donates 5 percent of its pretax income to charities, whereas employees both select and volunteer in many of these community-based organizations.

- Philippine Business for Social Progress, a foundation established and funded by more than 160 companies, provides organized, professional, and sustainable assistance to the Filipino poor.

- Scientists at Bell Laboratories are involved in making recommendations for grants to universities in areas of teaching and research that are of current interest to the company.

- Through the company's foundation, executives at AT&T are strongly encouraged to join nonprofit organizations' boards of directors.

- Employees of Boardwalk Equities, Inc., a Canadian owner and operator of multifamily apartment buildings, travel to Mexico to build homes and apartment buildings for poor Mexican families.

- Customers of Hanna Andersson, a manufacturer of high-quality children's clothes, can return worn clothing for credit toward their next purchase, with the used clothing donated to needy children.

- Kraft Foods donates about half of its corporate giving dollars to hunger relief and school nutrition programs.

- Businesspeople from the toy industry in Brazil created the Abrinq Foundation for Children's Rights, which is dedicated to promoting the rights of children and youth at risk in Brazil.

- Seafirst Bank's partnership with Indian Nations in the state of Washington resulted in education programs for Native Americans in financial management and tribal economic development and helped Seafirst employees to better understand cultural issues related to business relationships and development.

- More than 6,000 companies sponsor matching-gift programs, where an employee's personal donation to an educational institution is matched by the employer.

Sources: Peggy Dulany and David Winder, "The Status of and Trends in Private Philanthropy in the Southern Hemisphere," Synergos Institute, http://www.synergos.org/globalphilanthropy/02/philanthropyinsouthern hemisphere.htm, accessed January 28, 2003; Reynold Levy, *Give and Take: A Candid Account of Corporate Philanthropy* (Boston: Harvard Business School Press, 1999); "Better To Give and To Receive," *Hemispheres* (January 1997); Luba Krekhovetsky, "Charity Begins With Homes," *Canadian Business*, December 30, 2002: 91–93; Glen Peters, *Waltzing with the Raptors: A Practical Roadmap to Protecting Your Company's Reputation* (New York: Wiley, 1999); Ann Svendsen, *The Stakeholder Strategy* (San Francisco: Berrett-Koehler, 1998).

business. Additionally, through the establishment of core values and ethical cultures, most firms are recognizing the many benefits of good ethics. As we saw in Chapter 1, evidence is accumulating that there is a positive relationship between social responsibility and performance, especially with regard to customer satisfaction, investor loyalty, and employee commitment. Strategic social responsibility can reduce the cost of business transactions, establish trust among stakeholders, improve teamwork, and preserve the social capital necessary for an infrastructure for doing business. In sum, these efforts improve the context and environment for corporate operations and performance.[8]

When Noah's Bagels began expanding beyond its original Berkeley, California, location in the late 1980s, the company focused not only on opening new retail stores but also on helping surrounding neighborhoods. Noah's sought to be a positive, dynamic force in its local communities because it "recognizes the importance of giving the community more than just exhilarated taste buds." Thus, the company began to link its philanthropic efforts directly with the core operations and skills required to run the business. For example, Noah's donates bagels and other foods to fight community hunger. The company also gives employees paid time off to work on service projects that benefit surrounding neighborhoods. Store managers can choose a local charity and apply for matching funds from corporate headquarters. Customers are encouraged to comment on the company's bagels, coffee, and community affairs. All of these efforts directly link Noah's philanthropy to issues that positively affect, and reflect, its operations and marketing. Because the company carefully chooses projects and charities that are aligned with its core competencies, Noah's Bagels is taking a strategic approach to its philanthropy.[9] Many companies consider philanthropy only after they have met their financial, legal, and ethical obligations. As companies strive for social responsibility, their ability to meet each obligation lays the foundation for success on other responsibilities. In addition, there is synergy in corporate efforts directed at the four levels of responsibility. As one of the most voluntary dimensions of social responsibility, philanthropy has not always been linked to profits or business ethics. In fact, the traditional approach to philanthropy disconnects giving from business performance and its impact on stakeholders. Before the evolution of strategic philanthropy, most corporate gift programs separated the company from the organizations, causes, and individuals that its donations most benefited.[10]

Research has begun to highlight organizations' formalization of philanthropic activities and their efforts to integrate philanthropic goals with other business strategies and implementation. A Conference Board survey of 463 U.S. companies found that those adopting a more businesslike approach to philanthropy experienced a better image, increased employee loyalty, and improved customer ties. Another Conference Board report indicated that strategic community involvement, global giving, and stakeholder engagement, which involve many aspects of company operations, are replacing the traditional corporate philanthropy model.[11] Because philanthropy involves using organizational resources, formal methods should deliver more effective and professional results to the effort. In this case, philanthropy is viewed as an investment from which a company can gain some type of value.[12]

The traditional approach to corporate philanthropy is characterized by donations and related activities that are not purposefully aligned with the strategic goals and resources of the firm. For instance, employees may be encouraged to volunteer in the community but receive little direction on where or how to spend their time. Employees of Fuji Bank of Japan, for example, may apply for leaves of absence to take part in volunteer opportunities.[13] After the September 11, 2001, terrorist attacks, companies and employees became quite creative in their philanthropic efforts. One result was "leave-based donation programs," which allow employees to donate the value of accumulated vacation and sick- and personal-leave days to a nonprofit cause. The U.S. Treasury Department approved the idea and clarified regulations to benefit employees, companies, and nonprofits.[14] Indeed, there are numerous examples of companies supporting community involvement. Although these actions are noble, they are not always considered in tandem with organizational goals and strengths.

In some cases, corporate contributions may be made to nonprofit organizations in which top managers have a personal interest. Ben & Jerry's Homemade, for example, traditionally gave 1 percent of its pretax profits to programs supporting peace initiatives because this cause is dear to its founders; it also donated an overall 7.5 percent of pretax profits to support environmental and social causes. Ben & Jerry's successfully tied "caring capitalism" to its company image and mission to clearly differentiate its products in the marketplace.[15] Finally, many companies will match employees' personal gifts to educational institutions. Although gift-matching programs instill employee pride and assist education, they are rarely linked to company operations and competencies.[16] In the traditional approach to corporate philanthropy, then, companies have good intentions, but there is no solid integration with organizational resources and objectives.

In the social responsibility model that we propose, philanthropy is only one focal point for a corporate vision that includes both the welfare of the firm and benefits to stakeholders. This requires support from top management, as well as a strategic planning structure that incorporates stakeholder concerns and benefits. Corporate giving, volunteer efforts, and other contributions should be considered and aligned not only with corporate strategy but also with financial, legal, and ethical obligations. The shift from traditional benevolent philanthropy to strategic philanthropy has come about as companies struggled in the 1980s, 1990s, and 2000s to redefine their missions, alliances, and scope, while becoming increasingly accountable to stakeholders and society.

History of Corporate Philanthropy

Downsizing, mergers, divestitures, growing international competition, consumer activism, and investor demands have led many firms to reassess their business practices and outcomes. As we discussed in previous chapters, organizations are experiencing increasing pressure to demonstrate responsibility at many levels, including financial and social performance. As a result, companies integrating a strategic philanthropy approach now blend both organizational and social needs. Under this approach, neither philanthropy nor business objectives have a dominant role, as both collaborate to benefit and inform the other. This is a relatively recent phenomenon, as most companies are just beginning to realize the benefits of "caring as fiercely as you compete."[17] Table 11.2 traces the evolution of corporate philanthropy in the United States.

Tax law implemented in 1935 allowed companies a tax deduction on donations made up to 5 percent of their domestic pretax income. Until the middle of the twentieth century, however, corporate donations were virtually outlawed in the United States unless it could be proven that the donations were linked to stockholder interests. Companies began making contributions when laws were changed in the 1950s, so that charitable contributions did not necessarily have to be strictly related to stockholder interests. Many firms began to establish separate foundations to make donations in the 1960s. Most large corporations in the United States allocated much less than 5 percent of pretax profits to their foundations. Under this model, the founda-

TABLE 11.2	Evolution of Corporate Philanthropy in the United States

TIME PERIOD	GENERAL CHARACTERISTICS
Through 1950s	Federal law prohibits corporate donations unless they are closely linked to stockholders interests.
1960s and 1970s	Public begins to believe companies should donate some of their profits to social causes.
	Large corporations set up foundations.
	There are few criteria for choosing philanthropic projects.
1970s and 1980s	Stagnant economy slows corporate philanthropy.
	Public and government lower expectations of business.
	Merger and acquisition strategies leave little room for philanthropic effort and donations.
Early 1990s	There is pressure to formalize corporate governance and accountability.
	Public reacts to "greed" of 1980s by raising expectations of business.
	Companies take more active role in community and societal causes.
Mid-1990s and Beyond	Philanthropy model is expanded to include time and human resources.
	Corporations recognize the relationship between philanthropy and corporate benefits with customers, employees, business partners, and community.
	There is collaboration between business and other groups to resolve social problems.
	The focus moves to aligning business goals to philanthropic activity through overall corporate vision.

Sources: Craig N. Smith, "The New Corporate Philanthropy," *Harvard Business Review* 72 (May–June 1994); Ann Svendsen, *The Stakeholder Strategy: Profiting from Collaborative Business Relationships* (San Francisco: Berrett-Koehler, 1998).

tions were deliberately kept distinct from business interests and goals. These foundations continue to contribute millions of dollars to the nonprofit and charitable sector of the United States, as demonstrated in Table 11.3.

During the 1960s, the public began to question the role of business in society, and many individuals called for corporations to give some of their profits back to society. This sentiment continued throughout most of the 1970s. However, corporate philanthropy remained a low priority for many businesses through the 1980s. This era of acquisitions and cost cutting stripped away many of the incentives for philanthropy, although some financially sound and progressive organizations began formalizing their efforts during this time. By the early 1990s, attitudes about the responsibilities of business in society had shifted again.[18] Today, most company leaders understand the benefits of well-managed corporate philanthropy initiatives, even if they have not

TABLE 11.3	Ten Largest Corporate Foundations by Total Giving

RANK	NAME/(STATE)	TOTAL GRANTS	AS OF FISCAL YEAR END DATE
1.	Ford Motor Company Fund (MI)	$169,100,475	12/31/00
2.	Bank of America Foundation, Inc. (NC)	$ 85,755,841	12/31/00
3.	Wal-Mart Foundation (AR)	$ 75,301,122	01/31/01
4.	SBC Foundations (TX)	$ 68,678,574	12/31/00
5.	The J. P. Morgan Chase Foundation (NY)	$ 44,656,806	12/31/00
6.	AT&T Foundation (NY)	$ 43,539,963	12/31/00
7.	General Motors Foundation, Inc. (MI)	$ 43,280,242	12/31/00
8.	Citigroup Foundation (NY)	$ 41,779,503	12/31/00
9.	Aventis Pharmaceuticals Health Care Foundation (NJ)	$ 41,558,325	12/31/00
10.	Verizon Foundation (NY)	$ 41,205,556	12/30/00

Source: "50 Largest Corporate Foundations by Total Giving," The Foundation Center, http://fdncenter.org/research/trends_analysis/top50giving.html, accessed August 22, 2003.

fully formalized their approach in this area. For example, Cadbury Schweppes, along with other firms in the United Kingdom, donates money to Crisis, a national charity that relieves poverty and homelessness, every holiday season. Instead of sending holiday greeting cards to thousands of customers, vendors, and other business partners, these firms donate their greeting card and postage budget to Crisis.[19]

Strategic philanthropy emerged as a management practice to support social responsibility in organizations in the 1980s. AT&T was one of the first organizations to formalize strategic philanthropy when it appointed Reynold Levy to head its foundation to provide leadership in this area. Levy's ideas altered the link between organizational and social needs by tying AT&T's foundation activities to its business goals and objectives and by emphasizing that such activities could advance business interests.[20] Levy, reflecting on his role at AT&T and in the strategic philanthropy movement, noted, "What I soon discovered was that the special value of corporate philanthropy resides in the business perspectives and array of resources it brings to addressing societal needs."[21] Large corporations such as AT&T have been fundamentally responsible for shaping our understanding of strategic philanthropy. Although some companies have advanced toward strategic philanthropy, most firms are still developing their efforts.

Once organizations become interested in philanthropy, they have a number of options for providing contributions and other resources. For instance, sponsorships provide an opportunity to associate a company's name and brands to a particular event. This business activity is normally considered a marketing tactic rather than a philanthropic act, as sponsorships may have little effect on a social cause or issue. Although sponsoring a sports stadium may assist team and venue owners, it is not fully linked to bettering some aspect of society.[22] One common method for tying the business purpose and philanthropy to society and community concerns is through the implementation of cause-related marketing campaigns. British Petroleum (BP) recently launched a pan-European project with the Red Cross, where customers at

BP's gas stations across Europe can donate money to the Red Cross. The cause-related marketing effort is part of an overall strategy to reposition BP as socially responsible.[23]

Strategic Philanthropy Versus Cause-Related Marketing

The first attempts by organizations to coordinate organizational goals with philanthropic giving emerged with cause-related marketing in the early 1980s. Whereas strategic philanthropy links corporate resources and knowledge to address broader social, customer, employee, and supplier problems and needs, **cause-related marketing** ties an organization's product(s) directly to a social concern. Table 11.4 compares cause-related marketing and strategic philanthropy. With cause-related marketing, a percentage of a product's sales is usually donated to a cause appealing to the relevant target market. The Avon Breast Cancer Crusade, for example, generates proceeds for the breast cancer cause through several fundraising efforts, including the sale of special "pink ribbon" products by Avon independent sales representatives nationwide (see Figure 11.3). Gifts are awarded by the Avon Products Foundation, Inc., a nonprofit 501(c)(3) accredited public charity, to support five vital areas of the breast cancer cause with a focus on medically underserved women, biomedical research, clinical care, financial assistance and support services, educational seminars and advocacy training, and early detection and awareness programs nationwide. Both the cause and Avon Crusade "pink ribbon" products appeal to Avon's primary target market, women. Between 1993 and 2002, the Avon Breast Cancer Crusade generated $250 million net in total funds raised worldwide to fund access to care and finding a cure for breast cancer.[24]

American Express was the first company to use cause-related marketing widely, when it began advertising in 1983 that it would give a percentage of credit-card charges to the Statue of Liberty and Ellis Island Restoration Fund.[25] In a more recent alliance, Regis Hair Salons offered $10 haircuts during its "Clip for the Cure" campaign, which raised more than $200,000 for breast cancer research.[26] As is the

cause-related marketing
business strategy that ties an organization's product(s) directly to a social concern through a marketing program

TABLE 11.4	Strategic Philanthropy Contrasted with Cause-Related Marketing	
	STRATEGIC PHILANTHROPY	**CAUSE-RELATED MARKETING**
Focus	Organizational	Product or product line
Goals	Improvement of organizational competency or tying organizational competency to social need or charitable cause	Increase of product sales
Time frame	Ongoing	Traditionally of limited duration
Organizational members involved	Potentially all organizational employees	Marketing department and related personnel
Cost	Moderate—alignment with organizational strategies and mission	Minimal—alliance development and promotion expenditures

FIGURE 11.3   The Avon Breast Cancer Crusade

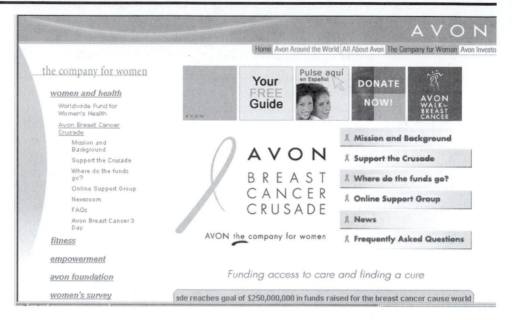

Source: "Avon Breast Cancer Crusade," http://www.avoncompany.com/women/avoncrusade/, accessed January 28, 2003. Courtesy of Avon Products, Inc.

case with Avon, American Express, and Regis, companies generally prefer to support causes that are of interest to their target markets. In a single year, organizations paid more than $500 million for the rights to support various social programs, ultimately raising roughly $2.5 billion for these causes.[27] Thus, a key feature of cause-related marketing is the promise of donations to a particular social cause based on customer sales or involvement. Whereas strategic philanthropy is tied to the entire organization, cause-related marketing is linked to a specific product and marketing program. The program may involve in-store promotions, messages on packages and labels, and other marketing communications.[28]

Although cause-related marketing has its roots in the United States, the marketing tool is gaining widespread usage in other parts of the world. A study by Saatchi & Saatchi found that about 40 percent of European senior marketers were aligning their cause-related marketing budgets with brand communication programs. For example, the New Covent Garden Soup Co. recently partnered with a homeless charity in Great Britain. During the Christmas season, portions of sales of New Covent Garden's pea and ham soup were donated to help renovate the charity's kitchens. Tesco, a large European grocery chain, also joined the cause by donating funds based on every soup carton sold in the six-week holiday season.[29] Business in the Community, a nonprofit group in the United Kingdom, sponsors annual awards for British firms that demonstrate excellence in cause-related marketing. Walkers, a manufacturer of cookies and biscuits, is a recent winner, due to its distribution of more than 2.3 million books to schools in the United Kingdom. Bettys and Taylors of Harrogate Yorkshire Tea also received an award, for its cause-related marketing program to plant trees and slow forest degradation in regions where it sources its teas and commodities.[30]

Cause-related marketing activities have the potential to affect buying patterns. In order for cause-related marketing to be successful, consumers must have awareness and affinity for the cause, the brand and cause must be associated and perceived as a good fit, and consumers should be able to transfer feelings toward the cause to their brand perceptions and purchase intentions. Studies have found that a majority of consumers said that, given equal price and product quality, they would be more likely to buy the product associated with a charitable cause. Eighty percent of customers say they have more positive perceptions of firms that support causes about which they personally care. These surveys have also noted that most marketing directors felt that cause-related marketing would increase in importance over the coming years.[31] Through cause-related marketing, companies first become aware that supporting social causes, such as environmental awareness, health and human services, education, and the arts, can support business goals and help bolster a firm's reputation, especially those with an ethically neutral image. However, firms that are perceived as unethical may be suspected of ulterior motives in developing cause-related campaigns.[32] One of the main weaknesses with cause-related marketing is that some consumers cannot link specific philanthropic efforts with companies.[33] Consumers may have difficulty recalling exact philanthropic relationships because many cause-related marketing campaigns have tended to be of short duration and have not always had a direct correlation to the sponsoring firm's core business. Because strategic philanthropy is more pervasive and relates to company attributes and skills, such alliances should have greater stakeholder recognition, appreciation, and long-term value.

Robins Bush Foods and Coles supermarkets of Australia sell "outback products" and contribute a portion of each sale to funds that aid the development of Aboriginal enterprises by improving the cultivation, harvest, and marketing of native foods. (Robins Bush Foods)

Stakeholders in Strategic Philanthropy

Although more businesses are moving toward adopting a strategic philanthropy model, others are still focusing only on the needs of individual stakeholders. Although these efforts are important and commendable, companies may not be realizing the full benefits for themselves and their stakeholders. For example, the implementation of cause-related marketing efforts may not reinforce employee skills and competencies. Instead, such campaigns usually focus on generating product sales and donations to a specific cause. Volunteer programs may benefit the community and employee morale, but the value of this service could be greatly enhanced through synergies between current and future job-related aptitude and nonprofit needs.

In this section, we offer examples of organizations that have effectively collaborated with various stakeholders in the pursuit of mutual benefits. Their efforts serve as examples of best practices in implementing and managing strategic philanthropy by engaging, not just managing, stakeholder relationships. Arnold Hiatt, former CEO of Stride Rite Corporation, noted, "Look at a well-run company and you will see the needs of its stockholders, its employees, and the community at large being served simultaneously."[34] The following strategic philanthropic efforts demonstrate a dual concern for meeting stakeholder needs while strengthening organizational competencies.

Employees

A key to organizational success is the ability of organizations to attract, socialize, and retain competent and qualified employees. Through strategic philanthropy initiatives, companies have the opportunity to increase employee commitment, motivation, and skill refinement. For example, United Airlines Foundation adopted four focus areas for its philanthropic strategy. One of those focus areas was education and careers, with a global emphasis. Using the professional expertise of United Airlines employees, the foundation helped develop the Virtual Trade Mission, a collaboration between the U.S. federal government, labor groups, and private companies to teach high school and middle school students the importance of the United States's export economy. This educational program, which has been implemented in more than thirty communities around the world, employed multimedia technology to simulate a trade mission. United Airlines employees contributed expertise on world geography, global economic conditions, and cross-cultural communication to the Virtual Trade Mission. These elements were not only effective for student learning but also mirror the skills and knowledge necessary for the airline to operate effectively on a daily basis. United Airlines's core competencies include the ability to transfer knowledge and best practices between countries in which it operates.

BE&K, an international construction and engineering firm headquartered in Birmingham, Alabama, has mobilized its retirees for supporting special community service projects. Because these retirees have years of experience in the construction business, they are particularly suited for philanthropic efforts that involve renovation, design, and related skills. For example, one retired employee heads up a YWCA effort to renovate housing for disabled and low-income women.[35] BE&K has also extended its employee safety and drug abuse programs into the philanthropic realm.

The Bell Foundation supports initiatives that benefit the community, including an after-school tutoring program. (Tom Herde/The Boston Globe via www.Merlin-Net.com)

These programs were originally designed to assist employees, reduce accidents, and help the business perform more effectively. After taking this experience and program to others in the industry and beyond, the company received the FBI Director's Community Leadership Award for outstanding contributions to the community in the prevention of drug abuse.[36]

Customers

As industries become increasingly competitive, companies are seeking ways to differentiate themselves in customers' minds. Home Depot, for example, has been progressive in the way it approaches philanthropy. The company has aligned its expertise and resources to address community needs. Its relationship with Habitat for Humanity gives employees a chance to improve their skills and bring direct knowledge back into the workplace to benefit customers. It also enhances Home Depot's image of expertise as the do-it-yourself center. Home Depot also responded to customers' needs when Hurricane Andrew hit the Miami area. Many home building supply and hardware stores were taking advantage of customers by inflating prices on emergency materials, but Home Depot opened its stores twenty-four hours a day and made materials available at reduced costs to help customers survive the disaster.

Bankers Trust Private Bank, part of German-headquartered Deutsche Bank AG, introduced its Wealth with Responsibility program to assist wealthy families in planning for philanthropy. In addition to financial experts, the bank employs consultants and advisers who help families set goals, invest for future wealth, and provide funds to charities and other groups. Thus, the bank is providing services that not only benefit wealthy clients but also direct assets into philanthropic directions to benefit society. The program targets clients around the world, with a focus on Europeans who are just beginning to become interested in philanthropy.[37]

GTE, through its philanthropic foundation, distributed more than $30 million nationwide in 1999, much of which supported the literacy movement. The merger of GTE and Bell Atlantic in 2000 created Verizon, and the company's foundation still considers literacy and technology education two of its greatest concerns. The Verizon Reads program is multifaceted to affect the largest number of stakeholders. With an estimated 40 million U.S. citizens classified as illiterate, Verizon feels it can influence customers' quality of life with such broad-based initiatives, most of which is chronicled on www.verizonreads.net. Employees are encouraged to volunteer in education-related programs and to take part in initiatives that will strengthen their own literacy and technology use.[38] Target is another firm that contributes significant resources to education, including direct donations of $14 million to schools as well as fundraising and scholarship programs to assist teachers and students. Through the retailer's Take Charge of Education program, customers using a Target Guest Card can designate a specific school to which Target donates 1 percent of that customer's total purchase. This program is designed to make customers feel that their purchases are benefiting their community while increasing the use of Target Guest Cards.[39] As Figure 11.1 showed earlier, education is the second-largest category of philanthropic donations (behind religion) that appeals to Verizon's and Target's broad target markets.

Business Partners

More companies are using philanthropic goals and social concerns as a measure of with whom they would like to do business. Companies are increasingly requiring social audits and the adoption of industry codes of ethics on the part of their business partners. The Freeplay Group, based in South Africa, is an example of a company founded on the principle of "making money and making a difference." The company manufactures and markets wind-up radios that were originally intended for use in poor nations where electricity and batteries are scarce. For example, these radios have been used to transmit elementary school lessons in South Africa and election results in Ghana. The radios now sell in many countries at retailers such as Sharper Image, Radio Shack, and Harrod's. Freeplay's investors include the General Electric Pension Trust and Liberty Life, a South African insurance firm. Rotary International and other community organizations are using the radios to implement programs that benefit society and communities. These investors and customers have chosen Freeplay for its solid business plan founded on broader social goals.[40]

BJC Health System is working with other area health care systems to make health insurance available to St. Louis, Missouri, residents who cannot afford it. BJC manages Care Partners and ConnectCare. Care Partners offers twenty-four-hour emergency care and primary-care facilities to anyone in need, whether they are insured or not. ConnectCare was launched by city officials and community leaders with the same goal of providing health services to all citizens. BJC has won praise for its ability to work with insurers, other systems, and the public in supporting health insurance initiatives with the collective goal of improving people's lives. These collaborative ventures allocate the costs of caring for indigent and uninsured patients across the community, a strategy that benefits all hospitals and care providers representing suppliers and business partners' best interests.[41]

Finally, nonprofit organizations are finding innovative ways to raise money and partner with business firms. For example, Social Venture Partners, founded in 1997 by a former software entrepreneur, brings together business professionals with an interest in solving social and community problems. These partners pool their financial and business expertise to assist nonprofit organizations. This model includes high expectations for measurable change and impact in the community. The Austin Social Venture Partners (ASVP) developed from the rapid growth of technology firms in central Texas. Founders and executives of companies such as Dell Computer Corporation are committed to improving the prospects for nonprofit activity in Austin.[42]

Community and Society

Society expects businesses to be socially responsible and to contribute to the well-being of the communities in which they operate. The Coca-Cola Company takes a strategic view of its role in society by linking its company resources and operating practices to stakeholder issues. Although it acknowledges the profusion of problems in today's world, Coca-Cola has chosen to focus its energies and resources on environmental issues where the company has an impact and relevant expertise. Water quality, water conservation, and waste reduction are therefore key considerations in its packaging and operational decisions.[43] Coca-Cola has also contributed funds and expertise around the world to support collaborations that respond to these environmental concerns. These projects involve bottlers, employees, suppliers, regulators, customers, and other corporations interested in building strategies for environmental excellence.

Merck developed a drug to combat river blindness, a disease afflicting more than 18 million people worldwide. Merck's expertise as a pharmaceutical laboratory allowed it to develop Mectizan to treat river blindness, and its humanitarian orientation led it to donate the drug to nearly 25 million people at risk in thirty-one countries in Africa, Latin America, and the Middle East. A Merck scientist who worked on the project noted, "I've received more mail based on this decision than anything else we've done as a company. Not only was it positive, more important than our shareholders, I thought, was the effect on the people at Merck, . . . about what a fantastic move this was for the company."[44] The benefits of the decision to develop and donate the drug to heavily afflicted areas demonstrates Merck's understanding of strategic philanthropy and the positive effects on society, as well as on employees, investors, and even customers.

LensCrafters has pledged to give 3 million pairs of glasses to the needy. Not wanting the firm's motives questioned, the CEO directed employees not to seek publicity. He states, "I do not want anyone thinking the company is doing this for any reason other than it's the right thing to do." Employees can engage in other philanthropy, but this effort makes more sense because it leverages LensCrafters's eye care provision skills and competencies.[45]

Finally, groups of companies and industry associations are also working to extend the philanthropic efforts of their member companies. For example, the American Apparel Manufacturers Association assists manufacturers in donating surplus apparel to the needy, homeless, and disaster victims. More than $54 million of surplus has been donated to more than 250 charitable organizations in sixteen countries.[46]

Global Initiatives

Global Change Through Social Venture Capital and Entrepreneurship

The "New Economy" made millionaires of many entrepreneurs, stockholders, and even employees. Many of these individuals look for opportunities to invest in the well-being of their communities, neighborhoods, and even global society. Other individuals, though less wealthy, are just as concerned about social conditions. Today, many types of citizens are looking for opportunities to give their time and money to organizations that engage in socially responsible programming. One promising global tool to support philanthropy applies the concept of venture capital, which once funded many of the start-up companies that made some people wealthy, to socially responsible initiatives through charitable organizations.

Social venture capital and the resulting social entrepreneurship are emerging as alternative forms of philanthropy for both individuals and corporations. Hundreds of social venture capital funds and related philanthropic opportunities have sprouted around the world. This type of philanthropy is more personalized, engaged, and directed than simply writing a check. These philanthropists also donate their time, know-how, and connections to enhance the worthy cause. Moreover, they expect solid outcomes from their time and investments. Whereas the traditional venture capital approach funds new businesses, the social venture model backs individuals and organizations dedicated to changing some aspect of society. This approach can be implemented in a number of ways.

Founded in 1980, Ashoka is a global nonprofit organization that spends roughly $7 million a year supporting social entrepreneurs who are dedicated to making significant changes and contributions to society. Ashoka's mission is to "develop the profes-

sion of social entrepreneurship around the world" and it uses a venture capital approach to fulfill its mission. The organization's social entrepreneurship fellows are provided with a living stipend, other financial support, and training to promote a fundamental change in human rights, education, health care, education and youth development, the environment, human rights, economic development, and access to technology. For example, Ashoka Fellow Veronica Khosa brought the concept of home health care to South Africa after she became frustrated with the poor health services there. In a few short years, the South African government had adopted her approach. Dani Mungguro, another Ashoka Fellow, developed Indonesia's Center of Excellence for Community Forestry to create a paradigm shift in the management of rain forests. His approach brought together many stakeholders, including companies and government and citizens groups, to redefine their approach to logging and other uses of precious natural resources. Within five years of becoming Ashoka Fellows, over 80 percent report that national policy has changed as a direct result of their efforts and projects. Thus, social entrepreneurship replaces profit maximization with social impact as its primary goal. Companies, individuals, foundations, and others make donations to Ashoka, which in turn finds and cultivates social entrepreneurs and dramatic change around the world. Ashoka does not accept government funds.

Social venture capital organizations donate funds and other resources to nonprofit organizations that support the community and charitable works. These organizations typically require their donors (or partners, as many organizations refer to them) to contribute $5,000 to $10,000 a year for a minimum of two years and to participate in selecting and overseeing the charitable organizations to which they contribute. Although these organizations apply the concepts of traditional venture capital, they often feel more like neighborhood investment clubs. Partners' funds are pooled and "invested" in organizations that fit with the social venture capitalists' goals. In addition to money, partners in these organizations donate their talents, contacts, and other resources in order to serve as strategy consultants, media advisers, tech experts, and even headhunters to help targeted nonprofit organizations reach their objectives. The nonprofit organizations receiving the funds are treated like start-up organizations, with expectations for accountability, risk taking, and ultimately, an exit strategy through financial self-sufficiency.

One of the best-known social venture capital organizations is the Social Venture Partners International, which was established in 1997 by Paul Brainerd, the founder of Aldus Corporation. The first SVP was created in Seattle, and within its first two years of offering grants, the partnership awarded thirteen nonprofit organizations a total of about $1 million. SVP Seattle grew rapidly, from 30 members to more than 260, about half of whom are current or former Microsoft employees. To date, the original organization has spawned chapters in twenty-four communities in several countries with other chapters under consideration. The Calgary chapter of Social Venture Partners, for example, gave $100,000 over a two-year period to Calgary Community Support for Young Parents. This program assists young families struggling with poverty, lack of education, isolation, and other conditions that can create an environment of neglect and child abuse. The chapter's partners also make in-home visitations with families in the support program. The Israel Venture Network requires $25,000 annually from each partner, and its first project is the Education Initiative in Tiberias, a three-year partnership that involves the Israeli Ministry of Education, the Tiberias municipality, and others.

Through the investments and assistance of individual donors, nonprofit organizations, social venture capitalists, and other philanthropic arms, innovative social entrepreneurs can enhance their positive impact around the world. Despite such efforts, applying the venture capital logic to philanthropy and charity raises some concerns with critics who are skeptical of a business approach to social change. Others are uncomfortable with the hands-on approach adopted by these groups, which demand accountability but may not be well versed in all aspects of a charity's work and environment. Finally, there is question about whether an exit strategy is meaningful to nonprofits. Although the global debate on venture capital philanthropy is just beginning, most charities and activists generally welcome the experience, connections, oversight, and other resources that can help them achieve their goals more efficiently and effectively. One entrepreneur calls social venture capitalism the "new philanthropy for the new economy."

Sources:
"Ashoka," http://www.ashoka.org/home/index.cfm, accessed January 24, 2003; "Philanthropy As Start-Up," *Globes–Israel's Business Arena*, December 10, 2002, accessed via LexisNexis; Lawrence Bush and Jeffrey Decko, "Social Venture Philanthropy," *Tikkun* 17 (March–April 2002): 48; John Byrne, "The New Face of Philanthropy," *Business Week*, December 2, 2002, pp. 82–86; William Drayton, "The Citizen Sector: Becoming As Entrepreneurial and Competitive As Business," *California Management Review* 44 (Spring 2002): 120–132; Alisa Gravitz, "Soul into Money: Four Tools," *Whole Earth*, Spring 1998: 177; Colin James, "Social Entrepreneurs," *New Zealand Management* 48 (October 2001): 58; Edward Skloot, "The Promise of Venture Philanthropy," Surdna Foundation, http://www.surdna.org/venture.html, accessed August 22, 2003; "A New Kind of Giving," Social Venture Partners Calgary, http://www.svpcalgary.org/index2.html, accessed January 24, 2003; "A Community of Social Investors," Social Venture Partners International, http://www.svpintl.org/, accessed January 24, 2003; John L. Thompson, "The World of the Social Entrepreneur," *International Journal of Public Sector Management* 15 (April–May 2002): 412–431; Carol Tice, "Social Venture Partners Sharpens Mission, Values," *Puget Sound Business Journal*, August 4, 2000, p. 8; David Whitford, "The New Shape of Philanthropy," *Fortune*, June 12, 2000, pp. 315–316; S. L. Wykes, "San Jose, Calif.–Area Venture Capital Group Helps Low-Income Become Savers," *San Jose Mercury News*, September 20, 2000.

By working with their trade association, apparel manufacturers have been able to benefit from strategic philanthropy.

Natural Environment As we saw in Chapter 9, environmental causes have become increasingly important to stakeholders in recent years. Environmental abuses have damaged company and industry reputations and resulted in lost sales. 3M is one company that has been very aggressive in implementing environmentally friendly processes and procedures throughout its operations. This commitment extends to employees, as the company provides van transportation to work for employees within a 15-mile radius of the corporate office. If a van has only a few riders, each rider pays a minimal monthly fee to help offset some of the costs of the program. If the number of employees using the program increases to a specified level, 3M drops the monthly fee. The van-pooling initiative has minimized pollution levels.[47] 3M is able to coordinate its commitment to various stakeholders, including employees, customers, the natural environment, and the community. For this reason, 3M recently ranked second among the top fifty chemical manufacturers and users in the world for environmental performance.[48] The company also scores very highly on *Fortune* magazine's annual "Most Admired Companies" list.

Benefits of Strategic Philanthropy

To pursue strategic philanthropy successfully, organizations must weigh both the costs and benefits associated with planning and implementing it as a corporate priority. Companies that assume a strategic approach to philanthropy are using an investment model with respect to their charitable acts and donations. In other words, these firms are not just writing checks; they are investing in solutions to stakeholder problems and corporate needs. Such an investment requires the commitment of company time, money, and human talent in order to succeed. Companies often need to hire staff to manage projects, communicate goals and opportunities throughout the firm, develop long-term priorities and programs, handle requests for funds, and represent the firm on other aspects of philanthropy. In addition, philanthropy consumes the time and energy of all types of employees within the organization. Thus, strategic philanthropy involves real corporate costs that must be justified and managed.

Most scholars and practitioners agree that the benefits of strategic philanthropy ultimately outweigh its costs. The positive return on strategic philanthropy is closely aligned with benefits obtained from strong social responsibility. First, in the United States, businesses can declare up to 10 percent of pretax profits as tax-deductible contributions. Most firms do not take full advantage of this benefit, as 10 percent is viewed as a very generous contribution level. In fact, corporate giving has averaged just over 1 percent of pretax profits in the last several decades and has never exceeded 2.1 percent. Whereas corporate profits increased threefold in the 1990s, charitable contributions rose only 70 percent. In addition, just 25 percent of all U.S. firms claim any charitable tax deductions.[49]

Second, companies with a strategic approach to philanthropy experience rewards in the workplace. Employees involved in volunteer projects and related ventures not only have the opportunity to refine their professional skills; they also develop a stronger sense of loyalty and commitment to their employer. A national survey of employees demonstrated that corporate philanthropy is an important driver in employee relations. Those who perceive their employer as strong in philanthropy were four times as likely to be very loyal as those who believed their employer was less philanthropic. Employees in firms with favorable ratings on philanthropy are also more likely to recommend the company and its products to others and have intentions to stay with the employer. Positive impressions of the executives' role in corporate philanthropy also influenced employees' affirmative attitudes toward their employer.[50] Results such as these lead to improved productivity, enhanced employee recruitment practices, and reduced employee turnover, each contributing to the overall effectiveness and efficiency of the company.

As a third benefit, companies should experience enhanced customer loyalty as a result of their strategic philanthropy. By choosing projects and causes with links to its core business, a firm can create synergies with its core competencies and customers. For example, Rosie O'Donnell used her celebrity status and television talk show to establish the For All Kids Foundation to support the social and cultural development of disadvantaged children. The foundation has been funded by a number of creative projects, including *Kids Are Punny,* a compilation of riddles, puns, and drawings sent by kids to the *Rosie O'Donnell Show.* Warner Books, the publisher, agreed to contribute its net profits to the foundation. Warner-Lambert, the manufacturer of Listerine Antiseptic mouthwash, donated $500,000 for kisses ($1,000 a kiss) Rosie received from guests on her show. In addition to grants from corporations, the foundation is also funded through celebrity charity auctions on eBay.[51] To the benefit of Warner Brothers studio and production, these creative projects not only support hundreds of children's causes and charities but also earned the show critical praise and customer loyalty. Because a majority of Rosie O'Donnell's viewers were women with children, her For All Kids Foundation was a natural and strategic vehicle.

The For All Kids Foundation grew out of the Rosie O'Donnell show. Although the show is off the air, Ms. O'Donnell and the foundation continue to support a number of initiatives to benefit children. (www.forallkids.org. Copyright © 2003. Reprinted with permission.)

Rosie's For All Kids Foundation is just that - for all kids, because every child deserves to feel loved, to be safe, to have opportunities for a better future, to know that there will always be someone to care for them, no matter what. Every child deserves a bright beginning and a chance to make his or her own dreams come true.

Rosie O'Donnell established her For All Kids Foundation, Inc. in 1997 to provide financial support to nonprofit programs serving economically disadvantaged and at-risk children and their families. Since its inception, the foundation has helped thousands of children across the country through grant awards to child care, after-school, education and other essential programs. The foundation's main focus is center-based child care, and first priority is given to programs serving low-income, urban areas, where many families struggle to find quality child care and early childhood education programs.

TABLE 11.5	Perceived Benefits of Corporate Philanthropy		

| | MEAN VALUE[a] | | |
POTENTIAL BENEFIT	UK	FRANCE	GERMANY
Building goodwill	6.1	5.6	5.9
Facilitating public relations	6.1	6.3	6.2
Involving the company in the community	5.9	6.0	5.5
Improving social and economic life and infrastructures	5.7	6.0	6.1
Improving the company's image	5.7	6.4	6.3
Improving the loyalty and motivation of employees	4.9	3.6	4.1
Increasing general public awareness of the firm and/or its products	4.5	5.9	5.1
Encouraging loyalty among existing customers	4.3	3.5	4.0

[a] Based on a seven-point scale: 1 = no contribution whatsoever; 7 = vitally important contribution.

Source: Adapted from Roger Bennett, "Corporate Philanthropy in France, Germany, and the UK," *International Marketing Review* 15 (June 1998): 469. © MCB University Press, 2000. Reprinted with permission.

Finally, strategic philanthropy should improve a company's overall reputation in the community and ease government and community relations. Research indicates a strong negative relationship between illegal activity and reputation, whereas firms that contribute to charitable causes enjoy enhanced reputations. Moreover, companies that contribute to social causes, especially to problems that arise as a result of their actions, may be able to improve their reputations after committing a crime.[52] If a business is engaged in a strategic approach to contributions, volunteerism, and related activities, a clear purpose is to enhance and benefit the community. By properly implementing and communicating these achievements, the company will "do well by doing good." Essentially, community members and others use cues from a strategic philanthropy initiative, along with other social responsibility programs, to form a lasting impression—or reputation—of the firm. These benefits, together with others discussed in this section, are consistent with research conducted on European firms. Table 11.5 highlights the perceived benefits of corporate philanthropy to companies located in France, Germany, and the United Kingdom. The table suggests that companies in these countries believe that their charitable activities generally have a positive effect on goodwill, public relations, community relations, employee motivation, and customer loyalty.[53]

Implementation of Strategic Philanthropy

Attaining the benefits of strategic philanthropy depends on the integration of corporate competencies, business stakeholders, and social responsibility objectives to be fully effective. However, fruitfully implementing a strategic philanthropy approach is not simple and requires organizational resources and strategic attention. In this section, we examine some of the key factors associated with implementing strategic philanthropy.

Although some organizations and leaders see beyond economic concerns, other firms are far less progressive and collaborative in nature. To the extent that corporate leaders and others advocate for strategic philanthropy, planning and evaluation practices must be developed just as with any other business process. Almost all effective actions taken by a company are well-thought-out business plans. However, although most large organizations have solid plans for philanthropy and other community involvement, these activities typically do not receive the same attention that other business forays garner. A study by the American Productivity and Quality Center found that many organizations are not yet taking a systematic or comprehensive approach in evaluating the impact of philanthropy on the business and other stakeholders.[54]

Top Management Support

The implementation of strategic philanthropy is impossible without the endorsement and support of the chief executive officer and other members of top management. Although most executives care about their communities and social issues, there may be debate or confusion over how their firms should meet stakeholder concerns and social responsibility. When Al Dunlap became CEO of Sunbeam, for example, he eliminated the company's annual giving program of $1 million. He was very clear that he felt that Sunbeam's primary responsibility was to shareholders, noting that the company was giving to society by making money for shareholders.[55] In contrast, Robert Allen, chair of the board for AT&T, observed that although some corporations

Employees at The Gymboree Corporation, a retailer of children's clothing and a leader in parent/child developmental play programs, demonstrate strategic philanthropy by supporting the March of Dimes, a charity devoted to innovative research and programs that save babies from prematurity, birth defects, and other health problems. (Gymboree Corporation)

are solely motivated by financial returns, he is confident that "the men and women who guide AT&T firmly believe that our business has the responsibility to contribute to the long-term well-being of the society."[56]

Top managers often have unique concerns with respect to strategic philanthropy. For example, chief executive officers may worry about having to defend the company's commitment to charity. Some investors may see these contributions as damaging to their portfolios. A related concern involves the resources required to manage a philanthropy effort. Top managers must be well versed in the performance benefits of social responsibility that we discussed in Chapter 1. Additionally, some executives may believe that less philanthropic-minded competitors have a profit advantage. If these competitors have any advantage at all, it is probably just a short-term situation. The tax benefits and other gains that philanthropy provides should prevail over the long run.[57] In today's environment, there are many positive incentives and reasons that strategic philanthropy and social responsibility make good business sense.

Planning and Evaluating Strategic Philanthropy

As with any initiative, strategic philanthropy must prove its relevance and importance. In order for philanthropy and other stakeholder collaborations to be fully diffused and accepted within the business community, a performance benefit must be evident. In addition, philanthropy should be treated as a corporate program that deserves the same professionalism and resources as other strategic initiatives. Thus, the process for planning and evaluating strategic philanthropy is integral to its success.

To make the best decisions when dealing with stakeholder concerns and issues, there should be a defensible, workable strategy that ensures that every donation is wisely spent. The author Curt Weeden, CEO of the Contributions Academy, has developed a multistep process for ensuring effective planning and implementation of strategic philanthropy.

1. **Research** If a company has too little or inaccurate information, it will suffer when making philanthropic decisions. Research should cover the internal organization and programs, organizations, sponsorship options, and events that might intersect with the interests and competencies of the corporation.
2. **Organize and Design** The information collected by research should be classified into relevant categories. For example, funding opportunities can be categorized according to the level of need and alignment with organizational competencies. The process of organizing and designing is probably the most crucial step in which management should be thoroughly involved.
3. **Engage** This step consists of engaging management early on so as to ease the approval process in the future. Top managers need to be co-owners of the corporate philanthropy plan. They will have interest in seeing the plan receive authorization, and they will enrich the program by sharing their ideas and thoughts.
4. **Spend** Deciding what resources and dollars should be spent where is a very important task. A skilled manager who has spent some time with the philanthropy

program should preferably handle this. If the previous steps were handled appropriately, this step should go rather smoothly.[58]

Evaluating corporate philanthropy should begin with a clear understanding of how these efforts are linked to the company's vision, mission, and resources. As our definition suggests, philanthropy can only be strategic if it is fully aligned with the values, core competencies, and long-term plans of an organization. Thus, the development of philanthropic programs should be part of the strategic planning process.

Assuming that key stakeholders have been identified, organizations need to conduct research to understand stakeholder expectations and their willingness to collaborate for mutual benefit. Although many companies have invested time and resources to understand the needs of employees, customers, and investors, fewer have examined other stakeholders or the potential for aligning stakeholders and company resources for philanthropic reasons. Philanthropic efforts should be evaluated for their effects on and benefits to various constituents.[59] Although philanthropists have always been concerned with results, the aftermath of September 11 brought not only widespread contributions but also a heightened sensitivity to accountability. For example, the American Red Cross suffered intense scrutiny after its leaders initially decided to set aside a portion of donations received in response to the terrorist strikes. The rationale for setting aside $200 million was that a long-term program on terrorism response needed to be developed and funded. Other funds were earmarked for expansion, maintenance, and other purposes not directly related to September 11. Many donors rejected this plan and the Red Cross reversed its decision. There were outright scams after the attacks, including people who claimed loved ones were killed in the World Trade Center in order to collect money, entrepreneurs who sold patriotic items supposedly for charitable reasons, and fake charities for police and fire personnel. A survey in late 2002 indicated that 42 percent of Americans have less confidence in charities than they did before the September 11 attacks. Major philanthropists are also stepping up their expectations for accountability, widespread impact, strategic thinking, global implications, and results.[60] Figure 11.4 lists ten guidelines that potential donors should use in evaluating and choosing organizations with which to partner or provide funding.

Methods used to evaluate strategic philanthropy should include an assessment of how these initiatives are communicated to stakeholders. Vancouver City Savings and Credit Union of Canada (VanCity) initiated the process of increasing its social accountability to its various stakeholders when its executives and board of directors recognized that VanCity's level of disclosure, not necessarily its social responsibility, was below many other financial institutions in Canada. By increasing its disclosure and reporting, VanCity improved awareness of its commitment to social responsibility and ultimately refined its corporate strategy to meet other stakeholder concerns.[61] Such reporting mechanisms not only improve stakeholder knowledge but also lead to improvements and refinements. Although critics may deride organizations for communicating their philanthropic efforts, the strategic philanthropy model is dependent on feedback and learning to create greater value for the organization and its stakeholders, as we shall see in the next chapter.

| FIGURE 11.4 | A Donor Bill of Rights |

Philanthropy is based on voluntary action for the common good. It is a tradition of giving and sharing that is primary to the quality of life. To assure that philanthropy merits the respect and trust of the general public and that donors and prospective donors can have full confidence in the not-for-profit organizations and causes they are asked to support, we declare that all donors have these rights:

1. To be informed of the organization's mission, of the way the organization intends to use donated resources, and of its capacity to use donations effectively for their intended purposes
2. To be informed of the identity of those serving on the organization's governing board and to expect the board to exercise prudent judgment in its stewardship responsibilities
3. To have access to the organization's most recent financial statements
4. To be assured their gifts will be used for the purposes for which they were given
5. To receive appropriate acknowledgment and recognition
6. To be assured that information about their donations is handled with respect and with confidentiality to the extent provided by law
7. To expect that all relationships with individuals representing organizations of interest to the donor will be professional in nature
8. To be informed whether those seeking donations are volunteers, employees of the organization, or hired solicitors
9. To have the opportunity for their names to be deleted from mailing lists that an organization may intend to share
10. To feel free to ask questions when making a donation and to receive prompt, truthful, and forthright answers

The text of this statement in its entirety was developed by the American Association of Fundraising Counsel (AAFRC), Association for Healthcare Philanthropy (AHP), Council for Advancement and Support of Education (CASE), and the Association of Fundraising Professionals (AFP).

Source: American Association of Fundraising Counsel, "A Donor Bill of Rights," http://www.aafrc.org/choose_counsel/donor.html, accessed August 22, 2003. The Donor Bill of Rights is developed by the American Association of Fundraising Counsel (AAFRC), the Association for Healthcare Philanthropy (AHP), the Council for Advancement and Support of Education (CASE), and the Association of Fundraising Professionals (AFP), and endorsed by Independent Sector, National Catholic Development Conference (NCDC), National Committee on Planned Giving (NCPG), National Council for Resource Development (NCRD), and United Way of America.

Summary

Generally, philanthropy involves any acts of benevolence and goodwill. Strategic philanthropy is defined as the synergistic use of organizational core competencies and resources to address key stakeholders' interests and to achieve both organizational and social benefits. Strategic philanthropy involves both financial and nonfinancial contributions to stakeholders, but it also benefits the company. As such, strategic philanthropy is part of a broader philosophy that recognizes how social responsibility can help an organization improve its overall performance. Research suggests that those companies that adopt a more businesslike approach to philanthropy will experience a better image, increased employee loyalty, and improved customer ties.

Corporate giving, volunteer efforts, and other philanthropic activities should be considered and aligned with corporate strategy and financial, legal, and ethical obligations. The concept of strategic philanthropy has evolved since the middle of the twentieth century, when contributions were prohibited by law, to emerge as a management practice to support social responsibility in the 1990s. Whereas strategic philanthropy links corporate resources and knowledge to address broader social, customer, employee, and supplier problems and needs, cause-related marketing ties an organization's product(s) directly to a social concern. By linking products with charities and social causes, organizations acknowledged the opportunity to align philanthropy to economic goals and to acknowledge stakeholder interests in organizational benevolence.

Many organizations have skillfully used their resources and core competencies to address the needs of employees, customers, business partners, the community and society, and the natural environment. In order to pursue strategic philanthropy successfully, organizations must weigh the costs and benefits associated with planning and implementing it as a corporate priority. The benefits of strategic philanthropy are closely aligned with benefits obtained from social responsibility. Businesses that engage in strategic philanthropy often gain a tax advantage. Research suggests that they may also enjoy improved productivity, employee commitment and morale, and reduced turnover and experience greater customer loyalty and satisfaction. In the future, many companies will devote more resources to understand how strategic philanthropy can be developed and integrated to support their core competencies.

The implementation of strategic philanthropy is impossible without the support of top management. To integrate strategic philanthropy into the organization successfully, the efforts must fit with the company's mission, values, and resources. Organizations must also understand stakeholder expectations and propensity to support such activities for mutual benefit. This process relies on the feedback of stakeholders in improving and learning how to better integrate the strategic philanthropy objectives with other organizational goals. Finally, companies will need to evaluate philanthropic efforts and assess how these results should be communicated to stakeholders.

Key Terms

strategic philanthropy (p. 333)
cause-related marketing (p. 339)

Discussion Questions

1. What are some of the issues you might include in a defense of strategic philanthropy to company stockholders?
2. Describe your personal experiences with philanthropy. In what types of activities have you participated? Which companies that you do business with have a philanthropic focus? How did this focus influence your decision to buy from those companies?
3. How have changes in the business environment contributed to the growing trend of strategic philanthropy?
4. Compare cause-related marketing with strategic philanthropy. What are the unique benefits of each approach?
5. What role does top management play in developing and implementing a strategic philanthropy approach?
6. Describe the four-stage process for planning and implementing strategic philanthropy.

Experiential Exercise

Choose one major corporation and investigate how closely its philanthropic efforts are strategically aligned with its core competencies. Visit the company's web site, read its annual reports, and use other sources to justify your conclusions. Develop a chart or table to depict how the company's core competencies are linked to various philanthropic projects and stakeholder groups. Finally, provide an analysis of how these efforts have affected the company's performance.

 ## What Would You Do?

As a new vice president of corporate philanthropy, Jack Birke was looking forward to the great initiatives and partnerships the company could create through his office. During his eighteen-year career, Jack worked for several large nonprofit organizations and earned an excellent reputation for his ability to raise funds, develop advisory boards, and in general, work well with the business community.

About a year ago, Jack decided to investigate other opportunities within the fundraising industry and started looking at companies that were formalizing their philanthropy efforts. He was hired as VP less than a month ago and was in the process of developing an office structure, getting to know the organization, and creating a strategic plan. His charge over the next year was to develop a stronger reputation for philanthropy and social responsibility with the company's stakeholders, including employees, customers, and the community. An executive assistant, director of volunteerism, and director of community relations were already on board and Jack was looking for additional staff.

The position and office were new to the company, and Jack had already heard dissent from other employees, who openly questioned how important philanthropy was to the business. After all, the economy was slowing, and it seemed that customers were more concerned about price and value than any "touchy feely" program. About half of the company's employees worked on the manufacturing line, and the other half was employed in administrative or professional positions. Both groups seemed to be equally suspicious of Jack and his office. The company developed an employee volunteer program two years ago, but it was never very successful. A program to gather food, gifts, and money to support needy families at Christmas, however, drew strong support. The firm had fairly good relationships in the community, but these were primarily the top executives' connections through the chamber of commerce, industry associations, nonprofit boards, and so forth. In sum, while Jack had the support of top management, many employees were unsure about philanthropy and its importance to the company. Jack was starting to think about short-term tactics and long-term strategy for "marketing" his office and goals to the rest of the organization. What would you do?

The Social Audit

CHAPTER OBJECTIVES

- Define social auditing
- Identify the benefits of social auditing
- Discuss the potential limitations of social auditing
- Compare the process of social auditing with that of financial auditing
- Explore the stages of the social auditing process
- Explore the strategic role of social auditing

CHAPTER OUTLINE

The Nature of Social Auditing

The Auditing Process

The Strategic Importance of Social Auditing

Vancouver City Savings Credit Union (VanCity) is Canada's largest credit union, with 290,000 members and forty branches in the Greater Vancouver area, Victoria, and the Fraser Valley. The credit union has long valued ethical and responsible practices and good relationships with its stakeholders. To further its social responsibility efforts, the firm began reporting information about its impact on members, staff, the community, and the environment in its annual report in 1992. In 1998, the firm extended this effort by publishing its first "Social Report," later changed to accountability report. On their web site, VanCity states:

> Being accountable to our members, employees and communities for the results of our decisions and actions is one of our key values as laid out in our Statement of Values and Commitments. One of the ways we are accountable is through our social audit process and the release of our Accountability Report (formerly Social Report). Our Accountability Report is the final product of our social audit process and is externally verified to provide assurance that it is a reliable, balanced and reasonable account of our social and environmental performance.

VanCity's 2000–2001 Accountability Report communicated both quantitative and qualitative information about the firm's social and environmental performance on issues its customers, staff, the community, and other credit unions had identified as important. The Accountability Report also compared the credit union's performance with several external benchmarks established by the Canadian Centre for Philanthropy, Michael Jantzi Research Associates, and an industry benchmarking study conducted by EthicScan Canada on VanCity's behalf. In addition to reporting information about the credit union's performance, the report pinpointed areas where the credit union could improve. Among the areas cited as needing improvement were communications with members, staff, other credit unions, and community organizations; implementation and communication of a comprehensive ethical policy to guide decisions and business strategies; and support of staff seeking balance between the pressures of work and family life.

To indicate its seriousness about being responsible, accountable, and transparent with regards to its social performance, VanCity had its first, internally drafted, "Social Report" independently verified by the U.K.-based New Economics Ltd. in collaboration with a local firm, Solstice Consulting. Solstice Consulting also independently verified the second and third reports. The credit union had the 1998–1999 and 2000–2001 reports reviewed, post-publication and before they were released to the public, by key stakeholders and community leaders from business, labor, academia, nonprofit, and environmental organizations. The feedback was then used to inform the next report.

VanCity's social audit has had positive benefits for the firm's image, and public support for continuing the auditing effort is strong. Within the firm, the social audit has increased knowledge about important nonfinancial issues, helped further integrate corporate responsibility into core areas of the business, and become a valuable tool for staff training, planning, and governance. As one executive says, "This report gives us the information we need to set benchmarks and track our progress."[1]

Just as VanCity did, more companies around the globe are beginning to audit their social performance and report the results of those assessments as a means of demonstrating their commitment to social responsibility. According to Investor Responsibility Center, 61 percent of S&P 500 companies have published an assessment of their environmental impact, and many more firms have announced their intention to provide environmental reports in the future. A similar study by EthicScan found that 60 percent of major Canadian corporations had voluntarily begun to incorporate sustainable development management and reporting into their operations.[2] Since the mid-1990s, more organizations are reporting about their impact on and relationships with a variety of stakeholders as well as their performance on social issues ranging far beyond the environment. These reports are often called "social audits," "social responsibility reports," or "corporate citizenship audits."

Regardless of what name they go by, the reports of such auditing efforts are important for demonstrating a firm's commitment to and ensuring the continuous improvement of its social responsibility efforts. Without reliable measurements of the achievement of social objectives, a company has no concrete way to verify their importance, link them to organizational performance, justify expenditures to stockholders and investors, or address any stakeholder concerns.[3] Because the well-conducted social audit has the ability to do all these things, we devote this chapter to this leading-edge social responsibility tool. We begin by defining the social audit and explore the reasons for conducting the audit and its benefits and limitations. Next we compare the social audit to financial audits in order to derive standards that may be applied to social auditing and reporting. We also describe an auditing procedure that can be used to measure and improve the social responsibility effort. Finally, we look at the strategic importance of social auditing.

The Nature of Social Auditing

social auditing
the process of assessing and reporting a business's performance on fulfilling the economic, legal, ethical, and philanthropic social responsibilities expected of it by its stakeholders

Social auditing is the process of assessing and reporting a business's performance on fulfilling the economic, legal, ethical, and philanthropic social responsibilities expected of it by its stakeholders. Social audits are tools that companies can employ to identify and measure their progress and challenges to stakeholders—including employees, customers, investors, suppliers, community members, activists, the media, and regulators—who are increasingly demanding that companies be transparent and accountable for their commitments and performance.[4] The auditing process is important to business because it can improve financial performance, increase attractiveness to investors, improve relationships with stakeholders, identify potential liabilities, improve organizational effectiveness, and decrease the risk of misconduct and adverse publicity.[5]

The social audit provides an objective approach for an organization to demonstrate its commitment to improving strategic planning, including showing social accountability and commitment to monitoring and evaluating social issues. Thus, it is critical that top managers understand and embrace the strategic importance of the social audit. Key stakeholders of the company should also be involved in the audit to ensure the integration of their perspectives into the firm's economic, legal, ethical, and philanthropic responsibilities.[6] Companies are working to incorporate accountability into actions ranging from long-term planning to everyday decision making, including corporate governance, financial reporting, and diversity. The strategic responsibility goals and outcomes measured in the social audit need to be communicated throughout the organization and to all of its stakeholders, so that everyone is aware of what the company would like to achieve and what progress has been made in achieving its goals. The social audit should provide regular, comprehensive, and comparative verification of the views of stakeholders. Disclosure is a key part of auditing to encourage constructive feedback. Directions for finding best practices and continuous improvement on legal, social, ethical, philanthropic, and other issues can come from all stakeholders.

Reasons for Social Audits

Throughout this book we have examined the various forces affecting social responsibility. There are many reasons why companies choose to understand, report on, and improve their social performance. The increased visibility of corporate social responsibility has encouraged companies to better account for their actions in a wide range of areas, including human resources, environmental policies, ethics programs, and community involvement. At one extreme, a company may want to achieve the best social performance possible, whereas at the other extreme, a firm may desire to project a good image to hide misconduct. Still other companies may see the auditing process as a key component of organizational improvement. Thus, the reasons that companies exceed their legally prescribed duties lie along a vast spectrum, as the social responsibility continuum in Chapter 1 indicated.[7] For example, it is common for firms to conduct audits of business practices with legal ramifications, such as employee safety and environmental impact. Although these concerns are important to a firm's social responsibility, they are also legally prescribed and indicative of minimal social responsibility. Stakeholders are demanding increased transparency and are taking a more active role through external organizations representing the interests of these groups. Government regulators are calling on companies to increase the quantity and quality of information disclosed aimed at increasing the companies' accountability to society. For example, the 2002 Sarbanes-Oxley Act requires top financial officers to file their company's code of ethics with the Securities and Exchange Commission. A number of financial and auditing decisions must also be reported on a regular basis.

Benefits of Social Auditing

Social auditing provides benefits for both organizations and their stakeholders. For example, regular audits permit stockholders and investors to judge whether a firm is achieving the goals it has established and whether it abides by the values it has specified as important. Moreover, it permits stakeholders to influence the organization's behavior.[8] Increasingly, a broad range of stakeholder groups are seeking specific, often quantifiable, information from companies. These stakeholders expect companies to take a deeper look at the nature of their operations and to publicly disclose both their progress and problems in addressing these issues. Some investors, for example, are using their rights as stockholders to encourage companies to modify their plans and policies to address specific social issues. Tyco International Ltd. shareholders voted to eliminate some benefits to top executives on the basis of the reported scandal that occurred in the past. Greater transparency related to social auditing assists stakeholders in making decisions related to corporate governance.[9] Every year, managers of Shell companies worldwide are required to write and sign three different letters covering performance in business integrity; health, safety, and environment; and executing the Statement of General Business Principles. Writing the letters is a mandatory part of a senior manager's duties and the task is taken seriously, since managers are held personally responsible for the accuracy of the contents. Those who give false information or fail to reveal the truth can be dismissed. Shell has also opened communications to stakeholders through an annual series of Shell Reports.[10]

The Royal Dutch/Shell Group of Companies publishes the independently verified Shell Report, *which details the firm's commitment to social responsibility. The report includes information on Shell's environmental, economic, and social goals and performance. (http://www.shell.com, downloaded March 21, 2003. Reproduced with the permission of Shell International Petroleum Company Limited.)*

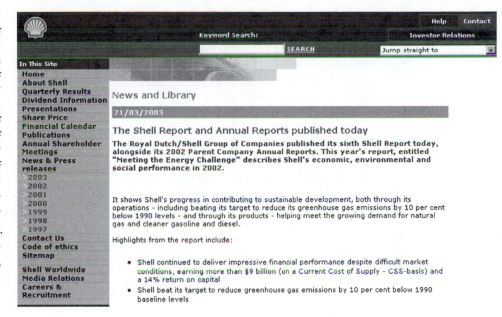

For organizations, one of the greatest benefits of the auditing process is improved relationships with stakeholders. Many stakeholders have become wary of corporate public relations campaigns. Verbal assurances by corporate management are no longer sufficient to gain the trust of stakeholders. Independent verification of social and environmental reports is one way in which companies are addressing this lack of trust. Verification can provide readers with a measure of assurance that the company has reported honestly and fairly, together with an assessment of the quality of its social reporting systems. Accessibility and distribution of the report, as well as its direct relevance to stakeholders, help to facilitate a more beneficial, ongoing relationship between a company and its stakeholders.[11] When firms and their suppliers trust each other, the costs of monitoring and managing contracts are lower. Companies experience less conflict with their suppliers, resulting in fewer lawsuits, and there is a heightened capacity for innovation. In addition, social auditing and reporting can identify the effectiveness of programs and policies, often improving operating efficiencies and reducing costs. For example, Qwest Communications International Inc. spent over $7 million per month in 2003 for outside lawyers to defend the company over allegations about accounting irregularities and fraud. A social audit and report could have helped prevent that situation.

As an investor-owned telecommunications company, Qwest's Board of Directors and top management have been able to limit transparency and more recently antagonize stakeholders. Qwest was fined $20.3 million for switching customer's long-distance accounts without permission and adding unauthorized charges to their bills. To inflate its earnings, it devised a scheme to generate $33 million in revenue on a purchase order. In addition, Qwest is facing a potential bankruptcy and scandal over incorrectly booking sales of over $2 billion of telephone communication capacity. Top management and the board are taking a reactive approach by spending millions of dollars on outside attorneys to defend Qwest. Investors, customers, and regulatory agencies feel that Qwest restrained communications and there was no openness about many events that led to the destruction of stakeholders' interest.[12] Information from audits and reports can also help identify priorities among corporate social responsibility activities to ensure the company is achieving the greatest possible impact with available resources.

The process of social auditing can also help an organization identify potential risks and liabilities and improve its compliance with the law. Accountable companies may be better prepared to address the concerns of customers or other stakeholders who might otherwise take negative action on social issues. For example, by engaging in a dialog with stakeholders about their interests and concerns and addressing those concerns in business implementation processes, companies may be able to head off or minimize the impacts of boycotts organized by consumer groups. Similarly, companies that proactively address the concerns of shareholders can reduce the risk of adverse publicity stemming from high-profile shareholder disputes.[13] Furthermore, the audit report may help to document the firm's compliance with legal requirements as well as to demonstrate its progress in areas of previous noncompliance, including the systems implemented to reduce the likelihood of recurrence.[14] Shareholders and investors welcome the increased disclosure that comes with corporate accountability. A growing number of investors are including new nonfinancial metrics in their analysis of the quality of their investments. New metrics include legal compliance, the board of directors' independence, corporate governance, employee assistance through help lines, and a wide variety of other social responsibility concerns. Research suggests investors may be willing to pay higher prices for the stock of companies considered to be accountable. Every year, *Fortune* magazine conducts a study to find the "Top Ten Most Admired Companies." The chosen companies for 2003 were

1. Wal-Mart
2. Southwest Airlines
3. Berkshire Hathaway
4. Dell Computer
5. General Electric
6. Johnson & Johnson
7. Microsoft
8. FedEx
9. Starbucks
10. Procter & Gamble[15]

There seems to be a correlation between companies that are judged to treat their stakeholders well and how those companies rate among peers as having superior management. Stakeholders, including government regulators, may look more favorably on a company that identifies such problems through an audit, especially when the firm publicly reports the problems, demonstrates that it is attempting to resolve them, and implements systems that will reduce the likelihood of their recurrence.[16] Thus, the social audit is a form of due diligence that provides evidence of a strategic attempt to benchmark and comply with standards.

Social auditing may also help a company coordinate its social responsibility initiatives throughout the firm, resulting in more effective and efficient use of company resources to address community and social concerns. Information from audits and reports can help identify priorities among corporate social responsibility activities to ensure the company is achieving the greatest possible impact with available resources. Because a well-designed audit can document the effectiveness and efficiency of social and accountability initiatives, the audit process may uncover areas where operations can be made more efficient (e.g., through recycling) and thereby reduce costs and increase profits.[17] Indeed, many companies are finding that the audit reduces operating costs while at the same time creating social benefits. One study, by Smith O'Brien, a leader in the social audit industry, found dramatic savings for some companies conducting social audits. Examples of these savings ranged from nearly $200,000 from lower production costs in a small manufacturing plant to $1.7 million from a 10 percent decline in paper use in a company switching to electronic communication.[18] The auditing process helps organizations establish priorities for social responsibility, thereby allowing them to focus on those that will generate the greatest economic and social impact.[19]

Reporting on social responsibilities also allows a company to quantify the nonfinancial aspects of its community involvement. To illustrate, consider the fact that many organizations commit significant resources to activities such as providing volunteers for community activities. Sometimes volunteers engage in activities during regular work hours. The time and effort an organization's staff spends on projects such as providing dinners at a homeless shelter or painting a youth center do not appear on a company's balance sheet. In addition, many companies donate products to help their communities. Bottled water companies, for example, often donate their products after disasters such as hurricanes.[20] Microsoft, IBM, and Hewlett-Packard have a reputation for donating their products to educational institutions.

Investors view companies that engage in social reporting more favorably. According to the Dow-Jones Sustainability Indexes (DJSI), in 2002 the average sustainability performance of companies has improved significantly. Reasons for this include the integration of economic, environmental, and social issues moving up on the business agenda in all sectors and reaching a high level of sophistication in particularly exposed industries. The DJSI also recognized an increase in the number of sustainability-driven investors. People are realizing that sustainability trends have an impact on their investment decisions. Recent corporate scandals have emphasized the need for greater transparency and accountability on all social issues. As a result, investors are turning to the concept of sustainability to identify well-managed and future-oriented companies.[21]

Risks of Social Auditing

Although social audits provide many benefits for individual organizations and their stakeholders, they do have potential risks, which could create as many problems as the audits solve. A firm may uncover a serious problem that it would prefer not to disclose until it can remedy the situation. An audit could discover an environmental problem or an employee who is creating an antitrust violation. For example, special-interest groups may be concerned about the amount of fat in fast-food meals. The audit may find that one or more of the firm's stakeholders' criticisms cannot be dismissed or easily addressed. Occasionally, the process of conducting a social audit may foster stakeholder dissatisfaction instead of stifling it. Asking employees about discrimination or other unethical conduct in the workplace can create employee complaints and dissatisfaction. Moreover, the auditing process imposes burdens (especially with regard to record keeping) and costs for those firms that undertake it. Finally, the process of auditing and reporting a firm's social efforts is no guarantee that the firm will not face challenges to its social responsibility.[22] In addition, because this type of auditing is relatively new, there are few common standards to judge disclosure and effectiveness or to make comparisons.[23] In environmental auditing, it has been noted that some assurance providers engage in what is called selective disclosure; that is, they deliberately fail to give an opinion or judgment on so-called gray areas or activities that could be negative to the client's interests. The need for organizations to be seen by the public as being audited can be the motivating factor for conducting the audit, and in this case, of signaling that something is wrong.[24]

Although social responsibility is defined and perceived differently by various stakeholders, a core of minimum standards for corporate social performance is evolving. These standards represent a fundamental step in the development of a socially responsible company. The minimum standards are specific and measurable, and they are achievable and meaningful in terms of business impact on communities, employees, consumers, the environment, and economic systems. These standards help companies set measurable and achievable targets for improvement and form an objective foundation for reporting the firm's efforts to all stakeholders. There may still be disagreements on key issues and standards, but through these standards, progress should be made.[25]

Crisis Management and Recovery

A significant benefit of social auditing is that it may help prevent public relations crises associated with ethical or legal misconduct, which can potentially be more devastating than traditional natural disasters or technological disruptions. Just as companies develop *crisis management* plans to prepare to respond to and recover from natural disasters, they should also prepare for social responsibility disasters, which can not only result in substantial legal and financial costs but also disrupt routine operations, paralyze employees and reduce productivity, destroy organizational reputation, and erode stakeholder confidence. Ethical and legal crises have resulted in the demise of a number of well-known companies including Enron and Arthur Andersen. Many other companies—Colombia/HCA, Firestone, Waste Management, Sunbeam, WorldCom, Rite Aid, Mitsubishi Motors, Xerox, Daiwa Bank of Japan, Archer Daniels Midland, and Microsoft to name but a few—survived ethical and legal crises but paid a high price not only financially but also in terms of compromised reputation and declining stakeholder trust. The previous Qwest example illustrates such a demise of public and stakeholder trust. One study found that publicity about unethical corporate behavior lowers stock prices for at least six months.[26] A poll by Harris Interactive found many scandal-plagued firms at the bottom of its annual survey of perceived corporate reputation, including Enron, Global Crossing, WorldCom, Andersen Worldwide, and Adelphia. The most recent survey, which ranks companies according to how respondents rate them on twenty attributes, also found that public perceptions of trust had declined considerably as a result of the accounting scandals of the early twenty-first century. Joy Sever, a Harris vice president, reported, "The scandals cost many companies their emotional appeal, the strongest driver of reputation."[27]

Despite the high costs of misconduct, a Pricewaterhouse Coopers survey indicates that U.S. companies are failing to identify and manage ethical, social, economic, and environmental issues of concern. Although most companies recognize that these issues have the potential to harm corporate reputation and threaten relationships with customers, suppliers, and other stakeholders, few are taking steps to identify, evaluate, and respond to them.[28] Table 12.1 indicates areas of concern that some companies consider in contingency planning for crisis management. Social audits could help companies identify potential risks and liabilities in order to implement plans to eliminate or reduce them before they reach crisis dimensions.

Ethical misconduct can be caused by organizational members who engage in questionable or even illegal conduct. These rogue employees can threaten the overall integrity of the organization. Top leaders in particular can bring ethical misconduct to disastrous dimensions. For example, the stock of Martha Stewart Living Omnimedia crashed after CEO and founder Martha Stewart was indicted for alleged insider trading. Other examples of organizational disaster that resulted from individual misconduct include the disasters from the conduct of the Rigas family members at Adelphia Communications, Andrew Fastow at Enron, and Dennis Kozlowski at Tyco.[29] A social audit can help discover rogue employees who are violating the firm's ethical standards and policies, or laws and regulations.

There are recognizable phases of escalation from a social responsibility decision to disaster including a mistake or infraction, organizational discovery, and organizational response. Without appropriate anticipation and intervention, these can lead to organizational disaster. Contingency planning is tied to risk assessment and planning for these potential occurrences. Contingency planning also provides ready tools for

TABLE 12.1	Ethical Misconduct Readiness/Preparedness
SOCIAL MISCONDUCT DISASTER READINESS	COMPANIES' READINESS, RATED LOW TO NONE
Ethnic/sexual harassment	35%
Regulatory violations	39%
Criminal conduct	36%
Fraud	37%
Unethical behavior	36%
Unlawful discrimination	35%
Falsifying records	39%
Criminal charges	41%
Deception of customer	42%
Public relations disaster	44%
Bribery	45%

Source: Robert C. Chandler and J. D. Wallace, Pepperdine University Ethical Misconduct Disaster Recovery Preparedness Survey conducted at DRJ Spring World 2001, San Diego, California. Copyright © 2001. Reprinted with permission of *Disaster Recovery Journal* and the authors.

responding to crises. The process of social responsibility disaster recovery planning involves an assessment of the organizations' values, development of social responsibility programs, a social audit, and the ability to develop contingency plans for potential disasters. The social audit provides the key link to preventing disasters related to social responsibility.

Social Auditing Versus Financial Auditing

The social audit is much like the internal auditing companies have used for years to verify the accuracy of their financial reports. In many cases, the standards used in financial auditing can be adapted to provide an objective foundation for social reporting. Thus, it is constructive to compare the financial audit and the social audit to better understand the reasons for and benefits of the social auditing process. With major scandals in accounting, such as WorldCom's and Global Crossing's, fraud is so visible that the reforms to prevent fraud in financial reporting provide some guidance in conducting a social audit.

Whereas a financial audit is concerned primarily with a company's claims about its financial performance, a social audit is interested in a company's assertions about its social responsibility. Financial auditing focuses on all systems related to money flows and financial assessments of value for tax purposes and managerial accountability. Social auditing deals with nonfinancial aspects of operations from both their internal and external impacts. Issues such as diversity, privacy, human resource decisions, and environmental impact are included in a social audit.

Another significant difference is that social auditing is a voluntary process, whereas financial auditing is required of public companies that issue securities. Because social

President and CEO of WorldCom John Sidgemore announces the company's bankruptcy despite the message communicated in the hanging banner. (AP Photo/ Diane Bondareff)

audits are voluntary, there are few standards that a company can apply with regard to reporting frequency, disclosure requirements, and remedial actions that a company should take in response to results. A variety of organizations and initiatives are attempting to standardize social and environmental reporting procedures to let stakeholders more easily compare companies across facilities, sectors, and borders. For example, the Global Reporting Initiative, an alliance of international organizations headed by the U.S.-based organization CERES, was established in 1998 to streamline the numerous initiatives on corporate environmental reporting that have developed independently around the world and to shape them into a set of consistent global standards. Also, the Institute of Social and Ethical Accountability introduced standards that aim to help companies understand and improve their social and ethical performance, describing how to identify key issues and report on them in a way that outsiders can rely on and suggesting how those reports should be audited. The AA1000 standard sets out principles for ensuring that social reports are comprehensive, meaningful, and reliable. Even without such initiatives, many companies have been steadily improving the quality and quantity of information featured in their annual reports, voluntarily including greater amounts of data related to their environmental and social performance. A wide variety of standards are emerging that apply to corporate accountability. These include industry benchmarking tools and frameworks, legislation, and voluntary codes developed by nongovernmental organizations and private-sector consultancies. In 1997, the Global Reporters report analyzed the social reports of 14 companies. In 2000, this number had grown to 202 (SustainAbility 2000). The Global Reporting Initiative (GRI) estimates there are now some 4,000 current social or environmental reports. In relative terms, this is a large increase, but in absolute terms, it remains small.[30]

Social auditing is similar to financial auditing in that both employ the same procedures and processes in order to create a system of integrity with objective reporting. An independent expert must verify both types of audits. The financial auditor will employ external sources to certify the assertions in financial statements, such as comparing the company's accounts receivable with its accounts payable. To vouch for a company's claims about its social performance, a social auditor will contact customers and other stakeholders and compare their perceptions of the firm's social performance with the company's assessments. As in financial audits, social audits are often performed by certified public accountants. Table 12.2 illustrates the social responsibility auditing standards established by one of these accounting and consulting firms.

Both financial and social audits begin with planning. In each audit, planning involves collecting information to understand the company's industry, determining the scope of the audit, and documenting the details of the audit program. This information must be of high quality, consistent, complete, material, segregated, and collected in a controlled environment. The auditor cannot start the program assuming management is in compliance with legal and ethical standards. Nor can the auditor assume management is not in compliance with standards. It is a practice that is based on judgment with use of professional skepticism. The failure to use professional skepticism in financial audits created the accounting audit fraud scandals that are associated with WorldCom and Enron.

The quality of information gathered affects management's capacity to direct the company's social responsibility activities and therefore influences the social auditor's

| TABLE 12.2 | Social Auditing Standards |

COMPETENCE

The engagement shall be performed by a practitioner having adequate technical training and proficiency

The engagement shall be performed by a practitioner having adequate knowledge in the subject matter

The practitioner shall perform an engagement only if he or she has reason to believe that the following two conditions exist:

- The assertion is capable of evaluation against reasonable criteria that have been established by a recognizable body or are stated in the presentation of the assertion in a sufficiently clear and comprehensive manner for a knowledgeable reader to be able to understand them

- The assertion is capable of reasonably consistent estimation or measurement using such criteria

INDEPENDENCE

An independence in mental attitude shall be maintained by the practitioner who shall not have participated in the assertion

DUE CARE

Due professional care shall be exercised in the performance of the engagement

PLANNING

The work shall be adequately planned and assistants, if any, shall be properly supervised

CONTROL STRUCTURE

A sufficient understanding of the communications and control structures is to be obtained to plan the audit and to determine the nature, timing, and extent of tests to be performed

EVIDENCE

Sufficient evidence shall be obtained to provide a reasonable basis for the conclusion that is expressed in the report

STANDARDS OF REPORTING

The report shall identify the assertion being reported on and state the character of the engagement

The report shall state the practitioner's conclusion about whether the assertion is presented in conformity with the established or stated criteria against which it was measured

The report shall state all of the practitioner's significant reservations about the engagement and the presentation of the assertion

The report on an engagement to evaluate an assertion that has been prepared in conformity with agreed-upon criteria or on an engagement to apply agreed-upon procedures should contain a statement limiting its use to the parties who have agreed upon such criteria or procedures

Source: "Social Responsibility Auditing Standards," Vasin, Heyn & Company, www.vhcoaudit.com/SRAarticles/SRAStandards.htm, accessed November 5, 2001. Reprinted by permission of Vasin, Heyn & Company.

ability to conduct the audit. The auditor is primarily concerned with how the company records, processes, summarizes, and reports on its social responsibilities and how the company communicates these responsibilities to involved stakeholders. Accuracy in measurement and due diligence and professionalism in reporting are required to ensure quality.

Consistency is also essential in both financial and social audits. For example, an auditor of financial statements will use analytical procedures, such as comparing current-year account balances to those of prior years, to test specific claims. The methods of reporting must be consistent in order to be meaningful. Thus, a company is not permitted to change its method of reporting without adequate disclosure. A common example of this would be an announcement of a change in the method of valuing inventory accounts from "last in, first out" (LIFO) to "first in, first out" (FIFO). For the same reasons, a company should not alter its method of reporting about social responsibility results for a particular stakeholder group from one year to the next without disclosing that fact. For example, if the sample size of community groups surveyed in a subsequent social audit is significantly reduced, the auditor should question whether this reduction provides consistency with the results of the prior year's audit. Perhaps more favorable results were obtained in a prior year because the company surveyed more community groups that responded positively than negatively in the prior audit. Although this type of practice undermines the purpose and continuous improvements that a company can gain from a social responsibility effort, its possibility should not be overlooked. For these reasons, a social balance sheet has been created. It is defined as a representation of a given enterprise's social and socioeconomic development. Modern versions attempt to cover not only the point of view of owners and shareholders but also that of other stakeholders. The social balance sheet and the provision of socioeconomic information in general have come into being as a result of the change in the traditional notion of the enterprise, which is no longer identified solely with the interest of its owners (maximizing profit) and is seen as a coalition of interests of various stakeholders. This means that greater attention has to be paid to the interests and concerns of all stakeholders.[31]

Both social and financial auditors are particularly concerned about the completeness of the records used to document a company's assertions. In a financial audit, the auditor will trace from the source documents to the financial statements to ensure that accounts are complete. Likewise, a social audit must include all aspects of the company's "social footprint," including all the places, people, and stakeholders that are affected by the firm and all the company's activities, standards, and perceived organizational culture as related to social performance. Did the company record all of its responsibilities and performance related to social responsibility?

The concept of materiality is related to the audit's completeness. In a financial audit, something is deemed material if it is probable that the judgment of a reasonable person relying on the information would have been changed or influenced by its omission or misstatement. Materiality applies to social audits as well because users of a social audit could be misled if the audit fails to include material measures of stakeholders' perspectives, such as those of the company's customers. It is important for materiality that research methods and measurement procedures provide an accurate and timely audit. For example, Enron concealed off–balance sheet partnerships that materially influenced the value of the corporation.

To avoid misstatements in the social report, it is important for social auditors to clearly segregate certain functions. For example, the individual responsible for gathering stakeholder perspectives should not be the same individual who records the results. Obviously, if the duty of gathering evidence, as well as recording the findings, is conducted by the same person, there is no way to independently verify the accuracy of the recorded perspectives. The segregation of audit activities is facilitated by assigning accountants or consultants responsibility for certain audit functions. Even financial audits need to be conducted by an independent auditor that does not have conflicts of interest related to consulting income.

Perhaps the most significant component of the auditing process is the control environment, which relates to the attitude or philosophy, and operating style of management. The control environment facilitates establishing standards and reducing differences between desired and actual performance. The control environment represents the collective effect of both formal and informal methods to achieve desired results. Does management strongly emphasize the need for controls to ensure that the firm's social responsibility claims can be trusted? Are the ethical values of management in question? In a financial audit, it is standard procedure for an audit firm to determine if management lacks integrity before accepting an auditing engagement. Auditors lend credibility to a company's assertions, and this credibility can never be compromised. It is better for an outside audit consultant to decline an engagement than to be associated with a company that lacks integrity. Arthur Andersen made the mistake of being the auditor of clients such as Enron, WorldCom, Qwest, Sunbeam, Waste Management, and others that wanted to manipulate expenses and revenues to inflate earnings. If there is limited commitment to the auditing process, then the company may plan to use the audit for public relations rather than for improvement.

Skewed financial results appear in financial statements primarily because management's compensation is often tied to the financial results and management feels pressure to meet analyst expectations. In 2002, 330 U.S. firms restated earnings, indicating attempts to distort financial results.[32] As the demand for social responsibility grows in importance, the temptation for management to conceal and perpetuate social irregularities will also grow. The unavoidable result will be for social audits to emphasize internal control variables in a manner similar to financial audits. When internal control is overemphasized, there is a movement away from proactive value-driven activities that are hard to measure to emphasizing required, objective, legalistic audits.

The Auditing Process

There are relatively few standards available for companies to follow in conducting a social audit, such as what standards of performance should be used, how often to conduct an audit, whether and how to report an audit's results to stakeholders, and what actions should be taken in response to audit results. A survey conducted by one of the Big Four accounting firms found that only a few social reports contained any form of external verification. Such a general lack of third-party assurance has probably contributed to the general critique that social reporting is simply about corporate spin and public relations. However, the number of outside verified reports is growing. Thus, corporate approaches to social auditing are as varied as their approaches to social responsibility.[33]

It is our belief that a social audit should be unique to each company based on its size, industry, and corporate culture, as well as the regulatory environment in which it operates and the commitment of its top management to social responsibility. For this reason, we have mapped out a framework that is somewhat generic and can therefore be expanded on by all companies that want to conduct a social audit. The steps of this framework are presented in Table 12.3. As with any new initiative, companies may choose to begin their effort with a smaller, less-formal audit and then work up to a more comprehensive social audit. For example, a firm may choose to focus on primary stakeholders in its initial audit year and then expand to secondary groups in subsequent audits.

When creating a framework, companies should be aware of the development of standards such as the AA1000 Series. Although no regulation exists, AA1000 lays out guidelines that can be used to judge the quality of the audit. The guidelines build on the core principle of inclusivity and are based on three propositions: Stakeholder engagement remains at the core of the accountability processes of accounting, embedding, assurance, and reporting; accountability is about organizational responsiveness, or the extent to which an organization takes action on the basis of stakeholder engagement; and responsiveness requires the organizational capacities to learn and innovate effectively on the basis of stakeholder engagement. The AA1000 Series includes a statement on its use of this principle and the level of assurance its guidelines are able to provide, a statement of independence, and a statement about its professional competences. By using these guidelines, a company can better assess its goals in the social audit.[34] Table 12.4 lists some other do's and don'ts of social auditing.

TABLE 12.3	Framework for a Social Audit

- Secure commitment of top management and/or board of directors.
- Establish an audit committee.
- Define the scope of the audit process, including subject matter areas important to the social audit (e.g., environment, discrimination, employee rights, privacy, philanthropy, legal compliance, etc.).
- Review organizational mission, policies, goals, and objectives.
- Define the organization's social priorities as they relate to stakeholders.
- Identify the tools or methods the organization can employ to measure its achievement of objectives.
- Collect relevant information in each designated subject matter area, including internal data and data from concerned stakeholders.
- Summarize and analyze the data collected and compare the internal information to stakeholder expectations.
- Have the results verified by an independent agent (i.e., a social audit consultant, accounting firm that offers social auditing services, or nonprofit special-interest organization with social auditing experience).
- Report the findings to the audit committee and, if approved, to managers and stakeholders.

Sources: These steps are compatible with the social auditing methods prescribed by Warren Dow and Roy Crowe, *What Social Auditing Can Do for Voluntary Organizations* (Vancouver: Volunteer Vancouver, July 1999); "Social Audits and Accountability," Business for Social Responsibility, www.bsr.org/resourcecenter/index.html, accessed January 10, 2001; Sandra Waddock and Neil Smith, "Corporate Responsibility Audits: Doing Well by Doing Good," *Sloan Management Review* 41 (Winter 2000): 79.

TABLE 12.4	Do's and Don'ts of Social Auditing

Do's

- Do recognize that social auditing is specific to each organization's stakeholders, business purposes, and responsibilities.
- Do get departments, managers, and staff involved. This is especially true when deciding the scope of the audit.
- Do set up an internal audit system or department to report to the board of directors or other executive group.
- Do be careful in selecting an independent verifier, for they will have great access to the "heart and soul" of the company.
- Do allow a good amount of time for drafting and finalizing the final audit report.
- Do report formally and informally, publicly and internally.

Don'ts

- Don't start the audit without talking to someone who has performed one and reading other similar audits.
- Don't forget to focus on the benefits and the business case for social responsibility performance measurement and disclosure for all stakeholders.
- Don't forget to publicize the role of the audit team and its purpose. This allows for less fear and greater acceptance of the audit team.
- Don't forget that you may need other sources of expert advice such as survey design and analysis.
- Don't allow one stakeholder's issues to outweigh the others.
- Don't be afraid to include good and bad aspects of performance. It is better to point out your own faults than to have critics expose these on their terms.

Source: Based on Maria Sillanpaa and David Wheeler, "Integrated Ethical Auditing: The Body Shop International, UK," in *Building Corporate Accountability: The Emerging Practices in Social and Ethical Accounting, Auditing and Reporting,* ed. Simon Zadek, Peter Pruzan, and Richard Evans (London: Earthscan Publications, 1997), pp. 102–128.

Our framework encompasses a wide range of business responsibilities and relationships. The audit entails an individualized process and outcomes for a particular firm, as it requires the careful consideration of the unique issues that face a particular organization. For example, the auditing process at Kellogg Company includes the following:

> The Social Responsibility Committee of the Board of Directors shall identify, evaluate and monitor the social, political, environmental, occupational safety and health trends, issues, and concerns, domestic and foreign, which affect or could affect the Company's business or performance.
>
> The Committee shall make recommendations to assist in the formulation and adoption of policies, programs and practices concerning the matters set forth above including, but not limited to, environmental protection, employee and community health and safety, ethical business conduct, consumer affairs, alcohol and drug abuse, equal opportunity matters, and government relations, and shall monitor the Company's charitable contributions.[35]

FIGURE 12.1	Framework for Social Auditing and Disclosure at The Body Shop International

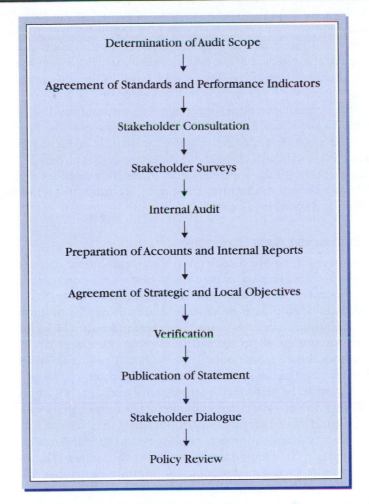

Source: Maria Sillanpaa and David Wheeler, "Integrated Ethical Auditing: The Body Shop International, UK," in *Building Corporate Accountability: The Emerging Practices in Social and Ethical Accounting, Auditing and Reporting,* ed. Simon Zadek, Peter Pruzan, and Richard Evans (London: Earthscan Publications Ltd., 1997), p. 116.

Figure 12.1 depicts The Body Shop's framework for its social auditing and disclosure process. Thus, although this chapter presents a structure and recommendations for a social audit, there is no generic approach to satisfy every firm's circumstances. However, the benefits and limitations that companies derive from social auditing are relatively consistent.

Secure Commitment of Top Management and/or Board of Directors

The first step in conducting any audit is securing the commitment of the firm's top management and/or its board of directors. In some cases, the push for a social audit may come directly from the board of directors in response to stakeholder concerns.

Changes in corporate governance associated with the 2002 Sarbanes-Oxley Act would suggest that the board of directors should be providing oversight for all auditing activities. In other cases, pressure for an audit may come from top managers looking for ways to create a competitive advantage for their firm by publicizing its social efforts. Some companies now have a senior officer in charge of social responsibility, and this individual may campaign for a social audit as a means of demonstrating the effectiveness of the firm's social initiatives. Regardless of where the impetus for an audit comes from, its success hinges on the full support of top management, particularly the CEO and the board of directors. In addition, court decisions related to the Federal Sentencing Guidelines for Organizations hold board members responsible for the ethical and legal compliance programs of the firms they oversee.

The Sarbanes-Oxley Act requires the board's financial audit committee to examine ethical standards throughout the organization as they relate to financial matters and to deal with the implementation of the code of ethics from top financial officers. Many of these issues relate to corporate governance issues as compensation, stock options, and conflicts of interest.

Establish an Audit Committee

The next step in our framework is the establishment of a committee to oversee the audit process. This committee works best when it establishes the scope of the audit and monitors its progress to ensure that it stays on track. On the basis of the best practices of corporate governance, audits should be monitored by an independent board of directors committee. The committee should include some members that have knowledge about the nature and role of social audits. The internal or external auditors should report directly to the board audit committee. The company being audited must get all services, other than the audit, approved by the audit committee if they are to be performed by the external auditors. It is important that external consultants do not have conflicts of interest or relationships with top management that may affect their independence. Companies may consider inputs from stakeholder members such as customers, employees, and shareholders in determining the scope of the audit. It is important to document the scope of the social audit in the beginning stages, even if modifications of the preliminary scope are made later.

Define the Scope of the Audit Process

The next step after establishing an audit committee is to define the scope of the audit process, including subject matter areas that are important to the social audit. The scope of an audit depends on the type of business, the risks faced by the business, and the available opportunities to manage social responsibility. The scope will determine the key subject matter areas of the company's social responsibilities (e.g., environment, governance, discrimination, employee rights, privacy, philanthropy, and legal compliance) that the audit should cover and on what basis they should be assessed. Assessments can be made on the basis of direct consultation, observation, surveys, or focus groups.[36] For example, the Chris Hani Baragwanath Hospital (CHBH) in Johannesburg, South Africa, conducted an audit that included focus groups with hospital management, doctors, nurses, related health professionals, support staff, and patients. On the basis of the trends uncovered in these focus groups, CHBH then developed a questionnaire for a survey, which it administered to a larger group of in-

TABLE 12.5	Sample Subject Matter and Stakeholder Audit Items

Please check the response (yes or no) that best answers the following questions:

YES	NO	HUMAN RESOURCE ISSUES
○	○	Does the company have a formal training program that focuses on social responsibility issues?
○	○	If training sessions exist, are they designed to cover legal, ethical, and subject matter social concerns that relate to daily operations?
○	○	Has someone been appointed to provide oversight for training and compliance of ethical, legal, and social issues?
○	○	Do employees have an independent mechanism, such as an 800 number or e-mail address to report social responsibility concerns?
○	○	Does the company have programs for helping employees manage work-related stress and conflict?

YES	NO	CUSTOMER RELATIONS ISSUES
○	○	Does the company have a feedback mechanism to obtain customer concerns/complaints?
○	○	Has the company established policies and a shared value system of fairness and honesty toward customers?
○	○	Is there a long-term focus on all aspects of customer welfare at the expense of short-run profits?
○	○	Are product quality, pricing, and service designed to deliver customers' expectations of value?
○	○	Are all the laws and legal rights related to customers communicated to employees?

YES	NO	COMMUNITY ISSUES
○	○	Does the company achieve its goals without compromising community ethical norms?
○	○	Are there environmental impact considerations for operations and organizational activities?
○	○	Does the company contribute resources to the community?
○	○	Are there programs to empower or reward employees who contribute to recognized community activities?
○	○	Does top management express organizational commitment to improving the quality of life and the general welfare of society?

YES	NO	DIVERSITY ISSUES
○	○	Are all laws protecting specific classes of employees and customers properly communicated?
○	○	Are systems in place to ensure compliance with all discrimination laws?
○	○	Does the company value and proactively embrace diversity in the workplace?
○	○	Is all communication designed to incorporate a philosophy of culture and diversity?
○	○	Has the company developed special educational or employment opportunities to contribute to diversity objectives?

dividual stakeholders.[37] The greater the number of stakeholders included in this stage, the more time and resources will be required to carry out the audit; however, a larger sample of stakeholders may yield a more useful variety of opinions about the company. Table 12.5 lists some sample subject matter areas and audit items for each of those areas.

Review Organizational Mission, Policies, Goals, and Objectives

Because social audits generally involve a comparison of organizational performance to the firm's policies and objectives, the audit process should include a review of the current mission statement and strategic objectives. The company's overall mission may incorporate social responsibility objectives, but these may also be found in separate documents focused on social responsibility. For instance, the Furniture Resource Centre states:

> Founded in 1988 by Nic Frances, we have grown from having a small community based response to poverty in inner city Liverpool to being today one of Britain's best known social businesses turning over millions of pounds. We are about personal and social change. We have a passion about all we do, aspire to be professional in all areas, and believe that our ambitious goals require relentless creativity and bravery.[38]

For example, the firm's ethics statement or statement of values may offer guidance for management on the transactions and human relationships that support the firm's reputation, thereby fostering confidence from stakeholders outside the firm.[39] This step should examine the formal documents that make explicit commitments to environmental or social responsibility, as well as less formal documents, including marketing materials, workplace policies, and ethics policies and standards for suppliers or vendors. Such a review may reveal a need to create additional statements or a new comprehensive mission statement or ethics policy to address deficiencies uncovered during this step.[40]

It is also important to examine all of the firm's policies and practices for the specific areas covered by the audit. For example, in an audit that includes environmental issues in its scope, this step would consider the company's goals and objectives on environmental matters, the company's environmental policies, the means for communicating these policies, and the effectiveness of this communication. This assessment should also look at whether and how managers are rewarded for meeting their goals and the systems available for employees to give and receive feedback. An effective social audit should review all these systems and assess their strengths and weaknesses.[41]

Define the Organization's Social Priorities

The next step in the auditing process is defining the organization's social priorities. Determining a company's social priorities is a balancing act, as it can be difficult to identify the needs and assess the priorities of each stakeholder. Because there are no legal requirements for social priorities, it is up to the board of directors's and management's strategic planning processes to determine appropriate duties and required action to deal with social issues. It is very important in this stage to articulate these priorities and values as a set of parameters or performance indicators that can be objectively and quantitatively assessed. Because the social audit is a structured report that offers quantitative and descriptive assessments, actions should be measurable by quantitative indicators. However, it is sometimes not possible to go beyond description.[42]

At some point, the firm must demonstrate action-oriented responsiveness to those social issues given top priority. Wells Fargo, for example, believes that education, jobs, and housing are fundamental community issues and therefore are the focus of the

firm's philanthropy programs. In line with these priorities, the bank has donated $300 million to nonprofit organizations and made $45 billion in loans for community reinvestment projects, including affordable housing development, commercial economic development, and small-business loans, especially to firms owned by women and minorities.[43] Likewise, Home Depot has identified affordable housing, at-risk youth, and the natural environment as social priorities. To address its environmental priority—and satisfy stakeholders' concerns about deforestation—the world's largest home-improvement retailer recently pledged to stop selling lumber and other products made from wood from endangered forests and to focus instead on wood products that have been certified as having come from responsibly managed forests. Also, www.HomeDepot.com has a social responsibility report on their web site to account for how they strive to be the best neighbor by contributing to local communities.[44]

Identify Tools or Methods for Accurate Measurement of Social Objectives

The sixth step in our framework is identifying the tools or methods that can be employed to measure the firm's achievement of social responsibility objectives. In this age of globalization and intense competitive pressures, such measurement tools are important to ensure that corporate social responsibilities are not compromised for higher profitability. Performance indicators can be used to quantitatively and qualitatively measure an organization's social as well as its financial performance. Some organizations, for example, have found that quantifying their community involvement can lead to more efficient and effective use of company resources to address community needs. The London Benchmarking Group has developed a template for companies to monitor and measure community involvement activities. This template helps companies to assess their community efforts and make continual improvement.[45]

Smith OBrien, a leading social audit firm, has identified some useful measurement techniques for social audits. The social balance sheet assigns dollar values to social impact as well as financial performance. The social performance index uses a numerical ranking system relating to corporate social performance. Stakeholder surveys incorporate the perceptions of the company from the stakeholders' point of view. The Body Shop has conducted such surveys based on interviews with its key stakeholders. Disclosure audits are similar to those provided in a company's financial statements, but relate to a firm's social responsibilities. Ben & Jerry's (owned by Unilever) has employed disclosure accounts in its social audit.

Collect Relevant Information

The next step in the auditing process is to collect relevant information for each designated subject matter area. To understand employee issues, for example, the auditing committee will work with the firm's human resources department in gathering employee survey information and other statistics and feedback. A thorough audit will include a review of all relevant reports, including external documents sent to government agencies and others. The information collected in this step will help determine baseline levels of compliance as well as the internal and external expectations of the company. This step will also identify where the company has, or has not, met its commitments, including those dictated by its mission statement and other policy documents. The documents reviewed in this process will vary from company to company, depending on the firm's size, nature of its business, and the scope of the audit process.[46]

Some techniques of evidence collection might involve examination of both internal and external documents, observation of the data-collection process (such as stakeholder consultation), and confirmation of information in the organization's accounting records. Ratio analysis of relevant indicators may also be used to identify any inconsistencies or unexpected patterns. The importance of objective measurement is the key consideration of the social auditor.[47] As with the financial audit, reliability depends on the source of all information collected. A document or acknowledgment that has been generated and circulated externally provides the most objective evidence. For example, New Belgium Brewing Company received the Better Business Bureau Marketplace Ethics Award and the Annual Business Ethics Award, granted by *Business Ethics* magazine. In response to this, an NBC *Today Show* segment about New Belgium's environmental stewardship provided evidence of how these actions can be favorable for a company. Another example of such a document might be the minutes of a focus group taken by an external stakeholder group that is sent directly to the social auditor. Documents that are internally generated and circulated are more subjective because they can more easily be altered. Sometimes internal documents are used for publicity or to motivate employees. In the context of a social audit, an example of the least-objective document would be an internally generated and circulated report on the hours of staff spent in community volunteering. This document might count hours that are questionable.[48]

Because stakeholder integration is so crucial to the social audit, a company's stakeholders need to be defined and interviewed during the data-collection stage. For

Jeff Lebesch and Kim Jordan founded New Belgium Brewing Company on a strategic philosophy of social responsibility. This philosophy includes a commitment to continuous improvement and the evaluation of programs related to the natural environment, philanthropy, employees, and other areas. (Courtesy, New Belgium Brewing Company)

most companies, stakeholders include employees, customers, investors, suppliers, community groups, regulators, nongovernmental organizations, and the media. Social audits typically include interviews and focus groups with these stakeholders to gain an understanding of their perceptions of the company. The greater the number of stakeholders included in this stage, the more time and resources will be required to carry out the audit; however, a larger sample of stakeholders may yield a more useful variety of opinions about the company. In multinational corporations, a decision must also be made on whether to include only the main office or headquarters region or to use all facilities around the globe in the audit.[49] Coca-Cola must be concerned about the hundreds of independent bottlers and distributors around the world. All of these relationships are a part of Coca-Cola's social performance.

Because employees carry out a business's operations, including its social initiatives, understanding employee issues is vital. Indicators that are useful for assessing employee issues include staff turnover and employee satisfaction. High turnover rates could indicate poor working conditions, an unethical climate, inadequate compensation, or general employee dissatisfaction. Companies can analyze these factors to determine key areas for improvement.[50] For example, Wild Planet Toys, as part of its annual social assessment, surveys employees on a range of issues including company mission, product quality, diversity, the workplace, the environment, and community outreach. The results of this process, which are provided to employees, have led to clearer priorities and better internal coordination, as well as to a revised mission statement and the addition of long-term disability insurance to the benefits package.[51] Most companies recognize that employees will behave in ways that result in recognition and rewards and avoid behavior that results in punishment. Thus, companies can design and implement human resources policies and procedures for recruiting, hiring, promoting, compensating, and rewarding employees to encourage behaviors that further social responsibility efforts.[52]

Customers are another primary stakeholder group because their patronage determines financial success. Providing meaningful feedback through a number of mechanisms is critical to creating and maintaining customer satisfaction. Through surveys and customer-initiated communication systems such as response cards, e-mail, and toll-free telephone systems, an organization can monitor and respond to customer issues and social performance. Sears, for example, surveyed more than 2 million customers to investigate attitudes toward products, advertising, and the social performance of the company.

A growing number of investors is seeking companies that conduct social audits to include in their investment portfolios. They are becoming more aware of the financial benefits desired from socially responsible management systems—as well as the negative consequences of a lack of responsibility. One study found that publicity about unethical corporate behavior lowers stock prices.[53] Additionally, many investors simply do not want to invest in companies that engage in certain business practices, such as cigarette production, or in companies that fail to provide adequate working conditions, such as sweatshops. Thus, it is critical for companies to understand the issues that this very important group of stakeholders have and what they expect from corporations they have invested in, both financially and socially.

The community is another significant stakeholder group. Community groups such as local business chambers, schools, and hospitals, as well as environmental groups, can be asked to comment on the social responsibility initiatives of an organization. As with customers, surveys can be used to obtain community feedback. Such surveys may be administered on a random basis (e.g., every tenth listing in the local telephone book) or through regular contact with various groups. Web sites and e-mail also provide opportunities for interaction with community stakeholder groups.

Social responsibility should be assessed from the vantage point of each of the previously mentioned stakeholders. Their respective assessments can be broken down into four main components—economic, legal, ethical, and philanthropy. Table 12.6 provides sample questions that ensure a company is assessing its social responsibility from each stakeholder perspective and should be modified to meet the unique attributes of each company.

Feedback from these stakeholders may be obtained through standardized surveys, interviews, and focus groups. Companies can also encourage stakeholder exchanges by inviting specific groups together for discussions. Such meetings also may include an office or facility tour or a field trip by company representatives to sites in the com-

TABLE 12.6	Sample Stakeholder Social Responsibility Concerns			
STAKEHOLDERS	**SOCIAL RESPONSIBILITIES**			
	ECONOMIC	**LEGAL**	**ETHICAL**	**PHILANTHROPIC**
Employees	Are salary, benefits, and promotions perceived to be fair and equitable to all employees?	Does the organization train employees on effective legal compliance?	Have the company's ethical standards been communicated to employees?	Does the organization encourage and enable employees to contribute to the community?
Customers	Does the company adhere to fair pricing and maintain acceptable product quality?	Does the company participate in deceptive or unfair marketing activities?	Are customers' rights and concerns about products considered in all decisions?	Does the company seek to share in philanthropic activities important to customers?
Investors	Has the organization increased its profitability through socially responsible business practices?	Are there any potential illegal activities that could damage investors?	Is there an effective values program to enhance organizational performance?	Is the company using its resources to strategically improve its philanthropic efforts?
Community Groups	Does the community benefit from the economic impact of the company?	Are the legal rights of all community stakeholders considered?	Are the ethical standards of the company consistent with those of the community?	Does the company invest in the community through grants, fundraising, and community service?

The questions on the chart are mere examples of potential questions that can be asked of the stakeholders. Stakeholder perceptions related to each component of social responsibility should be obtained through additional questions.

munity. Regardless of how information about stakeholder views is collected, the primary objective is to generate a variety of opinions about how the company is perceived and whether it is fulfilling stakeholders' expectations.[54]

Analyze the Data

The next step in the auditing process is to compare the company's internal perceptions to those discovered during the stakeholder assessment stage and then to summarize these findings. During this phase, the audit committee should draw some conclusions about the information obtained in the previous stages. These conclusions may involve descriptive assessments of the findings, including the costs and benefits of social responsibility, strengths and weaknesses in the firm's policies and practices, and feedback from stakeholders, as well as issues that should be addressed in future audits. In some cases, it may be appropriate to weigh the findings against standards identified earlier, both quantitatively and qualitatively.[55]

Data analysis should also include an examination of how other organizations in the industry are performing in the designated subject matter areas. The audit committee can investigate the successes of some other firm that is considered the best in a particular area and compare the auditing company's performance to the benchmark established by that firm. Some common examples of benchmark information available from most corporate social audits include employee or customer satisfaction, the perception of the company by community groups, and the impact of the company's philanthropy. For example, the Ethics Officer Association (EOA) conducts research on legal and ethical issues in the workplace. The studies allow members of the EOA to compare their responses to the aggregate results obtained through the study.[56] Such comparisons can help the audit committee identify best practices for a particular industry or establish a baseline of minimum requirements for ethical compliance programs. It is important to note that a wide variety of standards are emerging that apply to social corporate accountability. The aim of these standards is to create a tool for benchmarking and a framework for businesses to follow.[57]

Verify the Results

The next step is to have the results of the data analysis verified by an independent party, such as a social audit consultant, a financial accounting firm that offers social auditing services (e.g., KPMG), or a nonprofit special-interest group with auditing experience (e.g., the New Economics Foundation). The international consulting firm Arup is committed to social responsibility and discusses with clients and governments the promotion of more sustainable performance. From this, the company identified the need for a robust and accepted high-quality social responsibility reporting system for organizations. They created a program called Corporate SpeAR, which is an independent, auditable, transparent reporting tool. It measures and records an organization's sustainable performance and guides development of strategic policy. The tool is groundbreaking in the way that it will provide the financial community with a transparent and verifiable means of analyzing a company's performance, which will also help support their inclusion into ethical frameworks.[58]

Business for Social Responsibility, a nonprofit organization supporting social responsibility initiatives and reporting, has defined verification as an independent assessment of the quality, accuracy, and completeness of a company's social report. Independent verification offers a measure of assurance that the company has reported its performance fairly and honestly, as well as providing an assessment of its social and environmental reporting systems.[59] As such, verification by an independent party gives stakeholders confidence in a company's audit and lends the audit report credibility and objectivity.[60]

Although independent validation of social audits is not required, many companies choose to have their social auditing efforts verified, much as they have their financial reports certified by a reputable auditing firm. Many financial auditors believe that an independent, objective assessment of an audit can be provided only if the auditor has

played no role in the reporting process; in other words, consulting and auditing should be distinctly separate roles. The subject of auditor independence has been controversial. In 2002, the Sarbanes-Oxley Act established a requirement for preventing conflicts of interest by financial auditors, prohibiting most consulting work's being done by the same firm that conducts the audit.[61]

The process of verifying the results of an audit should involve standard procedures that control the reliability and validity of the information. As with a financial audit, auditors can apply substantive tests to detect material misstatements in the social audit data and analysis. The tests commonly used in financial audits—confirmation, observation, tracing, vouching, analytical procedures, inquiry, and recomputing—can be used in social audits as well. For example, positive confirmations can be sent to the participants of a stakeholder focus group to affirm that the reported results are consistent with those of the focus group. Likewise, a social auditor can observe the actual working conditions in a company's manufacturing plant to verify statements made in the report. And, just as a financial auditor traces from the supporting documents to the financial statements to test their completeness, a social auditor or verifier may examine customer complaints in order to attest to the completeness of the reporting of such complaints. The auditor can examine canceled checks paid to local charities to vouch for the stated amounts of donations. A social auditor can employ analytical procedures by examining plausible relationships, such as the prior year's employee turnover ratio or the related ratio that is commonly reported within the industry. With the reporting firm's permission, an auditor can contact the company's legal counsel to inquire about pending environmental or civil rights litigation. Finally, a social auditor can recompute salaries reported to attest to the equal pay assertion that companies report.[62]

Global Initiatives

Social Reporting at Johnson & Johnson

Johnson & Johnson (J&J), based in New Brunswick, New Jersey, has achieved the enviable position of being one of the most respected companies in the world. The company sells $32 billion worth of consumer, professional, and pharmaceutical/diagnostic products in more than 175 countries through 198 companies operating in 54 countries. In 2003, J&J was acknowledged for having the best corporate reputation in the United States for the fourth straight year. In fact, the firm has been widely recognized as one of *Fortune* magazine's "Most Admired Companies," *Industry Week* magazine's "World's 100 Best Managed Companies," and *Working Mother* magazine's "100 Best Companies for Working Mothers," and it has won numerous awards for its diversity, philanthropy, and environmental initiatives over its 117 years of operation.

The company's strong reputation stems in part from its credo, written in 1943 by then-chair Robert Wood Johnson. The credo begins, "We believe our first responsibility is to the doctors, nurses and patients, to mothers and fathers, and all others who use our products and services. In meeting their needs, everything we do must be of high quality." Not only is this document displayed in company offices worldwide, posted prominently on J&J's web site, and etched on an eight-foot-tall limestone structure at corporate headquarters, it is the topic of a full day in executive training programs, and its impact is assessed regularly through extensive employee surveys. The credo provides guidance for even the toughest corporate decision, including two recalls of Tylenol during the 1980s after some bottles of the product were found to be contaminated with cyanide, causing eight deaths. The company's rapid and intense response to the crisis helped it retain consumer's trust, and Tylenol remains a leading brand today.

Johnson & Johnson's credo specifies that the company is "responsible to the communities in which we live and work and to the world community as well." To communicate its efforts to fulfill this responsibility, J&J has begun to release annual reports detailing its citizenship initiatives in specific areas. One of these reports, the *Worldwide Contributions Program Annual Report,* details the company's philanthropic activities around the world. In a recent re-

---

Additionally, the financial auditor may be asked to provide a letter to the company's management to highlight inconsistencies in the reporting process. The auditor may request a reply from management regarding particular points raised in the letter, indicating actions that management intends to take to address problems or weaknesses. The financial auditor is required to report to the internal audit committee (or equivalent) any significant adjustments found during the audit, disagreements with management, and difficulties encountered during the audit. In reference to the social guidelines on reportable conditions, it seems unlikely that a social auditor would be requested by the company's management to highlight reporting inconsistencies if they had any true consequence on the auditor's report. Therefore, social auditors should be required to report to the company's audit committee the same issues that a financial auditor would report.[63]

Report the Findings

The final step is in our framework is issuing the social audit report. This involves reporting the audit findings to the relevant internal parties and, if approved, to exter-

port, the company highlighted its efforts to collaborate with a variety of organizations "to implement programs that create healthy futures for many people in need." The report detailed J&J's contributions, in grants and products, to a variety of health initiatives around the world, such as a diabetes-education program in Zimbabwe, a burn-treatment center in South Africa, a children's hospital in France, and a hospital infection-control program in Vietnam. In sum, the company donated $230 million to health-related organizations, community-development organizations, disaster-relief efforts, and university programs around the world in 2002.

Since 1996, J&J has also produced an annual report highlighting its activities in the areas of the environment, health, and safety. The 2001 *Environmental, Health, and Safety Report,* which adopted the theme, "Healthy People, Healthy Planet Explorer," presented case studies that demonstrate the company's commitment to the environment, health, and safety around the world. The report summarized the firm's performance in all three areas and compared these results to its goals. Although the firm exceeded its goals on most measures, the report also clearly indicted where the company failed to do so, thereby pinpointing areas for improvement.

Johnson & Johnson's annual social reports allow the company to demonstrate its commitment to social responsibility and achievement of associated objectives, identify areas for improvement, justify expenditures to stockholders and investors, and address stakeholder concerns. These efforts also help the company's venerable brands maintain their trusted image with consumers. For example, in the reputation survey by Harris Interactive and the Reputation Institute, J&J ranked first overall, first in emotional appeal, and first in products and services. This level of trust provides evidence that J&J's half-century-old credo is far more than a poster on the wall of corporate headquarters.

Sources:
Ronald Alsop, "Corporate Reputations Are Earned with Trust, Reliability, Study Shows," *Wall Street Journal Interactive,* September 23, 1999, http://interactive.wsj.com; Ronald Alsop, "Johnson & Johnson Turns Up Tops Thanks to Its Credo, and to Babies," *Wall Street Journal Interactive,* September 23, 1999, http://interactive.wsj.com; "Awards and Recognition," Johnson & Johnson, http://www.jnj.com/wo_is_jnj/awards.html, accessed March 28, 2003; "Social & Environmental Responsibility," www.juj.com, accessed March 28, 2003; "Johnson & Johnson Ranks #1 in National Corporate Reputation Survey for the Fourth Year," *Harris Interactive,* www.harrisinteractive.com, accessed March 28, 2003.

nal stakeholders in a formal report. Although some companies prefer not to release the results of their auditing efforts to the public, more companies are choosing to make their reports available to a broad group of stakeholders. Some companies, including U.K.-based Co-operative Bank, integrate the results of the social audit with their annual report of financial documents and other important information. Other companies, including The Body Shop, Shell, and VanCity, also make their social audit reports available on the World Wide Web.[64] Based on the guidelines established by the Global Reporting Initiative and AccountAbility, the social report should spell out the purpose and scope of the audit, the methods used in the audit process (evidence gathering and evaluation), the role of the (preferably independent) auditor, any auditing guidelines followed by the auditor, and any reporting guidelines followed by the company.[65]

As mentioned earlier, the social audit may be similar to a financial audit, but their forms are quite different. In a financial audit, the statement of auditing standards dictates literally every word of a financial audit report in terms of content and placement. Based on the auditor's findings, the report issued can be, among other modifications, an unqualified opinion (i.e., the financial statements are fairly stated), a qualified opinion (i.e., although the auditor believes the financial statements are fairly stated, an unqualified opinion is not possible because of limitations placed on the auditor or minor issues with disclosure or accounting principles), an adverse opinion (i.e., the financial statements are not fairly stated), or a disclaimer of opinion (i.e., the auditor didn't have full access to records or discovered a conflict of interest). The technicality of these various opinions has enormous consequences to the company.

Figure 12.2 depicts the standard (unqualified opinion) independent auditor's disclaimer issued at the end of a financial audit report. Every word has significant meaning. Notice, for example, that the introductory paragraph explicitly states the responsibilities: Management is responsible for the financial statements, and the auditors are responsible only for offering an opinion as to their veracity and validity. Another paragraph discusses the generally accepted auditing standards and states that the auditors can provide only "reasonable assurance" with regard to the financial statement assertions. Such disclaimers never express absolute assurance due to the many limiting factors such as collusion, error, and cost. The last paragraph of the disclaimer begins, "In our opinion." Here, the auditors acknowledge the risks associated with an audit. They simply state their opinion, but they do not say, "We guarantee," "The fact is," or "We have no reason to believe." The end of the report includes the firm's signature and the date of the report. Social audit reports have not yet reached even this level of scrutiny, but it is desirable to move toward more-objective social audits, using the standards typically applied to financial audits. Figure 12.3 provides an example of an ideal standard social audit report.

FIGURE 12.2 **Standard Independent Auditor's Disclaimer**

To the Board of Directors and Stockholders of XYZ Company:

We have audited the accompanying balance sheet of XYZ Company as of December 31, 2004, and the related statements of income, retained earnings, and cash flows for the year then ended. These financial statements are the responsibility of the company's management. Our responsibility is to express an opinion on these financial statements based on our audit.

We conducted our audit in accordance with generally accepted auditing standards. Those standards require that we plan and perform the audit to obtain reasonable assurance about whether the financial statements are free of material misstatement. An audit includes examining, on a test basis, evidence supporting the amounts and disclosures in the financial statements. An audit also includes assessing the accounting principles used and significant estimates made by my management, as well as evaluating the overall financial statement presentation. We believe that our audit provides a reasonable basis for our opinion.

In our opinion, the financial statements referred to above present fairly, in all material respects, the financial position of XYZ Company as of December 31, 2004, and the results of its operations and its cash flows for the year then ended in conformity with generally accepted accounting principles.

Firm's Signature and Report Date

FIGURE 12.3	Ideal Independent Auditor's Disclaimer

To the Board of Directors and Stakeholders of XYZ Company:

We have audited the social responsibility assertions of XYZ Company as of December 31, 2004. These assertions are the responsibility of the company's management. Our responsibility is to express an opinion on these assertions based on our audit.

We conducted our audit in accordance with *generally accepted social auditing standards.* Those standards require that we plan and perform the audit to obtain reasonable assurance about whether the social assertions, relating to the economic, legal, ethical, and philanthropic responsibilities of the company, are free of material misstatement. An audit includes examining, on a test basis, evidence supporting the social responsibility assertions of the company. An audit also includes an independent assessment of the stakeholders' perspectives, as well as the methods used by management to report on such perspectives. We believe that our audit provides a reasonable basis for our opinion.

In our opinion, the social responsibility assertions referred to above present fairly, in all material respects, the position of social responsibility of XYZ Company as of December 31, 2004, in conformity with *generally accepted social responsibility principles.*

Firm's Signature and Report Date

The Strategic Importance of Social Auditing

Although the concept of auditing implies an official examination of social performance, many organizations audit their performance informally. Any attempt to verify outcomes and to compare them with standards can be considered an auditing activity. Many smaller firms probably would not use the word *audit*, but they do perform auditing activities.

The social audit, like the financial audit, should be conducted regularly instead of only when there are problems or questions about a firm's priorities and conduct. In other words, the social audit is not a control process to be used during a crisis, although it can pinpoint potential problem areas and generate solutions. A social audit may be comprehensive and encompass all of the social impact areas of a business, or it can be specific and focus on one or two areas. One specialized audit could be an environmental-impact audit in which specific environmental issues, such as proper waste disposal, are analyzed. Other areas for specialized audits include diversity, ethical conduct, employee benefits, and workplace conditions. Table 12.7 lists some issues related to quality and effectiveness in social auditing.

Social audits can present several problems. They can be expensive and time-consuming, and selecting the auditors may be difficult if objective, qualified personnel are not available. Employees sometimes fear comprehensive evaluations, especially by outsiders, and in such cases, social audits can be extremely disruptive.

| **TABLE 12.7** | Quality and Effectiveness in Social Responsibilitiy |

- Inclusivity means that the audit process must include the views of all the principal stakeholders, not just the "noisy" stakeholders. Therefore, the assessment is based on many different views rather than just one.
- Comparability is the ability to compare the organization's performance from one audit period to another.
- Completeness means that no area of the company is excluded from the audit. This eliminates any "choice" picking of the best areas of the company, and it gives a more accurate and honest view.
- Evolution is what the company goes through when it fully commits to the social responsibility audit.
- Management policies and systems are needed to ensure that the process of auditing is done in a controlled manner.
- Disclosure of the information obtained from the social responsibility audit is necessary if it is to truly be effective. The question of how many people the information should be disclosed to is a continual debate.
- External verification is to ensure that the audit is done appropriately and that nothing is hidden in the information.
- Continuous improvement makes sure that the audit process is not just retrospective, but uncovers areas for change and improvement.

Source: "How to Do It," in *Building Corporate Accountability: The Emerging Practices in Social and Ethical Accounting, Auditing and Reporting,* ed. Simon Zadek, Peter Pruzan, and Richard Evans (London: Earthscan Publications Ltd., 1997), pp. 35–49.

Despite these problems, however, auditing social responsibility performance can generate many benefits, as we have seen throughout this chapter. Hundreds of companies all over the world have been issuing social responsibility reports since the 1970s to accrue these benefits.[66] The social audit provides an assessment of a company's overall social performance as compared to its core values, ethics policy, internal operating practices, management systems, and, most important, the expectations of key stakeholders.[67] As such, social responsibility reports are a useful management tool to help companies identify and define their social impacts and facilitate improvements in vital areas.[68] This assessment can be used to reallocate resources and activities as well as to focus on new opportunities for social contributions. The audit process can also help companies fulfill their mission statements in ways that boost profits and reduce risks.[69] More specifically, a company may seek continual improvement in its employment practices, environmental responsibilities, customer and community relations, and ethical behavior in its general business practices.[70] Thus, the audit can pinpoint areas where improving operating practices can improve both bottom-line profits and stakeholder relationships.[71]

Most managers view profitability and social responsibility as a trade-off, which prevents them from moving from an "either/or" mindset to a more proactive "both/and" approach.[72] However, the auditing process can demonstrate the positive impact of social responsibility efforts on the firm's bottom line, convincing managers—and other primary stakeholders—of the value of more socially responsible business practices.[73]

Summary

Social auditing is the process of assessing and reporting a business's performance in fulfilling the economic, legal, ethical, and philanthropic social responsibilities expected of it by its stakeholders. The social audit provides an objective approach for an organization to demonstrate its commitment to improving strategic planning, including social accountability. There are many reasons why companies choose to understand, report on, and improve their social responsibility performance.

A social audit can satisfy stakeholder demands for increased transparency and greater disclosure; this can help amend and advance relationships with investors, customers, suppliers, regulators, the media, and the community while helping these stakeholders better understand the firm's goals and operations. Dialogs established with stakeholders during the audit process may contribute insight about a firm's current situation, how various stakeholders perceive it, issues that could create threats for the company in the future, and opportunities (or weaknesses) of which the company is not yet aware. The process of social auditing can also help an organization identify potential risks and liabilities and improve its compliance with the law. A significant benefit of social auditing is that it may help prevent public relations crises associated with ethical or legal misconduct.

Although social audits provide many benefits for companies and their stakeholders, they do have the potential to create risks. In particular, the process of auditing cannot guarantee that the firm will not face challenges related to its efforts. Nonetheless, a core of minimum standards for corporate social performance is evolving.

Whereas a financial audit is concerned primarily with a company's claims about its financial performance, the social audit is interested in a company's assertions about its social responsibility. Unlike financial audits, social auditing is voluntary. Both social auditing and financial auditing employ the same procedures and processes in order to create a system of integrity and objective reporting. Both types of audits begin with collecting information to understand the company's industry, determining the scope of the audit, and documenting the details of the audit program. This information must be of high quality, consistent, complete, material, segregated, and collected in a controlled environment.

A social audit entails an individualized process and individualized outcomes for each firm, as it requires the careful consideration of the unique issues that face a particular organization. The first step in this process is securing the commitment of the firm's top management and/or its board of directors. The second step involves establishing a committee to oversee the audit process. In the third step, the audit committee, or an outside consultant, defines the scope of the audit process, including important subject matter areas. The scope depends on the type of business, the risks faced by the business, and available opportunities to manage social responsibility. The fourth step involves a review of the current mission statement, strategic objectives, and organizational policies, goals, and objectives. The fifth step defines the organization's social priorities. These should be articulated as a set of measurable parameters or performance indicators.

The sixth step involves identifying the tools or methods that can be employed to measure the firm's achievement of social objectives. The seventh step involves collecting relevant information for each designated subject matter area. Collection techniques might include examination of internal and external documents, observation of the data-collection process, and confirmation of information in the organization's accounting records. Social audits typically include interviews and focus groups with stakeholders to gain an understanding of their perceptions of the company. The eighth step compares the company's internal perceptions to those discovered during the stakeholder assessment stage and then summarizes these findings. This analysis may also include benchmarking, or comparing organizational performance in designated subject matter areas to other organizations or industry standards.

The ninth step is verification by an independent party. Verification offers a measure of assurance that the company has reported its social performance fairly and honestly, as well as an assessment of its social and environmental reporting systems. The process of verifying the results of an audit should involve standard procedures that control the reliability and validity of the information. The final step in the auditing process is issuing the social audit report.

Although the concept of auditing implies an official examination of social performance, many organizations audit their performance informally. The social audit should be conducted regularly. Although social auditing may present problems, it can generate many benefits. Through the auditing process, a firm can demonstrate the positive impact of social responsibility efforts on its bottom line, convincing stakeholders of the value of more socially responsible business practices.

Key Term

social auditing (p. 359)

Discussion Questions

1. What is a social audit? Should a firm conduct an audit before or after developing a social responsibility initiative?
2. Name some benefits and limitations of reporting the social audit. How should a company address negative issues that are discovered in an audit?
3. What are the major differences between a financial audit and a social audit? How are they similar? Should financial audit rules always be applied to a social audit?
4. Why should top management be involved in and committed to developing a social audit?
5. How should the scope of the social audit be defined?
6. Why should social priorities be translated from abstract principles and values into performance indicators that offer a minimum of objectivity?
7. What types of data should be collected during a social audit? Where can a company obtain this information?
8. What is the difference between a qualified opinion, an unqualified opinion, and an adverse opinion and disclaimer of opinion in a financial audit? How are these opinions relevant to a social audit?
9. Should the organization or individual who verifies the results of the audit be independent? Why or why not?
10. Should a company release audit results that disclose negative information?

Experiential Exercise

Visit Vancouver City Savings Credit Union's (VanCity) web site (http://www.vancity.com) and find its most recent social audit. Review the audit document. What reasons for conducting the audit are given? Where are VanCity's strengths and opportunities for growth with stakeholders? Provide three recommendations on how VanCity could improve its auditing process and report.

What Would You Do?

The situation seemed crystal clear to Karey Ponds. Why, then, was the rest of the department willing to look the other way? Karey worked for United Foods, a company that owns and operates 142 restaurants in sixteen states. The restaurants use one name, specialize in pizza and Italian food, and are themed according to local culture. The restaurant's primary target markets are families and large groups, so they are located in cities that attract conventions and tourists.

United Foods was participating in a new program advocated by the National Food and Restaurant Association. An industry council organized through the association was focused on social responsibility and recently completed a position paper on the importance of social auditing. United Foods was very active in the association and agreed to participate in a pilot program for social auditing in the food and restaurant industry. Top managers selected a consulting firm to perform the external audit. The audit team was visiting the company this week to meet with various departments and individuals. The audit team was determining successes and problems that existed with primary stakeholders, including customers, employees, and suppliers.

As a quality manager, Karey's job was to monitor the quality, freshness, and taste of food prepared and served at the restaurants. Karey was in charge of restaurants in five states. The company recently implemented formal and standardized guidelines for all aspects of restaurant operations, including designated suppliers, kitchen equipment, recipes, plate presentations, em-

ployee training, electronic systems, and so forth. Two assistant managers, who reported to Karey, traveled to restaurants and conducted both scheduled and non-scheduled site visits.

After their latest trips, the assistant managers shared their informal reports and were surprised to learn that a trend was developing with a new product being served at the restaurants. The entree was not meeting sales projections, so many kitchens had "expired" entrees in their freezers. The expired entrees were supposed to be discarded within two days. Restaurant managers were slowing their wholesale orders of the entree through the electronic system, but retail sales figures did not mesh with the situation. Karey and the assistant managers assumed that some restaurants were serving expired entrees instead of ordering new ones. Unsold entrees were a drain on restaurant profitability. In Karey's mind, this was the only explanation for the discrepancies between retail sales and wholesale orders.

At a weekly meeting of all quality managers, Karey expressed concerns about this new finding. Other managers felt that, at this point, it was conjecture and recommended multiple, unannounced site visits before the violation became "official." Karey was firm in her belief, but valued her colleagues' insights and experiences. They went on to discuss the importance of documentation and verification. They reminded Karey that the Information Technology group was still working out problems with the electronic procurement and sales reporting system. Karey was scheduled to meet with two people from the social audit team this afternoon. What would you do?

Cases

I. Successful Management of Social Responsibility

1. Coca-Cola Company: Crisis and Reputation Management

2. Wainwright Bank & Trust: Banking on Values

3. Conoco's Decision: The First Annual President's Award for Business Ethics

4. Home Depot: Commitment to Social Responsibility

5. New Belgium Brewing Company: Environmental and Social Concerns

6. DoubleClick: Privacy on the Internet

II. Challenges in Social Responsibility

7. Enron: Questionable Accounting Leads to Collapse

8. WorldCom: Actions Lead to Corporate Reform

9. Martha Stewart: Insider-Trading Scandal

10. Arthur Andersen: Questionable Accounting Practices

11. Tyco International: Leadership Crisis

12. Global Crossing: Inflated Sales Lead to Bankruptcy

Coca-Cola Company: Crisis and Reputation Management

This case was prepared by Debbie Thorne McAlister and Kevin Sample for classroom discussion, rather than to illustrate either effective or ineffective handling of an administrative, ethical, or legal decision by an individual or management.

Retirement after just two years at the helm of one of the most-recognized companies in the world is not a commonplace occurrence in business today. However, Doug Ivester did just that when he announced he was resigning and retiring as chair and chief executive officer of the Coca-Cola Company in 1999. He did so with the "encouragement" of Warren Buffett and Herbert Allen, two of Coca-Cola's most powerful board members. Ivester's tenure was short, and his earlier boast of being able to "generate so much cash I could make everybody's head spin" proved to be wishful thinking.

Before he took the reins at Atlanta-based Coca-Cola, Ivester was heralded for his ability to handle the financial flows and details of the soft-drink giant. Former chief executive Roberto Goizueta had carefully groomed Ivester for the top position, which he assumed in October 1997 after Goizueta's untimely death. However, Ivester seemed to lack leadership in handling a series of crises that hurt Coca-Cola in many ways, causing some to doubt "Big Red's" reputation and its prospects for the future. For a company with a rich history of marketing prowess and financial performance, Ivester's departure represented a high-profile glitch on a relatively clean record in 100 years of business. In April 2000, Doug Daft, the company's former president and chief operating officer, replaced Ivester as the new chief executive at Coca-Cola. Although Daft's tenure has been occasionally rocky, the company has largely rebounded from the negative events that occurred in the late 1990s. For example, the company's performance in 2002 included its highest operating income ever and product sales that far outpaced industry averages. In a 2002 survey of business leaders, Daft was named the twenty-ninth most respected business leader in the world.

History of the Coca-Cola Company

The Coca-Cola Company is the world's largest beverage company, and it markets four of the world's top five leading soft drinks: Coke, Diet Coke, Fanta, and Sprite. The company also operates the largest distribution system in the world, which enables it to serve customers and businesses in more than 200 countries. Coca-Cola estimates that more than one billion servings of its products are consumed every day. For much of its early history, Coca-Cola focused on cultivating markets within the United States.

Coca-Cola and its archrival, PepsiCo, have long fought "cola wars" in the United States, but Coca-Cola, recognizing additional market potential, pursued international opportunities in an effort to dominate the global soft-drink industry. By 1993, Coca-Cola controlled 45 percent of the global soft-drink market, while PepsiCo received just 15 percent of its profits from international sales. By the late 1990s, Coca-Cola had gained more than 50 percent of the global market share in the soft-drink industry. Pepsi continues to target select international markets in order to gain a greater foothold in international markets. Although Coke and Pepsi are almost neck and neck in the United States, 60 percent of Coca-Cola's sales now come from outside the United States. As the late Roberto Goizueta once said, "Coca-Cola used to be an American company with a large international business. Now we are a large international company with a sizable American business."

Coca-Cola has been a successful company since its inception in the late 1800s. PepsiCo, although it was founded about the same time as Coca-Cola, did not become a strong competitor until after World War II, when it began to gain market share. The rivalry intensified in the mid-1960s, and the "cola wars" began in earnest. Today, the duopoly wages war primarily on several international fronts. The companies are engaged in an extremely competitive—and sometimes personal—rivalry, with occasional accusations of false market share reports, anticompetitive behavior, and other questionable business conduct. These accusations are not commonplace, however, and in all actuality, PepsiCo and Coca-Cola appreciate one another. Without this fierce competition, neither would be as good a company as it is today.

Coca-Cola's Reputation

Coca-Cola is the most-recognized trademark and brand name in the world today. The company has always demonstrated a strong market orientation, making strategic decisions and taking actions to attract, satisfy, and retain customers. During World War II, for example, then company president Robert Woodruff committed to selling Coke to members of the armed services for just a nickel a bottle. As one analyst said later, "Customer loyalty never came cheaper." This philosophy helped make Coke a truly global brand, with its trademark brands and colors recognizable on cans, bottles, and advertisements around the world. The advance of Coca-Cola products into almost every country in the world demonstrated the company's international market orientation and improved its ability to gain brand recognition. These efforts contributed to the company's strong reputation.

In 1999, Coca-Cola ranked second in a survey by Harris Interactive and the Reputation Institute, which employed a standardized measure based on twenty perceived attributes from which they derived a reputation quotient for each company. The rankings grouped these attributes into six main areas of reputation. Within these areas, consumers perceived Coca-Cola as second in emotional appeal (how much the company is liked), third in financial performance, and fourth in vision and leadership (demonstrated strong leadership and clear vision).

The following year, however, Coca-Cola failed to make the top ten of *Fortune*'s annual "America's Most Admired Companies" list for the first time in ten years, although it still ranked first in the beverage industry. Problems that the company experienced in 1999, including leadership issues, poor economic performance, and other upheavals, may have affected its standing in the *Fortune* list. The company also dropped out of the top 100 in *Business Ethics* magazine's annual list of "100 Best Corporate Citizens" in 2001. For a company that had spent years on both lists, this was disappointing, but perhaps it was not unexpected, given the recent crises.

The company rebounded by 2002, when it scored highest in the beverage industry on *Fortune* magazine's measure of social responsibility, and *Business Ethics* magazine's survey highlighted Coca-Cola's relationships with stakeholders. In the 2002 Harris Interactive Reputation Quotient survey, Coca-Cola ranked third in overall reputation. The company ranked fourth in the *Financial Times* World's Most Respected Companies poll in 2002. These gains are an important step in the company's efforts to reclaim its top reputation.

Coca-Cola's promise states that the company exists "to benefit and refresh everyone who is touched by our business." It has successfully done this by continually increasing market share and profits to a point to where Coca-Cola is one of the most-recognized brands in the world. Because the company is so well known, the industry in which it operates is so pervasive, and it has such a strong history of market orientation, the company has developed a number of social responsibility initiatives to further enhance its trademarks. These initiatives are guided by the company's core beliefs in the marketplace, workplace, community, and environment.

Social Responsibility Focus

Coca-Cola has made local education and community improvement programs a top priority for its philanthropic initiatives, some of which are implemented through various Coca-Cola foundations. These foundations "support the promise of a better life for people and their communities." For example, since reentering the Vietnamese market in 1994, Coca-Cola has invested time and money to help educate Vietnamese youth, in collaboration with the Ministry of Education and Training and the National Ho Chi Minh Communist Youth Union. These National Education Programs in Vietnam consist of fourteen Coca-Cola Learning Centers, which teach computer skills and an "English in Vietnam" language program and promote an annual national schools environmental awareness contest. Such programs are important in helping Coca-Cola aid the community, but they also foster long-term relationships with consumers, including possible future leaders of the country.

Coca-Cola also offers grants to various colleges and universities in more than half of the United States, as well as numerous international grants. In addition to grants,

Coca-Cola provides scholarships to more than 170 colleges, and this number will grow to 287 schools over the next four years. It includes 30 tribal colleges belonging to the American Indian College Fund. Coca-Cola has also been involved with the Hispanic Scholarship Fund. Such initiatives help enhance the Coca-Cola name and trademark, and thus ultimately benefit shareholders.

The company recognizes its responsibilities on a global scale and continues to take action to uphold this responsibility, such as taking steps not to harm the environment while acquiring goods and setting up facilities. The company is also proactive on local issues, such as HIV/AIDS in Africa. Because consumers rely on Coca-Cola, trust its products, and develop a strong attachment through brand recognition and product loyalty, Coca-Cola's actions also foster relationship marketing. For these reasons, problems at a firm like Coca-Cola can stir the emotions of many stakeholders.

Crisis Situations

Although 1998 was not a good year for Coca-Cola in terms of financial performance, 1999 proved problematic on both financial and nonfinancial fronts. The year brought a number of crisis situations that truly tested the mettle of Doug Ivester as well as various company stakeholders. Some of the crises continued to have effects even several years after they occurred.

Contamination Scare

Perhaps the most damaging of Coca-Cola's crises—and the situation that every company dreads—began in June 1999, when about thirty Belgian children became ill after consuming Coke products. Although the company recalled the product, the problem soon escalated. The Belgian government eventually ordered the recall of all Coca-Cola products, which led officials in Luxembourg and the Netherlands to recall Coke products as well. The company eventually determined that the illnesses were the result of a poorly processed batch of carbon dioxide. Coca-Cola took several days to comment formally on the problem, which the media quickly labeled a slow response. Ivester initially judged the situation to be a minor problem, not a health hazard, but by this time a public relations nightmare had begun. France soon reported more than 100 people sick from bad Coke and banned all Coca-Cola products until the problem was resolved. Soon thereafter, a shipment of Bonaqua, a new Coca-Cola water product, arrived in Poland contaminated with mold. In each of these instances, the company's slow response and failure to acknowledge the severity of the situation further harmed its reputation.

The contamination crisis was exacerbated in December 1999 when Belgium ordered Coca-Cola to halt its "Restore" marketing campaign in order to regain consumer trust and sales in Belgium. A rival firm claimed that the campaign strategy, which included free cases of the product, discounts to wholesalers and retailers, and extra promotion personnel, was intended to strengthen Coca-Cola's market share unlawfully. Under Belgium's strict antitrust laws, the claim was upheld, and Coca-Cola abandoned the campaign in an effort to avoid further problems. This decision, along with the previous crisis, reduced Coca-Cola's market standing in Europe even more.

Competitive Issues

Questions about Coca-Cola's market dominance and government inquiries into its marketing tactics plagued the company outside of Belgium as well. Because most European countries have very strict antitrust laws, all firms must pay close attention to market share and position when considering joint ventures, mergers, and acquisitions there. During the summer of 1999, when Coca-Cola became very aggressive in France, the French government responded by refusing to approve Coca-Cola's bid to purchase Orangina, a French beverage company. French authorities also forced Coca-Cola to scale back its acquisition of Cadbury Schweppes, another beverage maker. Moreover, Italy successfully won a court case against Coca-Cola over anti-competitive prices late in 1999, prompting the European Commission to launch a full-scale probe of the company's competitive practices. PepsiCo and Virgin accused Coca-Cola of using rebates and discounts to crowd their products off the shelves, thereby gaining greater market share. Coca-Cola's strong-arm tactics proved to be in violation of European laws, and once again demonstrated the company's lack of awareness of European culture and laws. What action will result from these charges remains uncertain at this time, but any litigation carries the risk of additional damage to the company's reputation as well as financial penalties.

Despite these recent legal tangles, Coca-Cola products, along with many other U.S. products, have pervaded and dominated foreign markets throughout the world. According to some European officials, the pain U.S. automotive manufacturers felt in the 1970s because of Japanese imports is the same pain that U.S. firms are meting out in Europe. The growing omnipresence of U.S. products, especially in highly competitive markets, is why corporate reputation—both perceived and actual—is so important to relationships with business partners, government officials, and other stakeholders.

Racial Discrimination Allegations

In the spring of the same year, 1,500 African American employees sued Coca-Cola for racial discrimination. Their lawsuit, which eventually grew to include 2,000 current and former employees, accused the company of discriminating against them in pay, promotions, and performance evaluations. For example, plaintiffs charged that the company grouped African American workers at the bottom of the pay scale, where they typically earned $26,000 a year less than white employees in comparable jobs. The suit also alleged that top management had known about companywide discrimination since 1995, but had done nothing about it. Coca-Cola had pledged in 1992 to spend $1 billion on goods and services from minority vendors, an action designed to show the public that Coca-Cola did not discriminate, but this apparently was not the case in the workplace.

Although Coca-Cola strongly denied the allegations of racial discrimination, the lawsuit evoked strong reaction within the company. In response to the suit, Ivester created a diversity council and asked Carl Ware, a respected senior vice president and an African American, to lead it. However, during a management shuffle several months later, Ivester moved Ware to a position reporting to another senior vice president. The reorganization and perceived demotion did not sit well with Ware, who promptly announced his intention to retire. Coca-Cola's board members were puzzled by Ivester's management shuffle: Ware was not only capable and respected, he was also the firm's highest-ranking African American and thus could aid Ivester in reinforcing a corporate culture based on diversity and equal opportunity. Eventually, the company paid $193 million to settle the racial discrimination lawsuit.

Problems with Bottlers and Concentrate Prices

Throughout the crises of 1999, the media focused primarily on their effect on Coca-Cola's reputation rather than on the company's relations with bottlers, distributors, suppliers, and other partners. Without these strategic partnerships, Coca-Cola would not have been able to develop the relationships it has with consumers today. Such partnerships involve sharing in risks and rewards, and headaches like the contamination scare and racial discrimination allegations, especially when handled poorly, can therefore reflect on other business relationships beyond the firm's core business. When the reputation of one of these companies suffers, all the firms within the supply chain suffer in some way or another. This is especially true because Coca-Cola adopted an enterprise resource system that linked Coca-Cola's once almost classified information to a host of partners. Thus, the company's less-than-stellar handling of the crises of 1999 may have introduced a lack of integrity in its partnerships. Although some of the crises had nothing to do with the information shared across the new system, the partners still assume greater risk because of their closer relationships with the giant company. The interdependence between Coca-Cola and its partners requires a diplomatic and considerate view of the business and its effects on various stakeholders. Thus, these crises harmed Coke's partner companies, their stakeholders, and eventually, their bottom lines.

Coca-Cola further damaged relations with bottlers when Ivester announced in November 1999 that it would raise concentrate prices. This decision angered the bottlers, many of which had ties to Coca-Cola's board of directors. Consequently, this decision was one of the last that Doug Ivester made as CEO.

Post-Crises Management

Doug Daft, the new chief executive, quickly drafted plans designed to help Coca-Cola regain its financial footing and improve its tarnished reputation. Some of these plans included downsizing the workforce, creating a new office devoted to global relations, renewing its commitment to diversity, and launching a new marketing campaign. These decisions were designed to help Coca-Cola's stock price recover from its decline from $89 to $64 per share in late 1999. Sales volume, revenue, profits, and growth all fell in 1999. Some analysts even speculated that Goizueta's leadership before Ivester may have left the company "more broken than practically anyone had realized." Thus, Daft faced an incredible rebuilding task with many key stakeholders, including bottlers and investors.

Early in 2000, Coca-Cola announced that it would lay off nearly one-fifth of its global workforce. Not since 1988 has the company made significant workforce reductions, except in overseas operations, such as in Brazil and Russia, where troubled economies forced the layoffs. The new layoffs slashed about 5,000 jobs, half of them in Atlanta. To ease the trauma of the layoffs, Coca-Cola offered one of the more generous severance packages seen in recent history. The severance package for a ten-year employee, for example, included at least forty weeks of pay and eighteen months of company-paid health benefits. Some employees were even eligible for early retirement if they were at least fifty-two years old and had worked for the company for at least seven years.

In a surprise about-face of his earlier decision to retire, Carl Ware decided to remain with the company and assumed a new role within the post-Ivester corporation. He took charge of Coca-Cola's new Global Public Affairs and Administration division, which was given responsibility for the company's global public issues, including communications, external affairs, and government relations. According to CEO Daft, the new division should help the company respond to a growing number of stakeholders and ensure that Coca-Cola is welcomed around the world as a community member.

Daft also took great strides to counter diversity protests. The racial discrimination lawsuit, along with the threat of a boycott by the NAACP, led to this correction in Coca-Cola's reputation. Daft's plan to counter racial discrimination tied his success and compensation to company diversity goals. This plan applied to all Coca-Cola managers, and was designed to help Coca-Cola greatly improve employment of minorities.

Coca-Cola introduced a new marketing campaign in January 2000, the first new campaign in seven years. Most experts believe it represented the beverage giant's attempt to rebuild its once untarnishable reputation. Rather than having just one message targeted at all consumers, the campaign was designed to appeal to different regions of the globe. Top executives hoped the message would instill a desire to enjoy Coca-Cola in consumers. The slogan "Coca-Cola.enjoy" was an invitation for everyone to experience Coke. Although Coca-Cola has experienced enormous success with some advertising campaigns, like the "I'd Like to Buy the World a Coke" campaign of the 1970s, marketing analysts labeled more-recent advertising efforts as fragmented. Although the "Coca-Cola.enjoy" campaign did not address the problems that Coca-Cola faced, the company planned to regain its reputation by focusing on selling its product and connecting with consumers.

After a few months, Belgian officials closed their investigation of the health scare involving Coca-Cola and announced that no charges would be filed against the company. A Belgian health report indicated that no toxic contamination had been found in Coke bottles. Although the bottles were found to have contained tiny traces of carbonyl sulfide, which produced a rotten-egg smell, the amount of carbonyl sulfide would have to have been a thousand times higher to be toxic. Officials also reported that they found no structural problems with Coca-Cola's production plant, and that the company had cooperated fully throughout the investigation.

When Coca-Cola settled the racial discrimination lawsuit, the agreement stipulated that Coke donate $50 million to a foundation to support programs in minority communities; hire an ombudsman, who would report directly to CEO Daft, to investigate complaints of discrimination and harassment; and set aside $36 million for a seven-person task force and authorize it to oversee the company's employment practices. The task force, which includes business and civil rights experts, was to have unprecedented power to dictate company policy with regard to hiring, compensating, and promoting women and minorities. Despite the unusual provision to grant such power to an outside panel, Daft said, "We need to have outside people helping us. We would be foolish to cut ourselves off from the outside world."

Despite the company's problems in 1999, consumers surveyed after the European contamination scare indicated that they felt Coca-Cola would still behave correctly during times of crises. The company also ranked third globally in a Pricewaterhouse-Coopers survey of the most respected companies. Coca-Cola even managed to retain its strong ranking in this survey even while other companies facing setbacks, including Colgate-Palmolive and Procter & Gamble, dropped from it or fell substantially in the ranks. Thus, even after a series of crises and missteps, Coca-Cola seemed to retain a relatively positive reputation.

Reputation Management

According to a Burston-Marsteller study, 40 percent of a company's reputation is based on the CEO's reputation. Although a CEO's reputation will not boost short-term sales, it can enhance a company's ability to attract investors and employees, and it can allow the company the benefit of the doubt by stakeholders in times of crisis. Although Doug Ivester may have had the business background to assume ultimate responsibility for Coca-Cola, crisis and reputation management proved to be as important during his two-year tenure. While some critics have questioned whether Doug Daft personally communicates enough with the media and other stakeholders, Daft's tenure has brought improvements in stakeholder relations and company performance. For a leading firm like Coca-Cola, the CEO's decisions reverberate through the media and affect a number of stakeholders. As one columnist put it, "The real secret of Coca-Cola is not its concentrate formula. The real secret is in the marketing . . . [of] an emotional attachment to an experience." To this end, the company launched the "Coca-Cola . . . Real" marketing campaign in early 2003. This focus on and understanding of relationships, along with an eye toward social responsibility, will be pivotal to twenty-first-century leadership and management at Coca-Cola. As this case demonstrates, the transparency and accountability of business have reached new heights and require top managers to develop strong skills in crisis and reputation management.

Questions

1. What factors led to the public relations and financial crises that Doug Daft inherited after Doug Ivester resigned from the chair and CEO positions at Coca-Cola? Is there a common theme throughout the various crisis situations that developed? If so, discuss this theme and its relationship to social responsibility.

2. What role does corporate reputation play within organizational performance and social responsibility? Develop a list of factors or characteristics that different stakeholders may use in assessing corporate reputation. Are these factors consistent across stakeholders? Why or why not?

3. Assume it is 2000 and you have just become CEO at Coca-Cola. Outline the strategic steps you would take to remedy the concerns emanating from the company's board of directors, consumers, employees, and business partners; governments; and the media. What elements of social responsibility would you draw from in responding to these stakeholder issues?

Sources

Elise Ackerman, "It's the Real Thing: A Crisis at Coca-Cola," *U.S. News & World Report,* October 4, 1999, pp. 40–41; Ronald Alsop, "Corporate Reputations Are Earned with Trust, Reliability, Study Shows," *Wall Street Journal,* September 23, 1999, http://interactive.wsj.com; "America's Most Admired Companies," *Fortune,* February 8, 2000, www.pathfinder.com/fortune; "America's Most Admired Companies," www.fortune.com/fortune/mostadmired/, *Fortune,* accessed December 17, 2002; Paul Ames, "Case Closed on Coke Health Scare," *Associated Press,* April 22, 2000; Coca-Cola Company, www2.coca-cola.com/ accessed August 21, 2003; "Coca-Cola Introduces 'Real' Marketing Platform," *PR Newswire,* January 9, 2003, accessed via LexisNexis; "Coke Rapped for Restore," *The Grocer,* December 4, 1999, p. 14; "Corporate Reputation in the Hands of Chief Executive," *Westchester County Business Journal,* May 18, 1998, p. 17; Sharon Foley, "Cola Wars Continue: Coke vs. Pepsi in the 1990s," Harvard Business School Press, Case 9-794-055, April 10, 1995; "FYI," *Incentive* 176 (June 2002): 67; Ann Harrington, "Prevention Is the Best Defense," *Fortune,* July 10, 2000, p. 188; Constance Hays, "Coca-Cola to Cut Fifth of Workers in a Big Pullback," *New York Times,* January 27, 2000, p. A1; Ernest Holsendolph, "Facing Suit, Coca-Cola Steps Up Diversity Efforts," *Atlanta Journal and Constitution,* May 27, 1999, p. F1; Anita Howarth, "Coca-Cola Struggles to Refurbish Image after Recent European Troubles," *Daily Mail,* January 16, 2000, accessed via Lexis Nexis Academic Universe; Tammy Joyner, "Generous Severance Packages," *Atlanta Journal and Constitution,* January 27, 2000, p. E1; Jeremy Kahn, "The World's Most Admired Companies," *Fortune,* October 11, 1999, pp. 267–275; Scott Leith, "Where Has Daft Been?" *Atlanta Journal and Constitution,* December 1, 2002, p. 1Q; Betty Lui, "Think of Us as a Local Company," *Financial Times,* January 20, 2003, p. 6; Betsy Morris and Patricia Sellers, "What Really Happened at Coke," *Fortune,* January 10, 2000, pp. 114–116; Dan Morse and Ann Carrns, "Coke Rated 'Acceptable' on Diversity," *Wall Street Journal,* September 26, 2002, p. A9; Jon Pepper, "Europe Resents That Europeans Much Prefer to Buy American," *Detroit News,* November 10, 1999, http://detnews.com/1999/business/9911/10/11100025.htm; Jordan T. Pine, "Coke Counters Protests with New Diversity Commitment," *DiversityInc,* March 13, 2000, www.diversity-inc.com/; V. L. Ramsey, "$1 Billion Pledged to Vendors," *Black Enterprise,* July 1992, p. 22; Maria Saporta, "Transition at Coca-Cola: Ivester Paid a Price for Going It Alone," *Atlanta Journal and Constitution,* December 8, 1999, p. E1; "Second Annual List of '100 Best Corporate Citizens' Quantifies Stakeholder Service," www.business-ethics.com/newpage24.htm, *Business Ethics,* accessed December 17, 2002; Patricia Sellers, "Coke's CEO Doug Daft Has to Clean Up the Big Spill," *Fortune,* March 6, 2000, pp. 58–59; Christopher Seward, "Company Forewarned: Meaning of Goizueta's '96 Letter Echoes Today," *Atlanta Journal and Constitution,* January 27, 2000, p. E4; "Top 75: The Greatest Management Decisions Ever Made," *Management Review,* November 1998, pp. 20–23; Henry Unger, "Revised Suit Cites Coca-Cola Execs," *Atlanta Journal and Constitution,* December 21, 1999, p. D1; Greg Winter, "Bias Suit Ends in Changes for Coke," *Austin American-Statesman*, November 17, 2000, http://austin360.com/statesman.

Wainwright Bank & Trust: Banking on Values

This case was prepared by Debbie Thorne McAlister and Kevin Sample for classroom discussion, rather than to illustrate either effective or ineffective handling of an administrative, ethical, or legal decision by individuals or management. The research assistance of Shannon Yohe is gratefully acknowledged.

ainwright Bank & Trust Company, founded in Boston, Massachusetts, in 1987, is a $500 million commercial bank that is known for its progressive social agenda. During its brief history, the bank has demonstrated sound financial standing, earnings, and security and, under the guidance of President Jan Miller, has become a leader in socially responsible community development. Examples of Wainwright's community commitment include the financing of more than 50 percent of Boston-area housing projects for people living with AIDS as well as the creation of more than 500 affordable housing units in Boston and Cambridge. Nearly 40 percent of Wainwright's commercial lending portfolio finances community development initiatives, like environmental improvements, health services, and food banks. The bank also donates significant funds to many charities, including the Boston Foundation. Wainwright Bank is deeply involved and committed to its role as a socially responsible corporate citizen, working to build relationships across its community in an effort to uphold a practice of "banking on values." Wainwright's social responsibility is integral to daily and strategic decisions, resulting in a truly collaborative focus on social and financial objectives. Figure C2.1 provides an overview of the bank's philosophy.

The mission statement of Wainwright Bank reads, "With a sense of inclusion and diversity that extends from the boardroom to the mailroom, Wainwright Bank & Trust Company resolves to be a leading socially responsible bank. The Bank is equally committed to all its stakeholders—employees, customers, communities and shareholders." From this mission statement, the bank employs the "banking on values" slogan on its web site and other communication media. The bank also uses the slogan, "the conventional bank doing the unconventional." Wainwright's business purpose stands in contrast to that of many other companies, including banks.

FIGURE C2.1 Wainwright Bank's Philosophy

In the one-dimensional corporate world where shareholder concerns have always reigned supreme, Wainwright Bank prefers the concept of stakeholders. In our model of inclusion, employees, customers and communities have an equal place at the table alongside of stockholders. We believe each of these constituencies is best served when all are served.

With an active commercial lending operation and products such as Debit Cards and Telebanking, Wainwright Bank (www.wainwrightbank.com) outwardly resembles most other banking institutions both large and small. However, the resemblance to other banks becomes blurred as we are now increasingly seen as part of the vanguard of the social investment movement. The Bank's social justice agenda has become a unifying theme that embraces our mission statement, literature, and products while providing a unique identity to a publicly traded corporation.

As the bank has expanded we have consciously created an environment that provides all our employees freedom to be themselves; the benefits to the organization and to the community have been immense. For example, some years ago the introduction of domestic partner benefits at our bank was perhaps less significant than the cultural leverage it provided to the entire banking industry.

The twenty-two languages spoken at Wainwright Bank are a source of pride and reflect the diversity of the communities we serve. Indeed there are some among us who while speaking only English, hear the strong cadences of social justice that resonate from other cultures.

The Bank's progressive agenda includes a commitment to affordable housing, community development, women's rights and the gay and lesbian community. While these initiatives have been honored by awards and recognition they have also brought to the Bank a committed, indeed passionate, customer constituency.

Our recent acquisition of a 30% equity interest in Trillium Asset Management provides an affiliation specializing in socially responsible investing. A unique dimension is its use of shareholder activism. Whether in support of diversity in the corporate workplace or in coalitions with trade union movements to oppose sweatshops in Haiti and Indonesia, Trillium Asset Management has repeatedly taken courageous positions on economic justice issues.

The Bank has attempted to use both its cultural and financial capital to further a vision of a just, tolerant and sustainable society. Over the years we have seen the same voices of intolerance arrayed against the civil rights movement, the women's movement, gay rights and the civil liberties of people with AIDS. For us, the rights of these groups are all connected threads that weave the fabric of a just society. Indeed none of us journeys alone.

Source: "Mission and Philosophy," Wainwright Bank, www.wainwrightbank.com/site/m2A.asp, accessed November 12, 2003.

Current Trends in the Banking Industry

Banks have traditionally been viewed as very conservative institutions. Their primary role has been to provide checking, savings, loans, and related financial services. In the past, bank managers and executives consisted primarily of white males, and their institutions' missions typically focused more on financial issues than on the community. However, many traditional banks have attempted to evoke a community and neighborly image, often through volunteer efforts, board memberships, and giving programs. For example, U.S. Bank of Pennsylvania won a grant from the Community Development Financial Institution Bank Enterprise Award Program for its community efforts. This grant is awarded to the institution that most exemplifies a strong commitment to expanding traditional financial institution services to underserved markets.

Other trends are also changing the face of traditional banking. For example, technology and information systems have altered many aspects of customer interaction. Although the larger banks are gaining a foothold on the Internet, some are focusing less on their neighborly feel and community relationships. In response to this strategic shift, smaller and new independent banks looking for a competitive edge have focused even more on their "neighborliness." However, the surge of Internet banks has also reminded the big banks that they need to retain a friendly community atmosphere. Although many banks are now promoting their neighborhood or community orientation, few have mastered it yet.

Another significant trend in the banking industry is consolidation. Many large banks merged with or acquired competitors in the late 1990s and early 2000s. While bank employees focus on completing these mergers and combining facilities, systems, and methods into one business, some consumer advocates warn that higher banking fees, job losses, and a potential lack of customer focus will result from this trend. For example, after Bank of America acquired 342 NationsBank branches in Texas in 1999, managers were involved in decisions related to changing bank colors, logos, and slogans, as well as which of several branches would be closed at a later date. The company's announcement that it would cut 8,000 jobs left many employees in limbo, worrying about whether their jobs or branches would be among those eliminated. Bank executives also deliberated whether to raise the fees NationsBank customers were paying and dealt with consolidating a multitude of systems. Bank of America planned to continue its community involvement, even in the newly acquired branches, by investing in low-income communities and other programs.

Although Wainwright Bank & Trust provides the same financial services as other banking firms, it breaks sharply from the traditional banking mold with its progressive agenda and focus on nontraditional markets. Of course, Wainwright is but one example of institutions around the world that have chosen a nontraditional market position. Citizens Bank of Canada is another example of an institution that looks beyond the monetary aspects of banking. This Canadian firm has a policy of investing in and doing business only with companies that have strong employee relations, do not trade or manufacture weapons, do not significantly profit from tobacco products, treat animals humanely, and do not harm the environment.

Wainwright Bank in Action

Wainwright Bank has been designated a Community Development Financial Institution (CDFI), which indicates that it makes loans and other investments in low-income communities. The bank has received an "Outstanding" Community Reinvestment Act rating, which means it is in the top 10 percent of all financial institutions serving low-to-moderate-income neighborhoods in their market areas. Wainwright was also recognized for its Financial Empowerment program that innovatively promotes financial literacy to inner-city teens and adults. To support its community development initiatives, Wainwright has chosen to focus on several areas, including homelessness, affordable housing, health care services, diversity, and the natural environment. Its partners in these efforts have high praise for Wainwright, some of which is chronicled in Figure C2.2.

Homelessness and Hunger

The founders of Wainwright believe that the health of society can be judged by how its members provide for the well-being of those most often discriminated against, including those lacking income, housing, and food. Since 1991, the bank has provided more than $15 million in loans to nationally recognized service providers for the homeless and the hungry, including the Pine Street Inn, the Greater Boston Food Bank, and the Committee to End Elder Homelessness. The Greater Boston Food Bank helps to feed 465,000 a month—72 percent of those in need in the nine counties of eastern Massachusetts. Lawrence D. Lowenthal, the executive director of the American Jewish Committee, says, "I think it is admirable that a bank would devote important resources to the needs of disadvantaged people, and I personally applaud [Wainwright's] enlightened policy."

| FIGURE C2.2 | Quotes About Wainwright Bank |

"The fact [clients'] deposits are being lent into the community follows their missions and extends their own practices." *Banker & Tradesman,* December 23, 2002.

"If you want your banking dollars to directly benefit the environment, you need a traditional but progressive bank such as . . . Wainwright Bank & Trust Company in Boston." *E, The Environmental Magazine,* November 1995.

"Wainwright's stock has experienced record earnings since the beginning of the year. Sometimes, nice guys really do finish first." *Improper Bostonian,* July 10, 2002.

"When Robert Glassman and John Plukas decided to transform their small, private financial institution into a traditional retail bank, they asked staff about their thoughts. What they came up with was hardly traditional. When Wainwright Bank opened its first branches in 1992, it operated under three guiding principles: financial value, personal service and social responsibility." Greater Boston Business Council, March 2000.

Source: "What People Are Saying About Us," Wainwright Bank, www.wainwrightbank.com/site/m2E.asp, accessed November 12, 2003. Copyright © 2003 by Wainwright Bank. Reprinted with permission.

Affordable and Special-Needs Housing

Wainwright executives believe that there is a great need for safe, clean, affordable rental housing in the inner city, not only for low-income residents but also for those who are often discriminated against, such as the homeless, the elderly, and the mentally disabled. The bank has therefore committed $51 million in financing to many affordable housing projects in the Greater Boston area, including Cortes Street, Brookview House, Cambridge YMCA and YWCA, 270 Huntington Avenue, and Rockport School Elder Housing. Cortes Street was developed by Boston Aging Concerns Young and Old United to serve the needs of the low-income elderly, whereas Brookview House was established to provide housing for homeless women and children. Wainwright also issued a real estate loan to add a new wing to an existing building for forty-three single-room-occupancy units for homeless women and provided construction financing to create thirty-one units of low-income housing for the elderly at Rockport School Elder Housing. Wainwright has also provided financing for Pine Street Inn shelters for the homeless throughout Boston.

AIDS and Health Services

Labeling the HIV/AIDS crisis one of the "defining social issues of our times," Wainwright has committed more than $11 million to finance housing for individuals and families living with HIV/AIDS. This commitment covers 50 percent of these projects in the Greater Boston area. Larry Kessler, the executive director of the AIDS Action Committee of Massachusetts, sums up the significance of Wainwright's efforts in this area: "If there was a Nobel Prize for business involvement in the needs of the community, Wainwright Bank would be up there as a top nominee. [Wainwright's] corporate and philanthropic support in the community is a bold act of leadership." The bank has also financed organizations involved in researching breast cancer and counseling addicts. A number of nonprofit organizations have formed relationships with Wainwright Bank, including the AIDS Action Committee of Massachusetts, AIDS Housing Corporation, the Boston Living Center, Fenway Community Health Center, and the Men of Color.

Diversity and Nondiscrimination

Executives of Wainwright Bank believe that issues of race, religion, gender and sexual orientation, and immigration will increasingly define communities and workplaces in the United States. They also believe the diversity of communities enhances and strengthens society as a whole. Because of this increase in diversity, Wainwright has established relationships with many nonprofit organizations that focus on diversity and discrimination issues. Some of these include the Association of Affirmative Action Professionals (AAAP), the New England Work & Family Association (NEWFA), and the Black-Jewish Economic Roundtable. According to Gary Buseck, the executive director of the Gay Lesbian and Affirming Disciples (GLAD), "Your [Wainwright's] contributions to the gay and lesbian community in New England have been unparalleled, and the way in which you combine business with community activism and personal integrity is a model for society."

Women's Issues

Addressing women's issues is also a priority for Wainwright Bank & Trust. Wainwright's board of directors shatters the proverbial "glass ceiling" by including a significant number of women and other minorities, and about half of the bank's officers are women. This is especially significant considering the predominately male banking industry. The bank strives not only to include women in its workforce but also to help address their needs as customers. To this end, the bank developed Personal Financing Planning for Women seminars to help women become financially independent. Seminar topics have included proper uses of credit, understanding risk, inflation, and tax deferral.

The bank has also established relationships with area nonprofit agencies including the Boston Women's Health Book Collective, Massachusetts Breast Cancer Coalition, Center for Women in Enterprise (CWE), and Massachusetts National Organization for Women (NOW). Boston Women's Health Book Collective is a nonprofit health education, advocacy, and consulting organization that works to help individuals and groups make informed decisions about issues affecting women's health and medical care. Massachusetts Breast Cancer Coalition's goals are to increase public awareness, improve access to screening and care for all women, increase research funding, and ensure consumer participation in research priorities and public policy. The Center for Women in Enterprise is a nonprofit education organization that offers courses, workshops, one-on-one consulting, and assistance in securing loans. Wainwright Bank was also one of the first and largest Boston-area businesses to sign the Pledge to NOW in August 1997. This document covers policies on affirmative action, family leave, domestic partnership benefits, and strong anti-harassment policies. One example of Wainwright's fulfillment of this pledge is the low-interest loans that it makes available to help day care centers upgrade and expand their services. Along with six other financial institutions, Wainwright's loans allow more women to participate more effectively in the workforce, knowing that their children have quality care throughout the workday.

Environmental Issues

Wainwright Bank is particularly concerned about the intersection between environmental issues and social justice. The bank has established relations with many environmental nonprofit agencies, including the Environmental Diversity Forum, Trust for Public Land, Silent Spring Institute, and Coalition for Environmentally Responsible Economies (CERES). The Environmental Diversity Forum's mission is to protect the environment by advocating for all policies and programs of the environmental movement. In collaboration with the Trust for Public Land, Wainwright provided financial assistance for the preservation of the shores of Lake Tarelton in Piermont, New Hampshire. The bank endorsed the CERES Principles in September 1997, highlighting a commitment to an environmental ethics that goes beyond mere compliance with the law. Wainwright was recently recognized as one of ten leading banking organizations to provide financing for small businesses and nonprofit organizations that create environmentally sound goods and services. The bank has provided financing assistance to various organizations dedicated to preserving important tracts of land and also offers the Green Loan, a home equity loan at a discounted rate for funding the installation of solar energy systems.

Social Activism as a Corporate Value

The founders of Wainwright Bank believe that the management of financial affairs is not a socially or morally neutral practice. That is, where people choose to invest their money and from whom they choose to buy their goods and services can influence social conditions. Wainwright has extended this view to the corporate level. For example, the bank works with organizations such as Trillium Asset Management (formerly Franklin Research & Development Corporation); Kinder, Lydenberg, Domini & Company, Inc. (KLD); the Political Research Associates (PRA); and the Partners for the Common Good 2000 (PCG2000). Wainwright holds a 30 percent interest in Trillium, the oldest and largest firm that specializes in socially responsible investing, because it is profitable and because it coincides with Wainwright's strategy and social responsibility. KLD provides social research to money managers, whereas PCG2000 applies ethical principles to investment choices and directs loans and deposits, through intermediaries, to projects that promote economic justice and social change. Wainwright works with these companies by furnishing loans and other types of assistance for uniting financial and social goals.

Criticisms of Wainwright

Because banks usually fit a strict conservative mold, it should come as no surprise that some people in the banking business disagree with a number of Wainwright's practices. Most criticisms focus on its business and operation methods. Many traditionalists feel that Wainwright is too focused on affairs other than banking and warn that it could lose touch with how it should be transacting business and that this may hurt its customers and shareholders, regardless of who they are, in the long run. However, Wainwright has been listed as one of the most profitable independent banks created after 1984 by Danielson Associates Inc. The bank's financial standing has remained secure, with steady increases in both return on assets and return on equity.

Some critics have also suggested that Robert Glassman, the cochair of Wainwright Bank, chose to operate Wainwright in this way in order to achieve some ulterior motive. Others, including members of the press, have accused the bank of "window dressing," using its social and values orientation to attract customers without actually getting involved in the causes it champions. However, most customers believe that Wainwright's actions and record demonstrate that it does more than just talk about being socially responsible.

Other critics contend that Wainwright is missing out on some very lucrative options because of its adherence to certain beliefs. For example, consumers who oppose gay and lesbian lifestyles may not want to bank with Wainwright because of its social agenda. For several reasons, Wainwright has remained a relatively small bank in the Massachusetts area. Like many other banks, Wainwright now offers online banking services, and this option, coupled with the company's unique approach, may boost its customer base. Although Wainwright's philosophies and practices do generate criticism, the bank seems to respond with continuing exemplary performance. Robert Glassman says, "In the one-dimensional corporate world in which shareholder concerns have always reigned supreme, Wainwright Bank prefers the concept of stakeholders. In our model of inclusion, employees, customers, and communities have an equal place at the table alongside stockholders. We believe each of these constituencies is best served when all are served."

Wainwright Garners Awards

Glassman's stakeholder philosophy has helped Wainwright Bank win numerous awards for its endeavors to support the community. For example, *Business Ethics* magazine awarded the company its Business Ethics Award in 1998 on the basis of Wainwright's contributions to environmental, diversity, and nondiscriminatory practices. The Center for Responsibility in Business named Wainwright a recipient of its Fifteenth Annual Corporate Conscience Award for the bank's significant efforts and outcomes in community partnership. These contributions include the fact that community development loans make up one-fifth of the bank's loan portfolio. Wainwright supplies more than 60 percent of the financing for housing for people with HIV/AIDS in the Boston area. Wainwright Bank also practices diversity in the workplace in an exemplary manner. In addition to advancing women, Wainwright actively recruits many categories of minorities as employees, and the bank's staff now includes speakers of twenty-two different languages.

Robert Glassman has devoted time, money, and energy to creating several organizations and activities designed to improve the lives of people in need. Glassman says, "I believe it's important to use the platform the bank affords me to inform, educate, and introduce different constituencies to issues of social injustice. This work, alongside the culture of diversity we've developed at the Bank, is the most important legacy I contemplate I will leave my children." Glassman's statement and record demonstrate the importance of top management commitment to nonfinancial issues. Wainwright not only won the 1998 Business Ethics Award but also received the 1998 Institute of Human Relations Award from the American Jewish Committee, the CDFI Fund Award from the U.S. Treasury Department, the Small Business Award for Excellence from the Greater Boston Business Council, the Ray Frost Award from the Association of Affirmative Action Professionals, the Friend of the Community Award from the Lesbian and Gay Political Alliance of Massachusetts, and the Bank Honor Roll from the Massachusetts IOLTA Committee. These and many other awards indicate how important the bank has become to its community and the leadership it has shown in social responsibility.

Many people are surprised when they hear about Wainwright Bank because most do not think of banks as institutions that go out of their way to help the community. The "banking on values" concept at Wainwright has earned the bank and its employees a great deal of respect from community stakeholders. As Christine Connhalter, the executive assistant to the mayor of the city of Cambridge, Massachusetts, says, "Wainwright does not believe in 'Business as Usual.' Wainwright is 'Business as It Should Be'—community partnership, equality, and caring. Wainwright dares to be different—and succeeds." Such quotes sum up Wainwright Bank & Trust Company's mission and values very well and demonstrate the respect Wainwright has gained by doing what not every business will do.

Questions

1. What factors led the founders of Wainwright Bank to pursue the "banking on values" philosophy? What type of risks and rewards are associated with this nontraditional banking approach?
2. Contrast Wainwright Bank's mission statement with your own bank's mission statement. What are the similarities and differences? Would you consider banking with Wainwright? Why or why not?
3. Visit Wainwright Bank's web site. What is the company's financial standing? What social concerns and stakeholders is the bank now exploring and supporting? On the basis of your beliefs and Wainwright's own statements, delineate the bank's prospects for the future.

Sources

Citizens Bank of Canada, www.citizens.com, accessed April 12, 2000; "Exceptional Community Support by U.S. Bank Leads to Unique Government Grant," *PR Newswire,* November 4, 1999; Jay Fitzgerald, "Atlanta, Wainwright Make Honor Roll," *Boston Business Journal,* August 23, 1996, p. 4; Robert Glassman, "Wainwright Bank Finds Social Investment Pays," *Star Tribune,* November 30, 1998, pp. 3–4; Skip Kaltenheuser, "10th Annual Business Ethics Awards," *Business Ethics* 12 (November–December 1998): 12; Steve Klinkerman, "The Tie That Binds," *Banking Strategies,* March 25, 2000, www.bai.org/; Diane E. Lewis, "Financial Firms Make Loans to Boost Child Care in Massachusetts," *Boston Globe,* March 15, 2000; Heather MacKenzie, "Wainwright Banks on More Than Money," *Boston Globe,* June 28, 1998; Chris Mahoney, "Wainwright's Mensch," *Boston Business Journal,* January 15, 1999, p. 3; Chris Mahoney, "Wainwright Poised to Take Its Causes National," *Boston Business Journal,* November 26, 1999, p. 3; Charles Ornstein, "Merger Giving New Name to NationsBank," *Dallas Morning News,* October 2, 1998; Wainwright Bank, www.wainwrightbank.com, accessed February 3, 2003; "Wainwright Bank Participates in Over $2 Million in Loans Originated by the Boston Community Loan Fund," *PR Newswire,* December 20, 2002, accessed via LexisNexis; "Wainwright Bank Praised as One of 10 Best 'Green' Banking Firms in U.S.," *PR Newswire,* January 22, 2003, accessed via LexisNexis; "Wainwright Bank Receives 'Outstanding' CRA Rating," *PR Newswire,* December 9, 2002.

Case 3

Conoco's Decision: The First Annual President's Award for Business Ethics

This case was prepared by J. Brooke Hamilton III and Mark Smith of the University of Louisiana at Lafayette and Steve L. Scheck of ConocoPhillips for classroom discussion rather than to illustrate either effective or ineffective handling of an administrative, ethical, or legal decision by management. Paid-in-full members of NACRA are encouraged to reproduce any case for distribution to their students without charge or written permission. All other rights reserved jointly to the authors and the North American Case Research Association. This case is presented for discussion purposes only. In addition to company documents and other sources cited, the case is based on the personal experiences of two of the authors as members of the Selection Team. Dialog is meant to represent the substance of the discussion and is not a transcription of the meeting. The authors' notes did not allow attribution of remarks to individual committee members. Some material from the nomination forms is included in the dialog. ConocoPhillips has generously granted permission to use the company materials presented in this case. Reprinted with permission from the Case Research Journal. *Copyright 2004 by J. Brooke Hamilton III, Mark Smith, and Steve L. Scheck and the North American Case Research Association. All rights reserved.*

Introduction

On a December Friday in 1999, Steve L. Scheck, General Auditor for Conoco Inc., directed the other members of the award selection team toward lunch in the corporate dining room. They had spent the morning reviewing all the nominees for Conoco's first annual President's Award in Business Ethics. The heavy lifting would take place that afternoon. The team was charged with deciding who should receive the award and how the process should be improved for next year.

As they walked through the corridors of the headquarters campus in Houston, Steve reflected on the events that had brought this group together. He recalled the meeting with Archie Dunham, Conoco's president, chairman, and CEO, when the idea first surfaced. In their discussion, Dunham had indicated that he wanted to initiate a "President's Award for Business Ethics." "We have a President's award for the other core values of safety and health, environmental stewardship, and valuing all people," he stated. "Why don't we have an award for business ethics?" Steve had agreed to get started on the project right away. Now a year later and after a great deal of planning, the process was coming to fruition. The award recipient or recipients would be presented with a trophy at the company's honors banquet and featured in an awards video circulated internally and externally. All the nominees would receive a note of congratulations from the president, chairman, and CEO that certainly would provide some carryover in their annual performance evaluations. After the discussion of the candidates that morning, Steve had his own preliminary judgments on who should be selected. He was curious to see what the other members of the selection team thought.

Background and History of the Company

In 1999, Conoco was a large integrated oil company. The firm traced its origins back to the Continental Oil and Transportation Company first incorporated in Utah in 1875. At the time of the case, it was a global firm operating in more than forty countries in the oil exploration, transportation, refining, and marketing sectors of the industry. The company had approximately 16,700 employees plus contractors and joint venture partners.

The firm's history has not been without difficulties. During the oil shocks of the early 1980s, the company lost its independence. In 1981, DuPont acquired Conoco in order to ensure adequate feed stocks for DuPont's chemical business. In 1992, the international oil analyst Schroder and Co. rated Conoco last in overall exploration results among the fourteen firms it surveyed.

As the oil crisis abated, the need to secure feed stocks seemed less important to DuPont. Wall Street was pressuring the company to improve its performance. DuPont's response was to streamline its operations. In the early 1990s, Conoco's new president, Archie Dunham, began a program of rationalizing Conoco's assets and developing new sources of supply. The company was successfully spun off from DuPont in a complex public offering and stock swap in 1999. In 1999, the Schroder survey ranked the firm number one in exploration efficiency among the major oil companies.

The newly independent company had the task of reintroducing itself to the stock market and establishing its own identity. While retaining its decades-old retailing identity as "The Hottest Brand Going!" Conoco's new corporate identity campaign centered on Domino, the fast cat, emphasizing that in the new global energy environment speed and agility matter more than size. Internally, the company emphasized a culture based on Conoco's core values of safety, environmental stewardship, valuing all people, and business ethics. The company developed compensation plans that closely align employees' interests with those of their shareholders. Under these plans, a portion of an employee's pay was tied to the total shareholder return, as well as other performance objectives, including upholding Conoco's core values. Conoco maintained that upholding these core values provided a powerful advantage for a company intent on global growth and that they were one of the reasons Conoco was welcomed around the world by customers, partners, governments, and communities.

The management believed that this values focus was particularly important for a global oil producer. The nature of the product, business, and technology required that the company have a big footprint. The firm must go where the oil is, move it, refine it, and sell it where it is needed. Conoco employees are natives of many countries and expatriates in many countries. They deal with governments, suppliers, joint venture partners, contractors, workers, and civilian populations in many places in the world All of this means dealing with the environmental and moral hazards of the world community. The oil industry has a bad press, some of it, possibly, well deserved. However, the world economy depends on the flow of oil, and the industry is not going away anytime soon.

Conoco was proud to have avoided major disasters, such as the *Exxon Valdez* oil spill. In 1998, it was the first of the major oil companies to have converted completely to double-hulled tankers, a full seventeen years before the U.S. government's deadline in 2015. It promoted this and other safety and environmental accomplishments prominently in its annual report. One of the ways it did this is by having awards and contests in these areas. The winners received a letter from the president, and their accomplishments and pictures were published in the annual report.

Development of the Award

Conoco had formal programs throughout the company to ensure that employees understand and put into practice the company's core values of safety and occupational health, care for the environment, valuing all people, and business ethics (See 1999 Annual Report, pp. 22–24, Exhibit 1). The ethics program included a formal ethics policy, procedures for ensuring integrity and compliance with laws and ethics, and a twenty-four-hour ethics action line for employees to seek guidance and report possible violations. In developing the Business Ethics Award to complement this program, Steve had decided to work with a team of managers who were interested in the ethics process and who represented areas in which ethics questions would be a part of daily business. Debbie Tellez, Assistant General Counsel, Business Development; L. Cathy Wining, General Manager, Materials and Services; and Barbara Govan, Human Resources Generalist, formed the core team, which was completed by several key persons around the world to ensure inclusion of global perspectives. The team met over a period of several months, with a number of drafts circulated and revised, to design a process for soliciting and judging nominees for the award (see Award Guidelines, Exhibit 2).

Award Guidelines

The purpose of the award was to "support and recognize ethics as one of Conoco's four core values," to recognize "extraordinary examples" of "leadership" that demonstrate "excellence" in "conduct," and to provide "role models whose behavior embodies what Conoco stands for" (Exhibit 2). Rather than simply stating that the award was to be given for ethical conduct, the guidelines made a number of distinctions. The award was to reward individuals or groups for good conduct and to inspire it in the actions, attitudes, and opinions of others. It sought to reward both individuals and groups, to recognize both significant and sustainable activities, to include both business and personal conduct, to be concerned with both ethics and law, and to represent Conoco's values both internally and externally. Conoco's business

EXHIBIT 1 **Think Big, Move Fast: Delivering On Our Promises**

(Conoco 1999 Annual Report, pp. 22–24)

Our vision is to be recognized around the world as a truly great, integrated, international energy company that gets to the future first. Conoco operates in more than 40 countries worldwide and at year-end 1999 had approximately 16,700 employees. Conoco is active in both the upstream and downstream segments of the global petroleum industry.

Distinctive Corporate Culture Defines Conoco—Past, Present and Future Core Values—An Unwavering Commitment

Safety and Health: Conoco is dedicated to protecting the safety and health of our employees, who maintained an outstanding safety performance in 1999. The total recordable injury rate of 0.36 per 100 full-time employees was just slightly above the previous year's record low. During the past five years, employee safety performance has improved more than 60 percent. Conoco has achieved these outstanding results through the company's efforts to continuously improve safety systems and processes, and because employees take personal responsibility for their safety and the safety of their co-workers. This sense of shared concern was reflected in the safety performance of the thousands of contractors who work at Conoco facilities. Contractor safety performance improved 17 percent in 1999, and 64 percent during the last five years. . . . .

Environmental Stewardship: Conoco is working to minimize the impact of the company's activities on the environment. The number of significant environmental incidents was reduced to zero in 1998, with one occurring in 1999. "Significant" incidents are major releases or spills with the potential to affect our neighbors. Over the past five years, emissions of volatile organic compounds (which contribute to smog) have been reduced by an estimated one-third, while Conoco's global refining operations have continued to reduce flaring and sulfur emissions. Ernst & Young, a global accounting and auditing firm, is conducting an independent evaluations of Conoco's worldwide reporting processes for future data on safety, health and environmental performance. This audit will help us better measure the company's progress in these areas. In the communities where Conoco operates major facilities, we maintain a flow of information to local residents through Citizens Advisory Councils, which bring together community representatives and Conoco managers. . . . .

Valuing All People: Conoco operates in more than 40 countries and has a diverse global workforce. We draw on the different perspectives and cultures of our employees, along with their combined experience, knowledge and creativity, to gain a powerful business advantage around the world. Throughout the company, we strive to create an inclusive work environment that treats all people with dignity and respect. In such an environment, employees are recognized and valued for their experience, intellect and leadership.

Business Ethics: Conducting business with the highest ethical standards is critical to Conoco's continuing success. As Conoco becomes more global, the company is subject to an ever-widening variety of laws, customs and regulations. This requires us to be flexible and innovative in our business dealings, while at the same time resolute about doing what's right, both legally and ethically. Adherence to the highest ethical standards is a condition of employment at Conoco. The company has a formal ethics policy and procedures for conducting business with integrity and in compliance with all applicable laws. Employees are required to review the policies and procedures regularly and complete an annual certificate of compliance. A 24-hour telephone hot line also provides employees a way to seek guidance or report possible conflicts.

EXHIBIT 2 **Guidelines: President's Award For Business Ethics**

(Conoco Inc., 1999)

Purpose

The **President's Award for Business Ethics** was created to support and recognize this as one of Conoco's four core values. This award recognizes individuals or groups that make significant and sustainable contributions to this core value.

The award is designed to inspire others by recognizing extraordinary examples of individual and/or group leadership that demonstrates, on an ongoing basis, sustainable excellence in personal and business conduct. The people recognized are role models whose behavior embodies what Conoco stands for both internally and externally.

Definition/Judging Criteria

Living up to Conoco's core values in everything we do, individually and as a company, is fundamental to Conoco's success. Conoco must conduct its business with the highest ethical standards. As our activities grow and extend into new areas of the world, we are subject to an ever-widening variety of laws, customs and regulations. We need to be flexible and innovative, and at the same time absolutely unwavering in doing what is right, ethically and legally, so that we may enhance our corporate image, and still gain competitive advantage and increase shareholder value.

Conoco's business conduct guide, **Doing the Right Thing,** provides a summary of the company's policies and standards, and of significant laws relating to our business. Every employee is personally responsible for compliance with those laws and standards. However, this award is designed to recognize those individuals who go beyond simply complying with company policies or the applicable laws.

It is designed to recognize those individuals who seek to change the actions, attitudes or opinions of others with regard to what constitutes ethical behavior, both internally and externally. This may be done through the role modeling of a significantly higher standard of ethical conduct; through the implementation of policies and practices that drive our actions, or the actions of others externally, beyond the minimally acceptable standard or customary behavior; or through decision making that demonstrates that "doing the right thing" from an ethical perspective increases shareholder value.

Nominations should represent extraordinary behavior and will be judged according to specific criteria described below.

1. The significance of the achievement, effort or behavior. Significant improvement above the minimum required standard for ethical conduct; linkage to business objectives and implementation of policy and standards; and/or successful performance in spite of difficult and challenging circumstances such as location, language, culture and/or alignment with and cooperation between Conoco and an external party.
2. The degree of innovation/creativity displayed. Proactive assessment of and response to a need; implementation of new approaches to address ethical business conduct.
3. The degree of extent of employee involvement or support with respect to the higher standard or expectation role modeled or implemented. A work environment exists that encourages employees to conduct themselves ethically at all levels; employees

(continued)

EXHIBIT 2   *(Continued)*

recognize the value of strong ethical behavior and are accountable for their conduct; employees are actively involved in the administration of company standards and training others; and/or rewards and recognition programs reinforce the desired behavior at all levels across the company.

4. The leadership qualities exhibited in challenging norms or customary practices. Persistence in implementing improvement programs or new approaches that lead to outstanding ethical performance.

5. The impact on the company's image/value; internally (with employees) and/or externally (with stakeholders such as partners, governments, suppliers, customers, and communities) in a way that creates shareholder value over time.

Eligibility

Nominees for this award may be an individual employee (regular or temporary), a team, an entire work unit or retiree of Conoco, for leadership or conduct while in Conoco service in the year of nomination. Contractors may be included in team or work unit awards. There may be multiple recipients each year, dependent upon the number and quality of nominations received. An organization's size or a person's position within the company is not a deciding factor.

The Award

The President's Award for Business Ethics will be presented annually to award recipients or their representatives at a special recognition ceremony. This award will reflect a unique and globally symbolic representation of ethics and will be consistent in stature with that of other President's Awards. The award will remain with the group or individual. Any additional forms of recognition will be left to the discretion of the business units.

Selection Team

Conoco Leadership Center—Legal and Finance are jointly responsible for coordinating the selection process to determine award recipients. Input on selection team membership will be solicited from multiple sources, with final selection of the team made by the President and CEO. The Selection Team will be vested with the power to select a winner(s) and other finalists. The team's decision will be reviewed and endorsed by the President and CEO.

The Selection Team will consist of employees who are recognized as credible role models and able to provide an objective assessment. Team makeup will reflect a broad and global cross-section of the organization. Diversity of thinking styles, beliefs, cultures and backgrounds will be represented, as well as different salary grade, gender, ethnic and business perspectives.

To insure new perspective while maintaining continuity, we expect about one-third of the team's membership to transition in any given year. About one-third of the team will be comprised of former recipients of the award.

In addition to employees, global external resources will be invited to participate on the team to provide additional perspectives.

(continued)

| EXHIBIT 2 | (Continued) |

Nomination

Each year Conoco's President and CEO will send a communication to all employees inviting nominations. The communications will be combined with nomination requests for the other three Conoco core values.

Nominations shall be submitted using **this on-line form,** or follow the format described below:

- The name, address, phone number and e-mail of the person submitting the nomination and responsible for providing any additional information if necessary.
- The name of the individual(s) being nominated. Indicate the name of the nominated team or work group if applicable.
- **REASON/RESULTS**—briefly describe **WHAT** was accomplished. Include details of any measures or impact of the behavior or activity involved to the extent possible, the drivers and the significance of the accomplishment.
- **STRATEGY AND TACTICS**—briefly describe **HOW** the results were achieved. What obstacles had to be overcome? What new or innovative tools or processes were used?
- **PEOPLE**—describe **WHO** was involved in this achievement and why they made a difference. Describe the leadership criteria exhibited and the degree of teamwork and networking that was necessary.

Nominations should consist of no more than three pages, including a brief introductory summary. Clear and concise nominations are encouraged. The Selection Team will make judgments based upon "substance" of the achievement, not form or length of the nomination.

conduct guide, *Doing the Right Thing,* set the standards with which every employee was expected to comply. The Ethics Award was to recognize individuals who had gone beyond compliance.

Instead of simply assuming that good conduct is worthwhile, the award guidelines spelled out why this and the other core values were important to Conoco:

Living up to Conoco's core values in everything we do, individually and as a company, is fundamental to Conoco's continuing success. Conoco must conduct its business with the highest ethical standards. As our activities grow and extend into new areas of the world, we are subject to an ever-widening variety of laws, customs and regulations. We need to be flexible and innovative, and at the same time absolutely unwavering in doing what is right, ethically and legally, so that we may enhance our corporate image, and still gain competitive advantage and increase shareholder value (Exhibit 2).

According to the Guidelines, the specific criteria for judging the Award candidates were:

1. significance of the achievement
2. degree of innovation/creativity
3. degree of employee involvement

4. leadership qualities exhibited
5. impact on Conoco's image/value

The form on which all employees were invited to submit nominations asked for a description of:

1. the reason for the nomination, in terms of the results that were accomplished;
2. strategy and tactics, describing how the results were achieved, including obstacles and innovations; and
3. people involved and why they made a difference, including aspects of leadership and teamwork.

Those eligible for the award included individual employees (regular or temporary), a team, an entire work unit, or retiree of Conoco, for leadership or conduct while in Conoco service in the year of the nomination. Contractors could be included in work units. Multiple recipients were possible. The award winner(s) were to be decided by a selection team representing diverse constituencies, and confirmed by Archie Dunham, the president, CEO, and chairman. Persons outside the company (global external resources) were asked to participate in order to provide additional perspectives. For new perspective and continuity, one-third of the team was expected to change each year, and about one-third was to be made up of former recipients of the award (Exhibit 2).

The Selection Process

The Selection Team met at Conoco's corporate campus in Houston in December 1999. The team had been chosen by the president, after input from a variety of sources. After introductions, the team members heard comments on the importance of the process by one of the champions of the Ethics Award and a member of the president's top management team, Bob Goldman, Senior Vice President for Finance and CFO. The meeting facilitator then presented the ground rules for the deliberations, and the discussion began. A Conoco employee selector, called a validator, had been assigned by the team chair to do a workup of each nominee before the meeting. Each validator gave a ten-minute summary of this background information on his/her nominee to the group. The validator then placed that nominee into one of three categories: outstanding, good, or weak. The "outstanding" nominees were to constitute an initial short list of potential award winners, though other candidates could be added to this list by the committee. After each validator's presentation, the selectors asked questions and discussed the nominee, but no comparative rankings were made by the committee at this phase of the discussion.

Presentation of the Nominees by the Validators

Twelve nomination forms had been submitted by employees, with one nominee receiving two separate nominations. After each nominee was described to the committee by a validator, committee members were allowed to ask for clarifications regarding the facts presented or to add facts that not been mentioned. Then the validator was asked to rank the nomination as "outstanding," "average," or "weak," in order to develop a short list for discussion of the relative strengths of the nominees.

(1) Patrick R. Defoe, Asset Manager, Grand Isle, Louisiana

The first nomination presented was Patrick R. Defoe, Asset Manager, Grand Isle, Gulf Coast & Mid-Continent Business Unit, Lafayette, Louisiana. "Patrick Defoe is an example of ethical leadership in a very unexciting business unit," his validator began.

> The Grand Isle asset (50+ platforms and associated pipelines situated in the Gulf of Mexico) was a mature field, destined to be sold off within several years. The reservoir was depleting, making the property no longer internally competitive for development funding. That information gets around, and the tendency is for everyone involved, from the bottom to the top, to get lax on dotting the i's and crossing the t's. Everyone is worried about his/her own future with the company. Especially toward the end, as people begin transferring out or retiring, it's difficult to uphold the value of the asset for sale. Patrick would not let that happen. He let people know that there was work to be done and that it would be done according to Conoco standards. His persistent and sustained leadership approach over a six-year period turned around the performance of Grand Isle in every respect. He introduced new programs in vendor convergence, alliance contracting, and a proactive maintenance, and began to actively manage the unit's relationships with regulatory bodies such as the Minerals Management Service. He would not tolerate ethical or other core value lapses from employees or from contractors. When computer equipment on some of the platforms was missing, phones were stolen, and employees' cars were vandalized, he followed up with a thorough investigation rather than looking the other way. These could have been considered minor incidents since the monetary value was small and the unit would soon be sold. Patrick felt business ethics involved the small things as well as the big things. When there were allegations of environmental misconduct and unethical behavior involving documents, he called in Legal/Security and gave them a free hand to investigate no matter who was involved. As it turned out, both allegations were essentially unfounded, but he implemented the minor changes recommended by the investigators.
>
> Pat Defoe motivated his people to deliver, and they did in terms of costs per barrel, safety, and environmental stewardship. As the description on the nomination form indicates, platform fires decreased from 17 in 1996 to none in 1999, and incidents of regulatory noncompliance dropped from 42 to 2 in the last year. The continuous improvement in the asset's performance was crucial to the successful sale, which realized some $47M for the company's bottom line.

"How did he keep his employees motivated when they knew the property was up for sale?" one selector asked. "Usually employees just want to retire or get transferred out and leave the problems to someone else."

"He took it upon himself to actively network for other employment opportunities throughout Conoco," replied the validator. "While getting rid of an asset of this size inevitably results in some layoffs, he found places throughout Conoco, in Downstream, Natural Gas and Gas Pipelines, in Venezuela, Dubai, Indonesia, and U.S. Upstream, for high-performing individuals, while at the same time maintaining the quality of work at Grand Isle. He carved out several 'win-win' solutions for Conoco. I can close by saying that this is a strong nomination. Because of his good work, Pat has been put in charge of assimilating an acquisition in Canada."

"A good example of the fact that no good deed goes unpunished!" one of the outside selectors noted.

(2) Georgian LPG Terminal Project Team, Georgia and Russia

The next nomination presented was the Georgian LPG Terminal Project Team. The team members included David Huber, Lead, Conoco Energy Ventures, Istanbul & Batumi; Roy Mills, Finance, London & Batumi; Harry Crofton, Development Engineering, London; Mikhail Gordin, Supply Logistics, Moscow; Asuman Yazici, Marketing Manager, Istanbul; Fiona Braid, Legal, London; and Pat Cook, Human Resources, London. "This nomination represents ethical conduct in very difficult circumstances by employees some of whom were fairly new in their positions with Conoco," the validator began.

> It is an Indiana Jones story. You arrive at the airport in an exotic regional capital with a briefcase full of $100 bills and you have to open a bank account, find a hotel room, and start doing business there.
>
> Conoco saw an opportunity to become the first western oil company to establish offices and a hydrocarbon operation in Batumi by refurbishing a liquefied petroleum gas terminal there for transshipment and sale of LPG gas in Turkey and the eastern Mediterranean. The idea was to buy the product in Russia and ship it by rail to the terminal. This was Conoco's first venture into the area so it was critical that the team set the proper ethical tone for future business and that all employees, expatriate and native, uphold the Conoco values. The target was to have the first trainload of gas arrive at the terminal just as the repairs were completed. They were financing the remedial work on the terminal; purchasing the LPG; arranging for transportation through customs in Russia, Azerbaijan, and Georgia; making terminal arrangements in Adjaria; and reselling the product in Turkey. Roy Mills was overseeing the transfer of funds that had to be coordinated with the rebuilding of the terminal by a Turkish contractor based on engineering work monitored by Harry Crofton. Mikhail Gordin, who at that time was based in Moscow, was scouring the country to secure a supply of natural gas and negotiating a transportation agreement with both a freight forwarder and the local refinery management. There were many setbacks at both ends, frequently created by pressure to sweeten deals and alter scheduled work plans. Though bribes and kickbacks are illegal in these areas, many companies who operate there accept them as distasteful necessities because the legal infrastructure is often insufficient to stop such practices. There was a lot of pressure on the team members to go along with these types of payments in order to keep the project on schedule. By their refusal to make any "extraordinary" payments and their constant reminder to local employees, suppliers, and local customs and tax officials that business would have to be done according to Conoco standards or not at all, the project now operates successfully without constant harassment for such payments.
>
> David Huber, the team lead, used his persistence and experience of working in Russia to convince the local government of Adjaria that LPG terminaling and transportation via Batumi would be an attractive business opportunity. The nominator points out that through his vision setting and understanding of the cultural differences and language barriers, David was able to assemble a multinational, multilingual team capable of working across all of the countries involved: Mikhail, who was responsible for finding the gas and transporting it through customs in Russia, Azerbaijan, and Georgia; David

and Harry, who made the terminal arrangements workable in Adjaria; and resale of the product in Turkey by Asuman. It is also important to mention the financial, legal, and human resources services provided by Roy, Fiona, and Pat.

There was one other positive aspect of this story. In order for governments and businesses to understand the Conoco way of doing business, it was crucial to hire local employees who would adhere to Conoco values that ran contrary to some local practices. In an area where personal references are practically worthless, Human Resources, through Pat Cook, checked all references and used a special interview process to vet all new hires. Integrity was a prime concern and a killer factor in hiring. Team members reinforced this concern through advice regarding expected behavior, auditing, and recognition. In addition, in order to assure that good conduct was rewarded by salary schedules appropriate to the region, the team sought salary advice from the United Nations Development Program, a first for an energy company. The UNDP praised the company's treatment of employees in the region. Overall, I think this is a strong nomination.

"What worries me about this situation is that we would be rewarding employees for doing what was expected of them," objected a selector. "The company policy is clear about not paying bribes. These guys did what they were supposed to do."

"Were there any extra pressures from within the company," asked one of the outside selectors, "other than the usual concern to meet targets with a profitable project? That might make their behavior extraordinary. Remember, the guidelines talk about 'overcoming obstacles.'" (See Exhibit 3.)

Well, these employees were relatively new in these particular jobs and new to that area, so even a failure caused by a conflict of Conoco's ethical practices with local practices could have been perceived as more serious than for a more experienced person. In a company like ours that really stands behind its values, failure on those grounds would have been accepted as the right way to do business, but the perception of danger might still be there for newer employees. From a business standpoint, however, there were no more than the usual pressures to succeed.

"There was no pressure directing them to violate the company's ethical standards, but there was extra pressure," another selector said. "Remember that our primary project in the region had already gone under, so the LPG terminal was our only active effort. We needed the terminal to succeed in order to have a platform from which to launch other projects. The team members knew that if they failed, Conoco would likely pull out of the region entirely."

(3) Eric Johnson, EXCEL Paralubes, Lake Charles, Louisiana

"This may not be as dramatic a story," began the validator, "but it represents behavior that deserves recognition just as well. It involves day-to-day ethical leadership that set the tone for the employees of one of our joint ventures. EXCEL Paralubes is an effort to leverage technology and personnel from Conoco and Pennzoil in the creation of a product and profits that neither organization could realize alone. Conoco is the managing partner in the venture, which is sited next to the Conoco facility in Lake Charles."

EXHIBIT 3	**Organizational Structures That Block Ethical Action**

Note: This exhibit is not a Conoco document but is included by the authors to facilitate case discussion.

Are Illegal and Unethical Activities Common in the Workplace?

The 2000 National Business Ethics Survey (NBES'00) conducted by the Ethics Resource Center showed that in comparison to their 1994 survey data, companies are doing more in terms of their ethics programs—more have written standards, ethics training programs, and means for employees to get ethics advice. Many ethics indicators have improved, and a majority of employees are positive about ethics in their organizations. Many employees believe that their supervisors and organizational leaders talk about and model ethical behavior at work. Interestingly, there are relatively few differences in the ethics perceptions of employees in the government, for-profit, and nonprofit sectors.

In a 1997 survey (hereafter "EOAS'97") conducted by the Ethics Officer Association and the American Society of Chartered Life Underwriters and Chartered Financial Consultants, **48%** of American workers admitted to illegal or unethical actions in the past year.

The NBES'00 reported that **33%** of American workers observed behaviors that violated either their organization's ethics standards or the law. [This report was based on a nationally representative telephone survey of 1,500 U.S. employees conducted between November 1999 and February 2000.]

A 1999 survey (hereafter KPMGS'99) conducted by KPMG LLP, a professional services firm, indicated that greater than **75%** of U.S. workers surveyed had observed violations of the law or company standards in the previous twelve months. Nearly **50%** said their company "would significantly lose public trust" if the observed infraction had been reported by the news media. [This report is based on questionnaires sent to the homes of 3,075 randomly selected U.S. working adults in October and November 1999; 2,390 completed questionnaires were returned, for a response rate of 78%.]

What Are the Most Common Illegal and Unethical Activities?

The top five types of unethical/illegal activities in the EOAS'97 were:

1. cutting corners on quality control,
2. covering up incidents,
3. abusing or lying about sick days,
4. deceiving or lying to customers, and
5. putting inappropriate pressure on others.

Others mentioned included cheating on an expense account, discriminating against coworkers, paying or accepting kickbacks, secretly forging signatures, trading sex for sales, and ignoring violations of environmental laws.

The five types of misconduct observed most frequently according to the NBES'00 were:

1. lying,
2. withholding needed information,

(continued)

| EXHIBIT 3 | *(Continued)* |

3. abusive or intimidating behavior toward employees,
4. misreporting actual time or hours worked, and
5. discrimination.

Common infractions cited in the KPMGS'99 were sexual harassment and employment discrimination, while other offenses mentioned included deceptive sales practices, unsafe working conditions, and environmental breaches.

What Are the Factors That Lead to Illegal and Unethical Activities in the Workplace?

The top ten factors that workers reported in EOAS'97 as triggering their unethical activities are: balancing work and family, poor internal communications, poor leadership, work hours and workload, lack of management support, need to meet sales, budget or profit goals, little or no recognition of achievements, company politics, personal financial worries, and insufficient resources.

Mid-level managers most often reported a high level of pressure to act unethically or illegally (20%). Employees of large companies cited such pressure more often than those at small businesses (21% versus 14%). High levels of pressure were reported more often by high school graduates than by college graduates (21% versus 13%).

The NBES'00 indicated that one in eight employees feels pressure to compromise their organizations' ethics standards. Almost two-thirds who feel this pressure attribute it to internal sources—supervisor, top management, and coworkers. Employees with longer tenure in their organizations feel more pressure to compromise their organizations' ethics standards. Employees who feel this pressure to compromise observe more misconduct in the workplace.

The KPMGS'99 reported that nearly three-fourths of the respondents blamed cynicism and low morale as the reason for employee misconduct. Fifty-five percent of respondents said their CEO was unapproachable if an employee needed to deliver bad news; 61 percent thought their company would not discipline individuals guilty of an ethical infraction.

An Organizational Focus Is as Important for Understanding Ethical Behavior as an Individual Focus

Since many of the causes cited as triggering unethical behavior are organizational factors, an organizational focus is as important as an individual focus for understanding the obstacles to ethical behavior. By focusing on structure, it is possible to identify certain common features of business organizations that act as organizational blocks to ethical behavior. These ways of organizing business activity can make it difficult for individuals to act in an ethical way, even if the corporation's ethics code requires ethical behavior. James A. Waters ("Catch 22; Corporate Morality As an Organizational Phenomenon," *Organizational*

(continued)

EXHIBIT 3 *(Continued)*

Dynamics, Spring 1978. Reprinted in Donaldson & Werhane, *Ethical Issues in Business,* 3rd Edition, 1988) identifies seven such blocks to ethical action:

(a) Strong role models who follow unethical practices make it difficult for new employees trained by them to imagine how the assigned tasks could be done without unethical practices. Corporations must pay careful attention to the messages that new employees get during their training about the importance of following the firm's ethics code.

(b) The strict line of command followed in many organizations makes it difficult for individuals down the chain to resist an immediate supervisor's order to do something unethical. The employee must assume that the order has come from higher up the chain and represents company policy. If there are no channels of communication for questioning the ethics of an action without going to the higher-ups who presumably originated the order, the employee is unlikely to risk retribution by going above his/her supervisor's head. Thus, compliance in unethical activities can often be enforced by lower-level supervisors without the higher company officials ever knowing about it.

(c) The separation of policy decisions from their implementation can be a strong block to ethical action. In most organizations, policy is set by upper management without discussion with lower-level employees. Lower-level employees may then be forced to resort to unethical activities in order to carry out unreasonable policies or goals set by the top management or risk losing their jobs.

(d) The division of work necessary to accomplish the goals of large organizations also makes reporting unethical activities difficult. Employees in one channel do not see it as their responsibility to report wrongdoing in other channels, nor do they usually have enough information about what is going on throughout the organization to be certain that the activities are unethical.

(e) Task group cohesiveness can frustrate even well-structured internal reporting procedures. Members of a work group who are engaged in unethical activities will exert strong pressure on every member to be loyal to the group rather than report the activities to the company.

(f) Loyalty to the company can lead to protection from outside intervention by the law or adverse public opinion. Employees can avoid investigating reported unethical activities for fear that word will get out that wrongdoing has occurred.

(g) Another organizational block is constituted by ambiguity about priorities. Corporate ethics codes may not make it clear to employees how conflicts between performance criteria and ethical criteria should be resolved. Companies may reward employees only on the basis of the "hard" measurable criteria of meeting sales goals or profit projections, with no consideration given to the means used to achieve these ends.

Two further blocks that Waters does not mention are time pressure, which may make unethical shortcuts seem like the most expedient solution to a workload that cannot be completed in the time permitted. Inadequate resources to complete the job with ethical means may also pressure employees into unethical shortcuts. Overcoming these organizational blocks in meeting the expected standards of behavior would qualify as "extraordinary" and worthy of recognition.

The nomination came from a Conoco manager working as the Organizational Development Coordinator for Petrozuata Upgrader, another joint venture in Venezuela. The nominator had been part of the EXCEL startup and knew that EXCEL had developed innovative work processes that had contributed to the success of EXCEL and would be readily adaptable to help with organizational development in Petrozuata. He asked Eric to share them with Petrozuata. Eric responded that he would be happy to help but that certain of these processes represented a competitive advantage to the EXCEL joint venture. Though these processes would certainly add to the bottom line at Conoco through its Venezuela venture, they could not be given out in fairness to the joint venture partner, Pennzoil. This response from a loyal Conoco employee who was conscious of his ethical and legal obligations to his joint venture so impressed the nominator that he submitted Eric for the award. The nominator also stated that, following Eric Johnson's leadership in this area, he has conveyed this standard of conduct to his peers at Petrozuata so that they are aware of their obligation to protect not only Conoco's interests but those of their joint venture partners as well.

As I looked into Eric's activities at EXCEL, I was more and more impressed that this was not an isolated incident and that Eric was modeling ethical conduct crucial to the success of Conoco joint ventures. If we are the managing partner in the venture, the other partner needs to be confident that the Conoco employees in charge will not show any favoritism to Conoco in cost sharing. And to hear tell from the EXCEL and Conoco people on the site, Eric is fair to a fault. The EXCEL operation is right next to the Conoco plant in Lake Charles, Louisiana, and the two plants jointly use some of the facility. Eric has gotten flak from his counterparts at the Conoco plant for not cutting them any slack on sharing costs for these joint facilities. They would rather not have these costs show up in their budgets, but he reminds them that he is wearing his EXCEL hat and needs to look out for the interests of EXCEL. On one occasion, for example, he made Conoco pay for its share of grading the road that borders both plant sites. While that may seem unimportant, it sets a tone for all of the Conoco employees lent to the venture and has given Pennzoil such confidence in the fairness of the operation that they are planning additional ventures with Conoco. I think this nomination is another strong one.

"But again, isn't this conduct that we expect of all employees? Does it arise to an award level?" asked a selector.

"Well, you need to realize that his long-term career is with Conoco and that most managers after several years with the joint venture return to work with their parent company. By upholding these standards he is risking burning some bridges with managers at Conoco that he might be working for or with in the future," replied the validator.

"We also have to consider that joint ventures of this kind are important to a company the size of Conoco, and we haven't been doing them for that long. We need models for how to make those ventures work, and an award might help to get the message out as to our company's expectations," another selector added.

(4) Terry Beene, Retail Marketing, Houston, Texas

"When Conoco, for competitive reasons, elected to include convenience stores in our retail stations," the validator began, "the company found itself with a whole new kind of employee."

Instead of the salaried engineers, managers, and support staff who make up most of the workforce, we were responsible for recruiting, training, motivating, and monitoring a group of not very highly paid hourly workers who were our retail face to the public. In addition, these not very highly paid workers were surrounded by all kinds [of] temptations in the form of merchandise and cash, in a situation where direct supervision was too costly. Looking at this problem, Terry decided that there were two main options. One was to assume that a small percentage of employees were going to steal and concentrate on catching and punishing them. The other was to assume that the great majority of employees were honest and that a program that spent time and money recognizing their honesty in the face of temptation would motivate them to continue their good conduct. Such a program could convert or drive out the bad actors as well.

Terry decided to emphasize "keeping honest people honest." The program was designed to "catch people being honest and reward them for it." The first step was a strong training program for new employees that began with a unit that explained all the ways that employees can steal from a convenience store. Employees who expect to steal were thereby warned that the company knew all of their methods and most of the dropouts occurred in this early phase of the training. Honest employees understood what the temptations were and were taught how to avoid them. They understood that the company uses extensive control measures and that one of the purposes of these was to "catch them doing something right." Once on the job, the employees were continually motivated to be honest with visits by mystery shoppers who rewarded them on the spot for good behavior and reported on store procedures to management.

A second phase of the program involved systemized operational practices designed to decrease the opportunity for theft to occur. There are extensive control measures to manage inventory and track sales through scanning technology and regular and surprise audits. Security cameras have been installed in virtually all stores within the last two years. Honest employees were encouraged to be honest by knowing that dishonest behavior would be caught and punished. But the emphasis even in the audits was to reward people whose inventory and cash are all properly accounted for rather than focusing on the threat that controls pose to those who do wrong. The desire to accurately measure inventory and control losses was the catalyst in the decision to employ new and innovative scanning technology. The data resulting from this Loss Control Program has also proved valuable in the development of trend reports and standardized operations reports that can highlight loss control problems before they become critical.

The results of this approach to managing retail sales have been significant. While the standard rate of losses in the industry is 2% to 4% of gross revenue per year, Conoco's loss percentage has averaged 1.13% over the past three years. This difference translates into additional revenues of $1.5MM and $2.5MM per annum over the past two years. The turnover rate for employees is also significantly lower than the industry average, which contributes to lower recruitment and training costs.

In his position as Director of Security in Retail Operations, Terry was the sole employee in the retail sector assigned to Loss Control. His work designing and selling this program throughout the sector resulted in a functionwide commitment to the Retail Loss Control Program at all levels. Because of his efforts, loss control focused not on fixing problems by firing dishonest employees but on training personnel to recognize the importance of honesty and on implementing sustainable processes to prevent problems from occurring. All in all, I think this nomination warrants serious consideration.

(5) Raymond S. Marchand, Upstream Aame, Damascus, Syria

"Raymond Marchand is a unique individual."

Born a French-Algerian, Raymond has translated his dual nationality into a unique understanding of how to preserve Conoco values in some of the most complex and challenging business cultures in the world. As a young man he fought the Algerians as a member [of] the French Foreign Legion's "Blackfoot" brigade, a group that planned to parachute into Paris to assassinate French president De Gaulle for granting Algerian independence. After his military service, Raymond began working for Conoco as a laborer in the 1960s and quickly advanced into management responsibility. He has been in charge of the company's operations in Chad, Egypt, the Congo, Somalia, Angola, and Nigeria, and is now heading operations in Syria. His leadership in doing business the Conoco way or not doing business at all involved relationships both outside and inside the company. By his own example he established a clear policy of integrity in all dealings with government officials and contractors, and taught both native and expatriate employees that requests for "exceptional" payments could be refused continually without insulting the person making the request.

Raymond is most masterful in difficult business environments. In Somalia, the U.S. government employed his experience in negotiating in a corrupt environment without compromising his standards. As the situation there deteriorated, Raymond was forced to leave the country to the sound of gunfire. In Nigeria, his high ethical standards and personal negotiating style changed the paradigm of what was acceptable business conduct for Conoco's Nigerian employees, our Nigerian indigenous partners, and our Nigerian government contacts. His approach took the risk of losing business opportunities. The respect he garnered for his way of operating, however, gained opportunities for Conoco, especially as a new government under President Obasanjo made the ideal of integrity fashionable in that country.

Nigeria was a particularly challenging environment because 95% of the Conoco workforce was native-born and had grown up in an atmosphere in which companies bought their way into whatever situation they wanted to be in. Marchand taught the whole organization from top to bottom that business could be conducted without such payments. His alternative to bribes was establishing relationships based on trust and dependability, an approach that requires spending the time to build personal relationships. Actions speak louder than words in establishing trust, and as his nominator put it, "You can see his heart behind everything he says and does." With the company's indigenous partners he was successful in resolving contractual problems and educating them about Conoco's core values, especially ethical behavior. In doing so he earned not only their respect but a wider recognition within the business community and the government that Conoco's integrity is second to none in Nigeria.

Because of his leadership, many of our operating costs have been lowered by newly empowered, bright young native Nigerian employees. Throughout Nigeria, I am told, all the Conoco employees respond to requests for "extraordinary" payments with Marchand's characteristic smile, two raised and waving hands, and the phrase "No can do!"

delivered in a loud friendly voice. This behavior has become so standard that most people do not even request payments from Conoco employees.

Inside the company, Marchand has shown an equally high level of integrity. Whenever accusations have surfaced about irregularities in his operations, he has immediately requested a full company investigation of the matter and has ensured the full cooperation of all employees in his shop. When notified that he was being posted to Syria, he requested a meeting with a management committee from Auditing and Legal Affairs to map out strategies for dealing with the business environment in that country. I think his career achievements set a standard against which future award nominations can be measured.

"That mention of career achievement raises some interesting points regarding the award criteria," observed an outside selector. "Should the President's Ethics Award recognize only heroic ethical conduct that goes beyond the standard expected of every employee, or should employees be rewarded for meeting the expected standards? And if employees are recognized for meeting the expected standard, should this be only for consistent behavior over time (a lifetime of ethical action), or for behavior in difficult circumstances (pressures to meet other performance criteria)? Or would the company's objectives be furthered in giving awards sometimes for behavior that shows how the standards can be followed in ordinary circumstances (a good example, or 'Charlie Brown' award)?"

"It seems that we have examples of all of these possibilities in this group of nominees," another selector said. "In giving this first award, the company will be setting some kind of a standard for future nominations, though an evolution of the standards is certainly possible. But I think it is important to keep in mind that our decision may encourage some and discourage other types of nominations from being submitted in the future."

"We might want to consider giving more than one award this first year, since we are reviewing conduct from several prior years rather than one prior year," one selector said.

"It is interesting," another selector noted, "that we have some real diversity among the nominees. We have overseas and domestic. We have upstream (exploration and production), midstream (transportation and refining), and downstream (retailing). We have career nominations and specific project nominations, and we have individuals and a team. The only kind of nomination missing is for a single action that was unique enough, had such important consequences, or was done under such difficult circumstances that it was significant enough for a nomination."

Making the Decision

The morning passed quickly as the nominees were presented. "These five nominees have made the short list based on the validators' evaluations," the facilitator said as she stood up to indicate that the descriptive phase of the work was concluded. "But any of the others can be considered as we begin to make judgments this afternoon. Archie [President Dunham] considers this award to be important for Conoco. We have a real task ahead of us. Steve has promised us an excellent lunch before we decide who to recommend for the first President's Award for Business Ethics."

Questions

1. What purposes does the Conoco ethics award serve?
2. By arguing that Conoco is committed to ethics and legal compliance because they are good for business, do the award guidelines suggest that ethics and the law should be followed only when they can be shown to affect the bottom line?
3. How should the company evaluate the success of the award program?

Case 4

Home Depot: Commitment to Social Responsibility

This case was prepared by Gwyneth V. Walters for classroom discussion, rather than to illustrate either effective or ineffective handling of an administrative, ethical, or legal decision by individuals or management.

When Bernie Marcus and Arthur Blank opened the first Home Depot store in Atlanta in 1979, they forever changed the hardware and home-improvement retailing industry. Marcus and Blank envisioned huge warehouse-style stores stocked with an extensive selection of products offered at the lowest prices. Today, do-it-yourselfers and building contractors can browse from among 35,000 different products for the home and yard, from kitchen and bathroom fixtures to carpeting, lumber, paint, tools, and plants and landscaping items. Some Home Depot stores are open twenty-four hours a day, but customers can also order products online and pick them up from their local Home Depot stores or have them delivered. The company also offers free home-improvement clinics to teach customers how to tackle everyday projects like tiling a bathroom. For those customers who prefer not to "do it yourself," most stores offer installation services. Well-trained employees, recognizable by their orange aprons, are always on hand to help customers find just the right item or to demonstrate the proper use of a particular tool.

Today, Home Depot employs 315,000 people and operates approximately 1,700 Home Depot stores, EXPO Design Centers, and Villager's Hardware stores in the United States, Canada, and Mexico. It also operates four wholly owned subsidiaries: Apex Supply Company, Georgia Lighting, Maintenance Warehouse, and National Blinds and Wallpaper. The company racks up more than $58 billion in annual sales, making it the second-largest retailer in the United States. Now the world's largest home-improvement retailer, Home Depot continues to do things on a grand scale, including putting its corporate muscle behind a tightly focused social responsibility agenda.

Environmental Initiatives

Just because Home Depot is a big corporation doesn't mean it is an uncaring and impersonal one. In fact, cofounders Bernard Marcus and Arthur Blank nurtured a corporate culture that emphasizes social responsibility, especially with regard to the company's impact on the natural environment. Home Depot began its environmental program on the twentieth anniversary of Earth Day in 1990 by adopting a set of Environmental Principles (see Figure C4.1). These principles have since been adopted by the National Retail Hardware Association and Home Center Institute, which represents more than 46,000 retail hardware stores and home centers.

Guided by its Environmental Principles, Home Depot has initiated a number of programs to minimize the firm's—and its customers'—impact on the environment. In 1991, the retailer began using recycled content materials for store and office supplies, advertising, signs, and shopping bags. It also established a process for evaluating the environmental claims made by suppliers. The following year, the firm launched a program to recycle wallboard shipping packaging, which became the in-

---

FIGURE C4.1   **Home Depot's Environmental Principles**

At the Home Depot, we realize how vitally important it is to conserve our environment. The following principles help to guide us in our actions and lead us down a path of sustainability.

- We are committed to improving the environment by selling products that are manufactured, packaged and labeled in a responsible manner, that take the environment into consideration and that provide greater value to our customers.

- We will support efforts to provide accurate, informative product labeling of environmental marketing claims.

- We will strive to eliminate unnecessary packaging.

- We will recycle and encourage the use of materials and products with recycled content.

- We will conserve natural resources by using energy and water wisely and seek further opportunities to improve the resource efficiency of our stores.

- We will comply with environmental laws and will maintain programs and procedures to ensure compliance.

- We are committed to minimizing the environmental health and safety risk for our associates and our customers.

- We will train our employees to enhance understanding of environmental issues and policies and to promote excellence in job performance and all environmental matters.

- We will encourage our customers to become environmentally conscious shoppers.

Source: "The Home Depot Environmental Principles," Home Depot, www.homedepot.com/HDUS/EN_US/ corporate/corp_respon/environ_principles.shtml, accessed May 5, 2003. Reprinted by permission from The Home Depot Headquarters, Homer TLC.

dustry's first "reverse distribution" program. It also opened the first drive-thru recycling center, in Duluth, Georgia, in 1993. In 1994, Home Depot became the first home-improvement retailer to offer wood products from tropical and temperate forests certified as "well-managed" by the Scientific Certification System's Forest Conservation Program. The company also began to replace wooden shipping pallets with reusable "slip sheets" to minimize waste and energy use and to reduce pressure on hardwood resources used to make wood pallets.

In 1999, Home Depot announced that it would endorse independent, third-party forest certification and wood from certified forests. The company joined the Certified Forests Products Council, a nonprofit organization that promotes responsible forest product buying practices and the sale of wood from Certified Well-Managed Forests. Despite this action, environmentalists picketed company stores to protest Home Depot's practice of selling wood products from old-growth forests. Led by the Rainforest Action Network, environmentalists have picketed Home Depot and other home center stores for years in an effort to get companies to stop selling products from the world's old-growth forests, of which just 20 percent survive. Later that year, during Home Depot's twentieth anniversary celebration, Arthur Blank announced,

> Our pledge to our customers, associates, and stockholders is that Home Depot will stop selling wood products from environmentally sensitive areas. . . . Home Depot embraces its responsibility as a global leader to help protect endangered forests. By the end of 2002, we will eliminate from our stores wood from endangered areas—including lauan, redwood, and cedar products—and give preference to "certified" wood.

To be "certified" by the Forest Stewardship Council (FSC), a supplier's wood products must be tracked from the forest, through manufacturing and distribution, to the customer, and harvesting, manufacturing, and distribution practices must ensure a balance of social, economic, and environmental factors. Blank also challenged competitors to follow Home Depot's lead, and within two years, Lowe's, the number two home-improvement retailer; Wickes, a lumber company; and Andersen Corp., a window manufacturer, had met that challenge. By 2003, Home Depot reported that it had reduced its purchases of Indonesian lauan, a tropical rain forest hardwood used in door components, by 70 percent, and it continued to increase its purchases of certified sustainable wood products.

Home Depot has also been very generous to environmental organizations and causes, donating $1.5 million in 2002 to nonprofit groups like Keep America Beautiful, the Tampa Audubon Society, the World Wildlife Fund Canada, and the Nature Conservancy. The company also established a carpooling program for more than 3,000 employees in the Atlanta area. Home Depot remains the only North American home-improvement retailer with a full-time staff dedicated to environmental issues. These efforts have yielded many rewards in addition to improved relations with environmental stakeholders. Home Depot's environmental programs earned the company an A on the Council on Economic Priorities Corporate Report Card, a Vision of America Award from Keep America Beautiful, and, along with Scientific Certification Systems and Collin Pine, a President's Council for Sustainable Development Award. The company was also voted *Fortune* magazine's "America's Most Admired Retailer" for six years in a row.

Corporate Philanthropy

In addition to its environmental initiatives, Home Depot focuses corporate social responsibility efforts on disaster relief, affordable housing, and at-risk youth. The company has an annual philanthropic budget of $25 million, which it directs back to the communities it serves and to the interests of its employees through its Matching Gift Program. The company also posts a Social Responsibility Report on its web site detailing its annual charitable contributions and the community programs in which it has become involved over the years.

Home Depot works with more than 350 affiliates of Habitat for Humanity, a nonprofit organization that constructs and repairs homes for qualified low-income families. The company also works with Christmas in April, a nonprofit organization that rehabilitates housing for the elderly and disabled. Through such programs, thousands of Home Depot associates volunteer, using products supplied by the company, to help build or refurbish affordable housing for their communities, thereby reinforcing their own skills and familiarity with the company's products. Home Depot also provides support to dozens of local housing groups around the country, as well as specific community events, like Hands on San Francisco Day.

Home Depot also supports YouthBuildUSA, a nonprofit organization that provides training and skill development for young people. YouthBuildUSA gives students the opportunity to help rehabilitate housing for homeless and low-income families. Home Depot contributes to many at-risk youth programs, including Big Brothers/Big Sisters, KaBOOM!, and the National Center for Missing and Exploited Children.

In recent years, Home Depot has also tackled the growing need for relief from disasters such as hurricanes, tornadoes, and earthquakes. When Hurricane Floyd devastated parts of North Carolina, the company donated nearly $100,000 in cleanup and rebuilding supplies to relief agencies, sent more than 50,000 gallons of water to storm victims, extended credit to more than fifty communities, and sponsored clinics on how to repair damage resulting from the storm. After the terrorist attacks on September 11, 2001, the company set up three command centers with more than 200 associates to help coordinate relief supplies such as dust masks, gloves, batteries, and tools to victims and rescue workers. When a deadly tornado struck Oklahoma City, Home Depot helped by rebuilding roofs, planting trees, and clearing roads. The company has contributed emergency relief funds, supplies, and labor to American Red Cross relief efforts. Home Depot also partners with the Weather Channel in Project SafeSide, a national severe weather public awareness program.

Employee Relations

On a more personal level, Home Depot encourages employees to become involved in the community through volunteer and civic activities. On any given day, a small army of Home Depot volunteers may be found swinging hammers and waving paintbrushes to fix up a family shelter, planting trees to spruce up an inner-city park, or framing a Habitat for Humanity house for a deserving family. In 2002, employees volunteered 7 million hours to community causes. Such contributions allow employees to make a real difference in their communities while enhancing their skills along with their employer's reputation.

Home Depot also strives to apply social responsibility to its employment practices, with the goal of assembling a diverse workforce that truly reflects the population of the markets it serves. However, the company recently settled a class-action lawsuit brought by female employees who claimed they were paid less than male employees, awarded fewer pay raises, and promoted less often. The $87.5 million settlement represented one of the largest settlements of a gender discrimination lawsuit in U.S. history at the time. In announcing the settlement, the company emphasized that it was not admitting to wrongdoing and defended its record, saying it "provides opportunities for all of its associates to develop successful professional careers and is proud of its strong track record of having successful women involved in all areas of the company."

The settlement required Home Depot to establish a formal system to ensure that employees can notify managers of their interest in advancing to a management or sales position. The company's Job Preference Program (JPP), an automated hiring and promotion computer program, opens all jobs and applicants to the companywide network, eliminates unqualified applications, and helps managers to learn employee aspirations and skills in a more effective manner. The JPP has also brought positive changes for the many women and minority managers working at Home Depot. Despite these efforts, the company faced a new sexual discrimination lawsuit brought by the U.S. Equal Employment Opportunity Commission in 2002 on behalf of a woman who claimed that she had been rejected for several positions at a Los Angeles–area store in favor of less-qualified men. Denying the accusations, a spokesperson for Home Depot declared, "The company has a zero tolerance for discrimination of any kind. The company plans to defend itself vigorously."

A Strategic Commitment to Social Responsibility

Knowing that stakeholders, especially customers, feel good about a company that actively commits resources to environmental and social issues, company executives believe that social responsibility can and should be a strategic component of Home Depot's business operations. The company remains committed to its focused strategy of philanthropy and volunteerism. This commitment extends throughout the company, fueled by top-level support from the cofounders and reinforced by a corporate culture that places great value on playing a responsible role within the communities it serves.

Questions

1. On the basis of Home Depot's response to environmentalists' issues, describe the attributes (power, legitimacy, urgency) of this stakeholder. Using the Reactive-Defensive-Accommodative-Proactive Scale in Chapter 2, assess the company's strategy and performance with environmental and employee stakeholders.
2. As a publicly traded corporation, how can Home Depot justify budgeting more than $25 million annually for philanthropy? What areas other than the

environment, disaster relief, affordable housing, and at-risk youth might be appropriate for strategic philanthropy by Home Depot?

3. As part of its settlement of the gender discrimination suit brought against it, Home Depot established a formal system for employees to inform managers of their interest in advancement. What other steps might Home Depot take to strengthen the rights of its employees to equal treatment in the workplace?

Sources

1999 Annual Report, Home Depot, 2000; Jim Carlton, "How Home Depot and Activists Joined to Cut Logging Abuse," *Wall Street Journal,* September 26, 2000, pp. A1+; John Caulfield, "Social Responsibility: Retailer's Community Affairs Agenda Includes Disaster Relief, Housing, Youth and the Environment," *National Home Center News,* December 17, 2001, via www.findarticles.com; Cora Daniels, "To Hire a Lumber Expert, Click Here," *Fortune,* April 3, 2000, pp. 267–270; Kirstin Downey Grimsley, "Home Depot Settles Gender Bias Lawsuit," *Washington Post,* September 20, 1997, p. D1; "Hands on San Francisco Announces Fifth Annual Citywide Day of Volunteerism on May Tenth," *Business Wire,* April 30, 2003, www.businesswire.com; Home Depot, www.homedepot.com/, accessed May 5, 2003; "Home Depot Faces Federal Sex Discrimination Suit," *USA Today,* September 6, 2002, www.usatoday.com/money/industries/retail/2002-09-06-home-depot-sued_x.htm; "Home Depot Lambasted for Attempt to Go Green," *Environmental News Network,* March 15, 1999, www.enn.com/; "The Home Depot Launches Environmental Wood Purchasing Policy," *Rainforest Action Network,* August 26, 1999, www.ran.org/ran_campaigns/old_growth/news/hd_pr.html; "Home Depot Retools Timber Policy," *Memphis Business Journal,* January 2, 2003, www.bizjournals.com/memphis/stories/2002/12/30/daily12.html; Susan Jackson and Tim Smart, "Mom and Pop Fight Back," *Business Week,* April 14, 1997, p. 46; Janice Revell, "Can Home Depot Get Its Groove Back?" *Fortune,* February 3, 2003, www.fortune.com/fortune/investing/articles/0,15114,409691,00.html.

Case 5

New Belgium Brewing Company: Environmental and Social Concerns

This case was prepared by Nikole Haiar for classroom discussion, rather than to illustrate either effective or ineffective handling of an administrative, ethical, or legal decision by individuals or management.

lthough most of the companies frequently cited as examples of ethical and socially responsible firms are large corporations, it is the social responsibility initiatives of small businesses that often have the greatest impact on local communities and neighborhoods. These businesses create jobs and provide goods and services for customers in smaller markets that larger corporations often are not interested in serving. Moreover, they also contribute money, resources, and volunteer time to local causes. Their owners often serve as community and neighborhood leaders, and many choose to apply their skills and some of the fruits of their success to tackling local problems and issues that benefit everyone in the community. One such small business is the New Belgium Brewing Company, Inc., based in Fort Collins, Colorado.

History of the New Belgium Brewing Company

The idea for the New Belgium Brewing Company began with a bicycling trip through Belgium. Belgium is arguably the home of some of the world's finest ales, some of which have been brewed for centuries in that country's monasteries. As Jeff Lebesch, an American electrical engineer, cruised around that country on his fat-tired mountain bike, he wondered if he could produce such high-quality beers back home in Colorado. After acquiring the special strain of yeast used to brew Belgian-style ales, Lebesch returned home and began to experiment in his Colorado basement. When his beers earned thumbs up from friends, Lebesch decided to market them.

The New Belgium Brewing Company (NBB) opened for business in 1991 as a tiny basement operation in Lebesch's home in Fort Collins. Lebesch's wife, Kim Jordan, became the firm's marketing director. They named their first brew Fat Tire Amber Ale in honor of Lebesch's bike ride through Belgium. New Belgium beers quickly developed a small but devoted customer base, first in Fort Collins and then throughout Colorado. The brewery soon outgrew the couple's basement and moved into an old railroad depot before settling into its present custom-built facility in 1995. The brewery includes an automated brew house, two quality assurance labs, and numerous technological innovations for which New Belgium has become nationally recognized as a "paradigm of environmental efficiencies."

Today, New Belgium Brewing Company offers a variety of permanent and seasonal ales and pilsners. The company's standard line includes Sunshine Wheat, Blue Paddle Pilsner, Abbey Ale, Trippel Ale, 1554 Black Ale, and the original Fat Tire Amber Ale, still the firm's bestseller. Some customers even refer to the company as the Fat Tire Brewery. The brewery also markets two types of specialty beers on a seasonal basis. Seasonal ales include Frambozen and Abbey Grand Cru, which are released at Thanksgiving, and Christmas and Farmhouse Ales, which are sold during the early fall months. The firm occasionally offers one-time-only brews, such as LaFolie, a wood-aged beer, which are sold only until the batch runs out.

Since its founding, NBB's most effective form of advertising has been its customers' word of mouth. Indeed, before New Belgium beers were widely distributed throughout Colorado, one liquor store owner in Telluride is purported to have offered people gas money if they would stop by and pick up New Belgium beer on their way through Fort Collins. NBB continues to expand, most recently into California, and is currently the fifth largest craft brewer in the United States. Although New Belgium beers are distributed in just one-third of the United States, the brewery receives numerous e-mails and phone calls every day inquiring when its beers will be available elsewhere.

New Belgium's Purpose and Core Beliefs

New Belgium's dedication to quality, the environment, and its employees and customers is expressed in its mission statement: "To operate a profitable brewery which makes our love and talent manifest." The company's stated core values and beliefs about its role as an environmentally concerned and socially responsible brewer include:

- Producing world-class beers
- Promoting beer culture and the responsible enjoyment of beer
- Continuous, innovative quality and efficiency improvements
- Transcending customers' expectations
- Environmental stewardship: minimizing resource consumption, maximizing energy efficiency, and recycling
- Kindling social, environmental, and cultural change as a business role model
- Cultivating potential: through learning, participative management, and the pursuit of opportunities
- Balancing the myriad needs of the company, staff, and their families
- Committing ourselves to authentic relationships, communications, and promises
- Having Fun

David Kemp, a longtime brewery employee, believes that these statements help communicate to customers and other stakeholders what New Belgium, as a company, is about.

Employee Concerns

Recognizing employees' role in the company's success, New Belgium provides many generous benefits. In addition to the usual paid health and dental insurance and retirement plans, employees get a free lunch every other week as well as a free massage once a year, and they can bring their children and dogs to work. Employees who stay with the company for five years earn an all-expenses-paid trip to Belgium to "study beer culture." Perhaps most importantly, employees can also earn stock in the privately held corporation, which grants them a vote in company decisions. New Belgium's employees now own one-third of the growing brewery.

Environmental Concerns

New Belgium's marketing strategy involves linking the quality of its products, as well as their name and look, with the company's philosophy toward affecting the planet. From leading-edge environmental gadgets and high-tech industry advancements to employee-ownership programs and a strong belief in giving back to the community, New Belgium demonstrates its desire to create a living, learning community.

NBB strives for cost-efficient energy-saving alternatives to conducting its business and reducing its impact on the environment. In staying true to the company's core values and beliefs, the brewery's employee-owners unanimously agreed to invest in a wind turbine, making New Belgium the first fully wind-powered brewery in the United States. Since the switch from coal power, New Belgium has been able to reduce its CO_2 emissions by 1,800 metric tons per year. The company further reduces its energy use by employing a steam condenser that captures and reuses the hot water that boils the barley and hops in the production process to start the next brew. The steam is redirected to heat the floor tiles and de-ice the loading docks in cold weather. Another way that NBB conserves energy is by using "sun tubes," which provide natural daytime lighting throughout the brew house all year long.

New Belgium also takes pride in reducing waste through recycling and creative reuse strategies. The company strives to recycle as many supplies as possible, including cardboard boxes, keg caps, office materials, and the amber glass used in bottling. The brewery also stores spent barley and hop grains in an on-premise silo and invites local farmers to pick up the grains, free of charge, to feed their pigs. NBB even encourages its employees to reduce air pollution by using alternative transportation. As an incentive, NBB gives its employees "cruiser bikes"—like the one pictured on its Fat Tire Amber Ale label—after one year of employment and encourages them to ride to work.

Social Concerns

Beyond its use of environment-friendly technologies and innovations, New Belgium Brewing Company strives to improve communities and enhance people's lives through corporate giving, event sponsorship, and philanthropic involvement.

One way that New Belgium demonstrates its corporate citizenship is by donating $1 per barrel of beer sold to various cultural, social, environmental, and drug- and alcohol-awareness programs across the thirteen western states in which it distributes beer. Typical grants range from $2,500 to $5,000. Involvement is spread equally among the thirteen states, unless there is a special need that requires more participation or funding.

NBB also maintains a community bulletin board in its facility where it posts an array of community involvement activities and proposals. This community board allows tourists and employees to see the different ways they can help out the community, and it gives nonprofit organizations a chance to make their needs known. Organizations can even apply for grants through the New Belgium Brewing Company web site, which has a link designated for this purpose.

NBB also sponsors a number of events, with a special focus on those that involve "human-powered" sports that cause minimal damage to the natural environment. Through event sponsorships, such as the Tour de Fat, NBB has raised more than $15,000 for various environmental, social, and cycling nonprofit organizations. In 2000, New Belgium also sponsored the MS 150 "Best Damn Bike Tour," a two-day, fully catered bike tour, from which all proceeds went to benefit more than 5,000 local people with multiple sclerosis. In the same year, NBB also sponsored the Ride the Rockies bike tour, which donated the proceeds from beer sales to local nonprofit groups. The money raised from this annual event funds local projects, such as improving parks and bike trails. In the course of one year, New Belgium can be found at anywhere from 150 to 200 festivals and events, across all thirteen western states.

Organizational Success

New Belgium Brewing Company's efforts to live up to its own high standards have paid off with numerous awards and a very loyal following. It was one of three winners of *Business Ethics* magazine's 2002 Business Ethics Awards for its "dedication to environmental excellence in every part of its innovative brewing process." It also won an honorable mention in the Better Business Bureau's 2002 Torch Award for Outstanding Marketplace Ethics competition. Kim Jordan and Jeff Lebesch were named the 1999 recipients of the Rocky Mountain Region Entrepreneur of the Year Award for manufacturing. The company also captured the award for best mid-sized brewing company of the year and best mid-sized brewmaster at the Great American Beer Festival. In addition, New Belgium took home medals for three different brews, Abbey Belgian Style Ale, Blue Paddle Pilsner, and LaFolie specialty ale. One member of the staff of the Association of Brewers commented that Fat Tire is one of the only brews he'd pay for in a bar.

According to David Edgar, director of the Institute for Brewing Studies, "They've created a very positive image for their company in the beer-consuming public with smart decision-making." Although some members of society do not believe that a company whose major product is alcohol can be socially responsible, New Belgium has set out to prove that for those who make a choice to drink responsibly, the company can do everything possible to contribute to society. Its efforts to promote beer culture and the connoisseurship of beer has even led it to design a special "Worthy

Glass," the shape of which is intended to retain foam, show off color, enhance the visual presentation, and release aroma. New Belgium Brewing Company also promotes the responsible appreciation of beer through its participation in and support of the culinary arts. For instance, it frequently hosts New Belgium Beer Dinners, in which every course of the meal is served with a complementary culinary treat.

Every six-pack of New Belgium Beer displays the phrase, "In this box is our labor of love, we feel incredibly lucky to be creating something fine that enhances people's lives." Although Jeff Lebesch has "semiretired" from the company to focus on other interests, the founders of New Belgium hope this statement captures the spirit of the company. According to employee Dave Kemp, NBB's environmental concern and social responsibility give it a competitive advantage because consumers want to believe in and feel good about the products they purchase. NBB's most important asset is its image—a corporate brand that stands for quality, responsibility, and concern for society. Defining itself as more than just a beer company, the brewer also sees itself as a caring organization that is concerned with all stakeholders, including the community, the environment, and employees.

Questions

1. What environmental issues does the New Belgium Brewing Company work to address? How has NBB taken a strategic approach to addressing these issues? Why do you think the company has chosen to focus on environmental issues?
2. Are New Belgium's social initiatives indicative of strategic philanthropy? Why or why not?
3. Some segments of society vigorously contend that companies that sell alcoholic beverages and tobacco products cannot be socially responsible organizations because of the nature of their primary products. Do you believe that New Belgium Brewing Company's actions and initiatives are indicative of an ethical and socially responsible corporation? Why or why not?
4. What else could New Belgium do to foster ethical and responsible conduct?

Sources

These facts are from Peter Asmus, "Goodbye Coal, Hello Wind," *Business Ethics* 13 (July/August 1999): 10–11; Robert Baun, "What's in a Name? Ask the Makers of Fat Tire," *[Fort Collins] Coloradoan,* October 8, 2000, pp. E1, E3; Rachel Brand, "Colorado Breweries Bring Home 12 Medals in Festival," *Rocky Mountain News,* www.insidedenver.com/news/1008beer6.shtml, accessed November 6, 2000; Stevi Deter, "Fat Tire Amber Ale," The Net Net, www.thenetnet.com/reviews/fat.html, accessed April 29, 2003; DirtWorld.com, www.dirtworld.com/races/Colorado_race745.htm, accessed November 6, 2000; Robert F. Dwyer and John F. Tanner Jr., *Business Marketing* (Irwin McGraw-Hill, 1999), p. 104; "Fat Tire Amber Ale," Achwiegut (The Guide to Austrian Beer), www.austrianbeer.com/beer/b000688.shtml, accessed January 19, 2001; "Four Businesses Honored with Prestigious International Award for Outstanding Marketplace Ethics," Better Business Bureau, press release, September 23, 2002, www.bbb.org/alerts/2002torchwinners.asp; Julie Gordon, "Lebesch Balances Interests in Business, Community," *Coloradoan,* February 26, 2003; Del I. Hawkins, Roger J. Best, and Kenneth A. Coney, *Consumer Behavior: Building Marketing Strategy,* 8th ed. (Irwin McGraw Hill, 2001); David Kemp, Tour Connoisseur, New Belgium Brewing Company, personal interview by Nikole Haiar, November 21, 2000, 1:00 P.M.; New Belgium Brewing Company, Ft. Collins, CO, www.newbelgium.com, accessed April 29, 2003; New Belgium Brewing Company Tour by Nikole Haiar, November 20, 2000, 2:00 P.M.; "New Belgium Brewing Wins Ethics Award," *Denver Business Journal,* January 2, 2003, http://denver.bizjournals.com/denver/stories/2002/12/30/daily21.html; and Dan Rabin, "New Belgium Pours It on for Bike Riders," *Celebrator Beer News,* August/September 1998, www.celebrator.com/9808/rabin.html.

Case 6

DoubleClick: Privacy on the Internet

This case was prepared by Tracy A. Suter, Oklahoma State University, for classroom discussion rather than to illustrate either effective or ineffective handling of an administrative situation.

DoubleClick Inc. is an information revolution phenomenon. What started out as an outgrowth of self-proclaimed computer "geeks" and savvy advertising agency executives has grown into a high-tech heavyweight providing advertising services and information about Internet users for advertisers, web site operators, and other companies. The nature of its business has also put DoubleClick in the center of a brewing controversy over the issue of a person's right to privacy on the Internet. DoubleClick, which contends that it is committed to protecting the privacy of all Internet users, views its role as important in maintaining the Internet as a free medium driven by highly targeted advertising. Consumer activists see it differently, noting that DoubleClick's actions loom larger than its words regarding access to personal information. Opponents, which include the Michigan attorney general Jennifer Granholm, regard DoubleClick's business practices as little more than a "secret, cyber wiretap." To understand how DoubleClick found itself in this uncomfortable position, it is helpful to examine the firm's history, key strategic business units, and the issue of Internet privacy.

Merge onto Silicon Alley

Like many entrepreneurs in recent years, Kevin O'Connor and Dwight Merriman, two Atlanta-based engineers, saw an opportunity to cash in on the growing popularity of the Internet. O'Connor and Merriman had observed the challenges faced by niche-driven, subscription-based content web sites attempting to compete with America Online's growing mass audience. They reasoned that they could capitalize on this situation by creating a single network to bring together numerous online publications to create a critical mass of information. With the idea of multiple publications forming a larger online network, it became crucial to address a significant issue for each of the various publications: advertising. After substantial research, O'Connor and Merriman decided to move forward with a network concept. However, they determined that the advertising, rather than publishing, industry could be better served with such a network. Thus, they founded the DoubleClick Network in January 1996.

Although O'Connor and Merriman's engineering backgrounds helped them tremendously with the technology issues associated with their concept, their engineering experiences provided little insight into the world of sophisticated advertising. To resolve this issue, the software-based startup formally merged with a division of the ad agency Poppe Tyson. O'Connor believed the marriage of nerd and Madison Avenue cultures was possible because of a common bond—the love of the Internet. However, as O'Connor admitted, "The two cultures are completely ignorant of each other's ways." The "offspring" of this union set up shop in the heart of Silicon Alley in New York City—the location, coincidentally, where some of New York's first advertising agencies sprang up a century ago.

Like traditional advertising agencies, DoubleClick's focus is to get the right advertisement to the right person at the right time. The difference between DoubleClick and offline ad agencies is the use of technology to track Web surfing activities more directly as compared to older media such as magazines. A magazine publisher, for instance, can detail the number of subscribers as well as the number of issues sold at newsstands. Unfortunately, the publisher does not have a very clear picture as to which articles in a magazine issue have been read, by whom, and when. Online, however, technology developed by DoubleClick can track traffic to a given customer's web site and identify specific articles selected. Moreover, DoubleClick can trail traffic to and from the web site to establish a surfing portfolio of site visitors. This breadth and depth of information quickly made DoubleClick a valuable service provider to online advertisers trying to make advertising work on the Internet.

Throwing Darts

The heart of DoubleClick's technology is its DART—Dynamic Advertising Reporting and Targeting—system. DART works by reading twenty-two criteria about web site visitors' actions such as their cyber location and time of visit. This technology also leaves, often without the user's knowledge, a "cookie" on his or her computer. Cookies are simply bits of information sent to a Web browser to be saved on the user's hard drive. Cookies are helpful for Internet users because they can contain important information like login information and user preferences that make return visits to subscription-based web sites more manageable. Cookies are also useful for web site operators because they can include additional information such as evidence of repeat visits or advertisements viewed. The information provided by the cookie about a web site visitor's activities and interests helps DoubleClick tailor advertisements to specific users. It should be noted, however, that cookies do not collect personally identifiable information such as a user's name, mailing address, telephone number, or e-mail address, so individual profiles are essentially anonymous. Instead of tracking an identifiable individual, cookies track users' digital footsteps.

The wealth of information DoubleClick could provide for its network members fueled the company's rapid growth. By the end of its first year of business,

TABLE C6.1	DoubleClick Inc. Financial Performance: Six Fiscal Years Ending December 31, 2002*

	2002	2001	2000	1999	1998	1997
Net sales	300.2	405.6	505.6	258.3	80.2	30.6
Cost of sales	64.7	132.2	194.6	90.4	51.1	19.7
Selling, general & admin. expenses	187.7	301.9	355.3	168.3	47.2	18.4
Net income (loss)	(117.9)	(265.9)	(156)	(55.8)	(18.2)	(8.4)
Earnings/share	(0.87)	(2.05)	(1.29)	(0.51)	(0.29)	(0.20)

*All figures in millions of dollars except per share amounts.

Source: "DoubleClick, Inc.," *MSN MoneyCentral,* http://moneycentral.msn.com/investor/, accessed February 1, 2001, and May 5, 2003.

DoubleClick had secured the business of twenty-five web sites. Today, the company has 5,000 customers and handles ad sales for 715 web sites. As Andy Jacobson, regional vice president for sales, says, "We set a goal: sell $500,000 of advertising in a week, and we'll buy lunch for everyone in the room." By 2000, the firm had achieved revenues of almost $507 million—an average of nearly $10 million a week. That figure declined after the high-tech industry went into a recession, stifling ad spending online for a time (Table C6.1).

This growth and increasing volume have allowed DoubleClick to command fees of 35 to 50 percent of advertising expenditures compared to the 15 percent fee structure charged by more traditional offline advertising agencies. Consider as well that the DoubleClick network has the capability to add hundreds of thousands of anonymous consumer profiles per day. Thus, it becomes clear that its technological capabilities make it an increasingly attractive ad-servicing option.

Despite the phenomenal sales growth DoubleClick has achieved, executives believe there is further potential available from the DART system. In fact, the expectation is for DART technologies alone to account for 50 percent of future revenues. However, those revenue expectations are not limited to the DoubleClick network alone. The company is intent on servicing clients outside of its own network and growing complementary businesses in the ad-servicing business. For example, the company recently launched a new service called ChannelView, which helps online, catalog, and store retailers tailor promotions to particular shoppers, determine whether the promotions are effective, and make quick adjustments as necessary. Like traditional companies, DoubleClick has used its growing clout to develop and acquire important worldwide subsidiaries both on- and offline.

Key Subsidiaries

Despite the prevalence of technology today, targeting remains surprisingly low-tech. According to Jim Nail, a Forrester research analyst,

To get advertisers to continue to pay the big premiums, DoubleClick will have to tell advertisers more than just where you are and the kind of site you visit. It might have to tell them whether you are married or single, what your income is, and whether or not you have kids. What it needs to do above all is predict, with greater accuracy, how likely you are to buy an advertised product.

To that end, DoubleClick acquired offline catalog database company Abacus Direct in 1999, shortly after buying NetGravity, Inc., a direct competitor. The idea behind the Abacus acquisition was the potential to merge the database company's personally identifiable offline buying habits with DoubleClick's nonpersonally identifiable online habits to provide even greater depths of information to current and future clients. The trend toward collecting more personally identifiable information continued with DoubleClick's development of Flashbase, an automation tool that allows DoubleClick clients a means of collecting personal information by running contests and sweepstakes online. Additionally, DoubleClick web sites such as www.Net-Deals.com and www.IAF.net collect personally identifiable information online. However, DoubleClick argued that it provides ways for consumers to limit communication only to prize- or deal-specific information. In other words, consumers have the ability to "opt out" of future communications not specific to the instance when and where they entered their personal data.

The Controversy

The only problem with these developments and acquisitions was that their intended use signaled a significant philosophical shift in the way DoubleClick had always done business. Specifically, they created a drastic change in the company's consumer privacy position, a fact that consumer privacy groups and the Federal Trade Commission (FTC) did not take long to notice. According to Jason Catlett of Junkbusters, an Internet privacy activist, "Thousands of sites are ratting on you, so as soon as one gives you away, you're exposed on all of them. For years, [DoubleClick] has said (their services) don't identify you personally, and now they're admitting they are going to identify you."

In the face of growing public concern, Kevin O'Connor, now chair of the company, defended its plans: "The merger with Abacus Direct, along with the recent closing of the NetGravity merger, will allow us to offer publishers and advertisers the most effective means of advertising online and offline." Kevin Ryan, DoubleClick's CEO, took the defense a step further: "What we continue to hear from consumers is that they'd like to be in a position to have better content, greater access for everyone in the United States, and they would love it all to be free and advertising-served." Ryan pointed out that the Internet is driven by advertising, and that advertisers need to know their substantial investments are being targeted to the right audience or individual. Without more accurate information, Ryan asserted, much of the gratis content on the Internet would no longer be free.

Initially, the merger announcements were well received as shares of DoubleClick traded as high as $179 per share in early December 1999. Unfortunately, the comments of O'Connor and Ryan failed to stem the stock's decline after privacy concerns were voiced by Junkbusters and others in the aftermath of the Abacus Direct merger.

At the time, DoubleClick's posted privacy policy stated that online users are given *notice* about the data collection and the *choice* not to participate or to opt out.

However, Internet users had to read carefully to understand that granting permission, or failing to deny permission, at even one DoubleClick- or Abacus-serviced web site allowed the company to select personal information across all sites. Consequently, the Center for Democracy and Technology (CDT), a Washington-based watchdog organization, launched a hard-line campaign against DoubleClick. The focus of the campaign centered around a "Websit" under the slogan, "I Will Not Be Targeted," where users can opt out of DoubleClick's profiling activities. According to Deirdre Mulligan, CDT's staff counsel, "You may have already been double-crossed by DoubleClick or you may be next in line. In either case, if you care about your privacy and want to surf the Web without your every move being recorded in a giant database connected to your name, its time to opt-out."

The CDT campaign was just one of the challenges DoubleClick faced as public concerns about Internet privacy escalated. A California woman brought a lawsuit against DoubleClick, alleging the company had unlawfully obtained and sold her private personal information. Additional lawsuits accused the company of invading privacy and misrepresenting itself. Media critics labeled DoubleClick an online "Big Brother" that passed information about employees' Internet surfing behavior onto their employers. Attorneys general in Michigan and New York also launched investigations into DoubleClick's business practices. One of the most publicized challenges was the Electronic Privacy Information Center (EPIC) complaint filed with the FTC regarding DoubleClick's profiling practices. The complaint led to a full-scale investigation of DoubleClick's business practices by the federal watchdog. EPIC and similar privacy groups preferred an opt-in mechanism as opposed to DoubleClick's opt-out platform. EPIC executive director Marc Rotenberg said, "Several years ago, DoubleClick said it would not collect personally identifiable information and keep anonymous profiles. Privacy experts applauded that approach." But as a result of the Abacus merger, "DoubleClick has changed its mind and they're trying to convince users they should accept that [new] model."

DoubleClick attempted to defuse the growing controversy (and plummeting stock price) by announcing a program to protect consumers it tracks online. The program included a major newspaper campaign, 50 million banner ads directing consumers to the privacy rights information and education site PrivacyChoices (http://www.privacychoices.org/), the appointment of a chief privacy officer, the hiring of an external accounting firm to conduct privacy audits, and the establishment of an advisory board. The board, in particular, was less than well received. Calling the board a "facade," Jeffrey Chester, executive director of the Center of Media Education, said, "This is a public relations ploy to ward off federal and state scrutiny." Chester and other privacy organizations expressed dismay that the advisory board included no true privacy advocates and, worse, it included a DoubleClick customer. Moreover, that customer advocated technologies called "Web bugs" or "clear-gifs" that some consider even more intrusive than cookies. These sentiments prompted O'Connor to state, "It is clear from these discussions that I made a mistake by planning to merge names with anonymous user activity across web sites in the absence of government and industry privacy standards."

Another attempt to regain consumer goodwill is DoubleClick's participation in the Responsible Electronic Communication Alliance (RECA) along with fifteen of the nation's leading online marketers. The purpose of the RECA is to give consumers greater choice and notice regarding their online activities. To identify companies that subscribe to the RECA's proposed standards, the alliance is developing a "seal of approval" program in the spirit of *Good Housekeeping*'s. According to Christopher Wolf, RECA president, "Our ultimate goal is to phase in a set of firm standards on privacy, notice, access, and choice."

A New Era

On January 22, 2001, the Federal Trade Commission announced that it had completed its investigation of DoubleClick. In a letter to the company, the commission said, "It appears to staff that DoubleClick never used or disclosed consumers' PII [personally identifiable information] for purposes other than those disclosed in its privacy policy." On news of the announcement, the company's stock price jumped 13 percent, although it remained well below the company's historic high. However, the FTC also warned that its decision "is not to be construed as a determination that a violation may not have occurred" and reserved the right to take further action. Needless to say, the privacy advocates were not happy with the announcement. EPIC, for example, contended that the FTC never addressed its allegations. CEO Kevin Ryan, however, felt that DoubleClick had been vindicated: "We felt from the beginning that our privacy policy and practices are solid. We never felt there was any substantial problem with them."

A little more than a year later, DoubleClick settled the lawsuits, which were consolidated into a single federal suit, and agreed to create an easy-to-read privacy policy that outlines the company's use of cookies and other technologies. The settlement required the company to regularly purge various information that it has collected on consumers and to post 300 million banner ads across the Internet to explain how consumers can protect their privacy, how to opt out of having DoubleClick cookies placed on their computers, and how cookies and data are collected. DoubleClick was also required to engage an accounting firm to audit its compliance with the terms of the settlement and to pay $1.8 million in attorneys' fees. Although it seems that the storm has quieted for now, Internet consumers, privacy advocates, and government officials will be watching DoubleClick closely, and the issue of Internet privacy will almost certainly continue.

Questions

1. Why did DoubleClick's decision to merge Abacus Direct's database of personally identifiable offline buying habits with DoubleClick's nonpersonally identifiable online habits so upset privacy advocates and arouse the attention of federal and state officials? What other ethical issues exist in this situation?
2. How has DoubleClick taken a strategic approach to addressing these issues?
3. What else could or should DoubleClick do to address stakeholders' concerns about personal privacy protection?

Sources

2002 Annual Report, DoubleClick; Eryn Brown, "The Silicon Alley Heart of Internet Advertising," *Fortune*, December 6, 1999, pp. 166–167; Jeanette Brown, "DoubleClick, Take Two," *Business Week Online*, February

18, 2002, www.businessweek.com:/print/magazine/content/02_07/b3770615.htm?tc&sub=eb; Lynn Burke, "A DoubleClick Smokescreen?" *WiredNews,* May 23, 2000, www.wirednews.com/news/print/0,1294,36404,00.html; Tom Conroy and Rob Sheffield, "Hot Marketing Geek," *Rolling Stone,* August 20, 1998, p. 80; "Crisis Control @ DoubleClick," *Privacy Times,* February 18, 2000, www.privacytimes.com/*New*Webstories/doubleclick_priv_2_23.htm; "DoubleClick Accused of Double-Dealing Double-Cross," *News Bytes News Network,* February 2, 2000, www.newsbytes.com; "DoubleClick Completes $1.8 Bil Abacus Direct Buyout," *News Bytes News Network,* November 30, 1999, www.newsbytes.com; "DoubleClick, Inc.," *MSN MoneyCentral,* http://moneycentral.msn.com/investor/, accessed May 5, 2003; "DoubleClick Outlines Five-Step Privacy Initiative," *News Bytes News Network,* February 15, 2000, www.newsbytes.com; "DoubleClick Tracks Online Movements," *News Bytes News Network,* January 26, 2000, www.newsbytes.com (originally reported by *USA Today,* www.usatoday.com); Jane Hodges, "DoubleClick Takes Standalone Route for Targeting Tools," *Advertising Age,* December 16, 1996, p. 32; "I Will Not Be Targeted," Center for Democracy and Technology, www.cdt.org/action/doubleclick.shtml, accessed January 29, 2001; Chris Oakes, "DoubleClick Plan Falls Short," *WiredNews,* February 14, 2000, www.wirednews.com/news/print/0,1294,34337,00.html; Chris O'Brien, "DoubleClick Sets Off Privacy Firestorm," *San Jose Mercury News,* February 26, 2000, www.mercurycenter.com/business/top/042517.htm; "Online Marketing Coalition Announces Proposals for Internet Privacy Guidelines," *MSN MoneyCentral,* September 25, 2000, http://news.moneycentral.msn.com/; "Privacy Choices," DoubleClick, Inc., www.privacychoices.org/, accessed January 29, 2001; "Privacy Policy," DoubleClick Inc., www.doubleclick.net/, accessed May 5, 2003; "Privacy Standards Proposed," MSNBC, September 25, 2000, www.msnbc.com/news/467212.asp; Randall Rothenberg, "An Advertising Power, but Just What Does DoubleClick Do?" *New York Times,* September 22, 1999, E-Commerce Special Section, www.nytimes.com/library/tech/99/09/biztech/technology/22roth.html; Brian Sullivan, "Privacy Groups Debate DoubleClick Settlement," CNN, May 24, 2002, www.cnn.com; Allen Wan and William Spain, "FTC Ends DoubleClick Investigation," CBS MarketWatch.com, January 23, 2001, www.aolpf.marketwatch.com/pf/archive/20010123/news/current/dclk.asp.

Enron: Questionable Accounting Leads to Collapse

This case was prepared by Neil Herndon, University of Missouri–Columbia, for classroom discussion, rather than to illustrate either effective or ineffective handling of an administrative, ethical, or legal decision by management.

O nce upon a time, there was a gleaming headquarters office tower in Houston, with a giant tilted "E" in front, slowly revolving in the Texas sun. Enron's "E" suggested to Chinese *feng shui* practitioner Meihwa Lin a model of instability, which was perhaps an omen of things to come. The Enron Corporation, which once ranked among the top *Fortune* 500 companies, collapsed in 2001 under a mountain of debt that had been concealed through a complex scheme of off-balance-sheet partnerships. Forced to declare bankruptcy, the energy firm laid off 4,000 employees; thousands more lost their retirement savings, which had been invested in Enron stock. The company's shareholders lost tens of billions of dollars after the stock price plummeted. The scandal surrounding Enron's demise engendered a global loss of confidence in corporate integrity that continues to plague markets, and eventually it triggered tough new scrutiny of financial reporting practices. To understand what went wrong, we'll examine the history, culture, and major players in the Enron scandal. (See Figure C7.1 for a brief timeline.)

The Enron Corporation was created out of the merger of two major gas pipeline companies in 1985. Through its subsidiaries and numerous affiliates, the company provided products and services related to natural gas, electricity, and communications for its wholesale and retail customers. Enron transported natural gas through pipelines to customers all over the United States. It generated, transmitted, and distributed electricity to the northwestern United States, and marketed natural gas, electricity, and other commodities globally. It was also involved in the development, construction, and operation of power plants, pipelines, and other energy-related projects all over the world, including the delivery and management of energy to retail customers in both the industrial and commercial business sectors.

Throughout the 1990s, Chairman Ken Lay, chief executive officer (CEO) Jeffrey Skilling, and chief financial officer (CFO) Andrew Fastow transformed Enron from

| FIGURE C7.1 | A Brief Timeline of the Enron Scandal |

1985	Houston Natural Gas merges with Omaha-based InterNorth; the resulting company is eventually named Enron Corp. Ken Lay, who had been CEO of Houston Natural Gas, becomes chairman and chief executive officer the following year.
2000	Annual revenues reach $100 billion, and the Energy Financial Group ranks Enron as the sixth-largest energy company in the world, based on market capitalization.
Feb. 2001	Jeff Skilling takes over as chief executive officer. Ken Lay remains chairman.
Aug. 2001	Skilling unexpectedly resigns "for personal reasons," and Ken Lay steps back into the CEO job. That same month, a letter from an Enron executive raises serious questions about the company's business and accounting practices.
Oct. 2001	Enron releases third-quarter earnings, showing $1 billion in charges, including $35 million related to investment partnerships headed by Andrew Fastow, Enron's former chief financial officer. Fastow is replaced as CFO.
Oct. 22, 2001	Enron announces that the Securities and Exchange Commission has launched a formal investigation into its "related party transactions."
Nov. 8, 2001	Enron restates earnings for 1997 through 2000 and the first three quarters of 2001.
Dec. 2, 2001	Enron files for protection from creditors in a New York bankruptcy court.
Dec. 3, 2001	Enron announces that it is laying off 4,000 employees.
Jan. 9, 2002	The Justice Department announces that it is pursuing a criminal investigation of Enron.
Jan. 14, 2002	U.S. House and Senate lawmakers return campaign contributions from Enron.
Jan. 24, 2002	Ken Lay resigns as chairman and chief executive of Enron. The first of at least eight congressional hearings on Enron begins.
Jan. 30, 2002	Enron names Stephen Cooper, a restructuring specialist, as acting chief executive officer.
Feb. 4, 2002	A report by a special committee of Enron's board investigating the energy trader's collapse portrays a company riddled with improper financial transactions and extensive self-dealing by company officials.
May 2, 2002	Enron announces plans to reorganize as a small company with a new name.
Oct. 2, 2002	Andrew Fastow voluntarily surrenders to federal authorities after prosecutors indicate they will file charges for his role in the company's collapse.

(continued)

| **FIGURE C7.1** | *(Continued)* |

Oct. 31, 2002	Fastow is indicted on seventy-eight counts of masterminding a scheme to artificially inflate the energy company's profits.
Feb. 3, 2003	Creditors of Enron sue Ken Lay and his wife, Linda, to recover more than $70 million in transfers.
July 11, 2003	Enron finally announces a plan to restructure and pay off creditors after five deadline extensions.

Sources: "A Chronology of Enron's Woes: The Accounting Debacle," *Wall Street Journal*, March 20, 2003, http://online.wsj.com; "A Chronology of Enron's Woes: The Investigation," *Wall Street Journal*, March 20, 2003, http://online.wsj.com; and "Enron Timeline," *Houston Chronicle*, January 17, 2002, http://www.chron.com/cs/CDA/story.hts/special/enron/1127125; Kristen Hays, "16 Cents on $1 for Enron Creditors," *Austin American-Statesman*, July 12, 2003, http://statesman.com.

an old-style electricity and gas company into a $150 billion energy company and Wall Street favorite that traded power contracts in the investment markets. From 1998 to 2000 alone, Enron's revenues grew from about $31 billion to more than $100 billion, making it the seventh-largest company of the *Fortune* 500. Enron's wholesale energy income represented about 93 percent of 2000 revenues, with another 4 percent derived from natural gas and electricity. The remaining 3 percent came from broadband services and exploration. However, a bankruptcy examiner later reported that although Enron claimed net income of $979 in that year, it really earned $42 million. Moreover, the examiner found that despite Enron's claim of $3 billion in cash flow in 2000, the company actually had a cash flow of negative $154 million.

Enron's Corporate Culture

When describing the corporate culture of Enron, people like to use the word *arrogant,* perhaps justifiably. A large banner in the lobby at corporate headquarters proclaimed Enron "The World's Leading Company," and Enron executives blithely believed that competitors had no chance against it. Jeffrey Skilling even went so far as to tell utility executives at a conference that he was going to "eat their lunch." There was an overwhelming aura of pride, carrying with it the deep-seated belief that Enron's people could handle increasing risk without danger. The culture also was about a focus on how much money could be made for executives. For example, Enron's compensation plans seemed less concerned with generating profits for shareholders than with enriching officer wealth. Enron's corporate culture reportedly encouraged flouting, if not breaking, the rules.

Skilling appears to be the executive who created a system in which Enron's employees were rated every six months, with those ranked in the bottom 20 percent forced out. This "rank and yank" system helped create a fierce environment in which employees competed against rivals not only outside the company but also at the next desk. Delivering bad news could result in the "death" of the messenger, so problems in the trading operation, for example, were covered up rather than being communicated to management.

Enron chairman Ken Lay once said that he felt that one of the great successes at Enron was the creation of a corporate culture in which people could reach their full potential. He said that he wanted it to be a highly moral and ethical culture and that he tried to ensure that people did in fact honor the values of respect, integrity, and excellence. On his desk was an Enron paper weight with the slogan "Vision and Values." Some of the people behind Enron, however, believed that nearly anything could be turned into a financial product and, with the aid of complex statistical modeling, traded for profit. Short on assets and heavily reliant on intellectual capital, Enron's corporate culture rewarded innovation and punished employees deemed weak.

Enron's Accounting Problems

Enron's bankruptcy in December 2001 was the largest in U.S. corporate history at the time. The bankruptcy filing came after a series of revelations that the giant energy trader had been using partnerships, called *special-purpose entities (SPEs),* to conceal losses. In a meeting with Enron's lawyers in August 2001, the company's then chief financial officer, Andrew Fastow, stated that Enron had established the SPEs to move assets and debt off its balance sheet and to increase cash flow by showing that funds were flowing through its books when it sold assets. Although these practices produced a very favorable financial picture, outside observers believed they might constitute fraudulent financial reporting because they did not accurately represent the company's true financial condition. Most of the SPEs were entities in name only, and Enron funded them with its own stock and maintained control over them. When one of these partnerships was unable to meet its obligations, Enron covered the debt with its own stock. This arrangement worked as long as Enron's stock price was high, but when the stock price fell, cash was needed to meet the shortfall.

After Enron restated its financial statements for fiscal 2000 and the first nine months of 2001, its cash flow from operations dropped from a positive $127 million in 2000 to a negative $753 million in 2001. In 2001, with its stock price falling, Enron faced a critical cash shortage. In October 2001, after it was forced to cover some large shortfalls for its partnerships, Enron's stockholder equity fell by $1.2 billion. Already shaken by questions about lack of disclosure in Enron's financial statements and by reports that executives had profited personally from the partnership deals, investor confidence collapsed, taking Enron's stock price with it.

For a time it appeared that Dynegy might save the day by providing $1.5 billion in cash, secured by Enron's premier pipeline, Northern Natural Gas, and then purchasing Enron for about $10 billion. But when Standard & Poor downgraded Enron's debt below investment grade on November 28, some $4 billion in off-balance-sheet debt came due, and Enron didn't have the resources to pay. Dynegy terminated the deal. On December 2, 2001, Enron filed for bankruptcy. Enron now faces 22,000 claims totaling about $400 billion.

The Whistle-blower

Assigned to work directly with Andrew Fastow in June 2001, Enron vice president Sherron Watkins, an eight-year Enron veteran, was given the task of finding some assets to sell off. With the high-tech bubble bursting and Enron's stock price slipping, Watkins was troubled to find unclear, off-the-books arrangements backed only by Enron's deflating stock. No one seemed to be able to explain to her what was going on. Knowing she faced difficult consequences if she confronted then CEO Jeffrey Skilling, she began looking for another job, planning to confront Skilling just as she left for a new position. Skilling, however, suddenly quit on August 14, saying he wanted to spend more time with his family. Chairman Ken Lay stepped back in as CEO and began inviting employees to express their concerns and put them into a box for later collection. Watkins prepared an anonymous memo and placed it into the box. When CEO Lay held a companywide meeting shortly thereafter and did not mention her memo, however, she arranged a personal meeting with him.

On August 22, Watkins handed Lay a seven-page letter she had prepared outlining her concerns. She told him that Enron would "implode in a wave of accounting scandals" if nothing was done. Lay arranged to have Enron's law firm, Vinson & Elkins, look into the questionable deals, although Watkins advised against having a party investigate that might be compromised by its own involvement in Enron's scam. Near the end of September, Lay sold some $1.5 million of personal stock options, while telling Enron employees that the company had never been stronger. By the middle of October, Enron was reporting a third-quarter loss of $618 million and a $1.2 billion write-off tied to the partnerships that Watkins had warned Lay about.

For her trouble, Watkins had her computer hard drive confiscated and was moved from her plush executive office suite on the top floors of the Houston headquarters tower to a plain office on a lower level with a metal desk. That desk was no longer filled with the high-level projects that had once taken her all over the world on Enron business. Instead, now a vice president in name only, she faced meaningless "make-work" projects. In February 2002, she testified before Congress about Enron's partnerships and resigned from Enron in November.

The Chief Financial Officer

Chief Financial Officer Andrew Fastow was indicted in October 2002 by the U.S. Justice Department on seventy-eight federal counts for his alleged efforts to inflate Enron's profits. These charges included fraud, money laundering, conspiracy, and one count of obstruction of justice. Fastow faces up to 140 years in jail and millions of dollars in fines if convicted on all counts. Federal officials say they will try to recover all of the money Fastow earned illegally. Having already seized some $37 million of Fastow's gains, they are now seeking their forfeiture.

Federal prosecutors argue that Enron's case is not about exotic accounting practices but fraud and theft. They contend that Fastow was the brains behind the partnerships used to conceal some $1 billion in Enron debt and that this led directly to Enron's bankruptcy. The federal complaints allege that Fastow defrauded Enron and its shareholders through the off-the-balance-sheet partnerships that made Enron appear to be more profitable than it actually was. They also allege that Fastow made about $30 million both by using these partnerships to get kickbacks that were disguised as gifts from family members who invested in them and by taking income himself that should have gone to other entities.

Fastow, who has denied any wrongdoing, says that he was hired to arrange the off-balance-sheet financing and that Enron's board of directors, chairman, and CEO directed and praised his work. He also claims that both lawyers and accountants reviewed his work and approved what was being done and that "at no time did he do anything he believed was a crime." Jeffrey Skilling, chief operating officer (COO) from 1997 to 2000 before becoming CEO, reportedly championed Fastow's rise at Enron and supported his efforts to keep up Enron's stock prices.

The case against Fastow is largely based on information provided by Managing Director Michael Kopper, a key player in the establishment and operation of several of the off-the-balance-sheet partnerships. Kopper, a chief aide to Fastow, pleaded guilty to money laundering and wire fraud. He faces up to fifteen years in prison and has agreed to surrender some $12 million he earned from his dealings with the partnerships. Others charged in the Enron affair include Timothy Belden, Enron's former top energy trader, who pleaded guilty to one count of conspiring to commit wire fraud. He could receive five years in prison, three years' probation, and a $250,000 fine. David Bermingham, Giles Darby, and Gary Mulgrew were indicted in Houston on wire-fraud charges related to a deal at Enron. They were able to use secret investments to take $7.3 million in income that belonged to their employer, according to the Justice Department. The three, employed by the finance group Greenwich NatWest, have not yet been arrested.

Fastow has also been served with a civil lawsuit by the Securities and Exchange Commission (SEC), which claims that Fastow violated securities laws and defrauded investors. The SEC is seeking unspecified penalties and, as mentioned, the return of Fastow's allegedly improperly obtained profits.

The Chief Executive Officer

Former CEO Jeffrey Skilling, widely seen as Enron's mastermind, will probably be the most difficult case to prosecute. He was so sure he had committed no crime that he waived his right to self-incrimination and testified before Congress that "I was not aware of any inappropriate financial arrangements." However, Jeffrey McMahon, who took over as Enron's president and COO in February 2002, told a congressional subcommittee that he had informed Skilling about the company's off-the-balance-sheet partnerships in March 2000, when he was Enron's treasurer. McMahon said that Skilling had told him "he would remedy the situation."

Calling the Enron collapse a "run on the bank" and a "liquidity crisis," Skilling said that he did not understand how Enron went from where it was to bankruptcy so quickly. He also said that the off-the-balance sheet partnerships were Fastow's creation.

Prosecutors may try to convict Skilling for perjury, but they have reportedly widened their probe to investigate his role in Enron's broadband venture. Skilling is said to have joked that Enron could make "a kazillion dollars" through an exotic new accounting scheme. Skilling is also reported to have sold 39 percent of his Enron holdings before the company disclosed its financial troubles.

The Chairman

Kenneth Lay became chairman and CEO of the company that was to become Enron in February 1986. A decade later, Lay promoted Jeffrey Skilling to president and chief operating officer and then, as expected, Lay stepped down as CEO in February 2001, to make way for Skilling. Lay remained as chairman of the board. When Skilling resigned in August, Lay resumed the role of CEO.

Lay, who holds a Ph.D. in economics from the University of Houston, contends that he knew little of what was going on even though he had participated in the board meetings that allowed the off-the-balance-sheet partnerships to be created. He said he believed the transactions were legal because they were approved by attorneys and accountants. But by late summer 2001, while he was reassuring employees and investors that all was well at Enron, he had already been informed that there were problems with some of the investments that could eventually cost Enron hundreds of millions of dollars. On February 12, 2002, on the advice of his attorney, Lay told the Senate Commerce Committee that he was invoking his Fifth Amendment rights not to answer questions that could be incriminating.

Ken Lay is expected to be charged with insider trading. Specifically, prosecutors are looking into why Lay began selling about $80 million of his own stock beginning in late 2000, even while he encouraged employees to buy more shares of the company. It appears that Lay drew down his 4-million-dollar Enron credit line repeatedly, then repaid the company with Enron shares. These transactions, unlike usual stock sales, do not have to be reported to investors. Lay says that he sold the stock because of margin calls on loans he had secured with Enron stock and that he had no other source of liquidity.

Vinson & Elkins

Enron was Houston law firm Vinson & Elkins' top client, accounting for about 7 percent of its $450 million revenue. Enron's general counsel and a number of members of Enron's legal department came from Vinson & Elkins. Vinson & Elkins seems to have dismissed Sherron Watkins's allegations of accounting fraud after making some inquiries, but this does not appear to leave it open to civil or criminal liability. Of greater concern are allegations that Vinson & Elkins helped structure some of Enron's special-purpose partnerships. Watkins, in her letter to CEO Ken Lay, indicated that the law firm had written opinion letters supporting the legality of the deals. In fact, Enron could not have done many of the transactions without such opinion letters. Although the law firm denies that it has done anything wrong, legal experts say the key question is whether or not Vinson & Elkins approved deals that it knew were fraudulent.

Merrill Lynch

The prestigious brokerage and investment banking firm of Merrill Lynch faces scrutiny by federal prosecutors and the SEC for its role in Enron's 1999 sale of Nigerian barges. The sale allowed Enron to improperly record about $12 million in earnings and thereby meet its earnings goals at the end of 1999. Merrill Lynch allegedly bought the barges for $28 million, of which $21 million was financed by Enron through Fastow's oral assurance that Enron would buy Merrill Lynch's investment out in six months with a 15 percent guaranteed rate of return. Merrill Lynch went ahead with the deal despite an internal Merrill Lynch document that suggested that the transaction might be construed as aiding and abetting Enron's fraudulent manipulation of its income statement. Merrill Lynch denies that the transaction was a sham and said that it never knowingly helped Enron to falsify its financial reports.

There are also allegations that Merrill Lynch replaced a research analyst after his coverage of Enron displeased Enron executives. Enron reportedly threatened to exclude Merrill Lynch from a coming $750 million stock offering in retaliation. The replacement analyst is reported to have then upgraded his report on Enron's stock rating. Merrill Lynch maintains that it did nothing improper in its Enron business dealings. However, the firm agreed to pay $80 million to settle SEC charges related to the questionable Nigerian barge deal.

Arthur Andersen LLP

In its role as Enron's auditor, Arthur Andersen was responsible for ensuring the accuracy of Enron's financial statements and internal bookkeeping. Andersen's reports were used by potential investors to judge Enron's financial soundness and future potential before they decided whether to invest and by current investors to decide if their funds should remain invested there. These investors would expect that Andersen's certifications of accuracy and application of proper accounting procedures were independent and without any conflict of interest. If Andersen's reports were in error, investors could be seriously misled. However, Andersen's independence has been called into question. The accounting firm was a major business partner of Enron, with more than 100 employees dedicated to its account, and it sold about $50 million a year in consulting services to Enron. Some Andersen executives even accepted jobs with the energy trader.

Andersen was found guilty of obstruction of justice in March 2002 for destroying Enron-related auditing documents during an SEC investigation of Enron. As a result, Andersen has been barred from performing audits.

It is still not clear why Andersen auditors failed to ask Enron to better explain its complex partnerships before certifying Enron's financial statements. Some observers believe that Andersen was unduly influenced by the large consulting fees Enron paid it. However, an Andersen spokesperson said that the firm had looked hard at all available information from Enron at the time. But shortly after she spoke to Enron CEO Ken Lay, Vice President Sherron Watkins had taken her concerns to an Andersen audit partner, who reportedly conveyed her questions to senior Andersen management responsible for the Enron account. It is not clear what action, if any, Andersen took.

The Fallout

Enron's demise caused tens of billions of dollars of investor losses, triggered a collapse of electricity-trading markets, and ushered in an era of accounting scandals that precipitated a global loss of confidence in corporate integrity. Now companies must defend legitimate but complicated financing arrangements, even legitimate financing tools tainted by association with Enron. On a more personal level, 4,000 former Enron employees are struggling to find jobs, while many retirees have been forced to return to work in a bleak job market because their Enron-heavy retirement portfolios were wiped out. One senior Enron executive committed suicide.

In July 2003 Enron announced its intention to restructure and a plan to pay off its creditors. Pending creditor and court approval of the plan, most creditors would receive between 14.4 cents and 18.3 cents for each dollar they were owed—more than most expected. Under the plan, creditors would receive about two-thirds of the amount in cash and the rest in equity in two new companies, neither of which would carry the tainted Enron name. According to the plan, CrossCountry Energy Corp. would retain Enron's interests in three North American natural gas pipelines, while Prisma Energy International Inc. would take over Enron's nineteen international power and pipeline holdings. It remains unclear who owns what, whether assets are available that are free and clear of encumbrances, and what value these assets might have given that Enron now has no auditor, has not issued a financial report for 2001, and is saying that its financial reports after 1997 cannot be relied upon.

Enron's auditor, Arthur Andersen, faces some forty shareholder lawsuits claiming damages of more than $32 billion. Andersen closed its doors, leaving clients and employees to adjust. Enron itself faces many civil actions. A number of current and former Enron executives face federal investigations and possible criminal action, as well as civil lawsuits. The company is also being investigated in California for allegedly colluding with at least two other power sellers in 2000 to obtain excess profits by submitting false information to the manager of California's electricity grid. And, finally, the company is under investigation for tax evasion. As for the giant tilted "E" logo so proudly displayed outside of corporate headquarters, it was auctioned off for $44,000.

Questions

1. How did the corporate culture of Enron contribute to its bankruptcy?
2. What role did Enron's stakeholder relationships play in its demise? Examine the company's relationships with employees, customers, investors, the media, auditors, and attorneys.
3. How did the Enron scandal change expectations of corporate social responsibility?

Sources

Alexei Barrionuevo, Jonathan Weil, and John R. Wilke, "Enron's Fastow Charged with Fraud," *Wall Street Journal,* October 3, 2002, pp. A3–A4; Eric Berger, "Report Details Enron's Deception," *Houston Chronicle,* March 6, 2003, pp. 1B, 11B; Christine Y. Chen, "When Good Firms Get Bad *Chi*," *Fortune,* November 11, 2002, p. 56; Peter Elkind and Bethany McLean, "Feds Move Up Enron Food Chain," *Fortune,* December 30, 2002, pp. 43–44; "Enron Whistle-Blower Resigns," MSNBC News, www.msnbc.com/news/835432.asp, accessed December 2, 2002; Greg Farrell, "Former Enron CFO Charged," *USA Today,* October 3, 2002, p. B1; Greg Farrell, Edward Iwata, and Thor Valdmanis, "Prosecutors Are Far from Finished," *USA Today,* October 3, 2002, pp. 1B–2B; "Fastow Indicted on 78 Counts," MSNBC News, www.msnbc.com/news/828217.asp, accessed November 6, 2002; O. C. Ferrell, "Ethics," *BizEd,* May/June 2002, pp. 43–45; Jeffrey A. Fick, "Report: Merrill Replaced Enron Analyst," *USA Today,* July 30, 2002, p. B1; Daren Fonda, "Enron: Picking over the Carcass," *Fortune,* December 30, 2002–January 6, 2003, p. 56; "Finger-Pointing Starts As Congress Examines Enron's Fast Collapse," *Investor's Business Daily,* February 8, 2002, p. A1; Mike France, "One Big Client, One Big Hassle," *Business Week,* January 28, 2002, pp. 38–39; Bryan Gruley and Rebecca Smith, "Keys to Success Left Kenneth Lay Open to Disaster," *Wall Street Journal,* April 26, 2002, pp. A1, A5; Tom Hamburger, "Enron CEO Declines to Testify at Hearing," *Wall Street Journal,* December 12, 2001, p. B2; Kristen Hays, "16 Cents on $1 for Enron Creditors," *Austin American-Statesman,* July 12, 2003, http://statesman.com; Edward Iwata, "Merrill Lynch Will Pay $80M to Settle Enron Case," *USA Today,* February 20, 2003, www.usatoday.com; Jeremy

Kahn, "The Chief Freaked Out Officer," *Fortune,* December 9, 2002, pp. 197–198, 202; Kathryn Kranhold and Rebecca Smith, "Two Other Firms in Enron Scheme, Documents Say," *Wall Street Journal,* May 9, 2002, pp. C1, C12; Bethany McLean, "Why Enron Went Bust," *Fortune,* December 24, 2001, pp. 58, 60–62, 66, 68; Jodie Morse and Amanda Bower, "The Party Crasher," *Fortune,* December 30, 2002–January 6, 2003, pp. 53–56; Belverd E. Needles Jr. and Marian Powers, "Accounting for Enron," *Houghton Mifflin's Guide to the Enron Crisis* (Boston: Houghton Mifflin, 2003), pp. 3–6; Mitchell Pacelle, "Enron's Creditors to Get Peanuts," *Wall Street Journal,* July 11, 2003, http://online.wsj.com; "Primer: Accounting Industry and Andersen," *Washington Post,* www.washingtonpost.com, accessed October 2, 2002; Miriam Schulman, "Enron: What Ever Happened to Going Down with the Ship?" Markkula Center for Applied Ethics, www.scu.edu/ethics/publications/ethicalperspectives/schulman0302.html, accessed September 11, 2002; Chris H. Sieroty, "3 Ex-Bankers Charged in Enron Scandal," *Washington Times,* www.washtimes.com, accessed October 2, 2002; William Sigismond, "The Enron Case from a Legal Perspective," *Houghton Mifflin's Guide,* pp. 11–13; Elliot Blair Smith, "Panel Blasts Enron Tax Deals," *USA Today,* February 13, 2003, www.usatoday.com; Rebecca Smith and Kathryn Kranhold, "Enron Knew Portfolio's Value," *Wall Street Journal,* May 6, 2002, pp. C1, C20; Rebecca Smith and Mitchell Pacelle, "Enron Plans Return to Its Roots," *Wall Street Journal,* May 2, 2002, p. A1; Jake Ulick, "Enron: A Year Later," CNN/Money, www.money.cnn.com/2002/11/26/news/companies/enron_anniversary/index.htm, accessed December 2, 2002; Joseph Weber, "Can Andersen Survive?" *Business Week,* January 28, 2002, pp. 39–40; Winthrop Corporation, "Epigraph," *Houghton Mifflin's Guide,* p. 1; Wendy Zellner, "A Hero—and a Smoking-Gun Letter," *Business Week,* January 28, 2002, pp. 34–35.

Case 8

WorldCom: Actions Lead to Corporate Reform

This case was prepared by Linda Ferrell and Nichole Scheele, University of Wyoming, and Reneé Galvin, Colorado State University, for classroom discussion, rather than to illustrate either effective or ineffective handling of an administrative, ethical, or legal decision by management.

The story of WorldCom began in 1983 when businessmen Murray Waldron and William Rector sketched out a plan to create a long-distance telephone service provider on a napkin in a coffee shop in Hattiesburg, Mississippi. Their new company, Long Distance Discount Service (LDDS), began operating as a long-distance reseller in 1984. Early investor Bernard Ebbers was named CEO the following year. Through acquisitions and mergers, LDDS grew quickly over the next fifteen years. It changed its name to WorldCom, achieved a worldwide presence, acquired telecommunications giant MCI, and eventually expanded beyond long-distance service to offer the whole range of telecommunications services. It seemed poised to become one of the largest telecommunications corporations in the world. Instead, it became the largest bankruptcy filing in U.S. history to date and another name on a long list of those disgraced by the accounting scandals of the early twenty-first century. (See Figure C8.1.)

Financial Implications of Accounting Fraud

Unfortunately, for thousands of employees and shareholders, WorldCom used questionable accounting practices and improperly recorded $3.8 billion in capital expenditures, which boosted cash flows and profit over all four quarters in 2001 as well as the first quarter of 2002. This disguised the firm's actual net losses for the five quarters because capital expenditures can be deducted over a longer period of time, whereas expenses must be immediately subtracted from revenue. Investors, unaware of the alleged fraud, continued to buy the company's stock, which accelerated the stock's price. Internal investigations uncovered questionable accounting practices stretching as far back as 1999.

Even before the improper accounting practices were disclosed, however, by 2001 WorldCom was already in financial turmoil. Declining rates and revenues and an ambitious buying spree had pushed the company deeper into debt. In addition, chief executive Bernard Ebbers received a controversial $408 million loan to cover margin calls on loans that were secured by company stock. In July 2001, WorldCom signed a credit agreement with multiple banks to borrow up to $2.65 billion and repay it within a year. According to the banks, WorldCom tapped the entire amount six weeks before the accounting irregularities were disclosed. The banks contend that if they had known WorldCom's true financial picture, they would not have extended the financing without demanding additional collateral.

On June 28, 2002, the Securities and Exchange Commission (SEC) directed WorldCom to detail the facts underlying the events the company had described in a June 25, 2002, press release. That press release had stated that WorldCom intended to restate its 2001 and first-quarter 2002 financial statements and that Scott Sullivan—who reported to Bernard Ebbers until he resigned in April 2002—had prepared the financial statements for 2001 and the first quarter of 2002. On February 6, 2002, a meeting had been held between the board's audit committee and Arthur Andersen, the firm's outside auditor, to discuss the audit for fiscal year 2001. Andersen assessed WorldCom's accounting practices to determine whether it had adequate controls to prevent material errors in its financial statements and attested that WorldCom's processes were, in fact, effective. When the audit committee asked Andersen whether its auditors had had any disagreements with WorldCom's management, Andersen replied that they had not; they were comfortable with the accounting positions WorldCom had taken.

FIGURE C8.1	Bankruptcy Timeline

Early 2001	WorldCom shows signs of financial troubles: Rates and revenues decline and debt rises.
July 2001	WorldCom receives $2.65 billion in loans from twenty-six banks—to be repaid by the end of 2001.
Feb. 6, 2002	Arthur Andersen LLP and WorldCom's audit team meet to discuss the 2001 audit. Everything is deemed correct, and Andersen gives its approval.
Mar. 11, 2002	The U.S. Securities and Exchange Commission (SEC) requests more information concerning accounting procedures and loans to officers.
Apr. 30, 2002	Bernard Ebbers resigns as CEO of WorldCom and is replaced by vice chairman John Sidgmore.
June 25, 2002	CFO Scott Sullivan is fired after improper accounting of $3.8 billion in expenses is discovered, which covered up a net loss for 2001 and the first quarter of 2002.
June 28, 2002	WorldCom fires 17,000 employees to cut costs.
July 8, 2002	John Sidgmore testifies before a congressional committee to explain how internal investigations uncovered the accounting problems.

(continued)

FIGURE C8.1	*(Continued)*

July 21, 2002	WorldCom files for reorganization under Chapter 11 bankruptcy, an action that affects only the firm's U.S. operations, not its overseas subsidiaries.
Aug. 9, 2002	Continued internal investigations uncover an additional $3.8 billion in improperly reported earnings for 1999, 2000, 2001, and the first quarter of 2002, bringing the total amount of accounting errors to more than $7.6 billion.
Aug. 13, 2002	WorldCom names Greg Rayburn as chief restructuring officer and John Dubel as chief financial officer to lead the company through the reorganization process.
Sept. 10, 2002	WorldCom formally announces it is seeking a permanent chief executive officer.
Oct. 1, 2002	The U.S. Bankruptcy Court approves WorldCom's request to pay full severance and benefits to former employees, which had been limited under the company's Chapter 11 filing.
Oct. 15, 2002	The U.S. Bankruptcy Court approves up to $1.1 billion in debtor-in-possession (DIP) financing for WorldCom while it undergoes reorganization.
Nov. 8, 2002	WorldCom files additional bankruptcy petitions for forty-three of its subsidiaries.
Nov. 15, 2002	Michael D. Capellas, former president of Hewlett-Packard Company, is named chairman and CEO.
July 8, 2003	WorldCom, now operating under the name MCI, agrees to pay $750 million to settle the SEC's civil fraud charges.
Oct. 18, 2003	MCI sets up enhanced Code of Conduct and zero-tolerance policy.

WorldCom did not have the cash needed to pay $7.7 billion in debt, and therefore, filed for Chapter 11 bankruptcy protection on July 21, 2002. In its bankruptcy filing, the firm listed $107 billion in assets and $41 billion in debt. WorldCom's bankruptcy filing allowed it to pay current employees, continue service to customers, retain possession of assets, and gain a little breathing room to reorganize. However, the telecom giant lost credibility along with the business of many large corporate and government clients, organizations that typically do not do business with companies in Chapter 11 proceedings.

Who Is to Blame?

Naturally, no one has stepped forward to shoulder the blame for WorldCom's accounting scandal, not its auditors, executives, board of directors, or its analysts. As the primary outside auditor, Arthur Andersen—also under fire for alleged mismanagement of many other large scandal-plagued audits—has been faulted for failing to uncover the accounting irregularities. In its defense, Andersen claimed that it could not have known about the improper accounting because former CFO Scott Sullivan never informed Andersen's auditors about the firm's questionable accounting practices. But, in WorldCom's statement to the SEC, the company claimed that Andersen did know about these accounting practices, had no disagreement with World-Com's management, and was not uncomfortable with any accounting positions taken by WorldCom.

Several former WorldCom finance and accounting executives, including David Myers, Buford Yates, Betty Vinson, and Troy Normand, pleaded guilty to securities-fraud charges. They claimed that they were directed by top managers to cover up WorldCom's worsening financial situation. Although they protested that these directions were improper, they say they agreed to follow orders after their superiors told them it was the only way to save the company. However, Scott Sullivan, who worked above many of these employees, pleaded not guilty. Chief executive Bernard Ebbers stated that he did nothing fraudulent and has nothing to hide. WorldCom's lawyers have said that Ebbers did not know of the money shifted into the capital expenditure accounts. However, the *Wall Street Journal* reported that an internal WorldCom report identified an e-mail and a voice mail that suggested otherwise. Former CEO Ebbers has not been charged with any crime as of this writing.

John Sidgmore, who briefly replaced Bernard Ebbers as CEO, blames World-Com's former management for the company's woes. Richard Thornburgh, the independent investigator appointed by WorldCom's bankruptcy court, asserted that there was a "cause for substantial concern" regarding WorldCom's board of directors and independent auditors. The board has been accused of lax oversight, and the board's compensation committee has been attacked for approving Bernard Ebbers's generous compensation package. Moreover, Thornburgh's report claimed that Ebbers and Sullivan ran WorldCom "with virtually no checks or restraints placed on their actions by the board of directors or other management." Another report, prepared for the firm's new board of directors, also criticized Ebbers for bucking efforts to develop a code of conduct, which Ebbers was said to have called a "colossal waste of time."

Additionally, Jack Grubman, a Wall Street analyst specializing in the telecommunications industry, who rated WorldCom's stock highly, has admitted he did so for too long. However, he insists he was unaware of the company's true financial shape. Grubman was later fired by Salomon Smith Barney because of accusations that he hyped telecommunications stocks, including Global Crossing and WorldCom, even after it became public that the stocks were poor investments.

Many people have blamed the rising number of telecommunications company failures and scandals on neophytes who had no experience in the telecommunications industry. Among these telecom outsiders are a junk-bond financier (Gary Winnick of Global Crossing), a railroad baron (Phil Anschutz, who founded Qwest), and Bernard Ebbers, who operated a motel before he took the helm of WorldCom. They tried to transform their startups into gigantic full-service providers like AT&T, but in an increasingly competitive industry it was unlikely that so many large companies could survive.

Effect on Investors

A Chapter 11 reorganization bankruptcy filing means different things to different investor groups, but the reality is that in the end, few investors will get back what they put into WorldCom. In a bankruptcy proceeding, shareholders have a legal right to some money, but because they essentially sit at the bottom of the list of creditors, they will not likely see anything at all.

In 2001, WorldCom created a separate "tracking" stock for its declining MCI consumer long-distance business in the hopes of isolating MCI from WorldCom's Internet and international operations, which were seemingly stronger. WorldCom announced the elimination of the MCI tracking stock and suspended its dividend in May 2002 in the hopes of saving $284 million a year. The actual savings was just $71. The S&P 500 cut WorldCom's long-term and short-term corporate credit rating to "junk" status on May 10, 2002, and the NASDAQ de-listed WorldCom's stock on June 28, 2002, when the price dropped to $0.09.

Likewise, holders of WorldCom's bonds, which include banks' investment departments, insurance companies, and pension funds, are not expected to receive interest and principal payments on those bonds. Although they may receive new stock, new bonds, or a combination of stocks and bonds in exchange for the bonds they hold, any new stock is unlikely to be worth nearly as much as investors lost. Various state funds alone lost $277 million when WorldCom's stock tanked.

After WorldCom emerges from bankruptcy, shareholders may be able to exchange current stock for new stock in the reorganized company, but, as with bonds, any new shares may be fewer and worth less. Of course, if WorldCom's attempt to reorganize proves futile and is declared insolvent, then both bond and shareholders will be left with nothing at all.

Effect on Consumers

The greatest effect on consumers could be any change in service by MCI, the long-distance giant acquired by WorldCom years ago. MCI, touted as the second-largest long-distance carrier, is continuing service during WorldCom's Chapter 11 bankruptcy reorganization. If WorldCom's reorganization ultimately proves unsuccessful, its assets would be liquidated, thus ending MCI's long-distance service. In that event, the FCC would have to receive a thirty-day warning from MCI before any service is cut, which hopefully would give consumers sufficient time to find another long-distance carrier.

The potential termination of MCI's long-distance services brings up a historical debate about the relative merits of having a single network provider versus having two or more carriers. Many WorldCom customers, along with Qwest and Global Crossing customers, may wish they had implemented a backup provider. Ted Chamberlin, a networking analyst for the research firm Gartner, believes that "For any customer of a network service provider, the potential is there for gloomy times. So we tell our customers that having a dual-carrier strategy is essential." Gartner has also advised all information technology (IT) decision makers to delay signing up for new services with WorldCom, to extend expiring contracts for only six months, to consider a second Internet service provider for Internet access, to research alternative Web-hosting sites, and to document all their WorldCom services and networking needs.

Where Now? Reorganization

In March 2003, WorldCom announced that it would write down close to $80 billion in goodwill, write off $45 billion of goodwill as impaired, and adjust $39.2 billion of property-and-equipment accounts and $5.6 billion of other intangible assets down to a value of about $10 billion. These figures join a growing list of similar write-offs and write-downs by companies in the telecom, Internet, and high-tech industries, which have admitted that they overpaid for acquisitions during the booming 1990s. Such charges also reflect downturns in various sectors. Deutsche Telekom recently took $21 billion in charges; France Telecom, $20 billion; AOL Time Warner, $45.5 billion; Qwest Communications, $41 billion; and JDS Uniphase took $50 billion. A few months later, WorldCom filed its plan for restructuring its debt in order to emerge from bankruptcy proceedings. Among other provisions, the plan included changing the firm's name to MCI. In July, the company agreed to settle the SEC's civil fraud charges and to pay $750 million in cash and stock to investors who lost money as a result of the fraud.

Will WorldCom survive restructuring in bankruptcy court? Many signs point to yes, but there are skeptics who don't think the telecom giant can be pulled out of the hole it has found itself in. WorldCom's greatest problem is accountability. It has taken many steps toward a successful reorganization, including securing $1.1 billion in loans and appointing Michael Capellas as chairman and CEO. WorldCom has also taken many actions to restore confidence in the company, including replacing the board members who failed to prevent the accounting scandal, firing many managers, reorganizing its finance and accounting functions, and making other changes designed to help correct past problems and prevent them from reoccurring. The hiring of four line controllers to oversee revenue accounting, operational accounting, financial accounting, and financial controls and procedures is also in process. Additionally, the audit department staff is being increased and will now report directly to the audit committee of the company's new board. "We are working to create a new World-Com," John Sidgmore said. "We have developed and implemented new systems, policies, and procedures."

Questions

1. What actions could have been taken by WorldCom executives to prevent the accounting and business scandal?
2. How could an emphasis on corporate governance and business ethics have played a part in this failure? How could they help to bring about a new and successful WorldCom?
3. Give a thorough update on WorldCom's struggle to reorganize. What penalties have WorldCom executives paid for their part in the fiasco? Do you think these penalties are sufficient?

Sources

"02 CV 8083 (JSR) Complaint (Securities Fraud)," Securities and Exchange Commission, October 31, 2002, www.sec.gov/litigation/complaints/comp17783.htm; "Accounting Fraud," WorldCom News, http://Worldcomnews.com/accountingfraud.html, accessed April 3, 2003; Andrew Backover, "Overseer Confident WorldCom Will Come Back," *USA Today*, December 31, 2002, p. 8A; "Bankruptcy," WorldCom News, http://WorldComnews.com/bankruptcy.html, accessed April 3, 2003; Andrew Barakat, "Reports Detail How Ebbers, Officers Ran Wild at WorldCom," *Austin American-Statesman*, June 10, 2003, http://statesman.com; Rebecca Blumenstein and Ken Brown. "Scrapped WorldCom Merger Sparked Sprint Tax Shelter," *Yahoo! News*, February 27, 2003, http://story.news.yahoo.com/news?tmpl=story&u=/dowjones/20030207/bs_dowjones/200302070218000057; "Capellas Close to Leading WorldCom," CNN/*Money*, November 13, 2002, http://cnnmoney.printthis.clickability.com/pt/cpt?action=cpt&expire=&urlID=4597701&fb; "Corporate Scandals: WorldCom," MSNBC, www.msnbc.com/news/corpscandal_front.asp?odm=C2ORB, accessed April 4, 2003; Nora Devine, "WorldCom to Write Off $45B Goodwill, Adjust Intangibles," Dow Jones Newswires, March 13, 2003, http://story.news.yahoo.com/news?tmpl=story&u=/dowjones/20030313/bs_dowjones/200303131736001097; "Ebbers Reportedly Knew of Fraud," MSNBC, March 12, 2003, www.msnbc.com/news/884175.asp; "Effect on Consumer," WorldCom News, http://Worldcomnews.com/effectonconsumer.html, accessed April 3, 2003; "Effect on Investors," WorldCom News, http://Worldcomnews.com/effectoninvestors.html, accessed April 3, 2003; Janet Elliott, "AG Would Have More Investigative Power—Bill Focuses on Integrity in Business," *Houston Chronicle*, March 11, 2003, www.chron.com/cs/CDA/story.hts/metropolitan/1812842; "Enron & WorldCom Scandals Inspire Movie and National Ethics Scholarship For Students," *Yahoo! News*, March 12, 2003, http://biz.yahoo.com/prnews/030312/daw022_1.html; "Former WorldCom CEO, CFO Take the Fifth," *eWeek*, July 8, 2002, www.eweek.com/article2/0,3959,362703,00.asp; Charles Gasparino, "Grubman Informed Weill of AT&T Meetings," *Wall Street Journal*, November 15, 2002, pp. C1, C13; "Investment and Litigation," WorldCom News, http://Worldcomnews.com/investmentandlitigation.html, accessed April 3, 2003; Carrie Johnson, "More Guilty Pleas from WorldCom Managers," *Washington Post*, October 11, 2002, http://nl12.newsbank.com/nl-search/we/Archives?p_action=list&p_topdoc=126; "Judge Outlines Budget Plan for WorldCom," *Yahoo! News*, March 6, 2003, http://story.news.yahoo.com/news?tmpl=story2&cid=509&ncid=509&e=41&u=/ap/20030306/ap_on_bi_ge/worldcom_budget_1; Gina Keating, "U. of Calif. Files $353 Million WorldCom Lawsuit," *Yahoo! News*, February 13, 2003, http://story.news.yahoo.com/news?tmpl=story&u=/nm/20030213/tc_nm/telecoms_worldcom_lawsuit_dc_1; Peter Kennedy, "WorldCom Puts Ebbers' B.C. Ranch Up for Sale," *Globe and Mail*, January 28, 2003, p. B5, http://www.globeandmail.com/servlet/ArticleNews/PEstory/TGAM/20030128/RANCH/Headlines/headdex/headdexBusiness_temp/52/52/58/; Stephanie Kirchgaessner, "WorldCom Mulls Further $16Bn Write-off," *Yahoo! News*, January 30, 2003, http://story.news.yahoo.com/news?tmpl=story2&cid=1106&ncid=1106&e=5&u=/ft/20030130/bs_ft/1042491347715; Matt Krantz, "Capitalizing on the Oldest Trick in Book: How WorldCom, and Others, Fudged Results," *USA Today*, June 27, 2002, www.usatoday.com/tech/techinvestor/2002/06/27/worldcom-whatdo.htm; Adam Lahinsky, "WorldCom: Picking Up the Pieces," *Business 2.0*, May 2, 2002, www.business2.com/articles/web/print/0,1650,40140,FF.html; Joseph McCafferty, "Scott Sullivan," *CFO Magazine*, September 1998, www.findarticles.com/cf_0/m3870/n9_v14/21119225/print.jhtml; Jack McCarthy, "WorldCom Woes," *InfoWorld*, August 2, 2002, www.infoworld.com/article/02/08/02/020805cttelco_1.html; Stephanie Mehata, "Birds of a Feather," *Fortune*, October 2002, www.business2.com/articles/mag/print/0,1643,43957,00.html; Adrian Michaels, "SEC Extends Charges Against WorldCom," *Financial Times*, November 6, 2002, http://news.ft.com/servlet/ContentServer?page name=Synd/StoryFT/FTFull&artid=10358730; Susan Pulliam, "Ordered to Commit Fraud, A Staffer Balked, Then Caved," *Wall Street Journal*, June 23, 2003, http://online.wsj.com; Amanda Ripley, "The Night Detective," *Time*, December 22, 2002, www.time.com/time/personoftheyear/2002/poycooper.html; Simon Romero, "WorldCom to Write Down $79.8 Billion of Good Will," *New York Times*, March 14, 2003, www.nytimes.com/2003/03/14/technology/14TELE.html; Mathew Secker, "WorldCom (Company Operations)," *Telecommunications*, March 2001, www.mobilepayment forum.org/pdfs/TelecommunicationsIntlEd.pdf; Ben Silverman, "WorldCom Waits for Blame Game," *New York Post*, March 10, 2003, www.nypost.com/business/70283.htm; Christopher Stern, "6 Resign from WorldCom Board," *Washington Post*, December 18, 2002, p. E04, http://www.washingtonpost.com/ac2/wp-dyn?pagename=article&node=&contentId=A3966-2002Dec17&notFound=true; Christopher Stern, "Cost-Cutting WorldCom Considers More Layoffs," *Washington Post*, February 2, 2003, p. A02, www. washingtonpost.com/ac2/wp-dyn?pagename=article&node=&contentId=A16324-2003Feb2&notFound=true; David Teather, "Former WorldCom Controller Admits Fraudulent Entries," *The Guardian*, September 27, 2002; David Teather, "To Ebber's Wedding, on Expenses," *The Guardian*, August 30, 2002; Steven Titch, "Deconstructing WorldCom: A Revealing Autopsy of the 1998 Mega-Merger," *America's Network*, May 1, 2001, www.findarticles.com/cf_0/m0DUJ/6_105/74651470/print.jhtml; John Van and Michael Oneal, "$750 Million WorldCom Settlement Is Approved," *Austin American-Statesman*, July 8, 2003, http://statesman.com; Lingling Wei, "More WorldCom Restatements?" *Wall Street Journal*, November 4, 2002, http://www.msnbc.com/news/83048.asp; "Who Is to Blame?" WorldCom News, http://Worldcomnews .com/whoistoblame.html, accessed April 3, 2003; "WorldCom Announces Its Post-Restructuring Management Plan," WorldCom, press release, September 10, 2002, www1.worldcom.com/infodesk/news/news2 .xml?newsid=4392&mode=long&lang=e; "WorldCom Finances," WorldCom News, http://Worldcomnews .com/worldcomfinances.html, accessed April 3, 2003;

"WorldCom Issues July and August 2002 Operating Results," WorldCom, press release, October 22, 2002, www.worldcom.com/global/about/ news/news2.xml?newsid=4870&mode=long&lang=en&width=530& root=global/about/; "WorldCom's Latest Development," CNN/*Money,* November 11, 2002, www.cnn money.printthis.clickability.com/pt/cpt?action=cpt&expire=urlID=4580252&fb; "WorldCom Milestones," *Washington Post,* August 9, 2002, www.washingtonpost.com/ac2/wp-dyn/A491562002Jun26?language= printer; "WorldCom Report Suggests Ebbers Knew of Accounting Fraud," Quicken Brokerage, March 12, 2003, www.quicken.com/investments/news_center/story/?story=NewsStory/dowJones/20030312/ON2003031 20406000594.var&column=P0DFP; "WorldCom Report Suggests Ebbers Knew of Fraud," *Forbes,* March 12, 2003, www.forbes .com/technology/newswire/2003/03/12/rtr904375.html; "WorldCom Revised Statement Pursuant to Section 21 (a)(1) of the Securities Exchange Act of 1934," Securities and Exchange Commission, July 8, 2002, www.sec.gov/news/extra/wcresponserv.htm; "WorldCom, SEC to Settle Charges," CNN, November 5, 2002, www.cnn. com/2002/BUSINESS/11/05/worldcom.reut/index.html; "WorldCom to Cut 2,000 Jobs," CNN, September 16, 2002, www.cnn.com/2002/BUSINESS/09/16/worldcom/index.html.

Case 9

Martha Stewart: Insider-Trading Scandal

This case was prepared by Leyla Baykal and Debbie Thorne McAlister for classroom discussion, rather than to illustrate either effective or ineffective handling of an administrative, ethical, or legal decision by an individual or management.

artha Stewart is one of the latest chief executive officers to become embroiled in a widening series of corporate scandals across the United States. She founded Martha Stewart Living Omnimedia Inc., a company with interests in publishing, television, merchandising, electronic commerce, and related international partnerships. Along the way, she became America's most famous homemaker and one of its richest women executives. In late 2001, however, she became the center of headlines, speculations, and eventually a federal investigation and indictment on charges related to her sale of 4,000 shares of ImClone stock one day before that firm's stock price plummeted. Although Stewart's case had not come to trial at the time of this writing, the scandal harmed the empire she created in her name.

Evolution of a Media Empire

Born in 1941, Martha Kostyra grew up in Nutley, New Jersey, in a Polish-American family with six children. During her childhood years, she developed a passion for cooking, gardening, and home keeping. She learned the basics of cooking, baking, canning, and sewing from her mother; her father introduced her to gardening at a very early age. While earning a bachelor's degree in history and architectural history at Barnard College, she worked as a model to pay her tuition. She became Martha Stewart when she married in her sophomore year. Although she became a successful stockbroker on Wall Street, she left to open a gourmet-food shop that later became a catering business in Westport, Connecticut. She used the distinct visual presentations and stylish recipes she developed for her catering business as a source for her first book, the best-selling *Entertaining*, which was first published in 1982.

Stewart's natural business instincts and leadership skills helped her make smart choices as she transformed her small business into a media empire and her name into a well-recognized brand. She joined Kmart as an image and product consultant in 1987, and persuaded the retailer to sell her growing line of products. She eventually became partners with the firm. This partnership helped her gain the capital necessary to break free of Time Warner, publisher of her highly successful *Martha Stewart Living* magazine. When Stewart and Time Warner disagreed over her plan to cross-sell and market her publishing, television, merchandising, and Web interests, she used everything she owned to buy back the brand rights of her products and publishing for an estimated $75 million. In 1999, she took her rapidly growing business public. Martha Stewart Living Omnimedia, the company she created, now owns three magazines, a TV and cable program, thirty-four books, a newspaper column, a radio program, a web site, and a merchandising line, as well as the Martha by Mail catalog business. The company earns 65 percent of its revenues from publishing, and its media properties reach 88 million people a month around the world, which allows Martha Stewart Living Omnimedia to command top advertising rates.

Martha Stewart's successes have been widely recognized. Her television show has won an Emmy, and *Adweek* named her "Publishing Executive of the Year" in 1996. She has been named one of "New York's 100 Most Influential Women in Business" by *Forbes* 400, one of the "50 Most Powerful Women" by *Fortune,* and one of "America's 25 Most Influential People" by *Time*. In 1998, she was the recipient of an Edison Achievement Award from the American Marketing Association, among many other national awards and honors.

Martha Stewart Living Omnimedia is clearly a classic success story: the small catering business transformed into a well-known brand, in the process making its founder synonymous with stylish living and good taste. Even those who have ridiculed Stewart's cheery perfect-housewife image acknowledge her confidence and business acumen. One author commented, "To the degree that her business partners were prepared to help advance the success of Martha Stewart, she was prepared to work with them. To the degree that they got in her way, she was willing to roll right over them." Another admired her hard-working nature by saying, "Anyone who spends more than a few minutes with America's most famous homemaker learns that she is one heck of a juggler."

The Insider-Trading Scandal

Despite her reputation and business successes, Stewart was indicted in 2003 on criminal charges and faced several civil lawsuits related to her sale of the ImClone stock. Stewart sold the stock on December 27, 2001, one day before the Food and Drug Administration refused to review ImClone System's cancer drug Erbitux; the company's stock tumbled following the FDA's announcement. The scandal also touches a number of other ImClone insiders, including the company's counsel, John Landes, who dumped $2.5 million worth of the company's stock on December 6; Ronald Martell, ImClone's vice president of marketing, who sold $2.1 million worth of company stock on December 11; and four other company executives who cashed in shares between December 12 and December 21.

Developments in the Scandal

After learning that that FDA would refuse to review Erbitux, Sam Waksal, the CEO of ImClone and a close friend of Stewart's, instructed his broker Peter Bacanovic, who is also Stewart's broker, to transfer $4.9 million in ImClone stock to the account of his daughter Aliza Waksal. His daughter also requested that Bacanovic sell $2.5 million of her own ImClone stock. Sam Waksal then tried to sell the shares he had transferred to his daughter, but was blocked by brokerage firm Merrill Lynch. Phone records indicate that Bacanovic called Martha Stewart's office on December 27 shortly after Waksal's daughter dumped her shares. Stewart's stock was sold ten minutes later.

Sam Waksal was arrested on June 12, 2002, on charges of insider trading, obstruction of justice, and bank fraud in addition to previously filed securities fraud and perjury charges. Although he pleaded innocent for nine months, Sam Waksal eventually pleaded guilty to insider trading and another six out of thirteen charges. In his plea, Waksal said, "I am aware that my conduct, while I was in possession of material non-public information, was wrong, I've made some terrible mistakes and I deeply regret what has happened." He was later sentenced to more than seven years in prison—the maximum allowed by federal sentencing guidelines—and ordered to pay a $3 million fine. Prosecutors continue to investigate whether he tipped off others, including family members and an individual who sold $30 million in the biotechnology company's shares. Sam Waksal's father and daughter also face a criminal investigation and the possible forfeiture of nearly $10 million that the government contends were obtained from illegal insider trading.

Martha Stewart denied that she engaged in any improper trading when she sold her shares of ImClone stock. On December 27, Stewart says she was flying in her private jet to Mexico for a vacation with two friends. En route, she called her office to check her messages, which included one from her broker Peter Bacanovic, with news that her ImClone stock had dropped below $60 per share. Stewart claims she had previously issued a "stop-loss" order to sell the stock if it fell below $60 per share. Stewart called Bacanovic and asked him to sell her 3,928 shares; she also called her friend Sam Waksal, but could not reach him. Stewart's assistant left a message for Sam Waksal saying, "Something's going on with ImClone, and she wants to know what it is. She's staying at Los Ventanos." Waksal did not call her back. Investigators are also looking into the sale of another 10,000 shares of ImClone stock by Dr. Bart Pasternak, a close friend of Stewart. At about the time Stewart made her sale, she was on her way to Mexico with Pasternak's estranged wife, Mariana.

However, Stewart's explanation that she unloaded her stock because of a prearranged sell order collapsed when Douglas Faneuil, the broker's assistant who handled the sale of the ImClone stock for Stewart, told Merrill Lynch lawyers that his boss, Peter Bacanovic, had pressured him to lie about a stop-loss order. Although Faneuil initially backed Stewart's story, he later told prosecutors that Bacanovic prompted him to advise Stewart that Waksal family members were dumping their stock and that she should consider doing the same. During interviews with law enforcement officials, Faneuil said, "I did not truthfully reveal everything I knew about the actions of my immediate supervisor and the true reason for the sales." He reportedly received money or other valuables for hiding his knowledge from investigators.

Faneuil pleaded guilty to a misdemeanor charge on October 2 and is expected to testify against Stewart, who resigned from her board membership of the New York Stock Exchange a day after Faneuil pleaded guilty. Merrill Lynch fired Faneuil after he pleaded guilty; Bacanovic was also fired for declining to cooperate with investigators looking into trading activity of ImClone's shares.

The Probe

In August 2002, investigators requested Stewart's phone and e-mail records on the ImClone stock trade and her Merrill Lynch account as well as those of her business manager. Stewart and Bacanovic have yet to provide investigators with proof that a stop-loss order existed. Congressional investigators for the U.S. House of Representatives' Energy and Commerce Committee could not find any credible record of such an order between Stewart and her broker. However, portions of the documents presented to the committee were unreadable because they were blacked out. Stewart's lawyers later agreed to return to Capitol Hill with unedited documents. The committee did not call Martha Stewart to testify as her lawyers had made it clear that she would invoke her Fifth Amendment right to remain silent. Investigators, who had been negotiating unsuccessfully with Stewart's lawyers to arrange for her voluntary testimony, came to believe that Stewart was "stonewalling" and would not cooperate. Many wondered, "If Ms. Stewart has been straight about her story, then why wouldn't she tell it under oath?" After the scandal broke, however, Stewart and her spokespeople declined to comment or could not be reached. The House Energy and Commerce Committee ultimately handed the Martha Stewart/ImClone investigation over to the U.S. Justice Department, with a strong suggestion that it investigate whether Stewart had lied to the committee.

Additionally, the SEC indicated that it was ready to file civil securities fraud charges against Stewart for her alleged role in the insider-trading scandal and her public statement about the stop-loss arrangement with her broker. Federal prosecutors soon widened their investigation to include determining whether Stewart had tampered with a computerized phone log to delete a message from her broker as well as whether she had made her public statements about why she sold ImClone shares in order to maintain the price of her own company's stock. Federal law bars officers of public corporations from knowingly making false statements that are material in effect—meaning they have the potential to shape a reasonable investor's decision to buy or sell stock in a particular company. If prosecutors could prove that Stewart made a deceptive statement to repair her credibility and keep her firm's stock price from falling, it could charge her with securities fraud. Already, one shareholder has filed suit against Stewart.

The Charges

Finally, on June 4, 2003, a federal grand jury indicted Stewart on charges of securities fraud, conspiracy (together with Peter Bacanovic), making false statements, and obstruction of justice. Although the forty-one-page indictment did not specifically charge Stewart with insider trading, it alleged that she lied to federal investigators about the stock sale, attempted to cover up her activities, and defrauded Martha Stewart Living Omnimedia shareholders by misleading them about the gravity of the situation and thereby keeping the stock price from falling. The indictment further accused Stewart of deleting a computer log of the telephone message from Bacanovic informing her that he thought ImClone's stock "was going to start trading downward." Peter Bacanovic was also indicted on charges of making false statements, making and using false documents, perjury, and obstruction of justice. The indictment alleged that Bacanovic had altered his personal notes to create the impression of a prior agreement to sell Stewart's ImClone shares if the price fell below $60/share. Both Stewart and Bacanovic pleaded "not guilty" to all charges. If convicted, Martha Stewart could be sentenced to up to thirty years in prison and fined up to $2 million.

Additionally, the SEC filed a civil lawsuit accusing both Stewart and Bacanovic of insider trading, demanding more than $45,000 in recompensation, and seeking to bar Stewart from being an officer or director of a public company. Although Stewart denied the charges, she resigned her positions as chief executive officer and chairman of the board of Martha Stewart Living Omnimedia just hours after the indictment, avowing, "I love this company, its people and everything it stands for, and I am stepping aside as chairman and CEO because it is the right thing to do." She retains a seat on the firm's board of directors and remains its chief shareholder. Sharon Patrick, the company's president and chief operating officer, replaced Stewart as CEO, while Jeffrey Ubben, the founder of an investment group that owns Omnimedia stock, was named chairman.

Ironically, Martha Stewart could have sold her ImClone stock on December 31 instead of December 27 and collected $180,000 in profit without raising any concerns. That's just $48,000 less than what she gained through the earlier sale. That $48,000 gain has already cost Stewart $261,371,672 plus legal fees, an amount that grows daily due to the damage the scandal may create for her image and brand. Despite Stewart's denials of any wrongdoing, the scandal has sliced more than 70 percent off the stock price of Omnimedia and, according to one estimate, washed away more than a quarter of her net worth. Before the scandal Stewart had an estimated net worth of $650 million.

After the indictment and Stewart's resignation, she took out a full-page newspaper ad in which she reiterated her innocence and appealed to her customers to remain loyal. Stewart insisted in the ad, "I simply returned a call from my stockbroker. . . . Based in large part on prior discussions with my broker about price, I authorized a sale of my remaining shares in a biotech company called ImClone. I later denied any wrongdoing in public statements and voluntary interviews with prosecutors. The government's attempt to criminalize these actions makes no sense to me." Stewart also retained a public-relations firm to help her firm weather the crisis and set up a web site, www.marthatalks.com, to update her customers and fans about the case.

Implications of the Scandal

After the scandal became public, Martha Stewart began a campaign to detach herself from the events. However, she couldn't escape questions about the insider-trading scandal. Even in her regular weekly cooking segment on CBS's *The Early Show*, host

Jane Clayson attempted to ask about the scandal, but Stewart responded: "I want to focus on my salad. . . ." Her appearances on the morning program have since been put on hold.

If convicted on all charges, Stewart could face a prison sentence and be forced to give up her seat on the board of directors. Separating Martha Stewart from Omnimedia, the company she personifies, would be no simple task. Her most important role in the company is as its highly recognizable spokesperson, brand, and television personality. Finding someone to replace her in that role would be far more difficult than finding a replacement chairwoman and CEO.

The Future of Stewart's Image and Business

There are few companies so closely identified with their founders as Martha Stewart Living Omnimedia Inc. Although many companies have survived scandals and the exit of their founders, Martha Stewart has a one-of-a-kind relationship with her company, its brands, and products. Regardless of whether she is convicted, the insider-trading scandal has affected Stewart's company: The stock price has fallen by 50 percent, and magazine revenues and subscription renewals have declined. Many wonder whether the firm can truly recover without Stewart's presence. Organizational psychologist Ken Siegel, commenting for *CBS News*, suggested that, "Even if she is legally exonerated, her image as the mistress of homeyness is significantly tarnished. She's playing this a little too close to the vest. It's a contradiction of the marketplace image of open, warm, and domestic." On *CBS News*, Steven Fink, president of Lexicon Communications, likewise questioned Stewart's choice of avoiding the questions: "Someone as culturally prominent as Stewart would be expected to address the public, and she has not really done that, resulting, rightly or wrongly, in the perception that she has something to hide. She branded herself as the ultimate last word on perfect living but now her image is looking like a complete act, and the dishonored reputation of its creator is sure to have severe costs for Omnimedia."

The scandal occurred at an unfortunate time for Martha Stewart Living Omnimedia. The company's publishing arm was in its mature stage, its television show was suffering declining ratings, and the Internet operation was taking heavy losses. Moreover, some market analysts have expressed concern that the company depends too heavily on the name and image of its celebrated founder. One shareholder voiced the concern felt by many: "Without Martha, the company is only a shell. She's it." Stewart personifies the brand that is associated with her credibility and honesty—traits the public and investigators now question. In this case, the strength of the brand also becomes its weakness, as it is hard to tell where the person ends and the brand begins. Market analysts agree that Stewart needs to take steps to ensure that the brand can go beyond the person. With the tremendous growth of her company, Stewart has surrounded herself with a group of trustworthy professionals to deal with the fine points who are as detail oriented as she is. She believes that her business can live on without her because it is now a combination of her artistic philosophy and spirit and the creativity of others.

Although Stewart has taken strides to make the brand more independent, there are lingering doubts about the long-term effects of the scandal.

Others, however, believe that Martha Stewart's drive and spirit will help her overcome this setback. Jerry Della Femina, an advertising executive, said, "The brand will survive because Martha has gone beyond being a person who represents a brand." She built an empire and became famous by making the most discouraging circumstances seem neat and elegant. The question now is whether the billionaire "diva of domesticity" can survive an insider-trading scandal that has already resulted in the convictions of two people. Before the scandal broke, Stewart was asked about her close ties with her brand. She replied, "I think that my role is Walt Disney. There are very few brands that were really started by a person, with a person's name, that have survived as nicely as that. Estee Lauder has certainly survived beautifully, despite Mrs. Lauder's absence from the business in the last, maybe, 15 years. I would like to engender that same kind of spirit and same kind of high quality."

Questions

1. Martha Stewart has repeatedly denied any wrongdoing, despite the indictment. Why is her company being damaged by the scandal?
2. What role has Stewart's image played in the insider-trading scandal?
3. Will Martha Stewart Living Omnimedia survive if Stewart is convicted? In order to survive, what changes will need to be made at the company?

Sources

These facts are from Christopher M. Byron, *Martha Inc.: The Incredible Story of Martha Stewart Living Omnimedia* (New York: John Wiley & Sons, Inc., 2002); Diane Brady, "Martha Inc. Inside the Growing Empire of America's Lifestyle Queen," *Business Week,* January 17, 2000; Julie Creswell, "Will Martha Walk?" *Fortune,* November 25, 2002, pp. 121–124; Mike Duff, "Martha Scandal Raises Questions, What's in Store for Kmart?" *DSN Retailing Today,* July 8, 2002, pp. 1, 45; Anne D'Innocenzio, "Charges Imperil Stewart Company," *[Fort Collins] Coloradoan,* June 5, 2003, pp. D1, D7; Shelley Emling, "Martha Stewart Indicted on Fraud," *Austin American-Statesman,* June 5, 2003, www.statesman.com; Shelley Emling, "Stewart Defends Her Name with Ad," *Austin American-Statesman,* June 6, 2003, www.statesman.com; "Feds Tighten Noose on Martha," CNN/*Money,* February 6, 2003, http://money.cnn.com/2003/02/06/news/companies/martha/index.htm; Charles Gasparino and Kara Scannell, "Probe of Martha Stewart's Sale of Stock Enters Its Final Phase," *Wall Street Journal,* January 24, 2003, p. C7; Constance L. Hays, "Stiff Sentence for ImClone Founder," *Austin American-Statesman,* June 11, 2003, http://www.statesman.com; "ImClone Founder Pleads Guilty," CBS News, October 15, 2002, www.cbsnews.com/stories/2002/08/12/national/main518354.shtml; "ImClone Probe Costly for Martha Stewart," MSNBC, January 27, 2003, http://stacks.msnbc.com/news/864675.asp; Charles M. Madigan, "Woman Behaving Badly," *Across the Board,* July/August 2002, p. 75; Jerry Markon, "Martha Stewart Could Be Charged As 'Tippee,'" *Wall Street Journal,* October 3, 2002, pp. C1, C9; "Martha Stewart Enters Not Guilty Plea to Charges," *Wall Street Journal,* June 4, 2003, http://online.wsj.com; "Martha's Mouthpiece: We'll Deliver," CBS News, August 20, 2002, www.cbsnews.com/stories/2002/08/20/national/main519320.shtml; "Martha Stewart Living Slides into Red, Expects More Losses," *Wall Street Journal,* March 4, 2003, http://online.wsj.com/article/0,,SB1046721988332486840,00.html; Erin McClam, "Martha Stewart Indicted in Stock Scandal," *Coloradoan,* June 5, 2003, p. A1; Amy Merrick, "Can Martha Deliver Merry?" *Wall Street Journal,* October 8, 2002, pp. B1, B3; Keith Naughton, "Martha's Tabloid Dish," *Newsweek,* June 24, 2002, p. 36; Keith Naughton and Mark Hosenball, "Setting the Table," *Newsweek,* September 23, 2002, p. 7; "New Witness in Martha Probe," CBSNews, August 9, 2002, www.cbsnews.com/stories/2002/08/12/national/main518448.shtml; Marc Peyser, "The Insiders," *Newsweek,* July 1, 2002, pp. 38–53; Thomas A. Stewart, "Martha Stewart's Recipe for Disaster," *Business2.com,* July 3, 2002; Jeffrey Toobin, "Lunch at Martha's," *New Yorker,* February 3, 2003, pp. 38–44; Thor Valdmanis, "Martha Stewart Leaves NYSE Post," *USA Today,* October 4, 2002, p. 3B.

Arthur Andersen: Questionable Accounting Practices

This case was prepared by Heather A. Stein for classroom discussion, rather than to illustrate either effective or ineffective handling of an administrative, ethical, or legal decision by management.

rthur Andersen LLP was founded in Chicago in 1913 by Arthur Andersen and partner Clarence DeLany. Over a span of nearly ninety years, the Chicago accounting firm would become known as one of the "Big Five" largest accounting firms in the United States, together with Deloitte & Touche, PricewaterhouseCoopers, Ernst & Young, and KPMG. For most of those years, the firm's name was nearly synonymous with trust, integrity, and ethics. Such values are crucial for a firm charged with independently auditing and confirming the financial statements of public corporations, whose accuracy investors depend on for investment decisions.

In its earlier days, Andersen set standards for the accounting profession and advanced new initiatives on the strength of its then undeniable integrity. One example of Andersen's leadership in the profession occurred in the late 1970s when companies began acquiring IBM's new 360 mainframe computer system, the most expensive new computer technology available at the time. Many companies had been depreciating computer hardware on the basis of an assumed ten-year useful life. Andersen, under the leadership of Leonard Spacek, determined that a more realistic life span for the machines was five years. Andersen therefore advised its accounting clients to use the shorter time period for depreciation purposes, although this resulted in higher expenses charged against income and a smaller bottom line. Public corporations that failed to adopt the more conservative measure would receive an "adverse" opinion from Andersen's auditors, something they could ill afford.

Arthur Andersen once exemplified the rock-solid character and integrity that was synonymous with the accounting profession. But high-profile bankruptcies of clients such as Enron and WorldCom capped a string of accounting scandals that eventually cost investors nearly $300 billion and hundreds of thousands of people their jobs. As a result, the Chicago-based accounting firm was forced to close its doors after ninety years of business.

The Advent of Consulting

Leonard Spacek joined the company in 1947 following the death of founder Arthur Andersen. He was perhaps best known for his uncompromising insistence on auditor independence, which was in stark contrast to the philosophy of combining auditing and consulting services that many firms, including Andersen itself, later adopted. Andersen began providing consulting services to large clients such as General Electric and Schlitz Brewing in the 1950s. Over the next thirty years, Andersen's consulting business became more profitable per partner than its core accounting and tax services businesses.

According to the American Institute of Certified Public Accountants (AICPA), the objective of an independent audit of a client's financial statements is "the expression of an opinion on the fairness with which [the financial statements] present, in all material respects, financial position, results of operations, and its cash flows in conformity with generally accepted accounting principles." The primary responsibility of an auditor is to express an opinion on a client firm's financial statements after conducting an audit to obtain reasonable assurance that the client's financial statements are free of material misstatement. It is important to note that financial statements are the responsibility of a company's management and not the outside auditor.

At Andersen, growth became the priority, and its emphasis on recruiting and retaining big clients perhaps came at the expense of quality and independent audits. The company linked its consulting business in a joint cooperative relationship with its audit arm, which compromised its auditors' independence, a quality crucial to the execution of a credible audit. The firm's focus on growth also generated a fundamental change in its corporate culture, one in which obtaining high-profit consulting business seems to have been regarded more highly than providing objective auditing services. Those individuals who could deliver the big accounts were often promoted ahead of the practitioners of quality audits.

Andersen's consulting business became recognized as one of the fastest-growing and most profitable consulting networks in the world. Revenues from consulting began catching up with the auditing unit in the early 1980s, and surpassed them for the first time in 1984. Although Andersen's consulting business was growing at a rapid pace, its audit practice remained the company's bread and butter. Ten years later, Arthur Andersen merged its operational and business systems consulting units and set up a separate business consulting practice in order to offer clients a broader range of integrated services. Throughout the 1990s, Andersen reaped huge profits by selling consulting services to many clients whose financial statements it also audited. This lucrative full-service strategy would later pose an ethical dilemma for some Andersen partners, who had to decide how to treat questionable accounting practices discovered at some of Andersen's largest clients.

Thanks to the growth of Andersen's consulting services, many viewed it as a successful model that other large accounting firms should emulate. However, this same model eventually raised alarm bells at the Securities and Exchange Commission (SEC), concerned over its potential for compromising the independence of audits. In 1998, then SEC chairman Arthur Levitt publicly voiced these concerns and recommended new rules that would restrict the nonaudit services that accounting firms could provide to their audit clients—a suggestion that Andersen vehemently opposed.

Nonetheless, in 1999, Andersen chose to split its accounting and consulting function into two separate—and often competing—units. Reportedly, under this arrangement, competition between the two units for accounts tended to discourage a team spirit and instead fostered secrecy and selfishness. Communication suffered, hampering the firm's ability to respond quickly and effectively to crises. As revenues grew, the consulting unit demanded greater compensation and recognition. Infighting between the consulting and auditing units grew until the company was essentially split into two opposing factions.

In August 2000, following an arbitration hearing, a judge ruled that Andersen's consulting arm could effectively divorce the accounting firm and operate independently. By that time, Andersen's consulting business consisted of about 11,000 consultants and brought in global revenues of nearly $2 billion. Arthur Andersen as a whole employed more than 85,000 people worldwide. The new consulting company promptly changed its name to Accenture the following January. Later, the auditing unit, Arthur Andersen, changed its name to Andersen Worldwide in order to better represent its new global brand of accounting services.

Meanwhile, in January 2001, Andersen named Joseph Berardino as the new CEO of the U.S. audit practice. His first task was to navigate the smaller company through a number of lawsuits that had developed in prior years. They company paid $110 million in May 2001 to settle claims brought by Sunbeam shareholders for accounting irregularities and $100 million to settle with Waste Management shareholders over similar charges a month later. In the meantime, news that Enron had overstated earnings became public, sending shock waves through the financial markets. Over the following year, many companies, a number of them Andersen clients, were forced to restate earnings. The following sections describe a few of the cases that helped lead to Andersen's collapse.

Baptist Foundation of Arizona

In what would become the largest bankruptcy of a nonprofit charity in U.S history, the Baptist Foundation of Arizona (BFA), which Andersen served as auditor, bilked investors out of about $570 million. BFA, an agency of the Arizona Southern Baptist Convention, was founded in 1948 to raise and manage endowments for church work in Arizona. It operated like a bank, paying interest on deposits that were used mostly to invest in Arizona real estate. The foundation also offered estate and financial planning services to the state's more than 400 Southern Baptist churches, and was one of the few foundations to offer investments to individuals.

BFA invested heavily in real estate, a more speculative investment strategy than other Baptist foundations in the state traditionally used. Profits from investments were supposed to be used to fund the churches' ministries and numerous charitable causes. Problems began when the real estate market in Arizona suffered a downturn, and BFA's management came under pressure to show a profit. To do so, foundation officials allegedly concealed losses from investors beginning in 1986 by selling some properties at inflated prices to entities that had borrowed money from the foundation and were unlikely to pay for the properties unless the real estate market turned around. In what court documents would later label a "Ponzi scheme" after a famous swindling case, foundation officials allegedly took money from new investors to pay off existing investors in order to keep cash flowing. In the meantime, the foundation's top officers received six-figure salaries. With obligations to investors mounting, the scheme eventually unraveled, leading to criminal investigations and investor lawsuits against BFA and Andersen; more than half of the foundation's 133 employees were laid off. Finally, the foundation petitioned for Chapter 11 bankruptcy protection in 1999, listing debts of about $640 million against assets of about $240 million.

The investor lawsuit against Andersen accused the auditing firm of issuing false and misleading approvals of BFA's financial statements, which allowed the foundation to perpetuate the fraud. Andersen, in a February 2000 statement, responded that it sympathized with BFA investors but stood by the accuracy of its audit opinions. The firm blamed BFA management for the collapse, arguing that it was given misleading information on which to conduct the audits. However, during nearly two years of investigation, reports surfaced that Andersen had been warned of possible fraudulent activity by some BFA employees, and the firm eventually agreed to pay $217 million to settle the shareholder lawsuit in May 2002.

Sunbeam

Andersen's troubles over Sunbeam Corp. began when its audits failed to address serious accounting errors that eventually led to a class-action lawsuit by Sunbeam investors and the ouster of CEO Albert Dunlap in 1998. Boca Raton–based Sunbeam is the maker of such notable home appliance brands as Mr. Coffee, Mixmaster, Oster, Powermate, and others. Both the lawsuit and a civil injunction filed by the SEC accused Sunbeam of inflating earnings through fraudulent accounting strategies such as "cookie jar" revenues, recording revenue on contingent sales, and accelerating sales from later periods into the present quarter. The company was also accused of using improper "bill and hold" transactions, which involves booking sales months ahead of actual shipment or billing, temporarily inflating revenue through accounts receivable, and artificially boosting quarterly net income. As a result, Sunbeam was forced to restate six quarters of financial statements. The SEC's injunction also accused Phillip Harlow, then a partner at Arthur Andersen, of authorizing clean or "unqualified" opinions on Sunbeam's 1996 and 1997 financial statements despite his awareness of many of Sunbeam's accounting and disclosure improprieties.

In August 2002, a federal judge approved a $141 million settlement in the case. In it, Andersen agreed to pay $110 million to resolve the claims without admitting fault or liability. As of this writing, losses to Sunbeam shareholders have amounted to about $4.4 billion and job losses have totaled about 1,700.

Waste Management

Andersen also found itself in court over questionable accounting practices with regard to $1.4 billion of overstated earnings at Waste Management. A complaint filed by the SEC charged Waste Management with perpetrating a "massive" financial fraud over a period of more than five years. According to the complaint, the company's senior management itself violated and aided and abetted others' violations of antifraud, reporting, and recordkeeping provisions of federal securities laws, resulting in a loss to investors of more than $6 billion. Andersen was named in the case as having aided the fraud by repeatedly issuing unqualified audit opinions on Waste Management's materially misleading financial statements.

According to SEC documents, Waste Management capped the amount of fees it would pay for Andersen's auditing services, but it advised Andersen that it could earn additional fees through "special work." At first, Andersen identified improper accounting practices and presented them to Waste Management officials in a report called "Proposed Adjusting Journal Entries," which outlined entries that needed to be corrected to avoid understating Waste Management's expenses and overstating its earnings. However, Waste officials refused to make the corrections, and instead allegedly entered into a closed-door agreement with Andersen to write off the accumulated errors over a ten-year period and change its underlying accounting practices, but only in future periods. The SEC viewed this agreement as an attempt to cover up past frauds and to commit future frauds.

The result of these cases was that Andersen paid some $220 million to Waste Management shareholders and $7 million to the SEC. Four Andersen partners were sanctioned, and an injunction was obtained against the firm. Andersen, as part of its consent decree, was forced to promise not to sign off on spurious financial statements in the future or it would face disbarment from practicing before the SEC—a promise that it would later break with Enron. After the dust settled, Waste Management shareholders lost about $20.5 billion and about 11,000 employees were laid off.

Enron

In October 2001, the Securities and Exchange Commission announced that it was launching an investigation into the accounting of Enron, one of Andersen's biggest clients. Indeed, Andersen's new CEO, Joseph Berardino, had perhaps viewed the $1 million a week in audit fees Enron paid to Andersen, along with the consulting fees it paid to Andersen's spin-off firm, Accenture, as a significant opportunity to expand revenues at Andersen. And, with Enron as a client, Andersen had been able to make 80 percent of the companies in the oil and gas industry its clients. However, on November 8, 2001, Enron was forced to restate five years' worth of financial statements that Andersen had signed off on, accounting for $586 million in losses. Within a month, Enron filed for bankruptcy. The U.S. Justice Department began a criminal investigation into Andersen in January 2002, prompting both Andersen's clients and its employees to jump ship. The auditing firm eventually admitted to destroying a number of documents concerning its auditing of Enron, which led to an indictment for obstruction of justice on March 14, 2002. CEO Berardino stepped down by the end of the month.

As Andersen's obstruction-of-justice trial progressed, Nancy Temple, Andersen's Chicago-based lawyer, demanded Fifth Amendment protection and thus did not have to testify. Many others named her as the "corrupt persuader" who led others astray. She allegedly instructed David Duncan, Andersen's supervisor of the Enron account, to remove her name from memos that could have incriminated her. On

June 15, 2002, the jury found Andersen guilty of obstruction of justice, the first accounting firm ever to be convicted of a felony. The company agreed to stop auditing public companies by August 31, 2002, essentially shutting down the business.

Trouble with Telecoms

Unfortunately for Andersen, the accusations of accounting fraud did not end with Enron. News soon surfaced that WorldCom, Andersen's largest client, had improperly accounted for nearly $3.9 billion of expenses and had overstated earnings in 2001 and the first part of 2002. After WorldCom restated its earnings, its stock price plummeted, and investors launched a barrage of lawsuits that sent the telecom into bankruptcy court. WorldCom's bankruptcy filing eclipsed Enron's as the largest in U.S. history. Andersen blamed WorldCom for the scandal, insisting that the expense irregularities had not been disclosed to its auditors and that it had complied with SEC standards in its auditing of WorldCom. WorldCom, however, pointed the finger of blame not only at its former managers but also at Andersen for failing to find the accounting irregularities. The SEC filed fraud charges against WorldCom, which fired its CFO.

While the Enron and WorldCom scandals continued, more telecommunications firms, including Global Crossing and Qwest Communications, came under investigation for alleged accounting improprieties. Both firms had been issued unqualified or clean opinions on audits by Andersen. At the heart of both cases is the issue of fake asset swaps, in which the accused telecom companies allegedly exchanged fiber-optic broadband capacity at inflated prices in order to show huge gains. An investor lawsuit was filed against Global Crossing and Andersen alleging that Global Crossing had artificially inflated earnings and that Andersen had violated federal securities laws by issuing unqualified (positive) audit opinions on Global Crossing's financial statements, though it knew or failed to discover that they contained material misstatements. Global Crossing filed for Chapter 11 bankruptcy protection and fired Andersen as its auditor. Qwest, which thus far has avoided bankruptcy court, admitted to using improper accounting methods and will likely be forced to restate profits for 1999, 2000, and 2001, including $950 million in relation to the swaps and up to $531 million in cash sales of optical capacity.

Corporate Culture and Ethical Ramifications

As the details of these investigations into accounting irregularities and fraud came to light, it became apparent that Andersen was more concerned about its own revenue growth than where the revenue came from or whether its independence as an auditor had been compromised. One of the reasons for this confusion in its corporate culture may have been that numerous inexperienced business consultants and untrained auditors were sent to client sites who were largely ignorant of company policies. Another factor may have been its partners' limited involvement in the process of issuing opinions. As the company grew, the number of partners stagnated. There is also evidence that Andersen had limited oversight over its audit teams and that such visibility was impaired by a relative lack of checks and balances that could have identified when audit teams had strayed from accepted policies. Audit teams had great discretion in terms of issuing financials and restatements.

In February 2002, Andersen hired former Federal Reserve Board chairman Paul Volcker to institute reform and help restore its reputation. Soon after Volcker came on board, however, Andersen was indicted for obstruction of justice in connection with the shredding of Enron documents. During the investigations, Andersen had been trying to negotiate merger deals for its international partnerships and salvage what was left of its U.S operations. But amid a mass exodus of clients and partners and the resignation of Berardino, the company was forced to begin selling off various business units, and ultimately laid off more than 7,000 employees in the United States.

During this time, Alaska Air Group, an Andersen client, restated its 2001 results, which resulted in an *increase* in shareholder equity of $31 million. Alaska Air made the restatement on the recommendation of its new auditor, Deloitte & Touche, which had replaced Andersen in May 2002.

After Andersen was convicted of obstruction of justice, it was fined $500,000, among other penalties. Andersen agreed to cease auditing public corporations by the end of August, essentially marking the end of the ninety-year-old accounting institution. Accenture, its spin-off consulting unit, is free and clear of all charges, although the consulting firm seems reluctant to mention its origins and association with Andersen: Nowhere on Accenture's web site is the word *Andersen* to be found.

Implications for Regulation and Accounting Ethics

The accounting scandals of the early twenty-first century sent many Andersen clients into bankruptcy court and subjected even more to greater scrutiny. They also helped spur a new focus on business ethics, driven largely by public demands for greater corporate transparency and accountability. In response, Congress passed the Sarbanes-Oxley Act of 2002, which established new guidelines and direction for corporate and accounting responsibility. The act was enacted to combat securities and accounting fraud and includes, among other things, provisions for a new accounting oversight board, stiffer penalties for violators, and higher standards of corporate governance. Table C10.1 discusses some of the components of the act and how it could prevent these types of situations from occurring again.

For the accounting profession, Sarbanes-Oxley emphasizes auditor independence and quality, restricts accounting firms' ability to provide both audit and nonaudit services for the same clients, and requires periodic reviews of audit firms. All are provisions that the Arthur Andersen of the past would likely have supported wholeheartedly. Some are concerned, however, that such sweeping legislative and regulatory reform may be occurring too quickly in response to intense public and political pressure. The worry is that these reforms may not have been given enough forethought and cost-benefit consideration for those public corporations that operate within the law, which comprise the vast majority of corporate America.

TABLE C10.1	Sarbanes-Oxley Act Intended to Prevent Accounting Misconduct	
SARBANES-OXLEY ACT	**WHAT IT WILL DO**	**WHAT IT COULD PREVENT**
Section 104: Inspection of Registered Public Accounting Firms	Verify that financial statements are accurate	Use of questionable/illegal accounting practices
Section 201: Services Outside the Scope of Auditors; Prohibited Activities	Restrict auditors to audit activities only	Improper relationships, reduce likelihood of compromising good audit for more revenue
Section 203: Audit Partner Rotation	Rotate partners assigned to client, so fresh eyes see work papers	"Partner in Crime" relationship
Section 204: Auditor Reports to Audit Committees	Auditors must report to committee, who work for the board, not the company	Powerlessness of auditors by giving board power to investigate and rectify
Section 302: Corporate Responsibility for Financial Reports	Making executive personally liable for ensuring that statements are reported accurately	Companies from publishing misleading statements
Section 303: Improper Influence on Conduct of Audits	Removes power from company personnel	Withholding of information from auditors by making this illegal
Section 404: Management Assessment of Internal Controls	Gives auditor a voice outside of the audit to attest to policies demonstrated by the company	Information slipping by the SEC and stakeholders by giving more visibility to the firm
Title VIII: Corporate and Criminal Fraud Accountability Act of 2002	Makes it a felony to impede federal investigation, provides whistle-blower protection	Destruction of documents, will allow investigators to review work of auditors
Section 1102: Tampering with a Record or Otherwise Impeding an Official Proceeding	Persons acting to corrupt or destroy evidence liable for extended prison term	Others from attempting to interfere in an official investigation

Table adapted from Mandy Storeim, *Andersen LLP: An Assessment of the Company's Dilemmas in Corporate Crisis*, BG660 Final Project, Colorado State University, November 13, 2002.

Questions

1. Describe the economic, legal, and ethical issues surrounding Andersen's auditing of companies accused of accounting improprieties.
2. What evidence is there that Andersen's corporate culture contributed to its downfall?
3. How can the provisions of the Sarbanes-Oxley Act help minimize the likelihood of auditors' failing to identify accounting irregularities?

Sources

"$141M Sunbeam Fraud Case Settled; Andersen to Pay Bulk," New York State Society of Certified Public Accountants, August 9, 2002, http://nysscpa.org/home/2002/802/1week/article58.htm; "Alaska Air Restatement Adds Shareholder Value," *Seattle Times,* January 11, 2003, p. C1; "Andersen's Fall from Grace," BBC News, June 17, 2002, www.news.bbc.co.uk/1/hi/business/2049237.stm; John A. Byrne, "Fall from Grace," *Business Week,* August 12, 2002, pp. 50–56; Nanette Byrnes, Mike McNamee, Diane Brady, Louis Lavelle, Christopher Palmeri, et al., "Accounting in Crisis," *Business Week,* January 28, 2002, pp. 44–48; Dave Carpenter, "Andersen's WorldCom Story Familiar to Enron Excuse," *Houston Chronicle,* June 27, 2002, www.chron.com/cs/CDA/printstory.hts/special/andersen/1474232; "The Fall of Andersen," *Chicago Tribune,* September 1, 2002, www.chicagotribune.com/business/showcase/chi-0209010315sep01.story; Greg Farrell, "Jury Will Hear of Andersen's Past Scandals," *USA Today,* May 8, 2003, www.usatoday.com/money/energy/enron/2002-05-07-andersen-trial.htm; "First Trial of Arizona Baptist Foundation Case Starts This Week," *Baptist Standard,* March 4, 2002, http://baptiststandard.com/2002/3_4/print/arizona.html; Jonathan D. Glater, "Auditor to Pay $217 Million to Settle Suits," *Yahoo! News,* March 2, 2002, http://premium.news.yahoo.com/ews?tmpl=story&u=/nytp/20020302/880914; "Global Crossing Drops Andersen; Being Investigated by FBI, SEC," New York State Society of Certified Public Accountants, February 2, 2002, www.nysscpa.org/home/2002/202/1week/article45.htm; Floyd Norris, "$217 Million New Settlement by Andersen in Baptist Case," *Yahoo! News,* May 7, 2002, http://premium.news.yahoo.com/news?tmpl=story&u=/nytp/20020507/918059; Bruce Nussbaum, "Can You Trust Anybody Anymore?" *Business Week,* January 28, 2002, pp. 31–32; Barbara Powell, "Bankrupt WorldCom Says Financial Woes Persisting," *Yahoo! News,* October 22, 2002, http://story.news.yahoo.com/news?tmpl=story&u=/ap/20021022/ap_wo_en_po/us_worldcom_110/27/02; "Q&A: What Now for Andersen?" *BBC News,* June 16, 2002, http://news.bbc.co.uk/1/hi/business/2048325.stm; "Qwest Admits Improper Accounts," *BBC News,* July 29, 2002, http://news.bbc.co.uk/2/hi/business/2158135.stm; David Schepp, "Analysis: Verdict Signals Andersen's End," *BBC News,* June 15, 2002, http://news.bbc.co.uk/1/hi/business/2047381.stm; "SEC Sues Former CEO, CFO, Other Top Officers of Sunbeam Corporation in Massive Financial Fraud," U.S. Securities and Exchange Commission, May 15, 2001, www.sec.gov/news/headlines/sunbeamfraud.htm; Stephen Taub, "Andersen Pays $110 Million in Sunbeam Settlement," *CFO.com,* May 2, 2001, www.cfo.com/printarticle/0,53172947/A,00.html; "Telecoms Bosses Deny 'Fake' Swap Deals," *BBC News,* October 1, 2002, http://news.bbc.co.uk/2/hi/business/2290679.stm; Kathy Booth Thomas, "Called to Account," *Time,* June 18, 2002, pp. 43–45; "Waste Management Founder, Five Other Former Top Officers Sued for Massive Fraud," U.S. Securities and Exchange Commission, March 26, 2002, www.sec.gov/ews/headlines/wastemgmt6.htm; "WorldCom, Andersen Play Blame Game," *USA Today,* July 8, 2002, www.usatoday.com/money/telecom/2002-07-08-worldcom-hearings-ap.htm; "WorldCom Revelations Another Mark Against Andersen," *Atlanta Journal-Constitution,* June 27, 2002, www.accessatlanta.com/ajc/business/0602/worldcom/27andersen.html; Wendy Zellner, Stephanie Forest Anderson, and Laura Cohn, "A Hero—And a Smoking-Gun Letter," *Business Week,* January 28, 2002, pp. 34–35.

Case 11

Tyco International: Leadership Crisis

This case was prepared by Linda G. Mullen, Marketing Department, Southern Illinois University at Carbondale, for classroom discussion, rather than to illustrate either effective or ineffective handling of an administrative, ethical, or legal decision by management.

On September 12, 2002, Tyco International's former chief executive officer, L. Dennis Kozlowski, and former chief financial officer, Mark H. Swartz, were seen in handcuffs on national television after they were arrested and charged with misappropriating more than $170 million from the company. They were also accused of stealing more than $430 million through fraudulent sales of Tyco stock and concealing the information from shareholders. The two executives were charged in a Manhattan federal court with numerous counts of grand larceny, enterprise corruption, and falsifying business records. Another executive, former general counsel Mark A. Belnick, was also charged with concealing $14 million in personal loans. Months after the initial arrests, charges and lawsuits were still being filed in a growing scandal that threatened to eclipse the notoriety of other companies facing accounting fraud charges in the early 2000s.

Tyco's History

Tyco, Inc., was founded by Arthur J. Rosenberg in 1960, in Waltham, Massachusetts, as an investment and holding company focusing on solid-state science and energy conversion. It developed the first laser with a sustained beam to be used in medical procedures. After shifting its focus to the commercial sector, Tyco became a publicly traded company in 1964. It also began a pattern of acquisitions—sixteen different companies by 1968—that would continue through 1982 as the company sought to fill gaps in its development and distribution network. The rapidly growing and diversifying firm grew from $34 million in consolidated sales in 1973 to $500 million in 1982.

In 1982, Tyco reorganized into three business segments (Fire Protection, Electronics, and Packaging) to strengthen itself from within. By 1986, Tyco had returned to a growth-through-acquisitions mode. In the 1990s, Tyco maintained four core segments: Electrical and Electronic Components, Healthcare and Specialty Products, Fire and Security Services, and Flow Control. The company changed its name to Tyco International in 1993 to signal its global presence to the financial community. By 2000, the firm had acquired more than thirty major companies, including well-known firms such as ADT, Raychem, and the CIT Group.

The Rise of Dennis Kozlowski

Leo Dennis Kozlowski was born in Newark, New Jersey, in 1946. His parents, Leo Kelly and Agnes Kozlowski, were second-generation Polish Americans. His father worked for Public Service Transport (later the New Jersey Transport), and his mother was a school crossing guard in Newark's predominantly Polish neighborhood. Dennis Kozlowski attended public school and graduated from West Side High in 1964. He lived at home while he studied accounting at Seton Hall University in South Orange, New Jersey.

After brief stints at SCM Corp. and Nashua Corporation, Kozlowski went to work for Tyco in 1976. He soon found a friend and mentor in CEO Joseph Gaziano, whose lavish style—including company jets, extravagant vacations, company cars, and country club memberships—impressed Kozlowski. However, the luxurious lifestyle came to an end when Gaziano died of cancer in 1982. Gaziano was replaced by fellow MIT graduate John F. Fort III, who differed sharply in management style. Where Gaziano had been extravagant, Fort was analytical and thrifty, and Wall Street responded approvingly to his new course and direction for Tyco. Fort's goal was to increase the profits for the shareholders of Tyco and cut out the extravagant spending that had characterized Gaziano's tenure.

Kozlowski, who had thrived under Gaziano, had to shift gears to adapt to the abrupt change in leadership. However, Kozlowski's accounting background helped push him through the ranks at Tyco. He was very adept at crunching numbers and helping achieve Fort's vision of taking care of shareholders first. Fort soon noticed Kozlowski's talents.

Kozlowski's first major promotion within Tyco was to president of Grinnell Fire Protection Systems Co., Tyco's largest division. At Grinnell, Kozlowski cut out extras and reduced overhead, eliminated 98 percent of the paperwork, and reworked compensation programs. Although he slashed managers' salaries, he also set up a bonus compensation package that gave them greater control over the money they could earn. He gave public recognition to high achievers at a yearly banquet, but he also recognized the underachievers, giving out an award for the worst producing unit as well as the best. Perhaps most importantly, Kozlowski systematically began to buy out and acquire each of the fire protection division's competitors. As described in a *Business Week* article, he gained a reputation as a "corporate tough guy, respected and feared in roughly equal measure."

Over the next few years, Kozlowski continued his rise up Tyco's corporate ladder, becoming the company's president in 1987, before rising to CFO and eventually CEO in 1992. However, his aggressive approach to acquisitions and mergers during this period became a concern for then CEO Fort, who wanted to slow the rate of activity in Kozlowski's division. His largest acquisition was Wormald International, a $360 million global fire protection concern. However, integrating Wormald proved problematic, and Fort was reportedly not happy with so large a purchase. Fort and Kozlowski also disagreed over the rapid changes Kozlowski made in the fire protection division. Kozlowski responded by lobbying to convince Tyco's board of directors that the problems with Wormald were a "bump in the road" and that the firm should continue its strategy of acquiring profitable companies that met its guidelines. The board sided with Kozlowski, and Fort resigned as CEO and later as chairman of the board, although he remained a member of Tyco's board of directors until 2003.

Kozlowski's Tyco Empire

At the age of forty-six, Dennis Kozlowski found himself at the helm of Tyco International in 1992. He also moved out of his North Hampton home, leaving his wife and two daughters for a waitress, Karen Lee Mayo Locke, whom he eventually married in 2000. His new lifestyle—which included parties that were regular gossip-column fodder and homes in Boca Raton, Nantucket, Beaver Creek, and New York City—appeared to emulate that of Kozlowski's mentor, former CEO Joseph Gaziano. Indeed, Kozlowski's aggressive strategy of mergers and acquisitions made Tyco look more like the company it had been under Gaziano.

Kozlowski had learned Tyco and its businesses from the bottom up, which gave him an advantage in his determination to make Tyco the greatest company of the new century. Among other things, he recognized that one of the conglomerate's major shortcomings was its reliance on cyclical industries. Thus, he decided to diversify into more noncyclical industries. His first major acquisition toward that objective was the Kendall Company, a manufacturer of medical supplies, which had emerged from bankruptcy just two years before. Kozlowski quickly revived the business, which became very profitable and doubled Tyco's earnings. Although Tyco's board of directors had initially balked at the Kendall acquisition, the directors were pleased with the subsidiary's turnaround and contribution to profits. Kozlowski made Kendall the core of his new Tyco Healthcare Group, which quickly grew to become the second-largest producer of medical devices behind Johnson & Johnson. The board rewarded Kozlowski's performance by increasing his salary to $2.1 million and giving him shares of the company's stock.

Kozlowski's next strategic move was the acquisition of ADT Security Services, a British-owned company located in Bermuda, in 1997. By structuring the deal as a "reverse takeover," Tyco acquired a global presence as well as ADT's Bermuda registration, which allowed the firm to create a network of offshore subsidiaries to shelter its foreign earnings from U.S. taxes.

While Kozlowski continued to acquire new companies to build his vision of Tyco, he handpicked a few trusted people and placed them in key positions. One of these individuals was Mark Swartz, who was promoted from director of Mergers and Acquisitions to chief financial officer (CFO). Swartz, who had developed a strong financial background as an auditor for Deloitte & Touche and a reputation for being more approachable than Kozlowski, was aware of Kozlowski's business practices. Kozlowski also recruited Mark Belnick to become Tyco's general counsel.

By this time, Tyco's corporate governance system comprised Kozlowski as CEO and the firm's board of directors, which had eleven members, including Joshua Berman, a vice president of Tyco and former outside counsel; Mark Swartz, CFO; Lord Michael Ashcroft, a British dignitary who came with the ADT merger; James S. Pasman Jr., also from ADT; W. Peter Slusser, also from ADT; Richard S. Bodman, a venture capitalist; Stephen W. Foss, CEO of a textile concern; Joseph F. Welch, CEO of snack-food maker Bachman Co.; Wendy Lane, a private equity investor; John F. Fort III, former CEO and chairman of Tyco; and Frank E. Walsh Jr., director of the board. Kozlowski particularly liked the prestige of Lord Ashcroft being associated with his company. The majority of the directors had been on the board for ten to twenty years and were very familiar with Tyco's strategies and Kozlowski's management style. As directors, they were responsible for protecting Tyco's shareholders by disclosing any questionable situations or issues that might seem unethical or inappropriate, such as conflicts of interest. However, after the arrests of Kozlowski and Swartz, investigations subsequently uncovered the following troubling relationships among the board's members:

- Mark Swartz participated in loan-forgiveness programs.
- Richard Bodman invested $5 million for Kozlowski in a private stock fund managed by Bodman.
- Frank E. Walsh Jr. received $20 million for helping to arrange the acquisition of CIT Group without the knowledge of the rest of the board of directors.
- Walsh also held controlling interest in two firms that received more than $3.5 million for leasing an aircraft and providing pilot services to Tyco between 1996 and 2002.
- Stephen Foss received $751,101 for supplying a Cessna Citation aircraft and pilot services.
- Lord Michael Ashcroft used $2.5 million in Tyco funds to purchase a home.

With his handpicked board in place, Kozlowski decided to open a Manhattan office overlooking Central Park. However, the firm maintained its humble Exeter, New Hampshire, office, where Kozlowski preferred to be interviewed. According to *Business Week,* he bragged to a guest there, "We don't believe in perks, not even executive parking spots." The unpublicized Manhattan office essentially became the firm's unofficial headquarters, and Kozlowski lavished it with every imaginable perk. He also used Tyco funds to purchase and furnish apartments for key executives and employees in New York's pricey Upper East Side.

Meanwhile, Jeanne Terrile, an analyst for Tyco at Merrill Lynch, was not so impressed with Kozlowski's activities and Tyco's performance. Stock analysts like those at Merrill Lynch make recommendations to investors whether to buy, hold, or sell a particular stock. After Terrile wrote a less than favorable review of Tyco's rapid acquisitions and mergers and refused to upgrade Merrill's position on Tyco's stock, Kozlowski met with David Komansky, the CEO of Merrill Lynch. Although the subject of the meeting was never confirmed, shortly thereafter, Terrile was replaced by Phua Young, who immediately upgraded Merrill's recommendation for Tyco to "buy" from "accumulate." Merrill Lynch continued to be one of Tyco's top underwriters as well as one of its primary advisers for mergers and acquisitions.

Between 1997 and 2001, Tyco's revenues climbed 48.7 percent a year, and its pretax operating margins increased to 22.1 percent. The pace of mergers and acquisitions escalated with the able assistance of Mark Swartz, Tyco's CFO. In February 2002, Tyco announced that it had spent more than $8 billion on more than 700 acquisitions in the last three years. Among these were AMP Inc., an electronics maker for $11.3 billion in stock, and CIT Group, a commercial finance company. However, some of the merged companies were less than satisfied with the arrangement. Kozlowski forced acquired companies to scale back sharply and eliminate anything—and anyone—that did not produce revenue. The toll on human capital was enormous. Tyco shareholders and directors, however, were very happy with Kozlowski's performance, as demonstrated by his rapid salary increases from $8 million in 1997, to $67 million in 1998, to $170 million in 1999, which made him the second-highest-paid CEO in the United States.

During 1997–2002, Kozlowski's charismatic leadership style together with the firm's decentralized corporate structure meant that few people, including members of the board of directors, had a true picture of the firm's activities and finances. The company was organized into four distinct divisions—fire protection (53 percent); valves, pipes, and other "flow control" devices (23 percent); electrical and electronic components (13 percent); and packaging materials (11 percent)—and there was little interaction among them. Each division's president reported directly to Kozlowski, who in turn reported to the board.

Those who saw red flags at Tyco International were shot down, including Jeanne Terrile at Merrill Lynch and David W. Tice, a short seller who questioned whether Tyco's use of large reserves in connection with its acquisitions was obscuring its results. A nonpublic investigation by the Securities and Exchange Commission (SEC) resulted only in Tyco amending its earnings per share for 1999.

The Fall of Dennis Kozlowski

Everything began to fall apart in January 2002, when the board of directors learned that one of its members, Frank Walsh, had received a $20 million bonus for his part in securing and aiding in the CIT merger. Walsh promptly resigned from the board. Troubled by the idea that Kozlowski had made such a major payment without their knowledge, the remaining board members launched an investigation to determine whether other board members had earned such "commissions." The probe uncovered numerous expense abuses. Finally, after learning that he was about to be indicted for tax evasion, Kozlowski agreed to resign as CEO of Tyco on June 2, 2002.

Months earlier, the New York State Bank Department had observed large sums of money going into and out of Tyco's accounts. This would not have been unusual except that the funds were being transferred into Kozlowski's personal accounts. Eventually, authorities discovered that Kozlowski had allegedly avoided $3.1 million in New York state taxes by appearing to ship rare artwork to New Hampshire when in fact it was sent to New York. On June 3, Kozlowski was arrested for tax evasion, but the scandal was only just beginning.

On September 12, 2002, Dennis Kozlowski and Mark Swartz, who had also resigned from Tyco, were indicted on thirty-eight felony counts for allegedly stealing $170 million from Tyco and fraudulently selling an additional $430 million in stock options. Among other allegations, Kozlowski was accused of taking $242 million from a program intended to help Tyco employees buy company stock in order to buy yachts, fine art, and luxury homes. Together with former legal counsel Mark Belnick, the three face criminal charges, as well as a civil complaint from the SEC. Kozlowski was also accused of granting $106 million to various employees through "loan forgiveness" and relocation programs. Swartz was also charged with falsifying documents in this loan program in the amount of $14 million. Currently awaiting trial, Kozlowski and Swartz face up to twenty-five years in prison if convicted on the charges of enterprise corruption, grand larceny, falsifying documents, and conspiracy. Belnick was charged with larceny and trying to steer a federal investigation, as well as taking more than $26 million from Tyco.

In addition, several board members have been cited for conflict of interest and may yet face charges themselves. Frank Walsh, a former board member who received a $20 million bonus for the CIT merger, pleaded guilty and agreed to repay the $20 million plus an additional $2 million in court costs. Moreover, Jerry Boggess, the president of Tyco Fire and Security Division, was fired and accused of creating a number of "bookkeeping issues" that had a negative impact on earnings to shareholders. Richard Scalzo, the PricewaterhouseCoopers auditor who signed off on Tyco's 2002 audit, was removed.

Rebuilding an Empire

After Kozlowski's resignation, he was replaced as CEO by Edward Breen. The company filed suit against Dennis Kozlowski and Mark Swartz for more than $100 million. The SEC allows companies to sue for profits made by "insiders" who are profiting by buying and selling company stock within a six-month period. A statement by the company stated: "To hold him accountable for his misconduct, we seek not only full payment for the funds he misappropriated but also punitive damages for the serious harm he did to Tyco and its shareholders." Additionally, Tyco is suing for monies paid by Kozlowski to keep some of those closest to him from testifying against him.

Breen launched a review of the company's accounting and corporate governance practices to determine whether any other fraud had occurred. Although the probe uncovered no fraud, the firm announced in late 2002 that it would restate its 2002 financial results by $382.2 million. Tyco's new management declared in a regulatory filing that the firm's previous management had "engaged in a pattern of aggressive accounting which, even when in accordance with Generally Accepted Accounting Principles, was intended to increase reported earnings above what they would have been if more conservative accounting had been employed." Although Tyco's investigations found no further fraud, the company repeatedly restated its financial results or took accounting charges totaling more than $2 billion over the next six months.

Regardless of whether Kozlowski and Swartz are convicted, the scandal has had detrimental consequences, particularly for the company's shareholders. Tyco's stock plunged from $60 per share in January 2002 to $18 per share by December, and investors lost millions of dollars. Many of the firm's 260,000 employees were also shareholders and watched their savings dwindle. Tyco's retirees are worried that their savings and retirement plans, which were tied up in company shares, will plummet with the company's stock price.

To restore investors' faith in the company, Tyco's new management team is working to reorganize the company and recover some of the funds allegedly taken by Kozlowski. At its annual meeting, shareholders elected a completely new board of directors and voted to make future executive severance agreements subject to shareholder approval and to require the board chairman to be an independent person, rather than a Tyco CEO. However, the shareholders elected to keep the company incorporated in Bermuda.

Questions

1. What are the ethical and legal issues in this case?
2. What role did Tyco's corporate culture play in the scandal? What roles did the board of directors, CEO, CFO, and legal counsel play?
3. Have Tyco's recent actions been sufficient to restore confidence in the company? What other actions should the company take to demonstrate that it intends to play by the rules?
4. How will the implementation of the Sarbanes-Oxley Act of 2002 prevent future dilemmas in Tyco?

Sources

Bud Angst, "The Continuing Tyco Saga: December 2002," *[Valley View, PA] Citizen Standard,* January 1, 2003, via http://budangst.com/news/News763.htm; James Bandler and Jerry Guidera, "Tyco Ex-CEO's Party for Wife Cost $2.1 Million, but Had Elvis," *Wall Street Journal,* September 17, 2002, p. A1; Anthony Bianco, William Symonds, and Nanette Byrnes, "The Rise and Fall of Dennis Kozlowski," *Business Week,* December 23, 2002, pp. 64–77; Laurie P. Cohen, "Tyco Ex-Counsel Claims Auditors Knew of Loans," *Wall Street Journal,* October 22, 2002, http://online.wsj.com/article_print0,,SB1035524176089398951,00.html; Laurie P. Cohen and John Hechinger, "Tyco Suits Say Clandestine Pacts Led to Payments," *Wall Street Journal,* June 18, 2002, pp. A3, A10; Laurie P. Cohen and Mark Maremont, "Tyco Ex-Director Faces Possible Criminal Charges," *Wall Street Journal,* September 9, 2002, pp. A3, A11; Laurie P. Cohen and Mark Maremont, "Tyco Relocations to Florida Are Probed," *Wall Street Journal,* June 10, 2002, pp. A3, A6; "Corporate Scandals: Tyco, International," MSNBC, www.msnbc.com/news/corpscandal_front.asp?odm=C2ORB, accessed April 4, 2003; "Former Tyco Execs Face Fraud Charges," Canadian Broadcasting Corporation, September 12, 2002, www.cbc.ca/stories/2002/09/12/tyco020912; Charles Gaspaino, "Merrill Replaced Its Tyco Analyst After Meeting," *Wall Street Journal,* September 17, 2002, pp. C1, C13; Jerry Guidera, "Veteran Tyco Director Steps Down," *Wall Street Journal,* November 12, 2002, p. A8; "History," Tyco International, www.tyco.com/tyco/history.asp, accessed April 25, 2003; Arianna Huffington, "Pigs at the Trough Sidebars," Arianna Online, www.ariannaonline.com/books/pigs_updown.html, accessed April 25, 2003; Louis Lavelle, "Rebuilding Trust in Tyco," *Business Week,* November 25, 2002, pp. 94–96; Robin Londner, "Tyco to Consider Reincorporation, Auditor Removed," *[South Florida] Business Journal,* March 10, 2003, http://southflorida.bizjournal.com/southflorida/stories/2003/03/10/daily2.html; Loann Lublin and Jerry Guidera, "Tyco Board Criticized on Kozlowski," *Wall Street Journal,* June 7, 2002, p. A5; Mark Maremont, "Tyco May Report $1.2 Billion in Fresh Accounting Problems" *Wall Street Journal,* April 30, 2003, http://online.wsj.com/article/0,,SB105166908562976400,00.html?mod=home_whats_news_us; Mark Maremont, "Tyco Seeks Hefty Repayments from Former Financial Officer," *Wall Street Journal,* October 7, 2002, p. A6; Mark Maremont and Laurie P. Cohen, "Ex-Tyco CEO Is Likely to Face Charges over Unauthorized Pay," *Wall Street Journal,* September 12, 2002, pp. A1, A8; Mark Maremont and John Hechinger, "Tyco's Ex-CEO Invested in Fund Run by Director," *Wall Street Journal,* October 23, 2002, http://online.wsj.com/article_print0,,SB1035329530787240111,00.html; Mark Maremont and Jerry Markon, "Former Tyco Chief, Two Others Face New Charges and Lawsuits," *Wall Street Journal,* September 13, 2002, pp. A3, A6; Mark Maremont and Jerry Markon, "Former Tyco Executives Are Charged," *Wall Street Journal,* September 13, 2002, http://online.wsj.com/article_print0,SB1031836600798528755,00.html; Mark Maremont and Jerry Markon, "Tyco's Kozlowski Is Indicted on Charges of Tax Evasion," *Wall Street Journal,* June 5, 2002, pp. A1, A7; Samuel Maull, "Kozlowski Claims Tyco Owes Him Millions," *Real Cities,* March 14, 2003, www.realcities.com/mld/realcities/business/financial_markets/5395148.htm; Kevin McCoy, "Tyco

Acknowledges More Accounting Tricks," *USA Today,* December 31, 2002, p. 3B; Kevin McCoy, "Investigators Scrutinize $20M Tyco Fee," *USA Today,* September 16, 2002, p. 1B; Kevin McCoy, "Directors' Firms on Payroll at Tyco," *USA Today,* September 18, 2002, p. 1B; Gary Panter, "The Big Kozlowski," *Fortune,* November 18, 2002, pp. 123–126; Stephen Taub, "Tyco on Tyco: Errors Made, But No Fraud," CFO.com, December 31, 2002, www.cfo.com/article/1,5309,8596,00.html?f=related; "Tyco's History Under Kozlowski, *Washington Post,* June 3, 2002, www.washingtonpost.com; "Tyco's Shareholders Defeat Proposal to Leave Bermuda," *USA Today,* March 6, 2003, www.usatoday.com/money/industries/retail/2003-03-06-tyco_x.htm; "Tyco Smells Smoke at Fire Unit," TheStreet.com, March 12, 2003, www.thestreet.com/_yahoo/tech/earnings.10073763.html.

Case 12

Global Crossing: Inflated Sales Lead to Bankruptcy

This case was prepared by Neil Herndon, University of Missouri–Columbia, for classroom discussion, rather than to illustrate either effective or ineffective handling of an administrative, ethical, or legal decision by management.

G lobal Crossing began in 1997 as a grand idea. It was to become the fourth-largest bankruptcy in U.S. history just five years later. The road to that bankruptcy is a story of revenues inflated by what appears to be fraudulent accounting, in which senior executives enriched themselves while Arthur Andersen served as auditor and consultant. Global Crossing employees and shareholders seem to have been left holding the bag, much as in the Enron bankruptcy filed just two months earlier.

The Global Crossing Business Concept

Global Crossing was Gary Winnick's brainchild. Winnick was a former junk-bond financier who worked with Michael Milken at Drexel Burnham Lambert but escaped untarnished from a 1990s scandal at that firm. Together with a group of financial gurus and chief executive officers, he envisioned a global broadband network that would link continents with undersea fiber-optic cables. This was a risky proposition in 1997 because no such network existed, and no one knew exactly how profitable, or unprofitable, such a network would be. It has always been extremely difficult to forecast the profitability of new services or new technologies, and the Global Crossing proposal was no exception.

Demand for high-speed data services that could span continents exploded in the middle of the 1990s. The fiber-optic networks in the United States were owned by Sprint, AT&T, and MCI, with a few other relatively small players. None of these firms seemed able to keep up with the growing business demand for broadband capacity. Level 3, Qwest Communications International, and Williams Communications stepped in to add capacity by building fiber-optic networks that spanned the country, expecting that many businesses would pay extra just to have access to this

491

service. The creators of Global Crossing, as its name implies, envisioned a fiber-optic network that extended globally rather than just domestically.

Global Crossing faced one, not so small obstacle to executing its business plan: It effectively had no assets, and building such a high-tech, undersea network would be tremendously expensive, on the order of $2.7 billion. Fortunately, Wall Street investors valued the Global Crossing concept highly and offered Winnick and his management team about $40 billion in equity financing and $10 billion in debt financing. Investment analysts gave the stock a "strong buy" rating.

If demand for the services Global Crossing offered continued to exceed supply—in other words, creating a "seller's market"—then Global Crossing's plan to create additional fiber-optic broadband capacity had great profit potential because the company could set a high price for its service. However, if supply began to outstrip demand and prices dropped accordingly—a "buyer's market"—then Global Crossing's profits would drop, possibly taking profits into negative territory. In fact, the race to build fiber-optic networks quickly created excess capacity in the industry, which ultimately resulted in customers paying a lower price for broadband service, rather than the premium price executives had hoped for. The bottom line was that Global Crossing's profits could no longer pay the interest on its debt.

At its peak, Global Crossing had a market valuation of more than $50 billion, larger than General Motors on paper, and its fiber-optic telecommunications network connected 200 cities in twenty-seven countries. However, it amassed about $12.4 billion in debt establishing its global fiber-optic telecommunications network. So when Global Crossing's revenues dropped to $2.4 billion in the first three quarters of 2001, down from about $3.8 billion for the same period in 2000, the writing was on the wall. After finishing 2000 with a loss of some $1.67 billion, Global Crossing was forced to declare bankruptcy on January 28, 2002.

The Telecommunications Stock Analyst

Jack Grubman, a telecommunications stock analyst for investment house Salomon Smith Barney (owned by Citigroup, Inc.), was consistently "bullish" on Global Crossing after the company went public in August 1998. His support continued until November 2001, when it became clear that demand for broadband capacity was falling short of the demand Grubman and other telecommunications stock analysts had predicted in 1998 and 1999. Although he lowered his price target for Global Crossing stock in May 2001 by $40 per share, from $70 to $30, he also labeled the stock a "core holding" and maintained his "buy" recommendation.

It later emerged that Grubman, though employed by Salomon Smith Barney, helped Global Crossing make key business and management decisions for about two years after the company's initial public offering (IPO). In fact, Global Crossing chairman Gary Winnick and Grubman reportedly communicated almost daily for some time after Global Crossing's debut. Grubman allegedly advised Winnick on his personal stock sales and was reported to be involved in the recommendation to hire Robert Annunziata as Global Crossing's CEO. Grubman also allegedly helped to negotiate mergers with U.S. West, Inc. and Frontier Corporation on Global Crossing's behalf.

Grubman's extensive activities with Global Crossing were unusual given the traditional role of stock analysts, who are generally expected to provide only impartial advice to investors and shareholders. While Grubman's activities do not appear to violate federal securities law, investigators from the New York State Attorney General's Office are looking into the source of Grubman's bonuses. Was he being rewarded for his role as a telecommunications stock analyst or for his role as an advisor to Global Crossing's management?

Jack Grubman was certainly not the only Wall Street analyst enthusiastic about the prospects of the telecommunications industry, but he seems to have had more influence over the telecom sector than any of his peers. One former telecom CEO was quoted as saying that if Grubman didn't endorse a deal, the deal didn't happen. But, in order to get his endorsement, Salomon Smith Barney had to secure a major part of the investment business.

Concerns About Insider Trading

The laws regulating business in the United States emphasize fairness to all involved in commerce, regardless of wealth, fame, position of power, or role, such as consumer, producer, or investor. Some refer to these protections as "maintaining a level playing field," a metaphor that suggests that one team should not have to struggle to move the ball uphill while the other moves the ball easily downhill—aided by gravity. This fairness philosophy, enshrined in many facets of U.S. business law and associated regulations, is especially evident in the laws regarding insider trading.

Insider trading generally occurs when a person has nonpublic information that is material about a security or the company that issues it and then buys or sells that security based on that information. The Securities and Exchange Commission (SEC) requires that an individual who is privy to inside information that might affect a stock's price must not trade in that company's securities unless he or she discloses what is known before buying or selling the stock. The SEC and the courts use three sets of rules to determine whether insider trading has occurred. The traditional rule is that all partners and employees of a firm, including people whose professional activities put them in a relationship of trust or confidence with the firm or its shareholders, must not trade in the securities of the company in which they hold material, nonpublic information. Second, they are not permitted to disclose this information to others if they expect to profit in any way whatsoever from that disclosure. A person who receives a tip from an insider and then trades in that company's securities is generally guilty of insider trading. Finally, the misappropriation rule effectively extends insider liability to people who receive nonpublic, material information from insiders who have a duty to keep that information confidential, including people with whom the insider habitually shares confidential information, such as a spouse. Under tender-offer rules, traditional insiders and any others who obtain material information about the tender offer may not legally trade in that company's securities.

Penalties for insider trading are stiff. Making just over $10,000 in an illegal insider trade would draw a mandatory eight- to fourteen-month jail sentence if convicted. The combined maximum civil and criminal penalties for insider trading are even harsher. Civil penalties assessed to violators may be up to three times the amount of illegal profits gained or losses avoided by the act of insider trading. In addition, the maximum criminal penalties for individuals is twenty years in prison and a $5 million fine. Private parties may also sue the inside trader for damages.

There is evidence that top officials at Global Crossing knew that the company's business future appeared bleak before they sold company stock. These transactions resulted in millions of dollars of income for those involved. Chairman Gary Winnick is reported to have sold stock valued at $123 million on May 23, 2001, but a witness told a congressional committee investigating Global Crossing that he had seen an April forecast projecting a revenue fall of $300 million. A much earlier June 5, 2000, e-mail from then CEO Leo Hindery Jr. encouraged Winnick to offer the assets of Global Crossing for sale to other telecommunications companies. Winnick denies that he sold stock based on his inside information that the company was in financial trouble. Winnick's lawyer, Gary Naftalis, insists the stock sales were proper and had been approved by Global Crossing's counsel. Altogether, it appears that Winnick sold some $734 million in Global Crossing stock before the company filed for bankruptcy.

Other Global Crossing executives also profited from the sale of company stock. Between 1999 and the end of December 2001, they are reported to have sold some $1.3 billion worth. David Walsh, formerly the chief operating officer, sold stock worth $8.7 million on May 31, 2001; Global Crossing cochairman Lodwrick Cook sold stock worth $9.8 million on May 16, 2001. Cook said that he sold his shares to satisfy a margin call—that is, he had borrowed money to pay for Global Crossing shares and when share prices dropped, he needed to sell some of his shares to repay the margin loans.

The Capacity Swaps

During the "gold rush" fever of the telecommunications boom, start-up fiber-optic telecommunications companies like Global Crossing and Qwest would swap network capacity. In other words, the two companies would simultaneously sell each other the right to use some part of their respective fiber-optic networks, creating in effect a long-term lease that allowed one company to take control of part of the other company's network. The companies would then declare in their quarterly and annual reports the income from selling the rights to use a portion of the network, but would not declare the expense of purchasing the rights. This consequently "boosted" their revenues and overstated their profits, sending their stock price higher. This transaction, called a "capacity swap" or "swap," would have the effect of making the balance sheets of the two companies appear stronger than they actually were. Such deals added about $375 million to Global Crossing's bottom line in the first quarter of 2001.

Signing contracts to gain access to each firm's networks appears to be legal. The issue with such swaps is that one asset is replaced with another, virtually identical asset. It does not appear that any real economic value is created in the transaction, even though the financial statements of the telecommunications firms involved do not reflect this fact. This procedure tended to mislead shareholders and potential investors about the financial health of the company in which they were investing.

Global Crossing senior operations executive Carl Grivner commissioned an internal review of fiber-optic capacity that reported that most of the company's capacity purchases were of limited or no value. Less than 20 percent of the swapped assets could be cost-effectively added to Global Crossing's existing network. In some swaps, the assets were hundreds of miles from a Global Crossing connection point, making interconnection prohibitively expensive. It appears that engineers were sometimes consulted about the swaps and sometimes not, especially when the deals were being made in a quarter's closing minutes. Reportedly, the study was presented to the company's executive vice president of finance, Joseph Perrone, in September 2001.

The SEC looked into Global Crossing's accounting practices after it filed for bankruptcy protection and said that Global Crossing's accounting for these swaps did not comply with generally accepted accounting principles. It ordered Global Crossing to change its financial statements to reflect adherence to these principles, a ruling that would likely apply to other telecommunications companies that had adopted the practice of swapping capacity. Global Crossing indicated that restating its earnings from such capacity swaps to comply with the SEC order for the first nine months of 2001 would cost it about $19 million in revenue. This would lower the $2.44 billion booked in revenue for this period and thereby increase the company's net loss of $4.77 billion by about $13 million. Global Crossing also said that when it accounted for the swaps it had acted in accordance with information provided by Arthur Andersen, its accounting firm. Arthur Andersen reportedly had told Global Crossing that it did not agree with the SEC's interpretation of the accounting rule that Global Crossing used for the swaps.

The Congressional Investigation

The House of Representatives' Energy and Commerce Committee is looking into possible insider trading by Global Crossing executives. It is also investigating possible efforts by Global Crossing to increase revenues by acquiring other businesses and capacity swaps, which effectively misled investors. The probe was triggered by a former Global Crossing vice president of finance, Roy Olofson, who claimed publicly that the company had improperly increased revenues and underreported costs to improve earnings so it could meet Wall Street expectations and support its stock price. Olofson later lost his job and sued Global Crossing and key executives.

The committee released documents showing that Global Crossing bought 360networks, Inc. in something of a rush during March 2001. Some board members and top company officials objected, but Chairman Gary Winnick reportedly rammed the deal through even though there were limited opportunities for due diligence before the deal was consummated. It appears that the main reason for the rush purchase was to use 360networks' revenue to enhance Global Crossing's financial statements to avoid disappointing Wall Street investors' earnings expectations for Global Crossing.

Some members of Congress expressed concern that capacity swaps were used to inflate Global Crossing's revenue. Its chief financial officer, Dan Cohrs, told the House Financial Services Subcommittee on Oversight and Investigations that his company had not set out to inflate revenue by entering into some twenty-four deals or capacity swaps with other telecommunications companies. Rather, Cohrs said that Global Crossing wanted to expand the capacity and the reach of its global network.

But committee members noted that many of these deals dated from 2000 and 2001, a time when there was already overcapacity in the global telecommunications market. These deals added about $375 million to Global Crossing's bottom line in the first quarter of 2001. Qwest Communications International, also involved in deals for network capacity, said it was reversing some $950 million in revenue from capacity swaps and may have to make adjustments of another $531 million in revenue from other sales. The U.S. Justice Department and the Enforcement Division of the SEC are also probing Global Crossing and Qwest.

The committee is also investigating illegal insider trading. Winnick denied that he sold stock based on inside information that Global Crossing was in financial trouble and said that all of his stock transactions were appropriate. However, witnesses claim that top officials knew that Global Crossing's business outlook was weak before they sold company stock.

The subcommittee expressed concern that Global Crossing relied on nonstandard, pro forma numbers in reports circulated to investors but used generally accepted accounting principles in its public filings with the SEC. These pro forma reports claimed a 50 percent increase in revenues, about $531 million, over the statements filed by Global Crossing under generally accepted accounting rules.

There is also evidence that Global Crossing executives deliberately misled investors about the strength of the organization's finances. One report indicates that Winnick learned on February 26, 2001, that Global Crossing would fall some $200 million short of the first quarter financial targets expected by Wall Street investors. However, in April, then CEO Tom Casey told top stock analysts during a conference call that there were "record results in cash revenue" and that Global Crossing's results exceeded the estimates of the stock analysts themselves. This report led analysts to encourage investors to buy Global Crossing stock, sparking a surge in stock prices just before Winnick sold some $123 million of his shares. Winnick's lawyer, Gary Naftalis, said that Global Crossing did not mislead investors, but that it believed it would make its first quarter financial targets legitimately.

Jack Grubman, the telecommunications stock analyst for investment house Salomon Smith Barney, is also of interest to the committee. They would like to know more about the ties between Global Crossing and Salomon Smith Barney and also about the positive research reports Grubman was writing about telecommunications firms that later crashed.

After the Fall

Global Crossing hopes to emerge from bankruptcy protection in 2003. Its restatements of financial results related to its capacity swaps will have very limited impact on its continuing operations because it will use so-called "fresh-start" accounting procedures, which do not include any previous financial results. The company has also indicated that its use of nonstandard, pro forma numbers in reports to investors should be disregarded.

Global Crossing will have its debt load cut from about $6.6 billion to about $200 million and its workforce reduced from some 15,000 people to about 5,000. Some observers believe it will no longer be a market leader but rather exist as more of a niche player, with a network connecting about 200 cities. At least four other competitors are also emerging from bankruptcy proceedings at about the same time: Williams Communications, Flag Telecom, 360networks, and WorldCom. With excess network capacity available, it's a buyer's market now. Price wars, in which competitors compete away profits until, potentially, only those with the deepest pockets remain, could easily become a facet of telecom competitive life. And Global Crossing CEO John Legere has already said that his company could indeed cut prices after it emerges from Chapter 11 protection.

The bankruptcy process may be hastened by a bidding war for controlling interest in Global Crossing. Hutchison Whampoa of Hong Kong and Singapore Technologies Telemedia proposed a $250 million offer for Global Crossing, which was approved by the judge presiding over Global Crossing's bankruptcy case. However, a rival bid of $255 million from IDT Corporation may ultimately be successful because of the U.S. government's concern over potential national security issues resulting from Asian ownership of Global Crossing's fiber-optic network in the United States.

Global Crossing's creditors are owed about $12.4 billion; Global Crossing investors lost a total of about $54 billion. Some 14,000 current and former employees lost 401(k) funds and pension funds, as well as health and severance benefits. The employees' 401(k) funds alone appear to have declined in value about $191 million, from about $200 million to $8.9 million as of December 2001. Leo Hindery, Global Crossing's CEO from March to October 2000, is asking U.S. bankruptcy judge Robert Gerber to order Global Crossing to treat him as an administrative creditor. This would give his claims precedent over other creditors in the bankruptcy proceeding. Hindrey claims $817,714 dollars in unpaid severance benefits, which include $22,378 a month rent on his apartment in the Waldorf-Astoria Towers on Manhattan's Park Avenue. His claims are partly based on agreements that he stay on as the chairman and CEO of Global Center, Global Crossing's Web-hosting unit, for about a million dollars a year. Global Center was sold in January 2001 to Exodus Communications for $1.91 billion in stock.

Telecommunications stock analyst Jack Grubman would be banned for life from the securities industry and pay a $15 million fine for his role in the Global Crossing debacle under a tentative agreement with the New York State Attorney General's Office. Under this deal, Grubman neither admitted nor denied guilt, and he would remain subject to further investigations.

Global Crossing founder and chairman Gary Winnick resigned from the board on December 31, 2002, under pressure from investor groups. Altogether, it appears that Winnick profited by about $734 million from his sales of Global Crossing stock before the company filed bankruptcy. However, he and more than twenty Global Crossing executives and directors face a lawsuit filed in the federal district court in Manhattan that consolidates several class-action complaints on behalf of investors who lost billions of dollars on Global Crossing stocks and bonds.

The investigations of the events surrounding Global Crossing's bankruptcy continue. The Congress, SEC, U.S. Department of Justice, Federal Bureau of Investigation, and New York State Attorney General's Office could still bring civil or criminal proceedings against Global Crossing executives and other involved parties at any time. The scandal took a new twist when Richard N. Perle, who the firm retained to help overcome Defense Department concerns about the proposed sale to two Asian firms, was forced to resign as chairman of the Defense Policy Board after the press suggested that the two roles created a conflict of interest, perhaps violating ethics rules. Although Perle remained a member of the Defense Policy Board, which advises the Pentagon and secretary of defense on war matters including the recent conflict in Iraq, he withdrew from his role as advisor to Global Crossing.

Interestingly, Global Crossing shareholders were not the greatest beneficiaries of their risk-taking; they will lose almost all of their investment. The real beneficiaries are the customers of the telecommunications services market. They will have more fiber-optic broadband capacity connected to more locations at a lower price than would have been possible if Global Crossing and other telecommunications companies had not invested in the creation of these networks.

Questions

1. How did the pressure to meet earnings forecasts for Wall Street investors contribute to unethical conduct at Global Crossing?
2. What corporate governance mechanisms need to be implemented at Global Crossing?
3. Are there similarities between the bankruptcy at Global Crossing and the bankruptcy at Enron and other firms? If so, what are they? What are the differences?

Sources

Andrew Backover, "Global Crossing Plans Bold End to Chapter 11," *USA Today,* October 16, 2002, www.usatoday.com/money/industries/telecom/2002-10-16-global_x.htm; Andrew Backover, "Spring CEO Says Strong Will Survive," *USA Today,* October 21, 2002, www.usatoday.com/money/industries/telecom/2002-10-21-sprint_x.htm; Andrew Backover, "Telecom Executives Deny Wrongdoing," *USA Today,* October 2, 2002, p. B1; Dennis K. Berman, "Global Crossing's Accounting for 'Swap' Trades to Be Amended," *Wall Street Journal,* October 22, 2002, p. A10; Dennis K. Berman, "Global Crossing Faces More Accusations," *Wall Street Journal,* February 6, 2002, p. B6; Dennis K. Berman, "Hindery Wants Global Crossing to Give Him Pay," *Wall Street Journal,* October 14, 2002, p. B6; Dennis K. Berman, "Study Questioned Global Crossing Deals," *Wall Street Journal,* February 19, 2002, p. B6; Dennis K. Berman and Laurie P. Cohen, "SEC to Investigate Insiders' Trades at Global Crossing," *Wall Street Journal,* June 3, 2002, pp. A1, A8; Laurie P. Cohen and Dennis K. Berman, "How Analyst Grubman Helped Call Shots at Global Crossing," *Wall Street Journal,* May 31, 2002, pp. A1, A6; Julie Creswell, "The Emperor of Greed," *Fortune,* June 24, 2002, pp. 106–116; "Ex-Global Crossing CEO Seeks $821,714 in Severance Benefits," *Boston Globe,* October 15, 2002, p. D4; Harold Furchtgott-Roth, "Manager's Journal: Global Crossing's Bankruptcy Is a Success Story," *Wall Street Journal,* February 5, 2002, p. A18; "Global Crossing Exec Denies Insider Trading," *USA Today,* October 1, 2002, www.usatoday.com/money/industries/telecom/2002-10-01-global-crossing-hearing_x.htm; "Global Crossing Probe Eyes 2001 Accounts," *InfoWorld Media Group, Inc.,* October 14, 2002, http://staging.infoworld.com/articles; Tom Hamburger and Dennis K. Berman, "U.S. Adviser Perle Resigns As Head of Defense Board," *Wall Street Journal,* March 28, 2003, http://online.wsj.com; Jim Hopkins, "Winnick Quits Board at Global Crossing," *USA Today,* December 31, 2002, p. B03; Susan Ivancevich, Lucian C. Jones, and Thomas Keaveney, "Don't Run the Risk," *Journal of Accountancy* 194 (December 2002): 47–51; Siobhan Kennedy, "Global Crossing Restates Earnings," *Reuters,* October 21, 2002, http://reuters.com; Jonathan Krim, "Panel Widens Probe of Global Crossing," *Washington Post,* August 30, 2002, p. E01, www.washingtonpost.com; Stephen Labaton, "Pentagon Adviser Is Also Advising Global Crossing," *New York Times,* March 21, 2003, www.nytimes.com/2003/03/21/business/21GLOB.html; Stephanie N. Mehta, "Birds of a Feather," *Fortune,* October 14, 2002, pp. 197–202; "A Guide to Corporate Scandals," *The Economist Newspaper,* July 10, 2002, p. 1; Jeremy Pelofsky, "Ex-Global Crossing CEO Demands Rent Paid," *Reuters,* October 14, 2002, www.reuters.com; Simon Romero, "Adding to Claims Against Global Crossing," *New York Times,* January 30, 2003, p. C4; Simon Romero, "Technology; IDT Offers $255 Million to Control Global Crossing," *New York Times,* February 25, 2003, www.nytimes.com; Christopher Stern, "At Global Crossing, 'No Enron,'" *Washington Post,* March 22, 2002, p. E04; James Toedtman, "Telecom Head Pledges $25M," *Newsday,* October 2, 2002, www.newsday.com; "Under Fire: These Execs, Too, Are Embroiled in a Range of Investigations," *Business Week,* January 13, 2003, pp. 87, 89; Michael Weisskopf, "Global Crossing: What Did Winnick Know?" *Time,* October 7, 2002, p. 28; "Winnick Was Told of Telecom Risks," *Washington Post,* October 1, 2002, p. E03.

Appendix
Role-Play Exercises

A s highlighted throughout this text, the process of making decisions related to social responsibility is complex. In order to provide students with realistic experiences in decision making, the authors of this book developed five proprietary behavioral simulations for classroom use. These simulations, or role-play exercises, examine issues that affect multiple stakeholders, recreate the power and pressures that affect decision making, and give students an opportunity to practice making decisions that have social responsibility content and consequences.

Soy-DRI focuses on product misuse, *Videopolis* delves into cutting-edge intellectual property rights, *National Farm and Garden, Inc.,* examines product safety; the *Sexual Harassment Case* takes students through a difficult jury decision process; and *Deer Lake Marina: Forever Proud?* involves a complicated environmental situation. The exercises are written with some ambiguity and leave room for interpretation and creativity. Thus, students should use higher-level learning and reasoning methods, along with course concepts, to resolve the issues presented in the simulations. A summary of each exercise's core issues follows. Complete information on the simulations and their use in the classroom is located in the text's *Instructor's Resource Manual* and on the instructor's web site.

Soy-DRI Background

Two former employees of a large chemical manufacturer founded Soybean Derivative Research Initiatives (Soy-DRI) in 1985. One of the company's product lines consists of three soy-based powders with additives to enhance their moisture-absorbing properties. The products are used to absorb and eliminate excess moisture in a variety of consumer and organizational settings. In their powdered form, Soy-DRI products can absorb as much as ten times their weight in moisture. The products are environmentally friendly, a critical value of Soy-DRI. The company has been acknowledged for accomplishments in the area of environmental sensitivity.

Initially, Soy-DRI targeted the industrial market with the Slab-Dri brand. Slab-Dri is marketed primarily to commercial establishments for the purpose of eliminating moisture and oil from paved surfaces. The product soaks up spills and can then be swept dry. The product is white to enhance its visibility and ease of removal. Slab-Dri is distributed in 64-ounce tin containers with adjustable lids for application. The retail price of Slab-Dri is $2 per 64-ounce container, with a product cost of $1.50. The product is available to industrial buyers through catalogs and, more recently, through AutoZone, Discount Auto Parts, and other consumer automotive outlets. Slab-Dri generates the company's second-highest sales levels.

In 1990, Soy-DRI expanded its product line with two new products targeted at distinctly different end users. The first of these new products is Pet-Dri, which is used in pet litter boxes to facilitate moisture and odor absorption. Pet-Dri has the same formulation as Slab-Dri, but the product is beige so that it blends with other pet litter products. The product is available in a 32-ounce plastic container with an adjustable lid for application. Pet-Dri is distributed through major discount stores such as Wal-Mart, Target, and Kmart and supermarkets. The suggested retail price is $4 per 32-ounce container, with a product cost of $1.25. Pet-Dri has become Soy-DRI's best-selling product.

The final derivative product is Baby-Dri, which is used in place of traditional baby powder. As a relatively new addition to Soy-DRI's product line, Baby-Dri has the lowest sales. Because tests of Soy-DRI's first two products indicated that their high-moisture-absorption properties caused rashes and irritated babies' skin with prolonged use, Baby-Dri's moisture-absorbing properties were modified to make it absorb five times its weight in moisture. Baby-Dri is also purified to meet federal regulations for consumers' personal use. The product is white in color, the same as Slab-Dri. Baby-Dri is sold in 8-ounce plastic containers for a suggested retail price of $4, with a product cost of $2. Baby-Dri is distributed through major discount chains such as Target, Wal-Mart, Kmart, and Toys 'R' Us; supermarkets; and baby supply stores throughout the country.

Videopolis Background

Videopolis was founded as VideoNow in 1993 by two former employees of RCA, where they had learned television broadcasting, electrical engineering, satellite down-linking, and telephone networking applications. Today, Videopolis is a communications company that specializes in connecting videoconferencing equipment over digital telephone lines to cities around the world. The company does not produce meetings, conferences, or programs, but instead facilitates the videoconferencing process. Videopolis's most profitable product, the Broadcast Service, involves storing and playing prerecorded programs on its VCRs and broadcasting them through its computer equipment to clients' meeting rooms around the world. If a remote site is not immediately available to view a meeting or program from Videopolis, the client can record the program by connecting a VCR to a television monitor. Videopolis does not explicitly state that recording programs is forbidden. Company policy is that all viewing sites must obtain their own permissions from the owners of the content to record any copyrighted materials. There are some concerns that this policy may be facilitating the copying and distribution of copyrighted material.

VideoNow became Videopolis after it was acquired by TeleWide Corporation fifteen months ago. When VideoNow was started, the founders had a clear vision for growth, hiring only the best employees and purchasing the best equipment in more than sufficient quantities to ensure a high level of service and plenty of reserves for growth. Many of VideoNow's original employees joined the firm with high hopes of stock options, promotions, and bonuses based on future growth prospects. Many employees had purchased expensive homes and cars in anticipation of these bonuses and promotions. Unfortunately, the founding partners sold out directly to TeleWide before granting any options or bonuses to VideoNow employees. After the merger, TeleWide immediately instituted a hiring and equipment-purchasing freeze and virtually froze all salaries. The new corporate parent also set aggressive sales and growth goals for Videopolis and developed a highly incentive-based pay structure for upper managers who achieved their goals. This resulted in a considerable amount of turnover as those employees who could afford to leave promptly did so, placing tremendous stress on those who stayed and had to take up the slack. Many of the employees who remained after the buyout believe that promises have been broken and that they were misled about advancement opportunities.

Videopolis's chief legal counsel has sent an e-mail message to arrange a meeting with the CEO, vice president of operations, vice president of human resources, and vice president of marketing and sales to discuss a number of potential legal and ethical issues concerning the company.

National Farm and Garden, Inc., Background

National Farm and Garden, Inc. (NFG), was incorporated in Nebraska in 1935 and has been a leading supplier of farming equipment for more than sixty years. Over the last five years, however, demand for NFG's flagship product, the Ultra Tiller, has been declining. To make matters worse, NFG's market lead was overtaken by the competition for the first time two years ago.

Last year, NFG expanded its product line with the Turbo Tiller, a highly advertised and much anticipated upgrade to the Ultra Tiller. The product launch was timed to coincide with last year's fall tilling season. Due to the timing of the release, the research and development process was shortened, and the manufacturing department was pressed to produce high numbers to meet anticipated demand. All responsible divisions approved the product launch and schedule. In order to release the product as scheduled, however, the manufacturing department was forced to employ the safety shield design from the Ultra Tiller. When attached, the shield protects the user from the tilling blades; however, it is necessary to remove the shield in order to clean the product. Because of differences between the Ultra and Turbo models, the Turbo's shield is very difficult to reattach after cleaning and the process requires specialized tools. Owners can have the supplier make modifications on-site or at the sales location, or leave the shield off and continue operation. All product documentation warns against operating the tiller without the shielding, and the product itself has three distinct warning labels on it. Modifications are now available that allow for the shield to be removed and replaced quite easily, and these modifications are covered by the factory warranty. However, most owners have elected to operate the Turbo Tiller without the safety shield after its first cleaning.

Over the last year, a number of farm animals (chickens, cats, a dog, and two goats) have been killed by Turbo Tillers being operated without the guard. Two weeks ago, a seven-year-old Nebraska boy riding on the back of an unshielded tiller fell off. When the tiller caught the sleeve of his shirt, his arm was permanently mangled, requiring amputation. One of the child's parents owns the local newspaper, which ran a story about the accident on the front page the next day. NFG's CEO has called an emergency meeting with the company's divisional vice president, director of product development, director of manufacturing, director of sales, and vice president of public relations to discuss the situation and develop a plan of action.

Sexual Harassment Case Background

Read the following facts about sexual harassment:[1]

- Sexual harassment is a form of sex discrimination that violates Title VII of the Civil Rights Act of 1964.
- Unwelcome sexual advances, requests for sexual favors, and other verbal or physical conduct of a sexual nature constitute sexual harassment when submission to or rejection of this conduct explicitly or implicitly affects an individual's employment, unreasonably interferes with an individual's work performance, or creates an intimidating, hostile, or offensive work environment.
- Sexual harassment can occur in a variety of circumstances, including but not limited to the following:
  - The victim as well as the harasser may be a woman or a man. The victim does not have to be of the opposite sex.
  - The harasser can be the victim's supervisor, an agent of the employer, a supervisor in another area, a coworker, or a nonemployee.
  - The victim does not have to be the person harassed but could be anyone affected by the offensive conduct.
  - Unlawful sexual harassment may occur without economic injury to or discharge of the victim.
  - The harasser's conduct must be unwelcome.
  - It is helpful for the victim to inform the harasser directly that the conduct is unwelcome and must stop. The victim should use any employer complaint mechanism or grievance system available.
  - When investigating allegations of sexual harassment, the Equal Employment Opportunity Commission looks at the whole record: the circumstances, such as the nature of the sexual advances, and the context in which the alleged incidents occurred. A determination on the allegations is made from the facts on a case-by-case basis.

Read about recent court decisions. Recent U.S. Supreme Court decisions on sexual harassment cases indicate that

1. Employers are liable for the acts of supervisors.
2. Employers are liable for sexual harassment by supervisors that culminates in a tangible employment action (loss of job, demotion, etc.).
3. Employers are liable for a hostile environment created by a supervisor, but may escape liability if they demonstrate that they exercised reasonable care to

---

[1] "Facts About Sexual Harassment," U.S. Equal Opportunity Employment Commission, www.eeoc.gov/facts/fs-sex.html, accessed November 25, 2003.

prevent and promptly correct any sexually harassing behavior and that the plaintiff employee unreasonably failed to take advantage of any preventive or corrective measures offered by the employer.

4. Claims of hostile environment sexual harassment must be severe and pervasive in order to be viewed as actionable by the courts.

Read the actual case for deliberation.

Plaintiff: Michelle Cordoza, a former account executive with Creative Marketing Solutions, has filed a sexual harassment suit against the defendants named below. Before joining Creative Marketing Solutions, Ms. Cordoza worked in sales and marketing at several firms in another city. As an account executive with Creative Marketing Solutions, the plaintiff served as a liaison between her employer and several client accounts, including FoodService, Inc., one of the defendants. Ms. Cordoza's duties also included determining clients' marketing needs, designing proposals and projects to help them reach their marketing and business goals, and building professional relationships with key decision makers throughout the process. Like all account executives, Ms. Cordoza was expected to spend a great deal of time with client representatives, including socializing at dinners and other activities. Account executives at Creative Marketing Solutions handle about three major accounts at any one time and earn between $50,000 and $65,000 a year.

The plaintiff was employed by Creative Marketing Solutions for one year, during which time she received below-average evaluations. Specifically, supervisors documented instances in which Ms. Cordoza ignored company operating policy and directives. For example, she occasionally "overpromised" with respect to the delivery of marketing collateral and reports to clients. These promises created tension in the office.

Defendants: FoodService, Inc., John Harrison, and Creative Marketing Solutions. FoodService, Inc., is a distributor of fresh and prepared foods, kitchen equipment, supplies, and related products to restaurants, cafeterias, and other food service outlets in the United States. The company was founded in 1965 by William and Henry Creighton and went public in the mid-1990s. FoodService, Inc., has 755 employees and annual sales of approximately $58 million. The company has a sexual harassment policy that is discussed with all new employees during their initial orientation session (see attached document). All employees must certify that they have read and understand the sexual harassment policy.

John Harrison is currently the director of marketing at FoodService, Inc. He has been with the company for ten years and has received consistently favorable employment evaluations. He is considered a valued member of the FoodService "family," as his uncle worked with the company during the 1970s and early 1980s. As part of his duties, Mr. Harrison is expected to be active in community events, professional associations, and other client-building opportunities.

Creative Marketing Solutions, a marketing and business communications agency with seventy-five employees, is Ms. Cordoza's former employer. The company was established in 1984 and is owned by Anna Carlyle and Joseph Ruiz. Known as an aggressive competitor, Creative Marketing Solutions has received numerous awards for its marketing campaigns. The agency has also been recognized by the community for providing its services free of charge to several area nonprofit organizations. The company cites the importance of "respect for all persons" in its vision and mission statement (see attached document), but does not have a formal policy on sexual harassment.

Case Exhibits

FoodService, INC.

Sexual Harassment Policy

It is our policy to promote a productive and respectful workplace. We will not tolerate any employee conduct that harasses, disturbs, or interferes with another employee's performance or that creates an offensive or hostile environment. No harassment will be tolerated, including that based on race, religion, marital status, age, gender, ethnicity, or sexual overtones.

All employees have the responsibility to maintain a harassment-free workplace. Supervisors and managers carry additional accountability in this regard. For example, no supervisor or manager is ever to threaten or insinuate that an employee's refusal or willingness to submit to sexual advances will affect employment. Other sexually harassing or offensive conduct in the workplace, whether committed by supervisors, managers, or nonsupervisory employees, is also prohibited. Examples of prohibited conduct include: (1) Unwanted physical contact of any kind, (2) Verbal harassment of a sexual nature, and (3) Display of demeaning, insulting, or sexually suggestive objects or pictures.

An employee who experiences, witnesses, or learns of a potential violation of this policy must report it to the Human Resources office or through the confidential employee help line. Any of the above conduct, or other offensive conduct, may result in employment termination.

I have read the sexual harassment policy and agree to abide by its provisions as a condition of my employment at FoodService, Inc.

Employee Name (printed) _____

Signature _____

Date _____

Creative Marketing Solutions
Excerpt from Vision and Mission Statement

Effective communication is our business. This requires an unwavering trust between Creative Marketing Solutions and our clients, respect for all persons involved in the communication process, and a dedication to meeting client needs first.

Deer Lake Marina Background

Deer Lake Marina has been in existence since the late 1960s. The marina is located on Deer Lake, which connects to the Tennessee River. Residents of Alabama, Mississippi, and Tennessee enjoy the water and surrounding natural environment. Camping, boating, swimming, fishing, and other outdoor sports are very popular in this region. Deer Lake is located in a historic part of the United States, as the area has several Civil War battle sites. Because of the area's beauty, mild climate, interesting cultural history, and relatively modest cost of living, more and more retirees are moving to the area. In fact, Deer Lake was recently named to a list of "Best Places to Retire in America." Most of the county's development took place in the last twenty years, as the area was somewhat economically stagnant before that time. The county encouraged rapid real estate development during the last fifteen to twenty years and has been fairly "hands-off" with respect to environmental issues.

Today, Deer Lake Marina includes 150 in-water boat slips, dry storage for 125 boats, a fuel dock, and lifts for launching boats in the water. The owners of Deer Lake Marina hope to expand by building a large boating supply store, restaurant, and boat repair and service facility. Because the land and water space available for expansion includes a wetlands area, the marina owners obtained a permit from the Army Corp of Engineers. The next step is to secure business and building permits from the county. A public notice was issued to discuss the Deer Lake Marina application for permits. Two groups, the marina owners and the Deer Lake Forever Proud, a local conservation and historical group, have requested time to state their cases to the county council.

Wetlands are low-lying areas saturated with water that connect land with large bodies of water. In the last 200 years, the continental United States has lost over 50 percent of its wetlands. Flooding and poor water quality often follow the loss of wetlands. When the marina was originally built, environmental laws were virtually nonexistent. Environmental regulation has steadily increased since the 1970s, especially at the federal level. The U.S. Environmental Protection Agency (EPA) (http://www.epa.gov) provides information on wetlands and related projects to conserve and maintain the natural environment. The Clean Water Act provides most of the regulation on wetlands and waterways. According to its web site, the Army Corps of Engineers (http://www.usace.army.mil/) determines "which areas qualify for protection as wetlands . . . (and makes) decisions on whether to grant, deny, or set conditions on permits."

Notes

Chapter 1

1. "Cummins Inc. Receives Business Childcare Award," http://www.cummins.com/na/pages/en/mediare-sources/pressreleases/index.cfm?view=10&year=2002, accessed September 28, 2003. Cummins Engine Company, www.cummins.com/na/pages/en/whoweare/cumminshistory.cfm, accessed September 25, 2003; Cummins Engine Company, www.investor.cummins.com, accessed December 18, 2002; Kevin Kelly, "A CEO Who Kept His Eyes on the Horizon," *Business Week,* August 1, 1994, p. 32; Boris Ladwig, "Cummins Plans Child Care Center," (Columbus, IN) *Republic,* www.therepublic.com, accessed March 8, 2000; "Profit Soars, Fueled By Sales of Engines Ahead of New Rules, *Wall Street Journal,* October 18, 2002, p. B2; "The 100 Best Corporate Citizens," *Business Ethics* 14 (March–April 2000): 12–17; "The 100 Best Corporate Citizens," www.business-ethics.com/100best.htm, accessed September 28, 2003; Lois Therrien, "Mr. Rust Belt," *Business Week,* October 17, 1988, pp. 72–77; *Marina v. N. Whitman, New World, New Rules* (Boston: Harvard Business School Press, 1999), pp. 112–115.

2. "How Business Rates: By the Numbers," *Business Week,* September 11, 2000, pp. 148–149.

3. "Conseco Seeks Protection," http://money.cnn.com/2002/12/18/news/companies/conseco/, accessed September 25, 2003.

4. Milton Friedman, *Capitalism and Freedom* (Chicago: University of Chicago Press, 1962).

5. Clive Crook, "Why Good Corporate Citizens Are a Public Menace," *National Journal,* April 24, 1999, p. 1087; Charles Handy, "What's a Business For?" *Harvard Business Review* 80 (December 2002): 49–55.

6. Nancy J. Miller and Terry L. Besser, "The Importance of Community Values in Small Business Strategy Formation: Evidence from Rural Iowa," *Journal of Small Business Management* 38 (January 2000): 68–85; James Knight and Mary Kate O'Riley, "Local Heroes," *Director* 55 (February 2002): 28.

7. Paul Willax, "Small Businesses Contribute in a Large Way to Economy," *Business First–Louisville,* February 18, 2000, p. 13.

8. Shimizu Corporation, http://www.shimz.co.jp/english/index.html, accessed August 28, 2003.

9. "Awards and Recognition," Herman Miller Inc., www.hermanmiller.com/CDA/award/0,1239,c21,00.html, accessed October 18, 2001.

10. "The 1997 Cone/Roper Cause-Related Marketing Trends Report," *Business Ethics* 11 (March–April 1997): 14–16; Ronald Alsop, "Corporate Reputations Are Earned with Trust, Reliability, Study Shows," *Wall Street Journal,* September 23, 1999; http://interactive.wsj.com; Dale Kurschner, "5 Ways Ethical Busine$$ Creates Fatter Profit$," *Business Ethics* 10 (March–April 1996): 21.

11. Jim Carlton, "Against the Grain: How Home Depot and Activists Joined to Cut Logging Abuse," *Wall Street Journal,* September 26, 2000, p. A1.

12. Ann E. Tenbrunsel, Zoe I. Barsness, and Paul M. Hirsch, "Sara Lee Corporation and Corporate Citizenship: Unity in Diversity," in *Corporate Global Citizenship,* ed. Noel M. Tichy, Andrew R. McGill, and Lynda St. Clair (San Francisco: New Lexington Press, 1997), pp. 197–213.

13. William H. Miller, "Citizenship: A Competitive Asset," *Industry Week,* August 17, 1998, pp. 104–108; *TOTO Annual Report,* 2001, www.toto.co.jp/en/about/annu2001/pdf/annu2001.pdf, accessed December 20, 2002.

14. Barbara W. Altman, "Transformed Corporate Community Relations: A Management Tool for Achieving Corporate Citizenship," *Business and Society Review,* March 22, 1999, p. 43; Archie Carroll, "The Four Faces of Corporate Citizenship," *Business and Society Review,* January 1, 1998, p. 1; Diane Swanson and Brian E. Niehoff, "Business Citizenship Outside and Inside Organizations," in *Perspectives on Corporate Citizenship,* ed. Jörg Andriof and Malcolm McIntosh (Sheffield, UK: Greenleaf Publishing, 2001), pp. 104–116.

15. "Facts and Figures on Corruption," Transparency International, www.transparency.org/contact/media_faq.html, accessed October 20, 2001.

16. "Judge Rules that Microsoft Violated U.S. Antitrust Laws," *Wall Street Journal,* April 3, 2000, http://interactive.wsj.com; Steven Levy, "Look, Ma, No Breaks," *Newsweek,* September 17, 2001, pp. 52–54; "Microsoft Begins Implementing Antitrust Settlement," *Computer & Online Industry Litigation Reporter,* November 19, 2002, p.11.

17. "Code of Ethics," Direct Selling Association, http://www.dsa.org/ethics/, accessed October 1, 2003; "World Codes of Conduct for Direct Selling," World Federation of Direct Selling Associations, www.wfdsa.org/world_codes/code.asp, accessed October 1, 2003; Thomas R. Wotruba, *Teaching Notes to Accompany Ethics and Success in Business* (Washington, DC: Direct Selling Education Foundation, 1999).

18. The Hitachi Foundation, www.hitachi.org/, accessed October 18, 2001.

19. Altman, "Transformed Corporate Community Relations," p. 43; Carroll, "The Four Faces of Corporate Citizenship," p. 1.

20. Malcolm McIntosh, Deborah Leipziger, Keith Jones, and Gill Coleman, *Corporate Citizenship: Successful Strategies for Responsible Companies* (London: Financial Times Management, 2000).

21. Betsy Morris and Patricia Sellers, "What Really Happened at Coke," *Fortune,* January 10, 2000, pp. 114–116; "America's Most Admired Companies," *Fortune,* February 21, 2000, p. 108; "America's Most Admired Companies," www.fortune.com/fortune/mostadmired/, accessed December 17, 2002; "Second Annual List of '100 Best Corporate Citizens' Quantifies Stakeholder Service," www.business-ethics.com/newpage24.htm, accessed December 17, 2002; "The 100 Best Corporate Citizens for 2001," www.business-ethics.com./100best.htm, accessed October 20, 2001.

22. Charles Handy, "What's a Business For?" *Harvard Business Review* 80 (December 2002): 49–55; Geoff Mulgan, *Connexity: How to Live in a Connected World* (Boston: Harvard Business School Press, 1997); Ann Svendsen, *The Stakeholder Strategy: Profiting from Collaborative Business Relationships* (San Francisco: Berrett-Koehler, 1998).

23. R. E. Freeman, *Strategic Management: A Stakeholder Approach* (Boston: Pitman, 1984).

24. Ken Green, Barbara Morton, and Steve New, "Green Purchasing and Supply Policies: Do They Improve Companies' Environmental Performance?" *Supply Chain Management* 3 (February 1998); B&Q web site, www.dig.com, accessed October 20, 2001.

25. Edward S. Mason, Introduction, in *The Corporation in Modern Society,* ed. Edward S. Mason (Cambridge, MA: Harvard University Press, 1959), pp. 1–24.

26. Michael McCarthy and Lorrie Grant, "Sears Drops Benetton After Controversial Death Row Ads," *USA Today,* February 18, 2000, www.usatoday.com.

27. Isabelle Maignan and O. C. Ferrell, "Measuring Corporate Citizenship in Two Countries: The Case of the United States and France," *Journal of Business Ethics* 23 (February 2000): 283; Robert J. Samuelson, "R.I.P.: The Good Corporation," *Newsweek,* July 5, 1993, p. 41.

28. Charles W. Wootton and Christie L. Roszkowski, "Legal Aspects of Corporate Governance in Early American Railroads," *Business and Economic History* 28 (Winter 1999): 325–326.

29. Ralph Estes, *Tyranny of the Bottom Line* (San Francisco: Berrett-Koehler, 1996); David Finn, *The Corporate Oligarch* (New York: Simon & Schuster, 1969).

30. Whitman, *New World, New Rules.*

31. Edward S. Mason, Introduction in *The Corporation in Modern Society,* Mason, pp. 1–24.

32. Carl Kaysen, "The Corporation: How Much Power? What Scope?" in *The Corporation in Modern Society,* Mason, pp. 85–105.

33. Whitman, *New World, New Rules.*

34. Ibid.

35. David M. Gordon, *Fat and Mean: The Corporate Squeeze of Working Americans and the Myth of Managerial "Downsizing"* (New York: Free Press, 1996).

36. Richard Leider, *The Power of Purpose: Creating Meaning in Your Life and Work* (San Francisco: Barrett-Koehler, 1997).

37. Mark Lilla, "The Big Extract: Does Anyone Remember '68?" (London) *Guardian Editor,* August 29, 1998, p. 12; Mark Lilla, "Still Living With '68," *New York Times Magazine,* August 16, 1998, p. 34; Michael Willmott and Paul Flatters, "Corporate Citizenship: The New Challenge for Business," *Consumer Policy Review* 9 (November–December 1999): 230.

38. Marjorie Kelly, "The Next Step for CSR: Economic Democracy," www.business-ethics.com/thenext.htm, accessed December 18, 2002.

39. Martin Wolf, "Comment and Analysis: The Big Lie of Global Inequality," *Financial Times,* February 9, 2000, p. 25.

40. Aaron Bernstein, "Too Much Corporate Power?" *Business Week,* September 11, 2000, pp. 144–158.

41. Bruce Horovitz, "Scandals Shake Public," *USA Today,* July 16, 2002, p.1A.

42. "Issue Library: Globalization 101," http://www.corpwatch.org/issues/PII.jsp?topicid=104, accessed October 1, 2003; Paul Magnusson, "Making a Federal Case Out of Overseas Abuses," *Business Week,* November 25, 2002, p. 78; "USA: Burma Human Rights Abuse Case Against Oil Giant to Go Ahead," www.corpwatch.com, accessed December 19, 2002.

43. M. N. Graham Dukes, "Accountability of the Pharmaceutical Industry," *The Lancet,* November 23, 2002, pp. 1682–1684; Elizabeth Olson, "Global Trade Negotiations Are Making Little Progress," *New York Times,* December 7, 2002, p. C3; Robert Pear, "Investigators Find Repeated Deception in Ads for Drugs," *New York Times,* December 4, 2002, p. A22.

44. John Dalla Costa, *The Ethical Imperative: Why Moral Leadership Is Good Business* (Reading, MA: Addison-Wesley, 1998).

45. "All About Nestlé: Global Commitment," Nestlé, http://www.nestle.com/html/about/global.asp, accessed August 28, 2003.

46. Lynda St. Clair, "Compaq Computer Corporation: Maximizing Environmental Conscientiousness Around the Globe," in *Corporate Global Citizenship,* ed. Noel M. Tichy, Andrew R. McGill, and Lynda St. Clair (San Francisco: New Lexington Press, 1997), pp. 230–244.

47. S. A. Anwar, "APEC: Evidence and Policy Scenarios," *Journal of International Marketing and Marketing Research* 27 (October 2002): 141–153; Richard Feinberg, "Two Leading Lights of Humane Globalisation," *Singapore Straits Times,* February 21, 2000, p. 50.

48. "The Millennium Poll on Corporate Social Responsibility," Environics International Ltd., September 1999, www.environics.net/eil/millennium/.

49. Frederick Reichheld, *The Loyalty Effect* (Cambridge, MA: Harvard Business School, 1996); Jeffrey S. Harrison and R. Edward Freeman, "Stakeholders, Social Responsibility, and Performance: Empirical Evidence and Theoretical Perspectives," *Academy of Management Journal* 42 (October 1999): 479.

50. Stephen R. Covey, "Is Your Company's Bottom Line Taking a Hit?" *PR Newswire,* June 4, 1998, www.prnewswire.com; Terry W. Loe, "The Role of Ethical Climate in Developing Trust, Market Orientation and Commitment to Quality," unpublished Ph.D. dissertation, University of Memphis, 1996.

51. Ethics Resource Center, *The Ethics Resource Center's 2000 National Business Ethics Survey: How Employees Perceive Ethics at Work* (Washington, DC: Ethics Resource Center, 2000), p. 85.

52. "The 1997 Cone/Roper Cause-Related Marketing Trends Report," *Business Ethics* 11 (March–April 1997): 14–16.

53. Rebecca Gardyn, "Philanthropy Post-Sept 11," *American Demographics* 24 (February 2002): 16–17; "The 1997 Cone/Roper Cause-Related Marketing Trends Report," p. 14.

54. Ronald Alsop, "Corporate Reputations Are Earned with Trust, Reliability, Study Shows," *Wall Street Journal,* September 23, 1999, http://interactive.wsj.com.

55. Bernard J. Jaworski and Ajay K. Kohli, "Market Orientation: Antecedents and Consequences," *Journal of Marketing* 57 (July 1993): 10.

56. "About Hershey Foods," www.hersheys.com/about/, accessed December 19, 2002; "Hershey Foods Philosophy and Values," Hershey Foods Corporation Videotape, 1990.

57. "Global Workforce Study Highlights Alarming Trends in Workplace Commitment and Ethics," Walker Information, press release, September 18, 2000, http://walkerinfo.com/news/9_18_00_gerr.cfm.

58. John Galvin, "The New Business Ethics," *SmartBusinessMag.com,* June 2000, p. 97.

59. John A. Byrne, "Chainsaw," *Business Week,* October 18, 1999, pp. 128–149.

60. "Mutual Funds to Boycott Mitsubishi over Proposed Mexican Salt Plant," CNN, October 25, 1999, www.cnn.com.

61. David Rynecki, "Here Are 8 Easy Ways to Lose Your Shirt in Stocks," *USA Today,* June 26, 1998, p. 3B.

62. "Investment Club Numbers Decline; Crisis of Confidence Caused Many to Take Their Money and Run," *Investor Relations Business,* September 23, 2002, p.1; Charles Jaffe, "Securities Industry Aims to Renew Trust; Leaders Face Challenge of Rebuilding Investor Confidence Amid Slump," *Boston Globe,* November 8, 2002, p. E1; Ronni L. Tapia, "Investor Loyalty Makes a 'Whale of Difference,'" *Philippine Daily Inquirer,* April 26, 1999, www.inquirer.net/issues/apr99/apr26/features/fea_4.htm.

63. Isabelle Maignan, O. C. Ferrell, and G. Thomas Hult, "Corporate Citizenship: Antecedents and Business Benefits," *Journal of the Academy of Marketing Science* 24, no. 4 (1999): 455–469.

64. S. B. Graves and S. A. Waddock, "Institutional Owners and Corporate Social Performance: Maybe Not So Myopic After All," *Proceedings of the International Association for Business and Society,* San Diego, CA, 1993; Ronald M. Roman, Sefa Hayibor, and Bradley R. Agle, "The Relationship Between Social and Financial Performance," *Business and Society* 38 (March 1999); W. Gary Simpson and Theodor Kohers, "The Link Between Corporate Social and Financial Performance: Evidence From the Banking Industry," *Journal of Business Ethics* 35 (January 2002): 97–109; Curtis Verschoor and Elizabeth A. Murphy, "The Financial Performance of U.S. Firms and Those with Global Prominence: How Do the Best Corporate Citizens Rate?" *Business and Society Review* 107 (Fall 2002): 371–380; S. Waddock and S. Graves, "The Corporate Social Performance–Financial Performance Link," *Strategic Management Journal* 18 (1997): 303–319.

65. Chris C. Verschoor, "A Study of the Link Between a Corporation's Financial Performance and Its Commitment to Ethics," *Journal of Business Ethics* 31 (October 1998): 1509.

66. Shawn L. Berman, Andrew C. Wicks, Suresh Kotha, and Thomas M. Jones, "Does Stakeholder Orientation Matter? The Relationship Between Stakeholder Management Models and Firm Financial Performance," *Academy of Management Journal* 42 (October 1999): 502–503.

67. Roman, Hayibor, and Agle, "The Relationship Between Social and Financial Performance."

68. Melissa A. Baucus and David A. Baucus, "Paying the Payer: An Empirical Examination of Longer Term Financial Consequences of Illegal Corporate Behavior," *Academy of Management Journal* 40 (1997): 129–151.

69. K. J. Arrow, *The Limits of Organization* (New York: Norton, 1974), pp. 23, 26; D. C. North, *Institutions: Institutional Change, and Economic Performance* (Cambridge: Cambridge University Press, 1990).

70. Shelby D. Hunt, "Resource-Advantage Theory and the Wealth of Nations: Developing the Socio-Economic Research Tradition," *Journal of Socio-Economics* 26 (1997).

71. North, *Institutions,* p. 9.

72. L. E. Harrison, *Who Prospers? How Cultural Values Shape Economic and Political Success* (New York: Basic Books, 1992), p. 16.

73. Hunt, "Resource-Advantage Theory and the Wealth of Nations."

74. Ibid., pp. 351–352.

75. "Global Corruption Report 2001," www.globalcorruptionreport.org, accessed December 19, 2002.

76. Carol Stavraka, "Ford Admits SUVs Harm Environment; Looks for Ways to Improve Record," ResponsibilityInc.com, May 17, 2000, www.responsibilityinc.com.

77. Jennifer Rewick, "Connecticut Attorney General Launches Probe of Priceline.com After Complaints," *Wall Street Journal,* October 2, 2000, p. E16.

78. Bernstein, "Too Much Corporate Power?"

79. "19th Annual Technical Excellence Awards," *PC Magazine,* November 19, 2002, www.pcmag.com, accessed December 20, 2002; Glenn R. Simpson, "Raytheon Offers Office Software for Snooping," *Wall Street Journal,* June 14, 2000, p. B1.

80. Bernstein, "Too Much Corporate Power?" p. 153.

81. Julia Angwin, "Credit-Card Scams: The Devil E-stores," *Wall Street Journal,* September 19, 2000, pp. B1, B4; Michelle Delio, "Cops Bust Massive ID Theft Ring," Wired.com, November 25, 2002, www.wired.com/news/privacy/0,1848,56567,00.html, accessed December 20, 2002.

82. VanCity Credit Union, *The Future of Corporate Social Responsibility,* http://www.vancity.com/downloads/Future_of_CSR.pdf, accessed August 7, 2003.

Chapter 2

1. Paige Albiniak, "FTC Sees Progress on Violence," *Broadcasting & Cable,* December 10, 2001, p. 16; Darren Carlson, "The Blame Game: Youth and Media Violence," *Gallup Tuesday Briefing,* January 22, 2002, pp. 1–2; "Hollywood Execs Admit Bad Judgment," Associated Press, September 27, 2000, via Netscape, http://dailynews.netscape.com/mynsnews/story.tmpl?table=n&cat=50800&id=200009271209; Louise Kennedy, "Movies; The Ratings Game with the Latest Summer Flicks," *Boston Globe,* June 30, 2002, p. N13; John King, "Federal Report Finds Entertainment Industry Aims Marketing at Children," CNN, September 11, 2000, www.cnn.com/2000/US/09/11/entertain.report/; "Lights, Camera, Action: Hollywood Must Rewrite Marketing Script," *Columbus Dispatch,* October 3, 2000, p. 6A, via http://web.lexis-nexis.com/universe/; "Under Fire from Lawmakers, Movie Makers Present Plan," CNN.com, September 27, 2000, via Netscape, http://dailynews.netscape.com/dailynews/cnnnews.tmpl?story=hollywood.violence0927.html; Jack Valenti, "Report on Violence in the Media and Children," *FDCH Congressional Testimony,* September 13, 2000, via http://ehostvgw15.epnet.com/ehost1.asp?key=204.179.122.140_8000_633481665&site=ehost&return=y.

2. Joanne B. Ciulla, *The Working Life: The Promise and Betrayal of Modern Work* (New York: Times Books, 2000).

3. Lee E. Preston, "Stakeholder Management and Corporate Performance," *Journal of Behavioral Economics* 19, no. 4 (1990): 361–375.

4. American Productivity & Quality Center, *Community Relations: Unleashing the Power of Corporate Citizenship* (Houston, TX: American Productivity & Quality Center, 1998); Thomas Donaldson and Lee E. Preston, "The Stakeholder Theory of the Corporation: Concepts, Evidence and Implications," *Academy of Management Review* 29 (January 1995): 65–91; Jaan Elias and J. Gregory Dees, "The Normative Foundations of Business," Harvard Business School Publishing, June 10, 1997.

5. Theodore Levitt, *The Marketing Imagination* (New York: Free Press, 1983).

6. Norman Bowie, "Empowering People as an End for Business," in *People in Corporations: Ethical Responsibilities and Corporate Effectiveness,* ed. Georges Enderle, Brenda Almond, and Antonio Argandona (Dordrecht, Holland: Kluwer Academic Press, 1990), pp. 105–112.

7. Chris Marsden, "The New Corporate Citizenship of Big Business: Part of the Solution to Sustainability?" *Business and Society Review* 105 (Spring 2000): 9–25; James E. Post, Lee E. Preston, and Sybille Sachs, *Redefining the Corporation: Stakeholder Management and Organizational Wealth* (Stanford, CA: Stanford University Press, 2002).

8. Donaldson and Preston, "The Stakeholder Theory of the Corporation."

9. Randy Brooks, "Why Loyal Employees and Customers Improve the Bottom Line," *Journal for Quality and Participation* 23 (March–April 2000): 40–44; Frederick F. Reichheld, *The Loyalty Effect: The Hidden Force Behind Growth, Profits, and Lasting Value* (Boston: Harvard Business School Press, 1996).

10. Max B. E. Clarkson, "A Stakeholder Framework for Analyzing and Evaluating Corporate Social Performance," *Academy of Management Review* 20 (January 1995): 92–117.

11. Kate Miller, "Issues Management: The Link Between Organization Reality and Public Perception," *Public Relations Quarterly* 44 (Summer 1999): 5–11.

12. Clarkson, "A Stakeholder Framework for Analyzing and Evaluating Corporate Social Performance."

13. "Firms Hit By Apartheid Charge," *Financial Management* (October 2002): 5; Matthew Miller, "Now, Apartheid Echoes in Bank Boardrooms," *U.S. Banker* 112 (October 2002): 16.

14. Walker Information, *Stakeholder Management Around the World* (Indianapolis, IN: Walker Information Global Network, 1999).

15. Donaldson and Preston, "The Stakeholder Theory of the Corporation"; Walker Information, *Stakeholder Management Around the World.*

16. Thomas Donaldson and Thomas W. Dunfee, *Ties That Bind: A Social Contracts Approach to Business Ethics* (Boston: Harvard Business School Press, 1999); Darryl Reed, "Employing Normative Stakeholder Theory in Developing Countries: A Critical Theory Perspective," *Business and Society* 41 (June 2002): 166–207.

17. Debbie Thorne LeClair, "Marketing Planning and the Policy Environment in the European Union," *International Marketing Review* 17, no. 3 (2000): 189–211.

18. Carol Stavraka, "FDA Proposes New Biotech Rules," ResponsibilityInc.com, May 3, 2000, www.

responsibilityinc.com/News/fdarules.html; David Stipp, "Is Monsanto's Biotech Worth Less Than a Hill of Beans?" *Fortune*, February 21, 2000, pp. 157–160.

19. Devin Leonard, "Bhopal Ghosts (Still) Haunt Union Carbide," *Fortune*, April 3, 2000, pp. 45–46; Amy Waldman, "Bhopal Seethes, Pained and Poor 18 Years Later," *New York Times*, September 21, 2002, p. A3.

20. This section is adapted from Isabelle Maignan, Bas Hillebrand, and Debbie Thorne McAlister, "Managing Socially Responsible Buying: How to Integrate Non-economic Criteria into the Purchasing Process," *European Management Journal* 20 (December 2002): 641–648.

21. Andrew L. Friedman and Samantha Miles, "Developing Stakeholder Theory," *Journal of Management Studies* 39 (January 2002): 1–21; Ronald K. Mitchell, Bradley R. Agle, and Donna J. Wood, "Toward a Theory of Stakeholder Identification and Salience: Defining the Principle of Who and What Really Counts," *Academy of Management Review* 22 (October 1997): 853–886.

22. Dana Frank, *Buy American: The Untold Story of Economic Nationalism* (Boston: Beacon, 1999); David Kaplan, "U.S. Goods Are Preferred, Says Poll," *Adweek*, June 24, 2002, p. 1.

23. Amitai Etzioni, *Modern Organizations* (Upper Saddle River, NJ: Prentice-Hall, 1964).

24. Aaron Bernstein, "Too Much Corporate Power?" *Business Week*, September 11, 2000, pp. 144–158.

25. Treasury Advisory Committee on International Child Labor Enforcement, "Notices," *Federal Register*, March 6, 2000, 65 FR 11831.

26. Andrew Ward, "McDonald's Eager for Talks with Critics," (London) *Financial Times*, May 3, 2000, p. 3.

27. Mark C. Suchman, "Managing Legitimacy: Strategic and Institutional Approaches," *Academy of Management Review* 20 (July 1995): 571–610.

28. Brad Knickerbock, "Activists Step Up War to 'Liberate' Nature," *Christian Science Monitor*, January 20, 1999, p. 4.

29. Joshua Kurlantzick, "Protestors Form Human Chain Outside ADB Meeting," *Agence France Presse*, May 8, 2000, via LEXIS®-NEXIS® Academic Universe.

30. Bennett Daviss, "Profits from Principles," *Futurist* 33 (March 1999): 28–33; Carol Stavraka, "Could Nike's College Pull-Out Hurt Its Bottom Line?" ResponsibilityInc.com, April 28, 2000, www.responsibilityinc.com/News/nikemoney.html.

31. Thomas Friedman, "Nike Boss Knight Is Right," *Denver Post*, June 21, 2000, p. B11.

32. "Diamond Trade Funding Wars," *African Business* 248 (November 1999): 28; James E. Post and Shawn L. Berman, "Global Corporate Citizenship in a Dot.com World," in *Perspectives on Corporate Citizenship*, ed. Jörg Andriof and Malcolm McIntosh (Sheffield, UK: Greenleaf Publishing, 2001): 66–82; "Shaming the Sanctions-Busters," *The Economist*, March 18, 2000, p. 47.

33. Ronald Alsop, "Corporate Reputations Are Earned with Trust, Reliability, Study Shows," *Wall Street Journal*, Sep-

tember 23, 1999, http://interactive.wsj.com; John F. Mahon, "Corporate Reputation: A Research Agenda Using Strategy and Stakeholder Literature," *Business and Society* 41 (December 2002): 415–445.

34. Timothy Aeppel, "Bridgestone/Firestone Set to Replace 6.5 Million Tires," *Wall Street Journal*, August 10, 2000, http://interactive.wsj.com; Robert L. Simison, Norihiko Shirouzu, Timothy Aeppel, and Todd Zaun, "Logistics of Tire Recall, Investigation Cause Increasing Corporate Clashes," *Wall Street Journal*, August 28, 2000, http://interactive.wsj.com; Rachel Wenger, "All Aboard: Bridgestone/Firestone Headed In Right Direction," *Rubber and Plastics News*, September 9, 2002, p. 10.

35. Alsop, "Corporate Reputations Are Earned with Trust, Reliability, Study Shows."

36. Manto Gotsi and Alan Wilson, "Corporate Reputation Management: 'Living the Brand,'" *Management Decision* 39, no. 2 (2001): 99–105; Jim Kartalia, "Technology Safeguards for a Good Corporate Reputation," *Information Executive* 3 (September 1999): 4; Prema Nakra, "Corporate Reputation Management: 'CRM' with a Strategic Twist?" *Public Relations Quarterly* 45 (Summer 2000): 35–42.

37. Jeanne Logsdon and Donna J. Wood, "Reputation As An Emerging Construct In the Business and Society Field: An Introduction," *Business and Society* 41 (December 2002): 365–270; "Putting a Price Tag to Reputation," Council of Public Relations Firms, www.prfirms.org, accessed December 20, 2002; Allen M. Weiss, Erin Anderson, and Deborah J. MacInnis, "Reputation Management as a Motivation for Sales Structure Decisions," *Journal of Marketing* 63 (October 1999): 74–89.

38. Christy Eidson and Melissa Master, "Who Makes the Call?" *Across the Board* 37 (March 2000): 16; Logsdon and Wood, "Reputation As An Emerging Construct In the Business and Society Field."

39. Alison Rankin Frost, "Brand vs. Reputation," *Communication World* 16 (February–March 1999): 22–25.

40. Glen Peters, *Waltzing with the Raptors: A Practical Roadmap to Protecting Your Company's Reputation* (New York: Wiley, 1999).

41. Aeppel, "Bridgestone/Firestone Set to Replace 6.5 Million Tires"; Simison, Shirouzu, Aeppel, and Zaun, "Logistics of Tire Recall, Investigation Cause Increasing Corporate Clashes."

42. Much of this section is adapted from Lisa A. Mainiero, "Action or Reaction? Handling Businesses in Crisis After September 11," *Business Horizons* 45 (September–October 2002): 2–10; Robert R. Ulmer and Timothy L. Sellnow, "Consistent Questions of Ambiguity in Organizational Crisis Communication: Jack in the Box as a Case Study," *Journal of Business Ethics* 25 (May 2000): 143–155; Robert R. Ulmer and Timothy L. Sellnow, "Strategic Ambiguity and the Ethic of Significant Choices in the Tobacco Industry's Crisis Communication," *Communication Studies* 48, no. 3 (1997): 215–233; Timothy L. Sellnow

and Robert R. Ulmer, "Ambiguous Argument as Advocacy in Organizational Crisis Communication," *Argumentation and Advocacy* 31, no. 3 (1995): 138–150; Peter V. Stanton, "Ten Communication Mistakes You Can Avoid When Managing a Crisis," *Public Relations Quarterly* 47 (Summer 2002): 19–22.

43. "Crisis Survival Tactics for HR," *HR Focus* 79 (April 2002): 1, 13; "Boss of IBM's Disaster Recovery Center Tells What He Learned from Last Week's Crisis," *InfoWorld.com*, http://www.infoworld.com/articles/hn/xml/01/09/19/010919hngordon.xml, accessed August 28, 2003.

44. "Jack in the Box's Worst Nightmare," *New York Times*, February 6, 1993, p. A35; Robert Nugent, Remarks before the U.S. Senate Subcommittee on Agricultural Research, Forestry, Conservation, and General Legislation (available from Jack in the Box Inc., San Diego, CA, 1993); Robert R. Ulmer and Timothy L. Sellnow, "Consistent Questions of Ambiguity in Organizational Crisis Communication: Jack in the Box as a Case Study."

45. Paul Argenti, "Crisis Communication: Lessons From 9/11," *Harvard Business Review* 80 (December 2002): 103–109; L. Paul Bremer, "Corporate Governance and Crisis Management," *Directors and Boards* 26 (Winter 2002): 16–20; Christine M. Pearson and Judith A. Clair, "Reframing Crisis Management," *Academy of Management Review* 23 (January 1998): 59–76.

46. Michael John Harker, "Relationship Marketing Defined?" *Marketing Intelligence and Planning* 17 (January 1999): 13–20; Robert M. Morgan and Shelby D. Hunt, "The Commitment-Trust Theory of Relationship Marketing," *Journal of Marketing* 58 (July 1994): 20–38.

47. "Hormel Plans Ahead with Oracle Internet Procurement," *Fortune*, May 1, 2000, p. S12.

48. Jörg Andriof and Sandra Waddock, "Unfolding Stakeholder Engagement," in *Unfolding Stakeholder Thinking: Theory, Responsibility and Engagement*, ed. Jörg Andriof, Sandra Waddock, Bryan Husted, and Sandra S. Rahman (Greenleaf Publishing, 2002): 19–42; James Coleman, "Social Capital in the Creation of Human Capital," *American Journal of Sociology* 94 (1988): S95–S120; Carrie R. Leana and Harry J. Van Buren III, "Organizational Social Capital and Employment Practices," *Academy of Management Review* 24 (July 1999): 538–555.

49. Chemical Manufacturers Association, *Improving Responsible Care Implementation, Enhancing Performance and Credibility* (Washington, DC: Chemical Manufacturers Association, 1993); "Details of Revamped *Responsible Care* Take Shape," *Chemical Week*, November 20, 2002, pp. 33–39; Jennifer Howard, Jennifer Nash, and John Ehrenfeld, "Standard or Smokescreen? Implementation of a Voluntary Environmental Code," *California Management Review* 42 (Winter 2000): 63–82.

50. Clarkson Centre for Business Ethics, *Principles of Stakeholder Management* (Toronto: Clarkson Centre for Business Ethics, 1999), http://mgmt.utoronto.ca/ ~stake/ Principles.htm; Malcolm McIntosh, Deborah Leipziger, Keith Jones, and Gill Coleman, *Corporate Citizenship: Successful Strategies for Responsible Companies* (London: Financial Times Management, 2000).

51. E. Scholes and D. Clutterbuck, "Communication with Stakeholders: An Integrated Approach," *Long Range Planning* 31, no. 2 (1998): 227–238.

52. Nick Wingfield and Glenn R. Simpson, "With So Much Subscriber Information, AOL Walks a Cautious Line on Privacy," *Wall Street Journal*, March 15, 2000, http://interactive.wsj.com.

53. McIntosh, Leipziger, Jones, and Coleman, *Corporate Citizenship*, p. 139.

54. Royal Dutch/Shell, *People, Planet & Profits—The Shell Report* (London: Royal Dutch/Shell, 2001); Royal Dutch/Shell Group, *The Shell Report 1999: People, Planet and Profits—An Act of Commitment* (London: Royal Dutch/Shell, 1999); Royal Dutch/Shell, *Shell Report 2000: How Do We Stand?* (London: Royal Dutch/ Shell, 2000); all available at www.shell.com.

55. Jon Entine, "The Body Shop: Truth and Consequences," *Drug & Cosmetics Industry* 156 (February 1995): 54; Jon Entine, "Body Shop's Packaging Starts to Unravel," *Australian Financial Review*, December 18, 2002, p. 52.

56. Clarkson, "A Stakeholder Framework for Analyzing and Evaluating Corporate Social Performance," p. 105.

57. Ibid., p. 109.

58. Ibid.

59. Ibid.

60. Ibid.

61. Jörg Andriof, "Managing Social Risk through Stakeholder Partnership Building," unpublished dissertation, Warwick Business School, 2000; Jörg Andriof, "Patterns of Stakeholder Partnership Building," in *Perspectives on Corporate Citizenship*, Andriof and McIntosh, pp. 215–238.

62. Nick Chaloner and David Brontzen, "How SABMiller Protects Its Biggest Asset—Its Reputation," *Strategic Communication Management* 6 (October–November 2002): 12–15.

Chapter 3

1. "I am Gorgeous, aren't I," Better Business Bureau press release, December 10, 2002, via http://www.bbb.org/alerts/model-talent.asp, accessed February 21, 2003.

2. George J. Siedel, "Six Forces and the Legal Environment of Business," *American Business Law Journal* 37 (Summer 2000): 717–742.

3. Paul Starr, "Liberalism after Clinton," *American Prospect*, August 28, 2000; Amy Borrus and Paula Dwyer, "Surprise: Bush Is Emerging as a Fighter for Privacy on the Net," *Business Week*, June 5, 2000, p. 63.

4. Julia Appleby, "Columbia Agrees to $745 Million Penalty," *USA Today*, May 19, 2000, p. B1; Graham Brink, "Court Clears Ex-HCA Executives,"

St. Petersburg Times, http://www.sptimes.com/2002/ 03/26/TampaBay/Court_clears_ex_HCA_e.shtml, March 26, 2002, accessed August 14, 2003.

5. G. Meirovich and A. Reichel, "Illegal But Ethical: An Inquiry into the Roots of Illegal Corporate Behavior in Russia," *Business Ethics: A European Review* 9 (July 2000): 126–135.

6. Pam King, Mountain States Better Business Bureau, February 2003.

7. Maureen McGrath, "Telemarketing Company Fined $300,000 for Deceptive Telemarketing Practice," Competition Bureau, Canadian Government, January 20, 2003, via http://strategis.ic.gc.ca/SSG/ct02492e.html, accessed March 1, 2003.

8. "Drug Firms Agree to Settle Lawsuit over Cardizem," *Wall Street Journal,* January 28, 2003, p. A1.

9. John Fialka, "Lockheed Faces Record Fine for Safety Violations," *Wall Street Journal,* August 29, 2000, p. A8.

10. David A. Vise, "AOL, Microsoft team up, ask government to help stop spam," *Commercial Appeal,* February 21, 2003, p. C2.

11. Lee Gomes, "Ruling in Copyright Case Favors Film Industry," *Wall Street Journal,* August 18, 2000, p. B6.

12. "Warning Signs," *Business Ethics* 15 (September–October 2001): 11.

13. Carol McKay, "Online Auction Fraud Skyrocketing in 2002," National Consumer League, August 2002, via http://www.nclnet.org/fraudweek2.htm, accessed March 1, 2003.

14. Jim Carlton and Pui-Wing Tam, "Online Auctioneers Face Growing Fraud Problem," *Wall Street Journal,* May 12, 2000, p. B2; Michael Pastore, "Online Fraud: How Bad Is It?" http://cyberatlas.internet.com/ markets/retailing/ article/0,,6061_464841,00.html, accessed October 20, 2001.

15. "The Sherman Antitrust Act," Antitrust Case Browser, www.antitrustcases.com/statutes/ sherman.html, accessed October 21, 2001.

16. Ibid.

17. Andrew J. Glass, "Judge Splits Microsoft," *Austin American-Statesman,* June 8, 2000, www.austin360. com/statesman/; Jennifer Jones, "Government Drops Breakup Bid," *InfoWorld,* September 10, 2001, http:// www.findartices. com, accessed October 20, 2001.

18. U.S. Department of Justice, "Antitrust Enforcement and the Consumer" (Washington, DC: U.S. Department of Justice, www.usdoj.gov/atr/public/ div_stats/1638.htm, accessed October 21, 2001.

19. "Miss Cleo Promoters to Forgive Approximately $500 Million in Outstanding Consumer Charges and Pay an Additional $5 Million to Settle FTC Charges," Federal Trade Commission Press Release, November 14, 2002, via http://www.ftc.gov/opa/2002/11/ars.htm, accessed March 1, 2003.

20. "Appeals Court Upholds FTC Ruling: Doan's Must Include Corrective Message in Future Advertising and Labeling," Federal Trade Commission Press Release, August 21, 2000, via http://www.ftc.gov/opa/2000/08/doans.htm, accessed March 1, 2003.

21. "FTC Approves Pact Allowing Toysmart's Customer-List Sale," *Wall Street Journal,* July 24, 2000, p. A28.

22. "Nine West Settles State and Federal Price Fixing Charges," Federal Trade Commission, March 6, 2000, www.ftc.gov/opa/2000/03/ninewest.htm.

23. "Price Fixing Suit Settled," ABCNews.com, September 7, 1999, www.abcnews.go.com/sections/ business/ dailyNews/vitamins_settle990907.html.

24. Albert A. Foer and Robert H. Lande, "The Evolution of United States Antitrust Law: The Past, Present & (Possible) Future," *American Antitrust Institute,* October 20, 1999, www.antitrustinstitute.org/recent/64.pdf.

25. Richard Waddington, "World Health Body Warns that Mad Cow Still a Risk," Reuters Newswire, January 30, 2003.

26. Ernest Beck, "Stores Told to Lift Prices in Germany," *Wall Street Journal,* September 11, 2000, p. A27.

27. Brandon Mitchener, "Global Antitrust Process May Get Simpler," *Wall Street Journal,* October 27, 2000, p. A17; Debbie Thorne LeClair, O. C. Ferrell, and Linda Ferrell, "Federal Sentencing Guidelines for Organizations: Legal, Ethical, and Public Policy Issues for International Marketing," *Journal of Public Policy and Marketing* 16 (Spring 1997): 30.

28. LeClair, Ferrell, and Ferrell, "Federal Sentencing Guidelines for Organizations," p. 31.

29. David Fairlamb, "Mega Europe," *Business Week,* November 25, 2002, p. 62.

30. LeClair, Ferrell, and Ferrell, "Federal Sentencing Guidelines for Organizations," p. 31.

31. "Today's Briefing," *Commercial Appeal,* February 12, 2003, p. C1.

32. Ted Bridis, "Computer-Crime Treaty," *Wall Street Journal,* October 26, 2000, p. B8.

33. "National Press Club forum explores controversial federal regulatory review process," Washington University in St. Louis Press Release, December 12, 2001, via http:// news-info.wustl.edu/news/nrindex00/npc.html, accessed February 18, 2003.

34. Weidenbaum Center on the Economy, Government, and Public Policy Press Release, June 5, 2002, via http://wc.wustl.edu/RegBudgetNewsRelease.htm, accessed February 18, 2003.

35. "The Ban on Youth Targeting" under "Responsible Marketing: Tobacco Settlement Agreement," Philip Morris web site, via http://www.philipmorrisusa.com, accessed March 1, 2003.

36. U.S. Department of Justice, "Antitrust Enforcement and the Consumer," 2003.

37. Mark Wigfield, "FCC to Diminish Role in Monitoring Phone Equipment," *Wall Street Journal,* May 15, 2000, p. B12.

38. Shawn Tully, "Friendly Skies Aren't Out of the Picture," *Fortune,* December 18, 2002, via http://www.fortune.

com/fortune/articles/0,15114,400967,00.html, accessed March 1, 2003.

39. William M. Pride and O. C. Ferrell, *Marketing: Concepts and Strategies,* 12th ed. (Boston: Houghton Mifflin, 2003), pp. 54–55.

40. "The Better Business Bureau System," via www.bbb.org/bnd/bbbsystem.asp, accessed February 21, 2003.

41. Jennifer Rewick, "Connecticut Attorney General Launches Probe of Priceline.com After Complaints," *Wall Street Journal,* October 2, 2000, p. B16.

42. Pride and Ferrell, *Marketing: Concepts and Strategies,* pp. 54–55.

43. David Hardesty, "Digital Signals Act Becomes Law," July 2, 2000, via http://www.ecommercefax.com/doc/070200.htm#_ftn1, accessed March 1, 2003.

44. Joint Committee on the Organization of Congress, "Historical Overview," *Organization of the Congress,* December 1993, www.house.gov/rules/jcoc2c. htm#b; Joint Committee on the Organization of Congress, "Reorganization in the Modern Congress," *Organization of the Congress,* December 1993, www.house.gov/rules/jcoc2o.htm; Marc A. Triebwasser, "Congressional Leadership and Reform: The Trends Toward Centralization and Decentralization," *American Politics,* www.polisci.ccsu.edu/trieb/Cong-9.html, accessed October 21, 2001; "Driving Mr. Gephardt," *Newsweek,* August 21, 2000, p. 48.

45. "About the FEC," Federal Election Commission, www.fec.gov/about.html, accessed August 14, 2003; John Scorza, "Business Group Vows to Fight New Government Contracting Rule," www.lycos.com/ business/cch/news.html, accessed May 3, 2000.

46. "Common Cause Victories," Common Cause, www.commoncause.org/about/factsuccess.htm, accessed October 21, 2001, March 1, 2003.

47. Don Corney, Amy Borrus, and Jay Greene, "Microsoft's All Out Counterattack," *Business Week,* May 15, 2000, pp. 103–106.

48. Declan McCullagh, "Cable Operators Pledge to Keep Net Open," C/Net news.com, February 24, 2003.

49. "Corporate Lobbying Becoming a Key Business Risk," Lifeworth.com Press Release, February 11, 2003, via America Online.

50. Corney, Borrus, and Greene, "Microsoft's All Out Counterattack."

51. "Election Regulators Seek Scrutiny of Presidential Hopefuls PACs," via http://www.cnn.com/2003/ALLPOLITICS/02/26/political.pacs.ap/index.html, accessed August 14, 2003.

52. "Supreme Court Rejects Former Governor's Appeal on Extortion Case," via http://www.cnn.com/2003/LAW/02/24/scotus.edwards.ap.index.html, accessed March 1, 2003.

53. U.S. Sentencing Commission, "Mean and Median Organizations Receiving Fines or Restitution Imposed on Sentenced Organizations by Primary Offense Category and Applicability of Chapter Eight Fine Guidelines,"

1999–2001 Sourcebook of Federal Sentencing Statistics, www.ussc.gov/ANNRPT/ 19992001/table 521.pdf.

54. Win Swenson, "The Organizational Guidelines Carrot and Stick Philosophy and Their Focus on Effective Compliance," in *Corporate Crime in America: Strengthening the Good Citizen Corporation* (Washington, DC: U.S. Sentencing Commission, 1993), p. 17.

55. *United States Code Service* (Lawyers Addition), 18 U.S.S.C. Appendix, Sentencing Guidelines for the United States Courts (Rochester, NY: Lawyers Cooperative Publishing, 1995), § 8A.1.

56. Brock N, Meeks, "Scandal Takes Center Stage in 2002," December 6, 2002, via www.msnbc.com/news/838696.asp.

57. Elliot Blair Smith, "Probe: Former Kmart CEO 'grossly derelict,'" *USA Today,* January 27, 2003, p. B1.

Chapter 4

1. Yuri Kageyama, "Mitsubishi Motors Says Massive Defect Cover-ups Were Intentional," *Boston Globe,* August 22, 2000, www.boston.com/; Yuri Kageyama, "Mitsubishi Motors Says Massive Defect Cover-ups Were Intentional," *SF Gate,* August 22, 2000, www.sfgate.com/; "Mitsubishi Cover-up May Bring Charges," *Detroit News,* August 23, 2000, www.detnews.com/2000/autos/0008/23/b03-109584.htm; Miki Tanikawa, with Katy Marquardt, "Mitsubishi Concealed Evidence of Defects," *Austin American-Statesman,* August 23, 2000, http://austin360.com/statesman/.

2. Wendy Zellner, "No Way to Treat A Lady?" *Business Week,* March 3, 2003, pp. 63, 66.

3. "Privacy for Sale," *Business Ethics* 13 (July–August 1999): 8.

4. Andrew Singer, "CEO's Focus on 'Reputation' Buoys Unisys' Ethics Program," *Ethikos* 13 (November–December 1999): 1–3, 8, 16.

5. Erin White, "Study on Teen Readership of Magazines May Step Up Pressure on Tobacco Firms," *Wall Street Journal,* October 31, 2000, p. A8.

6. "SEC Chief Donaldson pushes ethics," MSNBC News, February 28, 2003, via www.msnbc.com/news/878994.asp, accessed March 1, 2003.

7. *Business Ethics* 9 (January–February 1995): 13.

8. "Eye on Europe," *Business Ethics* 16 (January–February 2002): 9.

9. "The Best Managers," *Business Week,* January 13, 2003, p. 6.

10. "Sales Slump, Lawsuits Grow at Body Shop," *Business Ethics* 12 (July–August 1998): 8.

11. Debbie Thorne McAlister and Robert Erffmeyer, "A Content Analysis of Outcomes and Responsibilities for Consumer Complaints to Third Party Organizations," *Journal of Business Research* 56 (April 2003): 341–352.

12. http://money.cnn.com/news/specials/corruption, accessed January 31, 2003.

13. "Worth Noting," *Business Ethics* 13 (January–February 1999): 5.

14. Elisa Williams, "The Man Who Knows Too Much," *Forbes,* November 11, 2002, pp. 68–69.

15. Barry Newman, "An Ad Professor Huffs Against Puffs, but It's A Quixotic Enterprise," *Wall Street Journal,* January 24, 2003, p. A1.

16. Chris Adams, "Merck Is Accused of Inflating the Price of Heartburn Drug," *Wall Street Journal,* January 31, 2003, p. A1.

17. Vernon R. Loucks, Jr., "A CEO Looks at Ethics," *Business Horizons* 30 (March–April 1987): 4.

18. James Bandler, "Two Big Film Makers Strive to Crush Renegade Recycler," *Wall Street Journal,* December 4, 2002, http://online.wsj.com.

19. Eric H. Beversluis, "Is There No Such Thing as Business Ethics?" *Journal of Business Ethics* 6 (February 1987): 81–88. Reprinted by permission of Kluwer Academic Publishers, Dordrecht, Holland.

20. Ibid., p. 82.

21. Emily Nelson and Laurie P. Cohen, "Why Grubman Was So Keen to Get His Twins into the Y," *Wall Street Journal,* November 15, 2002, http://online.wsj.com.

22. John Byrne, "Fall From Grace," *Business Week,* August 12, 2002, pp. 50–56.

23. Jenny Summerour, "Bribery Game," *Progressive Grocer,* January 2000, pp. 2–5, 43.

24. "Warning Signs," *Business Ethics* 16 (Sept/Oct/Nov/Dec 2002): 8.

25. William T. Neese, O. C. Ferrell, and Linda Ferrell, "An Analysis of Mail and Wire Fraud Cases Related to Marketing Communication: Implications for Corporate Citizenship," working paper, 2003, Colorado State University, Fort Collins, Colorado.

26. "Snapshot: Co-workers Reporting Fraud," *USA Today,* October 3, 2002, p. 1D.

27. James Bandler and Susan Pulliam, "SEC to File Civil Fraud Case Against KPMG over Xerox," *Wall Street Journal,* January 23, 2003, p. A3.

28. "Post-Enron restatements hit record," MSNBC News, January 21, 2003, via www.msnbc.com/news/862325.asp, accessed January 29, 2003.

29. "Warning Signs," *Business Ethics* 16 (Sept/Oct/Nov/Dec 2002): 8.

30. Charles Piller, "Bell Labs Says Its Physicist Faked Groundbreaking Data," *Austin American-Statesman,* September 26, 2002, www.austin360.com/statesman/.

31. James Heckman, "Puffery Claims No Longer So Easy to Make," *Marketing News,* February 14, 2000, p. 6.

32. Archie B. Carroll, *Business and Society: Ethics and Stakeholder Management* (Cincinnati, OH: South-Western, 1989), pp. 228–230.

33. Sara Nathan, "Phony Jobs," *USA Today,* March 7, 2000, p. B1.

34. Russell Mokhiber, "Warning Signs," *Business Ethics* 13 (May–June 1999): 8.

35. "Mott's Will Rewrite Some Labels Blamed for Misleading People," *Wall Street Journal,* August 2, 2000, p. B7.

36. "AT&T Settles Lawsuit Against Reseller Accused of Slamming," *Business Wire,* via America Online, accessed May 26, 1998.

37. Neese, Ferrell, and Ferrell, "An Analysis of Mail and Wire Fraud Cases Related to Marketing Communication: Implications for Corporate Citizenship."

38. Annie Finnigan, "Different Strokes," *Working Woman,* April 2001, p. 44.

39. O. C. Ferrell and Geoffrey Hirt, *Business: A Changing World,* 4th ed. (Boston: McGraw-Hill Irwin, 2003), pp. 312–316.

40. Mary Miller, "Warning Signs," *Business Ethics* 16 (January–February 2002): 8.

41. See pp. 122–155 of this text.

42. Ferrell and Hirt, *Business,* pp. 298–301.

43. "$3.5 Million Settlement in Woolworth Age Discrimination Case," CNN.com, November 15, 2002, www.cnn.com.

44. Sue Shellenberger, "Work & Family," *Wall Street Journal,* May 23, 2001, p. B1.

45. "What Is Affirmative Action?" HR Content Library, October 12, 2001, www.hrnext.com/content/view.cfm?articles_id=2007&subs_id=32.

46. Ibid.

47. "What Affirmative Action Is (And What It Is Not)," National Partnership for Women and Families, www.nationalpartnership.org/content.cfm?L1=202&DBT=Documents&NewsItemID=289&HeaderTitle=Affirmative%20Action, accessed December 4, 2002.

48. Ibid.

49. *U.S. Equal Employment Opportunity Commission: An Overview* (Washington, DC: U.S. Equal Employment Opportunity Commission, 1997), www.eeoc.gov/overview.html.

50. "Jury Awards $13 Million in Disability Discrimination Case," Equal Employment Opportunity Commission, press release, November 6, 1999, www.eeoc.gov/press/11-06-99.html.

51. Mary Miller, "Warning Signs," *Business Ethics* 16 (January–February 2002): 8.

52. "Company Watch," *Business Ethics* 15 (September–October 2001): 6.

53. Kirk O. Hanson, "A Nation of Cheaters," Markula Center for Applied Ethics web site, http://www.scu.edu/ethics/publications/ethicalperspectives/cheating.html, January 19, 2003, accessed January 28, 2003.

54. "Company Watch," *Business Ethics* 16 (Fall 2002): 7.

55. John W. Schoen, "Split CEO-chairman job, says panel," MSNBC News, January 9, 2003, via www.msnbc.com/news/857171.asp, accessed January 29, 2003.

56. This section was adapted from O. C. Ferrell, John Fraedrich, and Linda Ferrell, *Business Ethics: Ethical Decision Making and Cases,* 5th ed. (Boston: Houghton Mifflin, 2002), pp. 54–68.

57. "Warning Signs," *Business Ethics* 16 (Sept/Oct/Nov/Dec 2002): 8.

58. "Police Warn of Phone Scam," *Inside Tucson Business,* November 11, 1999, p. 3.

59. Lawrence J. H. Schulze, "OSHA's Proposed Ergonomics Standard," *Professional Safety* 45 (August 2000): 8.

60. Joanne Silberner, "All Things Considered," National Public Radio, April 11, 2000.

61. Immanuel Kant, "Fundamental Principles of the Metaphysics of Morals," in *Problems of Moral Philosophy: An Introduction,* 2nd ed., ed. Paul W. Taylor (Encino, CA: Dickenson, 1972), p. 229.

62. Stefanie E. Naumann and Nathan Bennett, "A Case for Procedural Justice Climate: Development and Test of a Multilevel Model," *Academy of Management Journal* 43 (October 2000): 881–889.

63. Joel Brockner and P. A. Siegel, "Understanding the Interaction Between Procedural and Distributive Justice: The Role of Trust," in *Trust in Organizations: Frontiers of Theory and Research,* ed. R. M. Kramer and T. R. Tyler (Thousand Oaks, CA: Sage, 1995), pp. 390–413.

64. Ferrell, Fraedrich, and Ferrell, *Business Ethics,* p. 55.

65. John Fraedrich and O. C. Ferrell, "Cognitive Consistency of Marketing Managers in Ethical Situations," *Journal of the Academy of Marketing Science* 20 (Summer 1992): 245–252.

66. Debbie Thorne LeClair, O. C. Ferrell, and John Fraedrich, *Integrity Management: A Guide to Managing Legal and Ethical Issues in the Workplace* (Tampa, FL: University of Tampa Press, 1998), p. 37.

67. This section was adapted from Ferrell, Fraedrich, and Ferrell, *Business Ethics,* pp. 106–109; and LeClair, Ferrell, and Fraedrich, *Integrity Management,* pp. 37–39.

68. Lawrence Kohlberg, "Stage and Sequence: The Cognitive Developmental Approach to Socialization," in *Handbook of Socialization Theory and Research,* ed. D.A. Goslin (Chicago: Rand McNally, 1969), pp. 347–480.

69. Suein L. Hwang, "The Executive Who Told Tobacco's Secrets," *Wall Street Journal,* November 28, 1995, pp. B1, B6.

70. Kohlberg, "Stage and Sequence: The Cognitive Developmental Approach to Socialization," pp. 347–480.

71. Rebecca Goodell, *Ethics in American Business: Policies, Programs and Perceptions* (Washington, DC: Ethics Resource Center, 1994), p. 15.

72. Patricia Carlson and Mark S. Blodgett, "International Ethics Standards for Business: NAFTA, Caux Principles and Corporate Codes of Ethics," *Review of Business* 18 (Spring 1997): 20–24.

73. David McClelland, "The Urge to Achieve," in *The Great Writings in Management and Organizational Behavior,* ed. Louis E. Boone and Donald D. Bowen (New York: McGraw-Hill, 1987), p. 386.

74. O. C. Ferrell and Larry G. Gresham, "A Contingency Framework for Understanding Ethical Decision Making in Marketing," *Journal of Marketing* 49 (Summer 1985): 87–96.

75. Joseph W. Weiss, *Business Ethics: A Managerial, Stakeholder Approach* (Belmont, CA: Wadsworth, 1994), p. 13.

76. Daniel Lyons, "Bad Boys," *Forbes,* July 22, 2002, pp. 99–100.

77. Marjorie Kelly, "14th Annual Business Ethics Awards," *Business Ethics* 16 (Sept/Oct/Nov/Dec 2002): 11.

78. O. C. Ferrell, Larry G. Gresham, and John Fraedrich, "A Synthesis of Ethical Decision Models for Marketing," *Journal of Macromarketing* 9 (Fall 1989): 58–59.

79. Michael S. James, "What Is Ethical?" ABCNews.com, February 21, 2003.

80. David Oyama, "Mitsubishi Electric Reveals TV Dangers After 8-Year Silence," *Wall Street Journal,* September 13, 2000, p. A21.

81. "Lack of Formal Ethics Program Connected to Workplace Problems: Survey Looks at Why People Sometimes Bend the Rules," PRNewswire, February 3, 1998.

82. Ethics Resource Center, *The Ethics Resource Center's 2000 National Business Ethics Survey: How Employees Perceive Ethics at Work* (Washington, DC: Ethics Resource Center, 2000), p. 38.

83. "Fraud A Growing Problem, Wall Street Journal Reports," Bloomberg Newswire, November 3, 2000, via America Online.

84. Rebecca Smith and Alexei Barrionuevo, "Dynegy Ex-Trader Is Indicted on Criminal Fraud Charges," *Wall Street Journal,* January 28, 2003, via http://online.wsj.com/article/0,SB1043687255134893064,00.html?mod=home_whats_ne..., accessed January 27, 2003.

85. "Deception: Three Disturbing Case Studies," *Business Ethics* 13 (July–August 1999): 10.

86. Ferrell, Gresham, and Fraedrich, "A Synthesis of Ethical Decision Models for Marketing," pp. 58–59.

Chapter 5

1. Evelina Shmukler, "Back to School," *Wall Street Journal Online,* February 24, 2003; Joann S. Lublin, "More Work, More Pay," *Wall Street Journal Online,* February 24, 2003; Carol Hymowitz, "Changing the Rules," *Wall Street Journal Online,* February 24, 2003; "The Hot Seat," *Wall Street Journal Online,* February 24, 2003.

2. Constance E. Bagley, "The Ethical Leader's Decision Tree," *Harvard Business Review* 81 (February 2003): 18–19.

3. Kara Wetzel, "SEC Files Complaint Against ClearOne," *Wall Street Journal Online,* January 15, 2003, via http://online.wsj.com/article_prit/0,BT_CO_20030115_00691000.htm, accessed February 11, 2003.

4. "AmericaEconomia Annual Survey Reveals Ethical Behavior of Businesses and Executives in Latin America," *AmericaEconomia,* December 19, 2002 from http://www.prnewswire.com, accessed December 20, 2002.

5. Eric Hellweg, "Mopping Up After Merrill Lynch," via http://www.business2.com, accessed September 10, 2002.

6. "62% of Americans Tell CEOs 'You're Not Doing Enough to Restore Trust and Confidence in American Business,'" Golin/Harris News Release, June 20, 2002, via www.golinharris.com/news/releases.asp?ID=3788, accessed January 31, 2003.

7. Constance E. Bagley, "The Ethical Leader's Decision Tree," *Harvard Business Review* 81 (February 2003): 18–19.

8. Ethics Resource Center, *The Ethics Resource Center's 2000 National Business Ethics Survey: How Employees Perceive Ethics at Work* (Washington, DC: Ethics Resource Center, 2000), p. 16.

9. "Ethics Is the Cornerstone of TI," http://www.ti.com/corp/docs/company/citizen/ethics/brochure/index.shtml, accessed September 26, 2000. Courtesy Texas Instruments.

10. "The TI Ethics Quick Test," http://www.ti.com/corp/docs/company/citizen/ethics/quicktest.shtml, accessed September 26, 2000. Courtesy Texas Instruments.

11. Mark S. Schwartz, "A Code of Ethics for Corporate Code of Ethics," *Journal of Business Ethics* 41 (2002): 37.

12. Ibid.

13. "Corporate Information," Fidelity Investments, via http://www100.fidelity.com/about/world/ethics_code.html, accessed November 20, 2000.

14. Ethics Resource Center, *The Ethics Center's 2000 National Buiness Ethics Survey*, p. 22.

15. Allynda Wheat, "Keeping An Eye on Corporate America," *Fortune*, November 25, 2002, pp. 44–45.

16. Ibid.

17. Ibid.

18. "Top Corporate Ethics Officers Tell Conference Board That More Business Ethics Scandals Are Ahead; Survey Conducted at Conference Board Business Ethics Conference," *PR Newswire*, June 17, 2002, via http://www.find-articles.com/cf_0/m4PRN/2002_June_17/87469997/print.jhtml, accessed February 7, 2003.

19. "Eye on Europe," *Business Ethics* 16 (May–June, July–August 2002): 9.

20. Ethics Resource Center, *The Ethics Resource Center's 2000 National Business Ethics Survey*, p. 18.

21. http://ec.hcahealthcare.com.

22. *PR Newswire*, June 17, 2002.

23. Ibid.

24. Debbie Thorne LeClair and Linda Ferrell, "Innovation in Experiential Business Ethics Training," *Journal of Business Ethics* 23 (2000): 313–322.

25. "Boeing: Ethics and Business Conduct Program," http://www.boeing.com/companyoffices/aboutus/ethics/index.html, accessed June 6, 2000. Courtesy of Boeing Business Services Company.

26. O. C. Ferrell and Larry G. Gresham, "A Contingency Framework for Understanding Ethical Decision Making in Marketing," *Journal of Marketing* 49 (Summer 1985): 87–96.

27. Diane E. Kirrane, "Managing Values: A Systematic Approach to Business Ethics," *Training and Development Journal* 1 (November 1990): 53–60.

28. "Boeing: Ethics and Business Conduct Program," http://www.boeing.com/companyoffices/aboutus/ethics/index.htm.

29. Janet Wiscombe, "Don't fear whistle-blowers: With HR's help, principled whistle-blowers can be a company's salvation," *Workforce*, July 2002, via http://www.findarticles.com, accessed February 7, 2003.

30. Ibid.

31. Ibid.

32. Mael Kaptein, "Guidelines for the Development of an Ethics Safety Net," *Journal of Business Ethics* 41 (December 2002): 217.

33. "The Network: Hotlines & Helplines," via The Network web site, www.tnwinc.com/hotlines_overview.asp, accessed February 27, 2003.

34. Kaptein, "Guidelines for the Development of an Ethics Safety Net."

35. Ethics Resource Center, *The Ethics Resource Center's 2000 National Business Ethics Survey*, p. 7.

36. John M. Schoen, "Split CEO-chairman job, says panel," MSNBC, January 9, 2003, via http://www.msnbc.com/news/857171.asp, accessed February 24, 2003.

37. Jathon Sapsford and Paul Beckett, "The Complex Goals and Unseen Cost of Whistle-Blowing," *Wall Street Journal*, November 25, 2002, pp. A1, A10.

38. Paula Dwyer, Dan Carney, Amy Borrus, Lorraine Woellert, and Christopher Palmeri, "Year of the Whistleblower," *Business Week*, December 16, 2002, p. 108.

39. Ibid.

40. Curt S. Jordan, "Lessons in Organizational Compliance: A Survey of Government-Imposed Compliance Programs," *Preventive Law Reporter* (Winter 1994): 7.

41. Robert Howard, "Values Make the Company: An Interview with Robert Haas," *Harvard Business Review* 68 (September–October 1990): 134.

42. Thomas A. Stewart, Ann Harrington, and Maura Griffin Sol, "America's Most Admired Companies: Why Leadership Matters," *Fortune*, March 3, 1998, pp. 70–71.

43. "Corporate Culture Can Prevent Ethical Crises and Boost Profits, Study Says; Analysis by International Survey Research Provides Roadmap for Monitoring Ethics," *PR Newswire*, September 4, 2002, via http://www.findarticles.com, accessed February 7, 2003.

44. Daniel J. Brass, Kenneth D. Butterfield, and Bruce C. Skaggs, "Relationship and Unethical Behavior: A Social Science Perspective," *Academy of Management Review* 23, no. 1 (1998): 14–31.

45. J. M. Burns, *Leadership* (New York: Harper & Row, 1985).

46. Roysto Greenwood, Roy Suddaby, and C. R. Hinings, "Theorizing Change: The Role of Professional Associations in the Transformation of Institutionalized Fields," *Academy of Management Journal* 45 (January 2002): 58–80.

47. "WorldCom Chief Outlines Initial Turnaround Strategy," *Wall Street Journal,* January 14, 2003, via http://online.wsj.com.

48. Wiscombe, "Don't fear whistle-blowers."

49. http://www.starbucks.com/aboutus/recognition.asp, accessed February 7, 2003.

50. Nicholas Stein, "America's Most Admired Companies," *Fortune,* March 3, 2003, p. 81.

51. Ferrell and Gresham, "A Contingency Framework for Understanding Ethical Decision Making in Marketing."

52. Wiscombe, "Don't fear whistle-blowers."

Chapter 6

1. "2002 Developments in the Field of Risk Management," *Business Insurance,* January 6, 2003, p. 16; "Adelphia Suing Deloitte & Touche," *Business Insurance,* November 11, 2002, p. 1; "Adelphia Files Lawsuit Against John Rigas and other Former Executives and Board Members of Adelphia," http://www.adelphia.com/invest/pdf/ 7_24_02.pdf, July 24, 2002; "Adelphia Statement Regarding the Federal Indictment of the Rigas Family Members," http://www.adelphia.com/invest/pdf/09_23_02. pdf, September 23, 2002; "Century/ML Cable Venture Files Petition for Chapter 11 Reorganization," http://www.adelphia.com/invest/pdf/CMLCV_CH11_ 93002.pdf, press release, September 30, 2002; "Sabres File for Bankruptcy Protection," CNN Sports Illustrated, http://sportsillustrated.cnn.com/hockey/news/2003/01 /13/sabres_bankruptcy_ap/, accessed January 15, 2003; Mike Farrell, "Adelphia's Numbers Aren't All Bad," *Multichannel News,* December 2, 2002, pp. 6–7; Ronald Grover, "Adelphia's Fall Will Bruise a Crowd," *Business Week,* July 8, 2002, p. 44; Avital Louria Hahn, "The Jailed, the Probed, the Embarrassed: A New Who's Who of the Afflicted In the Business and Street Worlds," *Investment Dealers' Digest,* September 16, 2002, p. 4; Devin Leonard, "The Adelphia Story," *Fortune,* August 12, 2002, pp. 136–148.

2. Rafael LaPorta and Florencio Lopez-de-Silanes, "Investor Protection and Corporate Governance," *Journal of Financial Economics* 58 (October–November 2000): 3–38.

3. James McRitchie, "Ending the Wall Street Walk: Why Corporate Governance Now?" www.corpgov.net/forums/ commentary/ending.html, accessed September 16, 2003.

4. "The 2020 Vision Project," Institute of Chartered Accountants in England & Wales, www.icaew.co.uk/, accessed October 29, 2001.

5. "In Plain Sight, In Plain English," *Across the Board* 39 (November–December 2002): 24–27.

6. "Let's Call the Whole Thing Off . . . ," *Directors & Boards,* 1999 Special Report Issue, p. 4.

7. Keith Bradsher, "A Struggle over Culture and Turf at Auto Giant," *New York Times,* September 25, 1999, p. C1; "A Look at the History of AOL Time Warner,"
Associated Press Online, January 30, 2003, accessed via LexisNexis; Geraldine Fabrikant and David Kirkpatrick, "AOL's Need: A New Vision," *New York Times,* February 2, 2003, Sec. 3, p. 1.

8. Keith Bradsher, "A Struggle over Culture and Turf at Auto Giant," *New York Times,* September 25, 1999, p. C1; Joann Muller, "Lessons from a Casualty of the Culture Wars," *Business Week,* November 29, 1999, p. 198; Joann Muller, Kathleen Kerwin, and Jack Ewing, "Man with a Plan," *Business Week,* October 4, 1999, p. 34; Dorothee Ostle, "Daimler Could Have Examined Chrysler," *Automotive News Europe,* May 21, 2001, p. 1; Christine Tierney, Matt Karnitschnig, and Joann Muller, "Defiant Daimler," *Business Week,* August 7, 2000, pp. 90–94.

9. Christine Tierney and Ken Belson, "Mitsubishi: Conquest or Quicksand for Daimler?" *Business Week,* September 25, 2000, p. 62.

10. Maria Maher and Thomas Anderson, *Corporate Governance: Effects on Firm Performance and Economic Growth* (Paris: Organization for Economic Cooperation and Development, 1999).

11. A. Demb and F. F. Neubauer, *The Corporate Board: Confronting the Paradoxes* (Oxford: Oxford University Press, 1992).

12. Maher and Anderson, *Corporate Governance.*

13. Organization for Economic Cooperation and Development, *The OECD Principles of Corporate Governance* (Paris: Organization for Economic Cooperation and Development, 1999).

14. Edward A. Stolzenberg, "Governance Change for Public Hospitals," *Journal of Healthcare Management* 45 (September–October 2000): 347–350; Jeffrey A. Alexander, Bryan J. Weiner, and Richard J. Bogue, "Changes in the Structure, Composition, and Activity of Hospital Governing Boards, 1989–1997: Evidence from Two National Surveys," *Milbank Quarterly* 79 (May 2001): 253–279.

15. World Bank Group, "About Corporate Governance," http://www.worldbank.org/html/fpd/privatesector/ cg/, accessed January 16, 2003.

16. Clive Crook, "Why Good Corporate Citizens Are a Public Menace," *National Journal,* April 24, 1999, p. 1087.

17. Robert A. G. Monks, *Corporate Governance in the Twenty-First Century: A Preliminary Outline* (Portland, ME: LENS, Inc, 1996), available at www.lens-library.com/ info/cg21.html.

18. McRitchie, "Ending the Wall Street Walk."

19. David A. Cifrino and Garrison R. Smith, "NYSE and NASDAQ Propose to Review Corporate Governance Listing Standards," *Corporate Governance Advisor* 10 (November–December 2002): 18–25.

20. Ronald E. Berenbeim, *The Corporate Board: A Growing Role in Strategic Assessment* (New York: Conference Board, 1996).

21. Melvin A. Eisenberg, "Corporate Governance: The Board of Directors and Internal Control," *Cordoza Law Review* 19 (September–November 1997): 237.

22. "TD Bank Splits CEO and Chairman Roles," *Toronto Star,* December 21, 2002, p. D3; John A. Byrne, "This Corporate Reform Lacks Spine," *Business Week Online,* January 13, 2003, http://www.businessweek.com/bwdaily/dnflash/jan2003/nf20030110_4900.htm, accessed January 17, 2003; Joann Lublin, "Splitting Posts of Chairman, CEO Catches On," *Wall Street Journal,* November 11, 2002, pp. B1, B3.

23. Jennifer Reingold, "Dot.Com Boards Are Flouting the Rules," *Business Week,* December 20, 1999, pp. 130–134.

24. Louis Lavelle, "The Best and Worst Boards," *Business Week,* October 7, 2002, p. 104; McKinsey & Company, *McKinsey Director Opinion Survey on Corporate Governance, 2002,* http://www.mckinsey.com/practices/corporategovernance/PDF/DirectorOpinion.pdf, accessed January 17, 2003.

25. Louis Lavelle, "The Best and Worst Boards," *Business Week,* October 7, 2002, p. 104; Gretchen Morgenson, "Shares of Corporate Nice Guys Can Finish First," *The New York Times,* April 27, 2003, p. 1; Peter Stanwick and Sarah Stanwick, "The Relationship Between Corporate Governance and Financial Performance: An Empirical Study," *Journal of Corporate Citizenship* 8 (Winter 2002): 35–48.

26. Louis Lavelle, "The Best and Worst Boards," *Business Week,* October 7, 2002, p. 104.

27. Adrian Cadbury, "What Are the Trends in Corporate Governance? How Will They Impact Your Company?" *Long Range Planning* 32 (January 1999): 12–19.

28. "How Shareholder Proposals Work," The Equality Project, http://www.equalityproject.org/how.htm#do, accessed January 14, 2003; Barry Burr, "Shareholder Activism Hot in Poor Business Climate," *Pensions & Investments,* July 8, 2002, pp. 4, 32; Jake Ulick, "Anger Rising Over CEO Pay," *CNN/Money,* April 21, 2003, http://money.cnn.com/2003/04/21/news/proxy_season/, accessed August 7, 2003.

29. Mark Anderson, "W. R. Grace Settles Shareholder Suit Led by CalPERS," *Sacramento Business Journal,* October 29, 1999, p. 12; "CalPERS Settles Lawsuit with W. R. Grace & Co.," CalPERS, press release, October 13, 1999, www.calpers-governance.org/news/1999/1013a.asp.

30. "Shareholder Resolution Process," Calvert Group, Ltd, http://www.calvert.com/sri_649.html, accessed August 12, 2003.

31. Peter D. Kinder, Steven D. Lyndenberg, and Amy L. Domini, *The Social Investment Almanac* (New York: Holt, 1992).

32. "Companies Fail Social Investors, Most Investors Value Corporate Responsibility, Few Are Satisfied," *Investor Relations Business,* August 6, 2001, pp. 1, 13; SocialFunds.com/Motley Fool, "Investor Survey on Corporate Responsibility," http://www.socialfunds.com/page.cgi/fool_results.html, accessed September 16, 2003.

33. Susan Scherreik, "Following Your Conscience Is Just a Few Clicks Away," *Business Week,* May 13, 2002, pp. 116–118.

34. B. Langtry, "The Ethics of Shareholding," *Journal of Business Ethics* 37 (May 2002): 175–185.

35. R. Bruce Hutton, Louis D'Antonio, and Tommi Johnsen, "Socially Responsible Investing: Growing Issues and New Opportunities," *Business and Society* 37 (September 1998): 281–305.

36. William Baue, "Corporate Responsibility Ratings and SRI Screens Sometimes Differ," SocialFunds.com, http://www.socialfunds.com/news/article.cgi?sfArticleId=1007, accessed August 13, 2003.

37. Barry B. Burr, "Social Investing Tops $2 Trillion," *Pensions & Investments,* November 15, 1999, p. 8.

38. Robert A. G. Monks, "What Will Be the Impact of Active Shareholders? A Practical Recipe for Constructive Change," *Long Range Planning* 32 (January 1999): 20–27.

39. "An Institutional Investor Models Democratic Governance," *Business Ethics* 13 (September–October, November–December 1999): 29.

40. "Worth Noting: At Random," ibid., p. 5.

41. "Proposal for Socially Responsible Investment by Colleges and Universities," Student Alliance to Reform Corporations, http://www.starcalliance.org/assets/sri/starcsri.doc, accessed August 7, 2003. Reprinted with permission from the STARC Alliance.

42. "Annual Eaton Vance Investor Survey Shows Unshaken Faith In Capitalism; Confidence in Corporate Management and Wall Street Dips," *Business Wire,* January 7, 2003, accessed via LexisNexis; David Schepp, "US Urged to Lift Investor Confidence," *BBC News Online,* September 27, 2002, http://news.bbc.co.uk/2/hi/business/2285847.stm, accessed January 14, 2003.

43. "Baptist Leader's Conviction Implies Lack of Board Oversight," *Board Members* 8 (March 1999): 2; "Ex-National Baptist Convention Exec Gets 21-Month Sentence," *Jet,* November 15, 1999, p. 38; John Gibeaut, "Raising a Holy Racket," *ABA Journal* 85 (January 1999): 50; "Lyons Found Guilty," *Christian Century,* March 17, 1999, p. 302.

44. "Internal Auditors: Integral to Good Corporate Governance," *Internal Auditor* 59 (August 2002): 44–49.

45. Eisenberg, "Corporate Governance."

46. Kathy Hoke, "Eyes Wide Open," *Business First–Columbus,* August 27, 1999, pp. 27–28.

47. Ray A. Goldberg, "Kraft General Foods: Risk Management Philosophy," (Boston: Harvard Business School Press, 1994).

48. Jim Billington, "A Few Things Every Manager Ought to Know about Risk," *Harvard Management Update,* March 1997, pp. 10–11; Lee Puschaver and Robert G. Eccles, "In Pursuit of the Upside: The New Opportunity in Risk Management," *PW Review,* December 1996.

49. Scott Alexander, "Achieving Enterprisewide Privacy Compliance," *Insurance & Technology* 25 (November 2000): 53; M. Joseph Sirgy and Chenting Su, "The Ethics of Consumer Sovereignty in an Age of High Tech," *Journal of Business Ethics* 28 (November 2000): 1–14.

50. "How To Pay Bosses," *The Economist*, November 16, 2002, p. 60; Charles Elson, "What's Wrong With Executive Compensation?" *Harvard Business Review* 81 (January 2003): 5–12; Roger L. Martin, "Taking Stock," *Harvard Business Review* 81 (January 2002): 19.

51. "How Business Rates: By the Numbers," in "Too Much Corporate Power?" Aaron Bernstein, *Business Week*, September 11, 2000, pp. 148–149.

52. Don Bauder, "Study Blames Excessive Pay on Stock Options," *Copley News Service*, August 26, 2002, accessed via LexisNexis, January 16, 2003; Alison Grant, "Companies Now Under Suspicion Paid Well; CEOs Got 70 Percent More Than Average," *Plain Dealer*, August 26, 2002, p. E1.

53. "What We Learned in 2002," *Business Week*, December 30, 2002, p. 170.

54. Sarah Anderson, John Cavanagh, Ralph Estes, Chuck Collins, and Chris Hartman, *A Decade of Executive Excess: The 1990s Sixth Annual Executive Compensation Survey* (Boston: United for a Fair Economy, 1999).

55. Louis Lavelle, "CEO Pay, The More Things Change . . . ," *Business Week*, October 16, 2000, pp. 106–108.

56. Jeremy Kahn, "A CEO Cuts His Own Pay," *Fortune*, October 26, 1998, pp. 56–58.

57. Crystal Graef, "If Kodak Employees Have to Bite the Bullet, Why Not the CEO?" *South Florida Business Journal*, December 12, 1997, p. 23; Jake Ulick, "Anger Rising Over CEO Pay," *CNN/Money*, April 21, 2003, http://money.cnn.com/2003/04/21/news/proxy_season/, accessed August 7, 2003.

58. Carolyn Said, "Mutual Funds Forced to Be More Judicious," *San Francisco Chronicle*, August 3, 2002, http://seattlepi.nwsource.com/money/81188_fundstrategy03.shtml, accessed January 14, 2003; Gary Strauss, "Scandal Further Decimates Investor Confidence," *USA Today*, June 27, 2002, http://www.usatoday.com/money/general/2002/06/27/confidence.htm, accessed August 13, 2003.

59. Conference Board Commission on Public Trust and Private Enterprise, *Findings and Recommendations, Part 1: Executive Compensation* (New York: Conference Board, 2002), http://www.conference-board.org/pdf_free/756.pdf, accessed January 16, 2003; Lucian Bebchuk and Jesse Fried, "Improving Executive Compensation," *TIAA-CREF Investment Forum* (June 2003): 11–12.

60. Stephen M. Davis, "Global Governance: How Nations Compare," *Corporate Board* 20 (September–October 1999): 5–9.

61. "Measuring Corporate Governance Standards," *Asiamoney* 11 (December 2000–January 2001): 94–95.

62. Barbara Crutchfield George, Kathleen A. Lacey, and Jotta Birmele, "The 1998 OECD Convention," *American Business Law Journal* 37 (Spring 2000): 485–525; Ira Millstein, "Corporate Governance: The Role of Market Forces," *OECD Observer* (Summer 2000): 27–28; "What Is OECD," Organization for Economic Cooperation and Development, http://www.oecd.org/pdf/M00008000/M00008299.pdf, accessed January 10, 2003.

63. Davis Global Advisors, *Leading Corporate Governance Indicators™ 2002: An International Comparison*, Newton, MA, November 2002.

64. "Asian Capitalism: The End of Tycoons," *The Economist*, April 29, 2000, pp. 67–69; "The Importance of Corporate Governance," *Asiamoney* 10 (December 1999–January 2000): 92–94; "The Lost (Half) Decade—East Asian Economies," *The Economist*, July 6, 2002, via Lexis-Nexis.

65. "Cost of Workplace Regulation," *USA Today*, October 24, 2001, p. 1B.

66. Adam M. Brandenburger and Barry J. Nalebuff, *Co-opetition: 1. A Revolutionary Mindset That Redefines Competition and Cooperation; 2. The Game Theory Strategy That's Changing the Game of Business* (New York: Doubleday, 1997).

67. Maher and Anderson, *Corporate Governance*.

68. Monks, *Corporate Governance in the Twenty-First Century*.

69. "Three Skills for Today's Leaders," *Harvard Management Update* 4 (November 1999): 11.

70. Catherine M. Daily, Dan R. Dalton, and Albert A. Cannella, Jr., "Corporate Governance: A Decade of Dialogue and Data," *Academy of Management Review* 28 (July 2003): 371–382.

71. "The Way We Govern Now—Corporate Boards," *The Economist*, January 11, 2003, pp. 59–61; Carol Hymowitz, "How to Fix a Broken System," *Wall Street Journal*, February 24, 2003, pp. R1–R3.

72. Monks, *Corporate Governance in the Twenty-First Century*.

Chapter 7

1. Salesforce.com/foundation, http://www.salesforcefoundation.org/, accessed August 22, 2003; "The World Leader in CRM," salesforce.com, http://www.salesforce.com/us/company/, accessed January 3, 2003; Stewart Alsop, "A Bet on a Dead Business Model," *Fortune*, July 8, 2002, p. 46; Mark Benioff, "The End of Philanthropy: A New Model for Globalization," *Nonprofit World* 20 (September–October 2002): 31–35; Linda Tischler, "Vote of Confidence," *Fast Company* 65 (December 2002): 102.

2. Al Kelman and Barb Failer, "Sizing Up the Competition," *Chain Store Age* 78 (October 2002): 30; Jack Neff, "It's Not Trendy Being Green," *Advertising Age*, April 10, 2000, pp. 16–18; "Whole Foods Market Reminds Consumers That How Their Food Tastes Has Everything to Do with How It Is Grown," *CSR Newswire*, January 3, 2003, http://www.csrwire.com/article.cgi/1494.html, accessed January 3, 2003.

3. "Looking for Something to Get Angry About," *The Economist.com/Global Agenda*, November 29, 2002, p. 1; Debra Goldman, "Consumer Republic," *Adweek*, November 25, 2002, p. 16.

4. Consumers International, www.consumers-international.org/, accessed August 19, 2003.

5. "World Consumer Rights Day," Consumers International, http://www.consumersinternational.org/News_Events/world.asp?cat=22&regionid=135, accessed January 3, 2003.

6. "Consumer Charter for Global Business," Consumers International, www.consumersinternational.org/, accessed January 3, 2003.

7. M. Joseph Sirgy and Chenting Su, "The Ethics of Consumer Sovereignty in an Age of High Tech," *Journal of Business Ethics* 28 (January 2000): 1–14.

8. Lee E. Norrgard and Julia M. Norrgard, *Consumer Fraud: A Reference Handbook* (New York: ABC-Clio, 1998); Ernie Scarbrough, "Ethics in Business Is a 'Two-Way' Street," *Phoenix Business Journal*, September 3, 1999, p. 71.

9. David M. Gardner, Jim Harris, and Junyong Kim, "The Fraudulent Consumer," in *Marketing and Public Policy Conference Proceedings,* ed. Gregory Gundlach, William Wilkie, and Patrick Murphy (Chicago: American Marketing Association, 1999), pp. 48–54.

10. Richard C. Hollinger and Jason L. Davis, *2001 National Retail Security Survey,* 10th ed. (Gainesville: University of Florida, 2001).

11. Christine Doyle, "How to Beat Cellulite—Part Two: Do Anti-Cellulite Creams, Lotions and Massage Really Work, or Do Women Just Like to Think They Do?" *Ottawa Citizen,* May 23, 2000, p. D8; Kristin Hohenadel and Sasha Emmons, "Smoothing Away Age, Time," *Advertising Age,* September 9, 1996, p. 1; Anne Stein, "Can Anything Conquer Cellulite?" MSNBC, January 18, 2000, www.msnbc.com/news/357076.asp, accessed January 18, 2000.

12. "Top 10 Consumer Complaints in Survey," *Associated Press,* November 21, 2002, via LexisNexis; Sandy Kleffman, "Identity Theft Still No. 1 Consumer Fraud Complaint of Californians," *Contra Costa Times,* November 22, 2002, accessed via LexisNexis, August 19, 2003.

13. "Bureau of Consumer Protection," Federal Trade Commission, www.ftc.gov/bcp/bcp.htm, accessed September 30, 2003.

14. "Seven Internet Retailers Settle FTC Charges Over Shipping Delays During 1999 Holiday Season," Federal Trade Commission, July 26, 2000, www.ftc.gov/opa/2000/07/toolate.htm, accessed August 1, 2000; "FTC 'Surf' of 63 Internet Retailers Designed to Bolster Consumer Confidence During the Holiday Season," Federal Trade Commission, November 29, 2002, http://www.ftc.gov/opa/2002/11/2002holidaysurf.htm, accessed August 19, 2003.

15. Chris Tucker, "Welcome to the Cybermall," *Spirit,* November 2000, pp. 66–70, 168–169.

16. "Consumer and Governmental Affairs Bureau," Federal Communications Commission, www.fcc.gov/cib/, accessed January 6, 2003.

17. "Consumer Brochures," Iowa Attorney General, www.state.ia.us/government/ag/brochure.htm, accessed January 6, 2003.

18. Roger L. Miller and Gaylord A. Jentz, *Business Law Today* (Cincinnati, OH: West Legal Studies in Business, 2000).

19. Robert B. Downs, "Afterward," in *The Jungle,* Upton Sinclair (New York: New American Library, 1960).

20. "Manufacturers Pay $460,000 in Civil Penalties," *Consumer Product Litigation Reporter* 11 (June 2000): 15.

21. "Fair Housing 2000: An Interview with Eva M. Plaza," *Journal of Housing and Community Development* 57 (March–April 2000): 14–21.

22. "Sweepstakes Giant Agrees to $34 Million Settlement," CNN.com, June 27, 2001, http://www.cnn.com/2001/LAW/06/26/sweepstakes.lawsuit/index.html, accessed August 19, 2003; "Time Inc. Agrees to Refund $4.9 Million over Sweepstakes Mailings," CNN, August 24, 2000, www.cnn.com.

23. John Eggerton, "FTC Declares Diet Claims Have No Weight," *Broadcasting & Cable,* November 25, 2002, p.7; Travis E. Poling, "Body Solutions Maker Accused of Fattened Claims," *San Antonio Express-News,* December 6, 2002, p. 1A.

24. Monica Soto, "Federal Laws Have Wine Sellers Over a Barrel," *Seattle Times,* July 18, 2000, p. 5B.

25. Leslie Kane, "What to Do If Your New Car's a Lemon," *Medical Economics,* May 11, 1998, pp. 105–111.

26. Michael Bradford, "New South Korean Law May Bring Increased Product Liability Claims," *Business Insurance,* April 22, 2002, pp. 29–30.

27. Christine Gorman, "Diabetes Recall," *Time,* April 3, 2000, p. 94.

28. Thomas H. Kister, "General Aviation Revitalization Act: Its Effect on Manufacturers," *Defense Counsel Journal* 65 (January 1998): 109–115.

29. O. C. Ferrell and Geoffrey Hirt, *Business: A Changing World,* 3rd ed. (Boston: McGraw-Hill/Irwin, 2000), p. 38.

30. Sandra N. Hurd, Peter Shears, and Frances E. Zollers, "Consumer Law," *Journal of Business Law* (May 2000): 262–277.

31. Irene M. Kunii, "Stand Up and Fight," *Business Week,* September 11, 2000, pp. 54–55.

32. Suk-ching Ho, "Executive Insights: Growing Consumer Power in China," *Journal of International Marketing* 9 (Spring 2001): 64–84.

33. "Agreement Reached on EU-Wide Beef Labeling Rules," July 18, 2000, and "Final Conclusions on Geographical BSE Risk," *EUBusiness,* August 1, 2000, www.eubusiness.com/consumer/index.html, accessed August 1, 2000.

34. Kenneth J. Meier, E. Thomas Garman, and Lael R. Keiser, *Regulation and Consumer Protection: Politics, Bureaucracy and Economics* (Houston, TX: Dame Publications, 1998).

35. Allan Asher, "Going Global: A New Paradigm for Consumer Protection," *Journal of Consumer Affairs* 32 (Winter 1998): 183–203; Benet Middleton, "Consumerism: A Pragmatic Ideology," *Consumer Policy Review* 8 (November–December 1998): 213–217; Audhesh Paswan and Jhinuk Chowdhury, "Consumer Protection Issues and

Non-governmental Organizations in a Developing Market," in *Developments in Marketing Science,* ed. Harlan E. Spotts and H. Lee Meadow (Coral Gables, FL: Academy of Marketing Science, 2000), pp. 171–176.

36. "On the Left: What Makes Ralph Run," *Business Week,* September 25, 2000, pp. 82, 86.

37. Paul N. Bloom and Stephen A. Greyser, "The Maturing of Consumerism," *Harvard Business Review* 59 (November–December 1981): 130–139.

38. Consumers Union, www.consumersunion.org/, accessed January 6, 2003; Rhoda H. Karpatkin, "Toward a Fair and Just Marketplace for All Consumers: The Responsibilities of Marketing Professionals," *Journal of Public Policy and Marketing* 18 (Spring 1999): 118–123.

39. "Empowerment to the Consumer," *Marketing Week,* October 21, 1999, p. 3; Pierre M. Loewe and Mark S. Bonchek, "The Retail Revolution," *Management Review* 88 (April 1999): 38–44.

40. "Consumer Bill of Rights and Responsibilities: Report to the President of the United States," Advisory Commission on Consumer Protection and Quality in the Health Care Industry, November 1997, www.hcqualitycommission. gov/cborr/; Mary Jane Fisher, "Pressure Mounts for Patient Rights Agreement," *National Underwriter/Life & Health Financial Services,* May 22, 2000, pp. 3–4; Michael Pretzer, "New Mind 'Patient Relations': Get Ready for 'Consumer Rights,'" *Medical Economics,* February 23, 1998, pp. 47–55.

41. "Comprehensive Consumer Rights Bill Addresses Bank Fees, Identity Theft," *Consumer Financial Services Law Report,* May 15, 2000, p. 2.

42. Nichole Christian, "Domino's Reaches Deal on Accusations of Bias," *New York Times,* June 7, 2000, p. A28; T. J. Degroat, "Domino's Revises Delivery Policy," DiversityInc., June 6, 2000, www.diversityinc.com.

43. Marianne Lavelle, "The States Take the Lead on Gun Control," *U.S. News & World Report,* April 17, 2000, p. 24.

44. Steve Jarvis, "They're Not Quitting," *Marketing News,* November 20, 2000, pp. 1, 9; Marianne Lavelle, "Big Tobacco Rises from the Ashes," *U.S. News & World Report,* November 13, 2000, p. 50; Nancy Shute, "Building a Better Butt," *U.S. News & World Report,* September 18, 2000, p. 66.

45. www.diversityinc.com; "Pirate's Booty: Too Good to Be True," *Washington Post,* February 19, 2002, p. F3; Paige Smoron, "Is Booty-licious Diet Food Part of a Large Conspiracy?" *Chicago Sun-Times,* April 18, 2002, p. 42.

46. A. Ben Oumlil and Alvin J. Williams, "Consumer Education Programs for Mature Consumers," *Journal of Services Marketing* 14, no. 3 (2000): 232–243; Lauren Paetsch, "URAC Accreditation Provides Benchmark for Health Information Web Sites," *Employee Benefit Plan Review* 56 (June 2002): 10–18.

47. Lyuba Pronina, "Top Firms Team Up to Create Consumer Telephone Hot Line," *Moscow Times,* November 29, 2000.

48. "Dispute Resolution," Better Business Bureau, http://www.dr.bbb.org/, accessed January 6, 2003.

49. Federal Trade Commission, *Privacy Online: Fair Information Practices in the Electronic Marketplace: A Federal Trade Commission Report to Congress* (Washington, DC: FTC, May 2000), also available at www.ftc.gov/reports/privacy2000/privacy2000.pdf.

50. "CMC Properties," Better Business Bureau International Torch Award, http://www.bbb.org/torchaward/cmc.asp, accessed January 2, 2003; "Four Businesses Honored with Prestigious International Award For Outstanding Marketplace Ethics," *PR Newswire,* September 23, 2002, via LexisNexis.

51. "12-Point Plan: Airline Customer Service Commitment," *Sky,* June 2000, p. 183, also available at www.delta-air.com/care/service_plan/index.jsp.

52. "Wal-Mart Bucks for Education," *Home Textiles Today,* June 5, 2000, p. 11; Mike France and Joann Muller, "A Site for Soreheads," *Business Week,* April 12, 1999, p. 86; Wendy Zellner, "Wal-Mart: Why an Apology Made Sense," *Business Week,* July 3, 2000, pp. 65–66; Wendy Zellner and Aaron Bernstein, "Up Against the Wal-Mart," *Business Week,* March 13, 2000, p. 76.

53. Damien McElroy, "Chinese Shun Toshiba in Anti-Japan Protests," (London) *Sunday Telegraph,* June 4, 2000, p. 27.

54. Andy Altman-Ohr, "World Boycott of Transamerica Launched," *Jewish Bulletin News of Northern California,* January 21, 2000, www.angelfire.com/biz4/consumerama/transam.htm, accessed January 21, 2000.

55. "The 1997 Cone/Roper Cause-Related Marketing Trends Report," *Business Ethics* 12 (March–April 1997): 14–16.

56. Edwin R. Stafford and Cathy L. Hartman, "Environmentalist-Business Collaborations: Social Responsibility, Green Alliances, and Beyond," in *Advertising Research: The Internet, Consumer Behavior and Strategy,* ed. George Zinkhan (Chicago: American Marketing Association, 2000), pp. 170–192.

57. Ken Terry, "New Patients Will Rate You Online," *Medical Economics,* April 24, 2000, pp. 42–49; Foundation for Accountability, www.facct.org, accessed August 19, 2003.

58. Sandra A. Waddock and Mary Ellen Boyle, "The Dynamics of Change in Corporate Community Relations," *California Management Review* 37 (Summer 1995): 125–138.

59. Robin Lee Allen, "Restaurant Neighbor Honorees Break Barriers, Link Communities," *Nation's Restaurant News,* October 9, 2000, p. 146.

60. American Productivity and Quality Center, *Community Relations: Unleashing the Power of Corporate Citizenship* (Houston, TX: American Productivity and Quality Center, 1998); Edmund M. Burke, *Corporate Community Relations: The Principle of the Neighbor of Choice* (Westport, CT: Praeger, 1999).

61. Bradley K. Googins, "Why Community Relations Is a Strategic Imperative," *Strategy & Business* (Third Quarter

1997): 14–16, also available at www.strategy-business.com/briefs/97311.

62. Churchill Downs, Inc., Community Relations, http://www.churchilldownsincorporated.com/community_relations/, accessed August 19, 2003.

63. "Community Involvement," Business for Social Responsibility, www.bsr.org/resourcecenter/, accessed December 4, 2000; Sandra A. Waddock and Mary-Ellen Boyle, "The Dynamics of Change in Corporate Community Relations," *California Management Review* 37 (Summer 1995): 125–138; Barron Wells and Nelda Spinks, "Communicating with the Community," *Career Development International* 4, no. 2 (1999): 108–116.

64. Noelle Haner-Dorr, "Women Who Mean Business," *Orlando Business Journal*, March 24, 2000, p. 37.

65. Dirk C. Gibson, "The Cyber-Revolution in Product Recall Public Relations," *Public Relations Quarterly* 45 (Summer 2000): 24–26.

66. Royal Weld, "Great Expectations," *Industry Week*, September 4, 2000, pp. 30–34.

67. "Community Involvement," Business for Social Responsibility; Janelia Moreno, "More Casas for the Workers," *Houston Chronicle*, March 4, 2001, p. Business 1.

68. "Community Needs Assessment Survey Guide," Utah State University Extension, http://extension.usu.edu/coop/comm/survey/survey.htm, accessed January 6, 2003.

69. Mitchel Benson, "Insurers Test Investments in Housing," *Wall Street Journal Interactive*, August 9, 2000, http://interactive.wsj.com, accessed August 9, 2000.

70. Thomas A. Klein and Robert W. Nason, "Marketing and Development: Macromarketing Perspectives," in *Handbook of Marketing and Society,* ed. Paul N. Bloom and Gregory T. Gunlach (Thousand Oaks, CA: Sage, 2001), pp. 263–297.

71. Tim O'Brien, "VisionLand's Food Vision: Local Suppliers, Low Cost," *Amusement Business,* June 8, 1998, p. 13.

72. H. W. Becherer, "A More Cosmopolitan Way of Life: Why Local Economic Development Matters," in *Vital Speeches of the Day* 66 (May 15, 2000): 473–475.

73. Gavin Souter, "Carefully Handling Layoffs Could Head off Lawsuits," *Business Insurance,* May 8, 2000, pp. 3–4.

74. "What's So Bad About a Living Wage?" *Business Week,* September 4, 2000, pp. 68–70; Kelly Candaele and Peter Dreier, "Wage War; Despite a Setback, Momentum for a Living Wage Increases," *In These Times,* December 23, 2002, p. 8; Barry Chiswick, "Boosting the Living Wage No Cure-All for Worker Woes," *Crain's Chicago Business,* November 25, 2002, p. 11.

75. Zellner and Bernstein, "Up Against the Wal-Mart," pp. 76–78.

76. David Kaplan, "Plant for Recycling Food Waste Planned," *Houston Chronicle,* February 13, 2001, p. Business 2; Rebecca Mowbray, "Turning Trash into Profits: An Entrepreneur's Plans to Turn Waste into Animal Feed Take the Community into Consideration," *Houston Chronicle,* August 1, 1999, p. 4D.

77. "Pizza Corner Aims at 100 Outlets," *India Business Insight,* March 10, 2001, accessed via LexisNexis January 2, 2003; Vaani Anand, "Building Blocks of Corporate Reputation: Social Responsibility Initiatives," *Corporate Reputation Review* 5 (Spring 2002): 71–74; Anu Chalwa, "Home Run, Business India," *Business India,* March 17, 2000, p. 1.

78. New Belgium Brewing Company, Inc., www.newbelgium.com, accessed January 6, 2003.

79. Diane E. Lewis, "Volunteering Is a Way of Life for Some and at Some Firms, It Is Something That Is Expected," *Minneapolis Star Tribune,* April 26, 1999, p. D8.

80. "About Employee Volunteering," National Centre for Volunteering, http://www.employeevolunteering.org.uk/about/essentials.htm, accessed August 19, 2003.

81. Bill Leonard, "Supporting Volunteerism as Individual Americans Invest More Hours into Volunteer Activities," *HR Magazine,* June 6, 1998, p. 4.

82. Lewis, "Volunteering Is a Way of Life for Some."

83. Ibid.

84. D'Arcy Doran, "Village Women Paralyze Oil Giant in Nigeria," *Associated Press Worldstream,* July 12, 2002, via LexisNexis.

85. James L. Creighton, "The Utility as Civic Partner," *Public Utilities Fortnightly,* June 15, 2000, pp. 32–38.

Chapter 8

1. "SAS Marks 5th Straight Top 10 Ranking in FORTUNE's List of 100 Best Companies to Work For," SAS Institute, http://www.sas.com/news/preleases/012102/news2.html, accessed January 6, 2003; Michelle Conlin and Kathy Moore, "Dr. Goodnight's Company Town," *Fortune,* June 19, 2000, pp. 192–202; "Our Company," SAS Institute, www.sas.com/corporate/index.html, accessed January 6, 2003; Robert Levering and Milton Moskowitz, "The 100 Best Companies to Work For," *Fortune,* February 4, 2002, pp. 72–73; Karen Govel McDermott, "Walking the Talk at SAS Institute," *Nation's Restaurant News* 3 (June 2000): 38; Lance Secretan, "Customer Connections," *Industry Week,* May 15, 2000, p. 25; Thomas Watson, "Goodnight, Sweet Prince," *Canadian Business,* May 27, 2002, pp. 77–78.

2. Joanne B. Ciulla, *The Working Life: The Promise and Betrayal of Modern Work* (New York: Times Books, 2000).

3. Ciulla, *The Working Life;* Adriano Tilgher, *Work: What It Has Meant to Men Through the Ages,* trans. Dorothy Canfield Fisher (New York: Harcourt, Brace & World, 1958).

4. These facts are derived from Brenda Paik Sunoo, "Relying on Faith to Rebuild a Business," *Workforce* 78 (March 1999): 54–59.

5. Karen Sarkis, "Injured Workers File Claim with Malden Mills," *Occupational Hazards* 62 (February 2000): 16.

6. Sunoo, "Relying on Faith to Rebuild a Business"; Justin Pope, "Malden Mills Emerges from the Bankruptcy, Still

Under Financial Cloud," *Houston Chronicle,* August 15, 2003, p. B1. Janet B. Rodie, "Textile World News," *Textile World* 152 (January 2002): 12.

7. "Worldatwork Finds One-Third of Companies Downsized After 9/11," *Report on Salary Surveys* 2 (December 2002): 12; Stephanie Armour, "Companies Chisel Away at Workers' Benefits," *USA Today,* November 18, 2002, pp. 1B–3B; Michelle Conlin, Peter Coy, Ann Therese Palmer, and Gabrielle Saveri, "The Wild New Workforce," *Business Week,* December 6, 1999, pp. 38–44.

8. Ian Kessler, "Exploring Reciprocity Through the Lens of the Psychological Contract: Employee and Employer Perspectives," *European Journal of Work & Organization Psychology* 11 (March 2002): 69–86; Denise M. Rousseau, *Psychological Contracts in Organizations: Understanding Written and Unwritten Agreements* (Thousand Oaks, CA: Sage, 1995).

9. Jacqueline Coyle-Shapiro, "A Psychological Contract Perspective on Organizational Citizenship Behavior," *Journal of Organizational Behavior* 23 (December 2002): 927–946; William H. Turnley and Daniel C. Feldman, "The Impact of Psychological Contract Violations on Exit, Voice, Loyalty, and Neglect," *Human Relations* 52 (July 1999): 895–922.

10. Ibid.

11. "Formal Communication Boosts Shareholder Value," *IRS Employment Review,* October 21, 2002, p. 5; Kimberly D. Elsbach and Greg Elafson, "How the Packaging of Decision Explanations Affects Perceptions of Trustworthiness," *Academy of Management Journal* 43 (February 2000): 80–89; David E. Guest and Neil Conway, "Communicating the Psychological Contract: An Employer Perspective," *Human Resource Management Journal* 12, no. 2 (2002): 22–38.

12. Gillian Flynn, "Looking Back on 100 Years of Employment Law," *Workforce* 78 (November 1999): 74–77.

13. "A Guru Ahead of Her Time," *Nation's Business* 85 (May 1997): 24.

14. Steve Sayer, "Cleaning Up the Jungle," *Occupational Health & Safety* 66 (May 1997): 22.

15. Flynn, "Looking Back on 100 Years of Employment Law."

16. "Employee Relations in America," *IRS Employment Review* (March 1997): E7–E12; Roger LeRoy Miller and Gaylord A. Jentz, *Business Law Today* (Cincinnati, OH: West Legal Studies in Business, 2000).

17. C. Wright Mills, *White Collar: The American, Middle Classes* (New York: Oxford University Press, 1951).

18. Ciulla, *The Working Life;* William H. Whyte, *The Organization Man* (New York: Simon & Schuster, 1956).

19. *Work in America: Report of a Special Task Force to the Secretary of Health, Education, and Welfare* (Cambridge, MA: MIT Press, 1973).

20. Ciulla, *The Working Life.*

21. Taina Savolainen, "Leadership Strategies for Gaining Business Excellence Through Total Quality Management: A Finnish Case Study," *Total Quality Management* 11 (March 2000): 211–226.

22. "Younger Employees Want Security," *USA Today,* October 3, 2001, p. 1B.

23. This section is adapted from Debbie Thorne LeClair, "The Ups and Downs of Rightsizing the Workplace," *ABACA Profile,* November–December 1999, p. 25.

24. Priti Pradhan Shah, "Network Destruction: The Structural Implications of Downsizing," *Academy of Management Journal* 43 (February 2000): 101–112.

25. *New York Times Special Report: The Downsizing of America* (New York: Times Books, 1996); Victor B. Wayhan and Steve Werner, "The Impact of Workforce Reductions on Financial Performance: A Longitudinal Perspective," *Journal of Management* 26 (2000): 341–363; Jennifer Laabs, "The New Loyalty: Grasp It, Earn It, Keep It," *Workforce* 77 (November 1998): 34–39.

26. Harry J. Van Buren, III, "The Bindingness of Social and Psychological Contracts: Toward a Theory of Social Responsibility in Downsizing," *Journal of Business Ethics* 25 (January 2000): 205–219.

27. Steve Beigbeder, "Easing Workforce Reduction," *Risk Management* 47 (May 2000): 26–30; Matthew Camardella, "Legal Considerations of Workforce Reduction," *Employment Relations Today* 29 (Autumn 2002): 101–106.

28. Robert A. Nozar, "Nashville's Hot Job Market May Absorb Opryland Cuts," *Hotel and Motel Management* 214 (August 1999): 4, 40.

29. Angelo J. Kinicki, Gregory E. Prussia, and Francis M. McKee-Ryan, "A Panel Study of Coping with Involuntary Job Loss," *Academy of Management Journal* 43 (February 2000): 90–100.

30. Wayhan and Werner, "The Impact of Workforce Reductions on Financial Performance."

31. Nicholas Stein, "Winning the War to Keep Top Talent," *Fortune,* May 29, 2000, pp. 132–138.

32. Kathleen Melymuka, "Showing the Value of Brainpower," *Computerworld,* March 27, 2000, pp. 58–59; Milton Moskowitz and Robert Levering, "Best Companies to Work For: 10 Great Companies in Europe," *Fortune,* February 4, 2002, www.fortune.com/lists/bestcompanies/ ten_great.html, accessed November 22, 2002.

33. Carlyn Kolker, "Survivor Blues," *American Lawyer* 24 (October 2002): 116–118; Kyle Dover, "Watch the External Traps," *Management Review* 88 (January 1999): 54; Susan Reynolds Fisher and Margaret A. White, "Downsizing in a Learning Organization," *Academy of Management Review* 25 (January 2000): 244–251.

34. Susan Beck, "What to Do Before You Say 'You're Outta Here,'" *Business Week,* December 8, 1997, p. 6.

35. U.S. Department of Labor, Employment Law Guide. http://www.dol.gov/asp/programs/ EmpLawGuideFINAL.pdf, accessed October 2, 2003.

36. "Minimum Wage Laws in the States," U.S. Department of Labor, http://www.dol.gov/esa/minwage/america.htm, accessed August 21, 2003; Miller and Jentz, *Business Law Today.*

37. Flynn, "Looking Back on 100 Years of Employment Law."

38. Robert J. Nobile, "HR's Top 10 Legal Issues," *HR Focus* 74 (April 1997): 19–20.

39. Miller and Jentz, *Business Law Today.*

40. Flynn, "Looking Back on 100 Years of Employment Law."

41. Peter Elstrom, "Needed: A New Union for the New Economy," *Business Week,* September 4, 2000, p. 48; Tim Stentiford and David L. Young, "Case Study: Verizon Wireless Delivers On Its HR Web Site," *Employee Benefit Plan Review* 57 (November 2002): 43.

42. *The New OSHA: Reinventing Worker Safety and Health* (Washington, DC: U.S. Department of Labor, Occupational Safety and Health Administration, 1995), available at http://www.osha.gov/doc/outreachtraining/htmlfiles/newosha.html; Dana E. Corbin, "Speaking Their Language," *Occupational Health & Safety* 71 (July 2002): 32.

43. Judith N. Mottl, "Industry Fights OSHA's Proposed Ergonomic Rule," *Informationweek,* June 19, 2000, p. 122; Daniel R. Miller, "OSHA Goes Too Far with Ergonomics Rules," *National Underwriter,* May 8, 2000, p. 59; John D. Schulz, "Trucking Wants Out," *Traffic World,* May 29, 2000, pp. 21–22; Robin Suttell, "Healthy Work," *Buildings* 96 (October 2002): 56–58.

44. "Workplace Violence," Occupational Safety and Health Administration, http://www.osha-slc.gov/SLTC/workplaceviolence/index.html, accessed September 30, 2003.

45. Karen Sarkis, "Workplace Violence Top Concern for Employers," *Occupational Hazards* 62 (June 2000): 23; Sarah J. Smith, "Workplace Violence," *Professional Safety* 47 (November 2002): 34–43.

46. *Fear and Violence in the Workplace: A Survey Documenting the Experiences of American Workers* (Minneapolis, MN: Northwestern National Life Insurance Company, 1993).

47. Cal/OSHA Guidelines for Workplace Security (State of California, 1995), available at http://www.dir.ca.gov/dosh/dosh%5Fpublications/worksecurity.html.

48. Anonymous and Andrew R. Thomas, *Crisis in the Skies,* (Amherst, NY: Prometheus, 2001); Irene Korn, "Emergency Training," *Successful Meetings* 51 (November 2002): 35; Steve Rubenstein, "Flight Attendants Fight 'Air Rage,'" *San Francisco Chronicle,* July 7, 2000, p. A2;

49. "Suspect in Honolulu Shooting Spree Faces First-Degree Murder Charges," CNN, November 3, 1999, www.cnn.com; "Xerox Hawaii Cited Unsafe in Connection with Mass Shooting," CNN, November 7, 2000, www.cnn.com.

50. Richard V. Denenberg and Mark Braverman, *The Violence-Prone Workplace: A New Approach to Dealing with Hostile, Threatening, and Uncivil Behavior* (Ithaca, NY: Cornell University Press, 1999); Robert Grossman, "Bulletproof Practices," *HR Magazine* 47 (November 2002): 34–42; Bill Merrick, "Make Work a Safe Place," *Credit Union Magazine* 66 (June 2000): 19.

51. Carrie Coolidge, "Risky Business," *Forbes,* January 6, 2003, p. 54; John Leming, "New Product Covers Losses Related to Workplace Violence," *Journal of Commerce,* April 6, 2000, p. 15.

52. Judy Greenwald, "Employers Confront AIDS in Africa," *Business Insurance* 35 (July 23, 2001): 15.

53. "What Affirmative Action Is (And What It Is Not)," National Partnership, www.nationalpartnership.org/workandfamily/workplace/affirmact/aa_whatitis.htm, accessed November 1, 2001.

54. "What Is Affirmative Action?" HR Content Library, October 12, 2001, www.hrnext.com/content/view.cfm?articles_id=2007&subs_id=32.

55. "Facts About Sexual Harassment," U.S. Equal Employment Opportunity Commission, www.eeoc.gov/facts/fs-sex.html, accessed October 1, 2003.

56. Donald J. Petersen and Douglas P. Massengill, "Sexual Harassment Cases Five Years After *Meritor Savings Bank v. Vinson,*" *Employee Relations Law Journal* 18 (Winter 1992–1993): 489–516.

57. Maria E. Conway, "Sexual Harassment Abroad," *Workforce* 77 (September 1998): 8–9.

58. "EU Bids to Outlaw Sexual Harassment at the Workplace," European Commission, press release, June 7, 2000, www.eubusiness.com/employ/index.html; "EU Tightens Rules on Sexual Harassment at Work," EU Business, http://www.eubusiness.com/imported/2002/04/78499/view, accessed October 1, 2003.

59. Robert D. Lee and Paul S. Greenlaw, "The Legal Evolution of Sexual Harassment," *Public Administration Review* 55 (July 1995): 357–364.

60. Ibid.

61. George D. Mesritz, "Hostile Environment Sexual Harassment Claims: When Once Is Enough," *Employee Relations Law Journal* 22 (Spring 1997): 79–85; Laura Hoffman Roppe, "*Harris v. Forklift Systems, Inc.*: Victory or Defeat?" *San Diego Law Review* 32 (Winter 1996): 321–342.

62. Joann Muller, "Ford: The High Cost of Harassment," *Business Week,* November 15, 1999, pp. 94–96.

63. "Mitsubishi Agrees to $34 Million Sexual Harassment Settlement," *Business Week,* June 15, 1998, pp. 1–3; Samuel Greengard, "Zero Tolerance: Making It Work," *Workforce* 78 (May 1999): 28–34.

64. Jonathan W. Dion, "Putting Employers on the Defense: The Supreme Court Develops a Consistent Standard Regarding an Employer's Liability for a Supervisor's Hostile Work Environment Sexual Harassment," *Wake Forest Law Review* 34 (Spring 1999): 199–227; Darlene Orlov and Michael T. Roumell, *What Every Manager Needs to Know About Sexual Harassment* (New York: Amacom, 1999).

65. Richard Korman, David Kohn, Stephen H. Daniels, and Janice I. Dixon, "The Jokes Aren't Very Funny Anymore," *Engineering News Record,* September 7, 1998, p. 26.

66. This section is adapted from Randy Chiu, Richard Tansey, Debbie Thorne, and Michael White, "Is Procedural Justice the Dominant Whistleblowing Motive Among Employees?" submitted to *Journal of Applied Psychology,* June 2000.

67. J. P. Near and M. P. Miceli, "Organizational Dissidence: The Case of Whistleblowing," *Journal of Business Ethics* 4 (January 1985): 1–16.

68. Nancy Klingener, "Case Ends Utility Suit, but Plane Crash Still a Mystery," *Miami Herald,* May 8, 1991, p. B4.

69. Ron Ruggles, "Education, Training Is Beneficial to Employees 'Knowing It All' About Industry," *Nation's Restaurant News,* October 16, 2000, pp. 80, 162.

70. Jill Schachner Chanen, "You Rang, Sir?" *ABA Journal* 86 (October 2000): 82–84.

71. Jennifer Brown, "Employees Leave Managers, Not Organizations," *Computing Canada* 27 (April 6, 2001): 25.

72. Betsy Cummings, "Training's Top Five," *Successful Meetings* 49 (October 2000): 67–73; Adam J. Grossberg, "The Effect of Formal Training on Employment Duration," *Industrial Relations* 39 (October 2000): 578–599; Kathryn Tyler, "Extending the Olive Branch," *HR Magazine* 47 (November 2002): 85–89.

73. "ASTD Highlights International Training Trends in Its 2002 International Comparisons Report," American Society for Training and Development, http://www1.astd.org/pressRoom/pdf/ICRreport.pdf, accessed October 1, 2003.

74. "Diversity: A 'New' Tool for Retention," *HR Focus* 77 (June 2000): 1, 14.

75. Vijay Govindarajan and Anil K. Gupta, "Building an Effective Global Business Team," *MIT Sloan Management Review* 42 (Summer 2001): 63–71; Robin Kramer, "Managing Diversity: Beyond Affirmative Action in Australia," *Women in Management Review* 13, no. 4 (1998): 133–142.

76. "Use This Checklist To Rate and Improve Your Law Firm's Diversity Program," *Law Office Management & Administration Report* 3 (January 2003): 2–3; Peggy Layne, "Best Practices in Managing Diversity," *Leadership & Management in Engineering* 2 (October 2002): 28–30; Rose Mary Wentling and Nilda Palma-Rivas, "Current Status of Diversity Initiatives in Selected Multinational Corporations," *Human Resource Development Quarterly* 11 (Spring 2000): 35–60.

77. Marilyn Loden and Judith B. Rosener, *Workforce America! Managing Employee Diversity as a Vital Resource* (Burr Ridge, IL: McGraw-Hill Irwin Irwin/McGraw-Hill, 1991).

78. "Diversity Low Priority Reaps Low Numbers," *Editor & Publisher,* April 17, 2000, p. 16; Maryann Hammers, "Scripps Funds Media Diversity," *Workforce* 81 (December 2002): 16; Joe Strupp, "NAA: Diversity Under Review," *Editor & Publisher,* December 2, 2002, p. 6.

79. Ira Teinowitz, "Courting Change," *Advertising Age* 72 (May 14, 2001): 16–20.

80. Debby Scheinholtz, "Ernst & Young's New Leadership Vows Strong Commitment to Diversity," DiversityInc., July 5, 2000, www.diversityinc.com.

81. Cathy Lynn Crossman, "Wisconsin Restaurant Fills Staff with Workers Once Thought Unemployable," CNN, February 16, 2000, www.cnn.com.

82. "Verizon Takes the Lead in Business Network to Promote Employment of People with Disabilities," press release, November 1, 2000, Corporate Social Responsibility Newswire, CSRwire.com, www.csrwire.com/ article.cgi/ 490.html.

83. Jeffrey B. Cufaude, "Cultivating New Leadership," *Association Management* 52 (January 2000): 73; Scott Hays, "Generation X and the Art of the Reward," *Workforce* 78 (November 1999): 45; Jennifer Salopek, "Interview with Rom Zemke," *Training and Development* 54 (January 2000): 60; Ron Zemke, Claire Raines, and Bob Filipczak, *Generations at Work: Managing the Clash of Veterans, Boomers, Xers, and Nexters in Your Workplace* (New York: AMACOM, 2000).

84. Cora Daniels, "To Hire a Lumber Expert, Click Here," *Fortune,* April 3, 2000, pp. 267–270.

85. Judy Zhu and Brian Kleiner, "The Failure of Diversity Training," *Nonprofit World* 18 (May–June 2000): 12–14.

86. Robert D. Winsor and Ellen A. Ensher, "Choices Made in Balancing Work and Family: Following Two Women on a 16-year Journey," *Journal of Management Inquiry* 9 (June 2000): 218–231.

87. Jeffrey R. Edwards and Nancy P. Rothbard, "Mechanisms Linking Work and Family," *Academy of Management Review* 25 (January 2000): 178–199.

88. Douglas M. McCracken, "Winning the Talent War for Women: Sometimes It Takes a Revolution," *Harvard Business Review* 78 (November–December 2000): 159–167.

89. "Best In Class: Flexibility," *Working Mother,* http://www.workingmother.com/bestclass.shtml, accessed October 2, 2003.

90. Daniel Griffiths, "Japan's Workaholic Culture," *BBC News Online,* http://news.bbc.co.uk/1/low/world/asia-pacific/701458.stm, accessed August 22, 2003; Rebecca Segall, "Japanese Killer," *Psychology Today* 33 (September–October 2000): 10–11.

91. Lotte Bailyn, Joyce K. Fletcher, and Deborah Kolb, "Unexpected Connections: Considering Employees' Personal Lives Can Revitalize Your Business," *Sloan Management Review* 38 (Summer 1997): 11–20.

92. Michael A. Verespej, "Balancing Act," *Industry Week,* May 15, 2000, pp. 81–85.

93. Debby Scheinholtz, "Work/Life Professionals Discuss Trends for the 21st Century," DiversityInc., March 16, 2000, www.diversityinc.com/.

94. Pui-Wing Tam, "Silicon Valley Belatedly Boots Up Programs to Ease Employees Lives."

95. "For Organizations, Businesses and Volunteer Managers," Points of Light Foundation, http://www.pointsoflight.org/organizations/organizations.cfm, accessed August 22, 2003.

96. Alan J. Liddle, "McD Franchisees Make Online McStatement to Workers, Communities," *Nation's Restaurant News,* September 18, 2000, pp. 19, 94.

97. "Small Dog Gives Pet Perk," CNNfn, July 10, 2000, www.cnnfn.com.

98. Roger E. Herman and Joyce L. Gioia, *How to Become an Employer of Choice* (Winchester, VA: Oakhill Press, 2000).

99. Ibid; Daniel Koys, "How the Achievement of Human Resource Goals Drives Restaurant Performance," *Cornell Hotel and Restaurant Administration Quarterly* 44 (February 2003): 17–24.

100. "Employee Ownership and Corporate Performance," ESOP Association, http://www.the-esop-emplowner. org/media/corp_performance.html, accessed August 21, 2003; Dale Kurschner, "5 Ways Ethical Busine$$ Creates Fatter Profit$," *Business Ethics* 10 (March–April 1996): 21; Jacquelyn Yates and Marjorie Kelly, "The Employee Ownership 100," *Business Ethics* 14 (September–October 2000), http://www.business-ethics.com/employee.htm, accessed January 9, 2003.

101. Kris Frieswick, "ESOPs: Split Personality," *CFO*, July 7, 2003, p. 1; Ronald Mano and E. Devon Deppe, "We Told You So: ESOPs Are Risky," *Ohio CPA Journal* 61 (July–September 2002): 67–68; Matthew Mouritsen, Ronald Mano, and E. Devon Deppe, "The ESOP Fable Revisited: Employees' Exposure to ESOPs and Enron's Exit," *Personal Financial Planning Monthly* 2 (May 2002): 27–31.

102. Aaron Bernstein, "Sweatshop Reform: How to Solve the Standoff," *Business Week*, May 3, 1999, pp. 186–189; Kelley Holland and Aaron Bernstein, "Nike Finally Does It," *Business Week*, May 25, 1998, p. 46; Isabelle Maignan, Bas Hillebrand, and Debbie Thorne McAlister, "Managing Socially Responsible Buying: How to Integrate Non-economic Criteria into the Purchasing Process," *European Management Journal* 20 (December 2002): 641–648.

Chapter 9

1. "Fortune 500, 1999," *Fortune*, www.fortune.com; Herman Miller Furniture, www.hermanmiller.com, accessed December 16, 2000; Info Quotes Fundamentals, NASDAQ/AMEX Online, http://quotes.nasdaq.com/, May 10, 1999; David Woodruff, "Herman Miller: How Green Is My Factory," *Business Week*, September 16, 2001, http://bwarchive/businessweek.com.

2. "Gallup Poll: Public Supports Environmental Movement, But Not as a Priority," CNN, April 17, 2000, www.cnn. com/nature/specials/earthday, accessed September 10, 2003.

3. Alan K. Reichert, Marion S. Webb, and Edward G. Thomas, "Corporate Support for Ethical and Environmental Policies: A Financial Management Perspective," *Journal of Business Ethics* 25 (2000): 53–64.

4. "Air Quality," Office of Air Quality Planning and Standards, Environmental Protection Agency, February 20, 2003, www.epa.gov/oar/oaqps/cleanair.html, accessed September 10, 2003.

5. "The Plain English Guide to the Clean Air Act," Office of Air Quality Planning and Standards, Environmental Protection Agency, February 20, 2003, www.epa.gov/oar/oaqps/peg_caa/pegcaa01.html#topic1, accessed September 10, 2003.

6. "Environmental Effects of Acid Rain," Environmental Protection Agency, www.epa.gov/airmarkets/acidrain/effects/index.html, accessed September 10, 2003.

7. "Texaco Quits Global Warming Group," CNN, March 1, 2000, via http://edition.cnn.com/2000/NATURE/03/01/tex.climate/, accessed September 10, 2003.

8. www.newscientist.com/hottopics/climate/climatefaq.jsp., accessed September 10, 2003.

9. www.newscientist.com/hottopics/climate/climatetrends.jsp, accessed September 10, 2003.

10. www.CNN.com, January 14, 2002, accessed February 20, 2003.

11. "Global Warming FAQ: All You Ever Wanted to Know about Climate Change," http://www.newscientist.com/hottopics/climate/climatefaq.jsp, accessed September 30, 2003.

12. "Texaco Quits Global Warming Group."

13. Traci Watson, "Global Warming Good News?" *USA Today*, November 16, 2000, p. 16A.

14. "Canada Ratifies Kyoto Protocol," http://www.newscientist.com/news/news.jsp?id=ns99993188, accessed September 10, 2003.

15. Erin Kelly, "States Foul Out on Clean Water Act," *Coloradoan*, April 6, 2000, p. B1.

16. Ibid.

17. http://www.sierraclub.org/cleanwater/waterquality/, accessed September 10, 2003.

18. Kathleen Fackelmann, "Teen Discovers Antibiotics in Public Supplies; Scientists Fear 'Superbugs,'" *USA Today*, November 8, 2000, pp. 1D, 2D.

19. *Seattle Times*, December 17, 2002.

20. Kelly, "States Foul Out on Clean Water Act."

21. Dave Barry, *Charleston Daily Mail*, August 10, 2002, accessed February 20, 2003.

22. www.sierraclub.org/cleanwater/cleanwater_act/, accessed September 10, 2003.

23. Peter Jahrling, PRIMEDIA Business Magazines & Media Inc., January 8, 2003.

24. Mark H. Hunter, "Water, Harvest Cuts Urged at Conference: San Luis Valley Assesses Drought," *Denver Post*, January 20, 2003.

25. Robert Rosenblatt, "Man and Nature: All the Days of the Earth," *Time Earth Day 2000* 155 (Spring 2000): 12.

26. Gerald Urquhart, Walter Chomentowski, David Skole, and Chris Barber, "Tropical Deforestation," earthobservatory.nasa.gov/Library/Deforestation/, accessed September 10, 2003.

27. James Howard Kunstler, *The Geography of Nowhere: The Rise and Decline of America's Man-Made Landscape* (New York: Simon & Schuster, 1994).

28. Mark Walters, "Current Regulatory Environment and Impediments to the Establishment of a Compact City," directed research project, Southwest Texas University, San Marcos, Texas, November 1, 2001.

29. Sierra Club, "Roads and Highways," in *Sprawl Costs Us All: How Your Taxes Fuel Suburban Sprawl* (Sierra Club, 2000), www.sierraclub.org/sprawl/report00/roads.asp, accessed September 10, 2003.

30. Eugene Linden, "State of the Planet: Condition Critical," *Time Earth Day 2000* 155 (Spring 2000): 24.

31. "Tropical Forest Species Richness," World Resources Institute, www.wri.org/wri/biodiv/b01-koa.html, accessed September 10, 2003.

32. G. T. Miller, "Deforestation and Loss of Diversity," in *Living in the Environment: Principles, Connections and Solutions,* 8th ed. (Belmont, CA: Wadsworth Publishing, 1994).

33. "Monkey's Extinction May Be a Sign," CNN, September 13, 2000, www.cnn.com, accessed September 10, 2003.

34. Laura Tangley, "Keeping the Delicate Balance of Nature," *U.S. News & World Report,* November 15, 1999, p. 95, www.usnews.com, accessed September 10, 2003.

35. "Earth Matters: Pollinator Decline Puts World Food Supply at Risk, Experts Warn," CNN, http://www.cnn.com/2000/NATURE/05/05/pollinators.peril/, accessed September 10, 2003.

36. "Overcutting Costs More Timber Jobs than Owl, Study Says," *Idaho Statesman,* February 16, 1997.

37. Paul Magnusson, Ann Therese, and Kerry Capell, "Furor over Frankenfood," *Business Week,* October 18, 1999, pp. 50, 51.

38. "Biotech Food Safe, but More Tests Needed, Study Suggests," *Coloradoan,* April 6, 2000, p. B3.

39. Ellen Licking, "Tinkering with Genes: Time for a National Debate," *Business Week,* November 8, 1999, p. 44, www.businessweek.com, accessed January 27, 2003.

40. Jack Lewis, "The Birth of the EPA," *EPA Journal,* November 1985, www.epa.gov/history/topics/epa/15c.htm, accessed September 10, 2003.

41. "EPA's Mission, Goals, and Principles," *EPA Strategic Plan,* Office of the Chief Financial Officer, Environmental Protection Agency, www.epa.gov/ocfo/plan/plan.htm, accessed September 10, 2003.

42. Peter Eisler, "EPA to Phase out Popular Insecticide Diazinon," *USA Today,* December 5, 2000, p. 1A.

43. "EPA's Mission, Goals, and Principles," via http://www.epa.gov/history/org/origins/mission.htm, accessed September 11, 2003.

44. John J. Fialka, "Koch Industries' $30 Million Fine Is Biggest-Ever Pollution Penalty," *Wall Street Journal,* January 14, 2000, p. A10.

45. O. C. Ferrell, John Fraedrich, and Gwyneth Vaughn, "The Wreck of the Exxon Valdez," in *Business Ethics: Ethical Decision Making and Cases,* ed. O. C. Ferrell, John Fraedrich, and Linda Ferrell, 5th ed. (Boston: Houghton Mifflin, 2002), pp. 331–339.

46. "Major Environmental Laws: Clean Air Act," Environmental Protection Agency, www.epa.gov/region5/defs/html/caa.htm, accessed September 11, 2003.

47. Lewis, "The Birth of the EPA"; "Major Environmental Laws: Clean Air Act," http://www.epa.gov/history/topics/epa/15c.htm, accessed September 11, 2003.

48. "Major Environmental Laws: Clean Air Act."

49. "Major Environmental Laws: Federal Insecticide, Fungicide, and Rodenticide Act," Environmental Protection Agency, www.epa.gov/region5/defs/html/fifra.htm, accessed September 11, 2003.

50. "Major Environmental Laws: Endangered Species Act," Environmental Protection Agency, www.epa.gov/region5/defs/html/esa.htm, accessed September 11, 2003.

51. Ibid.

52. "How Has the ESA Impacted People," National Endangered Species Act Reform Coalition, www.nesarc.org/stories.htm, accessed September 11, 2003.

53. "Major Environmental Laws: Toxic Substances Control Act," Environmental Protection Agency, www. epa.gov/region5/defs/html/tsca.htm, accessed September 11, 2003.

54. "Major Environmental Laws: Clean Water Act," Environmental Protection Agency, www.epa.gov/region5/water/cwa.htm, accessed September 11, 2003.

55. "What Is the Toxics Release Inventory?" Environmental Protection Agency, www.epa.gov/tri/whatis.htm, accessed September 11, 2003.

56. "Major Environmental Laws: Pollution Prevention Act," Environmental Protection Agency, www.epa.gov/region5/defs/html/ppa.htm, accessed September 11, 2003.

57. "Food Quality Protection Act (FQPA) of 1996," Office of Pesticide Programs, Environmental Protection Agency, www.epa.gov/opppsps1/fqpa/, accessed September 11, 2003.

58. "The Food Quality Protection Act (FQPA) Background," Office of Pesticide Programs, Environmental Protection Agency, www.epa.gov/opppsps1/fqpa/ backgrnd.htm, accessed September 11, 2003.

59. Jeffrey Ball, "GM to Produce Hybrid Trucks, Buses in Scramble to Build 'Green' Vehicles," *Wall Street Journal,* August 3, 2000, p. A4, online.wsj.com, accessed September 11, 2003.

60. "Supporting Our National Parks," Parks Company, www.theparksco.com/support/onefortheparks.html, accessed January 27, 2003.

61. Nikki Sameshima, "Natural Born 'Burbs," *Coloradobiz* 27 (April 2000): 72, 74.

62. "The European Eco-label at a Glance," European Commission booklet; "The Eco-label and Exporting to Europe," *Business America,* November 29, 1993, p. 21.

63. "Saving the Forest for the Trees," *Business Week,* November 20, 2000, pp. 62–63, www.businessweek.com, accessed January 27, 2003.

64. Jim Carlton, "Chiquita to Take Part in Environmental Program," *Wall Street Journal,* November 16, 2000, p. A3, online.wsj.com, accessed February 20, 2003.

65. Jason Hopps, "Study Finds 'Green' Product Labeling Misleading," Reuters Newswire, www.ac-reunion.fr/pedagogie/anglaislp/Teaching_aids/readymade/rnvironmentally_friendly.htm, accessed September 11, 2003.

66. Paul Hawken and William McDonough, "Seven Steps to Doing Good Business," *Inc.,* November 1993, pp. 79–90, www.inc.com/magazine/19931101/3770.html, accessed September 11, 2003.

67. "Tire Recycling Gains Traction with Help from Business," CNN, April 25, 2000, www.cnn.com.

68. "AF and PA Recycling Programs," American Forest and Paper Association, www.afandpa.org, accessed September 11, 2003.

69. Helen Chung, "Starbucks Serves Up Coffee Grounds for Compost: Great Coffee Is Also Good for the Garden," *Business Wire,* March 20, 2000, www. businesswire.com/cnn/sbux.htm.

70. "Doing What It Takes to Be Wastewise," Environmental Protection Agency, April 1999, www.epa.gov/wastewise/about/id-bev.htm, accessed September 11, 2003.

71. Eric Peterson, "The Wal-Mart of Recycling," *Coloradobiz* 26 (October 1999): 66.

72. "Complete Recycling of Water Will Protect Environment, Resources at DaimlerChrysler Plant in Mexico," *PR Newsletter,* March 29, 2000, via America Online.

73. Sharon Begley, "The Battle for Planet Earth," *Newsweek,* April 24, 2000, pp. 50–53.

74. Duncan Austin and Craig Hanson, "Corporate Guide to Green Power Markets," World Resources Institute, July 2002, via http://pubs.wri.org/pubs_description.cfm?PubID=3771, accessed September 30, 2003.

75. Begley, "The Battle for Planet Earth."

76. John J. Fialka, "An Environment-Business Global-Warming Link," *Wall Street Journal,* November 22, 2000, p. A2.

77. Minette E. Drumwright, "Socially Responsible Organizational Buying: Environmental Concern as a Noneconomic Buying Criterion," *Journal of Marketing* 58 (July 1994): 1.

78. *Green Business Letter,* November 2002, via http://www.greenbizletter.com/archive_index.cfm, accessed September 11, 2003.

79. Isabelle Maignan and Debbie Thorne McAlister, "Socially Responsible Organizational Buying: Can Stakeholders Dictate Purchasing Policies?" working paper, Free University, Amsterdam, Netherlands, 2003.

80. A Guide to World Resources 2002–2004: Decisions for the Earth: Balance, Voice, and Power, World Resources Institute, 2003, via http://pubs.wri.org/pubs_description.cfm?PubID=3764, accessed September 30, 2003.

81. William M. Pride and O. C. Ferrell, eds., *Marketing: Concepts and Strategies,* 12th ed. (Boston: Houghton Mifflin, 2003), p. 89.

82. "BIO Statement Regarding Purported New Findings on Bt Corn and Monarch Butterflies," Life Sciences Knowledge Center, August 21, 2000, www.biotechknowledge.com/biotech/knowcenter.nsf/ID/4CE964D87D197F6E86256AF60052650E?OpenDocument&highlight=0,BT%20CORN,MONARCH%20BUTTERFLIES, accessed September 11, 2003.

83. Begley, "The Battle for Planet Earth."

84. "International Standard ISO 14000," Quality Network, www.quality.co.uk/iso14000.htm, accessed January 31, 2003.

85. "DaimlerChrysler Sets Registration Deadline," ISO 14000 Information Center, October 24, 2000, www.iso14000.com/WhatsNew/News02.htm; "Ford Requires Suppliers to Achieve ISO 14001 Certification," ISO 14000 Information Center, September 23, 1999, www.iso14000.com/WhatsNew/News01.htm, accessed September 11, 2003.

Chapter 10

1. Dawn C. Chmielewski, *Houston Chronicle,* January 21, 2003; Matthew Newman, "Music Industry Seeks Help from Companies on Piracy," *Wall Street Journal,* February 13, 2003; Anna Wilde Mathews, "Judge Orders Verizon to Name Song-Swapper," *Wall Street Journal,* January 22, 2003; "Napster Case," www.e-businessethics.com/napster.htm, accessed September 11, 2003; "Roxio Hopes to Revive Napster as Subscription-Based Service," *Wall Street Journal,* February 24, 2003; Bruce Orwall and Ethan Smith, "Music Industry Group Launches Legal Attack Against File Sharing," *Wall Street Journal Online,* September 8, 2003, accessed September 8, 2003.

2. Jason Dean, "China Issues 'Trial' Online Ad Licenses in First Step Toward Regulating Sector," *Wall Street Journal,* June 1, 2000, p. B18.

3. "China internet use grows," BBC News, July 23, 2002, news.bbc.co.uk/2/hi/business/2145865.stm, accessed September 18, 2003.

4. Kevin Bonsor, "How electronic ink will work," www.howstuffworks.com/e-ink1.htm, accessed September 18, 2003.

5. Dana James, "Broadband Horizons," *Marketing News,* March 13, 2000, pp. 1, 9.

6. "Supercomputers crack gene puzzles," www.msnbc.com/news/592898.asp# BODY, accessed January 31, 2003.

7. "Get ready for class warfare," Bill Saporito, January 13, 2003, www.cnn.com/2003/ALLPOLITICS/01/13/timep.classware.tm/index.html, accessed September 11, 2003.

8. Ibid.

9. Stacey Wells, "Across the Divide," *Business2.com,* December 12, 2000, pp. 186–204, www.business2.com/search?qt=Across+the+Divide&business2=on&expanded=, accessed September 11, 2003.

10. Jordan T. Pine, "Gateway to Help Bridge Technology Gap," DiversityInc.com, April 28, 2000, www.nafeo.org/index20.html, accessed September 11, 2003.

11. "Charting the Future of the Net," MSNBC, July 7, 2000, www.msnbc.com.

12. Leslie Walker, "The Lord of the Webs," *Washington Post,* January 30, 2003, p. E1.

13. "Supporting Research and Development to Promote Economic Growth: The Federal Government's Role," Council of Economic Advisers, Washington, DC, October 1995.

14. Alan Greenspan, Remarks to the Economic Club of New York, Federal Reserve Board, New York, January 13, 2000.

15. Elana Varon, "The ABCs of B2B," The E-Business Research Center, www.cio.com/research/ec/edit/b2babc.html, accessed September 18, 2003.

16. Greenspan, Remarks to the Economic Club of New York.

17. "Covisint Parts Exchange Officially Opens for Business," *Bloomberg Newswire,* December 11, 2000, via AOL.

18. Greenspan, Remarks to the Economic Club of New York.

19. Richard Karpinski, "Web delivers big results for Staples," November 11, 2002, www.btobonline.com/cgi-bin/article.pl?id=10088, accessed February 26, 2003.

20. Kimberly Hill, "Next Stop: Free Wireless Broadband?" Wireless News Factor, January 24, 2002, www.wirelessnewsfactor.com/perl/sotry/20557.html, accessed September 16, 2003.

21. Mark Hall, "Opinion: The Problem With Wireless Interoperability," *ComputerWorld,* December 16, 2002, www.computerworld.com/mobiletopics/mobile/story/0,10801,76667,00.html, accessed September 16, 2003.

22. John Cox, "Navy Set to Navigate with Wireless LANS," *Network World,* January 29, 2003, www.nwfusion.com/news/2003/0127navywireless.html, accessed September 16, 2003.

23. David Leiberman, "America's Digital Divide," *USA Today,* October 11, 1999, www.usatoday.com/life/ cyber/tech/ctg382.htm.

24. Michael Pastore, "One-third of online Americans surfing at high speeds," cyberatlas.internet.com/markets/broadband/article/0,1323,10099_790641,00.html, accessed September 11, 2003.

25. Ibid.

26. Anick Jesdanun, "Wiring Rural America," MSNBC, September 5, 2000, www.msnbc.com, accessed September 11, 2003.

27. Greenspan, Remarks to the Economic Club of New York.

28. Kyle Stock, "Internet tax loan efforts resume," *PC World.com,* January 14, 2003, www.computerworld.com/managementtopics/ebusiness/story/0,10801,77563,00.html?f+x010, accessed September 11, 2003.

29. "The Future of Purchasing and Supply: A Five and Ten Year Forecast," iPlanet, www.ism.ws/pubs/ismmag/090037.cfm, accessed September 11, 2003.

30. Karen Thomas, "An Early Education in Tech Toys," *USA Today,* December 6, 2000, pp. 1D, 2D.

31. David Field, "Some E-ticket Fliers Can Print Boarding Passes on PC," *USA Today,* December 5, 2000, p. 12B.

32. Glenda Chui, "Mapping Goes Deep: Technology Points the Way to a Revolution in Cartography," *San Jose Mercury News,* September 12, 2000, p. 1F.

33. "The World's Online Populations," *CyberAtlas,* March 21, 2002, http://cyberatlas.internet.com/big_picture/geographics/article/ 0,1323,5911_151151,00.html, accessed September 11, 2003.

34. Elizabeth Weise, "Web Users to Get More Places to Visit," *USA Today,* December 5, 2000, p. 3D.

35. William M. Pride and O. C. Ferrell, *Marketing: Concepts and Strategies,* 12th ed. (Boston: Houghton Mifflin, 2003), p. 493.

36. Julia Angwin, "Credit-Card Scams: The Devil E-stores," *Wall Street Journal,* September 19, 2000, pp. B1, B4.

37. Michael Pastore, "Market Retailing Fraud Continues to Haunt Online Retail," March 4, 2002, cyberatlas.internet.com/markets/retailing/article/0,,6061_984441,00.html, accessed September 11, 2003.

38. Jim Carlton and Pui Wing Tam, "Online Auctioneers Face Growing Fraud Problem," *Wall Street Journal,* May 12, 2000, p. B2.

39. Michael Pastore, "Consumers Remain Confident in Online Auctions," cyberatlas.internet.com/markets/retailing/article/0,,6061_578201,00.html, accessed September 12, 2003.

40. David H. Freedman, "Sleaze Bay," *Forbes ASAP,* November 27, 2000, pp. 134–140.

41. Steve Ulfelder "Online auctions offer IT bargains, risks," *ComputerWorld,* December 23, 2002, www.computerworld.com/hardwaretopic/hardware/story/0,10801,76944,00.html, accessed September 12, 2003.

42. Carlton and Tam, "Online Auctioneers Face Growing Fraud Problem."

43. Eve M. Caudill and Patrick E. Murphy, "Consumer Online Privacy: Legal and Ethical Issues," *Journal of Public Policy & Marketing* 19 (Spring 2000): 7–12.

44. "Survey shows security and privacy remain major concerns for online shoppers; Third Annual Internet Report also reveals that the Internet as become Internet users' most important source of information," *M2 Presswire,* January 31, 2003, accessed via Lexis-Nexis Academic Database.

45. peoplesearch.com, whowhere.com, accessed September 11, 2003.

46. "Internet Peaks as America's Most Important Source of Information, Reports Year Three of UCLA Internet Project; But Study Finds Doubts About Credibility, Privacy, Security," *AScribe Newswire,* January 30, 2003, accessed via Lexis-Nexis Academic Database.

47. "Privacy Initiatives," Federal Trade Commission, www.ftc.gov/privacy/index.html, accessed February 1, 2003.

48. "interMute Launches SpamSubtract to Bring an End to the Spam Epidemic; Maker of AdSubtract Introduces Family-Friendly Tool to Stop Junk E-mail," *Business Wire,* January 27, 2003, accessed via Lexis-Nexis Academic Database.

49. Pride and Ferrell, *Marketing: Concepts and Strategies,* pp. 600–601.

50. Brian Barber, *Tulsa World,* December 5, 2002.

51. Scott Wooley, "We Know Where You Live," *Forbes,* November 13, 2000, p. 332.

52. Nancy Weil, "Report Prompts Investigation of Health-Oriented Web Sites," CNN, April 3, 2000, www.cnn.com, accessed September 11, 2003.

53. "FTC Gets Complaints About Amazon.com's New Privacy Policy," *Wall Street Journal*, December 5, 2000, p. A10.

54. Edward C. Baig, "Progress in Online Privacy, But Critics Say Not Enough," *Business Week Online*, May 13, 1999, www.businessweek.com.

55. Heather Green, "Commentary: Privacy—Don't Ask Technology to Do the Job," *Business Week Online*, June 26, 2000, www.businessweek.com.

56. "Federal Web Sites Fail FTC Privacy Test," *USA Today*, September 12, 2000, www.usatoday.com.

57. "Survey: Kids Disclose Private Details Online," CNN, May 17, 2000, www.cnn.com.

58. Anne Reeks, "Electronic Sitters Evolve, But Some Still Beat Others," *Houston Chronicle*, January 23, 2003, p. 3.

59. Anick Jesdanun, "Survey: Users Consider Internet Important," *Associated Press Online*, January 31, 2003.

60. Jack McCarthy, "National Fraud Center: Internet Is Driving Identity Theft," CNN, March 20, 2000, www.cnn.com.

61. "Technology Briefing Internet: Senators Introduce Bill on Identity Theft," *New York Times*, January 28, 2003, p. C4.

62. "Georgetown Internet Privacy Policy Survey," E-Center for Business Ethics, www.e-businessethics.com/privacy/georgetown.htm, accessed September 11, 2003.

63. "Verizon Earns Top Telecom Ranking in Study of Online Services by Fortune 100 Companies, *PR Newswire*, January 30, 2003, accessed by Lexis-Nexis Academic Database.

64. Stepanek, "The Privacy Penalty on Dot-Coms," *Business Week Online*, June 13, 2000, www.businessweek.com.

65. "The Federal Trade Commission," E-Center for Business Ethics, January 18, 2000, www.e-businessethics.com/privacy/ftc.htm; "Internet Site Agrees to Settle FTC Charges of Deceptively Collecting Personal Information in Agency's First Internet Privacy Case," Federal Trade Commission, press release, August 13, 1998, www.ftc.gov/opa/1998/9808/geocitie.htm, accessed February 2, 2003.

66. "European Union Directive on Privacy," Banking & Financial Services Policy Report, December 2002.

67. Thomas E. Weber, "Views on Protecting Privacy Diverse in U.S. and Europe," *Wall Street Journal Interactive*, June 19, 2000, http://interactive.wsj.com, accessed September 11, 2003.

68. "A Private Sector Privacy Law," Privacy Commissioner of Canada, www.privcom.gc.ca/legislation/index_e.asp, accessed September 11, 2003.

69. "Privacy in Japan," E-Center for Business Ethics, www.e-businessethics.com/privacyJA.htm, accessed September 11, 2003.

70. Lorrie Cranor, "No Quick Fixes for Protecting Online Privacy," *Business Week Online*, March 14, 2000, www.businessweek.com.

71. "Privacy in Russia," E-Center for Business Ethics, www.e-businessethics.com/privacyRU.htm, accessed September 11, 2003.

72. "Customer Database Piracy Common in Russia," *Communications Today*, January 27, 2003, accessed via Lexis-Nexis Academic Database.

73. Guy Chazan, "A High-Tech Folk Hero Challenges Russia's Right to Snoop," *Wall Street Journal*, November 27, 2000, p. A28.

74. "Russia Regulators Clamp Down on Vodka Ads on the Internet," Agence France Presse, December 16, 2002, accessed via Lexis-Nexis Academic Database.

75. Catherine Siskos, "In the Service of Guarding Secrets," *Kiplinger's Personal Finance*, February, 2003, www.kiplinger.com/magazine.

76. "TRUSTe.com," www.truste.com, accessed September 11, 2003.

77. "American Education Services Sends One Million Trusted Sender Messages: Major Milestone in War Against Spam," *PR Newswire*, February 4, 2003, accessed via Lexis-Nexis Academic Database.

78. "Better Business Bureau Online," www.bbbonline.org, accessed September 11, 2003.

79. "Better Business Bureau and PlanetFeedback Will Help Companies Meet 'Whistleblower' Provision of Recent Corporate Reform Legislation: Two trusted organizations agree to create system for confidential reporting of alleged misconduct," *PR Newswire*, December 11, 2002, accessed via Lexis-Nexis Academic Database.

80. "FTC Sues Toysmart.com Over Customer Data," *USA Today*, July 10, 2000, www.usatoday.com/life/cyber/tech/cti204.htm, accessed February 23, 2003.

81. David G. McDonough, ". . . But Can the WTO Really Sock It to Software Pirates?" *Business Week Online*, March 9, 1999, www.businessweek.com, accessed September 11, 2003.

82. Patrick Thiibodeau, "Business alliance tool tracks software pirates," *ComputerWorld*, May 29, 2002, www.computerworld.com, accessed September 11, 2003.

83. McDonough, ". . . But Can the WTO Really Sock It to Software Pirates?"

84. Jim Duffy, "Cisco sues Huawei over intellectual property," *Network World*, January 23, 2003, IDG News Service, accessed via Lexis-Nexis Academic Database.

85. Rebecca Buckman, "Microsoft Steps Up Software Piracy War," *Wall Street Journal*, August 2, 2000, p. B6.

86. "Microsoft Missing Out Unnecessarily On Billion Dollar Revenues Due to Piracy," *Business Wire*, November 5, 2002, accessed via Lexis-Nexis Academic Database.

87. Stephen Wildstrom, "Can Microsoft Stamp Out Piracy?" *Business Week Online*, October 2, 2000, www.businessweek.com.

88. Rebecca Edelson and Adrienne D. Herman, "The Digital Millennium Copyright Act: A Tool to Limit Liability for Copyright Infringement and to Protect and Enforce Copyrights on the Internet," Alschuler, Grossman, Stein, and Kahan LLP, www.agsk.com/print/index.html, accessed September 11, 2003.

89. Elijah Cocks, "Internet Ruling: Hypertext Linking Does Not Violate Copyright," Intellectual Property and Technology Forum, Boston College Law School, Newton, MA, April 4, 2000.

90. William T. Neese and Charles R. McManis, "Summary Brief: Law, Ethics and the Internet: How Recent Federal Trademark Law Prohibits a Remedy against 'Cyber-Squatters,'" *Proceedings from the Society of Marketing Advances*, November 4–7, 1998.

91. Linda Rosencrance, "Ways to Verify Accuracy of Domain Name Data Sought," *Computer World,* December 9, 2002, www.computerworld.com.

92. William T. Neese and Charles R. McManis, "Summary Brief: Law, Ethics and the Internet."

93. Martyn Williams, "Update: ICANN president calls for major overhaul," IDG News Service, February 25, 2002, accessed via Lexis-Nexis Academic Database.

94. Thomas A. Guida and Gerald J. Ferguson, "Strategy ICANN Arbitration vs. Federal Court: Choosing the Right Forum for Trademark Disputes," *Internet Newsletter,* November 7, 2002.

95. Glenn McGee and Arthur Caplan, "An Introduction to Bioethics," Bioethics.net, www.bioethics.net/beginners/introduction.php, accessed September 11, 2003.

96. bioethics.net/bioethics_intro.php?task=view&articleID=98, accessed February 5, 2003.

97. Lucette Lagundo, "Drug Companies Face Assault on Prices," *Wall Street Journal,* May 11, 2000, p. B1.

98. Chris Adams, "Merck Is Accused of Inflating the Price of Heartburn Drug" Online.wsj.com/article_print/0,,SB1043981104443505544,00.html, January 31, 2003.

99. Lisa Stansky, "Drug Makers Could Face Wave Of Cases," *Connecticut Law Tribune,* January 24, 2003, pp. 123–128.

100. Lagundo, "Drug Companies Face Assault on Prices."

101. Christopher Oster, "Cracking the Code on Biotech Investing," *Wall Street Journal,* June 9, 2000, p. C1.

102. "Attention Business, Technology, Biotechnology, Health Care, Financial Services, Mutual Fund and Investing Special Report," *Canada NewsWire,* January 14, 2003, www.newswire.ca.

103. Mike Jensen, "A Modern Goldrush in Genetics," MSNBC, www.msnbc.com, accessed July 18, 2000.

104. "Activists take on gene patents," January 31, 2003, www.msnbc.com/news/697629.asp, accessed September 11, 2003.

105. "Avon Foundation Continues Commitment to Breast Cancer Cause; Awards Nearly $30 Million in Grants to Thirteen Organizations," *PR Newswire,* September 24, 2002, www.prnewswire.com.

106. Marilynn Marchione, "Study suggests setback in effort to morph stem cells into insulin-producing pancreas cells," *Milwaukee Journal Sentinel,* January 17, 2003, p. B8.

107. John Leavitt, "What Will Human Clones Be Like?" *Connecticut Law Tribune,* January 24, 2003, p. 5.

108. Andy Coghlan, "Cloning Special Report: Cloning Without Embryos," *New Scientist,* January 29, 2000, via www.newscientist.com/nsplus/insight/cone/cloningwithoutemb.html.

109. "Mini-pig Clone Raises Transplant Hope," www.newscientist.com/news/news.jsp?id=ns99993257, accessed September 11, 2003.

110. "Australia OKs human embryo research," www.newscientist.com/news/news.jsp?id=ns99993149, accessed September 11, 2003.

111. Jacqueline Stensen, "Gene Patents Raise Concerns," MSNBC, www.msnbc.com, accessed September 11, 2003.

112. Rebecca S. Eisenberg, "How Can You Patent Genes?" *American Journal of Bioethics* 2 (Summer 2002): 3–11.

113. "Controversies Surrounding the Risks and Benefits of Genetically Modified Food," scope.educ.washington.edu/gmfood/, accessed September 11, 2003.

114. Bill Gates, "Will Frankenfood Feed the World?" www.microsoft.com/presspass/ofnote/06-11time.asp, June 19, 2000, accessed September 11, 2003.

115. "Weighing the Future of Biotech Food," MSNBC, www.msnbc.com, accessed July 18, 2000.

116. Julia A. Moore and Gilbert Winha, "Let's not escalate the 'Frankenfood' war," www.csmonitor.com/2002/1220/p13s02-coop.html, accessed September 11, 2003.

117. "Green Groups Target Campbell Soup in GM Food Fight," CNN, July 20, 2000, www.cnn.com.

118. "Controversies Surrounding the Risks and Benefits of Genetically Modified Food," scope.educ.washington.edu/gmfood/, accessed September 11, 2003.

119. Paul Magnusson, Ann Therese, and Kerry Capell, "Furor over Frankenfood," *Business Week,* October 18, 1999, pp. 50, 51; "Japan Asks That Imports of Corn Be StarLink-Free," *Wall Street Journal,* October 30, 2000, p. A26.

120. Jennifer C. Davis, "Are Biotech Foods Really Safe?" February 6, 2003, www.healthwell.com/delicious-online/D_Backs/Feb_97/foodforthought.cfm?path=hw.

121. Magnusson, Therese, and Capell, "Furor over Frankenfood."

122. "Frankenfood," www.ecoworld.org/Home/Articles2.cfm?TID=23, accessed "Controversies Surrounding the Risks and Benefits of Genetically Modified Food," scope.educ.washington.edu/gmfood/, accessed September 11, 2003.

123. "McDonald's to Bar GMO Fries," CNNfn, April 28, 2000, www.cnnfn.com.

124. "EU's anti-GM stance under threat," Friday, January 10, 2003, www.cnn.com/2003/WORLD/europe/01/10/biotech.us.europe/index.html; "Controversies Surrounding the Risks and Benefits of Genetically Modified Food," scope.educ.washington.edu/gmfood/, accessed September 11, 2003.

125. "'Terminator' Victory a Small Step in Long War," CNN, October 7, 1999, www.cnn.com/NATURE/9910/07/terminator.victory.enn/index.html, accessed September 11, 2003.

126. Francesca Lyman, "Biotech Battle of Seattle, and Beyond, MSNBC, www.msnbc.com, accessed September 11, 2003.

127. Fred Guterl, "The Fear of Food," *Newsweek International,* January 27, 2003, accessed via Lexis-Nexis Academic Database.

128. Greg Farrell, "Police Have Few Weapons Against Cyber-Criminals," *USA Today,* December 6, 2000, p. 5B; Edward Iwata and Kevin Johnson, "Computer Crime Outpacing Cybercops," *USA Today,* June 7, 2000, www.usatoday.com/life/cyber/tech/cth404.htm.

129. Kevin Poulsen, "Feds seek public input on hacker sentencing," *SecurityFocus,* January 13, 2003, online. securityfocus.com/news/2028, accessed September 16, 2003.

130. Patrick Thibodeau, "DMCA," *ComputerWorld,* December 2, 2002, www.computerworld.com/governmenttopics/government/legalissues/story/0,10801,76301,00.html, accessed September 11, 2003.

131. "Websense Reports Record Billings, Revenue and Earnings for the 2002 Fourth Quarter and Year," Websense Press Release, www.websense.com/company/news/pr/Display.php?Release=03013058, accessed September 18, 2003.

132. Mathis Thurman, "Proxy Server Serves to Block Slacker," *ComputerWorld,* April 29, 2002, www.computerworld.com.

133. "Internet abuse costs big money," November 1, 2002, news.bbc.co.uk/1/hi/technology/2381123.stm, accessed September 11, 2003.

134. Michelle Conlin, "Workers, Surf at Your Own Risk," *Business Week Online,* www.businessweek.com/2000/00_24/63685257.htm, accessed September 11, 2003.

135. Michael J. McCarthy, "Keystroke Loggers Save E-mail Rants, Raising Workplace Privacy Concerns," *Wall Street Journal,* March 7, 2000, http://interactive.wsj.com.

136. Julene Snyder, "Should Overworked Employees Be Allowed to Surf the Web on the Job?" CNN online, May 11, 2000, www.cnn.com/2000/TECH/computing/05/11/job.surf.idg/, accessed September 11, 2003.

137. Roberta Fusaro, "Chief Privacy Officer: A Conversation with Richard Purcell," *Harvard Business Review* 78 (November–December 2000): 20–22.

Chapter 11

1. "Private Investments in Social Area Rose 15.7%," *O Globo,* May 22, 2001, accessed via LexisNexis; Peggy Dulany and David Winder, "The Status of and Trends in Private Philanthropy in the Southern Hemisphere," Synergos Institute, http://www.synergos.org/globalphilanthropy/02/philanthropyinsouthernhemisphere.htm, accessed January 28, 2003; Group of Institutes, Foundations and Enterprises, "Code of Ethics," http://www.gife.org.br/etica_ing.asp, accessed January 29, 2003; Group of Institutes, Foundations and Enterprises, "A Decade of History," http://www.gife.org.br/History_ing.asp, accessed January 29, 2003; Group of Institutes, Foundations and Enterprises, "Mission and Objective," http://www.gife.org.br/missao_ing.asp, accessed January 29, 2003.

2. American Productivity and Quality Center, *Community Relations: Unleashing the Power of Corporate Citizenship* (Houston: APQC, 1998).

3. "Money Woes May Close Russian Museum," *Associated Press Online,* November 24, 2000, via Comtex; "Our Partners," Moscow Center for Prison Reform, http://www.prison.org/english/mcprpart.htm, accessed August 22, 2003.

4. "Charity Holds Its Own in Tough Times: Giving in 2002 Nears $241 Billion, 1 Percent Above New Figures for 2001," AAFRC Trust for Philanthropy/Giving USA 2003, http://aafrc.org/press_releases/trustreleases/charityholds.html, accessed August 22, 2003.

5. Gifts in Kind International, http://www.giftsinkind.org/aboutus/default.asp, accessed August 22, 2003; Minette E. Drumwright and Patrick E. Murphy, "Corporate Societal Marketing," in *Handbook of Marketing and Society,* ed. Paul N. Bloom and Gregory T. Gundlach (Thousand Oaks, CA: Sage, 2001), pp. 162–183; Patricia MacInnis, "Dalhousie Keeps PACE With Automotive Advances," *Computing Canada,* November 15, 2002, p. 4.

6. Diane Lindquist, "Drug Companies' Rx for the Bottom Line," *Industry Week,* September 7, 1998, p. 25.

7. Noel M. Tichy, Andrew R. McGill, and Lynda St. Clair, *Corporate Global Citizenship: Doing Business in the Public Eye* (San Francisco: New Lexington Press, 1997).

8. Michael E. Porter and Mark R. Kramer, "The Competitive Advantage of Corporate Philanthropy," *Harvard Business Review* 80 (December 2002): 56–68; Robbie Shell, "Breaking the Stereotypes of Corporate Philanthropy," *Wall Street Journal,* November 26, 2002, p. B2.

9. Reynold Levy, *Give and Take: A Candid Account of Corporate Philanthropy* (Boston: Harvard Business School Press, 1999); Noah's Bagels, www.noahs.com, accessed August 22, 2003.

10. Tichy, McGill, and St. Clair, *Corporate Global Citizenship.*

11. Sophia A. Muirhead, Charles J. Bennett, Ronald E. Berenbeim, Amy Kao, and David J. Vidal, *Corporate Citizenship in the New Century: Accountability, Transparency, and Global Stakeholder Engagement* (New York: Conference Board, 2002); Nelson Schwartz and Tim Smart, "Giving—And Getting Something Back," *Business Week,* August 28, 1995, p. 81.

12. Drumwright and Murphy, "Corporate Societal Marketing."

13. "Corporate Citizen," Fuji Bank, www.fujibank.co.jp/eng/fb/topics/philan.html, accessed January 4, 2001.

14. Curt Weeden, "Leave-Based Donation Programs," Contributions Academy, www.contributionsacademy.com/html/news.html, accessed November 5, 2001.

15. Bob Nelson, *1001 Ways to Energize Employees* (New York: Workman Publishing, 1997).

16. Curt Weeden, *Corporate Social Investing* (San Francisco: Berrett-Koehler, 1998), pp. 116–123.

17. Hal F. Rosenbluth and Diane McFerrin Peters, *Good Company: Caring as Fiercely as You Compete* (Reading, MA: Perseus, 1998).

18. Craig N. Smith, "The New Corporate Philanthropy," *Harvard Business Review* 72 (May–June 1994) pp. 105–114; Ann Svendsen, *The Stakeholder Strategy: Profiting from Collaborative Business Relationships* (San Francisco: Berrett-Koehler, 1998).

19. "The Crisis Christmas Card Challenge," Cadbury Schweppes, www.cadburyschweppes.com/newsroom/crisis.html, accessed December 12, 2000.

20. Smith, "The New Corporate Philanthropy."

21. Levy, *Give and Take.*

22. Drumwright and Murphy, "Corporate Societal Marketing."

23. Mark Kleinman, "BP Set to Partner Red Cross Cause in European Deal," *Marketing,* September 20, 2001, p. 1.

24. Avon, "Avon Breast Cancer Crusade," www.avoncrusade.com/, accessed January 27, 2003.

25. Tichy, McGill, and St. Clair, *Corporate Global Citizenship.*

26. Tracy L. Pipp, "Corporate America Takes on Breast Cancer—and Both are Reaping the Benefits," Gannet News Service, October 21, 1996.

27. Daniel Kadlec and Bruce Voorst, "The New World of Giving: Companies Are Doing More Good, and Demanding More Back," *Time,* May 5, 1997, pp. 62–66.

28. Kevin T. Higgins, "Marketing With a Conscience," *Marketing Management* 11 (July–August 2002): 12–15; P. Rajan Varadarajan and Anil Menon, "Cause-Related Marketing: A Coalignment of Marketing Strategy and Corporate Philanthropy," *Journal of Marketing* 52 (July 1988): 58–74.

29. Allyson L. Stewart-Allen, "Europe Ready for Cause-Related Campaigns," *Marketing News,* July 6, 1998, p. 9.

30. "Business in the Community, Awards for Excellence," http://www.bitc.org.uk/awards/index.html, accessed January 27, 2003; Sue Adkins, "Why Cause-Related Marketing Is a Winning Business Formula," *Marketing,* July 20, 2000, p. 18.

31. Steve Hoeffler and Kevin Lane Keller, "Building Brand Equity Through Corporate Societal Marketing," *Journal of Public Policy & Marketing* 21 (Spring 2002): 78–89; Sue Adkins and Nina Kowalska, "Consumers Put 'Causes' on the Shopping List," *M2 PressWire,* November 17, 1997.

32. Jennifer Mullen, "Performance-Based Corporate Philanthropy: How 'Giving Smart' Can Further Corporate Goals," *Public Relations Quarterly,* June 22, 1997, p. 42; Michal Strahilevitz, "The Effects of Prior Impressions of a Firm's Ethics on the Success of a Catuse-Related Marketing Campaign," *Journal of Nonprofit & Public Sector Marketing,* 11, no. 1: 77–92.

33. Stan Friedman and Charles Kouns, "Charitable Contribution: Reinventing Cause Marketing," *Brand Week,* October 27, 1997.

34. Nelson, *1001 Ways to Energize Employees.*

35. Rosenbluth and Peters, *Good Company.*

36. BE & K, "BE & K Awards," www.BEK.com/awards.html, accessed January 28, 2003.

37. "BT Bolsters Wealth of Responsibility Program," *Private Asset Management,* January 24, 2000, p. 7; "Wealth with Responsibility," Deutsche Bank, http://www.pwm.db.com/com_en_philan_wealth.html, accessed January 27, 2003.

38. "America's Literacy Champion," Verizon Reads, http://www.verizonreads.net/, accessed August 22, 2003; Sharon Cohen-Hagar, "GTE Foundation Increases 1999 Contributions Budget to $30 Million to Support Education, Literacy, and Community Programs," *Business Wire,* February 17, 1999.

39. Peter J. Gallanis, "Community Support Is a Powerful Tool," *DSN Retailing Today,* July 24, 2000, pp. 57, 71; "Take Charge of Education," Target, http://target.com/common/page.jhtml?content=target_cg_take_charge_of_education, accessed August 22, 2003.

40. Richard Cree, "Cover Story: Rory Stear," *Director* 56 (November): 64–67; Cheryl Dahle, "Social Justice: The Freeplay Group," *Fast Company,* April 1999, pp. 166–182.

41. Don Babwin, "Gateway to Good Health," *Hospital and Health Networks,* November 20, 1998, p. 20.

42. David Whitford, "The New Shape of Philanthropy," *Fortune,* June 12, 2000, pp. 315–316; Austin Social Venture Partners, www.asvp.org, accessed January 28, 2003.

43. Coca-Cola Company, "Environment," http://www2.coca-cola.com/citizenship/environment.html, accessed August 22, 2003.

44. Alan Reder, *75 Best Business Practices for Socially Responsible Companies* (New York: Putnam, 1995); "Mectizan Program Removes the Darkness from an Ancient Disease," Merck, http://www.merck.com/about/cr/policies_performance/social/mectizan_donation.html, accessed January 28, 2003.

45. Anonymous, "Glasses Drive a Bug Success," *Florida Times-Union,* May 10, 2003, p. K4; Marianne Williams, "More Than Just Causes," *Chain Store Age* 76 (August 2000): 37–40.

46. "Associations Advance America," American Association of Association Executives, www.asaenet.org/AAA/, accessed September 30, 2003.

47. Reder, *75 Best Business Practices for Socially Responsible Companies.*

48. "3M Earns Second Place in Eco-Ranking of Major Companies," 3M, www.3M.com/us/about3M/innovation/eco/index.html, accessed January 28, 2003.

49. Levy, *Give and Take;* "What Do Crises Mean for Giving?" American Association of Fundraising Counsel, press release, http://www.aafrc.org/press5.html, accessed January 28, 2003.

50. Walker Information, *Corporate Philanthropy National Benchmark Study, Employee Report* (Chicago: Walker Information, 2002).

51. "For All Kids Foundation," http://www.4allkids. com/, accessed August 22, 2003.

52. Robert J. Williams and J. Douglas Barrett, "Corporate Philanthropy, Criminal Activity, and Firm Reputation: Is There a Link?" *Journal of Business Ethics* 26 (2000): 341–350.

53. Roger Bennett, "Corporate Philanthropy in France, Germany, and the UK," *International Marketing Review* 15 (June 1998): 469.

54. American Productivity and Quality Center, *Community Relations: Unleashing the Power of Corporate Citizenship* (Houston, TX: American Productivity and Quality Center, 1998).

55. John A. Byrne, "Chainsaw," *Business Week,* October 18, 1999, pp. 128–149.

56. Levy, *Give and Take.*

57. Weeden, *Corporate Social Investing.*

58. Reprinted with permission of the publisher. From *Corporate Social Investing,* copyright ©1998 by Curt Weeden, Berrett-Koehler Publishers, Inc., San Francisco, CA. All rights reserved. www.bkconnection.com.

59. Walter W. Wymer, Jr. and Sridhar Samu, "Dimensions of Business and Nonprofit Collaborative Relationships," *Journal of Nonprofit & Public Sector Marketing,* 11, no. 1: 3–22.

60. John A. Byrne, "The New Face of Philanthropy," *Business Week,* December 2, 2002, pp. 82–86; Stephanie Strom, "Ground Zero: Charity; A Flood of Money, Then a Deluge of Scrutiny for Those Handing It Out," *New York Times,* September 11, 2002, p. B5; Cheryl Wetzstein, "Americans' Generosity Runs Deep; $1.4 Billion Released, But Process Has Created Skepticism," *Washington Times,* September 9, 2002, p. A1.

61. Cathy Brisbois, "Ranking Disclosure: VanCity Savings & Credit Union, Canada," in *Building Corporate Accountability: The Emerging Practices in Social and Ethical Accounting, Auditing and Reporting,* ed. Simon Zadek, Peter Pruzan, and Richard Evans (London: Earthscan Publications, 1997).

Chapter 12

1. "Social Audits and Accountability," Business for Social Responsibility www.bsr.org/BSRResources/ WhitePaperDetail.cfm?, accessed September 9, 2003; "The VanCity Difference," Vancouver City Savings Credit Union, www.vancity.com/link?menuId=52709, accessed September 9, 2003; "The VanCity Social Report 1998/99," Vancouver City Savings Credit Union, www.vancity.com/menuId/52707, accessed September 9, 2003; "VanCity's First Comprehensive Social Report Indicates Direction for the Future," *Canada News Wire,* October 6, 1998, www. newswire.ca/releases/October 1998/06/c1357.html, accessed September 9, 2003; Simon Zadek, "Accountibility Report, 2000–2001 (Vancouver, WA: Vancouver City Savings Credit Union, 2001). Copyright © 2003 by VanCity. Reprinted with permission.

2. "Social Audits and Accountability."

3. "Why Count Social Performance," in *Building Corporate Accountability: The Emerging Practices in Social and Ethical Accounting, Auditing and Reporting,* ed. Simon Zadek, Peter Pruzan, and Richard Evans (London: Earthscan Publications, 1997), pp. 12–34.

4. "Accountability," Business for Social Responsibility, www.bsr.org/BSRResources/WhitePaperDetail.cfm? DocumentID=259, accessed September 9, 2003.

5. "Accountability."

6. Sandra Waddock and Neil Smith, "Corporate Responsibility Audits: Doing Well by Doing Good," *Sloan Management Review* 41 (Winter 2000): 75–83.

7. "Why Count Social Performance."

8. John Pearce, "Measuring Social Wealth" (London: New Economics Foundation, 1996) as reported in Warren Dow and Roy Crowe, *What Social Auditing Can Do for Voluntary Organizations* (Vancouver, WA: Volunteer Vancouver, July 1999), p. 8.

9. Mark Maremont, "Tyco Delayed Some Bonuses, Likely Boosting Cash Flows," *Wall Street Journal Online,* online.wsj.com, January 21, 2003.

10. "Accountability."

11. "Verification," Business for Social Responsibility, www.bsr.org/BSRResources/WhitePaperDetail. cfm?DocumentID=440, accessed September 9, 2003.

12. Dennis K. Berman, "Qwest Spends Top Dollar to Defend Its Accounting," *Wall Street Journal Online,* online.wsj.com, March 10, 2003.

13. "Accountability."

14. Trey Buchholz, "Auditing Social Responsibility Reports: The Application of Financial Auditing Standards," Colorado State University, professional paper, November 28, 2000, p. 3.

15. "Most Admired Companies of 2003," www.fortune.com, accessed September 9, 2003. From *Fortune* magazine. © 2003 Time Inc. All rights reserved.

16. "Accountability."

17. Ibid.

18. Louise Gordon, "An Update on SmithOBrien's CSR Audit —A Tool to Help Companies Measure Progress and Its Value," *Executive Citizen,* September–October 1996, p. 38.

19. "Social Audits and Accountability."

20. Buchholz, "Auditing Social Responsibility Reports," pp. 2–3.

21. "Results of the DJSI Review 2002," Dow-Jones Sustainability Indexes, www.sustainability-indexes.com/news/ pdf/press_releases/DJSI_PR_020904_Review2002.pdf, accessed March 27, 2003.

22. Warren Dow and Roy Crowe, *What Social Auditing Can Do for Voluntary Organizations* (Vancouver, WA: Volunteer Vancouver, July 1999), pp. 15–18.

23. Peter Raynard, "Coming Together: A Review of Contemporary Approaches to Social Accounting, Auditing and Reporting in Non-Profit Organizations," *Journal of Business Ethics* 17 (October 1998): 1471–1479.

24. Tracy Swift and Nicole Dando, "From Methods to Ideologies: Closing the Assurance Gap in Social and Ethical Accounting," *Journal of Corporate Citizenship* (Winter 2002): 81–90.

25. "What Is Corporate Social Responsibility?" Vasin, Heyn & Company, www.vhcoaudit.com/SRAarticles/WhatIsCSR.htm, accessed February 13, 2003.

26. "The Effect of Published Reports of Unethical Conduct on Stock Prices," reported in "Business Ethics," Business for Social Responsibility, www.bsr.org/BSRResources/WhitePaperDetail.cfm?DocumentID=270, accessed March 5, 2003.

27. Ronald Alsop, "Scandal-Filled Year Takes Toll on Firms' Good Names," *Wall Street Journal,* February 12, 2003, http://online.wsj.com, accessed February 12, 2003.

28. "U.S. Companies Risk Reputations and Finances Due to Broadening Public Concern with all Forms of Corporate Behavior," *PR Newswire,* August 19, 2002, via www.findarticles.com, accessed August 19, 2002.

29. Penelope Patsuris, "The Corporate Accounting Scandal Sheet," *Forbes,* August 26, 2002, www.forbes.com/2002/07/25/accountingtracker.html, accessed October 2, 2003.

30. Swift and Dando, "From Methods to Ideologies," p. 81.

31. "Social Balance Sheet," www.eurofound.eu.int/emire/SPAIN/SOCIALBALANCESHEET-ES.html, accessed March 3, 2003.

32. "Post-Enron Restatements Hit Record," www.msnbc.com/news/862325.asp, accessed January 29, 2003.

33. *Journal of Corporate Citizenship,* December 2002, p. 81.

34. "Introducing AA1000," www.accountability.org.uk/aa1000/default.asp, accessed March 27, 2003.

35. "CSR Governance Structures," www.bsr.org/BSRResources/IssueBriefDetail.cfm?DocumentID=190, accessed November 11, 2003. Copyright © 2003 by Business for Social Responsibility. Reprinted with permission.

36. "Accountability."

37. Johann Mouton, "Chris Hani Baragwanath Hospital Ethics Audit," Ethics Institute of South Africa, 2001, available at www.ethicsa.org/report_CHB.html.

38. "Who We Are and What Our Values Are," www.furnitureresourcesentre.com, accessed March 27, 2003. Copyright © 2003 by Furniture Resource Centre Ltd. Reprinted with permission.

39. "Ethical Statement," SocialAudit.org, www.socialaudit.org/pages/ethical.htm, accessed March 4, 2003.

40. "Verification."

41. Ibid.

42. "Ethical Statement."

43. "Wells Fargo's Community Reinvestment Leadership Commitment," Wells Fargo, www.wellsfargo.com/wfcra/index.jhtml, accessed March 5, 2003.

44. Community Involvement, www.homedepot.com, accessed March 5, 2003.

45. "Community Involvement," Business for Social Responsibility, www.bsr.org/BSRResources/WhitePaperDetail.cfm?DocumentID=264, accessed March 5, 2003.

46. "Verification."

47. Buchholz, "Auditing Social Responsibility Reports," p. 15.

48. Ibid., p. 16.

49. "Verification."

50. "Introduction to Corporate Social Responsibility," Business for Social Responsibility, www.bsr.org/BSRResources/WhitePaperDetail.cfm?DocumentID=138, accessed March 5, 2003.

51. Ibid.

52. Ibid.

53. "The Effect of Published Reports of Unethical Conduct on Stock Prices," reported in "Business Ethics," Business for Social Responsibility, www.bsr.org/BSRResources/WhitePaperDetail.cfm?DocumentID=270, accessed March 5, 2003.

54. "Accountability."

55. Ibid.

56. Ethics Officer Association, www.eoa.org, accessed March 5, 2003.

57. "Accountability."

58. Harriett Ryan, "Non-financial reporting more essential than ever, finds new survey by Arup," *M2 Presswire,* February 27, 2003.

59. "Verification."

60. Ibid.

61. Buchholz, "Auditing Social Responsibility Reports," pp. 18–19; "SEC Approves Conflict-of-Interest Limits for Auditors," Bloomberg LP, aol://4344:30.bloomberg.389091.602536905, accessed November 17, 2000.

62. Buchholz, "Auditing Social Responsibility Reports," pp. 16–18.

63. Ibid., pp. 19–20.

64. "Accountability."

65. Buchholz, "Auditing Social Responsibility Reports," pp. 19–20.

66. Ibid., p. 1.

67. Waddock and Smith, "Corporate Responsibility Audits."

68. Buchholz, "Auditing Social Responsibility Reports," p. 1.

69. Waddock and Smith, "Corporate Responsibility Audits."

70. Buchholz, "Auditing Social Responsibility Reports," p. 1.

71. Waddock and Smith, "Corporate Responsibility Audits."

72. J. C. Collins and J. I. Porras, *Built to Last: Successful Habits of Visionary Companies* (New York: HarperCollins, 1997).

73. Waddock and Smith, "Corporate Responsibility Audits."

Index

Page numbers followed by *n* refer to source notes.

Page numbers followed by *n* plus a number refer to endnotes, which are located at the back of the book.

AA1000 Series, 367, 371
Academy of Travel and Tourism, 333
AccountAbility, 385
Accountability
    demands for greater, 158
    explanation of, 159
    lack of mechanisms for, 164–165
Accounting scandals
    background of, 14–15
    conflicts of interest and, 104
    effects of, 105–106, 139, 145, 169, 294, 366, 459–461, 480
    as global issue, 84–85
    legislation to address, 88, 89
    whistle-blowers and, 145, 146, 244, 245
Acid rain, 260–261
Ackerman, Elise, 402*n*
ACORN principles, 248
Acquisitions, 160–161
Activism, shareholder, 169–171
Adadian Ambulance, 253
Adams, Chris, 515*n*16, 532*n*97
Adelphia Communications Corporation, 88, 157, 158, 364, 365
Adkins, Sue, 534*n*30, 534*n*31
Adobe Systems Inc., 312
Advertising
    fraud in, 107–108
    legal issues related to, 199–200
Aegon NV, 208
Aeppel, Timothy, 511*n*34, 511*n*41
Affirmative action programs
    explanation of, 109–110
    goals of, 239
African Americans, 109, 111
Age Discrimination in Employment Act, 109, 235
Agle, Bradley R., 36*n*, 509*n*64, 509*n*67, 511*n*21
Air Line Pilots Association, 43
Air pollution, 260–262
Albiniak, Paige, 510*n*1
Alcoa, 330
Alcoholic beverages, 200
Alexander, Jeffrey A., 518*n*14
Alexander, Scott, 520*n*49
Alibris, 214
Alien Tort Claims Act, 16
Allen, Herbert, 394

Allen, Robert, 351–352
Allen, Robin Lee, 522*n*59
Almond, Brenda, 510*n*6
Alsop, Ronald, 385*n*, 402*n*, 507*n*10, 509*n*54, 511*n*33, 511*n*35, 536*n*27
Alsop, Stewart, 520*n*1
Altman, Barbara W., 5*n*, 507*n*14, 508*n*18
Altman-Ohr, Andy, 522*n*54
Amazon.com, 81, 307
American Airlines, 181
American Apparel Manufacturers Association, 345
American Association for Retired Persons (AARP), 109
American Booksellers Association, 81
American Express, 120, 311, 333, 339
American Institute of Certified Public Accountants, 150
American Management Association, 323
American Medical Association, 114
American Productivity and Quality Center (APQC), 330, 351
American Society for Training and Development, 245
Americans with Disabilities Act, 109, 235, 239, 247
American Tobacco Company, 69
America Online (AOL), 54, 68, 311
AMR Corp., 181
Anand, Vaani, 523*n*77
Andersen, Arthur, 474, 475
Andersen Worldwide, 364
Anderson, Erin, 511*n*37
Anderson, Mark, 519*n*29
Anderson, Sarah, 520*n*54, 520*n*67
Anderson, Stephanie Forest, 482*n*
Anderson, Thomas, 518*n*10, 518*n*12
Anderson, Warren, 41–42
Andriof, Jörg, 507*n*14, 511*n*32, 512*n*48, 512*n*61
Andrx Corp., 67
Angst, Bud, 489*n*
Angwin, Julia, 510*n*81, 530*n*36
Anheuser-Busch Companies, 278
Annenberg Public Policy Center, 307
Anschultz, Philip, 106, 462
Anti-Cybersquatting Consumer Production Act, 314

Anti-Defamation League (ADL) of B'nai B'rith, 178
Antitrust Improvements Act, 70
Antitrust legislation
    benefits of, 76
    specific types of, 68, 71–72, 74
Anwar, W. A., 508*n*47
AOL/Time Warner, 160
Apartheid, 171
Appleby, Julia, 512*n*4
Apple Computer, 76, 81, 312–313, 331–332
Apria Healthcare, 168
Archer Daniels Midland, 320, 364
Argandona, Antonio, 510*n*6
Argenti, Paul, 512*n*45
Armour, Stephanie, 524*n*7
Arrow, K. J., 509*n*69
Arthur Andersen Case
    advent of consulting, 475–476
    Baptist Foundation of Arizona, 476–477
    corporate culture and ethical ramifications, 479–480
    Enron, 478–479
    implications for regulation and accounting ethics, 480
    introduction, 474
    Sunbeam, 477
    telecoms, 479
    Waste Management, 477–478
Arthur Andersen LLP, 104, 139, 143, 364, 370, 456, 457, 491, 495
Arup, 382, 383
Ashcroft, Michael, 486
Asher, Allan, 522*n*35
Ashoka, 346
Asian Americans, in workforce, 109
Asian Development Bank, 45
Asia-Pacific Economic Cooperation (APEC), 17
Asmus, Peter, 441*n*
Association of Equal Opportunity in Higher Education, 295
AT&T, 69, 84, 103, 108, 275, 311, 351–352, 491
AT&T Foundation, 338
Audits, 178, 366–370. *See also* Social audit process; Social audits
Austin, Duncan, 529*n*74

Austin Social Venture Partners (ASVP), 345
Aventis, 57, 67
Aventis Pharmaceuticals Health Care Foundation, 338
Avon, 98
Avon Breast Cancer Crusade, 317, 339, 340
Avon Products Foundation, 317, 339

Babwin, Don, 534n41
Baby boomers, in workplace, 248
Bacanovic, Peter, 469–471
Backover, Andrew, 107n, 465n, 498n
Bagley, Constance E., 516n2, 517n7
Bagwell, Kyle, 19n
Baig, Edward C., 531n54
Bailyn, Lotte, 526n91
Ball, Deborah, 85n
Ball, Jeffrey, 528n59
Banco Azteca, 201
Bandler, James, 489n, 515n18, 515n27
Bank of America Foundation, Inc., 338
Baptist Foundation of Arizona, 476–477
Barber, Brian, 531n50
Barclay's Bank, 39
Barrett, Amy, 245n
Barrett, J. Douglas, 535n52
Barrionuevo, Alexei, 457n, 516n84
Barry, Dave, 527n21
Barsness, Zoe I., 507n12
BASF, 72
Baucus, David A., 509n68
Baucus, Melissa A., 509n68
Bauder, Don, 520n52
Baue, William, 519n36
Baun, Robert, 441n
Bayer, 101
Baykal, Leyla, 467
BBBOnLine, 311
Beatty, Ted, 145
Bebchuk, Lucian, 520n59
Becherer, H. W., 523n72
Beck, Ernest, 513n26
Beck, Susan, 524n34
Beckett, Paul, 517n37
Beene, Terry, 426–428
Begley, Sharon, 529n73, 529n83
Beigbeder, Steve, 524n27
BE&K, 342
Belden, Timothy, 454
Bell Atlantic, 344
Bell Foundation, 343
Bell Labs, 107
Belnick, Mark A., 483, 485, 488
Belson, Ken, 518n9

Benetton, 12
Beniff, Mark, 520n1
Benioff, Marc, 192
Ben & Jerry's Homemade, 336, 378
Bennett, Charles J., 533n11
Bennett, Nathan, 516n62
Bennett, Roger, 350n, 535n53
Benson, Mitchel, 523n69
Berardino, Joseph, 478, 480
Berenbeim, Ronald E., 519n20, 533n11
Berger, Eric, 457n
Berkshire Hathaway, 362
Berman, Dennis K., 498n, 535n12
Berman, Joshua, 486
Berman, Melissa A., 5n
Berman, Shawn L., 509n66, 511n32
Bermingham, David, 454
Berners-Lee, 295
Bernstein, Aaron, 508n40, 510n78, 510n80, 511n24, 522n52, 523n75, 527n102
Besser, Terry L., 507n6
Best, Roger J., 441n
Better Business Bureau (BBB), 63, 65, 66, 78, 129, 207
Bettys and Taylors of Harrogate Yorkshire Tea, 341
Beversluis, Eric H., 102, 515n19, 515n20
Bhopal accident, 41–42, 49, 53
Bianco, Anthony, 489n
bigmailbox.com, 69
Bill and Melinda Gates Foundation, 82, 83
Billington, Jim, 519n48
Biodiversity, 267–268
Bioethics, 315
Biotechnology, 316–318
Birmele, Jotta, 520n62
BJC Health System, 344
Blank, Arthur, 431–433
Blodgett, Mark S., 516n72
Bloom, Paul N., 522n37, 523n70, 533n5
Blumenstein, Rebecca, 465n
Board of directors
    compensation for, 128
    expertise of, 166–167
    function of, 165
    independence of, 164, 166
    performance of, 167–168
    support for social audit by, 373–374
Bodman, Richard S., 486
The Body Shop International, 99, 373, 378, 385
Boeing, 141–143
Boggess, Jerry, 488

Bogue, Richard J., 518n14
Bonchek, Mark S., 522n39
Bonsor, Kevin, 529n4
Borrus, Amy, 245n, 512n3, 514n47, 514n50, 517n38, 517n39
Bower, Amanda, 458n
Bowie, Norman, 36, 510n6
Boycotts, 208
Boyle, Mary-Ellen, 522n58, 523n63
BP Amoco, 262
B&Q, 11, 276
Bradford, Michael, 521n26
Bradsher, Keith, 518n7, 518n8
Brady, Diane, 473n, 482n
Braid, Fiona, 421, 422
Brainerd, Paul, 347
Brand, Rachel, 441n
Brandenberger, Adam M., 520n66
Brass, Daniel J., 517n44
Braverman, Mark, 525n50
Breen, Edward, 488
Bremer, L. Paul, 512n45
Bribery, 104–105
Bridgestone Corporation, 46
Bridgestone/Firestone, Inc., 46, 48–49, 101
Bridis, Ted, 513n32
Brink, Graham, 512n4
Brisbois, Cathy, 535n61
Bristol-Myers Squibb Foundation, 333
British Petroleum (BP), 39, 338–339
Broadband technology, 292–293, 298
Brockner, Joel, 516n63
Brontzen, David, 512n62
Brooks, Randy, 510n9
Brown, James R., 157
Brown, Jeanette, 447n
Brown, Jennifer, 526n71
Brown, Ken, 465n
Brown-Dodson, Diana, 43
Brown University, 45
Brown & Williamson Tobacco Corporation, 116
Buchholz, Trey, 535n14, 535n20, 536n47, 536n61, 536n65, 536n68, 536n70
Buckman, Rebecca, 531n85
Buffalo Sabres, 157
Buffett, Warren, 174, 394
Bureau of Consumer Protection, 196
Burke, Edmund M., 522n60–523n60
Burke, Linda, 448n
Burns, J. M., 517n45
Burr, Barry, 519n28, 519n37
Bush, George W., 9, 79, 88, 237, 262
Bush, Lawrence, 347n

Business
  globalization of, 15–19
  influence of government on, 64–78
    (*See also* Government; Regulation)
  influence on government by, 78–85
    (*See also* Government)
  politics and, 79–80
  relationship between community and, 212–213
  rights and responsibilities of, 3–4
  technology and, 323–324
  trust in, 101–103
Business Discount Plan (BDP), 108
Business ethics. *See* Ethical decision-making process; Ethical issues; Ethics; Ethics programs
Business for Social Responsibility, 382
Business Software Alliance, 312–313
Business-to-business (B2B) e-commerce, 296–297
Butterfield, Kenneth D., 517*n*44
Byrne, John, 171*n*, 347*n*, 509*n*59, 515*n*22, 519*n*22, 535*n*55, 535*n*60
Byrnes, Nanette, 482*n*, 489*n*
Byron, Christopher M., 473*n*

Cadbury, Adrian, 168, 519*n*27
Cadbury Schweppes, 338, 398
Calgary Community Support for Young Parents, 347
California Public Employees' Retirement System (CalPERS), 170
Calloway Golf, 185
Calvert Group, Ltd., 172–174
Campbell v. Kansas State University, 240
Canada, 310, 358
Canadian Centre for Philanthropy, 358
Canadian Standards Association (CSA), 310
Canandella, Matthew, 524*n*27
Candaele, Kelly, 523*n*74
Cannella, Albert A., Jr., 520*n*70
Capell, Kerry, 528*n*37, 532*n*118, 532*n*120
Capellas, Michael, 151
Capitalism and Freedom (Friedman), 4
Caplan, Arthur, 532*n*94
Carlson, Darren, 510*n*1
Carlson, Jim, 436*n*
Carlson, Patricia, 516*n*72
Carlton, Jim, 507*n*11, 513*n*14, 529*n*64, 530*n*38, 530*n*42
Carlyle, Anna, 503
Carnegie, Andrew, 66, 164

Carney, Dan, 245*n*, 517*n*38, 517*n*39
Carns, Ann, 402*n*
Carpenter, Dave, 482*n*
Carrefour SA, 84
Carroll, Archie B., 5*n*, 9*n*, 507*n*14, 508*n*19, 515*n*32
Carson, Rachel, 269
Case, Steve, 160
Caudill, Eve M., 530*n*43
Caulfield, John, 436*n*
Cause-related marketing, 339–341
Caux Round Table Business Principles of Ethics, 116–119
Cavanagh, John, 520*n*54
CDNow, 196
Celler-Kefauver Act, 70
Cendant, 170–171
Center for Hope, 211
Centre for Board Effectiveness, 168
Certified public accountants (CPAs), 105
Chaloner, Nick, 512*n*62
Chalwa, Anu, 523*n*77
Chamberlin, Ted, 463
Chandler, Robert C., 365*n*
Chanen, Jill Schachner, 526*n*70
Chazan, Guy, 531*n*73
CheapTickets.com, 171
Chemical Manufacturers Association, 53
Chen, Christine Y., 457*n*
Chester, Jeffrey, 446
ChevronTexaco, 147, 148, 222, 275
Chief executive officers (CEOs)
  compensation for, 180–182
  roles of board and, 166
  support for social audits by, 373–374
Chief privacy officers (CPOs), 311
Child, Brandt, 273
Child labor, 235
Child Protection and Toy Safety Act, 197, 198
Children's Hospital (Seattle), 49
Children's Online Privacy Protection Act of 2000 (COPPA), 68–70, 197, 307, 309
Chmielewski, Dawn C., 529*n*1
China Consumers' Association, 203
Chiquita, 276
Chiswick, Barry, 523*n*74
Chiu, Randy, 526*n*66
Chomentowski, Walter, 527*n*26
Chowdhury, Jhinuk, 522*n*35
Chris Hani Baragwanath Hospital (CHBH), 374–375
Christian, Nichole, 522*n*42
Christy, Nancy, 247
Chrysler Corporation, 161, 180

Chubb Corporation, 166
Chuck E. Cheese, 111
Chui, Glenda, 530*n*32
Chung, Helen, 529*n*69
Churchill Downs, Incorporated, 211
Cifrino, David O., 518*n*19
Cigarette Labelling and Advertising Act, 198, 200
Cisco Systems Inc., 251, 313
Citigroup, 83, 84, 103, 311
Citigroup Foundation, 338
Ciulla, Joanne B., 228–229, 510*n*2, 523*n*2, 523*n*3, 524*n*18, 524*n*19
Civil Rights Act of 1964, Title VII, 109–111, 235, 239, 240, 246
Clair, Judith A., 512*n*45
Clarkson, Max B. E., 56, 57*n*, 510*n*10, 510*n*12, 512*n*56
Clayson, Jane, 472
Clayton Antitrust Act, 69–71
Clean Air Act Amendments of 1977, 271, 274
Clean Air Act Amendments of 1990, 271
Clean Air Act of 1970, 271, 272
Clean Water Act of 1972, 68, 263, 272
ClearOne Communications Inc., 130
Clinton, William J., 204
Cloning technology, 317–318
Closure Medical, 166
Clutterbuck, D., 512*n*51
CMC Properties, 208
Coalition for Environmentally Responsible Economies (CERES), 259, 260, 284, 367
Coca-Cola Company, 10–11, 49, 109, 147, 218, 278, 345, 379
Coca-Cola Company Case
  crisis situation, 397–399
  historical background, 395
  post crisis management, 399–401
  replacement of Ivester, 394
  reputation, 395–396
  reputation management, 401
  social responsibility focus, 396–397
Cocks, Elijah, 532*n*89
Codes of conduct
  development of, 131, 132, 136–137
  at Fidelity Investments, 134–136
  need for, 129
  at Texas Instruments, 132–134
Coercive power, 44
Coghlan, Andy, 532*n*107
Cohen, Laurie P., 489*n*, 498*n*, 515*n*21
Cohn, Laura, 482*n*
Cohrs, Dan, 495

Coleman, Gill, 11*n*, 54*n*, 508*n*20, 512*n*50, 512*n*53
Coleman, James, 512*n*48
Coles supermarkets, 341
Colgate-Palmolive Company, 214
Collins, Chuck, 520*n*54
Collins, J. C., 536*n*72
Colombia/HCA, 364
Colvin, Geoffrey, 245*n*
CommerceNet, 311
Commerce One, 297
Commission of the European Communities, 74
Common Cause, 80
Communication, 138–141
Communications Workers of America (CWA), 236
Community
  economic issues and, 217–219
  ethical issues and, 219–220
  legal issues and, 219
  philanthropic responsibilities to, 221–222, 345
  responsibilities to, 214–222
  as stakeholder, 210–214
  strategic implementation of responsibilities to, 222
Community mission statements, 213, 214
Community relations
  explanation of, 213–214
  myths about, 216–217
Compaq Computer Corporation, 17, 311
Compensation
  for board of directors, 128
  executive, 180–182
Compliance programs, 85–87
Comprehensive Environmental Response, Compensation, and Liability Act, 272
Computer and Communications Association, 74
Computer Matching and Privacy Protection Act, 309
Computers. *See also* Internet
  cybercrime and, 304–305
  for low-income families, 295
Computer Security Act, 309
Computer viruses, 304
Computer worms, 304–305
Conaway, Charles, 88, 150, 151
Cone-Roper, 20, 21
Coney, Kenneth A., 441*n*
Conference Board, 137, 139, 165, 335
Conflict, 55
Conflict of interest, 103–105
Congress, U.S., 80

Conhalter, Christine, 410
Conlin, Michelle, 523*n*1, 524*n*7, 533*n*133
Connecticut Better Business Bureau, 26–27
Conoco Case
  annual report, 415
  Award decision making, 429
  Award nominee presentation, 419–422, 426–429
  Award selection process, 419
  Business Ethics Award, 412–414, 416–419
  historical background, 413–414
  organizational structures blocking ethical action, 423–425
Conroy, Tom, 448*n*
Conry-Murray, Andrew, 305*n*
Conseco Inc., 4
Consequentialism, 113
Consolidated Gas Company, 164
Consumer Advisory Council, 204
Consumer Bill of Rights, 203
Consumer Charter for Global Business, 194
Consumer education programs, 204, 207
Consumer fraud, 194–195
Consumer Goods Pricing Act, 70, 198
Consumerism, 204
Consumer Product Safety Act, 197, 198
Consumer Product Safety Commission (CPSC), 73, 197
Consumer Protection Agency, 63
Consumer Reports, 204
Consumers
  discrimination against, 111
  economic responsibilities to, 194–196
  ethical responsibilities to, 203–209
  explanation of, 93
  legislation and regulations protecting, 196–203
  philanthropic responsibilities to, 210
  responsibilities to, 193–194
  strategic implementation of responsibilities to, 222
Consumers International, 193–194, 276
Consumer's rights
  to be heard, 207
  to be informed, 206–207
  to choose, 205
  explanation of, 203–205
  to privacy, 207–208
  to safety, 205–206
  to seek redress, 207
Consumers Union (CU), 204
Contingency planning, 365–366

Contracts, employee-employer, 229–231
Contributions Academy, 352
Conway, Maria E., 525*n*57
Conway, Neil, 524*n*11
Cook, Lodwrick, 494
Cook, Pat, 421, 422
Cookies, 306
Coolidge, Carrie, 525*n*51
Cooper, Cynthia, 145, 146, 244
Co-operative Bank, 281
Copyrights, 312–314
Corbin, Dana E., 525*n*42
Cordoza, Michelle, 503
Corney, Don, 514*n*47, 514*n*50
Corporate culture. *See* Organizational culture
Corporate governance
  boards of directors and, 165–168
  executive compensation and, 180–182
  explanation of, 159–161
  future outlook for, 185–187
  globalization and, 182–185
  historical background of, 163–165
  internal control and, 177–179
  as investment criteria, 176–177
  risk management and, 179–180
  shareholder model of, 162
  shareholders and investors and, 168–177
  social responsibility and, 161–163
  stakeholder model of, 162, 171
Corporations
  background of U.S., 12–15
  compliance programs in, 85–87
  influence on government by, 81–84
Corruption, national economy and, 24
Costa, John Dalla, 16, 508*n*44
Cotsakos, Christos M., 181
Council of Better Business Bureaus, 311
Council of Economic Advisors, 296
Covey, Stephen R., 20, 509*n*50
Cox, John, 530*n*22
Coy, Peter, 524*n*7
Coyle-Shapiro, Jacqueline, 524*n*9, 524*n*10
Craig, Andrea, 247
Crandall, Robert, 181
Cranor, Lorrie, 531*n*70
Creative Marketing Solutions, 503, 504
Cree, Richard, 534*n*40
Creighton, James L., 523*n*85
Creswell, Julie, 473*n*

Crime
    cyber, 304–305
    high-tech, 321–322
    workplace, 237, 239
Crisis management
    explanation of, 49–50
    social audits and, 364–366
    stages of, 50
    stakeholder communication
        during, 50–52
Crofton, Harry, 421–422
Crook, Clive, 507n5, 518n16
Crossman, Cathy Lynn, 526n81
Crouch, Gregory, 85n
Crowe, Roy, 371n, 535n8,
    535n22
CUC International Inc., 170, 171
Cufaude, Jeffrey B., 526n83
Culture. *See* Diversity; Organizational
    culture
Cummings, Betsy, 526n72
Cummins Engine Company, 2, 3, 10
Cunningham, Michael R., 122
Customers
    loyalty of, 349
    relations with, 35
    as stakeholders, 343–344
Customer satisfaction, social
    responsibility and, 21
Cybercrime, 304–305
Cyberterrorism, 322

Daft, Doug, 394, 399–401
Dahle, Cheryl, 534n40
Daily, Catherine M., 520n70
Daimler Benz, 161, 180
DaimlerChrysler, 95, 111, 161, 251,
    262, 279, 280, 284, 297
Daiwa Bank of Japan, 364
Daiwa Securities, 192
Dalhousie University, 332
Dalton, Dan R., 520n70
Damonti, John, 333
Dando, Nicole, 535n24, 536n30
Daniels, Cora, 436n, 526n84
Daniels, Stephen H., 525n65
D'Antonio, Louis, 519n35
Darby, Giles, 454
Davenport, Kim, 5n
Davis, Jason L., 521n10
Davis, Jennifer C., 532n119
Davis, Stephen M., 520n60
Daviss, Bennett, 511n30
Day, Julian, 151
Dean, Jason, 529n2
De Beers, 46

Decision making
    complexities of, 3
    process of ethical, 112–124 (*See also*
        Ethical decision-making process)
Decko, Jeffrey, 347n
Deer Lake Marina, 505
Dees, Gregory, 510n4
Defense Initiative on Business Ethics and
    Conduct, 150
Defoe, Patrick R., 420–421
Deforestation, 265, 267
Degroat, T. J., 522n42
DeLany, Clarence, 474
Dell Computer, 76, 147, 215, 295, 345,
    362
Della Femina, Jerry, 473
Deloitte & Touche, 157, 250
Delphi Automotive, 213–214
Delta Air Lines, 208, 209
Demb, A., 518n11
Democratic Party, 79, 82, 83
Denenberg, Richard V., 525n50
DePont, 268
Deppe, E. Devon, 527n101
Deregulation, 76–77
Deutsche Bank AG, 343
Devine, Nora, 465n
Diaz, Stephanie, 201
Digital Electronic Signatures Act of 2000,
    78
Digital Envoy, 306
Digital Millennium Copyright Act
    (DMCA), 68, 70, 290, 313, 322
Dilio, Michelle, 510n81
D'Innocenzio, Anne, 473n
Dion, Jonathan W., 525n64
Direct Marketing Association of Canada
    (DMAC), 310
Direct Selling Association (DSA), 10
Disabilities. *See* Individuals with
    disabilities
Disaster recovery, 364–366
Discrimination
    affirmative action programs and,
        109–110
    apartheid as, 171
    consumer rights and, 205
    in credit extension, 197–198
    employment, 110–111, 239
    legislation addressing, 109, 239
    racial, 398–400
    sexual harassment as, 239–242
Disinsection, 42–43
Distributive justice, 114
Diversity, workplace, 109–111, 246–249
Dixon, Janice I., 525n65

Dollar General, 181
Domini, Amy L., 519n31
Domini 400 Social Index, 172
Domini Social Investments, 172
Domino's Pizza, 205, 220
Donaldson, Thomas, 37n, 510n4,
    510n8, 510n15, 510n16
Donor Bill of Rights, 354
Doran, D'Arcy, 523n84
Dorazio, Sharon, 43
DoubleClick, 306
DoubleClick Case
    controversy, 445–447
    growth, 443–444
    introduction, 442–443
    new era, 447
    subsidiaries, 444–445
Dover, Kyle, 524n33
Dow, Warren, 371n, 535n8, 535n22
Dow Chemical, 41, 262
Dow-Jones Sustainability Indexes
    (DJSI), 363
Downs, Robert B., 521n19
Downsizing
    economic responsibility and, 218
    effects of, 232–234
Doyle, Christine, 521n11
Drayton, William, 347n
Dreamworks SKG, 34
Dreier, Peter, 523n74
Drexel Burnham Lambert, 491
Driver Privacy Protection Act, 309
Drumwright, Minette E., 280, 529n77,
    533n5, 533n12, 534n22
Dudley, Susan, 75n
Duff, Mike, 473n
Duffy, Jim, 531n84
Dukes, M. N. Graham, 508n43
Dulany, Peggy, 334n, 533n1
Duncan, David, 478
Dunfee, Thomas W., 510n16
Dunham, Archie, 412, 419, 429
Dunlap, Al, 351
Dunlap, Albert, 477
DuPont, 250, 279, 413
Dwyer, Paula, 245n, 512n3, 517n38,
    517n39
Dwyer, Robert F., 441n
Dynergy Inc., 124, 145

E. coli infection, 49
Eastman Kodak, 102, 210, 232, 280, 281
eBay, 81, 301, 311, 314
Ebbers, Bernard, 460, 462
Eccles, Robert G., 519n48–520n48
Eco-label (European Union), 276

e-commerce, growth of, 296–297

Economic growth
social responsibility and, 23–24
technology and, 294–298

Economic responsibilities
to consumers, 194–196
downsizing and, 218
to employees, 229–234

Edelson, Rebecca, 532n88

Edgar, David, 440

Edwards, Edwin, 83

Edwards, Jeffrey R., 526n87

Eggerton, John, 521n23

Egoism, 113

Ehrenfeld, John, 512n49

Eidson, Christy, 47n, 511n38

Eighteenth Amendment, 200

E Ink, 292

Eisenberg, Melvin A., 519n21, 519n45

Eisenberg, Rebecca S., 532n111

Eisler, Peter, 528n42

Elafson, Greg, 524n11

Elderly individuals, 109

Electronic Frontier Foundation, 311

Electronic Network Consortium (ENC) (Japan), 310

Elias, Jaan, 510n4

Eli Lily Pharmaceuticals, 215

Elkind, Peter, 457n

Elliott, Janet, 465n

Elsbach, Kimberly D., 524n11

Elson, Charles, 166, 520n50

Elstom, Peter, 525n41

Embryonic stem cells, 317, 318

Emergency Planning and Community Right-to-Know Act, 272, 274

Emissions reduction, 279

Emling, Shelley, 473n

Emmons, Sasha, 521n11

Employee-employer contact, 229–231

Employee Internet management (EIM), 323

Employee relations
importance of good, 28, 35
philanthropy and, 349

Employee Retirement Income Security Act (ERISA), 235–236

Employees
commitment of, 21–22
with disabilities, 109, 239, 247
economic responsibilities to, 229–234
ethical responsibilities to, 243–251
laid-off, 218
legal responsibilities to, 234–243
philanthropic responsibilities to, 251

as stakeholders, 227, 228, 342–343
strategic implementation of responsibilities to, 252–254

Employee satisfaction, 20

Employee stock ownership plans (ESOPs), 253

Employee training
benefits of, 243–245
deaf awareness, 55
ethics, 138–143
resources and commitment for, 245–246

Employers
of choice, 252–253
relationship between employees and, 230–231

Employment at will, 234

Endangered Species Act, 271–273

Enderle, Georges, 510n6

Energizer, 193

Enron Case
accounting problems, 452
Arthur Andersen, 456
chairman, 454–455
chief executive officer, 454
chief financial officer, 453–454
corporate culture, 451–452
fallout, 456–457
introduction, 449–451
Merrill Lynch, 455–456
Vinson & Elkins, 455
whistle-blower, 452–453

Enron Corporation, 14, 80, 84, 88, 104, 129, 139, 145, 146, 178, 244, 253, 364, 365, 367, 370, 478–479

Ensher, Ellen A., 526n86

Entertainment industry
stakeholders in, 35
violence in, 34

Entine, Jon, 512n54

Environmental initiatives
corporate, 348
emissions reduction, 279
green marketing, 275–277
recycling, 277–280
socially responsible buying, 280–281

Environmental issues
atmospheric, 260–262
biodiversity, 267–268
Bush administration and, 79, 262
business responses to, 274–281
explanation of, 28
genetically modified foods, 268
global, 259
insecticide use and, 42–43
land, 265–267

public interest in, 258–259
strategic approaches to, 281–285
water, 262–264

Environmental Protection Agency (EPA)
function of, 73, 269–270
goals of, 271–272
insecticide use and, 42
national air quality standards and, 271
water pollution and, 262–263

Episcopal Church, 170–171

Equal Credit Opportunity Act, 198

Equal Employment Opportunity Commission (EEOC)
function of, 73, 110–111
sexual harassment and, 241

Equal opportunity, 239

Equal Pay Act, 235

Erffmeyer, Robert, 514n11

Ergonomics, 237, 258

Ernst & Young, 170, 247, 311

Estee Lauder, 473

Estes, Ralph, 508n29, 520n54

Ethical climate, 121, 122

Ethical decision-making process
approach to, 112
individual factors in, 113–120
moral development stages and, 115–119
moral philosophy and, 113–115
motivation and, 119–120
opportunity and, 123–124
organizational culture and, 120–122
organizational relationships and, 120–123
significant others and, 122–123

Ethical formalism, 114

Ethical issues
conflict of interest as, 103–105
discrimination as, 109–111
explanation of, 101
fraud as, 105–109
genetically modified foods as, 320
honesty and fairness as, 101–103
information technology as, 111
recognition of, 111–112
related to community, 219–220
related to consumers, 204–209
related to workplace, 243–251

Ethical Leadership Group, 152

Ethics
codes of (*See* Codes of conduct)
conflict of interest and, 103–105
decision making and, 112–124
(*See also* Ethical decision-making process)
discrimination and, 109–111

explanation of, 96–97
foundations of, 98–101
fraud and, 105–109
honesty and fairness and, 101–103
information technology and, 111
issues in, 101
nature of, 97–98
overview of, 96
recognizing problems in, 111–112
EthicScan Canada, 358
Ethics Officer Association (EOA), 137,
138, 150, 382
Ethics officers
explanation of, 137–138
management of ethics training by,
139–140
responsibilities of, 146–147
Ethics Practitioner Forum, 138
Ethics programs
codes of conduct for, 132–137
continuous improvements in, 147
ethics officers for, 137–138
instituting training and communication initiatives for, 138–143
monitoring and enforcing standards
for, 143–145
need for, 129–132
role of ethical corporate culture in,
151–153
role of leaders in, 149–151
strategic approaches to, 128–129
whistle-blowers and, 145–147
Ethics Resource Center, 123, 132, 137,
139, 145, 152
Ethics training
explanation of, 138–139
goals of, 141
guidelines for, 140–141
influences on, 142–143
refresher programs in, 141–142
usefulness of, 139–140
Etzioni, Amitai, 511n23
European Union Directive on Data Protection, 99, 308
European Union (EU)
Eco-label, 276
function of, 74
genetically modified foods and, 319
health and consumer protection in,
203
privacy initiatives of, 308
sexual harassment legislation in, 240
Evans, Richard, 372n, 388n, 535n3,
535n61
Ewing, Jack, 518n8
Excite, 311

Executive compensation, 180–182
Exxon Corporation, 21, 46, 270–271
Exxon Valdez oil spill, 21, 46, 270

F. Hoffman La Roche, 72
Fabrikant, Geraldine, 518n7
Fackelmann, Kathleen, 527n18
Failer, Barb, 520n2
Fair, Isaac & Co., 100
Fair Credit Reporting Act, 198, 309
Fair Debt Collection Practices Act, 198
Fairechild, Diane, 43n
Fair Labor Association (FLA), 45
Fair Labor Standards Act (FLSA), 234,
235
Fairlamb, David, 513n29
Fairness, 101–103
Fair Packaging and Labeling Act, 70,
198
False Claims Act of 1986, 243, 316
Family and Medical Leave Act (FMLA),
235, 236
Faneuil, Douglas, 469–470
Fanning, Shawn, 322
Farber Blake Corporation, 67
Farrell, Greg, 107n, 457n, 482n,
533n127
Farrell, Mike, 518n1
Fastow, Andrew, 365, 449, 451, 453–454
Federal Bureau of Investigation (FBI),
145, 146, 321
Federal Communications Commission
(FCC), 76, 81, 197
Federal Election Campaign Act, 80
Federal Election Committee, 82
Federal Insecticide, Fungicide, and Ro-
denticide Act of 1972, 271, 272,
274
Federal regulatory agencies, 73
Federal Reserve Board, 73
Federal Sentencing Guidelines for Orga-
nizations (FSGO), 85–86, 128,
137, 146, 241, 322, 374
Federal Trade Commission Act, 70–72,
200
Federal Trade Commission (FTC)
fraud and, 108–109, 301–303
function of, 34, 68–69, 71–73, 196,
199
privacy issues and, 307–308
Federal Trademark Dilution Act, 70
FedEx, 152–153, 294, 362
Feinberg, Richard, 508n47
Feldman, Daniel C., 524n9, 524n10
Female Employment Initiative, 110
Ferguson, Gerald J., 532n93

Ferrell, Linda, 199n, 459, 513n27,
513n28, 513n30, 515n25,
515n37, 515n56, 516n64,
516n67, 517n24, 528n45
Ferrell, O. C., 199n, 457n, 508n27,
509n63, 513n27, 513n28,
513n30, 514n39, 514n42,
515n25, 515n37, 515n39,
515n42, 515n56,
516n64–516n67, 516n74,
516n78, 516n86, 517n26,
518n51, 521n29, 528n45,
529n81, 530n35, 531n49
Ferrellgas, 253
Feuerstein, Aaron, 229
Fialka, John, 513n9, 528n44, 529n76
Fick, Jeffrey A., 457n
Fidelity Investments, 134–136
Field, David, 530n31
FIFO (first in, first out), 369
Filipczak, Bob, 248n, 526n83
Financial audits, 178, 366–370
Financial Consumer's Bill of Rights Act,
204
Fink, Steven, 472
Finn, David, 508n29
Finnigan, Annie, 515n38
Firestone, 364
Fisher, Dorothy Canfield, 523n3
Fisher, Mary Jane, 522n40
Fisher, Susan Reynolds, 524n33
Fitzgerald, Jay, 411n
Flammable Fabrics Act, 197
Flatters, Paul, 508n37
Fletcher, Joyce K., 526n91
Flynn, Gillian, 235n, 524n12, 524n15,
525n37, 525n40
Foer, Albert A., 513n24
Foley, Sharon, 402n
FOLIOfn, 172
Fombrun, Charles J., 25n
Fonda, Daren, 457n
Food and Drug Administration (FDA),
73, 196–197, 202
Food Quality Protection Act, 273, 274
FoodService, Inc., 503
Foot Locker Specialty, 109
For All Kids Foundation, 349
Forbes, Walter A., 170
Ford, William Clay, Jr., 24–25
Ford Foundation, 331
Ford Motor Company, 24, 48–49,
111–112, 130, 241, 262, 284
Ford Motor Company Fund, 338
Forest Stewardship Council, 276
Forklift Systems, 241

Fort, John F., III, 484, 486
Foss, Stephen W., 486
Foundation for Accountability (FACCT), 210
Fox News, 157
Fraedrich, John, 199n, 515n56, 516n64–516n67, 516n78, 516n86, 528n45
France, Mike, 457n, 522n52
Frank, Dana, 511n22
Fraud
    accounting, 105–106
    consumer, 194–195
    explanation of, 105
    Internet, 301–303
    marketing, 107–109
Freedman, David H., 530n40
Freeman, R. E., 11, 508n23, 509n49
Freeman, Richard B., 44
Freeplay Group, 344
Fried, Jesse, 520n59
Friedman, Andrew L., 511n21
Friedman, Milton, 4, 507n4
Friedman, Stan, 534n33
Friedman, Thomas, 511n31
Frieswick, Kris, 527n101
Frito-Lay, 320
Frost, Alison Rankin, 511n39
Fuji, 102, 280, 281
Fuji Bank, 335
Furniture Resource Centre, 376
Fusaro, Roberta, 533n136
Future Solutions, Inc., 278–279
FX, 157

Gallanis, Peter J., 534n39
Galvin, John, 509n58
Galvin, Reneé, 459
The Gap, 16
Gardner, David M., 521n9
Gardyn, Rebecca, 509n53
Garman, E. Thomas, 521n34
Garten, Jeffrey, 19n
Gasparino, Charles, 465n, 473n, 489n
Gates, Bill, 83, 532n113
Gateway, Inc., 295
Gaziano, Joseph, 484, 485
Gebley, Sharon, 529n75
General Agreement of Tariffs and Trade (GATT), 18
General Electric, 362
General Electric Pension Trust, 344
General Motors, 16, 68, 147, 171, 275, 279, 284, 297
General Motors Foundation, Inc., 338
Generation X, in workplace, 248

Genetically modified foods
    background of, 268
    concerns regarding, 319–321
    research in, 318–319
    risk analysis and, 283
Genetic research, 318
GeoCities, 308
George, Barbara Crutchfield, 520n62
Gerber, Robert, 497
Giant Food Stores, 84
Gibson, Dirk C., 523n65
Gifts in Kind International, 332–333
Gilbeaut, John, 519n43
Gilbert, Lewis, 164
Gioia, Joyce L., 254n, 527n98, 527n99
girlslife.com, 69
Glass, Andrew J., 513n17
Glassman, Robert, 409–410, 411n
Global Climate Coalition, 262
Global Compact (United Nations), 17
Global Crossing, 104, 107, 177, 178, 364, 366, 463, 479
Global Crossing Case
    business concept, 491–492
    capacity swaps, 494–495
    congressional investigation, 495–496
    Grubman, 492–493
    insider trading concerns, 493–494
    outlook, 496–498
Globalization
    background of, 15–17
    corporate governance and, 182–185
    regulation and, 73–74
    stakeholders and, 40–43
    World Trade Organization and, 18–19
Global Reporters, 367
Global Reporting Initiative (GRI), 367, 385
Global warming, 261–262
Goizueta, Roberto, 394, 399
Goldberg, Ray A., 519n47
Goldman, Bob, 419
Goldman, Debra, 521n3
Golin/Harris Trust Survey, 131
Gomes, Lee, 513n11
Gonzalez, Jairo, 120–121
Goodell, Rebecca, 516n71
Good Housekeeping Institute, 206
Goodnight, James, 227
Googins, Bradley K., 523n61
Gordin, Mikhail, 421
Gordon, David M., 508n35
Gordon, Julie, 441n
Gordon, Louise, 535n18
Gorman, Christine, 521n27
Gotsi, Manto, 511n36

Govan, Barbara, 414
Governance, 158–159. See also Corporate governance
GovernanceMetrics International, 167
Government
    corporate governance and, 187
    influence on business of, 64–65
    legal and ethical compliance approaches of, 85–88
    regulation by, 65–78 (See also Regulation)
    technology and, 321–323
Govindarajan, Vijay, 526n75
Grace, E. Maria, 309n
Grace, W. R. & Co., 170
Graef, Crystal, 520n57
Granholm, Jennifer, 442
Grant, Alison, 520n52
Grant, Lorrie, 151n, 508n26
Graves, S. B., 509n64
Gravitz, Alisa, 347n
Green, Heather, 531n55
Green, Ken, 508n24
Greene, Jay, 514n47, 514n50
Greengard, Samuel, 525n63
Greenhouse gases, 261–262
Greenlaw, Paul S., 525n59, 525n60
Green marketing, 275–277
Green power, 279
Green Seal, 276
Greenspan, Alan, 530n14, 530n16, 530n18, 530n27
Greenwald, Judy, 525n52
Greenwood, Rysto, 518n46
Gresham, Larry G., 516n74, 516n78, 516n86, 517n26, 518n51
Greyser, Stephen A., 522n37
Griffiths, Daniel, 526n90
Grimsley, Kirstin Downey, 436n
Grivner, Carl, 494–495
Grossberg, Adam J., 526n72
Grossman, Robert, 525n50
Grover, Ronald, 518n1
Grubman, Jack, 103, 462, 492, 493, 496, 497
Gruley, Bryan, 457n
Grupo de Institutos Fundacoes E Empresas (GIFE), 330
Grupo Elektra S.A. de C.V., 201
GTE, 344
Guest, David E., 524n11
Guida, Thomas A., 532n93
Guidera, Jerry, 489n
Gulf Power, 243
Gundlach, Gregory, 521n9, 523n70, 533n5

Gupta, Anil K., 526*n*75
Guterl, Fred, 533*n*126
Gymboree, 351

Habitat for Humanity, 213, 343
Hackers, 304, 305
Hahn, Avital Louria, 518*n*1
Haiar, Nikole, 437, 441*n*
Hall, Mark, 297, 530*n*21
Hallmark Cards, 253
Hamberger, Tom, 457*n*
Hamilton, J. Brooke, III, 412
Hammers, Maryann, 526*n*78
Hampton University, 246
Handy, Charles, 507*n*5, 508*n*22
Haner-Dorr, Noelle, 523*n*64
Hanson, Craig, 529*n*74
Hanson, Kirk O., 515*n*53
Harallson, Darryl, 292*n*
Hardesty, David, 514*n*43
Harker, Michael John, 512*n*46
Harlow, Phillip, 477
Harrington, Ann, 402*n*, 517*n*42
Harris, Jim, 521*n*9
Harris, Teresa, 241
Harris Interactive Inc., 21, 301, 364,
    385, 396
Harrison, Jeffrey S., 509*n*49
Harrison, John, 503
Harrison, L. E., 24, 509*n*72
Harris v. Forklift Systems, 241
Hartman, Cathy L., 522*n*56
Hartman, Chris, 520*n*54
Harvard University, 174
Haverford College, 175
Hawaii Coffee Association, 81
Hawken, Paul, 529*n*66
Hawkins, Del I., 441*n*
Hayibor, Sefa, 509*n*64, 509*n*67
Hays, Constance, 151*n*, 402*n*
Hays, Kristen, 451*n*, 457*n*
Hays, Scott, 526*n*83
HCA-The Healthcare Company, 139
HealthNow New York, 311
Hechinger, John, 489*n*
Heckman, James, 515*n*31
Hellweg, Eric, 516*n*5
Help lines, ethics, 143–144
Herman, Adrienne D., 532*n*88
Herman, Roger E., 254*n*, 527*n*98,
    527*n*99
Herman Miller, Inc., 5–6, 258, 279
Herndon, Neil, 449, 491
Hershey Foods, 21
Hewlett-Packard, 17, 295, 363
HFS, 170

Hiatt, Arnold, 342
Higgins, Kevin T., 534*n*28
Hill, Kimberly, 530*n*20
Hillebrand, Bas, 511*n*20, 527*n*102
Hindery, Leo, Jr., 494
Hinings, C. R., 518*n*46
Hirsch, Paul M., 507*n*12
Hirt, Geoffrey, 515*n*39, 515*n*42, 521*n*29
Hispanics, 109
Hitachi, Ltd., 10
Hitachi Foundation, 10
HIV/AIDS, 239, 397
Ho, Suk-ching, 521*n*32
Hoechst, 57
Hoeffler, Steve, 534*n*31
Hofmeister, Joseph, 151
Hohenadel, Kristin, 521*n*11
Hoke, Kathy, 519*n*46
HolidaySmarts2.com, 196
Holland, Kelley, 527*n*102
Hollinger, Richard C., 521*n*10
Holsendolph, Ernest, 402*n*
Home Depot, 7, 27, 119, 168, 219, 249,
    276, 282, 343, 377
Home Depot Case
    commitment to social responsibility,
        435
    corporate philanthropy, 434
    employee relations, 434–435
    environmental initiatives, 432–433
    introduction, 431
Home Ownership and Equity Protection
    Act, 197–199
Honda Motor, 95
Honesty, 101–103
Hooker Chemical, 281–282
Hopkins, Jim, 498*n*
Hopps, Jason, 529*n*65
Hormel Foods, 52–53
Horovitz, Bruce, 508*n*41
Horton, Jacob F., 243
Hosenball, Mark, 473*n*
Hostile work environment sexual
    harassment, 240
Howard, Jennifer, 512*n*49
Howard, Robert, 517*n*41
Howarth, Anita, 402*n*
Huawei Technologies, 313
Huber, David, 421–422
Huffington, Arianna, 489*n*
Hult, G. Thomas, 509*n*63
Human Genome Project, 315
Hunt, Shelby D., 509*n*70, 509*n*73, 512*n*46
Hunter, Mark H., 527*n*24
Hurd, Sandra N., 521*n*30
Husted, Bryan, 512*n*48

Hutton, R. Bruce, 519*n*35
Hwang, Suein L., 516*n*69
Hymowitz, Carol, 516*n*1, 520*n*71
Hypercom Corp., 120–121

IBM, 49, 221, 232, 279, 293, 295,
    297, 311, 363
Identity theft, 307–308
Image, 48
ImClone, 15, 99, 468–471
In Demand, 157
Indianapolis Symphony Orchestra, 215
Individuals with disabilities
    employment discrimination against,
        109, 239
    employment opportunities for, 247
Information technology, 111, 294.
    See also Technology
Input-output model, 36–38
Insecticides, 42–43
Insider trading, 365, 493–494
insidetheweb.com, 69
Institute for Global Ethics, 130
Institute for Policy Studies, 180
Institute of Ethics, 114
Institute of Social and Ethical
    Accountability, 367
Intellectual property, 312–315
Interactional justice, 115
Interfaith Center on Corporate
    Responsibility, 170–171
Internal control, 178–179
International Brotherhood of Electrical
    Workers (IBEW), 236
International Data Corporation, 323
International Intellectual Property
    Alliance, 312
International Standards Organization
    (ISO), 276, 284
International Trade Commission, 281
Internet
    broadband access to, 298
    consumer education and protection
        resources on, 204, 207
    electronic signatures and, 78
    fraud and, 301
    historical background of, 300
    identity theft and, 307–308
    influence of, 299–301
    intellectual property issues and,
        312–315
    for low-income families, 295
    privacy issues and, 99, 207–208,
        304–312
    regulation of, 65, 68–69, 81
    shopping on, 294, 297, 301, 305

Internet Corporation for Assigned Names and Numbers (ICANN), 300–301, 314, 315
Investing, social, 171–175
Investor Responsibility Research Center, 175
Investors
confidence of, 175–177
expectations of, 168–169
loyalty of, 22–23
ISO 14000, 284
Israel Venture Network, 347
Italian Data Protection Commission, 308
Ivester, Doug, 394, 397, 399, 401
Iwata, Edward, 457n, 533n127

J. R. Simplot Co., 28
Jack in the Box restaurants, 49
Jackson, Thomas Penfield, 9, 69
Jacobson, Andy, 444
Jaffe, Charles, 509n62
Jahrling, Peter, 527n23
James, Dana, 529n5
James, Michael S., 516n79
Japan, 310
Jarvis, Steve, 522n44
Jaworski, Bernard J., 509n55
Jazz Photo Corporation, 102, 281
Jensen, Mike, 532n102
Jentz, Gaylord A., 199n, 235n, 521n18, 524n16, 525n39
Jesdanun, Anick, 530n26, 531n59
John Deere, 218
Johnsen, Tommi, 519n35
Johnson, Carrie, 465n
Johnson, Eric, 422, 426
Johnson, Kevin, 533n127
Johnson, Robert Wood, 384
Johnson Controls, Inc., 214
Johnson & Johnson, 35, 49, 109, 130, 279, 332, 362, 384–385
Jones, Jeffrey M., 103n
Jones, Jennifer, 513n17
Jones, Keith, 11n, 54n, 508n20, 512n50, 512n53
Jones, Lucian C., 498n
Jones, Thomas M., 509n66
Jordan, Curt S., 517n40
Jordan, Kim, 379, 437, 440
J.P. Morgan Chase Foundation, 338
Jung, Andrea, 98
Justice theory, 114–115

Kadlec, Daniel, 534n27
Kageyama, Yuri, 514n1

Kahn, Jeremy, 402n, 457n, 520n56
Kaiser Permanente, 108
Kaltenheuser, Skip, 411n
Kane, Leslie, 521n25
Kansas City Power & Light (KCPL), 222
Kant, Immanuel, 114, 516n61
Kao, Amy, 533n11
Kaplan, David, 511n22, 523n76
Kapner, Suzanne, 85n
Kaptein, Mael, 517n32, 517n34
Karnitschnig, Matt, 518n8
Karpatkin, Rhoda H., 522n38
Karpinski, Richard, 530n19
Kartalia, Jim, 511n36
Kawasoe, Katsuhiko, 95
Kaysen, Carl, 508n32
Keating, Gina, 465n
Keaveney, Thomas, 498n
Keiser, Lael R., 521n34
Keller, Kevin Lane, 534n31
Kellogg Company, 372
Kellogg Foundation, 330
Kelly, Erin, 527n15, 527n20
Kelly, Kevin, 507n1
Kelly, Marjorie, 508n38, 516n77, 527n100
Kelman, Al, 520n2
Kemp, David, 438, 441, 441n
Kennedy, John F., 203–204
Kennedy, Louise, 510n1
Kennedy, Peter, 465n
Kerwin, Kathleen, 518n8
Kessler, Ian, 524n8
Kessler, Larry, 407
KFC, 314
Khosa, Veronica, 346
Kim, Junyong, 521n9
Kinder, Peter D., 519n31
King, John, 510n1
King, Pam, 513n6
Kinicki, Angelo J., 524n29
Kirchgaessner, Stephanie, 465n
Kirkpatrick, David, 518n7
Kirrane, Diane E., 517n27
Kister, Thomas H., 521n28
Kleffman, Sandy, 521n12
Klein, Thomas A., 523n70
Kleiner, Brian, 526n85
Kleinman, Mark, 534n23
Klingener, Nancy, 526n68
Klinkerman, Steve, 411n
Kmart, 88, 150–151, 178
Knickerbock, Brad, 511n28
Knight, James, 507n6
Koch Industries, 270
Kohers, Theodor, 509n64

Kohlberg, Lawrence, 115, 116, 516n68, 516n70
Kohli, Ajay K., 509n55
Kohn, David, 525n65
Kolb, Deborah, 526n91
Kolker, Carlyn, 524n33
Komansky, David, 486
Kopper, Michael, 454
Koren, Irene, 525n48
Korman, Richard, 525n65
Kotha, Suresh, 509n66
Kotter, John, 149
Kouns, Charles, 534n33
Kowalska, Nina, 534n31
Koys, Daniel, 527n98
Kozlowski, Dennis, 131, 365, 483–489
KPMG, 105, 316, 382
Kraft Foods, 202
Kramer, Mark R., 533n8
Kramer, R. M., 516n63
Kramer, Robin, 526n75
Kranhold, Kathryn, 458n
Krantz, Matt, 465n
Krekhovetsky, Luba, 334n
Krim, Jonathan, 498n
Kropf, Susan, 98
Kunni, Irene M., 521n31
Kunstler, James Howard, 265, 528n27
Kurlantzick, Joshua, 511n29
Kurschner, Dale, 507n10, 527n100
Kwa, Aileen, 19n
Kyoto Protocol, 262, 279

Laabs, Jennifer, 230n, 524n25
Labaton, Stephen, 498n
Labor unions, 236
Lacey, Kathleen A., 520n62
Ladwig, Boris, 507n1
Lagundo, Lucette, 316n, 532n96, 532n99
Lande, Robert H., 513n24
Landes, John, 468
Land pollution, 265
Lane, Wendy, 486
Langtry, B., 519n34
Lanham Act, 70
LaPorta, Rafael, 518n2
Latham & Watkins, 243–244
Lauer, John, 181
Lavelle, Louis, 167n, 171n, 482n, 489n, 519n24–519n26, 520n55
Lavelle, Marianne, 522n43, 522n44
Lay, Kenneth, 143, 145, 244, 449, 451–455
Layne, Peggy, 526n76

Leadership
  ethical, 149, 151–153
  transactional, 150–151
  transformational, 149–150
Leana, Carrie R., 512n48
Leave-based donation programs, 335
Leavett, John, 532n106
Lebesch, Jeff, 379, 437, 440, 441
LeClair, Debbie Thorne, 510n17,
    513n27, 513n28, 513n30,
    516n66, 516n67, 517n24,
    524n23
Lee, Robert D., 525n59, 525n60
Legal issues. *See also* Legislation; Regula-
    tion
  related to advertising, 199–200
  related to community, 219
  related to employment, 234–243
Legislation. *See also specific legislation*
  antitrust, 69, 71–72
  consumer protection, 196–203
  employment, 234–243
  enforcement of, 72–73
  environmental, 271–274
  list of major, 70
  privacy, 309
  related to equality in workplace, 68
Legislative Reorganization Act Amend-
    ments of 1970, 80
Legitimacy, stakeholder, 45
Leiberman, David, 530n23
Leider, Richard, 508n36
Leipziger, Deborah, 11n, 54n, 508n20,
    512n50, 512n53
Leith, Scott, 402n
Lemon laws, 202
LensCrafters, 214, 345
Leonard, Bill, 523n81
Leonard, Devin, 511n19, 518n1
Levering, Robert, 523n1, 524n32
Levinson, Jay Conrad, 103
Levitt, Theodore, 36, 510n5
Levy, Reynold, 334n, 533n9, 534n21,
    534n49, 535n56
Lewis, Diane E., 411n, 523n79, 523n82,
    523n83
Lewis, Jack, 528n40, 528n47
Licking, Ellen, 528n39
Liddle, Alan J., 526n96
Lifeworth.com, 81
LIFO (last in, first out), 369
Lilla, Mark, 15, 508n37
Linden, Eugene, 528n30
Lindquist, Diane, 533n6
Lobbying, 81
Locke, Karen Lee Mayo, 485

Lockheed Martin, 141
Loden, Marilyn, 526n77
Loe, Terry W., 509n50
Loewe, Pierre M., 522n39
Logsdon, Jeanne, 511n37, 511n38
Londner, Robin, 489n
London Benchmarking Group, 377
Lopez-de-Silanes, Florencio, 518n2
Loucks, Vernon R., Jr., 515n17
Lowenthal, Lawrence D., 406
Lowe's, 253
Lublin, Joann, 489n, 516n1, 519n22
Lucent Technologies, 107, 292
Lui, Betty, 402n
Lutwak, Todd, 301
Lyman, Francesca, 532n125
Lyndenberg, Steven D., 519n31
Lyons, Daniel, 516n76
Lyons, Henry J., 177–178

MacInnis, Deborah J., 511n37
MacInnis, Patricia, 533n5
Mackay, Harvey, 103
MacKenzie, Heather, 411n
Macy's, 196
Madigan, Charles M., 473n
Magnuson-Moss Warranty (FTC) Act,
    70, 198, 200, 202
Magnusson, Paul, 508n42, 528n37,
    532n118, 532n120
Maher, Maria, 518n10, 518n12, 520n67
Mahon, John F., 511n33
Mahoney, Chris, 411n
Maignan, Isabelle, 508n27, 509n63,
    511n20, 527n102, 529n79
Mainiero, Lisa A., 511n42
Malden Mills Industries, 229
Manley, Walter W., II, 140n
Mano, Ronald, 527n101
Marchand, Raymond S., 428–429
Marchione, Marilynn, 532n105
Marcus, Bernie, 431, 432
Maremont, Mark, 489n, 535n9
Marketing
  cause-related, 339–341
  fraud in, 107–109
  green, 275–277
Markon, Jerry, 473n, 489n
Marquardt, Katy, 514n1
Marsden, Chris, 510n7
Martell, Ronald, 468
Martha Stewart Case
  future of image and business, 472–473
  historical background, 467–468
  implications of scandal, 471–472
  insider trading, 468–471

Martha Stewart Living Omnimedia, 365
Mason, Edward S., 12, 508n25, 508n31
Massengill, Douglas P., 525n56
Master, Melissa, 47n, 511n38
MasterCard, 301
MatchLogic, 311
Mathews, Anna Wilde, 529n1
Maull, Samuel, 489n
Mazetti, Mark, 254n
Mazurkiewicz, Gret, 214n
McAlister, Debbie Thorne, 394, 403,
    467, 511n20, 514n11, 527n102,
    529n79
McCarthy, Jack, 465n, 531n60
McCarthy, Michael, 508n26, 533n134
McClam, Erin, 473n
McClelland, David, 119, 516n73
McCoy, Kevin, 489n, 490n
McCracken, Douglas M., 526n88
McCullagh, Declan, 514n48
McDermott, Karen Govel, 523n1
McDonald's Corporation, 28, 44–45,
    203, 215, 251, 252, 320
McDonough, David G., 531n81, 531n83
McDonough, William, 529n66
McElroy, Damien, 522n53
McGee, Glenn, 532n94
McGill, Andrew R., 25n, 533n7, 533n10,
    534n25
McGrath, Maureen, 513n7
MCI, 151, 459, 463, 491
McIntosh, Malcolm, 11n, 54n, 507n14,
    508n20, 511n32, 512n50,
    512n53, 512n61
McKay, Carol, 513n13
McKee-Ryan, Francis M., 524n29
McLean, Bethany, 457n, 458n
McMahon, Jeffrey, 454
McManis, Charles R., 532n91
McNamee, Mike, 482n
McRitchie, James, 158, 518n3, 518n18
Meadow, H. Lee, 522n35
Meadow Ranch, 276
Mearian, Lucas, 305n
Media, 34, 39
Medicaid, 315
Medicare, 315
Medtronic, 168
Meeks, Brock N., 514n56
Mehta, Stephanie, 465n, 498n
Meier, Kenneth J., 521n34
Meirovich, G., 513n5
Mellon, Andrew, 66
Melymuka, Kathleen, 524n32
Menon, Anil, 534n28
Merck & Co., 101–102, 315, 345

Mergers, 160–161
Meritor Savings Bank v. Vinson,
   240
Merlino's Steak House, 211
Merrick, Amy, 473*n*
Merrick, Bill, 525*n*50
Merrill Lynch, 455–456
Merriman, Dwight, 442, 443
Mesritz, George D., 525*n*61
Metro-Goldwyn-Mayer, 34
Miceli, M. P., 526*n*67
Michael Jantzi Research Associates, 358
Michaels, Adrian, 465*n*
Michigan Beer and Wine Wholesalers
   Association, 81
Microsoft Corporation, 9, 68, 69, 74,
   81, 82, 84, 290, 311–313, 323,
   362–364
Midas, 166
Middleton, Benet, 522*n*35
Miles, Samantha, 511*n*21
Milken, Michael, 491
Millennium Poll, 17
Miller, Daniel R., 525*n*43
Miller, G. T., 528*n*32
Miller, Jan, 403
Miller, Kate, 510*n*11
Miller, Mary, 515*n*40, 515*n*51
Miller, Matthew, 510*n*13
Miller, Nancy J., 507*n*6
Miller, Roger L., 199*n*, 521*n*18
Miller, Roger LeRoy, 235*n*, 524*n*16,
   525*n*39
Miller, William H., 507*n*13
Mills, C. Wright, 231, 524*n*17
Mills, Roy, 421, 422
Millstein, Ira, 520*n*62
Minami, Chikara, 203
Minimum wage, 234
Minorities, 109–111
Mitchell, Ronald K., 36*n*, 511*n*21
Mitchener, Brandon, 513*n*27
Mitsubishi Motors, 22, 95, 111, 122,
   203, 241, 364
Mokhiber, Russell, 515*n*34
Monarch Watch, 283
Monks, Robert A. G., 174, 187,
   518*n*17, 519*n*38, 520*n*68,
   520*n*72
Monopolies
   explanation of, 66–67
   regulation of, 67, 76
Monsanto, 41, 268, 320
Montini, Enio, 151
Moore, Julia A., 532*n*115
Moore, Kathy, 523*n*1

Moral development
   corporate responsibility and, 129
   stages of, 115–116
Moral philosophies, 113–115
Moreno, Janelia, 523*n*67
Morgan, J. P., 66, 181
Morgan, Robert M., 512*n*46
Morgenson, Gretchen, 519*n*25
Morita, Hajime, 95
Morningstar, Inc., 172
Morris, Betsy, 402*n*, 508*n*21
Morse, Dan, 402*n*
Morse, Jodie, 458*n*
Mortgage Bankers Association
   of America, 150
Morton, Barbara, 508*n*24
Moskowitz, Milton, 523*n*1, 524*n*32
Motion Picture Association of America
   (MPAA), 34
Motivation, 119–120
Motorola, 46
Mottl, Judith N., 525*n*43
Mott's, Inc., 108
Mouritsen, Matthew, 527*n*101
Mouton, Johann, 536*n*37
Mowbray, Rebecca, 523*n*76
MTC, 314
MTV Networks, 214
Muirhead, Sophia A., 533*n*11
Mulcahey, Michael, 157
Mulgan, Geoff, 508*n*22
Mulgrew, Gary, 454
Mullen, Jennifer, 534*n*32
Mullen, Linda G., 483
Muller, Joann, 518*n*8, 522*n*52, 525*n*62
Mulligan, Deirdre, 446
Mungguro, Dani, 346
Murphy, Patrick, 521*n*9, 530*n*43,
   533*n*5, 533*n*12, 534*n*22
Murrah, Shailagh, 316*n*
Murzakhanov, Nail, 310
Myers, David, 462

Nacchio, Joseph, 106
Nader, Ralph, 68, 204, 318
Naftalis, Gary, 494
Nail, Jim, 444–445
Nakra, Prema, 47*n*, 511*n*36
Nalebuff, Barry J., 520*n*66
Napster, 290, 323
NASDAQ, 164, 181
Nash, Jennifer, 512*n*49
Nason, Robert W., 523*n*70
Nathan, Sara, 515*n*33
National Ambient Air Quality
   Standards (NAAQS), 271

National Association of Black Journalists,
   246
National Association of Corporate
   Directors, 166
National Association of Home
   Builders, 81
National Association of Theater
   Owners, 34
National Baptist Convention
   (NBC USA), 177
National Cable and Telecommunications
   Association (NCTA), 81
National Climatic Data Center, 264
National Consumers League, 204
National Environmental Policy Act,
   272, 274
National Farm and Garden, Inc.,
   501–502
National Federation of Independent
   Businesses, 81
National Fish and Wildlife Foundation,
   264
National Fraud Center, 308
National Highway Traffic Safety
   Administration, 46
National Hockey League, 157
National Infrastructure Protection
   Center, 305
National Institutes of Heath (NIH), 317
National Labor Relations Act (NLRA),
   235, 236
National Labor Relations Board
   (NLRB), 73
National Restaurant Association, 247
National Rifle Association, 83, 84, 205
National security, 79–80
National Wildlife Foundation, 264
Natural environment, 259
Naughton, Keith, 473*n*
Naumann, Stefanie, 516*n*62
Navran, Frank, 152
Near, J. P., 526*n*67
NEC, 295
Needles, Belverd E., Jr., 458*n*
Neese, William T., 515*n*25, 515*n*37,
   532*n*91
Neff, Jack, 520*n*2
Neighbor of choice, 211
Nelson, Bob, 533*n*15, 534*n*34
Nelson, Emily, 515*n*21
Nestlé Company, 17, 320
Netcom, 311
Netscape, 311
The Network, 144
Neubauer, F. F., 518*n*11
New, Steve, 508*n*24

New Belgium Brewing Company, 221, 378, 379
New Belgium Brewing Company Case
  employee concerns, 439
  environmental concerns, 439
  historical background, 437–438
New Covent Garden Soup Co., 340
  organizational successes, 440–441
  purpose and core beliefs and, 438
  social concerns, 439–440
New Economics Ltd., 358
Newman, Barry, 515*n*15
Newspaper Association of America, 246
New York Stock Exchange (NYSE), 128, 164, 181
Nexters, 248
Niehoff, Brian E., 507*n*14
Nike, 45–46, 253, 254
Nine West Group, 72
92nd St. Y nursery school, 103
Nissan, 111, 297
Nixon, Richard, 269
Noah's Bagels, 335
Nobile, Robert J., 525*n*38
Nokia, 311
Normand, Troy, 462
Norrgard, Julia M., 521*n*8
Norrgard, Lee E., 521*n*8
Norris, Floyd, 482*n*
North, D. C., 509*n*69, 509*n*71
North American Free Trade Agreement (NAFTA), 74
Nozar, Robert A., 524*n*28
Nuevo Energy Co., 128
Nugent, Robert, 512*n*44
Nussbaum, Bruce, 482*n*
Nutrition Labeling and Education Act, 70, 198, 206

Oakes, Chris, 448*n*
Oatis, Clyde, 219–220
O'Brien, Miles, 261*n*
O'Brien, Tim, 523*n*71
Occidental Petroleum Corporation, 162
Occupational Safety and Health Act (OSHA), 235–238, 272
Occupational Safety and Health Administration (OSHA), 73, 114, 236–238
O'Connor, Kevin, 442, 443, 445
Odometer Act, 198
O'Donnell, Rosie, 349
OECD Corporate Governance Principles, 183–184
Oekom Research, 174
Oglebay Norton, 181

Oil Pollution Act, 273
Olofson, Roy, 495
Olson, Elizabeth, 508*n*43
Oneal, Michael, 465*n*
Online auctions, 301
Opportunity, 123–124
Opryland Hotel, 233
Oracle Corporation, 192, 297, 323
Orangina, 398
Organisation for Economic Cooperation and Development (OECD), 183, 184, 186
Organizational culture
  ethics and, 130, 142–143, 151–153, 479–480
  explanation of, 120–122
Organizational identity, 48
Original Honey Baked Ham Company, 196
O'Riley, Kate, 507*n*6
Orlov, Darlene, 525*n*64
Ornstein, Charles, 411*n*
Orwall, Bruce, 529*n*1
Oster, Christopher, 532*n*100
Ostle, Dorothee, 518*n*8
Oumlil, A. Ben, 522*n*46
Oyama, David, 516*n*80

Pacelle, Mitchell, 458*n*
Pachard, Ben, 278
Paetsch, Lauren, 522*n*46
Palma-Rivas, Nilda, 526*n*76
Palmer, Ann Therese, 524*n*7
Palmeri, Christopher, 245*n*, 482*n*, 517*n*38, 517*n*39
Panter, Gary, 490*n*
Papa John's International, Inc., 107
Paramount, 34
Parks Company, 275
Pasman, James S., Jr., 486
Pasternak, Bart, 469
Pastore, Michael, 513*n*14, 530*n*24, 530*n*25, 530*n*37, 530*n*39
Paswan, Audhesh, 522*n*35
Patents, 312, 313, 317
Pathmark Stores, 166
Patient's Bill of Rights and Responsibilities, 204
Patrick, Sharon, 471
Patsuris, Penelope, 536*n*29
Peaple, Andrew, 245*n*
Pearce, John, 535*n*8
Pearl, Robert, 508*n*43
Pearson, Christine M., 512*n*45
Pelofsky, Jeremy, 498*n*
Pepper, Jon, 402*n*

PepsiCo, 278, 395, 398
Performance, 48
Perle, Richard N., 497–498
Personal Information Protection and Electronic Documents Act (Canada), 310
Pesticides
  on airplanes, 42–43
  genetically modified foods and, 321
  regulation of, 269–271
Peters, Diane McFerrin, 534*n*17, 534*n*35
Peters, Glen, 334*n*, 511*n*39
Peters, Thomas J., 231
Petersen, Donald J., 525*n*56
Peterson, Eric, 529*n*71
Pet Food Institute, 81
Petroleos de Venezuela, 214
Peyser, Marc, 473*n*
Pfizer Inc., 316
Pharmaceutical industry, 315–316
Philanthropy
  to community, 221–222, 251
  consumer interests and, 210
  examples of corporate, 334, 335
  explanation of, 331–333
  historical background of, 336–339
  strategic, 29, 333–354 (*See also* Strategic philanthropy)
Philip Morris, 9, 68, 69, 74, 81, 82, 84, 96
Piller, Charles, 515*n*30
Pine, Jordan T., 402*n*, 529*n*10
Pipp, Tracy L., 534*n*26
Pitofsky, Robert, 308
Pitt, Harvey, 15
Pizza Corner India, 220
Pizza Hut, 220
Points of Light Foundation, 251
Poling, Travis E., 521*n*23
Political action committees (PACs), 82
Political campaign contributions, 82–83
Politics, 79–80
Pollution. *See also* Environmental issues
  air, 260–262
  biodiversity and, 267
  land, 265
  water, 262–263
Pollution Prevention Act, 273, 274
Pope, Justin, 524*n*6
Porras, J. I., 536*n*72
Porter, Michael E., 533*n*8
Portland Trail Blazers, 214
Post, James E., 511*n*32
Poulsen, Kevin, 533*n*128
Powell, Barbara, 482*n*
Power, 44–45

Powers, Marian, 458*n*
Preston, Lee E., 37*n*, 510*n*3, 510*n*4, 510*n*7, 510*n*8, 510*n*15
Pretzer, Michael, 522*n*40
Price fixing, 72–73
Priceline.com, 26–27
Pricewaterhouse Coopers, 365
Pride, William M., 514*n*39, 514*n*42, 529*n*81, 530*n*35, 531*n*49
Priest, Steve, 152
Primary stakeholders, 39
Privacy
    business policies regarding, 311, 312
    consumer, 207–208
    international initiatives on, 308, 310–311
    Internet and, 304–308
    legislation addressing, 309
Privacy Act, 309
Privacy offices, 311
Procedural justice, 114–115
Procter & Gamble (P&G), 193, 253, 277–278, 297, 311, 362
Product liability, 202–203, 206
Profits, 23
Project Too Late.com, 196
Pronina, Lyuba, 522*n*47
Prudential Insurance, 311
Prussia, Gregory E., 524*n*29
Pruzan, Peter, 372*n*, 388*n*, 535*n*3, 535*n*61
Psychological contract, 230
Public Citizen, 318
Public Company Accounting Oversight Board, 14–15, 89, 164
Public Health Cigarette Smoking Act, 200
Publishers Clearing House, 199
Publix Supermarkets, 253
Pulliam, Susan, 465*n*, 515*n*27
Pure Food and Drug Act, 197, 198
Puschaver, Lee, 519*n*48–520*n*48

Quakers, 173
Quid pro quo sexual harassment, 240
Quova, 306
Qwest Communications, 104, 106–107, 361–362, 364, 370, 463, 479, 491, 494, 496

R. J. Reynolds, 206
Rabin, Dan, 441*n*
Racial discrimination, 398–400
Racketeer Influenced and Corrupt Organizations Act (RICO), 157
Rahman, Sandra S., 512*n*48

Raines, Claire, 248*n*, 526*n*83
Ramsey, V. L., 402*n*
Raynard, Peter, 535*n*23
Rayovac, 193
Reactive-Defensive-Accommodative-Proactive Scale, 57–58
Recording Industry Association of America (RIAA), 290
Rector, William, 459
Recycling
    initiatives in, 277–279
    single-use camera, 280–281
Red Cross, 338–339, 353
Reder, Alan, 534*n*44, 534*n*47
Reed, Darryl, 510*n*16
Reeks, Anne, 531*n*58
Regis Hair Salons, 339
Regulation. *See also* Legislation
    benefits of, 76–78
    corporate approaches to influencing, 81–83
    costs of, 74–76
    economic and competitive reasons for, 66–67
    global, 73–74
    rationale for, 65
    social reasons for, 67–69
Reichel, A., 513*n*5
Reichert, Alan K., 527*n*3
Reichheld, Frederick, 38, 509*n*49, 510*n*9
Reingold, Jennifer, 519*n*23
Relationships, 52–56
Renault, 297
Republican Party, 79, 82, 83
Reputation Institute, 21, 396
Reputation management
    at Coca-Cola, 401
    components of, 48–49
    explanation of, 46–47
Research and development (R&D), 295, 296
Resource Conservation Recovery Act, 272
Responsible Care, 53
Restructuring, 14
Retail shrinkage, 195–196
Revell, Janice, 436*n*
Rewick, Jennifer, 510*n*77, 514*n*41
Rhone-Poulene, 72
Rigas, Gus, 157
Rigas, James, 157
Rigas, John, 157
Rigas, Michael, 157
Rigas, Tim, 157
Right to Financial Privacy Act, 309
Ripley, Amanda, 245*n*, 465*n*

Risk analysis, 283–284
Risk management
    audits and, 178
    control systems and, 178–179
    explanation of, 178–180
Rissler, Jane, 320
RiteAid, 244, 364
Robert's American Gourmet Food, Inc., 206
Robins Bush Foods, 341
Robinson-Patman Act, 70
Rockefeller, John D., 66, 164
Rodie, Janet B., 524*n*6
Role-play exercises
    Deer Lake Marina, 505
    National Farm and Garden, Inc., 501–502
    sexual harassment, 502–504
    Soy-DRI, 499–500
    Videopolis, 500–501
Roman, Ronald M., 509*n*64, 509*n*67
Romero, Simon, 465*n*, 498*n*
Roosevelt, Franklin Delano, 295
Roppe, Laura Hoffman, 525*n*61
Rosenberg, Arthur J., 483
Rosenblatt, Robert, 527*n*25
Rosenbluth, Hal F., 534*n*17, 534*n*35
Rosencrance, Linda, 532*n*90
Rosener, Judith B., 526*n*77
Roszkowski, Christie L., 508*n*28
Rotary International, 344
Rotenberg, Marc, 446
Rothbard, Nancy P., 526*n*87
Rothenberg, Randall, 448*n*
Roumell, Michael T., 525*n*64
Round Rock Express, 215
Rousseau, Denise M., 524*n*8
Rowley, Coleen, 145, 146, 244
Royal Ahold, 84–85
Royal Dutch/Shell, 16, 56, 262, 279, 360, 361, 385
Rubeinstein, Bruce, 245*n*
Rubenstein, Steve, 525*n*48
Ruggles, Ron, 526*n*69
Ruiz, Joseph, 503
RunTex, 4–5
Rural Electrification Administration, 295
Russia, privacy policies in, 310–311
Ryan, Harriett, 536*n*58
Ryan, Kevin, 445, 447
Rynecki, David, 509*n*61

Saatchi & Saatchi, 340
SABMiller, 58
Sachs, Sybille, 510*n*7
Safe Drinking Water Act, 272

Safety
consumer's right to, 205–206
legislation related to employee, 236–239
Safeway, 239
Said, Carolyn, 520*n*58
Sainsbury's, 55
Sakharov, Andrei, 331
Sakharov Museum, 331
Salaries, 180–181
salesforce.com, 192
Salomon Smith Barney, 103, 174, 492, 493, 496
Salopek, Jennifer, 526*n*83
Sameshima, Nikki, 528*n*61
Sample, Kevin, 394, 403
Samu, Sridhar, 535*n*59
Samuelson, Robert J., 508*n*27
Saporta, Maria, 402*n*
Sapsford, Jathon, 517*n*37
Sara Lee Corporation, 8, 128
Sarbanes-Oxley Act
provisions of, 88, 89, 137, 168, 178, 383
purpose of, 14, 70, 97, 128–129, 145–146, 164, 374, 480, 481
whistle-blowers and, 243, 245
Sarkis, Karen, 524*n*5, 525*n*45
SAS Institute, 55, 227, 251
Saveri, Gabrielle, 524*n*7
Savolainen, Taina, 524*n*21
Sayer, Steve, 524*n*14
SBC Communications, 83, 84
SBC Foundation, 338
Scalzo, Richard, 488
Scannell, Kara, 473*n*
Scarbrough, Ernie, 521*n*8
Schaal, Dennis, 171*n*
Schacht, Henry, 2
Scheck, Steve L., 412, 429
Scheele, Nichole, 459
Scheinholtz, Debby, 526*n*80, 526*n*93
Schepp, David, 482*n*, 519*n*42
Scherreik, Susan, 519*n*33
Schoen, John, 515*n*55, 517*n*36
Scholes, E., 512*n*51
Schon, Jan Hendrik, 107
Schulman, Miriam, 458*n*
Schultz, Howard, 152
Schultz, John D., 525*n*43
Schulze, Lawrence J. H., 516*n*59
Schwab, Charles, 176–177
Schwartz, Mark S., 517*n*11
Schwartz, Nelson, 533*n*11
Scientific-Atlanta Inc., 157
Scorza, John, 514*n*45

Scott Paper, 275
Scripps Howard Foundation, 246
Sears, Roebuck & Co., 12, 35, 38, 143, 232
Secker, Matthew, 465*n*
Secondary stakeholders, 39, 42
Secretan, Lance, 523*n*1
Securities and Exchange Commission (SEC)
function of, 73, 128, 130, 151, 164
insider trading and, 493
investigations by, 22, 104–106, 495
Segall, Rebecca, 526*n*90
Self-regulation, 77–79
Sellers, Patricia, 402*n*, 508*n*21
Sellnow, Timothy L., 511*n*42, 512*n*44
Semantic Web, 295
Sen-lun, Yu, 19*n*
Serna, Joseph, 298
Service Employees International Union, 84
Service Merchandise Co., 219
Serwer, Andy, 171*n*
Sever, Joy, 365
Seward, Christopher, 402*n*
Sexual harassment
categories of, 240–241
court cases related to, 241
explanation of, 240, 502
legislation prohibiting, 239
prevention of, 241–242
role-play exercise on, 502–504
Shah, Priti Pradhan, 524*n*24
Shareholder model of corporate governance, 162
Shareholders
activism of, 169–171, 174
confidence of, 175–177
expectations of, 168–169
Shears, Peter, 521*n*30
Sheffield, Rob, 448*n*
Shellenberger, Sue, 515*n*44
Sherman Antitrust Act, 69–72, 74
Shimizu Corporation, 6
Shirouzu, Norihiko, 511*n*34
Shmukler, Evelina, 516*n*1
Shoplifting, 195–196
Shrinkage, 195–196
Shute, Nancy, 522*n*44
Sidgmore, John, 462, 464
Siedel, George J., 512*n*2
Siegel, Ken, 472
Siegel, P. A., 516*n*63
Sieroty, Chris H., 458*n*
Sierra Club, 263
Sigismond, William, 458*n*

Silberner, Joanne, 516*n*60
Sillanpaa, Maria, 372*n*
Silverman, Ben, 465*n*
Silverman, Henry R., 170, 171
Simison, Robert L., 511*n*34, 511*n*41
Simpson, Gary, 509*n*64
Simpson, Glenn R., 510*n*79, 512*n*52
Sinclair, Upton, 197, 230
Singer, Andrew, 514*n*4
Sirgy, Joseph, 520*n*49, 521*n*7
Siskos, Catherine, 531*n*75
Skaggs, Bruce C., 517*n*44
Skandia Assurance and Financial Services, 233
Skilling, Jeffrey, 449, 451, 453, 454–455
Skloot, Edward, 347*n*
Slusser, Peter, 486
Small Dog Electronics, 252
Smart, Tim, 533*n*11
Smith, Adam, 76
Smith, Craig N., 337*n*, 534*n*18, 534*n*20
Smith, Elliot Blair, 151*n*, 458*n*, 514*n*57
Smith, Ethan, 529*n*1
Smith, Garrison R., 518*n*19
Smith, Mark, 412
Smith, Neil, 371*n*, 535*n*6, 536*n*67, 536*n*69, 536*n*71, 536*n*73
Smith, Rebecca, 457*n*–458*n*, 516*n*84
Smith, Sarah J., 525*n*45
Smith O'Brien, 363, 378
Smoron, Paige, 522*n*45
Snyder, Julene, 533*n*135
Social audit process
analyzing data in, 381–382
collecting information in, 378–381
defining scope in, 374–375
defining social priorities in, 376–377
establishing audit committee for, 374
framework for, 370–373
identifying method of measuring social objectives in, 377–378
reporting findings for, 384–386
reviewing mission, policies, goals and objectives for, 376
securing commitment of top management and/or board for, 373–374
strategic importance of, 387–389
verifying results in, 382–384
Social audits
benefits of, 360–363
crisis management and recovery and, 364–366
explanation of, 29, 58, 344, 359
financial auditing vs., 366–370
reasons for, 360
risks of, 363–364

standards for, 368
Social capital, 53
SocialFunds.com, 172
Social investing
 by colleges and universities, 174–175
 examples of, 173–174
 explanation of, 171–173
 increases in, 174
Socially responsible buying (SRB), 280
Social responsibility
 applications for, 4–5
 assessment of, 380
 benefits of, 18–24
 corporate governance and, 161–163, 186–187
 customer satisfaction and, 21
 development of, 12–15
 employee commitment and, 21–22
 explanation of, 4, 5, 96, 364
 framework for studying, 24–29
 global nature of, 15–19
 investor loyalty and, 22–23
 national economy and, 23–24
 profits and, 23
 society's expectations for, 8–11
 stakeholders and, 11, 17, 25–27, 56–58, 222
 strategic focus of, 5–8
 strategic philanthropy and, 333–336
Social venture capital, 346–347
Social Venture Partners International, 345, 347
Society, business expectations of, 8–11
Software piracy, 312–313
Sol, Maura Griffin, 517n42
Solso, Tim, 2
Solstice Consulting, 358
Sonoma County Stable and Livestock, 278
Sony Corp., 34, 322
Soto, Monica, 521n24
Souter, Gavin, 523n73
Southwest Airlines, 362
Soy-DRI, 499–500
Spacek, Leonard, 475
Spain, William, 448n
Spam, 306
Special-interest groups
 power of, 80
 regulations from crusades by, 68
 as secondary stakeholders, 39
Spinks, Melda, 523n63
Sport utility vehicles (SUVs), 283, 284
Sprint, 491
St. Clair, Lynda, 25n, 508n46, 533n7, 533n10, 534n25

Stafford, Edwin R., 522n56
Stakeholder model
 of corporate governance, 162, 171
 explanation of, 37, 38
Stakeholder relations
 development of, 52–56
 link between social responsibility and, 56–58
Stakeholders
 attributes of, 43–46
 community, 210–214
 consumer, 193, 194
 crisis management and, 49–52
 employee, 227, 228, 342–343
 environmental issues and, 282–283
 explanation of, 11, 35–38
 global, 40–43
 historical perspectives on, 36
 primary and secondary, 38–39, 42
 regulatory, 42–43
 reputation management and, 46–49
 social responsibility and, 17, 25–27, 56–58
 in strategic philanthropy, 342–348
Stallkamp, Thomas T., 161
Standard & Poor, 183
Standard Mattress Co., 197
Standard Oil Company, 69
Stanford University, 175
Stansky, Lisa, 532n98
Stanton, Peter V., 512n42
Stanwick, Peter, 519n25
Stanwick, Sarah, 519n25
Staples, Inc., 280
Starbucks Corp., 6, 27, 128, 130, 152, 278, 362
Starr, Paul, 512n3
Stavraka, Carol, 509n76, 510n18, 511n30
Stein, Anne, 521n11
Stein, Heather A., 474
Stein, Nicholas, 518n50, 524n31
Stem cells, 317, 318
Stensen, Jacqueline, 532n110
Stentiford, Tim, 525n41
Stern, Christopher, 465n, 498n
Stewart, Martha, 15, 99, 365, 467–473
Stewart, Thomas A., 473n, 517n42
Stewart-Allen, Allyson L., 534n29
Stipp, David, 511n18
Stock, Kyle, 530n28
Stockholder relations, 35
Stolzenberg, Edward A., 518n14
Storeim, Mandy, 481n
Strahilevitz, Michal, 534n32

Straiger, Robert, 19n
Strategic environmental audit, 284–285
Strategic philanthropy. *See also* Philanthropy
 background of, 336–339
 benefits of, 348–350
 business partners and, 344–345
 cause-related marketing and, 339–341
 community and society and, 345–348
 customers and, 343–344
 Donor Bill of Rights and, 354
 employees and, 342–343
 explanation of, 29, 333
 implementation of, 350–351
 planning and evaluating, 352–353
 social responsibility and, 333–336
 top management support for, 351–352
Stratton, Jan, 213
Strauss, Gary, 520n58
Stress, job-related, 250–251
Strict liability, 202
Strom, Stephanie, 535n60
Strupp, Joe, 526n78
Student Alliance to Reform Corporations (STARC), 174–175
Su, Chenting, 520n49, 521n7
Suchman, Mark C., 511n27
Suddaby, Roy, 518n46
Sullivan, Brian, 448n
Sullivan, Scott, 145, 462, 465n
Summerour, Jenny, 515n23
Sunbeam Corp., 22, 104, 351, 364, 370, 477
Sun Microsystems, 137
Sunoo, Brenda Paik, 523n4, 524n6
Superfund Amendments Reauthorization Act, 272
Supreme Court, U.S.
 affirmative action and, 110
 sexual harassment and, 240, 241, 502–503
Surface Transportation Policy Project (STPP), 266
Suter, Tracy A., 442
Suttell, Robin, 525n43
Svendsen, Ann, 334n, 337n, 508n22, 534n18
Swanson, Diane, 507n14
Swartz, Jon, 305n
Swartz, Mark H., 483, 485–487
Swenson, Win, 514n54
Swift, Tracy, 535n24, 536n30
Sykes Enterprises, 212

Symbolic power, 44
Symonds, William, 489*n*
Syngenta, 269–270
Synovus, 247

Taco Bell, 202, 314
Taco Cabana restaurant chain, 243
Tam, Pui-Wing, 513*n*14, 526*n*94,
    530*n*38, 530*n*42
Tangley, Laura, 528*n*34
Tanikawa, Miki, 514*n*1
Tanner, John F., Jr., 441*n*
Tansey, Richard, 526*n*66
Tapia, Ronni L., 509*n*62
Target Corp., 8, 150, 344
Taub, Stephen, 482*n*, 490*n*
Taxes, 336–337
Teather, David, 465*n*
Technology. *See also* Internet
    biotechnology and, 316–318
    business and, 323–324
    characteristics of, 291–293
    economic concerns about use of,
      298–299
    economic growth and employment
      and, 295–298
    effects of, 28–29, 293–295
    explanation of, 291
    genetically modified foods and,
      268, 283, 318–321
    government and, 321–323
    health and, 315–316
    intellectual property and, 312–315
    Internet and, 299–303
    issues related to, 290–291
    privacy issues and, 304–311
Technology assessment, 324–326
Teinowitz, Ira, 526*n*79
Teixeira, Ruy, 15
Telemarketing, 113, 200
Telemarketing and Consumer Fraud and
    Abuse Prevention Act, 199, 200
Telephone Consumer Protection Act, 70,
    198, 309
Tellez, Debbie, 414
Temple, Nancy, 478
Templeton, Brad, 314*n*
Tenbrunsel, Ann E., 507*n*12
Terminator technology, 320
Terrile, Jeanne, 486, 487
Terrorist attacks of September 11, 2001
    crisis management and, 50
    diversity issues and, 249
    philanthropy following, 335, 353
    political environment following, 79
    security issues and, 77

    sense of community following, 211
    workplace risks and, 237
Terry, Ken, 522*n*57
Texaco, 109, 262
Texas Instruments, 130, 132–134
Therese, Ann, 528*n*37, 532*n*118,
    532*n*120
Therrien, Lois, 507*n*1
Thibodeau, Patrick, 531*n*82,
    533*n*129
Thomas, Andrew R., 525*n*48
Thomas, Edward G., 527*n*3
Thomas, Karen, 530*n*30
Thomas, Kathy Booth, 482*n*
Thompson, John L., 347*n*
Thornburgh, Richard, 462
Thorne, Debbie, 526*n*66
3M, 168, 348
Thurman, Mathis, 533*n*131
TIAA-CREF, 172
Tice, Carol, 347*n*
Tice, David W., 487
Tichy, Noel M., 25*n*, 507*n*12, 508*n*46,
    533*n*7, 533*n*10, 534*n*25
Ticketmaster, 313
Tickets.com, 313
Tierney, Christine, 518*n*8, 518*n*9
Time Inc., 199
Time Warner, 160, 221
Tischler, Linda, 520*n*1
Title VII, Civil Rights Act of 1964,
    109–111, 235, 239, 240, 246
Tobacco Institute, 81
Toedtman, James, 498*n*
Toobin, Jeffrey, 473*n*
Toronto Dominion Bank, 166
Toshiba, 208
Total quality management (TQM),
    231
Toto Ltd., 8
Toxics Release Inventory (TRI), 274
Toxic Substances Control Act of 1976,
    68, 272, 273
Toyota Motor, 95, 111, 221
Toy Safety Act, 198
Toysmart.com, 72, 312
Toys 'R' Us, 196
Trade, agreements to regulate, 74
Trademark Counterfeiting Act, 70
Trademark Law Revision Act, 70
Training. *See* Employee training
Transactional leadership, 149–151
Transamerica, 208
Transformational leadership, 149–150
Transparency International, 8, 24
Triebwasser, Marc A., 514*n*44

Trust
    in corporate leaders, 131
    investor, 22–23
    social responsibility and, 20–21
TRUSTe, 311, 312
Trusts
    explanation of, 66
    regulation of, 67, 69, 71–72
Tucker, Chris, 521*n*15
Tufts University, 175
Tully, Shawn, 513*n*38
Turner, Cal, Jr., 181
Turner, Ted, 160
Turnley, William H., 524*n*9, 524*n*10
Twain, Mark, 264
Twentieth Century Fox, 34
Twenty-first Amendment, 200
Tyco Case
    fall of Kozlowski, 487–488
    historical background, 483–484
    Kozlowski's empire, 485–487
    rebuilding an empire, 488–489
    rise of Kozlowski, 484–485
Tyco International, 131, 177, 365
Tyler, Kathryn, 526*n*72
Tyler, T. R., 516*n*63
Tyson, Poppe, 443
Tyson Foods, 65

Ulfelder, Steve, 530*n*41
Ulick, Jake, 458*n*, 519*n*28, 520*n*57
Ulmer, Robert R., 511*n*42, 512*n*42,
    512*n*44
Unger, Henry, 402*n*
Uniform Dispute Resolution Policy
    (UDRP), 314–315
Unilever, 320, 378
Union Carbide, 41, 42
Unita, 46
United Airlines, 43
United Airlines Foundation, 342
United Food & Commercial Workers
    Union, 84
United for a Fair Economy, 180
United Nations Global Compact, 17
United Parcel Service (UPS), 39,
    212, 294
United States Sales Corporation, 199
Universal Studios, 34, 213
University of Michigan, 45
University of Minnesota, 174–175
University of Oregon, 45
University of Washington, 175
University of Wisconsin, 174–175
Unocal, 16
Unum Provident Insurance Co., 113

Urban sprawl, 265–267
Urgency, of stakeholders, 45–46
Urquhart, Gerald, 527n26
U.S. Capital Visitors Center, 82
U.S. Chamber of Commerce, 81, 82
U.S. Custom Feed, 219–220
U.S. Fish and Wildlife Service, 271, 273
U.S. Sentencing Commission, 85, 86, 87n
Utilitarianism, 113–114
Utilitarian power, 44
Uyesugi, Bryan, 239

Valdmanis, Thor, 457n, 473n
Valenti, Jack, 34, 510n1
Van, John, 465n
Van Buren, Harry J., III, 512n48, 524n26
Vancouver City Savings Credit Union (VanCity), 353, 358, 385
van der Hoeven, Cees, 84
Vanguard, 172
Van Putton, Mark, 263
Varadarajan, P. Rajan, 534n28
Varon, Elana, 530n15
Vaughn, Gwyneth, 528n45
Veen, Maaike, 85n
Venture capital, social, 346–347
Verespej, Michael A., 526n92
Verizon Communications, Inc., 236, 247, 290
Verizon Foundation, 338, 344
Verschoor, Curtis, 509n65
Vesting, 236
Veterans, in workplace, 248
Vidal, David J., 533n11
Vidal, Humberto, 201
Videopolis, 500–501
Video Privacy Protection Act, 309
Vinson, Betty, 462
Vinson & Elkins, 455
Violence
  in media, 34
  workplace, 237, 239
Visa, 301
Vise, David A., 513n10
VisionLand Theme Park, 218
Volcker, Paul, 480
Volunteerism
  benefits of, 348–349
  explanation of, 221–222, 251
Volvo, 95
Voorst, Bruce, 534n27

Waddington, Richard, 513n25
Waddock, Sandra A., 371n, 509n64, 512n48, 522n58, 523n63, 535n6, 536n67, 536n69, 536n71, 536n73
Wainwright Bank & Trust Case
  banking industry trends, 405
  community programs, 406–408
  criticisms, 409–410
  introduction, 403
  philosophy, 404
  recognition, 410
  social activism, 409
Waksal, Sam, 15, 99, 469
Waldman, Amy, 511n19
Waldron, Murray, 459
Walker, Leslie, 530n12
Walker Information, 22, 38, 39n, 40
Walkers, 340–341
Wallace, J. D., 365n
Wallner, George, 121
Wal-Mart Foundation, 338
Wal-Mart Stores, 16, 27, 74, 84, 95, 150, 208, 215, 219, 281, 362
Walsh, David, 487, 494
Walsh, Frank E., Jr., 486
Walt Disney Company, 34, 275
Walters, Gwyneth V., 431
Walters, Mark, 528n28
Wan, Allen, 448n
Ward, Andrew, 511n26
Ware, Carl, 400
Warner Brothers, 34, 221, 349
Warner-Lambert, 202, 349
Warranties, 200–201
Warren, Melinda, 75n
Waste management, 265, 278
Waste Management, Inc., 104, 364, 370, 477–478
WasteWise, 278
Waterman, Robert H., Jr., 231
Water pollution, 262–263
Water quantity, 264
Waters, James A., 424
Watkins, Sherron, 145, 146, 452–453, 455, 456
Watson, Thomas, 523n1
Watson, Traci, 527n13
Wayhan, Victor B., 524n25, 524n30
Weber, Joseph, 458n
Weber, Thomas E., 531n67
Websense, 323
Weeden, Curt, 352, 533n14, 533n16, 535n57
Wei, Lingling, 465n
Weil, Jonathan, 457n

Weil, Nancy, 531n52
Weill, Sanford, 103
Weiner, Bryan J., 518n14
Weise, Elizabeth, 530n34
Weiss, Allen M., 511n37
Weiss, Joseph W., 516n75
Weisskopf, Michael, 498n
Welch, Joseph F., 486
Weld, Royal, 523n66
Wells, Barron, 523n63
Wells, Stacy, 529n9
Wells Fargo, 376–377
Wenger, Rachel, 511n34
Wentling, Rose Mary, 526n76
Werner, Steve, 524n25, 524n30
Wetzel, Kara, 516n3
Wetzstein, Cheryl, 535n60
Wheat, Allynda, 517n15–517n17
Wheeler, David, 372n
Whistleblower Protection Act, 243, 245
Whistle-blowers
  explanation of, 145–147, 242–243
  legal and regulatory issues related to, 244, 245
  protections for, 164, 245
White, Erin, 514n5
White, Margaret A., 524n33
White, Michael, 526n66
White Dog Café, 121–122
Whitford, David, 347n, 534n42
Whitman, Marina N., 507n1, 508n30, 508n33
Whole Foods Markets, 193
Wholesome Meat Act of 1967, 68
Whyte, William H., 231
Wicks, Andrew C., 509n66
Wicks, Judy, 121–122
Wigand, Jeffrey, 116
Wigfield, Mark, 513n37
Wild Planet Toys, 380
Wildstrom, Stephen, 531n87
Wilke, John R., 457n
Wilkie, William, 521n9
Willax, Paul, 507n7
William, Alvin J., 522n46
Williams, Elisa, 515n14
Williams, Marianne, 534n45
Williams, Martyn, 532n92
Williams, Robert J., 535n52
Williams Communications, 491, 497
Willmott, Michael, 508n37
Wilson, Alan, 511n36
Wilson Street Grill, 247
Winder, David, 334n, 533n1
Wingfeld, Nick, 512n52
Winha, Gilbert, 532n115

Wining, L. Cathy, 414
Winnick, Gary, 462, 491, 492, 494–496
Winsor, Robert D., 526n86
Winter, Greg, 402n
Wireless technology, 297–298
Wiscombe, Janet, 517n29, 518n48, 518n52
Woellert, Lorraine, 245n, 517n38, 517n39
Wolf, Christopher, 447
Wolf, Martin, 508n39
Women
    career and family issues for, 249–250
    in workforce, 109
Wood, Donna J., 36n, 511n21, 511n37, 511n38
Wood, Robert, 35–36
Woodruff, David, 527n1
Woodruff, Robert, 395
Woodyard, Chris, 43n
Wooley, Scott, 531n51
Woolworth's, 109
Wooton, Charles W., 508n28
Work-at–home business ventures, 108
Worker Adjustment and Retraining Notification Act (WARN), 233
Worker's Rights Consortium (WRC), 45, 46

Workforce reduction
    community impact of, 218
    explanation of, 231–232
Work/life programs, 250–251
Workplace
    discrimination in, 109–111
    diversity in, 109–111, 246–249
    equality in, 68
    safety and health standards in, 114
    sexual harassment in, 239–241
    values applied to, 96, 97
WorldCom, 14, 80, 88, 104, 145, 146, 151, 157, 244, 364, 366, 367, 370, 479
WorldCom Case
    assigning blame, 461–462
    effect on consumers, 463–464
    effect on investors, 463
    financial implications of accounting fraud, 459–461
    reorganization, 464
World Consumer Rights Day, 204
World Federation of Direct Selling Associations (WFDSA), 10
World Health Organization, pesticide use and, 43
World Jewish Congress, 208
World Resources Institute, 281

World Trade Organization (WTO)
    explanation of, 18–19
    genetically modified foods and, 319, 320
World Wide Web, 299. *See also* Internet
World Wildlife Fund, 210
Wotruba, Thomas R., 507n17
Wykes, S. L., 347n
Wymer, Walter W., Jr., 535n59

Xerox Corporation, 105, 239, 292, 364

Yahoo!, 81
Yates, Buford, 462
Yates, Jacqueline, 527n100
Yazici, Asuman, 421
Yohe, Shannon, 403
Young, David L., 525n41
Young, Phua, 486

Zadek, Simon, 372n, 388n, 535n3, 535n61
Zaun, Timothy, 511n34, 511n41
Zellner, Wendy, 458n, 482n, 514n2, 522n52, 523n75
Zemke, Ron, 248n, 526n83
Zhu, Judy, 526n85
Zimmerman, Ann, 85n
Zinkhan, George, 522n56
Zollers, Frances E., 521n30